I0225376

Testimonies - Experiences

Real life stories have always spoken to me louder than just concepts or theory, so it's very inspiring to read a book where many different people get to tell their own stories about their experience with the heart. I'm amazed by all the different ways that people's lives have been touched and changed by their hearts. There's a real treasure to be found here.

Thomas Croger, Bachelor of Business, Hobart

This book does not just talk about the non-physical heart as a theory, but shares practical ways to activate and strengthen your heart and use your heart more in daily life. If you are able to implement just a fraction of what is shared in this book, your life will change forever.

Dave Gale, Lawyer, Hobart/Melbourne

Not only is the book great, but the practices Klaus is discussing are profound. I have struggled with my mental health for about 15 years, but through the heart practices I have finally got off medication completely (first day without any drugs for the best part of seven years was a few days ago) and I feel incredible. I am happy, stable and for the most part, very calm. None of this would have happened without me being shown how to open my heart. Our hearts can indeed guide us! It happened in my life and I have seen it help and guide others too - to a much better place. I can't recommend this book enough.

Dr Ivan Zwart, Founder, 'Happy Ground Wellbeing', Hobart

Reading 'Your Heart Can Help - The Answer Is Within You' is a like meeting an old friend you have never met before: at the same time both familiar and wondrously new. The book's beautiful, step-by-step approaches, anecdotes and stories are perfectly interwoven to help readers remember how life really can be very simple and joyful and what they can do to help this be the case. It is a book for the times. Thank you for sharing it with us all, Klaus.

Stuart Hayes, Team Performance, Team and Culture Coach, Melbourne

I certainly recommend this book. It has so many practical ideas and ways to help us to access the wisdom of our hearts. For me personally, accessing the wisdom in my heart has helped me in so many ways. My relationship with my husband has improved the quality of our life together to having more understanding and connection and a deeper love for each other. At work I am also happier and more productive.

Lynda Stellamaris, Small Business Owner, Hobart

The best you can do ... is to follow your heart.

Paula Moreike, Naturopath for Psychotherapy, Berlin

Highly recommended! 'Your Heart Can Help' has just published a book and education program to help people find a sense of peace and calmness and feel connected.

Donna Ellerton, Health and Wellness Professional, Melbourne

National Library of Australia Cataloguing-in-Publication entry

Creator: Baur, Klaus, author.

Title: Your heart can help - the answer is within you: discover the complete guide to joy, health, love, success and fulfilment/Klaus Baur.

ISBN: 9780648062509 (paperback)

Subjects: Heart--Symbolic aspects.
Heart--Mythology.
Conduct of life
Health.
Quality of life.
Relationship quality.
Spiritual formation.

© Your Heart Can Help

This publication is copyright. Individual readers have permission to reproduce parts of this book as per the guidelines given within the book and as part of the exercises, such as the KHHs and PHTs, introduced.

Parts of this document can be quoted and re-printed for research and/or personal use, if the original meaning is retained and proper credit is given to Your Heart Can Help. All other persons and organisations wanting to reproduce material from this book should obtain permission from the publisher/author.

ISBN: 978-0-6480625-0-9

For further information, please contact:
Your Heart Can Help
@ Lotus Centre, Hobart CBD
45 Victoria Street
Hobart Tasmania 7000
E.:   connect@yourheartcanhelp.org
W.:   www.yourheartcanhelp.org
S.:   www.facebook.com/yourheartcanhelp

Your Heart Can Help

Discover the complete guide to joy, health, love, success and fulfilment

Klaus Baur

Heartfelt Thankyous

Thankyou to you, for opening the book, with interest in your own heart towards what your heart can offer. It seems that the world can do with more heart. Every heart that opens more, shares more heart-to-heart, is like a beacon of light that guides, brings joy, shares less conditional love and carries heartfelt calmness into families, friendship or work. Thankyou.

Deeply heartfelt gratitude must go to the many individuals who, knowingly or not, shared, commented, attended events and assisted in countless ways over the years for 'Your Heart Can Help', and its resources to come together.

Thankyou to Kristiina and Marko where it all began. Everyone's heart is so profoundly capable that to 'relax and smile' is the best assistance we can offer it. This is a book about relaxing and smiling. The first words were written at 'Santai Bali' cottages. 'Santai' in Indonesian means 'relax'. The most beautiful accommodation, peaceful surroundings and your 'big hearts' inspired and helped the early pages.

One of the biggest thankyous must go to my immediate family members, my dear and much-loved children Alex and Rebekka and my dearly loved partner Elle. They have been amazingly understanding, encouraging and patient. You are the book's heart! Thank you for your love, extraordinary support and active contributions! I feel honoured and humbled to be in so much heart and ever growing, shared love in this life with you.

Hobart, and with it other locations in Tasmania, has become a thriving heart learning centre. Thankyou Kent and Amanda! You followed your heart in letting the Lotus Centre become a 'heart centre'. One weekly heart evening has turned into over 40 weekly heart-related practice sessions. You have been immensely generous in making space available for meetings, sessions and recordings.

Thank you to the loving, joyful and wonderfully helpful community around the Lotus Centre. It is from this wonderful group of heart-friends, that most of the editors emerged. Thank you, Thomas, Linda, Vonni, Ivan, Su, Rachel, Dave, Yvonne, Gennifer, Diana, Steve, Wendy, Stuart, Carolyn and Susan! This special thank you is for your enthusiasm, hearty criticism or feedback for the many moments of discussions, exploration, wonder and joy.

In the most generous way clients, workshop participants, friends and family members offered to share their experiences of being helped by the heart. This is the essence of the book. The book would not exist, have its current depth or heart-touching nature, without your personal experiences or accounts. Your heart and the heart's help shines through these. In many instances the depth or significance of this heart help seems to be even beyond words shared - thankyou from the bottom of the heart!

The 'heart book' became so much more than solely a book. The most joyful lawyer turned artist Claire has been inspirational from the early days. Jonathan, who also shares a powerful journey of healing in the health section, wrapped the book in love and creativity via the front and back cover and other graphic inserts throughout. Your unwavering presence also were invaluable as all got towards the finishing line. A most heartfelt thankyou to you both.

I am extraordinarily grateful also to the team from Inner Heart Solutions Australia and the Canada Head Office. What a wonderful team of colleagues and what incredible insights the existence of your program has offered, experiencing better 'bridged hearts and minds' in the workplace.

Thankyou dear Ed (Dr Ed Rubenstein) and team from the Heart Based Institute in the US for the foreword and much more. Ed has published several heart books as a psychologist and facilitator and has been ever present with advice, publishing information and more. Thankyou also for developing the Heart Based Therapeutics training program for allied health professionals. This has offered another expanded spectrum of what is possible when help is facilitated through the heart.

The list of gratitude is not complete without a profoundly heartfelt thank you to dear Irman, Irmansyah Effendi, author of several heart books and tireless advocate of the importance and meaning of using our heart more. Your generosity of spirit, your loving and caring approach, and embodiment of what it can mean to live a heart-centred life, has 'turned so many hearts around', in our family, families around us, friends and a wider heart community, inspiring this book.

The list of gratitude ends with a huge thankyou to my dear heart teachers, teacher peers, peers, colleagues and heart-learning facilitators Vincent, Steve, Sunny, Rama, Tetty, Yvonne, Djoko, Kim, Krissan and others who teach in Australia and around the globe. Your tireless work, friendship and counsel around this natural heart-learning approach has been invaluable.

Contents

Preface

At the age of seventeen I was given a book on 'how to become more self-centred' as a fun gift and as a way to become happy and successful. What happened, though, was the beginning of an unfolding of much-needed inner peace and centredness at that early stage of my life. I loved the relaxation exercises and simple meditations in the book so much that I did them daily. Once at university, I attended meditation, seminars on Buddhism, psychology classes and first yoga sessions as I wanted to learn about the practices in the book from their source.

Whilst completing a Master's degree in social services I also became a meditation, yoga teacher and a Shiatsu practitioner - with Shiatsu drawing from the depths of Japanese/Chinese Medicine and Zen Buddhist practice. Over the years, my relationship with my wife, family and young children were affected in very positive ways ... yet suddenly it all came to a grinding halt.

After almost 20 years of welfare-related work, daily practice and teaching of yoga and meditation, the marriage went through a long and challenging time, eventually leading to separation. The experience was beyond heart-wrenching and outside everything I had ever imagined possible. The greatest pain felt was not my own distress and emotions but the pain that I could feel in others, especially our two quite young children.

Several extraordinary 'heart events' happened. One day, with the children, we watched Disney's 'Pocahontas' movie. When it came to one of the songs 'listen with your heart ... you will understand', my whole body began to tingle and feel incredibly light and beautiful with nurturing, calming and exquisite feelings. I had no idea what was going on, yet a deep memory of that experience remained.

There was one additional moment where a clear inner realisation suddenly appeared, almost like a voice, but nothing was said or heard, and it was something like 'everything will be ok ... there will be enough love to take care of all, for the children to experience so much love'.

The counsel from a wise and dear friend, after listening to my heart-ache, and in looking at me lovingly was 'it seems like you need better guidance, Divine guidance'. It was at that time of deep despair, I remember looking up to the sky realising that whatever I thought to have understood by then, through meditation and a working life of helping others, had not been enough. There was a dire need for help. Help came in the form of the heart.

Feeling back to it now, that looking up was like a prayer from deep within, from the heart. Yet, at the time, I had no practice of praying at all, even though open to the notion of prayer, I was a 'meditator'. Not long after these events I happened to bump into the same lovely person several times, on public transport, coming home from work and in a city where over one million people go to work via public transport every day. Eventually we became friends and one day she said, 'I feel to do this heart workshop'. This didn't make sense to me at all, as she had already done two similar programs, and how can anyone feel what to do and give it meaning? On the evening after the workshop we met and I clearly felt that she had changed, something deep, something profound had happened. It was her first full-day heart workshop. So I willingly joined her in going to a first 'introduction to the heart' evening event. Feeling my own heart the very first time, during a guided heart strengthening session and a heart meditation, was a very profound experience. I still recall the feeling of a vortex-like inward pulling sensation as if I was being pulled into the heart by the heart. A special journey of learning about and with this newly discovered heart began.

Why the book? There is so much that is positive about this other heart or feeling centre that can help. For instance, couples in similar situations, with difficulties or doubts, who start to use the heart, are in a better position to work things out, with one extra 'tool'. After all, one thing the heart is associated with is love. Through the heart love flows, an opening to love can happen and this love has an infinite ability to expand. Love needs the heart. Love and care underpin so many aspects of life. When the heart is used love for dear ones, siblings, parents, children, relatives, colleagues, clients and friends expands, deepens, becomes sweeter and at the same time becomes light and free, less wanting, clearer, more giving or flowing.

Over the first year of heart-learning I experienced all the changes, all the depth and also the 'holding on' that is shared in the book. I realised how powerful, dominant and active my mind/brain had become over the years and how it often cancelled out opportunities to love, to connect, to feel, to grow, and to learn. The impact of negative or limiting emotions and how they were major interferences in feeling content, joyful and loving became clearer. A new way of being and interacting at home, at work and in social circles opened up. It was humbling to admit to this. There was not one promising course or book that I had not tried or 'searched for'. And often there were several meaning-giving books in the bag or on bed-side table trying to find answers and growth. Yet, a deeper opening only happened when looking at life, starting to live life, with an active, clearing and helping heart.

'Your Heart Can Help' came about because of those early experiences. Then there were the experiences of friends, family, colleagues, children and young adults attending practice sessions opening and blossoming in feeling the calmness, lightness, radiance and joy: everyone experiencing gentle yet profound positive shifts in life; the young ones improving their relationships at home or their performance at school or university.

I also saw that there was no comparable training program available and that deep inside people are looking for feeling, for experiences that provide positive feeling or calmness, joy, love or fulfilment. It became clearer that the often chosen or normal way, to try and get there was through purchases, holidays or learning for the brain. It became clear that mind-based learning approaches, for thought to translate into feeling or a state of being, was like climbing on top of the roof of your home on a chilly night, clinging on and looking around in the hope to find the exquisite, warm bathroom and ready-made warm nurturing, relaxing and rejuvenating bath in the centre of your home. There is 'dirt' or impurity in this bathroom, in the heart, and yet the structure or design is beyond exquisite. The key to learn about the heart and to begin to use its profound abilities is to step into it, to splash around, to be there. Any clearing will easily and naturally happen; often in a light and even joyful way.

Heart learning started in Melbourne in early 2003. I was amongst a small group of Australians to first complete intermediate to advanced heart-learning workshops. Realising the gem that is in all of us, I ended up speaking at wellbeing fairs, expos, conferences, in meetings, and had endless discussions with friends. This led to an active involvement in the establishment of heart-centres in Melbourne and Hobart and being able to assist in other locations. The experiences of friends in Europe, mainly Germany and Austria, also contributed to first workshops in locations around the world.

What also flowed into the book are the experiences of thousands of individuals who have used this approach, who attended and shared at informal or therapeutically motivated one-on-one heart practices or structured heart-learning workshops around the world. I had the pleasure to sit in workshops and seminars in Asia, Europe, the US and in Australia.

Through the depth of my own experiences, I felt drawn to become actively involved in helping with the early, first Australian heart activities in 2003. Never planning to, I became one of the coordinators in 2004. A major occurrence was the first workshops in Tasmania in 2005. Since then Hobart has grown into one of the most active heart centres in Australia and the entire Western world. Many individuals assisted to help this growth. Now there are regular workshops, over 40 weekly informal heart practice sessions with over 50 volunteer practice leaders.

Realising the importance and significance of heart-centred work, I developed a work-based heart-centred wellbeing program and included heart-guided elements into my therapeutic one-on-one work. Since 2009 I have had the honour to teach Open Heart Workshops offered by the Padmacahaya Institute. Since then I have become a Heart Based Therapeutics practitioner and a facilitator for Inner Heart Solutions, offering inner-heart intelligence programs to large organisations and businesses. This book is the distilment of all these years of learning, teaching and realising about the heart.

This is also not 'my' book. The help and generousity experienced in pulling all this together, a book, a training program and associated resources involved many dear friends, colleagues and my family. It feels more like being the conductor of an orchestra, waving some sticks, fingers on a keyboard and bringing all together. It is only because all the musician are seamlessly working together that it all works. And, ultimately, it is the unseen part, the music, that is the reason, joy, passion or love why we are here.

In sections of the book some of the stories or comments or testimonies may seem impossible or not even real. This is because the heart's ability to help is so profound. Your heart is just as amazing and beautiful in its essence and in its capability to help. You solely need to stop balancing on the roof top, go to the bathroom, jump into the bath, start splashing and enjoy.

Your heart may or may not be directly available to you now, you may hope it is or you may not exactly know. Everyone has a heart, and even what you think you know what 'full use' of the heart means, your heart very likely has a different 'idea'. Regardless of what your heart ability is right now, in a comparatively short time, guided by this book and daily practice, its innate wisdom and intelligence will become more available to you. I have met several thousand individuals over the past years during heart workshops around the globe. Their happiness and heartfulness was very apparent and infectious, accompanied with many stories of how the heart has profoundly transformed their lives. Some of these you find in this book.

With heartsmiles, love and gratitude,

Klaus

Foreword

Advancements in modern technology have helped us in many ways. We have a variety of comforts in our daily lives that our ancestors never had. Yet technology cannot bring us true happiness. Technology has not been able to cure the burdens, problems and existential distress that many people face in their daily lives. The medical establishment has attempted to use technology in the form of medication to cure the anxiety, depression, anger, fears or distress that so many people experience. Developing newer drugs to alleviate mental suffering has failed to solve the problems ailing society. The traditional medical paradigm assumes that if we find the right medication to fix the 'brain chemistry' then we can alleviate the distress that so many people are suffering from.

In society, we now have a growing epidemic of people on prescription drugs in an attempt to solve the problems of anxiety, depression, or other mental challenges. This does not apply only to adults, but to young adults and even children. The abuse of prescription drugs for pain is also very alarming. Many people are attempting to numb their emotional pain. Finding the next best drug will not solve this huge problem that is facing our communities.

I do not mean to create a grim view of the challenges society is facing. Though my comments on these matters are meant to reinforce the understanding that trying to 'fix our brain', as if this is the route to healing the root of human suffering, is an outdated paradigm. In most cases, the real problem is that the heart and mind are not in alignment, working together as a team. When the mind/brain is the captain running the show, our heart is not able to be opened. A closed heart has negative effects on the physical, mental, emotional and social aspects of our being. The key to alleviating the mental anguish and suffering that so many people are experiencing, can only be accessed through the doorway of our heart. Our heart is the key to living a life of greater peace, calm, joy and gratitude. This book captures the essence of what it means to live with the heart, with more heart or within a natural mind/brain and heart balance.

As this book so clearly states, 'we look for love, happiness, meaning and purpose ... through planning (mind/brain based) or hope, etc. and yet these feelings or states of being can only be felt ... felt by the heart'. This book is written in a way that is simple to read and easy to assimilate. Do not let the simplicity fool you, because being easily assimilated is the gift that this book offers. Concepts that are deep in nature will touch your heart and gradually make the full potential of your heart available.

You will learn about the real-life stories of over forty people and how learning to properly connect to their heart has transformed and greatly enhanced the quality of their lives. It will become clear how living a heart-cantered life is the key to bringing out the best of us in all that we do. It will become evident how our being properly connected to our hearts allows us to experience deep contentment, fulfilment in our relationships, gratitude for even small things, and an ability to manage the challenges and stressors that we face in our daily lives.

This book will also help you learn about the functions and unique abilities of the heart. In addition, you will learn about the role of the heart in regard to nine life aspects: family, children, relationship, friendships, wellbeing, health, work, personal growth and spiritual growth.

Learning about the multifaceted ways in which our heart can touch and benefit every aspect of life is inspiring. However, as you will realize, understandings and realisations about your heart are just the beginning of what this book offers. Through a number of proven 'Key Heart Helpers' and other heart supporting practices, you will learn how to experience the gifts of the heart. You will also learn 'Practical Heart Tips' that will support you in integrating these key learnings into your daily life. What will help you to easily assimilate the theoretical and practical teachings are the Summary Sections which will allow you to effectively integrate the key concepts, understandings and practices.

Even if you think you are the type of person that is unable to relax, or that there is no way you can learn to enjoy your heart with all the stressors you are facing, just trust that the beauty of your heart awaits you. I believe you will be pleasantly surprised how easy and natural it is to have an enhanced experience of peace, calm, joy and gratitude. This book will guide you to enjoy your heart in a way that you may have never experienced before.

Dr Ed Rubenstein - Psychologist, Author, Facilitator

Introduction

We all talk and know about the heart and, at some level, we know about the depth and meaning that is associated with it. When a friend suggests 'a heart-to-heart' we realise it is important. There is sweetness and something special when your child, partner or a friend says, 'I love you from the bottom of my heart'.

The heart has been discussed by poets, saints and mystics for thousands of years. It is used in hundreds of common sayings, such as 'my heart is in it', 'follow your heart' or 'in the heart you know', indicating that something very profound is happening within. You may have been told that you 'have a big heart' or that you are a 'heartful' person. You know that when you 'are happy in your heart' or 'have peace in your heart' that it is deeply felt or really so.

There has been a rediscovery and resurgence of interest in the heart in recent years. People talk more openly and freely about the heart. But what is this heart? The suggestion 'we need a change of heart' points to something deep, mouldable.

'Your Heart Can Help - The Answer is Within You' is about the second heart, the non-physical or true heart. It is about the heart that knows, is able and can help when it is accessed and used. Your heart is a profound part of you, and, like your mind/brain or physical body, it is designed to work for you, to be a tool that helps you live this life, engage with it and to love and enjoy it.

I come across more people now who say and feel that they use the heart. Some even say that they long to live more with their heart or even to live a 'heart-centred life'. They intuitively know that with more heart life is more complete, full and meaningful and that the heart is there to help. Knowing about the heart or wanting to use it more is a first step, but on its own it will not be sufficient.

To invite you to use your heart and to offer experience-based discussion about the heart is unique about this book. In using mind/brain to read through the chapters and its content and in letting heart-mind-brain engage with the exercises, a deeper 'learning by heart' can open. This learning will also be with and for your heart. The invitation is supported by the people who share their stories or heart-experiences in the book showing that heart learning, 'a change of heart', can have positive impacts on others.

The first six chapters discuss the importance of the heart, what the heart is and how it works. They also explore the relationship between the mind/brain and heart as the two governing forces within, the centres of intelligence and ability. The first practical heart exercises are introduced to help you to experience your heart and to recognise the heart's abilities. The offered exercises, in particular the 15 'Key Heart Helpers' may look simple for the head's understanding. They are, however, a proven and natural approach that offer direct experiences of the transformative power of the heart and how to use the heart's direct guidance towards depth of wisdom and capability within.

From these introductory chapters, the book leads the reader through various aspects of life: family, children, relationships, friendships, health, work, personal and spiritual growth. These are all areas where there is potential for joy, love and fulfilment, and, equally, significant challenges. These chapters are a combination of discussions, stories and practical heart-helping exercises, all showing how the heart, when directly utilised, can offer significant help in positively navigating these aspects of life. Through all the chapters, 'Your Heart Can Help - The Answer is Within' offers a practical, gentle, personal and natural approach to heart-learning, making this book a uniquely comprehensive resource.

May your own heart lead you to a life with 'a heart that is bursting with joy', and more.

Klaus

Terms and Definitions

You will find the use of certain words in 'Your Heart Can Help' at times more free than in general usage. There will also be new or rarely used words like 'heartful' or 'feelable'. When achieving a stronger presence of the heart, one's perception, thoughts and, most importantly, how one feels changes. This is directed by the heart, working in tandem with the mind.

'The heart' in the way it is introduced in this book will be new for some readers. To share about the heart and the powerful, positive and at times surprising ways your heart can help you is the intention of this book. Particular words that are used somewhat differently in this book are explained at relevant sections. To assist working with the book, they are also explained here:

Your Heart

The heart talked and shared about in this book is the non-physical heart or true heart. It is also the centre of feeling. Positive and pleasant feelings spring from this heart and any burdensome, unpleasant feelings can be felt by it. On rare occasions where the other heart, the physical pump of the blood through the body, is referred to, this is clearly stated. It is your primary centre from which life is felt, directed and experienced.

Collection, Blockages and Negativities

In the book and the stories shared you will find these terms used interchangeably. They refer to the heavy and burdening deposits that are made by negative thoughts and negative emotions. They limit the heart's ability to help and the support for you to feel light, free, loving, calm, beautiful and joyful. They are no reason to be concerned either. The practices shared in 'Your Heart Can Help' have been shown to remove these over time, often faster than imagined.

Letting go

Letting go, does not mean giving away your property or money. To let go is an attitude or inner state, which, even by intention, will help you to connect more to the heart. It is about not holding on to burdens, emotions and negativities so that the heart and its functioning can be free and can come more to the surface. It will reduce other parts, like the mind/brain limiting the natural abilities of your heart.

Inner Heart ®

At the core of your non-physical heart is your inner heart. Your heart helps you to a bigger picture or greater truth and has the ability to help you in ways no other part of you can. The heart can have impurities which limit its functions. Your inner heart is the pure part at the core of the heart. As you attend to your heart in the way that it becomes light, pure and filled with love, joy and peace, naturally a connection to this core of the heart, your Inner Heart, can happen. If you are drawn to do so, attending any of the heart workshops referred to at the end of the book will accelerate this process.

Emotion

The definition and use of the words 'emotion' and 'feeling' in 'Your Heart Can Help' are in accordance with the function of the heart. Emotions are heavy or unpleasant feelings or experiences. According to this definition, when you have emotions or when someone is 'in emotion' when interacting with you, this is experienced as unpleasant or burdensome.

Feeling

Feelings are the positive or pleasant feelings that are facilitated by your heart. The more active and present the heart, the more a natural shift from 'emotion' towards 'feeling' occurs.

Mind/brain or head

The term mind/brain is used throughout the book as the second centre from which life is viewed, directed and experienced. Heart-learning and the building of your heart strength will always be a collaborative working between the two centres of intelligence: your mind/brain with its thinking abilities and your heart with the ability to feel.

Part A: The Foundations - Understanding Your Heart

Chapter I

Your Heart's Help

Have your best interest at heart.

Your heart can help. It is a part of you, everyone, it has depth, ability and wisdom. It is perhaps the most precious part of you, the aspect of you that will support you in life the most, giving meaning to it and enhancing your relationships with others in the most immediate and wonderful ways. When there is meaning, heartfelt, then there is also peace, joy, connectedness and love based on this meaning.

Letting your heart help you offers a new approach - and much more than just an approach - a path to happiness, love, purpose and more. Without the true and practical use of your heart, you may still be repeating the same actions, thoughts or habits in the hope that it will create new outcomes. In community meetings, workshops, heart meditations or introductions to the heart sessions, almost everyone knows that the heart in discussion here is the second, non-physical or energetic heart. Given its special qualities and abilities some also call it the 'true heart'.

If some of the challenges you face are in relationships with others at home, at work or in any situation, then your 'change of heart' will subtly, gently touch the lives of others, especially those dear to your heart. Hopefully the stories shared in this book will assist you to connect with the unique help from your own heart.

The book's intention is to offer new perspective, insights and practical tools and to invite you to experience the unique and amazing abilities of your own heart, ultimately to their full capacity.

Most of us can easily identify one area in life where we need help or where we may have severe challenges. I invite you to go to these areas in the book, browse and connect with the stories, or listen to the person's direct experience shared on www.yourheartcanhelp.org.

Will this book help you?

... when the heart has no care in the world.

What has been wonderful to hear, see and read over recent years is that people are increasingly talking about the heart. Once you tune in with it, you notice references on social media, on TV, in books and magazines or in business seminars. These heart references indicate a growing acceptance of living our life with more heart, no longer only through the mind/brain or other aspects of who we are.

You may wonder if the heart or this book can offer you something if your life is already good. You may be at a point in your life where you ...

- Have achieved all you ever wanted to achieve;
- Have found all you ever wanted to find; or
- Feel happy within your family, relationship, social circles, friends or work contacts.

The logical question may be 'is heart learning of any further advantage' or, 'can it deepen, enhance, or beautify these experiences?'

Clearly the answer is 'yes'. Unless you have a fully open heart and the full capacity of your heart available then there is room to improve in several aspects, such as:

- Inner calm and un-shakeable peace, whatever your surroundings present;
- Happiness and joy in every situation, every moment of your life;
- Connectedness to others and at the heart of it all deepest compassion, understanding and love for others; and
- Purpose and growth. Complete growth, development and purpose can only be achieved if all aspects of us are fully engaged - with your heart as driver, guide and facilitator. When your heart is present, more so the core of your heart or inner heart, then a clear sense of completeness in any growth and purpose will fill your life.

Your heart is a powerful resource

A person that helped me immensely to be more focussed, aware and successful in life once said to me: 'you are meant to be happy.' They were strange words and for a long time I connected with the essence of it in some way without really 'getting it'. Over the past ten years I have experienced and realised that the 'program' to be an individual who is happy, healthy, successful and at peace is written and ready to be installed in all of us. The hub, driver, core memory and main facilitator is the heart.

This program, however, can't be accessed through the mind or brain's understanding. This program can only be accessed through your heart and will naturally unfold as you become more 'heartful' and start to use your heart in a real way.

Using this analogy, your brain can initiate the connection, by understanding that a new program is available and making the decision to download. Your heart then has the ability to install the files and, similar to a sophisticated program, will continuously download updates, upgrades and bonuses.

But your own heart is much more than this, as it will help you to let go of old habits, traumas and resentments which you may or may not realise are there. It is the most powerful tool, which at the same time is gentle in its functioning.

At the core of who we are we long to be free: free to choose, free to love, free to live the life we feel deeper inside that it is possible to live.

Advertising often taps into this longing to be free. In an emotional sense, freedom is expressed in freedom from attachment, freedom from need and the freedom to love truly and deeply.

In a spiritual sense, freedom often describes an ultimate spiritual freedom, a return to Source, to the Divine, an ascension to a higher place, freedom from any attachment or earthly bond, and with it true, ultimate, unshakeable happiness and inner peace. All the innate or built-in functions of your heart are solely waiting to be accessed, are in the starting blocks to offer you freedom, whether for you this is freedom from burdens, emotional pain, and negativity, or freedom as a higher spiritual goal.

This freedom is inseparably tied with responsibility: making good decisions that will support your life and others. Freedom in the heart sense has qualities that nurture, support and attract people. In practising this more and more whole-heartedly, your life will be enriched beyond any plans, hopes or imagination. With a heart free from burdens or limitations, all life choices and decisions will help you to achieve a greater overall freedom.

When your heart is free, then you are free to say 'no'. This may be in situations where you may normally find it hard to say 'no'. For example, where it is normal for most people or close ones to say 'yes' or where in the past you said 'yes' and yet it wasn't supporting you. You will also feel free to say 'yes' in situations, where in the past you were reluctant to say 'yes', even though somewhere within you knew it would be right, helpful or suited to you, your situation or a next step in life.

Your heart will ultimately free you, your mind, your spirit, your emotional world from all the parts that block, limit and misguide you, for example those that make you trip up professionally or socially or that can hurt others whom you deeply love.

A word of caution too. While your heart has an immense, built-in ability to assist you in all areas of life, it is important to make any life changes step by step. In the same way you would not send a toddler or young child into the world to be on his/her own, you would not solely rely on your heart when learning to use your heart more.

Your heart is not only a profound resource for you. Most things we do in life are connected to interactions with others, at work, at home or in our social life. Every change that is happening to your heart will directly or indirectly impact on everyone around you too. Some of the stories refer to this and most chapters detail this unique phenomenon of the heart. When words do not work or when all has been said, 'let your heart speak' becomes a deepening and expanding reality.

There is more to your heart than the references that we use almost daily
... have best interest at heart.

You will find a lot of common sayings and words of wisdom from well-known people referring to the importance of our heart, and its amazing abilities, throughout the book.

The references are solely intended to point to this existing knowing, connection to or part-connection to the heart's potential. The book does not have a research or academic focus and the under-the-heading quotes are not referenced for this reason. And while they related to the heart, they also are not an immediate part of the direct heart helping approach introduced in the book. If some of the quotes speak to you, then please google the author or the well-known person to find out more.

The book has however one research element to it in the form of 'narrative inquiry'. It uses 'narratives', which are in stories and experiences shared by program participant or research subjects. Narrative inquiry offers readers to read, see and connect with impacts or outcomes of an intervention, here heart-learning, and even if the story or sharing is brief, the reader gets a comprehensive picture of the situation: what was there before, what are key change facilitators, and how is the situation and feeling now or afterwards. Even if short, narratives can offer a more holistic, more whole-of-person outcome picture.

Knowing about the heart is, however, only part of the picture and it is quite limited. It can be likened to someone reading out a menu in a good restaurant when hungry and looking forward to a meal. To have the meal served, to share it with someone close, to experience the richness of all its flavours is closer to the real experience of the heart.

You will tap into the healing ability of your heart and the profound joy, peace and inner freedom when you start to use it more in a practical way. The purpose of this book is to offer this practical use, to share practical insights and stories.

This book will help you to understand and put into practice how to have your, and others, best interests at heart, with the unique assistance from your heart.

Have you tried the heart yet?

Put your heart into it.

In my role as a therapist, heart-workshop facilitator and meditation teacher over many years, I have come across many people who had health problems, problems with those close to them, issues at work, mental health issues or other challenges.

Often they had tried numerous therapies, self-help methods or meditations to improve their situation or themselves. In some cases the improvement was enough; however, the vast majority of people looking for more help had not reached a satisfactory outcome.

What none of them had done up to then was use the immense ability of their own heart to help their situation or issue.

You may have heard about the heart, even know how important or beautiful it is to be more heartful. However, you may still have questions, such as:

- Do I know all that there is to know?
- Do I use my heart's near limitless potential to support me and my life the best?
- Is my heart in the situation, the path to a solution that will help myself and others in the truest, lightest and most practical ways?
- What will happen if I use my heart more: will I get hurt, become soft, become less strong?
- Is 'more heart' more an idea or a hope than a reality; or am I simply not too sure?

This book will offer you the answers to these questions. Some of the answers will be in the form of what you read and connect with. Others will be in the form of realisations bubbling up from within your heart, as your heart becomes stronger.

It is safe to use the heart

There is really no risk in using the heart more. The heart works in a gentle way. It will, at the very least, guide you through its innate, higher intelligence. Through this guidance and the step-by-step approach offered in the book, you can practically, and with feel-able results, put your heart into everything. You will also relate more to others from the heart, directly enhancing personal and professional outcomes.

The heart facilitates for you and others

Any good social or therapeutic work increasingly shifts the ownership to the recipient of a service: the client or patient. It empowers the consumer in terms of skills, abilities and choices. As improvements and solutions will be facilitated by your own heart's ability, intelligence and wisdom, the answers will gradually come from within you. In that way, all answers are inside you, accessible through your heart, realised as an inner knowing, feeling and truth.

Reading this book, you can begin to use your heart and to feel the immediate impact it can have on your wellbeing and happiness. You will also become aware of how others can be helped by your change of heart.

The heart offers another chapter in relation to the law of attraction. The clarity, strength and purity of your heart is another factor that determines what you attract. Your heart will also assist how successful you will be in your life, in accordance with your greatest inner truth, the bigger picture and the natural guidance and attraction that flows from these.

Whatever new ways of being and new directions that open for you, will only be in accordance with the 'program' that resides deep in your heart. Whatever these changes, they will come with growing feelings of calmness, rightness, joy, love and warmth around and within you.

How to use this book

The first sections I to VI of the book are an introduction to what our heart is and how, as the heart becomes stronger, it is revealed in greater depth how wonderful and helpful our heart really is.

The following sections 1 to 9 will then be an expansion into most areas of life, covering aspects of our interactions, relationships, home and working lives and the joys and challenges of these.

All the main sections about areas of life contain:

A. An outline of how the heart can work for you in each of these life aspects.

B. Key Heart Helpers (KHHs) which, if you follow them, are designed to connect you step by step, clearly and directly to your heart's capacity to help. The important KHHs start in the introductory chapter II.

C. Additional Practical Heart Tips (PHTs). These are supplementary practices that will, open, cleanse, activate and strengthen the heart for immediate help and clarity. There are over 80 PHTs throughout the book. Important ones, directly assisting your heart are marked with an *. Other PHTs are less essential and yet they can additionally assist in a shift from a dominant mind to an individual heart and mind balance.

D. 40 main personal accounts or stories, and additional shorter examples, how people have discovered and in some instances experienced immense help through using their heart more.

E. A summary section at the end of each chapter allowing you to use the booklet as a daily practice in relation to your e.g. goals in 'relationships', 'family' or any 'personal growth' or challenges in those areas of your life.

Every life-aspect chapter, and some of the early ones too, has a summary section at the end with the key practical heart helping steps.

Go to any chapter that interests you. The KHHs are more sequential, so if you do not read the chapters in order, it is recommended you go through the KHHs in sequence for your step-by-step heart learning.

You don't need to read all the chapters in the book. As a minimum, read Section II and then go systematically through the KHHs and any of the PHTs that you like. Then focus on life areas, aspects or challenges where you feel you want or need to improve with the help from your heart.

Starting in chapter II you also find the first PHTs. All KHHs and PHTs are designed to make your heart work more for you as soon as possible and in a step-by-step manner following the wisdom and logic of the heart. Practices will continue and deepen from here as you work through the remaining chapters of the book.

The end of the book, and the book's website, offer further useful links, resources and contacts. Through these you can obtain more information about the heart and deepen practices with more advanced resources like the 'Smiling to the Heart Meditation' book. The contacts will also help you with information towards joining an informal heart practice, heart meditation group or a workshop.

If you have a heart …
Follow your inner heart and the world moves in and helps.
Joseph Campbell

If you believe you have a heart, then it can feel like the world is moving in and helping. The full depth of your heart being opened and working for you is a wonderful possibility for you and everyone.

It is not a matter of belief. Every human being has a heart, both the physical heart which pumps blood and the non-physical heart or true heart. Everyone's true heart has the same immense ability and potential within.

The stories throughout the book and related clips on the web bring these possibilities close to you and your heart. Because the heart is deep and has a capacity to understand and realise beyond the mind/brain, with the help of your heart more is possible than one can imagine, dream or hope for.

The book has KHHs and other practical elements throughout because no matter how much studying or reading about the heart you do, it is only through the use of your heart that these abilities and full heart capacity unfold. It will happen because it is the in-built or pre-programmed nature of your heart.

And yes, you have this second or true heart - every human being has one. It is an immense treasure you have been given. How much of this depth and ability does the average human being use? Unfortunately, and this is my very practical and real experience, most people use only a small proportion of it, generally in an ad hoc way. Only in unusual instances is it used with intention, knowledge and awareness.

If all this sounds new to you, then please do not be concerned and do not put the book aside. The specialness of your heart will ensure that if you give it a go, keep reading and practically follow the heart-helpers, then the light, treasure and companionship of your heart will blossom.

I have spent over ten years attending to, working with my own heart and assisting countless others in similar ways … to connect more to the greater depth their heart's abilities. In that time, every person, with some perseverance and support, has been able to experience the heart.

If all this sounds very familiar, be invited through this resource to explore additional aspects, parts and chambers of your heart. There is a common saying … The heart is deeper than any ocean. Jokingly we have said many times in workshops or practice sessions that is not true; the heart is much deeper.

In fact, your heart has thousands of layers. At the same time, your heart's ability is so significant, that it does not take a thousand years to open or explore them. The more you commit to your heart and your own heart strengthening program, the quicker the journey can be.

The key feelings from the heart, deep calmness; radiant happiness and love for self and others, are like a well with no bottom. You can experience this bottomlessness if you are prepared walk on both legs, 'the head and the heart' and to find enough openness within to let your own heart help you.

Chapter II

Your Heart: Key to Happiness, Love, Purpose and More

When looking at essential goals in life, in many things we do there is the longing to be loved and the quest to find joy or happiness. At times this is clear, at other times it is a more hidden motivator.

In this section, the heart's role in finding deep and lasting levels of love, happiness and purpose will be explored, as well as the heart's role in healing and health. The heart is the centre of feeling, intuition and connection to others. Inner strength and everything related to it correlates to the condition and abilities of the heart. Also in this section is the heart's immense role in helping us through hard times.

The challenge is that the heart has not featured much in our upbringing or education. There are ideas or concepts about the heart that often make people shy away from it. The heart can wrongly be perceived as mushy, romantic, dreamy, soft or unsafe.

What I hope to show you, through the discussions and other parts of this section, is that the heart is an essential and real part of you and all of us. When active and being used, it becomes a skilled facilitator of deep, fulfilling qualities of life such as love, happiness, healing and special connections with others.

To share a fuller understanding and use of the heart is at the heart of this book, including the answers to the questions 'how much of the heart am I using? and can the heart show a truth that I can trust and follow'?

The search for love, happiness and fulfilment

Love is not written on Paper, for Paper can be erased.
Nor is it etched on Stone, for Stone can be broken.
But it is inscribed on a Heart and there it shall remain forever. Rumi

If you or your friends find it strange to read about the non-physical heart, then here is the mirror: much of what we do is in some way connected to the deep longing within us to find fulfilment in love, happiness or both. Both of these are non-physical. You may ask 'how can something physical, the mind/brain or material items, fulfil this deep-seated longing'?

About love

In this life, what many of us search for is love; to receive it, to exchange it, to feel it, to share it with others in connection or as a family. The love we seek fulfilment in is either a romantic or life partnership or another form of love, such as admiration, recognition or acceptance.

Love is discussed in the obvious sections such as 'family' and 'relationship', where the role, purpose and function of the heart is described. However, the search for purer, more complete love runs deep within. It is therefore natural that you will also find love discussed and referred to in most of the other sections such as 'friendship' or 'work'.

There are many forms of connections and relationships and yet there is only one unconditional love. You may feel a different kind of feeling towards each of your connections, friends or family members and yet the essence of what your heart is sharing is, at its core, one love, one feeling of growing joy, bliss and wonder.

You will find that, over the pages of the book, you will be able to feel what has often been referred to in poetic, spiritual or new age writings: the pure, unconditional love that flows to and through your heart, through the heart's natural connection to a source, Divine Being or Spirit greater than us.

About happiness, bliss, a deeply joyful life

Happiness is an inside job.
Unknown

Another major theme is the quest to be happy, to have joyful moments, within ourselves and with others. Many things we do, in our social and personal lives, are linked to this search.

You may, like I have many times, also have experienced that what we want, hope for or think is giving us happiness is often not the key. What we had hoped for, once it is near, is often not as fulfilling as we first thought. The heart offers a truer lens to look through on this eternal search.

The playful quote 'happiness is an inside job' refers to an age-old experience of highly-realised or enlightened people: there is a condition or state of being that can be achieved that offers feelings of happiness, in growing ways, as the right path is chosen. In this way, happiness is achieved by following our inner guidance and connecting to an inner centre where happiness is felt, your heart.

Fulfilment in life

When there is love in your life, when you are happy, then there is a chance that you are fulfilled also. Being fulfilled may also be a deeper felt longing or urge to give life meaning, to have a purpose that will fulfil an urge to be the part of something else, a greater mission, vision or set of goals that extends from self, from self-focus to something else. Being fulfilled, like feeling love or being loving with others, is ultimately a feeling which your brain can assist with yet can never hold this kind of feeling to give you the confidence that you are there, or moving in this direction.

It is hoped that the stories shared in this book help you to connect with what has become clear for me and a wonderful experience in working with many individuals over the past ten years. As the heart changes, opens and becomes lighter, profound feelings of love, happiness and of being fulfilled naturally and steadily grow.

One key theme for lack of happiness, love and fulfilment: emotions

Emotions, termed throughout the book 'negative emotions', are one of our behaviours or responses that don't support our journey towards a life filled with love, joy and fulfilment. This applies whether they are experienced when alone or in interactions with others. This is why 'emotions' feature throughout all chapters.

The book is divided into chapters that cover most, if not all, areas of life. In all these areas of life, whether you are a very social, outgoing person or quieter and withdrawn, your connections and relationships, and the heartfulness within them, give meaning to what you do. The condition and ability of the heart will determine the quality of every relationship and what levels of fulfilment, growth, love, happiness and joy will be in your life.

Negative emotions are behaviours, patterns or responses that do not support our journey towards a life filled with love, joy and fulfilment, within or in relations with others.

In all relations, emotions interfere: creating disconnection, distancing us, forcing outcomes in unpleasant ways or pushing us apart in business, friendship or partnership.

There are many ideas, concepts, even experiences expressed about the role of emotions, in particular negative emotions, and how best to be with them. In chapter IV emotions are discussed in greater depth; including the difference for your heart between emotion and feeling.

The practical exercises and Key Heart Helpers will allow you to experience how your heart is helping, supporting and enhancing your life with often immediate positive impact on how you feel.

In brief, negative emotions are anger, arrogance, jealousy or disappointment (a more complete list is in Figure 3 in section IV). When we experience emotion, in ourselves or others, the common understanding or feeling is that it does not feel so nice within or when receiving them. In contrary to this, a heart full of love can't have or express anything negative and our relations with others will not be burdened. You will find in each section the theme of 'emotions' resurfacing. When there is love in your heart and feeling, there is no room for anything negative.

However, no human being is perfect and whatever is still not pure or clear within the heart will impact on all our relationships in less than optimal ways. This may happen regularly in your life or may surface suddenly and create hurt, upset or disconnection. When this happens, it is often clear that it does not feel right or is a step out of line.

When you are at the receiving end of others' emotions, this may be much more obvious. It also will become clearer with a stronger, more alert heart, that when we burden others with our emotions, it also burdens us and makes our own heart heavy.

You will find from the moment you attend to your heart, that there is a greater, deeper love in your heart making other aspects of you less dominant. When this greater love surfaces, it will affect everyone and everything around you.

The missing link
Turn on your heart light.
From the movie 'ET'

In many ways the heart is the missing link in what can actively lead us towards greater happiness and love. In fact, not using the heart is more like not using the engine of a car. Instead of using the engine, you cut a hole through the car and push it with your feet.

In terms of who we are as human beings, not using your heart is quite significant. The heart has its own intelligence, in fact a greater knowing and as such, can greatly support every decision in every aspect of life. In addition, your heart can help you practically to get closer to a good, fulfilled and happy life and what this means to you, your heart.

Whether it is understood as intuition, awareness or gut feeling, the heart brings all this knowledge into one place and makes it learnable. In using this learning, you can bring the guidance from your heart to profound levels.

Your heart can guide you because at its centre is your higher self, true self or the real you. It is exactly this part that is referred to in religious writings, personal development books, and poetry. It is deep; it knows, and not only does it guide you, it is the very part that is required to be positively involved in your life. It is meant to influence your growth and development in the same way, if not more than the mind and emotional maturity.

The heart as a means to spiritual realisation and growth is referred to in poetry and many books or writings by people regarded by many as leaders. Some describe the heart as important, others describe it as the centre or core of our being. Yet others express the heart as the part within that can realise and complete the understanding of the Divine, as well as connect with the Divine world, heaven, nirvana, paradise or other non-physical places.

So, what is this heart? Is it the same heart that moves the blood through our body and is of great importance to our health? No, we have two hearts: the physical and the non-physical.

The heart discussed in this book, and referred to by friends, colleagues or clients throughout the book's chapters is our non-physical heart, centre of feeling, true or spiritual heart. This is further detailed in chapter III.

We have some knowledge about the physical heart. There is perhaps much less known about the non-physical heart or centre of feeling. It is hoped that the practical nature of this book will assist in making this missing link accessible to you and that your understanding and practical use of your heart will grow through this material.

Your heart's role in finding love and happiness

Straight from the heart.

Why a book about the heart? Whatever your age, you have been around for some time; living this life, looking for fulfilment, connection to others, love or happiness. In many things we strive for there are three drives or over-arching goals:

- Our search for love;
- Our search for happiness; and
- A search for purpose or fulfilment.

These refer to feelings, something we can't possess or pass to others. As the heart is the centre of feeling, they are felt and realised within the heart.

If the heart is of such integral importance, how have we lost the heart and this awareness? The principal limitation is that our education, and therefore our habit is to think, plan and analyse and we believe these qualities to be a foundation for a good, happy and purposeful life.

How then does this connect with the deeper yearning for love, happiness, purpose, inner calm, and other beautiful aspects of our life that are feel-able conditions?

This is one of the main dilemmas of modern life. Firstly, we hope that the use of mind/brain training and our intelligence or cleverness will offer a good life. Secondly, that intelligence, or a rational approach to planning and living life, will then magically bridge the gap between head and heart, between thinking and feeling.

Most, if not all, good aspects of life are ultimately feel-able and this is connected to the quality and strength of your heart. Happiness, love, kindness and genuine connection to others, as this book outlines, will always be straight from the heart, knowingly or not.

The mind can have some impact on how we feel, indirectly and only as much as it can trigger a feeling response in the heart. Your heart offers a more immediate and direct route to lasting happiness, love and other beautiful feelings.

Your heart has one other wonderful characteristic: its nature is to share. This can be with or without words and in the feelings you express in everything you do. In whatever progress you make with your heart, your entire environment will be within its radiance and glow, and the benefits will extend far beyond you.

Finding love

> *'How do you spell love?' Piglet*
> *'You don't spell it...you feel it.' Pooh*
> *A.A. Milne*

Looking for fulfilment in love or a loving relationship is a major theme in our society. The details and stories shared in this book will shed some light on the role of your heart in finding love, inside of you and in a growing number of relationships.

It will also point towards simple heart practices that can help you, whatever your relationship situation or challenge. Everything from your heart will always help, nurture and gently transform you and your relationships.

Falling in love with someone is something most have experienced in life as something very special. And for a very small number of couples, the same special, beautiful and love-is-all-embracing feeling remains throughout their relationship.

During this special time of falling in love, anything the other person does, says or shows is perfect. It is seen through what some say are the rose-coloured glasses of having fallen for someone so deeply.

What happens after this special period can go in many directions. Some say that after the period of falling in love, the real time for the relationship begins.

Unfortunately, in most relationships, after a time of wonderful love, acceptance and whole-hearted support, other aspects creep in and it seems hard to maintain a deep or growing love.

Demands, irritations, etc. emotions intrude and, as a therapist looking with some awareness around social and work circles, I've noted that the kindness, warmth, gentleness and loving tolerance towards each other often diminishes in equal proportions.

In the relationship section of the book this is explored in some depth. This is in the form of discussion, some examples and the most beneficial part of all: how to practically let your heart help you.

If you actually use your heart to its fuller ability, the glow of love will not only remain, it will deepen, become immensely beautiful and even extend beyond that one person.

The love your heart feels open to share will gradually expand to everyone around you, in ever widening circles. It will not stop.

And while the love for your soul or heart-mate may be a special and unique one, the vastness of all this love flowing through you will be beyond any dreams, hopes and words.

What your heart offers you is more and more love, in a purer, lighter, more unconditional form, whether for the romantic partner now in your life or one yet to come. And if there is no romantic partner, this vastness and depth of love will simply unfold for all, first for those close to you, then expanding wider and wider. In this way fulfilment is possible with or without a romantic partner.

This love exists and flows in all of us; it just needs the key to unlock it. This key is your heart. As your heart opens and is unburdened, there will be more love available for you.

The ocean of love with which your heart can flood every cell of your being is endlessly deep. Of course love is also what connects us to others close to us.

The natural radiance from your heart, as your heart begins to glow and share, will also affect others, opening their heart centre, and reminding their heart of a deeper love available there. This is a heart-to-heart exchange, where anything blocking the flow of love, such as brain, ideas, concepts or emotions can somehow be by-passed or released.

Finding more love, or a deeper love or sweeter love happens with the heart's opening to receive all the love the heart can receive, hold and share. The opening of your heart will lead to a merging of loving yourself and loving others. It will become one encompassing love while at the same time, within all this love, will be uniquely different and wonderful unfolding, healing and sharing.

Finding happiness

Looking for fulfilment or happiness can have a wide range of attempts and expressions. We plan, study or work hard to achieve something at home or work in order to find what is ultimately a feeling of fulfilment, purpose or happiness.

Sadly, it is often late in our lives that we realise happiness, purpose, fulfilment, whether in our work or our relationships to others is an 'inside job' We can only feel it, experience it and share it, if it is a genuine inside experience, based on the nurturing of our heart and, more than that, generated by our understanding of how our heart works and then putting it into practice.

What we do, such as doing good things or doing 'the right thing' will lead to some degree of happiness. In that way, right choice, right thinking and/or acting, in line with a good mind is important.

Your heart feels - it is your centre of feeling. Your heart will always want to support you, unburden you, free you, and make you feel good, happy and loved.

What your heart can give you is the ability to feel continuously deepening happiness, while at the same time naturally allowing parts around and within our heart that burden us to be removed. This enhances our ability to relate, feel connected to others and to nature and to be free, loving, kind, joyful and peaceful.

Letting the head or the heart 'rule'

Let your heart rule your head.

You may be afraid to let your heart rule your head. Or you may be concerned that your heart has ruled too much, for too long and you are unwilling to let it continue. In fact, it is not about one part ruling and the other being submissive.

It is about everyone one of us finding the right balance between when to use the heart and the head; when to have them work together and when to use one or the other.

This, however, can only start to take place as one learns equally about each part - head and heart.

Being concerned about letting the heart guide you more is justified. Past experiences where we thought we followed our heart have led to hurt or disappointment. This book will clarify how you can follow your heart and have a wonderful life. It will also clarify the difference between following the heart compared to following emotions, wants or desires, which may not be the heart's suggestion or choice. Following directions or choices the heart offers can be understood as 'following' the deeper knowing, or bigger picture.

Our mind and brain can't offer us happiness, peace or love. These are really only things we can feel. In the same way following the heart or letting the heart direct the head can only be done by learning to use the feeling from our heart.

A simple example is, on a day you don't feel good, tell yourself - from your brain - 'I am blissfully happy'. Will it work? Perhaps, but for some of us we would be equally likely to get annoyed or irritated. The example would be even clearer, if someone close to us or at work were to repeatedly tell us 'you are blissfully happy' on days like that. How many of us would react, snap or become worse? In comparison, feelings from the heart, such as compassion, understanding and care from others have often helped us in situations like the one above.

Our mind/brain is complex, special and offers an incredible tool for us to think, plan and have ideas. There is a flip side to the mind/brain too: it is the part of us that can worry or have negative thoughts about ourselves and others.

We are conditioned to use our brain, our logic, our rational way of thinking while in fact the heart is often under-utilised or ignored.

Your heart has a much greater ability to help you, to guide you and to bring about the change from within that is perfectly matched to your needs, deepest yearning, intuition or wisdom.

Every one of our hearts, has the built-in capacity to support, assist and transform us, not according to an outside model, such as someone's psychology, philosophy or belief. When used effectively and directly, as detailed in this book, the heart functions like the download and instalment of the most elaborate software, and has a continuously self-updating processor. And it is free, works beyond expectations and never breaks down!

The core 'program components' that your heart will always provide you with are deepening joy, bliss, happiness, compassion, unconditional love for others and profound inner peace, as well as healing energy that is waiting to be activated.

The very question as to whether to let the head or the heart rule is wrong. They ought to work together, like your left and right hands work together seamlessly when you eat with a knife and fork.

How many parts of who you are, are you using?

Your own heart is vast, with many layers to it and in some way endless. If your heart is an incredible and powerful tool to assist you, then how much you use right now is important.

Your heart's purpose is to remove all that is not love or joy and fill you with the sweetest yet deepest feelings of calm, joy and love.

It is good also to have a degree of openness to find out how much of your heart you are really and practically using.

Imagine you bought the most highly developed four-cylinder car, with all modern components available, a car that would even steer for you. However, unintentionally from the day of purchase, we only ever used three cylinders.

We use and train our body, mind and in some way our emotions. We hardly ever attend with conscious commitment to our heart.

What would you say to someone driving their car like this? This car is us and life is about much more than driving from A to B.

Another analogy may be that you plan to go for a relaxing walk with a dear friend or a loved one in a perfect part of nature, for example by a river or through a beautiful forest. If you only allowed yourself to use one leg, it would be very difficult to enjoy or even to do this walk. And yet in a similar way, we disable, ignore or only partially use the heart's ability.

The 'Key Heart Helpers'

Matters of the heart.

It is the intention of this book to be down-to-earth and practical. The following first 'Key Heart Helper' may assist you to feel the differences between when your mind/brain is working and when you are using your heart/feeling.

It is important to know and realise that the heart will always 'only' offer you a feeling. On the contrary the mind/brain will offer knowledge. The following table illustrates this in a simple way[1]:

Figure 1: Mind/brain and heart functions

MIND/BRAIN ...	HEART ...
Uses one of the five senses *[This includes physical feeling, like touching something soft, etc.]*	*Feels* *[Using the feeling ability is natural to your heart - it is the part in you that feels everything non-physical]*
Is thinking	*Is realising*
Is looking for something	*Is realising*
Is trying	*Is in its nature relaxed, a source of joy, smiling and connection to higher self*
If excessively used, the brain will become stronger and heavier *Excessive thinking in turn will create physical tension and can lead to burdening of the heart if thinking is negative*	*The more you use the heart the more beautiful and enjoyable your feeling will become*

The deeper nature of all of that we are is not an 'either-or' situation, a competition between the heart and the mind/brain, but the perfect balance that is right for you in how much, how often your mind/brain is used and how much, how often your heart is in use.

Several years of heart research and heart work has clearly indicated that most of us are trained to use the mind/brain very often, in fact in most of our daily doing, including when it is not necessary to use it. This has often resulted in an imbalance. In contrast, the true use of the heart, not in words or a romantic sense, is much rarer.

How much you will feel and how much your heart will initially assist you using this first Heart Helper depends on a number of issues:

- How high the level of tensions built up inside you are;
- How prepared and willing you are to really let go of the over-strength or control of your mind; and
- How the current overall strength of your heart is.

Do not be concerned if you do not feel much, or feel only a little at this point. Your heart has an immense capacity, which can be gradually unlocked. Continue reading the book step by step and follow the exercises in the form of the Key Heart Helpers.

Every single time you practice, your heart is engaged and will start to change and be able to help you. Initially you may feel only a little or nothing. A degree of perseverance is helpful here and if it feels right to keep going, do so. Often that very feeling is from that deeper place inside - your heart.

The next exercise and the first four Key Heart Helpers are immensely valuable warm-up exercises. These preparatory exercises offer a chance to start to use your heart and to feel more. Every time you intend to feel with your heart and use your heart, it becomes stronger and grows in its capacity to help you.

---

[1] The table is displayed with kind permission from the Padmacahaya Foundation of Inner Studies. It is an adaptation of the teaching material used in Padmacahaya's heart workshops.

It is very normal to feel, only a little or sometimes nothing. This does not matter, as the heart is participating and learning and underneath it all there will be progress.

You will start to feel with your heart and you will start to feel wonderful feelings from the heart as you go step by step through the book and exercises.

Key Heart Help 1: Feeling the heart2

This first KHH 'Feeling the heart', or realising the feelings from your heart, will assist you to start to feel, over time with growing clarity, the beautiful feelings from your heart and when your mind or your heart is at work.

This KHH will start to work for you best through the use of contrast learning. Do Part 1 first, then continue with Part 2. After a few times, feel free to do only Part 2.

Part 1: Sit somewhere quietly and think about your tasks for the day or the coming week. Work out exactly what you need to do. Make this list in your mind or on a piece of paper. Spend around two minutes doing this.

Part 2: Follow the instructions in the boxes below …

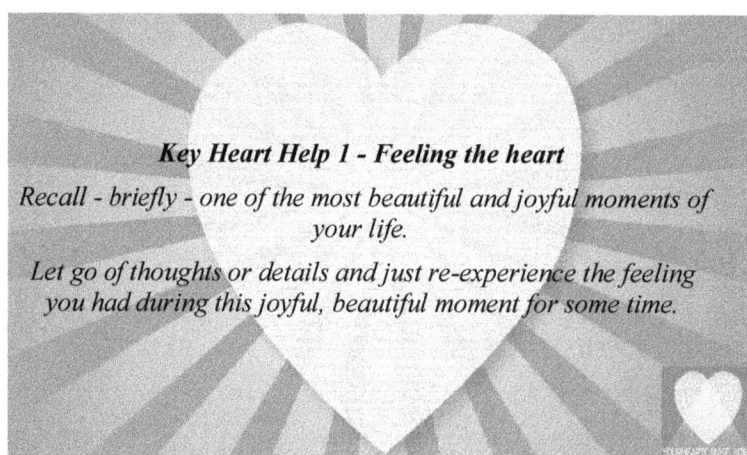

> ### Key Heart Help 1 - Feeling the heart
>
> *Recall - briefly - one of the most beautiful and joyful moments of your life.*
>
> *Let go of thoughts or details and just re-experience the feeling you had during this joyful, beautiful moment for some time.*

The full KHH 1 - Feeling the Heart

Spend a few moments to relax your body and your mind. If you have progressed further into the book already, use one of the PHT around 'relaxing' (PHT 19, 44 or 45).

Then close your eyes or keep them closed;

Relax your body and mind even further; then

- *Recall - briefly - one of the most beautiful and joyful moments of your life;*

- *Re-experience the beautiful, joyful or happy feelings that you had during that event; and*

- *Let go of any tendency to see or think. Let go of any thoughts or details that you remember, just feel and re-experience the feelings you had.*

Conclude the exercise by realising, feeling what kind of feelings you felt and where.

After doing Part 1 and Part 2 each time, realise and feel for a few moments which part of you is working. Where do you feel the feeling, where do you feel energy or pressure?

Then repeat Parts 1 and 2 three or four times. Because the feeling from the heart is subtle.

---

[2] I am very grateful for the permission given by the author of the 'Smiling to the Heart Meditations' Book, Irmansyah Effendi. The above exercise and elements of the exercises below are based on his sharings and insights.

When you do part 1 of the overall exercise you may feel that there is more energy, activity or busy-ness at the level of your mind/brain. This is normal, as you use your thoughts to make this list. However, tune in more to what you feel. This may be pressure, mental busy-ness or anything else.

When you do part 2 you may feel joy or happiness, but there may be other, additional feelings too, that your heart, which is triggered by this 'recall' generates beyond these. You may feel a radiant energy, warmth, tingly or other beautiful feelings in your chest area, where your heart is located or spreading through your whole body.

This may not be clear when you do it the first time. Repeat the KHH a few times. Make sure you are as relaxed as you can be. If you are not feeling anything, read on and do the next exercises. This will help and come back to it at a later point.

Starting to feel and feeling more

In sessions with individuals or in workshops, people often feel radiation of warmth, usually in the chest area, a sense of calmness, relaxation, peace, or tingling through the whole body. Sometimes this can be felt from the heart area. In the case where the feeling is in the whole body, it can often no longer be located in the chest area where the heart is.

It is best not to look for sensations in this exercise nor in any other heart exercises. The heart responds well when we let the heart do whatever the heart does. Just smile and enjoy the feeling.

The exact detail or feeling is not so important at this point. Repeat the practice on a regular or daily basis, together with the next KHHs. It is more important to do it, to intend to feel, be with the feeling where the heart is located. Enjoy the moments where you stop in your daily routine and if you start to feel, relax even more, smile and follow the feelings from within your heart or chest area.

Part 2 Variation:

Repeat the instructions of the KHH above. While starting to feel the gentle, pleasant feeling:

    A. Relax more and smile a little - feel what is happening when you do that; then
    B. Try to observe the feeling of calmness, gentleness - feel what is happening;
    C. Try to make the feelings stronger - feel what is happening; and
    D. Then relax again, smile again - feel what is happening.

Do each of these variations for around one minute. Without trying to do more or trying to have a particular result or effect, just feel what is happening.

Part 2 of this exercise is designed to allow you to connect with some of the key functions of the heart, or in other words, to feel more clearly what is supporting your heart-strength. If you relax and smile, your heart can relax too and open more, start to glow and radiate, so the feelings deepen and become more beautiful.

In terms of your heart - when you try to observe, when you try to help the heart or you try to make the feeling stronger, the growing beautiful feelings from your heart will be slowed down, even neutralised. It also means the ability for your heart to help you will be limited.

This is important to notice and to apply as best as possible during all the KHHs and heart exercises. At times it will not be easy to do this fully, as our conditioning and mind/brain tendency is to do, help and/or observe.

You use your heart already

The heart is deeper than any ocean.

You may say that you are living life through your heart and with an open heart already. No doubt you are, in some way and to some degree. However, how much have you opened your heart, how much of the vast landscape and depth of your heart are you using?

'Knowing' your heart is fully present, open and supporting you at full capacity is only one part of the reality. Fully realising these aspects is at a deeper level and only when you fully realise, through your heart's highest level of understanding, will you be there.

As long as we only 'know', there is a high risk that we are guessing, hoping and believing. Knowing is mainly the brain's function or ability. You can't read somewhere how open your heart is, nor can someone else tell you. You can only ever feel it, with the capacity of your own heart. Ultimately this is very empowering and safe.

In the past ten and more years of heart learning and teaching, working as a therapist and heart workshop facilitator, I have not come across one person whose heart could not become stronger, more open and more present, helping them achieve a better heart-mind balance.

Practical Heart Tip 1: Level of heart capacity

To get an indication of how present and active your heart already is, ask yourself:

Are there moments, situations or interactions in my life where small moments of irritation or other negative responses occur; or

Where or when am I taken out of a calm state of openness, acceptance and non-judgemental feeling towards the other at work, at home or in social situations?

It is quite normal to be taken out of it. Emotions associated with interactions with others that then follow are typically, but not limited to, irritation, resentment, grudges, anger or disappointment.

You can also use the more complete 'Heart Check' introduced as a PHT in section IV.

If your sincere answer to these two self-assessment questions is a clear 'no' then you are there and any further heart learning is perhaps not needed. If there is even a small 'yes' then the heart learning as offered in this book can significantly deepen your experiences, your feelings and overall positive engagement with others in life.

Be aware of the fact that this PHT is not to judge oneself either. It is good to realise and be more aware of one's emotional and heart strengths and to take action towards improving them.

In addition to knowing or believing your heart is already active, open and at work for you, there is a further aspect to realise. The heart has an almost infinite capacity to open and, in this way, to serve you, where ever you believe or feel you are already at in terms of living with an open heart.

Heart Myths - what the heart is and what it is not

If you could look into each other's hearts, and understand the unique challenges each of us faces,
I think we would treat each other much more gently, with more love, patience, tolerance and care.
Marvin J Ashton

It is important to dispel some of the myths you may have heard about the heart. Common knowledge, sayings, beliefs or hopes are different from what the heart truly is and how it functions for you.

Here are four of the main heart myths. Hopefully reading about them and connecting to them in some way creates a balanced view, as well as confidence to trust and follow your own heart more.

A more open heart will make you more vulnerable and open to being hurt

In fact, the opposite is the case with a stronger, more open heart. One of the key features you can receive from the feelings from your heart is guidance. This will make you much more alert to positive situations that will support you as well as making you aware of ones that will do the opposite.

A clearer and stronger heart presence will protect you more every moment, as well as helping you anticipate potential situations. Situations and interactions where you are being hurt will be reduced.

A further wonderful quality of the heart is the radiance of a deep and healing energy. This is important when it comes to our complete emotional healing.

It is this radiance, that not only can cleanse any burdens or negative emotions, but also, together with a stronger heart, can protect us from any negative energy or emotion coming towards us.

More heart will make you a soft person

There is a common perception that 'heart' equals being a soft person. Being kind and supporting your family members or colleagues are good qualities. If you are being kind out of principle or belief only, then you might be more likely to have difficulty saying 'no' or establishing clear boundaries.

If you really follow your heart, in the more direct way, you will be clear in your decisions and others will not only hear these decisions and see their impact, they will also feel the clarity and wisdom within their own hearts.

The heart will enable you to say 'yes' or 'no' with more clarity, from the heart, with others hearing you better. Any kindness or softness will naturally be present according to the situation.

You will not be strong

The greater strength in your heart will help you to be clearer within and to be more self-assured and confident in your interactions with others. This will be felt as a deeper knowing and give you strength that perhaps you did not know you had.

You are, with your heart's guidance, connected to a greater truth in all you do. An immense strength will radiate through all of you and it will be felt and perceived by others as a more authentic and genuine you, in what you say, do, think and even feel.

In work situations or at home, others will feel this truthfulness and clarity, will trust you more and find it easier to follow your guidance and directions. Shared learning and working together will not only bring success but also more joy and connection.

A new inner strength will attract others and engage them in fresh and positive ways.

Deciding from the heart will be a weak or 'romantic' option

Your heart is not only the centre of a greater, more integrative guidance. At the centre of your heart is your higher consciousness or your spirit, therefore your heart is the place from which you know things your mind/brain does not. From the first moment you connect more directly to your heart, this knowledge will support you. It will equally support all around you in a better way.

The heart will look for the best option in the short, medium and long term. At times the rightness or truthfulness of heart-decisions will be obvious, other times it may not seem logical or good, yet your heart pulls together a greater picture not yet known to you. It will take time for your trust in your heart's greater ability to grow.

Your heart will gently facilitate a shift towards more clarity, gentleness, love, patience, tolerance and care for others, as the above quote by Marvin Ashton implies.

Your heart knows

In your heart you know.

This short sharing about Anita's farewell is a simple example of how the heart can guide you, even if in the short term it looks wrong, weak or a soft option. At the time, Anita and her partner both had around one to two years of experience being and working with the heart and had enjoyed following and using it during that time.

A family story - Anita's farewell:

Anita, a young overseas student, had become a very dear friend of our family. Our son and daughter in particular had become very fond of her. She was an immensely positive and kind person and fond of our children, who at the time were five and nine years old.

Anita had to leave Australia and her boyfriend had kindly arranged a farewell dinner party for her.

When I felt with the heart there was pressure and I was drawn to call Anita. During the conversation the pressure remained. I said that, with the pressure, something felt wrong and, not knowing why at all, that we may not even come to the dinner. At the time I had already learned enough to know that the heart knows something not able to be perceived with the mind.

The conversation ended with both of us in some way upset and not knowing what to do. However, what happened afterwards was a conversation between Anita and her partner, prompted by the call and the heart-feeling.

A few hours later Anita rang. Her well-meaning partner had forgotten to invite more than half of her friends whom she really wanted to be at the party. 'I would have been heart-broken if I hadn't had a chance to properly say farewell' Anita later shared.

As a result, the date of the dinner was changed and everyone could be invited. It was one of the most joyful events of the past years for our children, for Anita, her partner and for all her dear friends who were able to attend after all.

I still remember the feeling more than the details during that conversation with Anita more than ten years ago. There were tears on both sides, as we really all wanted to see each other one more time and to say farewell to such a dear friend.

The heart equally remembers the joy, laughter and most wonderful evening we all had when it was resolved. There was so much gratitude in having been able to find out the not-quite-right arrangement for the evening and in having experienced the magical guidance from the heart. It clearly appeared to be something other than the mind/brain deciding. Logic had no real part in this, as the whole other group of friends were not known to me, nor was the state of who was or wasn't invited.

At some point, usually with some practice and growing confidence in your heart-feeling abilities, mind and heart work together in such a way that the greater, deeper intelligence of your heart can be accessed. This is available to everyone.

When you realise that your heart can perceive a much broader and deeper truth than the mind/brain, then it is logical and natural to follow this deeper truth.

In similar ways to following the gentle, pleasant feelings or movements your heart makes, you can follow your heart's answers to questions and even its comments on any situation arising. These comments will always be in the form of a feeling.

With growing experience and trust, these comments from your heart will support you all of your life, as well as supporting those dear to you in the best ways.

This is of great significance. To be healthy, happy and feel wonderful in many moments of your life, and eventually all the time, you need to start making the best decisions that fully support you in this direction: those guided by your heart.

Your heart is able to take you to a point where your purpose will start to surface and, through your heart, you can live this purpose in everyday life. This is immensely beautiful as with it comes the depth of joy, love and peace that poetry, songs and writing through the ages have indicated.

Your life has not been so good, recently or for some time

Life is up and down. Life events happen that are clearly difficult. Many are challenging and others are harder to classify, where some of us would react negatively while others would be less concerned.

Of course some events are clearly not so good. Some occurrences in life can be profoundly challenging, to the core of our ability to be able to deal with them.

The heart has an immense role to play here to make you stronger at a deep inner level where the feeling, and in this way the reality, by which you are being challenged is changing.

You may feel that life has not been so kind to you and you may be at a point where …

- You are experiencing deep distress, pain or trauma - or you feel held back by traumatic events in the past;
- Illness or pain are a burden or significant challenge;
- Other wounds have been cut and not healed;
- Despite all positives and achievements, there is emptiness;
- You feel flat or unmotivated;
- Things that gave you joy in the past don't anymore;
- Nothing seems to work or lead too much;
- There is a sense of resignation; and
- Whatever happens in your life … you don't feel much.

Help from your heart during hard times

A broken heart.

Your heart can help with current hard times or with experiences from the past. Over time, your heart's growing strength will make you somewhat 'immune' in the face of challenges, and it will dissolve all that does not feel good inside, regardless of the outer environment.

In response to difficult life events or situations, strength of heart means that you will be able to feel at peace, in a state of clarity and calm, instead of being swept away or deeply challenged.

The heart is the centre of peacefulness and calmness and will always bring these qualities to the surface, whatever situation we are in.

One of the resulting helpful aspects is that a more peaceful state of mind will allow you to respond with more reason, or heart, to your situation and you will be much more likely to make better decisions.

Strength of heart also means that feelings of understanding, kindness and love will be present. They will be feel-able in your own heart, even during very difficult interactions with close ones. They will, in the first instance, help you to respond more from the heart, with love and kindness. At the same time, whether they are held by you or expressed in some way, these feelings will be felt by the other person too.

It may take some time of consistently choosing your heart. Over time, love, kindness and genuine understanding from the heart will melt whatever is causing upset in others and burdening their heart. Every time you choose your heart or follow your heart in this way, your heart will become stronger, lighter and more open.

In relation to the broader function of the heart, it is also important to acknowledge and realise that any negative emotional response we may have to an external event, such as anger, frustration, jealousy or disappointment, will burden our own heart and close it over time.

Your heart is the direct route to happiness and more

I feel to cry my heart out.

This seems a big leap now - from challenging times to the direct route to happiness. Stay with it - the book, the direction, the route and most importantly with the immense help your heart offers.

The natural heart learning, as presented in the book, is very new. You may say 'I feel to cry my heart out', or 'I have a broken heart', indicating that depth of sorrow or pain experienced in the past or present.

The heart offers a new approach. If we repeat patterns, responses or approaches of the past, then …

'We repeat what we have been doing again and again, and yet we hope for and expect different outcomes.'

This quote is attributed to many people and by some described as a definition of 'insanity'. We need to try something new if we want a different result. This is very logical. Similarly, you will find that the heart will only do what is, at a deeper level of understanding and perceiving, 'logical'.

As soon as you attend to it using the simple methods introduced in this book, your heart will naturally lead you to deepening levels of happiness. This is a kind of happiness that will expand towards blissful moments where no external stimulus is required to bring you there … eventually you can be there always.

A word of caution too: while the heart-help is comparatively fast and the capacity of your heart is immense, it will take some time for the heart to make these subtle, gentle and yet profound changes and for happiness or joy to be felt clearly.

Experiences over the past ten or more years show that firstly there will be some form of letting go or cleansing and in most instances, some tears, sadness, or more rarely, anger arising. Stay with the instructions given on how to best work with these. It is better to let your heart do it as the KHHs describe it, and you will make steady and fast progress.

For most of us, our lives are a combination of good times and challenges or hardships. It is very difficult, over a longer period of time to find anyone who is exempt from this. It is common to think or believe that rich, healthy and beautiful people are outside these experiences of ups and downs. The reality, however, seems far from this.

Whatever your hardship or challenge has been, your heart has an immense ability to heal, whatever the depth of the wounds may be or whatever the challenge is now. The heart will facilitate profound change, in quite gentle, yet clearly feel-able ways.

All shared in the book is experience based - real stories
(Do something) to your heart's content.

I am not a writer and in some way I never planned to write a book … and then there was the time, mental clarity and heart to sit down and put it all together.

The wide range of stories and examples in this book show that, over the past years of learning, this new, practical and natural approach to opening and using the heart has touched the lives of many. Due to how fast and wide the heart learning spread, in a short time the lives of friends, patients, clients, workshop participants, and family members were impacted. Changes were often beyond any expectations, hopes or dreams.

It is my sole intention in these pages to share how everyone's heart is an 'Askenstone'[3] at the centre of your being, deep in the mountain of your own self. When discovered, mined and nurtured, it will assist in the most miraculous ways to gently, lovingly expand, heal and transform your life.

In your heart you are never alone
In the heart you know … the heart remembers.

We are not alone on this planet and we are not alone in our small units of family or friendship. Often we've had glimpses of pure joys, when 'the heart has no care in the world', when we were 'in love', just happy for no reason, or connecting with a friend or dear one in special moments of sharing. It is your heart that has the memory of all this, glimpses of what we not only can experience more of, but what can be a state of being filled with these feelings.

Your heart is waiting for you not only to re-experience these past feelings but for you to realise, through your heart's higher consciousness, that these past moments were only beacons, pointers for you to remember all of who you are and all of what is possible. They show the way to experience and share in this life in profoundly beautiful, purposeful and enriching ways … within yourself and with others.

Everything written and shared in this book by friends, colleagues, family members or clients or by myself is in no form 'a theory', or based on 'good ideas', 'hopes' or 'concepts'. Nor is it an analysis or synthesis of other books, or other materials read.

The suggested practices or approaches are based on experiences and stories by clients, friends, workshop participants or myself. They have been tested in group work and one-on-one exchanges over more than ten years.

---

[3] The Arkenstone, the term taken from the Hobbit/Lord of the Rings novels, was a great jewel discovered beneath the roots of the Lonely Mountain and prized as the 'Heart of the Mountain'.

The heart is learning with and through others

Immensely deep gratitude is due here to Irmansyah 'Irman' Effendi, who is a pioneer in terms of the heart learning as introduced in this book and related online pages. 'More heart' and access to his own innate heart wisdom has ensured continuous developments of these somewhat natural, unique and effective practices and techniques.

My own personal learning and that of others are based on his teaching, guidance and advice. These are repeated in many parts of this book with his kind permission. His vision is for everyone to learn about the heart more, to open it more and use it more. In doing so, the heart can remember the greater, deeper purpose of why we are here. This will in turn assist us in fulfilling a deeper level of our destiny.

Heart learning events, following this method, only started around 2000. The first Australian workshops took place in 2003. Workshops and more advanced, short retreats, expanded throughout the world, not through any sophisticated marketing but through sharing by people who had experienced the heart in a deeper way and felt to share with friends, in workshops and meditation meetings.

This deep gratitude is extended to the friends who have allowed for their experiences to be written or video-taped and to be available to you in this form. The Your Heart Can Help website and Facebook page allow you to directly and personally hear the stories, meet the storyteller and feel the profound, touching experiences within your heart. The sites will also offer some chance to interact with some of these wonderful and generous people.

There are over 40 stories or heart-experiences shared by a wide variety of individuals. Some have only very recently started to hear about the heart or started to use their heart. Others have been 'around' for several years. Some have been so deeply touched that they are now volunteers offering sessions here at the Lotus Centre in Hobart, Australia to assist others to learn to use their heart more.

Some of them have become very dear friends and some now operate Heart Learning Centres in different parts of Australia and around the world: Melbourne, Hobart, Launceston, Alice Springs, Berlin and Vienna.

Summary I & II: Your heart can help

To let your heart help you with the first practical heart-steps, and at this early stage to broaden knowledge and understanding about the heart, these are the first steps:

1. Your heart is an under-utilised resource. It is also often not fully understood or misunderstood. It is free to use, always available and limitless in its capacity.

2. In completely reading this first section, and answering the question 'am I using my heart to its full ability'? Commit to exploring your heart, at least to some degree.

3. Use the first KHH 'Feeling the Heart' as a proper practice to experience the heart. Repeat a few times if the feelings are not clear. You can then use it 'ad hoc' and throughout the day to bring you back into the gentle, pleasant heart-feeling, making you more centred and grounded and able to interact with others from this deeper, more connected and caring place.

4. Complete the PHT 'Level of heart capacity'. A greater awareness around emotions and their negative impact on the heart is essential to your heart capacity.

5. Read, even randomly, through the stories in the book. They may inspire and be in some way heart-touching. Reading the stories will positively and actively support your own heart journey. Alternatively visit www.yourheartcanhelp.org and watch some of them online.

6. Every time you intend to use any of the heart practices - when you really feel your heart, even in the smallest possible ways - you will be using and strengthening your heart. You will benefit from the unique and profound abilities your heart has.

Chapter III

What Is This Heart?

Close to my heart.

The heart at the centre of this book is not the commonly known heart, the physical heart or the important organ that pumps the blood through your body. This book is about your non-physical or true heart - the second, equally important heart that we all have.

This heart, everyone's second heart, is something very special. Even if you feel that you are using your heart already, the question is, are you using it to its full capacity; are you using the immense support, beauty and joy your heart can bring into your life?

In every one of us these two hearts are at work: the physical heart with all its known functions, and the non-physical heart, also known as the spiritual heart, our being, the true heart or centre of feeling.

Before explaining what the non-physical heart is and how it works in more detail, I would like to share a quite personal story, which is very 'close to my heart', about someone very dear to me, my younger brother.

Michael's story describes the two hearts that we have, the roles they play, and the important interplay that can happen between the physical and non-physical hearts.

Michael's Story:

My brother Michael was born five years after me. We both grew up in Germany, yet for the past 20 years my life has been in Australia. All my close family, parents and my siblings, are still in Germany. Thankfully, over the past years there have been enough opportunities to travel back to Germany and to spend time with dear family and friends.

For all those years, with friends too there has been regular and special contact and sharing. Since learning about the heart, almost ironically, my circle of dear friends has grown, despite the distance.

During the last time there, many friends came to visit our beautiful family home in the foot hills of the Swabian Alps. The backyard view shows a garden rich in flowers and useful plants, then meadows, scattered old fruit trees, hedges and then a forest reaching into the hills.

The friends who came to visit were all very interested to find out more about the heart. Almost every day was filled with some form of sharing about the heart and doing heart practices together.

Towards the end of the three weeks there my brother Michael, who had been at work during the weekdays but had been around enough to observe some of it closely, asked if he could have a session too.

The last afternoon, he returned from work at four and three friends - partially unannounced - were there too. One was Wolfgang, an incredibly caring and attentive psychiatrist who became a dear friend many years ago; Marianne, a high school friend, and another dear friend Edith (see her story in chapter IV 'the role of the mind/brain'). The afternoon was spent with heart practices followed by the evening meal.

Michael missed out on the session. I had said to Michael that we would try to find time and yet in the end we did not; the evening was too full and too unrelaxed for him and the early morning was departure and farewell time.

Not long after however, the family made contact and shared about Michael's emergency admission to hospital due to a serious form of 'cardiac arrhythmia'; irregularity in the way the heart was beating. He ended up staying several days in the emergency ward, at 45 years young.

His first priority was to rely on the advice from medical professionals and then take other steps. Eventually we talked on the phone and he said it was all okay and they had 'cleared' him and his physical heart.

For some reason, however, he continued in his request for help. He further shared that he had felt for some time he had been carrying a concrete wall around his heart, that he was not happy and, despite the clearance, did not feel healthy.

He agreed to some heart sessions over the phone and we started our work. He was not sure what to expect and yet he knew somehow, somewhere within, that the work with his non-physical heart would begin.

During this time he frequently said that he could not feel and that he wasn't too sure if it was working. At the same time, with further questioning, he recognised that every time he did the exercises he felt clearly that a deep calm was washing over him. He also felt his non-physical heart was opening, becoming bigger and starting to glow, like a golden, orange ball inside of his chest.

What helped him with this was his dog Anton, as each time Michael sat down on a chair by himself or during the phone sessions, Anton reverse-parked himself between his legs. Anton enjoyed the heart connecting, heart strengthening and the energy releasing together with his master. Through this, it became joyfully obvious to Michael that something was working, as his young and very energetic dog became a model pet for the duration of these sessions.

Michael did several weeks of practice. During one phone call he felt ready to try the full Open Heart Meditation. He could hardly hear it, yet he felt his heart joining and he clearly felt changes in his heart and overall feeling. He deepened his heart practice by adding the Open Heart Meditation.

> *After around six weeks and without much warning, I asked him to feel how the concrete wall was around his heart. With no hesitation he said it was no longer there, the concrete wall was gone and he and his heart felt free, light and more joyful.*
>
> *The second question was then to feel, with his heart, how the condition of his physical heart was compared to six weeks earlier. With an amazing clarity and in profound detail, he described his heart before as a black mass, small, shrivelled up, almost dead. In contrast, the feeling now was 'alive', and red in colour. He described it as red, larger, much lighter and radiant.*

The story about Michael offers a neat explanation of what our heart is and describes some of the qualities and aspects of it. You have two hearts and every human being is the same in this regard. When people talk about the heart, they can mean the non-physical or spiritual heart.

The two hearts

When pure sincerity forms within,
it is outwardly realized in other people's hearts. Lao Tzu

Michael's story illustrates the existence of the two hearts, one being the physical heart, where he experienced problems, and the other one the non-physical or spiritual heart that clearly started to help him. His experience also demonstrates that when a person attends to his/her heart, with sincerity, then more heart awareness, changes and healing are possible.

Modern medicine has made immense progress in understanding the physical heart more and in helping many with heart-related illnesses and problems. This knowledge and assistance is available to people in the Western world and, hopefully, increasing in every part of the world.

When Michael was admitted to hospital in an emergency and in the intensive care ward for almost a week, I was very grateful for the immediate care that could be provided to him.

As a therapist and his brother, I offered him some assistance immediately. He initially made the decision to let the hospital take care of him and to await a more detailed diagnosis and information. During this time, I was silently hopeful and grateful, knowing that the other heart could significantly help him to heal on all levels, should he be interested.

Everything was about medical issues surrounding his physical heart. Interestingly, not long after he was medically cleared and released from hospital, he recognised that his physical heart was still very fragile and weak.

It was around three weeks after his release that he made contact and openly said 'I need more help; I feel I have a concrete wall around my heart', clearly referring to qualities solely related to the non-physical heart.

When we started to talk more, it was all very natural and clear to him, even though these were some of our first conversations about the heart. This is how our regular sharing over the phone and work with the non-physical heart started to help his physical heart.

Only one heart can 'know'

Nothing like bereavement to keep the heart porous. Bono

It seemed that, in a time of hardship, Michael's feeling and his connectedness with his inner self were more pronounced and there was an openness to learning, and looking in new directions. This is one of the qualities of the heart which can guide and help you.

The knowledge of the heart, however, is often not so easily accessible. The physical heart can be impure in all the ways modern medicine can describe. However, it can't 'close'. Nor can it eliminate burdens or negativities related to our emotions, traumas and thinking in the same way that the non-physical heart can.

Learning to use the non-physical heart is one way we can experience relief. This energetic treatment will naturally extend first to the organs close by: the heart and the lungs.

The physical heart can have impurities which can be measured and may lead to problems such as heart failure or heart attack. In a similar way, the non-physical heart carries negativities not measurable in grams, atoms or matter. Rather, it carries negative non-physical deposits that are caused by our burdens, emotional reactivity, negative thinking and any other non-physical negative energy, such as memories or traumas, deposited at any point in our personal history.

In Michael's case, the challenges and hardships he experienced made some crust around his heart. However, by working on his non-physical heart, it became porous, allowed some light in and it started to work. Some of his heart-wisdom surfaced too. This assisted him to make new life and health choices he had not seen before.

The heart and your feeling

*The best and most beautiful things in the world
cannot be seen or even touched.
They must be felt with the heart. Helen Keller*

What is this heart, our spiritual heart? Firstly, the non-physical heart is best described as your centre of feeling. This may make perfect sense to you, yet for others it may not be so clear. You may use sentences like 'this feels right' or 'I don't feel to go there/do this' quite regularly in your life. You know at some level that most, if not all, wonderful events or experiences in life, are felt with our innate ability to feel.

Using the heart and using the feeling go hand in hand. As you use your ability to feel with the heart more, aided by the practices in this book, then your heart's condition and ability to help you will improve. You will also notice increasingly beautiful feelings.

Every time you use your heart, your ability to feel and the gentle, pleasant feelings from your heart will deepen. Every time you use your feeling, your heart will also improve, grow and become stronger.

The connection between this healthy way of feeling - feeling well, at peace, light or happy - and your heart and its natural feeling ability, is important to recognise. How you feel in daily life is the essence of how happy and fulfilled your life ultimately is. Events, people, things or milestones all mean very little if the feeling they give you is not positive or enhancing the quality of your life.

The more clearly and deeply you connect to your heart, the more you will recognise this. Within a comparatively short period of time, incredibly sweet and wonderful feelings from the heart will surface, and eventually and almost magically, they will blossom.

There is a journey to this. The heart will reveal these feelings at various times, particularly in moments where we might be more relaxed than usual, in a letting-go state. The journey to be fully within these feelings will take a sustained period of commitment to your heart.

In this way, talking about the heart is all about feeling ... feeling joyful, deeply calm, connected to life, others and our surroundings, being in love and more. This can be felt as love and joyfulness radiating through every cell and to others. It is not uncommon that after a longer time of committing to your heart and heart learning, there will be a constant feeling of joy and bliss flowing through all of you and all of your life.

Over time, if you use and open your heart, it will assist you to feel and perceive things, experiences and thoughts in a different way. Almost everything in your life becomes 'feel-able' by your non-physical heart. In return, every moment you use the feeling from your non-physical heart, your heart will be more open, it will be cleansed and it will help you even more.

Where exactly is your second heart?

*In your light I learn how to love, in your beauty, how to make poems.
You dance inside my chest, where no one sees you. Rumi*

Both your hearts are inside your chest. The physical heart is more towards the left and the other heart, your non-physical heart - is exactly at the centre of your chest. One way to feel it more easily and to stimulate it at the same time, is by gently touching it.

You find it easily by drawing a line - with one or two finger tips - from one arm pit to the other one. Exactly half-way you stop, on your sternum or central chest bone.

Figure 2 and 3: Location of the heart - side and front view

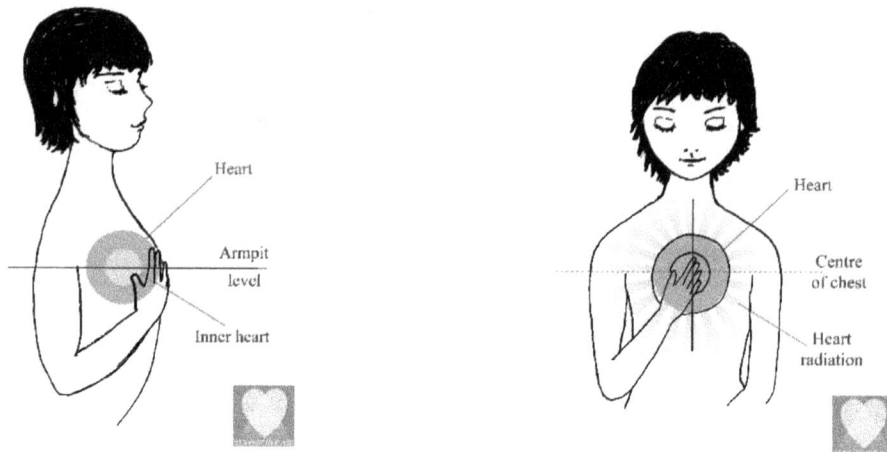

Key Heart Help 2: First casual try

You may know or experience the presence of your heart already you have felt it before. If you are not sure or if you would like to see whether you can feel it more clearly, even before the first heart strengthening practices are introduced, you can try this simple exercise:

Key Heart Help 2 - First casual try

Find a quiet moment to sit undisturbed. Gently smile and ...

- *Close your eyes and relax your body and mind*
- *Gently touch your heart with 1 or 2 fingers*
- *Intend to smile to your heart*
- *Keep relaxing and keep smiling*
- *Use your feeling to 'feel' where you touch your heart ... let go of everything else. Enjoy for a few minutes.*

The full KHH 2 - First casual try

Sit quietly and with no intention, gently smiling, not waiting or looking for anything ...

- *Gently touch your heart at the centre of your chest with one or two fingers;*
- *Use your feeling, just be there, where you touch. Close your eyes and relax your body and mind;*
- *Have only one intention- to smile to your heart (there is no need to think where the heart exactly is or how it may work);*
- *Now keep relaxing and smiling for some time;*
- *Use your feeling, feel the chest area, your heart and keep feeling;*
- *Let go of everything else; including any good ideas or intentions to help this along more;*
- *Thoughts naturally come up, do not follow them; let them pass; then*

> - *Sit for a few minutes. Enjoy peaceful or calming feelings from your heart for a few moments or minutes. In moments when you feel or realise your heart is moving and becoming active, smile even more freely ...*
>
> *As you sit, doing less and less, being relaxed and gently smiling, you may feel lightness, warmth or any of the feelings described below.*
>
> *If you are relaxed enough there is a chance for you to feel feelings from your heart or centre of your chest: these can include warmth, pressure, physical movement or any of the direct heart feelings: lightness, calmness, love towards self or others, gentle joy or the need to giggle or even laugh.*
>
> *If you are not sure or not feeling anything (yet), repeat this first KHH several times, or daily, and make sure you are as relaxed as possible and you smile freely and with feeling to your heart. Continue reading, do the next KHHs or practices and come back to this one later, even when you are half-way through the book.*

The gentle touch is not to do something to help your heart. Your heart knows what to do. Place the fingers gently at that point where your heart is, to bring more attention, feeling and focus there and it will work, either immediately or over time. For now it is important to detach from any outcomes and to let go of any ideas about how it should be or should feel.

There has been research that the physical heart, the blood 'pump' and important organ, also has some memory. I have heard of research being done into whether the physical heart has a memory. For example, recipients of heart transplants reported memories, thoughts and images surfacing that actually belonged to the donor. However, an example given was that of memories, thoughts or images from the previous owner of a heart surfacing in the recipient after a heart organ-transplant. It appears that this 'memory' is connected to physical or emotional memories in some form.

This heart function does not support you in ways that the non-physical or spiritual heart can. What your second heart offers is not only memories or good plans, but its full capacity to actively assist every moment and ultimately lead to a profoundly happy and deeply fulfilled life.

Intuition, gut feeling and the heart

Deep in my heart I knew it was true.

This common saying, even if it sounds more like a hunch or a sixth sense, suggests that the heart knows a greater truth. To a varying degree you may already be very comfortable with the notion of following your intuition, gut feeling or what 'feels' right to do.

Most of our education and learning, however, tells us that the part of us that 'knows' is our brain. Therefore, the more we train it and pack into it, the more we know. We are taught that thinking or knowing with the brain is the only way of knowing. Yet we also have 'intuition' - the heart - that can provide the same service, an additional and deeper version of it.

For this reason it is likely that some people find discussion of the heart rather fuzzy, unclear and even troublesome, particularly the idea that there is knowledge outside the comfort zone of the mind/brain. Remember though, that many things most people hope for, aspire to or long for are not 'knowable'. These are much more qualities that are feel-able, for example love or happiness. Even if what we want are consumer items or a better job, then behind these can often be the longing to be happy or to be loved.

For some of you 'knowing in your heart', therefore, rings true, and you may have been in this way with your heart for some time. It is, however, very normal if there are other good ideas that may equally work, such as 'instinct', 'gut feeling', 'intuition', 'sixth sense' and more. These other ways of referring to a deeper inner knowing have less clarity to them: there is 'something else somewhere'.

What you can do is to learn how to use the heart and how you can tap into this greater wisdom, knowing or insight. What is wonderful about the heart, which you will learn through your own clear heart experience, is that the depth of answers and guidance from your heart will wonderfully expand on any of these abilities.

Your heart will show you a greater, deeper and more helpful guiding truth. But it will greatly depend on your level of commitment to opening and unburdening your heart, so that you free the heart's ability to use all of the feeling and knowledge available. This includes feeling a truth way beyond the abilities of your mind/brain.

This will be covered in more detail throughout the book. However, if you feel encouraged to feel and to be guided by your heart, then do so: you are following something deep. In using your heart and feeling at the centre of your chest, if you feel a sense of pressure or contraction, then this means 'better not to follow' your current intentions or actions. In contrast, if you feel gentleness and a light feeling, coupled with expansion, then listen to your heart and trust, if you can, and follow what your heart is showing you.

The logic of your heart

In the heart of hearts you know.

Your mind/brain is often only capable of following sequential events. With some ability, it also uses processes or tools that will allow it to think outside the square. It becomes harder for the mind/brain to access information outside itself, however, such as the area you are exploring right now.

Your heart is much more capable of accessing any piece of information, any variable or data, including ones you did not think of, and making a wider range of information available for you. The stories about Anita's farewell (section II) and Barbecue (section IV) are two examples of this.

What the heart is showing you will always be in the form of a feeling, and yet at times these feelings will translate into thoughts or spontaneous ideas.

As your heart has this natural ability to pull in information from these additional sources, it will always give consideration to everyone involved. What your heart will show you, in terms of a truth or a decision to be made, will therefore always be more logical - to you and to others involved.

This is true for people who have experienced the heart in Melbourne, Tasmania and other locations where people have enjoyed the use of their heart more. All of them have gained clarity and insight from a more open and purer heart. This also naturally answers the question how safe and even logical is it to 'follow the heart'?

In the same way as your heart can open and can take you into greater depths of feeling, it can reveal a deeper and more expansive truth as your heart ability and condition improves.

Is it quite normal not to be sure about all this? Well, you can't lose, whatever your belief or experience. The heart does not have an either-or orientation. This means 'more heart', more real heart, will equally strengthen and support your mind/brain's abilities.

There is a naturalness to the heart learning; as you progress in your heart awareness and practical heart presence, it will be more and more natural to use it. There will also be growing trust in your heart with clear and convincing experiences. The KHH and PHT exercises are designed to facilitate this growing heart-opening and heart-presence within.

If you follow the guidance from this book, your heart will naturally open more, become lighter and start to glow. There will be a glow to your whole appearance too and you will become happier and more peaceful. Learning to follow the truth from your heart is more than a wonderful by-product; it is a chance to have profound inner guidance and insights.

Summary - Your second heart; feeling with your heart

First practical heart-steps in this brief section are:

1. You can read on or give the first heart-connecting, heart strengthening practice a try. The KHH 'First casual try' is intended to offer heart learning and natural heart work from the beginning of the book.

2. Use the KHH 'First casual try' several times. Then continue to use it and practice with it several times a day. Doing it 'casually' may have one significant benefit: you will not try too much to achieve something. Every time you 'try' or 'want to achieve' the mind and brain will do more than is needed and this will limit the heart's natural abilities. It will be beneficial if you maintain a casual and relaxed approach to working and being with your heart.

3. Let the reading up to here encourage you to feel with your heart area or heart centre in the middle of your chest, and to be guided by what you feel. If you feel a sense of pressure or contraction, it is better not to follow your current intentions or actions. However, if you feel gentleness, a light feeling, and expansion, listen to your heart and trust, by following what your heart is showing you. It shows a possible good course of action.

Chapter IV

How The Heart Works and Helps

The heart, like every other part of the body, is always there, always present and you can work with it in an active way for a better and more fulfilled life. Your heart can also function for you in a pro-active and preventative manner. As you attend to your heart, it will work for you, without doubt. It may take some time to feel this clearly and to fully realise it. The knowledge and natural techniques shared in this book are comparatively new and they are based on hundreds of people having deep and immensely helpful experiences, solely facilitated by their own hearts' abilities.

How does the heart work?

Now for some heartwork. Rainer Maria Rilke

How exactly does the heart work? As the mind/brain can think and the body can move, the heart has a built-in capacity to help us. During the early steps of opening, it will free itself from the collection or burdens around it that have limited its ability to work. Then, during phase two, it will do two things: it will continuously cleanse all the inner layers of the heart and- usually quite early in this phase - it will start to radiate outward.

This radiance outward will help you in terms of any health issues and burdens, whether they be physical, mental or emotional. Then it will start to radiate beyond your own body to others around you.

Depending on the purity, lightness and strength of your heart, this radiance to self and others will be quite deep. Over time, it will be immensely helpful in preventing and/or healing any health issues, as well as improving and beautifying relationships around you. It will also make relationships at work or with acquaintances smoother, more enjoyable and more effective.

Your heart will always work for you, but the extent to which it does so and the extent to which you can feel your heart depends on your heart condition. Common sayings, like the above quote from this famous European poet, have always indicated that, when we use our heart or do and say things from our heart, there is an ability to heal, and a greater truth at play than when the heart is not present. Whatever creative energies are within you, the heart will naturally unlock them and bring them to the surface too. You will see and feel how you can do things differently, in new and more effective ways, and in ways that the hearts and minds of others will also benefit.

Every human being has a heart and its natural way of helping is to bring us to a deeper centre of truthfulness, connectedness and peace. From this all our doing, especially our interactions with others, will become more beautiful, more creative and more effective.

The amount of heart use

How does the heart work? In some way it is always working. It is, however, important to realise whether you are using 1% of your heart or 99%. Once your heart is active and open, you will get answers to this from your own heart. This is very different to hoping for guessing how much of the heart you are really using.

Your heart does not only help and work for you, it will also show you things that are outside the abilities of the mind/brain. Most past students from clients get, after some time of practice, a clear answer from their own heart to the question 'how much of my heart am I using'?

There will be some people for whom living with the help of the heart is familiar, and many people make some use of their heart already. The heart is very, very deep, meaning that some use of it may only be a small proportion of its full potential. Generally, it looks like this: before you attend with clarity, understanding and commitment to your heart and use the correct natural techniques that support your heart, the percentage to which you use your heart is very likely quite small. This is an almost uniform picture running through all the heart workshops, one-on-one heart therapy sessions, and the more informal practices one can do to advance the practical availability and use of the heart.

Out of the last 1,000 clients what was the average use of the heart when they began? While the brain might be confused by this question, the heart can feel that it was less than 10%.

Because the heart is very special, even 10% regular use is already of benefit. Not many people use their hearts at much higher proportions. Even if you are strong in your heart, using your heart above 10% of its full ability, there is still around 90% available to you. It is good to realise here, also, that we often use far less of the brain than is available to us.

The heart helps the heart

Do not be concerned about how much of your heart you are using right now. If you are just starting to strengthen and use your heart, you will naturally progress and the best help for your heart is actually your heart itself. At first you may not clearly be aware that the heart is present or helping. This will change over time.

In similar ways to those in which the mind/brain works, if you intend to do something, there is an energy that is generated to then go and do it. For example, if you think about what to make for breakfast, you will start to think and plan and you will open the cupboard or fridge, go shopping or start cooking, etc.

The same moment you put attention to your heart, in the natural ways suggested through the KHHs and other practices, your heart will start to work.

The gradually deepening KHHs and other heart supporting practices will all lead to a radiance from within your heart that will cleanse, purify and open your heart more.

As soon as you connect to your heart with enough depth, the heart will start to radiate. This means having a letting-go attitude, while being relaxed and smiling freely enough. The radiance will then start to remove any 'collection' of burdens, accumulated negative emotions, etc. from your heart making it more and more available and present for you. Read the following chapters on what this 'collection' around and within the heart is.

Whether removing burdens or bringing to the surface beautiful feelings like joy, calmness and love for others, your heart is able to facilitate this. Indeed, this is the very nature of your heart. At the core of your heart is your spirit/true self/higher self/higher or pure consciousness. Many terms or names have been used in the past to describe this inner gem. This is the main reason why your heart is quite amazing and wonderful and will work naturally.

Heart - love - spirit - divine connection

There is no mistaking love. You feel it in your heart. It is the common fibre of life, the flame that heals our soul, energizes our spirit and supplies passion to our lives. It is our connection to God and to each other.
Elizabeth Kuebler-Ross

The quality within the radiance of the heart is similar to our experiences of love. This can be the love between a parent and a child, love between siblings or love between romantic partners.

For many, the healing, nurturing and peace-giving nature of a deeper love has been experienced before. The memory of such love may have been felt during a time of illness when being looked after by a caring family member. Whatever the impact of this love on the physical symptoms, it instills a deep comfort and inner peace, similar to a feeling of everything will be okay.

Much of this deeper, purer love is directly related to your heart and your heart's ability to help. We look for love and we know that love works. When we are being loved it is a very beautiful, amazing and wonderful feeling. During times like this we are at peace with the world.

The purity of the heart will make this love radiate in ever-deepening ways, for your health and wellbeing, as well as for the way you feel and the ways in which others perceive and connect with you. It will work, according to the higher, more profound nature of your heart.

For your heart to help you, there is no need to have any particular spiritual or religious belief. If spiritual learning or spiritual growth are not of your concern, then you can still fully utilise these qualities and let your heart work for you and your environment. If you have a belief or practice, then the heart will deepen and enhance it.

If you are interested in spiritual growth and learning, then the heart will deepen whatever you do or hope to achieve. As well-known author Elizabeth Kuebler-Ross demonstrates with the above quote, the heart is referred to in almost all spiritual and religious books as something of great depth and importance.

If, through your heart, you can connect to God, the Creator, the Divine, the High Spirit, then in reverse, the same being, entity or place can also connect to you. This is discussed in more depth, with stories and specific heart practices in chapter eight.

Your heart is always present and 'in the starting blocks' to help you. When you begin to access it the depth of help from your heart solely depends on how far you feel to go. The same goes for the depth of insight or guidance you want to get from your heart. It is up to you to what degree you want to access your heart and be helped by this marvellous key component within.

To make the best use of this book and all the exercises, practices and KHHs, it is important to be aware of:

- How the heart can help the heart the best;
- How the heart can directly and positively help you in all areas and aspects of life;
- How we tend to burden or negatively impact our hearts; and
- How there are natural techniques, practices or methods with which you can take care of your heart so that its full, incredible capacity can help you and others around you.

Burdening our heart ....

If your heart is a volcano, how shall you expect flowers to bloom? Kahlil Gibran

One reason why the heart may not work the best for you and perhaps has not helped you the best up to now, is that at times (maybe even most or all of the time) it is blocked out. In many cases, the heart is covered under layers of rubble: negativities or what I call the 'collection'.

The more you know about the heart, its function and its wonderful and very practical purpose, the more you can look after your heart and the more it will look after you. Knowing about the heart is really only the first step. As soon as you start to experience the deep and wonderful help, you pass from knowing to understanding and realising: deeper levels of 'knowing', which bring you to the field of wisdom, and very purposeful insight.

The next parts contain more on knowing about the heart and its function. Knowledge is important. The better you know, and the deeper your experiences with your heart, the more it can direct your actions in daily life not to burden the heart. Ultimately, you can let your heart remove your entire 'collection' over time.

Burdening your heart happens mainly in the following ways:

- Having negative thoughts or negative emotions;
- Experiencing significant personal events or traumas; and
- Exhibiting habits or behaviours that are not in accordance with the heart.

What are burdens? Burdens are everything that make the heart heavier and reduce feelings. They are a form of negative energy parts, blocks or layers that reduce the heart's natural function and access to it and its unique abilities.

Negative thoughts and negative emotions

... harden your heart.

Burdens are generated through occasional or regular negative thoughts or negative emotions.

Negative thoughts and negative emotions are the main culprits.

Negative emotions can be common or strong, such as anger. They can also be subtle, such as irritation, resentment or disappointment. Emotions, or negative emotions in terms of heart-learning and heart-capacity building, are experiences which, when going through them, don't feel pleasant for oneself or others. They are not-so-nice or negative experiences compared to the positive and clearing 'feelings' stemming from the heart.

Figure 3: List of 300 possible negative emotions

Abandoned	Abhorred	Abrasive	Abused	Adrift
Angry	Agitated	Agony	Aggression	Aggravation
Alone	Annoyance	Anxious	Arrogant	Angsty
Beaten Down	Bereft	Bewildered	Bitter	Blocked
Blue	Bored	Betrayed	Brokenhearted	Burdened
Cheated on	Careless	Confused	Conflicted	Conceited
Cynical	Critical	Crushed	Claustrophobic	Crazed
Deceitful	Defeated	Defiant	Deflated	Deprived
Deserted	Despair	Desperate	Devastated	Depressed
Deprived	Deserted	Dissatisfied	Distressed	Doubtful
Distrustful	Distorted	Down	Downcast	dreary
Embarrassed	Empty	Enraged	Envious	Estranged
Exasperated	Excluded	Exhausted	Exploited	Exposed
Faithless	Fatigued	Fearful	Feeble	Flustered
Foggy	Forgotten	Frantic	Frightened	Furious
Gloomy	Giddy	Grieved	Guilty	Gullible
Grudging	Grumpy	Gutless	Gutted	Gypped
Hatred	Hard-hearted	Heartless	Harmed	Hard
Heavy-hearted	Helpless	Hideous	Hopeless	Horrified
Hostile	Hurried	Humiliated	Hurt	Hysterical
Idiotic	Ignorant	Ignored	Impaired	Ill-tempered

Inferior	Insecure	Insulted	Isolated	Irritated
Jaded	Jealous	Jittery	Joyless	Judgmental
Kept apart	Kept away	Kept in	Kept out	Kept quite
Labelled	Lacking	Laughed at	Left out	Let down
Leaned on	Livid	Lonely	Lost	Low
Mad	Maligned	Manipulated	Masochistic	Mean
Messed up/with	Melancholic	Miserable	Misused	Misunderstood
Mixed up	Mocked	Molested	Moody	Mournful
Naïve	Nagged	Needy	Negative	Nervous
Neglected	Neurotic	Numb	Nuts	Nutty
Obnoxious	Obligated	Obsessed	Obstinate	Obstructed
Offended	On display	Oppositional	Oppressed	Outraged
Opinionated	Overlooked	Overwhelmed	Out-of-place	Over-controlled
Pained	Panic	Paralysed	Panic	Paranoid
Pathetic	Pissed off	Perplexed	Perturbed	Pessimistic
Poor	Powerless	Put down	Pushed	Puzzled
Quarrelsome	Queer	Querulous	Questioned	Quietened
Rage	Rattled	Rebellious	Regretful	Rejected
Resentful	Remorseful	Retarded	Ridiculed	Rotter
Robbed	Ruined	Rushed	Ruthless	Revengeful
Sad	Sarcastic	Scared	Screwed over	Screwed up
Scattered	Scorned	Selfish	Seething	Shy
Sick	Sinful	Slammed	Small	Smothered
Smug	Sorrowful	Spiteful	Stingy	Stressed
Stupid	Submissive	Suffocated	Spiteful	Stubborn
Stumped	Suffering	Suicidal	Suppressed	Superior
Tactless	Talkative	Tearful	Temperamental	Tense
Terrified	Thoughtless	Tired	Trapped	Threatened
Thwarted	Timid	Troubled	Tortured	Turned off
Unable	Unappreciated	Uncomfortable	Undecided	Undesired
Undisciplined	Uneasy	Undervalued	Ugly	Unforgiving
Unforgiveable	Unfriendly	Unhappy	Unmindful	Unpleasant
Unprotected	Unsettled	Unsure	Unthankful	Unwanted
Unwise	Upset	Uptight	Use	Useless
Vain	Vengeful	Vexed	Vicious	Victimized
Vindictive	Violent	Violated	Volcanic	Vulnerable
Warlike	Washed up	Wasted	Wavering	Weak
Weary	Weepy	Withdrawn	Worried	Worthless
Wounded	Worn out	Wretched	Wrong	Zealous

This is solely a sample list of 300 possible negative emotions. The important part to consider is whether the experience you have is 'emotional' and therefore burdening your heart. Some emotions are clearer in this category than others. For example, when you are 'angry' and experiencing anger then it will have a burdening effect. When you are 'wrong', you can be light, even jovial about it in which case it is very unlikely that burdening occurs. However, when thinking you are 'wrong' and you feel sad, anxious or worried then this is different.

In this way, also depending on your heart-strength, some of the listed qualities can move between have a burdening impact, being neutral or even positive.

The process of burdening the heart happens when you experience emotion, whether this is outwardly expressed or not. The result will be burdening or negative energy blocks around or even within the heart; in particular if it happens often or over a longer period. The size and heaviness of these blocks will depend on the severity, too.

Negative thoughts have less impact on the heart and yet they also create burdens and will, over time, limit the heart in its availability and ability. Negative thoughts can also be a path or stepping stone, if followed, leading to stronger, more emotional reactions.

Significant personal events or traumas

Traumas are some of the heavier and more burdensome experiences that life can present to any one of us. These can be separation from a loved one, the death or sudden passing of a loved one, natural disasters, emotional or physical harm, sustained mistreatment or loss of health or property.

Habits or behaviours that are not in accordance with the heart

Habits or behaviours that will burden your heart are not much different from the two main heart-burdening aspects above. They are often connected with burden-creating thoughts and emotions. However, habits and behaviours lie deeper and you will not find it so easy to recognise them at first. A habit can be a tendency to react to particular events in particular ways.

For example, your boss or spouse treats you in a dismissive way. A habit would then be to feel justified in being angry and to show this emotion in some way. Unfortunately this is often modelled by the media and, at a surface level, seems fair and fine to do. It is with growing heart awareness and heart intelligence that you may realise that this behaviour does not support you.

Practical Heart Tip 2: Scan and understand reactions, emotions and habits *

In your Heart Diary or personal diary make a simple table with three columns. The column headings can be similar to:

- *Column 1: 'Day' (allow space for 7 to 14 days) - you can do this on one page;*

- *Column 2: 'Current response/habit/emotion(s)'. Briefly detail here what type of reaction, emotion or habit you felt or displayed; and*

- *Column 3: 'New response/habit/emotion(s)'. Detail what heart exercise you used and what alternative responses or behaviours are available, including new responses you have chosen.*

As this is about your learning in how to let your heart support you, for now it is important to recognise that there are situations - and this is very normal - where you respond negatively in terms of your thoughts, actions or emotions.

If you have already started to use the heart, as suggested in KHH 1 and 2, you can make a short session of heart connecting and heart strengthening part of your new response or diary entry.

Do not be overly concerned and do not try to analyse every habit or behaviour in too much detail. For now it is about identifying a current tendency to react. This will allow you to monitor your changes more closely and to let the heart come in and help with more and more focus as you progress through the book.

Attend to your heart and your heart will first remove any parts of the collection along with more reactive dispositions or tendencies. Secondly, your heart will remove the underlying causes that 'drive' you to behave this way. So, by repeating PHT 'Scan and understand reactions, emotions and habits', over time you will see improvements, whether they be subtle or pronounced.

Your heart will also inform your mind/brain and clarify its role. This process will lead to the heart, in tandem with the mind/brain, choosing more heart-felt responses more often.

Choosing your heart more and more will involve removal work, and eventually lead to the full removal of negative dispositions, such as emotional reactivity and any other habits which do not support you or others.

While the heavier experiences or trauma are often known to us, the burdening of our heart, unfortunately, tends to happen in a less conscious way. This means that during the course of our life the heart's health is often neglected. The heart not only is less present or under-utilised as a result, but over time it loses strength and we stop being attuned to its natural helpfulness. Even worse, it can be buried under an accumulation of rubble and burdens, like the 'concrete wall' in Michael's case above.

The role of the mind/brain

Your mind/brain can either make your heart lighter and freer or the reverse: it can burden and cover your heart. This depends on your attitude, feelings and actions towards other people and situations. Your mind/brain, as the part of you that is most present and aware, has the amazing ability to work directly for you and your heart.

Mind and brain are essential tools and they can play an important role for our heart and whole-of-life development. The heart allows you to access an additional intelligence tool which can fully unfold, regardless of your level of mind/brain intelligence.

One of the main problems, however, is that in most of our upbringing and daily life, the overall focus is on using and training the brain.

This is not a problem as such; it means that the mind/brain are over-used and overly-strong. This tends to create an imbalance that does not reflect the complete nature of who we are: that is, able to exist in a state where all the elements of mind/brain, heart, body, soul and our emotional world are naturally and individually in balance.

Developments over the past 10, 20 years recognise the role of emotional and spiritual intelligence as aspects of our existing, functioning and living a good life. This has also found attention in business, research and training. The heart is more than solely another intelligence source.

When a greater brain-to-heart balance exists then your mind/brain can significantly support your heart opening and heart learning, leading to a more wholesome, complete life, in which you use all parts of you. This also means you access all possibilities that are given to you.

From the viewpoint of achieving a greater heart-to-brain balance, the functions of the mind/brain ideally are:

1. To help you to reflect upon actions or reactions in situations and to make adjustment to these (cognitive behavioural programs work with this ability);
2. To use these reflective abilities in conjunction with growing understanding and experience of how the heart can help; and
3. To help you to stay on course and not follow any negative thoughts or emotions, but instead to make more and more heart-supporting choices.

Let us look at examples for each of these three aspects. In the first scenario you look back at an interaction or situation where you have followed your emotion. Somebody has not done the right thing by you, disappointed you, or even done something that is commonly acknowledged as being unjust. You responded by reacting negatively to that person or by discussing the situation with others and expressing negative thoughts or even emotions such as anger.

While it may feel good to talk to others about a difficulty, there is a risk of re-experiencing some of the emotions. With more practical and felt understanding about the heart's functioning, you may reflect on this and in future situations choose not to go down the same track.

This interplay between the heart and your ability to reflect and learn can be illustrated further with an analogy of riding around on your bicycle or driving in your car with all the tyres slightly punctured. When you practice your heart, your ride becomes easier, freer and more enjoyable. The tyres are fully pumped and your ride is very smooth. If, however, you do not reflect on your actions and emotions towards others using your mind/brain, then it will be like pumping up the tyres again without fixing the puncture. There will be a short, pleasant ride and then the tyres will deflate again. You find yourself constantly in a cycle of pumping up, strengthening and cleansing your heart, and deflating it again by reacting with or following emotion. Reflection on behaviour and making heart-relevant adjustments will not only ensure a continuously pleasant ride, it will continuously improve it.

One example may be if your children leave their room messy. You tell them off, with emotion, and order them to clean it up. Reflection and a subtle change could lead to being within and feeling your heart, and then discussing tidiness with them and asking them, with care and love, to clean it up.

This may look small, but over time it is very significant. Will someone only have emotion when discussing something contentious, or only with the children? It is very likely there is a pattern here and it stretches into other areas of life and other interactions. Every time you have emotion you will also burden your heart. How your children react, in this moment and longer-term as you interact this way, is another matter altogether.

The second scenario where your mind/brain can help your heart looks similar. However, given the same scenario as above, with insight, awareness and a clear mind, you choose not to respond with negative thoughts or emotions.

Negative emotion may go first and then a negative thought may follow, or the other way around. For example, you see someone first, have some exchange and then react further with emotion by thinking 'I really don't like that person'. In the reverse situation, you may produce something at work, at home or for school, but in the end you are not happy with it. You begin with thoughts like 'that was very average' or 'that was the worst piece of work I've done in a long time'. In following these negative thoughts more and more emotions surface, for example disappointment in yourself, even feelings of self-doubt or anger.

Negative responses may not only be directed or related to the other person. They can also be directed toward yourself. Negative responses in these instances may be an inner dialogue such as 'this always happens to me, this is my fault, I am no good', or similar messages.

Thinking more about the issue or problem facing you is one way of dealing with it. Your heart offers another avenue: to let the heart help. This is particularly relevant when you feel that more thinking is going around in circles or taking you to places where emotions or negative thinking happens.

When using the brain correctly you make heart-supporting choices immediately, such as focussing on the heart more, connecting with it and even taking time out to do Heart Strengthening (KHH 6).

This ability to stay on course, as a short-term benefit, will mean that your reactions to an event or interaction will not harm relationships. It will also have medium to longer-term impacts as firstly, you will not react and burden your heart, and secondly, it will let the heart's abilities, over time, remove any disposition that makes you react with anything but kindness, understanding, care and love.

Alternatively, and as a shift towards a new approach and being helped by your heart, is the opportunity to be more positive, more heartful and kind to yourself. Thoughts may be more like 'this happens to me and to others at times', 'this was my fault, but I can improve' or 'in this situation I did not act in the best way'. It is exactly here that your mind/brain can assist, in quite important ways, not to turn a negative thought into another wave of negative burdens or negative emotions.

A heart of stone.

It is okay to say these things at some level. However, regardless of whether it is linked with a thought, or whether you express it, every time you feel a negative emotion, it will burden your heart. There is a risk, depending on the frequency or intensity of the emotion, that over time they will fully cover your heart.

This is best illustrated by the recent sharing of a close friend in which she reminisces about feeling lighter when she was younger. Edith is an attractive, professionally successful, socially active and very positive woman. When she was younger she worked as a model. She now works in a senior training and corporate coaching role at a large well-known German company. She had reached her 45th birthday and reflected on her life and the years ahead:

Edith's Story:

'I look around and notice myself and my friends ... I love them and in a way feel that amongst them I am still happy, perhaps the happiest, lightest.'

'However, I also clearly notice that the lightness and happiness that I felt 25 years or so ago is no longer there. I feel heavier, often burdened now and there is clearly less joy and happiness in my life compared to when I was a young adult.'

Edith shared also that she would love to claim this back, not wanting to be young again but to reconnect to the lighter feelings from that time. For the past years she has attended many personal development workshops and seminars in an effort to do so.

On the one hand, the story indicates how the heart works. Every time there is a negative thought or emotion, whether it is expressed or not, you are burdening your heart.

On the other hand, Edith's heart and feeling is still working for her, as she can clearly observe her changes over time.

One of the great abilities of the mind/brain is to know and understand the heart, so that you can practically apply this understanding to let the mind/brain's commitment to your heart assist you to receive all the help form your heart.

By following the natural heart steps suggested in this book, the KHHs and the PHTs, your heart and all your feeling that is connected to it can't go backwards or become heavier. Your own heart's profound ability will naturally, gradually and undoubtedly facilitate beautiful feelings and a positive, purposeful and love-filled life.

Emotions and emotional intelligence defined

You will find a different definition of 'emotional intelligence' in this book. For your mind/brain to choose your heart is one of the most emotionally intelligent choices available. It is ultimately your emotional response to every moment that will determine the quality or condition of your heart.

Below are two definitions: a common one for emotions, and one that is aligned with heart-learning and heart/spiritual/emotional intelligence. The definitions distinguish emotion, negative emotion and feeling and offer a shared understanding for the purpose of this book and your possible heart-journey.

Common definition of 'emotions':

The broadest possible arrangement of emotions and feelings, both negative and positive. This common definition is not so useful here, as it ranges from strong feelings deriving from one's circumstances, mood, or relationships with others, to sentimental feelings, as well as a range of possible sensations, reactions and responses such as passion, intensity, warmth, ardour, fervour, vehemence, fieriness, excitement, spirit, and soul. Common definitions also include an 'instinctive or intuitive feeling', as distinguished from reasoning or knowledge.

For our purposes and closely related to the heart's characteristics, this book will use the following definitions or understandings:

'Negative emotions', or just 'emotions':[4]

Emotions are negative drives such as anger, jealousy, arrogance, sadness or irritation.[5] Emotions can also be described as qualities that feel heavy or burdensome when we have them or when they are present between people; whether they are expressed or not.

Emotions stem from our centre of self or ego, and are associated with the solar plexus area in our abdomen. This is important to note, as sometimes, when your heart is active, you will feel sensations in this area too.

'Feelings':

Feelings are the positive, gentle feelings associated with the heart: calmness, inner peace, joyfulness or happiness, love for self or others, compassion, care, etc.

'Emotional intelligence':

With these slightly different definitions of 'emotion' and 'feeling', the term 'emotional intelligence' becomes a contradiction. In terms of the heart and its functions, it is best referred to as 'heart' or as 'heart-spiritual intelligence'.

This may be different from what you have read before. It is not my intention here to explore all of the different approaches or models available on emotional intelligence. Instead, this book's main intention is to share the stories of many individuals who, in attending to the heart, have experienced clear relief in terms of negative emotions held or felt. Many people have also experienced the foundations of their emotional intelligence being shifted from within, through their own heart's doing This has made them feel freer and better, as though being gently shifted in a more beautiful direction, and has found expression particularly in the relationships around them.

This is what the heart offers: instead of definitions, scientific ideas, theories or concepts, you have an experience that changes how you feel and how you interact emotionally and rationally with others. Further, the heart makes the experience of emotional relief and improvement of your emotional world accessible and often immediate in its positive impact.

Heart-emotional/heart-spiritual intelligence

Only the heart knows the correct answer.
It taps into the cosmic computer -
the field of pure potentiality,
pure knowledge, and infinite organising power
- and takes everything into account.
Deepak Chopra

One understanding of emotional intelligence is that you make choices that are positive, engaging and wise and that support you and, ideally, others around you. For me, this is to choose my heart and all my heart offers or 'knows'. From the perspective of the greater heart-knowing and your heart's innate ability, this means that action and choice of action is informed by your heart.

This offer from your heart-intelligence can be further refined by your mind/brain's ability to process and further develop the information the heart conveys as feelings. At its core, your source of emotional intelligence is connected to your heart.

The brain and everything connected to the brain, such as the amygdala, can hold emotional storage, trauma and hence a tendency to react in particular ways. The pure heart is the feeling centre that holds and generates at its deeper layers only beautiful feelings, both of itself and connected to our interactions with others. This is possible because your heart has, at its core, the real you or your spirit. Therefore, the term 'heart-spiritual intelligence' seems an equally natural description.

Your heart is the centre of only positive feelings, which happens in the absence of all negative emotions. Therefore, rather than 'emotional intelligence' a more accurate descriptor of its abilities would be heart intelligence or heart-spiritual intelligence.

Is it that simple? Yes, and no. The widespread usage of heart-themed quotes indicates that there are people out there who 'know' about the heart and its importance. It is however not what anyone *knows*, it is only in the practical use of the heart that this level of intelligence can be accessed.

For example, someone may be pleasant in a business transaction because it is expected that they deliver courteous customer service. When you add the heart to it, all aspects of this interaction become kind, polite, attentive and more. The customer will be able to feel it. It may only come across as a genuinely pleasant transaction and yet in these moments negative emotions are being cleared and the relationship, or at the very least the heart, will improve for whatever is next.

---

[4] 'Negative emotions' and 'emotions' are one and the same for the purposes of this book.
[5] The complete list of possible emotions is in the above section 'negative thoughts and negative emotions'.

No piece of knowledge, however smart or sophisticated is able to do this. Knowledge is connected solely to the mind/brain function. What is wonderful about your heart-spiritual intelligence is that it is not connected to your level of brain functioning and does not depend on your IQ (Intelligence Quotient).

Assuming that you are not a fully enlightened or holy being, or that you are not yet one hundred percent positive in thought, feeling or emotion, then your heart intelligence has room to improve.

Emotional reaction - a core problem

Based on the above definition of emotion, then it is the choice between our emotional response or our heart-guided response that can lead to either more or less rubble around or within our heart. Every time there is a negative emotion surfacing in us, there is some form of deposit being made on our heart, reducing our heart's ability to help us.

The following figure shows how with a weaker heart (a) and higher level/amount of existing heart-burdening deposits brings with it a tendency to react with emotion. The more the heart is strengthened (b), the more that emotional reactivity is lessened. Positive feelings become stronger and more continuously present.

Figure 4: Emotional reactivity and heart strength

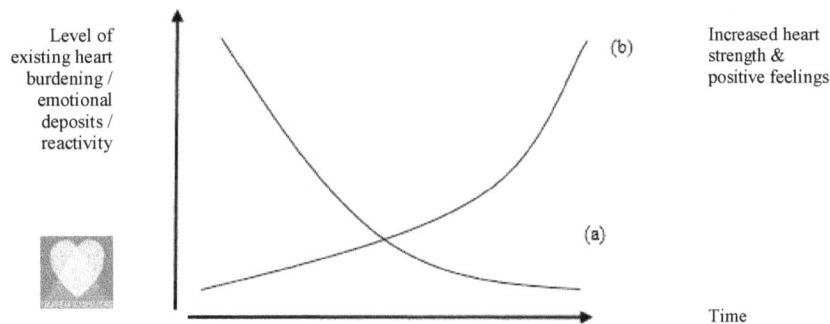

If a situation is difficult or very challenging, of course it is normal for emotions to surface.

Practical Heart Tip 3: Starting to choose the heart *

You can get an indication of a tendency in all of us to react emotionally using the following simple awareness-raising test. This makes it easier to start to choose the heart in some situations:

The harder one:

Something difficult or upsetting is happening and there is an emotional response:

- *Be aware of the fact that there is an outwardly expressed or unexpressed emotional reaction;*

- *In your Heart Diary make a brief note of the event and the reaction; and*

- *When you find yourself calmer, even only in a small way, attend to your heart. Do PHT 19 'Heart - breath - intention relaxation' as a warm-up followed by KHH 2 'First casual try'.*

The easier one: something less difficult, a smaller or medium challenge confronts you:

- *You are now aware of the emotional reaction or response, even if it is subtle or you have known it for some time;*

- *Realise the greater chance to be heartful and to let your let your heart help you; and*

- *Do this as often as possible. Use PHT 19, KHH 2 or KHH 6 'Heart Strengthening' whenever you can.*

It is normal that you might still experience or follow the emotional reaction for a bit. The key is to interrupt this flow or pattern and to choose the heart.

This PHT, as you include it into your heart practice routine, will gradually shift your inner response away from emotions felt and experienced, to a gentler, more relaxing and enjoyable way of being and interacting with others.

The purpose of this book is to share that there is an additional response available to every one of us, and that we all have a heart. How exactly you can use your heart in an emotionally challenging situation is detailed in several PHTs (7, 23, 28, 47, 53, 61 and 72).

As a minimum, let your heart begin to help you in those situations where there is a small to medium emotional challenge. Only after you have mastered your responses to the smaller to medium challenges to some degree, will you be more ready to let your heart help you with the more difficult challenges. This is more or less the logical approach. However, the heart is not limited by linear logic, that is, by events unfolding in a sequential manner. If you experience significant challenges now, let your heart help you the best now.

Soon, at least in the medium to longer-term, you will find yourself reacting less emotionally to situations that normally would have triggered an emotional response. Further, you will not find yourself becoming empty or anything similar. Instead, you will be naturally filled with beautiful feelings from your heart towards yourself and others, which in turn will support you immensely.

You will find yourself responding with more gentleness and kindness in new, beautiful, often creative ways that may surprise you and others around you.

One of the clients of a recent one-on-one heart-guided session shared about an accident that happened to her near-new computer.

> **Ursula's Sharing/Story**
>
> *This was a short conversation with Ursula via Facebook's messaging service:*
>
> *'One thing that struck me is that I found out yesterday that my Mac, which I spilt a glass of water on, is not going to come back to life. But I'm okay with that.'*
>
> *'Had this happened a month ago I'd have been distraught; it is brand new as well and cost me two months' saving up! But that's not a big deal for some reason.'*

This example (which probably rates 'small' to 'medium' on the scale of severity) is simple but poignant. It highlights that whether the damage is done by you or by another, it is ultimately your reaction to events, rather than the events themselves, that determines whether you become emotional or remain peaceful, calm and composed.

Life presents us with regular opportunities to react, to be upset or angry. You will find as you read through the book and as you do the suggested practice, you and your life will change in the gentlest of ways towards more joy and sharing with others in calmness and love.

Your heart is smarter - your heart's greater intelligence

If all the harps in the world were burned down,
still inside the heart there would be hidden music playing. Rumi

Let us talk a little more about everyone's in-built heart intelligence. Your intelligent heart, in simple terms, has two ways in which it helps:

- Through guidance, similar to intuition or inner knowledge, that you seek in a conscious and directed exchange with your heart; and
- By indirectly helping you through its stronger presence.

Your heart shows immediate responses every moment, whatever is happening in your life. These responses can initially be put into two categories: a 'yes, go and do it/pursue it' response or a 'no, not good' (for you or for others around you) response.

Even though it is a non-physical part of you, like a muscle that can tense and then relax, the heart has its own clear and precise functions. And it performs these functions for every human being.

The guidance you can have from your heart is through following this process consciously and with intent. You ask yourself a question while feeling your heart's response. This is the most real and direct way you can 'listen' to your heart.

Though it looks like a small matter, it is very important in these moments that you do not hold any intention or vision. The question is an impulse from the mind/brain which can be used to let the heart react and show something. It is a chance for the heart to take over, free from any brain domination or holding.

At a deeper level of guidance, after sufficient practice, you will be so deeply and permanently connected to your heart that this feedback mechanism from your heart will be permanently available to you.

The second level of intelligent help or guidance is from a naturally stronger and more present heart. As a source of wisdom and inner knowing the heart doesn't only function when you 'listen' to it with awareness, meaning when you feel its presence and reaction to events or thoughts. It will also inform your mind/brain function. Information from your heart is intuitive, one that is inclusive of a bigger picture and one that can surprise you and others around you.

When you follow your heart, the result of your actions, thoughts or decisions in the medium to long term will be immensely beautiful and always take into consideration the best for everyone around you.

A personal story I share at times in workshops or groups is from a time I had just started to learn about the heart and to use it.

Family invitation to a barbecue - Guidance from the heart

Some dear friends of the family, Tom and Marissa, had invited us to a barbecue. It was a hot summer day in Melbourne, meaning that temperatures were around 40 degrees Celsius.

These friends had attended meditation classes I had taught over several years and had greatly benefitted in terms of a serious and life threatening illness and other occasional disturbances.

Our children were excited to meet each other too and naturally, when the invitation arrived, I said 'yes' even though it was a two-hour drive across the city with a car that had no air conditioning.

On the afternoon before the barbecue, a dear heart friend reminded me to feel with the heart to see if there was a 'yes' or a 'no' feeling. As I was in the process of learning to follow the heart more, I felt again, with more peace and clarity. I was surprised to find there was a 'no' feeling - a contraction of the heart - and it was strong, meaning it was not good to go.

At the time I had enough trust in the heart to know there was a meaning behind it that the mind/brain did not yet know. I rang our friends and told them we would not be coming that night. The first surprise was that Marissa, who answered the phone, immediately offered her understanding, as I did not have any logical excuse.

That night my four-year-old son had a serious asthma attack. It is likely I would have forgotten the medical tools he needed if we had gone to the event.

It is beyond imagination how difficult it would have been to care for him at someone else's house, and on the way back home in the car, possibly without medication or breathing assistance.

In reality, we were at home. Everything was available and despite the severity of the attack, being in a relaxed atmosphere and able to apply Chinese medicine practices, shiatsu and reiki as he went to sleep, made it almost no issue at all. I remember to this day how grateful I felt for the guidance from the heart that afternoon, not for my own purpose but for the immense benefit to one of my children.

What this story hopefully shows is the refined knowing of the heart and how consciously seeking guidance from the heart was so valuable in this instance.

Assessing your growing heart function and heart intelligence

Always listen to your heart. It is on your left side but it will always be right.
Unknown

You know already that the heart is at the centre of your chest, it is your second, or non-physical, heart. It is time now to offer to you the Heart Check. The Heart Check is a self-assessment tool that will allow you to get a score for your current heart function and ability. It also makes you more aware of your current heart-emotional intelligence. This is really not to test you or for you to be concerned about your score but to offer you a reference point. It is suggested you visit the tool at set other times.

The Heart Check can become very meaningful and helpful to you if you do it now, note down your results somewhere, then follow the KHHs and other heart exercises, then redo as suggested.

The Heart Check is simple and should only take you a few minutes to complete. It covers the following four heart-emotional capacity and intelligence areas:

- Feeling within/for self and others;
- Emotional clarity or reactivity;
- Purpose, connectedness and positivity; and
- Guidance or inner knowing.

Practical Heart Tip 4: The 'Heart Check' - a heart function self-assessment tool *

Use the Heart Check as often as you like. It will give you a starting-point, regular feedback and show you how you progress, or at times go backwards. The score will give you a reference point and hopefully will assist you to be motivated, committed in attending to your heart.

Here are the suggested points in time/progress through the book and/or online program that you do the Heart Check by following the links to it on www.yourheartcanhelp.org:

- *At the end of reading the introductory chapters 1-6; or prior to beginning any of the PHTs or KHHs (if you have already started, then best do it now or soon);*

- *After KHH 6 or 7 (ideally after you practised at least KHH 6 for a minimum of two weeks several times daily; and*

- *After the completion of all or most KHHs and after practicing the deeper KHHs 10-15 for two to three weeks.*

- *Complete the Heart Check also after Unit 1 and/or Unit 2 of the online course.*

Each Heart Check will only cost you $1. Funds made from the selling the book and associated resources will be used to support additional heart help activities.

The online Heart Check is anonymous and yet it will give you a personal result/score. It will show you change and progress too. In filling it in, at the suggested intervals, scores are collected and later will allow a wider data analysis and will lead to heart book refinements.

You will help the book's intention and in turn encourage and help others:

- By filling in the online Heart Check at the suggested intervals or close to them (make a reminder note in your book, calendar or diary); and
- By sending any additional stories or experiences in via the web-site or linked social media pages.

Every test, self-assessment or inventory has its limitations. Hence the PHT Friends Check to go with the Heart Check.

A word of caution in using the test. There is a chance that you will score lower in your second test. This is for a very simple reason. The more attention you bring to your heart, the more you will be aware of your daily feelings, the good and the not-so-good. You will become more aware, which is very helpful, of any emotions, including their negative effect on you or others. And as you become more aware, you may score yourself more rigorously, with lower scores.

If this disturbs you, there are two things you can do:

- Do the test another time at one, two or three-month intervals, while you continue your heart practices; and
- Do the below 'Friends Check' as a second way to identify positive change.

Practical Heart Tip 5: The 'Friends Check'

The Friends-Check is simple, ad hoc and informal.

Ask people close to you, family or friends, what changes they have observed in you, in general and in terms of your emotional responses.

You can give them one or several pointers such as, how calm, attentive, caring, light, joyful or loving.

If you feel that you are, for example, more angry or irritable now, then ask others about this 'how angry or irritable did you perceive me to be six months ago, compared to now'? Write some of the comments from your friends or close ones into your Heart Diary.

The Friends Check can help to gain additional clarity around some of the changes that the heart is likely to facilitate. With more awareness you may become more aware of, for example, your anger. Yet, if you ask others, they may say 'you are still angry every now and then and yet, it is clearly less than before'.

If you find that your Heart Check score is worse than before or, in daily life you even feel that since learning about the heart and using the KHHs or heart practice you have become somewhat 'worse', then the Friends Check can help. Many people find that their perception of their progress is different from the feedback from loved ones.

Many people's experience, shared in workshops and casual practice groups, is that, more often than not, their loved ones comment that the changes have been positive over this period of time. Another facet of making progress is that you may now have more awareness of your negative emotions and their effects, and know that they still surface, whereas before you perceived them as 'normal' or didn't notice them at all.

More awareness also means more emotional intelligence; you can't express emotions as strongly, if at all, and most importantly you can eventually let your heart help you to remove the root causes and the inner disposition to have that emotion altogether.

How will your heart help you - what does it do?

The next two chapters offer more details and depth as to how your heart helps you. Firstly, what kind of help the heart facilitates and secondly, how the heart does it.

The essence as to how your heart helps can be explained in a simple analogy. Certain plants grow better when the weather is fine: there are few or no clouds, it is warm and in particular the sun shines for most of the day.

Your heart likes similar conditions. The overall fine weather is the initial lightness you can create in gently smiling more often. No clouds means fewer unnecessary thoughts and fewer dark clouds means fewer negative or burdensome thoughts. While the sun is out, you, your heart and your feeling will continue to grow and become more beautiful. In a similar way to people finding joy being in nature, as your heart-nature is blooming, people will enjoy your presence and feel relief, comfort and attraction. In this limited analogy, your heart is that sun inside your chest, waiting to shine more, waiting to be connected to, and this very heart-connectedness will make everything work.

Your heart removes everything burdening and limiting you

Your heart, when awakened and strengthened more, will radiate through whatever burdens, limitations, blockages or negativities are around your heart. This is not something theoretical. It is this freedom of your heart that will determine the depth of positive feelings in daily life. It will gradually change the tendency to respond with emotion, aggression, anger etc., which you know will severely challenge or hurt others and limit the depth, closeness, creativity and joy in all your relationships.

Your heart will change how you feel

Good things in life, such as warm friendships or special events, you will feel. In the same way you will feel the quality of all relationships close to you. An opening heart will always deepen and beautify these as profound inner experiences.

Often in all our striving or doing is the longing to be 'in love' or 'in happiness'. These are feelings that perhaps only your heart can feel. With an open heart these two feelings or experiences will always be in your heart, in a continuously evolving form.

Your heart will also guide you to express the feelings you have for others more freely and appropriately, according to your heart. It is not easy for some to say how much they care about someone, how much they appreciate someone or how deeply they love someone close. Things can be further complicated by when to say it and how to say it appropriately. How often have you thought 'I should have said how much I loved or cared about that person'?

At home or in your social circles, the qualities from your heart will gently and naturally make you feel more care, appreciation and love for others. The heart will prompt you when to say what: when to express a feeling of love or care. In addition, the warmth and radiance from your heart will accompany these feelings and make the other person feel what you feel more clearly and be touched by it. These are moments when we say 'I feel touched by what you say or it really touched me when you said or did this'.

One example of this was the relief experienced by the daughter of dear friends who, during a period of being unwell, listened to a radio interview about heart, and sent the following message:

> *... wonderful! So refreshing. I was having nightmares last night and then in my dream, I remembered you on the radio talking about the heart and it brought me out of them. Beautifully spoken.*

The impact that others feel will always be determined by their own heart quality, heart awareness and how they use their heart in daily life. When your heart is open, the full depth of all special feelings from the heart will always be felt by you. In your home environment you will naturally love and give more freely. You will also feel clarity around when to say 'no'. This will be with the warmth and strength from deep within your heart.

Opening the heart does not mean that you will allow people to walk all over you and in moments, when you need to be strong or firm, there will be an undercurrent or blanket of care and attention around you and the interaction.

This is very significant and helps build strong relationships all around you, every moment, even when you may need to say 'no' in the many ways this can be done in words or action. You will be able to do so with an open and light heart and others will feel and respect this more.

The more care and love you feel in your heart for others at work will not make you want to hug all your colleagues, superiors or your clients. This in fact, might not be the best career move. The ups and downs that happen at work will impact less on you. You will be calm in more situations which in the past threw you out of balance, even made you react with emotion.

The inner peace you feel will attract others. They will offer more to you and show more willingness to help and support you and your work. The natural joyfulness that will grow in you and radiate from you will engage others even more and natural successes will follow.

Your growing feeling of heartfulness and all it means for you and your wellbeing and whole-of-life will make you a better, more attentive team player and someone others respect and will naturally feel to work with and support.

'Following the heart' - to really be guided by your heart

It is built into your heart for you to know how to clearly and practically 'follow your heart'.

Following the heart is often frowned upon. It can be reduced to a romantic sentiment or a fluffy, unscientific, unclear way of making decisions.

This is often based on fear or experiences of past decisions that went wrong or did not support us. This is unfortunately commonplace. These so-called from-the-heart decisions were based on some half-clear sentimental intuition or 'gut-feel' loosely attributed to 'following the heart'.

This unclear following of the heart becomes something not logical and in turn your centre of logic, the mind/brain, allocates something similarly unclear to the experience of the heart or the concept of 'I followed the heart'. This association may be positive or negative, depending on what you have experienced in following your heart or intuition this way and how you value doing this.

In reality following the heart and having guidance from the heart is something very logical. It is also very clear and not 'romantic' in any way. It is, however, something very beautiful to do and feel every time you use the heart and you really follow the feeling from it.

Similar to the mind/brain, the heart is a seat of consciousness. It is more precise and has the ability to view everything, such as processes and decision-making environments more holistically.

Learning about the heart and using it as a source of more guidance, as an intelligence tool, is never about what is better, the heart or the mind/brain. It is about the seamless working together of these two wonderful aspects of every human being.

The book will guide you to learn how to be guided by your heart more accurately and practically and in this way to truly follow your heart. The innate ability of your heart to connect to a much greater picture will naturally assist you to make decisions that support you more.

At home or at work, as part of caring for others, many people want to make good decisions, not just for themselves but also with the best interests of others at heart, and thinking of the impact on them. Because of the bigger picture capacity of your heart, one of the most exciting parts is that your family, loved ones, colleagues and everyone around you will benefit from true heart decisions.

How will your heart help you - how does it do it?

There's nothing more inspiring than the complexity and beauty of the human heart. Cynthia Hand

What the above quote implies is that within the beauty and complexity of the heart there is a capacity far less explored than that of the mind/brain. And only a small percentage of the mind/brain is known to modern science.

The heart has its own unique way of functioning and working for you. This can be summarised in these ways:

1. Your heart naturally wants to open and enhance whatever you do to help or facilitate its opening. By following the instructions in the KHHs and most of the other practical, heart-helping exercises, this will simply happen. Even if, for example, you only do them 50% 'correctly', your heart will respond, open and be increasingly available for you.[6]

2. The heart only causes 'good problems'. You may say 'no' in a situation and experience some reaction from others. In the long run, people will see the heart's bigger picture. Look at your life and your heart practice more and more with your heart and feeling. There may be some letting go of emotions or of situations, even people. As things in your life begin to change, there will be more joy, love and gentleness. Things will run more smoothly and effectively. You or others may perceive some of the initial changes as not so good. Change is often a challenge in itself. You may feel to do things that others do not like, as it does not serve their perceived interests, wants or agendas.

3. Your heart only knows and generates good feelings. Any other experiences you may have along your heart-journey is some form of clearing, releasing or cleansing of things that need to go. Any negativities and blockages are released by an active heart. Anything not pleasant is not from your heart but a part of the collection of rubble and negativities accumulated over the years.

4. As you spend more time in your heart, using the step-by-step practices and KHHs offered in this book, the natural radiance from your heart will gently open and cleanse your heart to make it more available. It will also facilitate changes in your whole life which often happen unnoticed, including allowing those close to you to be helped by your heart and by their own hearts.

5. At the centre of the heart is the true or real you. Its beauty and ability are beyond words. The core of your heart, also referred to as the 'inner heart', will start to work from the first moment you use your heart. It will start to gently guide you and be the driver behind an ever-growing radiance from your heart. This also means increasingly wonderful feelings within, also surfacing in your exchanges with others.

The work of the heart, once it kicks in, is truly amazing and often it can facilitate desired changes very fast. This is particularly clear when niggling and disturbing health issues or emotional undercurrents that are hard to heal or let go of become less and less dominant in your life or miraculously disappear.

Then your heart will grow and glow

A few more words about how your heart works. Every time you work with the KHHs and practise your heart, your heart will grow and in a short time start to glow, whether you feel it initially or not.

---

[6] To do something only 50% correctly does not sound like much. It comes back to the nature of the heart, its wisdom and innate abilities. Looking at this 50% of other parts of us getting it 'right' is enough.

Early feelings will be similar to a feeling of expansion in the chest or a feeling of opening, widening, and also lightness and calmness.

As you pay more and more attention to your heart, even make bigger steps forward with regular heart strengthening, your heart will begin to radiate. Then you will clearly start to feel wonderful and immensely calm. It is not uncommon that others will notice your changed energy and a different, more radiant look.

You are on a direct path to continuously growing joy and happiness; keep going, only you can walk it. You heart is something extraordinarily special and so are you …

As you stay on your heart path, your heart will always support you in the now and changes to your heart will affect everyone around you and your future in all areas of life.

It will always naturally expand as you give it the right attention, in the same way you would look after your body, mind and emotional wellbeing.

Your heart is in the starting blocks … always

In some way all you need to say is 'go' and follow the KHHs and some or all of the other practical parts in this book. Your heart is always ready to begin its deeper journey.

The heart is immensely deep: one could even say it has an endless depth. No matter how much you feel or know your heart is open or present in your life already, it is very likely more is possible. The discussions and practices are designed to be a strong stepping stone in reaching the full potential of your quite amazing heart.

If you feel that life is difficult, that anything heart-related has been difficult and in the past living with an open heart did not work out, then it is hoped that the in-depth discussions, explanations, exercises and stories will help you to adjust your heart understanding and to reconnect to the trust that resides deep in your heart. The heart knows about itself and much more. The heart is also present, and highly competent, to assist you with any condition, situation or personal challenge no matter how big, old or immediate.

Whatever your situation or condition, your heart is in the starting blocks, willing, ready to help and waiting for you.

'Hearts that are alike attract each other'

I know I am but summer to your heart,
and not the full four seasons of the year.
Edna St. Vincent Millay

The heart is magical in terms of 'attraction'. This is another way in which the heart offers a profound level of help. The essence of what the heart does goes beyond attracting others, or assisting 'attraction'. In every moment that you are in your heart and relying on your heart, your entire life will be guided and assisted by it; including in relation to everyone you meet and connect with.

The beautiful saying above indicates how the heart works in all 'four seasons'. It points towards the quality of the heart, when the heart is actively present and involved it will create only 'summer': nice weather, emotions, interactions and, at a deeper inner level, a celebration of being together.

This happens regardless of what kind of relationship you have: at work, socially, at sport, even in ad hoc interactions with strangers. It also points towards a greater level of fulfilment that the heart knows, that even a wonderfully matched intimate or loving relationship will struggle to fulfil.

The full working of the heart, beyond knowing or attracting others, is the healing of relationships, whatever the level of intimacy, every moment you interact, and even outside these interactions.

In a more metaphysical way, when the heart is purer it will attract other situations, other people and overall more positive events and encounters. Your life will be enriched as your lighter and more beautiful heart will attract all of this naturally. However, the not-so-nice deposits or collection in our hearts is holding the heart and limiting it from using its full capacity.

In your heart there is a deeper recognition and wisdom about who to be with as a partner. Other parts of you also recognise this, yet ultimately not with the same depth. In any case, with a clearer understanding of what the heart offers, let your heart help you and guide you as to who to spend more time with professionally, socially and, if you are in this situation, romantically.

Some people talk about soul-mate. I prefer the term 'heart-mate'. They both imply a deeper level of knowing and which one is better is not clear to the mind. One way to look at it could be similar to a parent walking into a room full of happy children. If your heart and love are well developed, you would be naturally uplifted and it would be easy to squat down and hug any of the children - that is comparable to the quality of your soul's expression. The quality of your heart's expression and feeling is more similar to seeing your own child after a day in the office. The moment you hugged your child, you would feel the same sense of 'upliftment', plus deep feelings of love, connection and belonging together in a profound unity and bliss - this is your heart's recognition of others.

You will find more about this in the relationship and spiritual development sections. Sometimes, in the absence of knowing and experiencing exactly what the heart and what the soul is, people use these terms interchangeably.

The deep form of what you attract is connected to both your heart's condition and its ability to 'see', feel and recognise, similar to the above analogy. It will be clearer and stronger as your heart develops and follows these qualities. You will know and recognise with your own heart. Other parts of you, with your mind/brain as their expression, may blur this clarity and misguide you. It is good to be aware of this dynamic.

To have a heart-to-heart.

Attraction is very often associated with romantic attraction. However, the bigger picture is that attraction governs every aspect of life, at home, at work and socially. With your heart holding the summary of all experiences - as memory - and with your heart also being impacted by any negativities that hold and limit it, the need to improve the heart condition becomes a wonderful opportunity to naturally and easily attract goodness, support and wonderful experiences into our lives.

In summary, your open and radiating heart will make you more approachable, kinder and softer to the widest group of people; including your partner and family members. This softening is quite significant. There will be less competition in all relations, including very close ones. There will be less conflict or resistance in moving forward for a shared greater good or purpose.

Softness is not to be confused with weakness here either. More heart will not make you more passive or more of a pushover. On the contrary, clarity from the heart and a stronger heart supports assertiveness, firmness and strength, but from a place of love and calmness.

Heart-attracting means that people will naturally be more drawn to you, relate more with you and will be willing to spend more time with you. In terms of your work or home project successes, this is important; there is hardly any project we can accomplish better on our own than with the support and help of others.

Equally you will genuinely feel from your heart to help others more, to give more genuine support and care. This is different from fulfilling an obligation to help or do our home or work duties. Whatever you do whole-heartedly will bring joy to your own and others' lives.

The ageless heart

Young at heart.

In your heart, or somewhere deep inside, you feel young or even ageless, whatever your current age is. This has become more and more evident. Even during workshops prior to learning about the heart, I would invite people to feel inside without thinking of their physical age and a range between 16 and 25 would always emerge.

With this came a curiosity to find out what part in us makes people feel youthful or unaffected by age in some way. Earlier explanations talked about the soul, spirit or the part that is eternal, such as a part that is uplifted to heaven or other holy, special places.

Holy, religious or New Age books all talk about this journeying, through life, and beyond, implying an age-less or age-independent existence. Many of them talk about the heart, too, and that it has a special or key function in this age-independent journey.

Practical Heart Tip 6: Feel your inner age

Take time to sit somewhere undisturbed and relax.

If you have already done some of the KHHs, connect to your heart and be in the space, peace and energy of it all for a few minutes, then:

- *Have the intention to let go of your thoughts, including your knowledge of your age; and*
- *Feel how you feel deep inside about your age.*

What is your feeling, sense or awareness about this other, inner age?

This practice may only work for you if you are above the age of 25 or even older. You need to relax and let go and really trust your feeling. You may even know or feel this often in your daily life: you are 40, 50, 60 or older and yet inside you feel youthful and beautiful, with all the potential inside of you.

At the core of your heart is your true essence, your true self, who you truly are, your spirit. This is why some of you can connect to this and feel this way. While your body will age, there is an ageless part deeper within.

What does this imply or mean? In some way this means whatever your problems, challenges or life situation, at the core of your being is infinite beauty, radiant blissful energy, love, youthfulness, freedom and unlimited joy.

These are nice words and yet there are hundreds of people around me now for whom they are not just words or ideas, they are moment-to-moment feelings becoming a permanent stage of being. These are normal people, from all walks of life, professions, age groups, etc. They are clients, friends, family members, colleagues and workshop participants for whom all this is unfolding because of the specialness of the heart.

It is all in your heart

In your light I learn how to love, in your beauty, how to make poems.
You dance inside my chest, where no one sees you. Rumi

You are special; there is a part of you that is so beautiful, wonderful, loveable, childlike and playful, which all stems from your heart.

Be invited into the journey to discover fully the youthful, joyful and loving ability of your own heart. It is a gift beyond measure. The gift is for you and yet, as you change, guided by your heart, others will also feel and become a sweet, wonderful part of your life in ever-growing meaning and bliss. Happiness, joy and love alone have no depth; it is in your heart. You are the one that can decide to uncover this treasure. You need to make the start.

If this sounds too good to be true, too unrealistic, then all our experience attests to it, here at the health centre, the Lotus Centre in Hobart and around the globe in heart meditation groups, related workshops and one-on-one sessions. In only a little over ten years, heart learning as taught by the Padmacahaya Foundation has spread, mostly by word of mouth, and found a home on every continent and in many countries.

References to the fact that the heart is important are almost endless in literature, poetry, songs and religious writings. In the heading above, the 'all' is in brackets for one reason: you may look for other things or qualities in your life or have other experiences or beliefs.

However, regardless of what you believe, regardless of your experience to date, your heart will help you to take the next step, the next transition, to lift the next veil and see beyond.

Your very own heart will help you to reach new heights, penetrate greater depths or be gently moved along when times are difficult. It is part of the ultimate treasure within you, the Holy Grail, the Divine cup, that longs for filling and fulfilment, so that the most joyful dance within can unfold.

In an unwavering way, your heart has been patiently waiting for a welcoming 'hello' from you, to start forming a clear and strong relationship with you, with every part of you, not as a concept or good idea, but in simple, day to day actions towards more heart, more love, more joy, more purpose and blissful sharing.

Summary - the working of your heart

The practical heart learning steps in this section are:

1. Read the full section and, if you feel to, set up and complete the PHT 'Scan and understand reactions, emotions and habits' over a period of one or two weeks. Make a note in your calendar to re-do it in 3, 6 or 12 months, as you work through the book and actively start using your heart.

2. Use the understanding you gained though the above PHT exercise, or through reading the 'role of the mind/brain' section, to be more aware of your thinking patterns and any times when you react with emotion. Resolve, as you commit more to your heart's wellbeing and health, to do less negative thinking and reduce emotional actions or reactions.

3. Use PHT 'Starting to choose the heart' to shift you from emotionally reacting to situations, interactions with others and challenges to a more heart-centred approach. If you remember about the heart and relax more it will help. Emotional reactivity will be reduced, as will the deposits of negativities made in those moments. It is an important step towards a lighter, more joyful and beautiful life.

4. Complete the PHT 'The Heart Check', the book's heart-intelligence/heart-capacity self-assessment tool. You can get a better understanding of yourself now, improve from there and to continue to monitor changes.

5. Use the PHT 'The Friends Check' to get a more complete picture and to invite others into your heart program.

6. The PHT 'Feel your inner age' is one not to take too seriously. The main benefit is that you do yet another thing where you sit down and 'use the feeling' to try to feel and tune in. Whether you get the answer or not in this case is not really important. Much more important is that every time you stop and use your feeling, you also use the heart and strengthen the heart so that all the heart help and heart wonders become more and more available to you.

Chapter V

Practical Heart Understanding

The heart - mind relationship

Being logical is not the only way that the mind/brain can function. What is implied in this slightly controversial statement is that you need to ask yourself:

- Do you recall events where there was an instant 'do this' or 'don't do this' from the heart or your inner part/feeling/intuition and yet it was overruled by the mind/brain and did not work out so well in the end? The mind/brain resisted the message from the heart.
- What can the mind/brain know about something that is only felt, only accessible to your heart, such as happiness or love or feeling at peace?
- Are you aware of situations in your own life where perhaps you felt to do something and then looked in your mind/brain for the reasons, the explanations or justifications?

The practical ways in which the heart and mind/brain work together are fourfold:

- To commit to and support heart learning and all the working of the heart;
- To work in tandem with the heart;
- To be aware of when the mind/brain is resisting something that is a part of you, 'good for you' or will support you and your growth; and
- To also be aware of an over-thinking, overly-smart, over-analysing mind/brain.

The resisting, clever brain

The relationship between the mind/brain and heart is one where the mind/brain is resisting what the heart is gently trying to tell you, or even directly overruling it.

> *The situation is similar to that of a medium-to-large organisation where someone who solely uses the mind/brain has most of the decision-making power. At first glance this looks 'okay', even good. There are, however, uniquely innovative companies, such as The Body Shop or Zappos, who have realised that leadership is also about sharing a vision, combined with strong, unifying values. The outcomes are deeper levels of commitment and reciprocal support from staff and stakeholders for the whole organisation.*

> *If someone is highly-skilled or outstanding in creating an electronic product, in being a specialist nurse or in counselling people in need, should this person automatically be the General Manager, International Operations? No, it could potentially have very negative impacts. What is needed for such a senior role are strategic, visionary and other high level skills.*

> *Internally, as this analogy shows, is a similar dynamic. However, the skilled factory shop floor worker has been put in charge, while it is the heart or inner heart that has the higher level skills and should run the business: you.*

Let this not become too much of a concern. It is good to be aware of these dynamics within. The moment you practice the heart, follow your heart more, go through heart practices such as those in the book or follow the KHHs systematically, a new, refreshing and life-enhancing balance will naturally occur. Then your heart and mind/brain can have the relationship that they ought to have: one of mutual collaboration, of seamlessly working together.

Looking for more feeling

The mind/brain tends to look for feelings, for pleasant and meaningful experiences. Many things that people do to experience these feelings have particular drivers underneath. Often these fall under the following three headings: wanting to be happy, to find love or to give life meaning at a deeper, greater level.

While the brain can look for feeling and may have a lot of approaches, concepts, models and ideas about how to do this, if you do not feel any progress towards more feeling, it won't seem to be working very well.

All positive, pleasant or nice feeling is related to the quality of your heart and its ability to share the feeling with you, your mind/brain, your whole body, and beyond to your interactions with people around you. When this natural relationship is fully activated and functioning you are 'there', you reach these goals of happiness and fulfilment.

Feeling, then rationalising

Are you aware of a situation in your own life where you felt to do something or make changes and then looked in your mind/brain for the explanation for it? Some people are less aware of this existing relationship that allows the heart to direct the mind/brain, yet they follow it anyway. Wonderful! If this is already occurring, then everything in this book will support and balance this relationship in a way that is natural and perfect for you. Allowing more guidance from your heart will also beautify your life and feelings.

How you can help your heart

The previous section III was much about how the heart can help you and everyone. This section will begin to introduce attitudes, actions and approaches that will immensely support your heart's functions and growth.

You may have had experiences when your heart naturally 'raised its head', made itself better known to you and started to function for you. It is very likely that this has happened at some stage.

The core foundations: relax more and smile more

To be relaxed is something enjoyable. We look for it when we stop working, reach the peace of our home or spend some special time away on holiday.

Relax more, more often

It is important to realise that you can relax in daily life too. It will be helpful for your heart to find ways to balance aspects of your life that create tension and pressure. With knowledge, skill and practice, relaxing and de-stressing activities are key foundations for your heart. However, just relaxing more, on its own, will not work the best for your heart yet. There are other factors, and depth of relaxation can have differing levels.

There will also be a time when you feel that a stronger heart and the inner calmness generated by your heart will deepen the relaxation that you experience, while expanding into every moment of your life.

Smile more, more often

A random practice of smiling will directly assist your heart. A gentle introduction to smiling here and there will reduce the tendency to over-think issues, plans or difficulties.

Moments when your heart works, there are feelings of immense, gentle and deep joy that are almost overwhelming. There can be feelings of love spontaneously surfacing, touching you deeply and flowing as pure love, compassion and bliss toward others.

Sometimes when your heart is working for you, there can be experiences that attach to the cleansing or healing process and you follow the releasing of emotion in some way. You are likely to feel parts of the sadness, anger or other emotion that is being cleansed.

Whatever your heart does, whether you see it as positive, negative, good or bad, let go to the deeper and gentler feeling that comes from deep within your heart. If your heart is offering its beauty, love, joy, bliss and peaceful feelings to you and you let go, you will be taken to deeper places and feelings within; there is an endless depth.

Four heart-supporting attitudes and approaches

While your heart is in this removal or cleansing mode, be aware of and practise the following four attitudes and approaches, to best help your heart while your heart is helping you:

1. **Let go**
   Whatever is surfacing, when you use your heart or practise the deeper Heart Strengthening (KHH 6) or the Heart Meditations (KHH 12 or 13), let go! Do not hold any emotion, be natural. Most people at some point have a few tears flowing, or feel a need to cry or giggle or laugh. Whatever happens 'let go' is your best first response, for a few seconds at least.

2. **Be grateful**
   We value or judge in some way that a 'sad' or 'angry' response is worse than giggling or laughter.
   Whatever happens, it is the process of your heart starting to cleanse all that is not supporting you - all that is not joy, calmness, love, understanding and other beautiful feelings.

   Why be grateful? Your heart also likes to feel gratitude and be grateful. You will feel, over time, as you are more grateful for every time that your heart helps you, the special and deep feeling will increase, and cleansing of anything 'not-so-nice' or burdening you is much faster and smoother.

3. **Follow your heart**
   Or more correctly, follow the gentle, pleasant feeling from the deeper parts of your heart.

After an initial letting go, re-focus with your feeling on the heart again. There is a choice to follow the gentle feeling surfacing, flowing from your heart. You may initially follow the reaction, response or cleansing-associated 'feeling' such as sadness, laughing, or giggling. However, in doing this you will stay at the surface or in emotion. The best approach is: let go, to whatever happens while you work with the heart; and then make the choice to follow the deeper feelings you feel within your heart. Making this choice is 'following your heart'.

4. **Practise with a friend**
   The fourth way to help your heart is to get together with a friend and to practise together.
   It is even more helpful if that friend is a step ahead in terms of experience with the heart or s/he has completed exercises from the book, the online program on www.yourheartcanhelp.org or the community-based heart workshops.

These four approaches that YOU can practise and refine will help in both instances: when your heart is taking you to beautiful places within and when the heart is shaking off, cleansing some of the not-so-nice collection of negativities that have accumulated within and around it.

A few more words about practising with a friend. If you are given a gift of $100 or the equivalent in your currency, enough to have one of the best meals in one of the best restaurants in town: what would you enjoy more: having the meal on your own or sharing it with a friend? Most of the time people would say 'sharing with their best friend or partner'. This seems so clear. However, this analogy only partially describes the heart's function and what it wants to facilitate in all aspects of your life. This is feel-able in times when you do heart-practices with a friend.

Every time two or more hearts get together for practice, going through the KHHs or Heart Meditation, the depth of practice and the depth of help from the heart exponentially increase.

Being grateful for not-so-nice sensations or experiences may sound unusual. The key understanding here is that when your heart, with all its intelligence and capacity, is doing something, it is always good, helpful and for a longer-term goal.

If this is causing you difficulty to connect with or understand at this point, then perhaps make a note or leave a bookmark here. Come back to this section in two to four months after you have attended to your heart. You will very likely find another response when you re-visit it.

We know this. Gratitude is something very beautiful in normal day to day interactions. When someone expresses their gratitude for something we have said or done, it invites a part of us to do more, give more, help more. When you are grateful towards others they will be more inclined to help and support you.

In terms of the heart, when you are grateful from the heart, with your heart very naturally including and perceiving a much bigger picture, you could say the 'universe' moves in and helps.

What lies within all this is that, as your emotional/heart-spiritual intelligence and capacity grows you will find that a deep-seated gratitude for all of life grows. With it comes an ability to see or perceive challenges as a form of learning, as a chance to choose the heart. You may see or feel this shift in Jacqueline's sharing.

Jacqueline's Story

Jacqueline is a loving mother with two young children. I attended an alternative health and wellbeing expo and noticed a woman at the other end of the hall. It was much like the heart knew her and we ended up talking.

At that time Jacqueline had already done the first steps in learning about the heart and completed a workshop. Her life's journey then took a very challenging turn when her relationship with her partner, the father of her two children, ended. It was a difficult separation and there were additional and quite serious issues that had been present for some time.

Recently Jacqueline and I met for a heart session. These meetings were not booked therapy sessions, they were more like a meeting between friends. They consisted of a catch-up chat and then of some heart practice together.

One of the reasons for catching up was her feeling of heaviness and she described it as a 'deeply rooted sadness' within her. It was clearly a concern for her.

Once we started the heart practice, it took a mere ten minutes for her to smile freely and to feel the radiant energy of her heart flowing through her whole body.

What seemed like an insurmountable burden, heaviness and emotional medley that she was experiencing started to shift, as soon as two hearts connected for some practice.

The gentle encouragement and reminders to 'let go' as soon as we started some Heart Strengthening worked instantly. Her smile soon became a genuine smile of happiness and joy and when asked after twenty minutes about her problems, she could no longer remember them nor could she feel any burden, heaviness or sadness.

Jacqueline's story is an example of two of the suggested attitudes, actions and approaches: letting go and the benefit of practising with a friend.

The swiftness by which your heart can help you to remove deeply felt heaviness or burdens is surprising and surreal. There is something like an expectation that suffering is normal and should be for an extended time if there has been grief, trauma or other serious events in our life.

To be accurate in relation to the above story, it is necessary to add that Jacqueline already had some familiarity with her heart and had practised intermittently for around two years. It was enough for her heart to be responsive and able to help very quickly in this transition.

Emotions and feelings
... with a heavy heart.

In Section four we took a closer look at emotions. Following the definition of emotion offered: emotions are negative drives such as anger, jealousy, arrogance or sadness.

Feelings, in contrast, are beautiful feelings that give us joy and pleasure and are clearly recognised by others as positive, pleasant, gentle or beautiful.

Following these definitions, emotions are not so helpful, whereas feelings are a positive and integral part of your heart.

One of the key functions of the heart was also discussed: every negative emotion or thought that you have makes a deposit in or around your heart, making it heavier, more burdened and less able help you.

While this may sound a bit heavy, the more the heart is used, the stronger it becomes and the less you will be influenced by these negative drives. Firstly the heart is instantly being purified, secondly any emotional reactivity is lessened, and thirdly all positive feelings become stronger and will eventually dominate.

To offer you the best heart-help, it is important to share a common understanding or 'definition' about what is emotion and what is feeling. The aim of this book is to make heart learning simple, easy and accessible.

All of this is to simplify heart practice and heart learning, to make it easy for the mind/brain to have clarity, to be able to focus on the heart.

Emotions can vary from subtle negative drives to strong experiences that take over or at times override the control and reasoning of the mind/brain. Emotions feel heavy for you and for others who are exposed to it. When held or more so when expressed they tend to burden or damage relations.

Looking at this list of possible emotion in the earlier section IV (Figure 3), you may say that some of them are okay or good to have; you may disagree with this list or say that they aren't negative. This is normal and even good. Whatever your opinion, belief or experience, ultimately you have the opportunity to let your heart work and remove, cleanse, purify or bring more to the surface whatever your heart knows is not supporting you. It is between you and your heart.

In addition you will begin to recognise, as your heart becomes lighter and clearer, what emotions are, what some of your more typical emotions are and how in fact they burden you, your heart and others close to you.

What exactly do emotions do? Emotions carry a negative energy. You can feel this, either when you go through a phase of having one of them, or when someone else is in the emotion.

The emotions you hold or experience, expressed or not, generate negative deposits that:

- Burden your heart; and
- Are likely to also burden or hurt others.

With a stronger heart there is less energy, disposition or tendency of us hurting others during times when emotions surface or take over.

In terms of the condition of your own heart and your growth with your heart, it is solely the emotions you experience that will cause negative, heart-limiting burdens.

For example, when someone is angry around you or towards you and in your heart is only understanding and care, as true and real heart-feelings, then there is no burdening of your heart. There is more clarity and even ability to assist that person, now, or after some cooling down time.

Repetitive emotions, whether expressed or not, in the same way as negative thoughts, will make deposits within or around your heart, similar to when you sneeze or cough and particles are thrown in a particular direction. These particles are physical even though they are invisible to the eye.

Negativities generated by emotions or thoughts are invisible too. However, they are non-physical. They have a level of reality, as they burden the heart either instantly or progressively and limit any positive feelings coming from the heart.

Emotions can have varying degrees of strength. They can be subtle in how they have become part of our normal daily life, or they can be powerful and overwhelming. A friend told a simple story from times when the family sat around the dinner table:

> *I remember as a child and teenager sitting at the lunch and dinner table and I would feel an irritation rising between my Mum and Dad. It was shown in how they interacted and subtle expressions on their faces.*

> *For example, Mum would blow her nose and it was perceived as being too loud or too often. Dad would make a regular suppressed-sounding coughing sound. This was all very subtle. It was also not spoken about. Often the only ways in which it was expressed was in facial movements of disapproval. What was clearly there, however, was the emotion of 'irritation' from both of them. I remember it was disturbing and we felt uncomfortable; something was not right, flowing or 'normal'.*

Looking at this simple example one may say, yes, but it is annoying, or what is 'normal'?

Most aspects in life can be viewed as something flowing, something that is able to change, be fluid or dynamic. Interactions and feelings between people at home can flow into an increasingly beautiful, attentive and loving direction or the other way. This is the help that the heart offers and it will always make these dynamics flow in a positive direction.

A child that does not get what s/he wants will often have a strong emotional reaction and is very likely to show it instantly. As grown-ups we become more sophisticated. In either case, the burdening of the heart is happening, whether these emotions are expressed or not. To be on a journey of living life with a more open heart, strengthening our heart ability more, we need to realise and remember that and, more importantly, make the adjustments needed for 'more' heart.

From the perspective of you starting to take more care of your heart, when someone else or their behaviours are annoying you, disregard whether it is directed toward you or not. Their actions or behaviours are much less important than your response or reaction.

> *In the above situation, the irritation and the reaction to the irritation, that is, following or staying in the emotion, can become a habit for days, weeks and years. It is in the emotional reaction to external life events where the burdening of the heart occurs, bit by bit.*

While the burdens for the heart may not be big each time, if they are constant, regular and happen over a long time they will make the heart very heavy. Depending on responses and reactions to a wide range of events in life, this burdening can happen over a shorter period or quite a long time. It has the potential to take you to a point where you have closed your heart.

It is important to know this and to start to be aware of this. One thing people have said in the past:

> *What if I had a very difficult childhood, with a lot of negative events, large amounts of emotional interactions and also emotional reactions and responses?*

In a situation such as this, it is very likely the heart is already quite burdened at a young age, for example as a teenager or young adult. However, remember the heart is a new ingredient here, a very resourceful and strong one. Whatever the burdens, whatever the experiences, even traumas, they are no match for the capabilities of your heart. You may need to pay more attention to your heart more regularly or be more diligent in practising the KHHs or other suggested practices if you have experienced these kinds of difficulties.

For people new to the heart and its functioning, this may sound strange or very unusual. While the events that led to the burdening of the heart may not have been pleasant at all, the journey of unburdening it is in fact very enjoyable, assuring and beautiful.

This may not sound logical or normal. It is and will become your experience as you follow your heart and the exercises. As it starts to become your experience then validation occurs. It will become your experience and it will be logical from both the perspective of your mind/brain and heart.

Negative thoughts, feelings and your heart

> *If instead of a gem, or even a flower, we should cast the gift of a loving thought into the heart of a friend,*
> *that would be giving as the angels give. George MacDonald*

In a very similar way to emotions, negative thoughts also generate negativities and burdens within your heart.

Every moment in life then becomes a moment where you can cast the gift of a kind, loving or positive thought, not only into the heart of a friend but into your own, too.

There are many books and resources on positive thinking. In relation to the heart, your positive thinking will have an impact in the following ways:

Figure 5: Positive thinking versus positive heart attitude

| | What happens ... | |
	In the moment	Long-term
Positive thinking	*Negativities are not placed in your heart* *Your heart is not burdened*	*Positive, life-enhancing feelings remain level*
Positive heart attitude	*Use of your heart in reality and action* *Help from your heart in the form of positive radiance, guidance and heart-to-heart connection ability* *Your heart is continuously unburdened.*	*Positive, life-enhancing feelings continuously deepen and improve.*

You can see positive thinking in principle is good. The only issue is that most people will at some point during a day or week have negative thoughts which in turn will burden the heart. This will mean that despite best possible positive thinking efforts you are likely to go backwards in some way (line (b) in the following figure).

Further to what this chart shows is the fact that any amount of positive thinking will not improve your heart's condition and your desire to enlighten your life, feel more beautiful, happier, lighter, freer, more attentive and loving to others and in love with life.

Positive thinking is important and to some extent will support the heart, in the same way as negative thinking will burden it. However, an over-emphasis on positive thinking will not necessarily improve your heart condition or the support from your heart. It is when your actual heart capacity is combined with positive thinking that a happy life and life purpose will be realised.

Figure 6: Positive thinking - positive impact - plateaux - over-thinking

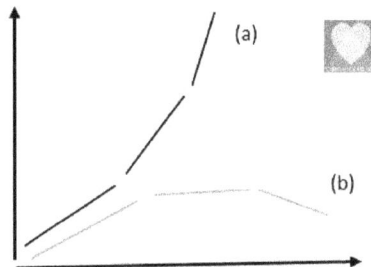

Line (a) indicates that positive thinking or more focus on positive thoughts can and will improve your heart and your life. Positive thinking alone however, the second line (b), will not have the ability to remove a disposition to react with emotions or negative thoughts or to have negative thoughts at set intervals; naturally you will reach a plateau.

If you over-emphasise positive thinking you will strengthen your mind/brain to the detriment of your heart. You are more likely to reach a plateaux (part 2 of line (b)) and even go backwards in how you feel overall in daily life (part 3 of line (b)).

Observe the thinking

From the perspective of the heart, however, it is good to observe your thinking habits. It is important, as you really do not want to burden your heart and reduce your ability to feel, whether you practise your heart with intent and clarity or not.

You also do not want to burden your heart in unnecessary ways once you start to use the very functions and natural abilities of your heart to make improvements.

Of course, if there is a tendency to have negative thoughts and emotional reactions or responses in day to day life, you will not change overnight, and not for some time to come.

It is important to be patient, kind and loving towards yourself here. Despite the wonderful, direct and often immediate help that your heart offers, changes of habits or patterns will take some time.

Emotions versus feelings - the role of the heart

When you start to feel and use the heart more, three things tend to happen in relation to stored emotions. This includes any emotions and their related burdens and negativities in your heart:

- Some of our stored emotions come to the surface;
- The majority of whatever is surfacing will be instantly cleansed; and
- Depending on your nature of letting go, or wanting to watch the process - both limiting the heart's nature to do a complete and instant job - there will be some holding back and incomplete cleansing.

The heart will, often within seconds, cleanse and remove some of the burdens around the heart, inside the heart and even deeper within the heart, including root causes that trigger us to react with emotions rather than in a lighter way: with compassion, understanding and love, or with no reaction.

To have no reaction is already very helpful for you and others. Every time you react with emotion or any form of negativity - expressed or not - you will burden your heart. If the reaction is with emotion or negativity, and this is expressed in your interaction with others, even more burdening occurs. You have perhaps experienced these negative impacts on family or work relations: trust is reduced and hurt feelings lead to distance.

Letting emotions help - not supressing emotions

When some of our stored emotions come to the surface, we may experience a fraction of what has been stored. Embrace this process as best as you can. Remember, in the above section we talk about only 2-5% of the responses and feelings from the heart possibly being experienced as challenging.

When emotions surface, even a comparatively small amount, for some people this is a challenge. Here are two scenarios and positive heart approaches:

'I do not want to supress my emotions' is something people often state or share. In letting your heart help you more there is only a small and subtle change to expressing emotions needed: let go of whatever emotion surfaces and let it find expression. Instead of following that emotion, shift attention to your heart and begin to focus on the heart. The heart's help will take over.

'This is unpleasant. My life is okay as it is; I prefer not to face or experience any (negative) emotion as part of the heart's cleansing, healing process.' The storage of burdens in your heart will impact primarily on your life, reducing the positive feelings you can have, every moment. Whatever is in each person's heart is directly related to behaviours, attitudes and the overall emotional past.

Even if you were to go and see a counsellor, psychiatrist or a life coach you would have to unravel, unpack and ultimately make all the changes. The same as in other modalities, whatever change your heart is experiencing and helping you with, will create wonders for others around you, at home, at work and socially.

Every health problem you have or do not yet have is also connected to the burdens or dark-spots in your heart. As the heart is opening and cleansing itself, current or future health issues are positively impacted on. Experiencing a small amount of what is actually cleansed will only happen on rare occasions. The more you relax, smile freely and feel the deeper heart-feelings, any cleansing experience will be minimal.

In an interesting way, and with more heart awareness, emotions can function as a positive in your life. Every time you still have some form of emotion or emotional experience you can let your heart help, cleansing the deposits from the past relating to this emotion along with the deeper-seated root causes.

This refers to an emotion surfacing within you, not triggered by others or when others do something and your reaction or response is with emotion. It is not uncommon that emotions are triggered more easily, if someone is 'in emotion' when interacting with us. The key, however, is to recognise when there is emotion in yourself, not the other, and to begin choosing not to follow it. A stronger, purer heart will help with this.

In terms of what you experience as part of the heart's clearing or cleansing process: yes, it will only ever be the 2-5% of what is being cleansed in total. For now, this is written here to set the scene. Later, when your heart is at a deeper level of functioning, you will easily be able to feel (1) what is being cleansed and (2) what you experience of this cleansing. This relationship will be shown to you by your heart. Your heart knows, in the same way as you know how much is '1' and how much is '9'. We don't need to argue or discuss any of the value of these two numbers. Your heart will show you this, my heart will show me this and we are in sync. In fact, if you have started to use your heart more and experienced cleansing, you may feel it now. Your heart will only ever show you things as a feeling.

What is important to note, however, is that whenever you experience this 2-5% of what is being cleansed, you will experience emotion at some level. It is really important to be aware of this and to make the transition now to choosing the heart and, after a few seconds of realising and feeling this emotion, to reconnect with the feelings from the heart as opposed to the emotion.

The best is to continually let the heart work, so that it can do the best for you and expand into the parts of your life that need attention and help. When you experience cleansing or any related emotion this will be more obvious and can appear out of proportion.

Every time we have and follow a negative thought or emotion we will burden and close our heart more. This applies to the times also when you practice your heart and when, during this practice, emotions surfaces.

Heightened heart awareness will make it clearer and clearer that every emotion adds to the heart's burdens and heaviness. This makes sense to the heart and to the mind/brain of who we are. Every minute you attend to the heart the experience will be, as the minutes add up, that you will gradually and consistently become lighter, and feel better and happier.

The more you start to feel all this it will become your experience, your insight and your understanding. Until then, try, give it some credit and enjoy this light way of personal growth, healing and development.

Once you learn and practise to follow the heart in this way, the full capacity of the heart will be developed every time you do so. Your heart will grow and open more, and more of it will be available for you.

Your Heart's Emotional Rescue Guide

Whilst learning to let your heart help you the best, the following is the best approach for working with your heart, both when emotions surface and when they are not present.

Practical Heart Tip 7: Emotional rescue guide *

This is your emotional rescue guide:

Realise an emotion is surfacing - as soon as the emotion surfaces, notice it, be aware of it (almost as when you see a common bird fly past your window: realise it, notice it, let it fly on. You would not get involved in the bird's flight, right?). Also realise now that you have another tool, a new approach. Before, you reacted or respond the 'normal' or old way, including being busy with the emotion, INSTEAD relax, smile, feel the heart and the BEST IS to use the heart more actively as described in, for example, KHHs 2 and 6.

Let go - means to have an attitude or approach of 'letting go'. It means not holding the emotional response or following it. For example, if some sadness surfaces, let the tears flow for a few seconds only, then immediately remember and focus more on the heart, similar to letting the bird fly on.

Remember the heart is always here, helping - just remembering will make the heart listen, respond and help in small ways. Similar to running a 100m race with only one leg, we use only the mind or brain or emotional response capacity. Use the other part of you: the heart!! It will make a significant difference to your whole life in a comparatively short time. After all, this is natural. The heart's nature is to do this, as good as, or even better than any other part of you.

Relax - be aware of any tension in your body, let go of any tension or holding, breathe naturally, freely. When your body is relaxed then your mind/brain can also be less active which means that your heart can be freer to do its job.

Smile - everyone loves a smile. If the person is close to your heart, you may even melt within. In the same way, your heart is strengthened and burdens melt away - it is part of the key function of the heart to work with the smile. This will be new to many. For example: sadness and tears come up, and you want me to smile? It is possible. You can have tears streaming down and still have some form of smile at the same time.

Feel your heart or heart area - use your feeling to be where your heart is and in the moments when something is happening to you, feel the heart 'connect' and be there with your feeling. If you can, stay there connected to your heart for a bit and whatever thought, emotion or action that the situation demands - let it be from your heart. Do not be busy trying to work out what is happening: just 'be there', be where the heart is. For that time, be a heart. Over time the feelings will become clearer and more refined.

Keep going - several parts of you may want to stop, to get a tissue, resolve some physical discomfort or respond to some compulsion. If possible, keep going for a few minutes with the heart focus/feeling or the KHH. If you have time, do the Heart Meditation for an even deeper opening and cleanse.

The more quality that you can bring to your heart practice, the quicker you will have a result and begin to feel more. As indicated above, similar to the Heart Strengthening or the KHHs previously mentioned, it is even better to follow the guidelines and then afterwards spend some quality time smiling to your heart, staying within and connected to your heart.

In the short term, at any moment, your mind/brain can stop action, reaction or emotion from growing and becoming more overpowering. This is one of the important functions of the mind/brain. It is your heart that can cleanse, heal and remove the disposition to be in that emotion. In the medium to longer term this is very significant and helpful for your heart and whole life.

Changes in how you feel, changes in heart strength and changes in how you respond will be the fastest if you do this each time an emotion surfaces. Be patient, too, depending on the depth of emotion, the depth of hurt that occurred, or the depth of trauma; it may take some time. When the heart is involved the end result will be the same: a complete cleanse and deep feelings of freedom and joy.

The heart is the direct route, the freeway or the short cut to any cleansing, clearing or healing.

Your heart is starting to work

The moment you bring your attention to your heart, it will start to work for your wellbeing and growth. In summary, and to keep it simple, when we have emotions there are two choices:

- To follow the emotion; or
- To follow the gentle, pleasant feeling from the heart, to connect to the heart and not to follow the emotion.

A nice, gentle or pleasant feeling will instantly be triggered and enlarged when you follow the above steps. It may be small, subtle and less strong than the emotions - let this nice feeling help you to relax and smile even more.

Your heart's expanding radiation carries within it a natural and immensely deep healing ability. It will remove negativities and blockages and free the positive feelings associated with the heart. These are feelings that we long for more, feelings that have often been locked away, buried under rubble or blocked by excessive use of our mind/brain energy.

It also means that when you are not following the emotion there is no negative reaction or response that is either burdening your heart or negatively impacting on a relationship that you have. This is an important choice to recognise and, ideally, to use more.

Use the above steps, even if you don't feel anything, even if you don't feel your heart. This is where the mind/brain can be very helpful, in making new choices and reminding you to choose the heart over following the emotion.

Learning about the heart, letting the heart help you towards a profoundly joyful and wonderful life, does not mean that you supress what is within, your emotions or feelings that surface. When emotions surface, try the heart approach and experience how quickly you can move through a period of sadness, disappointment, feeling hurt, being angry or any situation where negative emotions or thoughts surface in you.

Initial phases of heart help

Your heart ability is very likely to follow a similar pattern as shown above. The overall development and growth of your heart capacity will vary, as we have all had a different heart-past.

Overall, however, as you progress through the practical exercises in this book, you will progress in the following ways:

Figure 7: The growth of the beautiful feelings and help from the heart

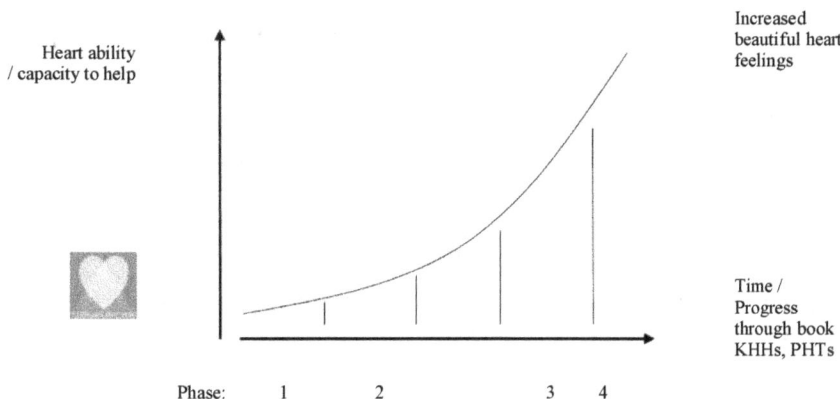

Let us have a closer look at the common four phases as the help from the heart unfolds:

Phase 1: Wondering and Doubting

You may or may not be aware of the constant availability and detailed functions of the heart. Either the heart is naturally used, yet not with clear intention or awareness; or it is not used in an active, direct and progressive way.

During the first phase most people start to feel the pleasant feelings of the heart irregularly. Naturally the mind/brain wonders about it all. The heart's ability to clearly help is still limited and though noticeable, the feelings from the heart are subtle. Doubt is normal during this phase. There can also be times when the wonderful heart feelings break through and are clearly present or discernible.

Phase 2: Response, Lightness and Up/Down

You start to attend to your heart and use the KHHs and PHTs from the book, including doing regular Heart Strengthening, or other heart exercises. Your heart begins to respond. The feelings from the heart are clearer and stronger, and have the ability to stay with you longer, even after you have finished your practices.

In situations where you use your heart as a new or additional choice, your heart is starting to help you and work for you. The first feelings after a heart session are often of lightness and relief. Some people feel this clearly, some a little, and some are not so sure or don't feel anything. You can be up and down in terms of trust. 'Is this working' and 'can I do it' are still normal thoughts here. While the heart's ability to help is still limited at this point, with regular practice it is not uncommon to feel lightness, calmness and bubbling joy.

Phase 3: Clarity and Joy

You are working with the heart practices and the KHHs and some of the PHTs and you regularly, or several times daily, attend to your heart. At times your heart is making the important shift from being active and present to radiating, particularly when you attend to your heart and your practice has good quality. Others start to notice your radiance and the positive changes in you.

The connection between using your heart and how you feel on a daily basis is very clear to you. There are lapses and times where you forget to practise with or use the heart.

You start to feel joyful with some clarity now. The feeling is also more burden-free and light. There is a growing sense of calm, and loving connectedness more frequently, with more people.

Phase 4: Connection, Deep Peace and Bliss

Life with your heart is becoming natural; the KHHs, PHTs and other heart-supporting practices have become part of your daily and weekly routine. Your heart is naturally shifting from being inactive in the morning when you get up, to active, to very active and radiating. Others clearly notice your radiance and the positive changes in you, and comment on them.

Forgetting the heart

Lapses, when you forget about your heart or do not practise at least something 'heartful' during the day, are rare. Even when you forget to be in the heart for a while, and get swept away by life's events, which is normal, the relative strength of your heart is helping you to reconnect. You feel connected to others, to the Divine, to the Being of your prayers or meditations in new ways. A deep peace is expanding through your heart, feeling, mind and all of you. Feelings of gentle, blissful joyfulness, lightness and inner calm are deepening, and the love of others is deepening and expanding in ever-widening circles.

You may notice that the heart progress curve is exponentially rising. Contrary to many things in life, the growth of your heart ability, when you attend to it, is exponentially fast and steep. There will be dents in the curve too, where you relapse, go back to old habits or follow emotion for some time. There may also be a time when your life demands the mind/brain to be comparatively stronger for a period at the expense of the heart.

Let this be of no concern to you. The heart is always present and always ready to re-emerge.

Over time a stronger heart will improve and beautify your emotional life immensely, and strengthen the function and creativity of your thinking processes, too.

Three layers of feeling from the heart

Working and enjoying with the heart involves the two simplified definitions about emotions and feelings. Look at the nature of feelings: what they are, the range of feelings you are likely to experience and how the depth of feeling is likely to unfold.

At the first layer of experiencing, feelings from the heart are the pleasant, assuring feelings listed below. At the second and the third layer of heart expansion and heart learning, feelings can also be the guidance that occurs through your heart's ability to feel a bigger picture, a deeper truth.

The second and third layers belong together. You may feel more of (II) or more of (III) at any point in time; or you feel, as your heart opens more, that the layers in fact overlap.

Figure 8: The three layers of heart-feeling

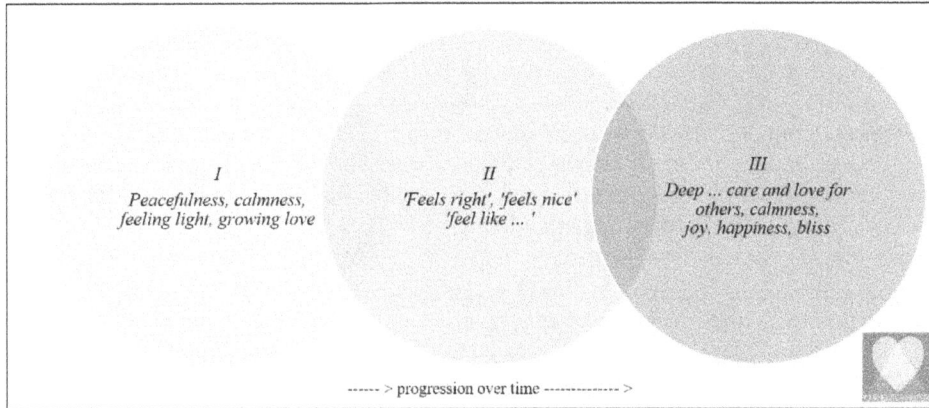

The chart also shows a natural progression that will occur over time. Your heart will gently take you from the first feelings of calm centredness (I) towards greater clarity of being guided by the heart-feeling (II), and towards deepening feelings of deep calmness, bliss and love for self and others (III).

Feelings are ...

A heart bursting with joy.

What are these feelings from our hearts? It has been commonly known through the ages that feelings from the heart come from a deeper place within and make us feel wonderful, beautiful and whatever is associated with this.

In heart teaching and heart learning, clients/students/workshop participants clearly experience that the core of pleasant feelings, contrary to 'emotions', is connected to the heart's natural function and ability, and that these feelings come from the heart.

The core feelings that your heart will generate and deepen will always be calmness, joyfulness and growing compassion, love and care for self and others.

Many of us strive for something in life, whether it is success at a personal, family or work level, or something that we hope to achieve or grow towards. Looking at any goal or deep wish in life, it is often connected to the feelings of happiness, love and inner peace that come as a result.

Alternative ways - the three 'Ws'

The heart naturally facilitates a love-filled, happy and fulfilled life. The dilemma is that often people hope that this can be achieved though the 3 'Ws':

- Work ... hard work or effort
- Wants ... our own knowing what we want
- Will .... our own will power or perseverance.

What's the dilemma? Feeling is feeling; why would any positive, life-enhancing feelings be related to any of the 3 Ws? Looking at it in this way, it is not logical to work at something or to want something a lot, or to use a lot of your will to get it.

In starting to learn to let your heart help you, the 3 Ws play a role and can help. They are, however, not the only solution to getting you there, and in fact they can reduce heart progress and negatively impact on the growth of the wonderful feelings and help from your heart.

Heart attitude

For any pleasant feeling to be present or to fully unfold, you will need to work on your heart, as opposed to any mental ideas, concepts, thoughts or beliefs. It is deeper understanding around heart attitude and an improved heart attitude that will support the heart and all that the heart means.

Willingness, commitment and a little letting go

Heart attitude is the attitude that will support you and your heart the best. The beginning of it is to be willing to try, to attend to the heart and to learn to follow it, to care for it and in turn to allow its care for you to unfold. It is then further finding the commitment to integrate the heart into your life, and to make space for some practice until you are more naturally connected to your heart again.

After that, be guided by the greater intelligence of your heart, and not by want or will or solely by good ideas or hopes.

The guidance from your heart will help. In fact, guidance may be very important. There is nothing more challenging than spending days, weeks, months or years trying to achieve or obtain something and then realising that it is not what 'your heart desired'.

There are, perhaps, examples of this around you, or some of your own life experience can help to illustrate this. Perhaps there has been hard work and a strong want or desire to obtain a nice physical item (house, car or special clothing) or an event (a holiday, a job, a special celebration, an engagement or a wedding) and at one level of your being you realise that the feeling of joy, happiness, peace or fulfilment is diminishing, even disappearing completely.

Anything external that does not resonate or connect to your heart and the deeper levels of feeling within, will not create lasting feelings, will not offer a growing heart feeling that satisfies a deep longing inside you.

That feeling from the heart will guide you. A stronger, lighter and expansive heart-feeling guides you towards what will help or support you. Heart-feelings occur all the time with or without mind/brain or conscious awareness that it is happening. With more familiarity, awareness will develop around this guidance and how it can be consciously used.

The range of feeling from the heart

In learning about the heart, when we talk about feelings, we refer to the pleasant feelings that you will increasingly feel as your heart gets stronger and opens more. These feelings stem from the heart, flow through it, and are facilitated by it.

The only way that you can have more of these pleasant feelings is by attending to your heart's ability to:

- Facilitate them for you;
- Naturally connect you to them; and
- Grow them to infinite depths of feeling by growing your heart.

These extended core feelings that you heart will generate and promote are:

- Calmness
- Joyfulness
- Peacefulness
- Lightness
- Freedom
- Feeling unburdened
- Happiness
- Care for self and others
- Love for self and others
- Connectedness - with others, close ones, colleagues, Divine, God, the universe, nature
- Gratefulness
- Contentment
- Being carefree
- Centredness, being grounded
- Feeling nurtured
- Feeling held, secure, protected
- Feeling at one, whole

These are the feelings from your heart, your centre of feeling. Everything gentle, beautiful or somewhat positive is a feeling from your heart, heart-related, heart-connected or heart-facilitated.

Do not look for any of these feelings as you practice or follow the natural progression of the KHHs. The heart will naturally generate and deepen them. 'Looking for' is closely related to your mind/brain's doing and will limit the natural ability of your heart to generate these feelings.

As you start to use and experience your heart more, it is natural that you will want to be within these beautiful and comforting feelings more. Your heart journey and heart opening will develop the best and the easiest when you follow the heart's natural support mechanisms:

- Relax and smile; and
- Enjoy whatever pleasant feelings you feel.

The heart helps everyone

Something about the heart and heart learning is that you are not required to be a certain character type, have certain IQ or intelligence scores, be of any particular socio-economic background or have particular prior experiences. Everyone can start immediately to have the help from their heart. Everyone can use the simplicity of the heart steps and heart strengthening techniques to personally grow, learn and have the full range of benefits available.

The simplicity of it all may appear too simple for some. The lack of familiarity may not make sense to others, or there may be a degree of wanting to know more, or be more in control. Here are some early practical tips.

Practical Heart Tip 8: Commit to your heart *

Just being relaxed and smiling will not be natural to everyone. However, as you commit to feeling your heart more and to practising, it will begin to feel more natural and the full capacity of your heart can unfold.

In terms of all your 'heart-work':

- *Give it some time and be patient. Do not work through the book or the practices in too serious a way; and*

- *Try to find an approach within you that combines commitment with lightness; not being too driven or focussed on a result.*

This will look different for everyone. It is good, however, to be aware of the qualities or attitudes that support heart opening, heart learning and the full development of your heart: one of them is to attend to it, to give it time and to commit to it.

When you share with others, form a small group or practice with your partner, family or loved ones. Many of the groups can be run in this way:

In group and one-on-one situations, we joke a lot, make light of things and situations where it is okay to do so. Lightness, smiling, and having a laugh helps our heart immensely. People who are naturally more like this tend to have a stronger, lighter heart. If this is not you, just practice a bit more, be a bit more dedicated - to your own heart learning and ability - and you will soon feel these feelings more every day.

It is not necessary to have a group to learn about the heart and to start using it more. A group can offer support, informal coaching and peer encouragement, which is helpful. A 'group' can be you and someone near or dear to you.

If you are from a similar cultural background to me, initially you may not like this approach very much. After more than eleven years of committed heart learning, now with a big grin on my face, I recall how eager and serious I was in learning how to meditate with the use of the heart. There was a tendency to be a serious German and at times this even made me annoyed or upset when people in workshops were laughing too much or not taking it seriously enough. I am so glad to have unlearned much of that.

What is additionally very logical, from the perspective of the heart and mind/brain, is the longing deep within to be blissfully and peacefully happy or, as a spiritual seeker, to enter the heights of deep 'anandam': cosmic bliss or ecstasy, neither of which are serious qualities. ☺

Practical Heart Tip 9: Be light *

When attending to your heart just be light, that is, in terms of your attitude. It is good to relax and then to smile and be light and joyful. For the time of your practice, stay in this lighter mood. Smile freely when possible!

Over time, your heart will inspire more lightness and even happiness. The difference between being light by intention - and with some of your effort - compared to being light naturally, generated through the heart, will become clearer.

Of course you do not want to pretend, to be fake or false. Lightness, to the extent that you can naturally be light, will support your heart. It allows the heart to be freer and less controlled by the learned activities of the mind/brain or by emotions that float around and have a hold on the heart.

Give the approach of being light and joyful a shot - it works and I encourage you to try. For the mind/brain and from the experience and background of most people, this is a paradox. If you are going through a challenge, working through issues and processing not-so-nice experiences or even traumas from the past, then this approach may be a challenge, and even bring up some resistance. If this is so, then take it easy.

If you find the suggestion to be intentionally a bit lighter or even to be more joyful than a normal challenge, then perhaps a compromise could be to be more serious during your routine life, and when you practise the KHHs or PHTs, be a little lighter.

The good thing about the heart is, that even if you feel, or your emotions are a bit denser or heavier, the heart will break through all, following some commitment on your part.

Gradual unfolding of the beautiful feelings from the heart
A heart full of joy.

The above listed beautiful, positive feelings will not be happening all at the same time. The gradual unfolding of the these feelings, related to the heart's help, can be for several reasons:

- Most people, whether aware of it or not, have used the mind/brain more than the heart;
- The collection and burdens accumulated around and within the heart, limiting its ability, will take some time to be changed: broken up, dissolved, altered or removed;
- While the beautiful or special feelings are all supported and triggered by the heart, we have a tendency to hold the heart. It will take time:
    - Until your heart is strong enough for the feelings to clearly shine through; and
    - Until a more natural letting go will support the heart opening.

If the feelings are not clear, tune in and feel how light you felt before and how light you feel after a heart session.

For this gradual unfolding to happen faster and more smoothly, the two qualities of 'letting go' and 'trusting the heart' can help significantly.

Let go
Are you crazy, let go.
Subtitle line in a foreign movie watch on a plane

The heart, of course, is always present, and as you are more aware of how it works, and use an initial 'letting go' attitude, pleasant feelings from your heart will gradually unfold.

'Letting go' is more than just an initial 'letting go' when you sit down and start to practise. The more complete approach is to have a continuous attitude of letting go every time your heart works. To let go is quite important for any heart work and for steady progress. There are three aspects that can be highlighted to illustrate this:

- 'Letting go' as an initial attitude, mindset and heart-set;
- An attitude of 'letting go' all the time during any heart practice, KHH or in daily life, when your heart is active and clearly present; and
- 'Letting go' of control where it is helpful - control we tend to hold over ourselves, others or over our heart.

To refine the ability to 'let go' is very important, in terms of heart learning, in our broader life.

You know that events from the past that are still bothering you or burdening you, were in the past. You perhaps also have quite clearly experienced that any amount of good advice 'just let it go' or any amount of reassuring words e.g. 'it was in the past, it is over now', or 'it was at work, you are at home now', do not do the job. The bother, the burden, remains.

You also know from past situations that there are moments when you have an issue, grudge or resentment with someone and yet you do not want to feel it, have it or hold it any more. Perhaps you like or love that person, or you just know/feel it is not helpful 'right now'. Despite all that wanting, it is still hard to let it go.

It is in the heart's working that 'letting go' occurs. It is when this attitude and approach becomes more natural, that the relief, the releasing of burdens, heaviness and everything-not-joy is taking place.

The opposite of 'letting go' is 'control'. You may have experienced someone telling you what to do, intending to control you, push their agenda or wishes onto you. It does not feel gentle, pleasant, beautiful, and when or if you are aware of it, there is a contraction, a withdrawing feeling in the other person, or in you.

In the same way, when you want the heart to do what you hope or what you 'think' is right for the heart, then there is some degree of holding or controlling the heart. It is normal, as the mind/brain likes to think it is pretty 'cool', clever, or even wise.

> **Practical Heart Tip 10: Let go I - 'just let go' ***
>
> *During any of your direct heart practices, like Heart Strengthening (KHHs 2 and 6), as you are aware of any tendency or habit of 'control', of controlling your heart, just 'let go'.*
>
> *Just 'let go' as a thought, or as an intention, will support the letting go at the level of the heart.*

This sounds simple. Yet, your attention to your heart, all your heart's working, will happen at least a little better than you let go before this short intervention. The moment you do so, have this intention, your heart and your higher self will assist and the natural letting go, programmed within, can kick in. The knowledge and intelligence in your heart knows how to let itself go/how to let go.

This natural 'letting go' cannot be forced. You can be aware of it, understand that it helps the heart, and simply have the attitude 'to let go' more freely, more fully. Then trust that it will happen in the way the heart knows. Every small amount of help from your heart will be significant.

Let your heart be free anytime you feel it, anytime you practise; having an attitude of just enjoying the feelings - however subtle they may be initially - will benefit you and your heart the most.

Give your heart and your heart practices time. Everyone's heart longs to be free. In this way, letting go a little more when practising the heart is moving in this direction.

It is also a freedom from us, the control that the mind/brain has had over the heart. It is in that freedom of heart, where infinite depths of joy, love and inner calm can be found, ultimately in ways and qualities so deep that they stay, no matter what the outside world presents.

It is good to let this quality of 'letting go' enter the mindset and ultimately become a 'heart-set' too. This will naturally happen. Whatever level of 'letting go' you are happy or comfortable with will be perfect. Your 'letting go' can be a little more relaxation, a slightly freer smile, or it can be a freer surrendering to the heart's capability and offering. Whatever letting go it is, the heart will appreciate it greatly.

Trusting your heart

In the small matters trust the mind,
in the large ones the heart.
Sigmund Freud'

Trusting your heart is a feeling. The more you use your heart and follow the examples and descriptions of how the heart is guiding and helping you, this trust will grow.

The key is for you to take the steps to be more committed to your heart in the first place, and to work with your heart more. The moment you pick up this book and start reading, you have already shown trust in your heart.

The more you progress through the book and its practices, growing degrees of trust will naturally develop. There is also nothing to be done to facilitate this: no affirmations or visualisations. It is when you notice your own personal experiences of your heart helping you, and gradually changing how you feel in situations or in daily life, that trust deepens and one day you will notice that it has deepened immensely.

The relationship with your heart is not dissimilar to the relationship that you have with a close friend or colleague. Trust grows as you create good experiences that nurture the friendship and the trust you feel within it.

The depth of feeling - the depth of your heart

The heart is deeper than any ocean.

The depth of an ocean can be imagined as a deep place and a place to explore. The nature of your heart means that almost all these positive feelings listed above, in particular the heart's core feelings, can have an incredible depth. However, your reaction, when you read or hear about comparing the heart to an ocean, may not be completely positive.

Everything physical, like an ocean or sea, can be 'good', enjoyable and pleasant, for example during a plunge on a hot summer day. Yet, it can also have deep, dark and dangerous parts within it for example, icy cold water or potentially harmful animals defending their territory.

The non-physical heart, on the contrary, will only offer you wonderful feelings and every time it is used it will open, expand, and offer you more of the beauty, joy and bliss of these expanding wonderful feelings.

In terms of the heart's ability to feel deeper your questions may be:

- How deep and unperturbable can someone's calmness or peacefulness be?
- How sweet and blissful can joy or happiness become?
- How much care or love can you have for one person or a growing number of people around you?

It is very difficult to measure these non-tangible, non-physical qualities. With modern technology the depth of an ocean can be measured, or at least estimated with some accuracy.

Often people share that they want to feel as light or as joyful as they felt when they were a particular age, or in particular circumstances. This is a good goal to have.

It is natural, especially for our mind/brain to want to find a reference or look for something it knows or has experienced before. However, the heart's way is outside and beyond these points of reference and knowing.

> *The heart's nature is not to look for any feelings, including feelings you once knew. It wants to take you to levels way beyond any qualities of past experiences.*

In fact, the depth and vastness of your heart is much deeper than any ocean and in some way infinite, which also means that the depth and exquisiteness of all feelings generated through your heart have an infinite quality to them.

Stories and experiences shared throughout the book are vibrant examples of this but they can only ever indicate it. Only you can have 'your experiences' and, as your heart quality, intentions and actions are gently changed by your own heart, this depth can also become your direct experience, joy and reality.

Sweetness and preciousness of feeling

The deliciousness of milk and honey is the reflection of the pure heart.
From that heart the sweetness of every sweet thing is derived.
Rumi

There is a sweetness and preciousness of feeling surfacing from your heart that gently opens the blissful depths hidden within your heart. These are ready to be accessed, to be used and to help you and ultimately to take you to the most exquisite expansiveness of being, and experiencing all your heart is waiting to offer you.

The sweetness is most closely described as the feeling of deep unconditional love, being held, being loved or being in love, where nothing can disturb these feelings. And all this is not caused by anything other than what your heart holds and is waiting for you to realise and fully access.

Someone whom others would describe as having a good heart or a heart of gold, is often not only a person whom you appreciate in your life, but someone who is consistently and convincingly good and generous in spirit or heart. People like this are precious in our lives. Your heart's very ability is the in-built tool, the gift that will enable you to become a person with a heart of gold.

> *This is the very preciousness and inner sweetness that you are. Everyone has been given this full potential within.*

Any goodness, as it grows in your heart, will not only be felt by others around you, it will be a sweet and soft, warm feeling in your heart, spreading through all of you as the heart opens more and becomes present within your perfect body-heart-mind balance.

Following your heart and feeling

My whole body was filled with a wonderful feeling
and I realised that I had to make my heart very wide,
to find compassion for all beings to reach the final goal. Detlef Kantowsky

It is natural to feel, and to want to feel, wonderful moments in life, every moment. Feeling and your ability to feel are essential to you and to the quality of life that you experience.

As you start to connect and work with your heart more, it is natural that you will feel your heart more, as you touch your heart, smile to it with intent and feel your heart area. In terms of time everyone is different; however, you will clearly feel it at some point.

> *From then on all that you feel will improve if you continue to treasure your heart, pay proper attention to it and nurture it.*

However long it takes, it will happen. Soon after you feel it, as you let go more of the control the mind has had and still wants to have over the heart, joy will naturally bubble up, fill your heart and radiate through you.

Any time from then on, as you start to feel, you have the ability, or choice, to follow these feelings. You can follow two other parts too: you can follow the mind/brain or you can follow your emotions. However, as previously mentioned, only following the heart feelings will lead you to experience the true joy, deep inner calmness, love for self and other and the growing bliss the heart wants to facilitate for you.

It is also possible to follow something different from that: intuition, a hunch, the sixth sense, gut feeling and other more esoteric directions. Often when we follow one of these, we follow something like a deeper feeling, driven by the urge to find or follow a deeper truth.

However, unfortunately, when we do so, there is a strong tendency to follow a mixed bag of everything: a bit of mind or good idea, some of the heart's clearer feeling, some emotion, or want/desire connected to emotion.

Perhaps this analogy can be explained more clearly: when you are in an upmarket restaurant and you are served the Chef's special, you know that you will get a high quality, delicious and in some way pure meal. On the contrary, if you had this meal all mixed together with the soup, with your juice or soft drink on the side, with the cake you have for dessert and with the espresso afterwards, it would not be such a desirable meal!

Mixing all different avenues of how we can perceive truth, make decisions or feel, will also blur the path ahead, the moment-by-moment living in truth and wonderful existence.

You may ask yourself 'how do I train these other ways of feeling deeper or of perceiving a higher truth'? There may be a lack of clarity about how to train these, or a belief that some are gifted with them and some are not. The heart, however, is in every human being, and that with the natural techniques the heart responds to, everyone can develop these abilities and qualities - to a profound depth.

For the mind/brain the notion of feeling, using the feeling more or even following the feeling may seem a small or even illogical matter. For your heart this is very significant.

Every moment that you feel your heart and follow these feelings, the heart will take you deeper and further, and the wonderful feelings from your heart will grow.

'Following your heart' is a common saying which, in terms of really being and working with the heart, has several aspects to it. One is, when practicing your heart, whatever 'movement' or feeling your heart shows you, you follow that feeling.

> ### Practical Heart Tip 11: Following heart and feeling I *
>
> *The moment that you start to embark on the KHHs and other heart practices, and you feel the heart responding, moving, reacting or anything pleasant: follow that feeling.*
>
> *This only makes sense - to heart and mind/brain - when you actually start to use the heart and feel a response.*
>
> *There is one deeper way to facilitate your heart's help even better:*
>
> - *In moments when you feel the heart responding, smile to whatever you are feeling (without thinking where to and how it may work); then*
>
> - *follow the feeling, whatever you feel.*

Within this simple practice are two profound aspects of your heart's working for you:

1. You make the choice to give priority to the heart, that part of you with an additional and immense ability to help you, and to nothing else, including the alternatives listed above (emotions or mind/brain); and
2. You make a choice to use your heart, and as you follow the feelings from your heart, they will continuously take you to deeper and more beautiful places of feeling and being.

Because of the unique qualities and abilities of your heart, once you feel some of the feelings described above and start to follow them, it means that your heart is opening and you are on a solid heart-learning path. WONDERFUL.

The heart is immensely deep and with layers, as has been indicated and discussed at a number of places above. The question is: how can you go to all its depth? How can you get to a point where you have all your heart's potential available to you?

Following your heart to all its depth

The step-by-step approach, the detailed descriptions, the KHHs and the experiences shared in the stories, reflect the stages of learning to use and follow your heart. At a deeper level of who we are, we are much more similar than we are different. Differences are in physical appearances, character, traits, habits, language, and personal qualities.

With the unfolding of the heart, an immense depth of feeling starts to unravel. While you will feel a widening connection and compassion for everyone, regardless of differences such as appearance and character, that essence-part of who you are will remain an individual.

Later there will be more exploration - in the relationship, family and spiritual sections - about the role of the heart in sharing/distributing care, attention and love; and the heart radiating good intention, energy and feeling, including into your environment.

To progress to the full depth of your heart, the above two points are very important: choose your heart and give priority to it over the choice to follow other parts of you, (especially your emotions or mind/brain); and make the choice to use your heart, and follow the feelings from your heart, both when you practise and in daily life, more often.

These two, in combination with the step-by-step KHHs, will take you to the heart's full depth. It will take quite some time; therefore, at the end of the book you will find the workshop suggestions that will speed up this process immensely.

When your heart is working

Every time you practise, or in daily life, when you feel your heart doing something, following this feeling - whatever else is going on - will take you to the greater depth and abilities of your heart. This will always combine with gentle, wonderful feelings that will flood your heart and increasingly every part of you.

To fully develop all the heart's abilities, it is important to know what else can be going on. This 'what else' can be:

1. An emotion surfacing;

2. A temporary thought;

3. A tendency to over-think issues; or

4. A physical sensation coming from the heart or chest area.

It is good to learn to distinguish between these and the deeper, clearer more direct heart feelings in order to follow the best or correct direction and feeling.

---

1. If you have emotions surfacing like sadness or anger, particularly as you do some of the heart practice, let go, let them surface and express themselves as your environment permits. However, as soon as you remember, or as soon as you can re-focus on your heart, do Heart Strengthening, so your heart can cleanse the causes, the surfacing emotion and everything related.

2. It is absolutely normal for thoughts to surface, at any time in our lives, when we meditate or pray or when we do heart practices. The best way, from the perspective of the heart, is to notice them, be aware and not follow them, to let them pass through without attaching to them.

3. The direct, immediate positive feeling your heart generates is the one you want to learn to recognise and follow. During or after experiencing an emotion, as you practice, follow the smallest and gentlest of feelings deep within your heart. In this way, you will follow the heart and nothing else and your heart will change, reduce or dissolve anything not pleasant that has arisen, along with the causes.

This understanding is very significant. There is always a choice to follow different parts of us. Every moment you follow or choose your heart with greater understanding and clarity, it will help you, and your heart ability and heart-spiritual intelligence will develop. In developing your heart, being connected to the wholeness of who you are, you will naturally also develop the fuller functions of your mind/brain.

It is normal to think while connecting more to the heart or doing heart practices.

It is when you practice that you ideally think less and are doing what helps to achieve this.

Any time you find yourself thinking, or find a thought surfacing, relax and smile more. Relaxing more will reduce the strength of your mind/brain. Smiling will do two important things: it will calm the mind and strengthen your heart in a natural, non-brain directed way. You can truly let go of your thought processes for some time in this way.

It is very normal to use the brain too often or excessively. It will take time to find your balance between these two possible drivers: mind/brain and heart. Give it time; practice some heart and the balance will naturally find itself from all the resources that you have within you.

Every time you use your mind/brain functions, you will actually strengthen and develop the habit of doing so more. From some angles it may look good to strengthen the brain. However, one may not necessarily develop the smart, analytical or creative aspects of your mind/brain in this manner.

It is good to realise that the heart always has a win-win orientation. For example: every time you follow your heart, as opposed to the tendency to think, not only will your heart develop, but also your clarity and creativity of thought and all your natural and given abilities to be creative and disciplined in your thinking.

Developing the 'following of your heart and feeling'

To develop a clearer sense of when you 'follow your feeling and heart' and when not, it is helpful to do the PHT below.

The same practice will greatly refine and enhance your clarity around when you use your feeling and when you follow it the best. This is helpful, as following the feeling is not normal to everyone, even though what you are invited to here is to follow what is naturally within.

How to follow the feeling? You follow the feeling from the heart by being present to the heart, by feeling with your heart and by learning how the heart is communicating through feeling.

To actually follow your heart to reach its full potential can only be understood or known to a certain degree. Following the heart is a feeling and only in doing the KHHs, PHTs and the other suggested practices can you learn to authentically 'follow your heart'. So, in a sense, it can only ever fully be understood by your heart and your heart's intelligence and knowing.

In workshops I often ask 'who can feel'? Some people in the group respond or raise the hand as a positive reply. Of course, not all hands go up for a number of reasons, one of them being that some do not feel the impact of a particular exercise or do not feel anything yet.

Trust; it is one of our natural abilities, and as your heart becomes stronger, your ability to feel and to follow the feeling will naturally become clearer, easier, stronger and more beautiful and at some point you will notice it.

Feeling from the heart and feeling the full depth of your heart is new in many ways. You can practice this and it can become clearer.

> **Practical Heart Tip 12: Following the heart and feeling II - following and not following ***
>
> *When you are connecting to your heart with intent, in particular doing heart strengthening, and you start to feel your heart, do the following:*
>
> - *Follow the feeling for a few moments (20, 30 seconds - as guide only); then*
> - *Stop following the feeling (for a shorter time - keep relaxing, smiling and touching your heart); then*
> - *Follow the feeling again; then*
> - *Stop following the feeling; then*
> - *Follow the feeling again.*
>
> *You can repeat it more times. The amount of repetition is, however, less important than the quality of attention, which really means the quality of feeling, you bring to this exercise.*
>
> *For this reason, it is best done in combination with Heart Strengthening or another quiet and direct heart-connecting practice.*

By way of analogy, as you intend to follow the feeling and not follow the feeling from your heart, it is like flexing and relaxing a muscle. In doing so, you strengthen the muscle. This is the way to strengthen your heart and it will happen naturally as you do this practice.

There is a naturalness in how your heart knows how to open, unfold and gradually offer more direct support.

A deeper level of learning and feeling will occur with some practice. As you come back to it when you are further into the book and the KHHs, you will more clearly know when you feel and follow the heart and feeling. Thus you will go deeper into the bliss, peace, help and guidance from your heart. A deeper surrender to your heart can occur.

The heart quality and recognition of 'surrendering'

Surrendering is a deeper form of 'letting go' that was touched on in the above section V and PHT 10. Your heart knows both these qualities and responds to them in different ways. The more that you relax and release into this deeper form of letting go, you will find it easier, lighter and more profound.

The qualities of 'surrendering' or 'letting go' into your heart and whatever is offered to you, step by step, moment by moment by your heart, can be facilitated and deepened by your heart.

This letting go and surrendering is part of the heart's learning, similar to 'surrendering to' the love of a dear one, a partner, family member or friend. Love can never be forced and will only grow to its full blossoming when we relax, let go, trust and be the truer self that we can be.

In a similar way, the heart feeling will grow, become more discernible and beautiful. It is the heart's nature and in this way, everyone's nature. Give it time. Let go, surrender to your heart and its natural abilities. It is very common to feel very little and at times nothing when you are practising or in your heart. Often this 'nothing' is the beginning or the stillness that eventually forms the foundation and spark of the peace we long to have every moment in life.

Like in other parts of the book, you will find practices, discussions, hints or stories where the mind/brain is not clear or does not know. This is normal. How your heart functions can be explained up to some point, then it is up to you to try, to experience and to let your heart take you there.

The heart, your heart, is more capable, has more depth, knows more and can 'do' more than the mind/brain. Therefore, you need to make a leap of faith into your heart, to trust.

It will only take some time until the sweetness and radiance of your heart will deeply move you and that trust or faith will become stronger - the faith in the beauty and wonder of your heart, based on your own experiences.

There is a sweetness and depth to 'surrendering' that you can discover along your heart journey. Remember too, surrendering is not to this book, a teacher, a guru or any other human, it is a deep form of surrendering to qualities, connections and wonderful feelings that only your heart recognises and feels.

Your heart's condition and memory
Learning by heart.

Your heart has the memory of everything that has occurred in your life. This is another indicator of the immense ability of your heart. This may sound a bit esoteric for now. However, as the heart opens more, and becomes freer, this ability is one of the treasures you can use more. The potential to remember and to access this memory is of no major importance; what is more important is the use of the heart's ability to feel now, for the heart to bring you into the here and now, to be wholeheartedly present.

For now, it is important to be aware of it and to know that the ease, lightness and speed of feeling with and opening your heart is somewhat connected to this memory. This memory will also only be available to you as a 'feeling' not as knowledge or even a vision. These are other functions of your mind/brain or ability to 'see' beyond the eye's physical sense of seeing.

The degree to which a person has followed or harboured emotion, the degree to which s/he has suffered hardship, pain or even trauma, will give some indication of what someone's present heart memory, condition and related ability is.

In other words, this means that if you scan through all of your life, at least the parts and aspects you remember, you will have an idea about the condition of your heart. The heavier the heart, the stronger, harder or more painful the memory, the more you will have a disposition to react and the more likely you may react with emotion in situations where these are triggered.

However, none of this should be of any concern. It is of no concern to your heart. Your heart has a far greater ability to cleanse, dissolve and remove any residue of heaviness, burden or trauma; up to or down to the very root causes of them.

Whatever you have experienced, whatever the severity of the hardship, the potential and ability of your heart to help will always be greater; and this is really quite amazing news.

Your heart's memory - its clearing and opening

One of the most wonderful and amazing aspects of the heart is that, despite the fact that emotions, other negativities and even traumas are stored in our hearts, letting the heart dissolve and remove them does not mean that they need to be experienced in any form as part of this cleansing process.

If you follow the book's guidance the entire process of clearing or cleansing will even be a predominantly joyful one.

There is no need to remember these events. In fact, if you tried to recall all of your particular positive or negative life events now, very likely you would miss even quite a few.

> **Practical Heart Tip 13: List of joyful moments**
>
> *For example, try to remember a time when you were really joyful and happy. Write the ten most joyful moments in your life on a list and keep it somewhere.*
>
> *As you do your heart practices, Heart Meditation or other meditations, and as you have directed your attention to it, there is a high likelihood that additional joyful moments will surface from your heart or other consciousness.*
>
> *Keep this list for one of the Practical Heart Tips (PHT 68) introduced later. In KHH 1, 'Feeling the heart', you can use one of the items from this list.*

When additional joyful moments surface, this is only one indicator of the greater memory of your heart.

In contrast, the limitation of the mind/brain is demonstrated by most of us not being able to remember any event from when we were zero to two or three years old. Exceptions to this are only possible when these events are made available, either through the heart's memory or other means, such as hypnosis or deep breath work.

The mind's forgetfulness is a good design feature too. Some of the unpleasant, or harder experiences, get forgotten. Time will reduce the presence of these events and more so the presence of any emotions being held.

How heavy or light your heart is will only determine how much cleansing you will experience during your heart journey. It is good to be aware of this. The very ability of your heart will do all that is needed to take care of everything, the whole condition, the entire collection (all negative deposits), in particular, everything that is not supposed to be within and around your heart.

You also need to be aware that you may experience some of these emotions when you practise, however, only for some of your heart session. In any session, whatever you will experience will only ever be 1-5% what is cleansed, compared to 99-95% pleasant, peaceful and even joyful feelings. Cleansing means the clearing, healing and removal of any negativities, blockages or closed-heartedness. This is the average experience over the past years in all one-on-one and group sessions.

Even the smallest amount of upset during cleansing or clearing experiences is not natural and not really required. It usually happens when there is holding or blocking in some way, often without clear or any awareness of it. Relax and smile more freely when anything not pleasant happens.

To really let go, to trust and believe that such cleansing and healing could be so easy, may not be easy to accept or do. In particular, the mind/brain will have quite a few perspectives as to how it should be. At the same time, you will very likely hold in some ways, as opposed to just giving the heart a 'pure heart time' by relaxing more and smiling really freely.

The current condition of your heart and the memories of your heart may not be easy 'concepts' to come to terms with. You are not required to fully understand, believe or trust it. Whatever unfolds through your own heart will be your experiences as time moves on.

It will be your empirical data and experience through all your channels of understanding. With some practice your heart will show you all this and it will begin to move you, your understanding and experience, from being aware of it to your own heart's full understanding or realisation.

More on clearing or cleansing

The work of your heart is overall gentle and beautiful, a nice experience. However, as it is not easy to smile very freely and to totally let go at the level of the heart, there will be clearing or cleansing experiences, such as some sadness or anger, surfacing. If you follow the instructions in the KHHs, PHTs and additional exercises on how to use and continuously strengthen your heart, there will be very few clearing or cleansing experiences. If there are moments, they will pass quite swiftly.

Everyone is a little different in the extent and nature of the collection around the heart and in letting go. The swift passing is an average, middle of the range experience.

> *When my own journey started, I did not experience this middle path. I also did not have a resource like this or an online support program. It was all quite new then. I simply had to use a lot of tissues and, at times, the kids' flannel nappies. It didn't bother me as, at some deep inner level, I was grateful for whatever was stored, heavy and burdensome to come out.*

Any clearing or cleansing should be much easier now and with this guide. To keep it as simple as possible, there are likely to be two experiences that will happen as your heart starts to work:

- You will feel lighter, freer and calmer, even if this is just a subtle or small feeling. A subtle feeling of joy will also surface; or
- You will feel part of the process of clearing or cleansing, that is, part of or a small amount of the emotion, like sadness, anger, or any of the other emotions. You will also, at the same time, feel the subtle and beautiful heart feelings.

Joy, clear feelings of the exquisiteness of the heart's presence, radiating beauty and love within, feelings of sweetness, tingling, bliss in the heart area or similar experiences are common.

What is really important is to remember that in either situation, these are the early responses or feelings of an incredibly special process unfolding: opening your heart.

They are clear indicators and signs that the heart is responding and starting to do its work. Either of the two scenarios are 'good'.

... and the best response is to be grateful, to realise something deep and wonderful is happening and any form of heartful or heartfelt gratitude will directly help your heart ... to help you even more.

This is not an easy process to understand, either in mind or as an experience.

One way to view it is to imagine you were carrying a heavy backpack all the time. It becomes normal to carry such a weight, even though you know how much better you would be without it. Your heart knows what baggage needs to go. When taking off the backpack, overly tense shoulders and arms may cause a little pain. The result, however, will be lighter travelling and lighter feeling almost instantly.

In the same way, it is not important to feel the process of how you become lighter - sometimes you do feel it and sometimes you don't. The key is to commit to letting the heart take off the extra baggage. Over some time of practice, in particular using the KHHs, the result will always be the same - directed and facilitated by your heart and initiated by your mind/brain: a wonderfully light feeling all the time, very similar to a physical release 'a load off your shoulders' and, more importantly, off your heart.

Your beauty is your heart's beauty

The only lasting beauty is the beauty of the heart. Rumi

The essence of your heart is beautiful, and, with your heart shining more, you are beautiful. You probably know and have experienced this, too; you may have felt people around you touched by a beauty not related to appearances such as looks, age or body shape. You would have felt a beauty deeper than whatever society may have said about the physical appearance.

In the same way as you have felt this about others, this beauty is not stagnant or locked into an aging process. The beauty that your heart determines is ageless and in fact it can improve immensely as you and your body age.

The beauty of your heart is a profound and unshakeable truth waiting to fully unfold as your heart qualities rise more to the surface: as your heart beautifies, so will you. You will feel more 'beautiful' and others will recognise a deeply touching beauty in you.

At times in your life you may have sensed about people you met, that their physical beauty was not something you noticed, and yet there was clearly another beauty shining through that attracted you and made it special to exchange, share or be with that person.

There is a beauty, not only within, but also from the heart, that you can recognise and perhaps already do recognise in others or yourself.

The more that your heart is present and shines, no matter what your physical appearance, age or 'beauty' is right now it will become more beautiful, gentler in appearance and radiant.

There is a beauty of the heart that can be felt in others around us, whatever the context. When the heart is light, open and present in someone's life, you enjoy their company and it is a joy to be around them.

How your heart will help you - even in unforeseen circumstances

Naturally, when starting to learn about the heart more, you may have ideas, or get some ideas from what is shared in the book, about how you can get help from the heart in this and that area of life.

The more that you attend to your heart, with deeper understanding and practice, the more it will start to help you. This may be conscious and you may feel the active involvement of your heart, or it may happen as the guidance and natural activity of your heart kicks in. At the same time, it is very likely that random and wonderful changes will happen in your life.

The following story that Jeremy shared shows this kind of unplanned and unforeseen heart help:

Jeremy's Story

Jeremy is the team leader of an ambulance service with around 20 staff. He was recently appointed team leader. People naturally respect him, his experience and expertise in the field.

New to supervision and leading a team, meetings were not his strength, and, at times what he had to communicate was not easy to say or pleasant for the team to hear. He remembered one meeting that he was not looking forward to. He had to communicate a difficult message to the team. He prepared and wrote out detailed notes as to what he had to say. He arrived early before any staff. He remembered the heart and, having extra time, did the Heart Strengthening before the meeting.

When the meeting began, he forgot all about his notes, conducted the meeting and felt an overwhelming sense of calm and peace during and after it. He later shared:

'I did not use any of my notes during the meeting. This was a total surprise to me, as I had spent a lot of time preparing for this meeting. The words just came, everything flowed and seemed just right.'

He further shared: 'Several staff members came up to him and said how good the meeting was, how well it was lead...[and] that it was a very difficult topic handled in a very positive way.'

Jeremy's story shows in some way how the heart will help even in unforeseen ways. It appears that his team connected with and felt his heart's presence and with it any genuineness and an overall heartfulness and care shining through.

My own work as a therapist is perhaps one of those examples ...

Heart-Guided Therapy - Klaus's Story

I am writing this with a big smile and deep feeling of joy. As a therapist and practitioner, commercially I am sometimes not as successful as I could be. From the range of treatment modalities offered, almost all clients choose the heart-guided therapy to complement the work that is being done.

The impact is so strong that the longest repeat client in the past five years has come for nine sessions only. The average is three sessions. In the beginning, this was a big challenge for me and I tried to keep clients for longer, hoping that they would commit to more sessions ... there was even some resentment.

Now I realise that the heart has opened up so many other areas of support which I could not have foreseen. Now I feel only joy when people find help and relief so easily through the heart.

What this means is that individuals looking for help with emotional, relationship, health or other problems, find the heart's abilities very impactful, so that, after a comparatively short time, they do not need regular treatment.

There is also quite a significant group of past clients who have found the heart and the rapid help from it so profound that they wanted to learn more. They attend the heart meditation groups or workshops as part of their ongoing journey.

It took me a while to realise, learn and trust. The heart's doing will always look for opportunity, balance and growth. Fewer hours in one-on-one client work has opened doors for more group sessions. The opportunities to run community-based and organisational heart-based workshops have grown significantly over the past few years - all with an income that, at the very least, has balanced out any reduced repeat sessions.

For me personally and for my family, there has been anything but a 'loss'. There is one group of clients and wonderful individuals, who, in situations where they continued the heart learning, have become dearest friends. Some of them generously shared their touching stories in this book.

In a small area of my work and life I can see and feel that the heart's help reaches beyond an initial purpose, to the connection we have with everyone, at home and at work.

People come for treatment and find out about the heart, learning about it in a practical way. Their issues are addressed, helped and even solved through it. Those who continue to practise and use what they learn expand the heart's help into other parts of their life, experiencing learning and growth above and beyond the initial issue. Friendships develop, health and wellbeing is facilitated, and a deeper life purpose is found.

To be part of these changes, developments and stories is an immense joy.

Getting started and staying on track

The key to any change or improvement program is to actually start. If the book, the stories and some of the heart's natural abilities interest you, then the best way is to experiment with the KHHs and other suggested heart-supporting practices.

'Experiment' sounds perhaps a little too casual or informal and yet it will only be when you *use* these natural techniques that you can truly experience the full capacity of what is possible to experience. Experiments create experiences. The experiment will be safe, too. Your heart is an integral part of you and an intelligent part; it will do things that support you and enhance your life.

Feel at peace when you start to use your heart. You would not say to anyone 'I am not using my mind or brain here in discussing this or in making this decision; it is not safe'. It is okay to use the heart and, for the first stretch of time, there is no need to let the heart take over and make decisions.

Remember also that in any situation you will be in charge. The mind/brain will always fully function and allow you to stop whatever is happening as part of your heart practices. This will not be needed but is perhaps good to know.

The heart has, as an integral part of you, always your best interest 'at heart', with its own ability to facilitate.

It gently creates changes, always also in harmony with your whole life's needs and direction, much of which is not known to your mind/brain.

As you give it a go, follow the hints and small, yet powerful, heart-freeing suggestions in the book's life sections and in the introductory chapters. The keys for a solid start and for staying on track are:

- Start with the KHHs and work from KHH 1 to KHH 15;
- Start a 'Heart Diary' (PHT 27) or any journal and write down your experiences, what you feel, and what you practised and for how long;
- Commit to either a small but regular routine of doing the practices and even better, of doing short heart-refreshers throughout the day that work together with the reminders (below); and
- You are likely, also, to have used your mind/brain more than your heart in the past. To achieve more balance, whatever that is for you, set yourself some reminders, on doors, mirrors or computer screens, to smile, relax more and do things that nurture your heartfulness.

Some of the small tips and hints you may do already in your daily life, so it will be easy to do them more regularly or more often. Growing wonderful feelings from your heart will affirm your direction.

Your heart is so special that you will progress to a deep level of heart help using the book and the online resources. The full depth of the heart can be explored through specific workshops offered by 'heart learning groups or centres' around the world (listed in the end of the book).

One of the key practices is the Heart Strengthening. Let the other parts of the book, stories and supporting practices be just that, support for your heart. The most impactful practice is to gain a deeper understanding by using Heart Strengthening as your core, daily (or quite regular) heart program.

Obtaining a copy of the 'Open Heart Meditation' will also deepen your experiences and improve your heart's condition and the feelings of deep inner beauty, calmness and joyfulness.

This greater the help that you will have from your heart, the more you develop your heart capacity, and the clearer it will bring improvements in all aspects of your life, including in areas of your life where you face some form of challenge, issue or problem now.

Summary - understanding the functions of the heart

The practical heart-reminders, heart supporting attitudes and approaches in this section are:

1. Commitment, willingness to try, and a little letting go, are all that is needed for your heart's work and attitude to steadily improve and for all the understanding and the heart's wonderful capacity to unfold gradually. Include PHT 'Commit to Your Heart' into a daily or weekly routine.

2. The next PHT 'Be light' discusses the benefits of being light and invites you to include it into your heart-day.

3. The PHT 'Let go I' outlines the importance of an attitude of 'just letting go'. It will help the mind/brain to be calmer and the heart naturally freer.

4. To be relaxed and to find ways to balance aspects of your life that create tension and pressure. The practice of relaxing, de-stressing activities is one of the key foundations for your heart. However, on its own it will not work the best for your heart … yet.

5. A random practice of smiling more will directly assist your heart. Once the smiling to heart connection is made and felt it will be even more effective. A gentle smile here and there will balance a tendency in most people to over-think issues or difficulties.

6. Additional heart-supporting approaches are to:
    -   Follow the heart/the gentle feeling from your heart once you start to feel it;
    -   Be grateful for small changes to the heart or feeling and for everything in life; and
    -   Practise KHHs or heart practices with a friend. It will help you to commit, to have regular check-ins and to have heart-to-heart practice. As soon as you practise the heart with someone else, the intensity, depth and help available increases.

7. The PHT 'Following heart and feeling I' is the beginning of several discussions/PHTs on this topic. Following the feeling is something your heart can do and that will improve your heart capacity. Good to be included in your routine!

8. No one is free from emotions or negative emotional reaction, whether this is shown or held back. Every time that a situation is irritating or triggering emotions, the heart can help. Realise, with a small shift, the full capacity of the heart can kick in and assist to cleanse and reduce emotional states and reactivity. Over time, the causes and any related matters will be cleansed, too. Your heart and the PHT 'Emotional rescue guide' are keys to change and improvement!

9. The PHT 'Emotional rescue guide' is the direct way to let your heart remove anything that is not gentle or positive as an experience and as a disposition. Disposition means: you feel not light or free in certain situations or you tend to react, leaving your heart burdened and often other people, too. The emotional rescue guide in brief is, when you find yourself in emotion or reactivity:
    -   Realise an emotion is surfacing;
    -   PHT 'Let go';
    -   Remember your heart;
    -   Relax;
    -   Smile;
    -   Touch and feel your heart area; and
    -   Keep going - with the focus on the heart and feeling your heart.

10. In a broader sense, not only when emotions surface, as you begin letting your heart be freer and start to help you, it is likely that you will experience the following four phases. Be aware of this, allow this natural progression to unfold and enjoy/be grateful for the subtle changes in feeling; you are improving/changing:
    - Phase 1: Wondering and Doubting;
    - Phase 2: Response, Lightness and Up/Down;
    - Phase 3: Clarity and Joy; and
    - Phase 4: Connection, Deep Peace and Bliss.

11. There is a list of positive, enjoyable and even blissful feelings that everyone's heart will reveal and deepen over time. One of the practical keys is, a bit paradoxically: feel only, follow the feelings from your heart only and do NOT look for them. Looking or observing is a function of the mind/brain and will limit these feelings from fully unfolding for you.

12. Whenever you practise or use your heart 'be light', not too serious, not too outcome-focussed. It will support the nature of the heart. Let go a little and be helped by your heart to find the right balance or approach, from within. Practise the PHT 'Be Light' several times until it becomes a habit or your second nature when you practice 'heart' and in life in general.

13. The PHT 'Following heart and feeling II' is a tool that invites you to experiment with this heart-ability of being able to feel in different ways. You can integrate this into your daily heart routine and into almost every heart practice.

14. Making a list of joyful, special moments is the essence of the PHT 'List of joyful moments'. You can use items from this list in later KHHs and PHTs, or ad hoc heart practices, to help your heart along in triggering joyful memories.

15. How to best get through all the practical aspects and exercises of the book:
    - Focus on the KHHs and work through them from 1-12 (skipping a maximum one or two is fine);
    - Start the Heart Diary (PHT 27) or an informal journal to write down when you practice and what you experience;
    - Commit to a small routine: for example, 3 x 10 minutes a day or 2 x 5 minutes and 1x 25 minutes, and
    - Give it a try for 2-3 weeks or more.

Note: There is a strong likelihood that you have predominantly used your mind/brain most of your life up until now. The heart will take some time to surface clearly and noticeably, even though it will function and work for you from the first moment on.

Chapter VI

First Heart Steps

This section is a continuation of some of the practices shared in the earlier parts. While KHH 3 'Relax more', below, is still heart preparation and not a complete heart practice yet, along with KHH 1 'Feeling the heart', your heart is already triggered, has become more active and is starting to help. If you have gone through these KHHs, you are already improving your heart condition and heart help. From the first steps onwards you can experience the subtle, yet clear and profound changes in your life that your heart can facilitate.

Take stock of your thoughts and emotions

A short stocktake is one way to find out how you are tracking in your life, in terms of generating negative thoughts or emotions. This is optional. You may already have some clarity around this. It is, however, a small exercise that allows you to evaluate and later see how, with the help of your heart, you can make significant improvements. It creates a point from which to start.

This PHT will assist you in looking at how you normally react, highlighting negative emotional reactions that are either displayed outwards or felt inside you.

Additionally, it is helpful in exposing thought patterns: when are you thinking negative thoughts, how often, and what triggers them. Tuning in to your emotional and thought patterns can be done in two ways:

- Take some time to make diary notes of how, in an average week, you have negative thoughts or emotions, for how long and to what depth. You can do this by writing one or two pages; or
- Draft a table, as suggested in the PHT below and then track negative thoughts or emotions for a few days.

It is very important to note that both of these steps can be helpful but they are not really that important. A third step is the more important one: to let the heart help. The main purpose of this exercise is to take stock now, before you work with your heart more intensively, then to take stock again in three to six months. Though this can be confronting initially, it is helpful to remember there are very few human beings around that have no negative thoughts or negative emotions. In all the group practices, workshops and one-on-one sessions I have been part of, there has not been one individual with no negative thoughts or negative emotions.

If you feel this exercise will burden you or cause you self-doubt, then just skip it. In some way this self-tracking will require you to make a courageous turn in perspective, by looking at others' behaviours that create a reaction in you, to analysing how you normally react and then making mind/brain choices to start changing these reactions.

This resolve will be significantly enhanced by your growing heart capacity. This stocktake can be purposeful for the following reason: as you become aware of emotions, patterns or habits of negative thinking, even subtle ones, you will want to use it as motivation to embark on the heart practices, as they will directly impact on these negative patterns, habits or expressions.

> **Practical Heart Tip 14: Negative Emotion and Thought Tracking (NETT)**
>
> *Create a simple table or spreadsheet on a sheet of paper or your pad, notebook, PC or phone. Track yourself for 3 to 7 days only. Across the top, list the days from Monday to Sunday. (Use an A4 sheet in landscape orientation)*
>
> *The very left column should have in each row the following three sub-rows: (1) Trigger situation (2) Emotion (3) Severity. To keep it simple, rate severity only from 1 to 3: 1 being mild emotion, 2 medium, and 3 strong emotional reaction.*
>
> *Now make an additional row for each event/reaction. Briefly note events when you have negative thoughts or emotions as a reaction to a situation or challenge or when existing habits or emotions surface. Total up the number of all events over the period. Do this for one week and for as many events in one day as you identify. To limit your work, only fill out one page. Keep every entry very brief.*
>
> *Note you can react at a 1, 2 or 3 level whether you show this outwardly or not. The key is how a situation makes you feel; whether you express negative thoughts or emotions is not important.*
>
> *After 3 or 6 months re-track.*

You can create this NETT table or find a free print-version of it in the resource section at www.yourheartcanhelp.org. The table and insight is only for you and only of importance to you. There is no need to share it with others. A clear and strong heart will lead to less entries and less heavy or strong reactions. After you have gained an insight into some of your behaviours, routine responses or emotional reactions, start to do the KHHs and other practices and let your heart directly or indirectly help you in this manner.

Ensure that you go through and complete at least KHHs 2-6, including the suggested practice pattern/time. It would be better to do KHHs 2-7, 12 and 13 and even better to practice all of them.

To see your progress after a set period of time you can do two things:

- Fill the table out again; and
- Ask others how you have improved in relation to your not-so-nice behaviours, routine responses or emotional reactions.

The benefits of this table are that, firstly, you start to identify that there are emotional reactions which do not support your heart and heart abilities, and which are very likely not supporting your relationships at work or home either.

Secondly, the insights from this table can assist you in your motivation to let your heart learning and growing heart capacity help you to remove these negative expressions and all root causes lying deeper within your heart that make you react. With your heart's help, they will naturally be cleared and replaced with understanding, insight, care and compassion from your heart.

Once you have designed and completed your table over three to five days, take note of what they are and, more importantly, use your mind/brain insights with growing heart strength to make a clear resolve to reduce your reactions or familiar emotional behaviours. This may involve not following thoughts, not engaging in any negative actions based on emotions, and not engaging in unnecessary conversations or any other forms of talk - to self or others - that is driven by these emotions or reactions. Do this as best you can. This is very much a mind/brain effort. However, heart and mind/brain work together on this and a stronger heart will make it increasingly easier.

If your heart is light and comparatively unburdened already, you will find this easier to do. If you are more burdened, however, or, when things are difficult or you are challenged by others or their behaviour, there is less inner control. You are more likely to react emotionally or even explode.

Never be concerned. It is good to realise where you are at. Though remember, it is not about the state of your heart but using the heart. With the help from your heart and following the practical guidelines in this book, you will make fast, easy and even joyful progress.

For your heart none of this is a concern or 'too much'. Your heart's ability far exceeds any patterns, behaviours and deeper issues or even traumas. All you need to do is pay proper attention to your heart, start using it more naturally, and have a mindset of letting it help you.

In all practices: do your best, ask for help, let go

It is important to look at yourself, and to reflect and, together with the additional heart knowledge you gain, to develop not only a growing understanding of how your heart can help with any challenges you face in life, but also how to use it in the best possible way.

With the active help from your heart, you are now starting to stand stronger on two legs. With less heart help or no heart at all you have largely one avenue available to you: the mind/brain. Now working as a team, there is the heart together with mind/brain.

If you are a more emotional or strong-thinking person, then be less focussed on this mind/brain activity and pay more attention to the KHHs. Read on, go from one KHH to the next and practice them wholeheartedly and diligently.

---

*Practical Heart Tip 15: A good approach ***

In all your KHHs, PHTs and broader areas of life, including all your heart-learning, the following approach can assist immensely:

- *Whatever you do in your life, heart-related or not, do it the best that you can;*
- *Make an affirmation from your heart-mind-brain; or*
- *Pray from your heart, asking for help; then*
- *Let go.*

Monitor your progress over time, starting here, now, in your personal diary, notebook, calendar or using the PHT table from above.

Standing on two legs: heart and mind/brain

When you look at a project at home or at work there are several ways that heart and mind/brain can interact. With a project there is always a beginning, a middle and an end. This makes it easier to see change or progress. In a project scenario the mind/brain might work in the following way:

Figure 9: Planning with a dominant mind/brain

Planning	Implementation	Review-Evaluation
Plan what you do through thinking ahead.	Think and do - at the same time.	Review - what you planned, how it went and what the outcome was.

Figure 10: Project character with heart and mind/brain working together

The heart, together with your mind/brain, works the best in these two ways:

Planning	Implementation	Review-Evaluation
Plan, and also Feel with your heart - how a planned action feels.	As above Feel and use the heart as you do/act Do what feels light; be guided by the heart feeling every moment.	As above In addition, feel the result of the outcomes.

What is hoped to be shown in these two tables is that the heart can further support the logical, linear way of the mind/brain in terms of planning, doing and reviewing something. Through 'feeling', your heart acts as a second intelligence and wisdom. The second table can be a project or note. You can use this approach in life, every day or during a 'project'.

There is a slightly more refined version which will take some heart practice to be comfortable with this, to trust this as an approach or way of life. In addition, bring the heart and mind/brain charts together, and the heart understanding gained, the following options available (next figure/table).

Figure 11: Heart and mind/brain work fully, seamlessly and continuously together

Planning	Implementation	Review-Evaluation
Plan what you do through thinking ahead	Think and do - at the same time	Review As in table 2.
Feel at the same time	Feel and use the heart as you do/act	
Make affirmation/pray for help (from the heart).	Do your best Let go Surrender.	

With the heart being a welcomed player in your life, there are more options and more choices.

What you may find is that the more you become familiar with the heart, the more you will trust your heart as a planner and decision-maker within. This trust will take time to build.

Naturally processes and outcomes will alter and, often miraculously, life will run more smoothly. It is common to get good results using your heart, though often surprising ones. The more you start to have these experiences, the more you will want to bring the heart into every part of your planning, doing and reviewing.

More letting go and surrendering

As shown in the last figure above there is an additional approach to use: let go or surrender. It is natural, with mainly the mind/brain at work, that good ideas are the main source of inspiration and direction. It is equally natural, when you do not get what you want or have planned for, to go back to the drawing board, the thinking process, feeling it, and starting again.

With your heart, there is another option now: let go and surrender. Both are aspects and abilities of your heart that help you to release the nagging or burdening unfulfilled dreams or hopes. The surrendering and letting go from the heart will allow for new ideas, new plans and often surprising new events to come into your life, unplanned by the mind/brain.

This process is not black and white. Even with limited awareness and skill in using the heart the best possible way, it is very likely that the heart plays a part when people talk about using their intuition or 'gut feel'. The heart is already helping, though it may sometimes be interpreted along these more familiar or common expressions.

How do I know I am using my heart?

You may have heard people say 'I am listening to my heart'. When your heart is really starting to work, or communicate with you, it will 'talk' to you as a feeling.

After over ten years of working intensively with people and the heart, 'feelings' fall into two categories: feelings on a scale from pleasant to wonderful plus sensations of cleansing, or not-so-nice feelings. To go deeper into the distinction between feelings and emotions, the following is a more thorough outline that can help you in all your practical heart work/joy.

This is particularly important if you already feel that you use your heart, or are starting to use the practical heart exercises, tips and the KHHs in this book.

First responses and feelings from the heart

Often it is not so easy to realise and feel that the heart is working. Every time you do one of the KHHs or other practices, the following five questions can be very helpful to refine your awareness and feeling. Ask yourself:

1. How do I feel now, overall?
2. How is the feeling from my heart or the chest now?
3. How busy is my mind (compared to normal)?
4. How calm and restful do I feel now?
5. How light and burden-free do I feel now?

You may only feel something in one or two areas. Or you may not feel anything for some time. That is all very normal. Still, memorising one or several of these questions, asking them and feeling the answers is helpful. You will continue to use your heart in these moments, which is helpful and over time it will move you forward and take you deeper.

'The good stuff'

You know that your heart is starting to work and your heart is improving when you have feelings or sensations like:

- Something opening
- Warmth, radiation, even heat
- Lightness
- Relief
- Emptiness
- Expansion

Feelings during your first weeks of practice can also be:

- Burning
- Intense heat

You may feel some of the above feelings as a physical sensation. From the non-physical heart the sensation can also be similar to a physical movement such as:

- Pressure
- Tightness in and around your heart or chest
- A feeling of opening, similar to your chest opening or widening.

It is very common that you also feel inclined to:

- Grin
- Giggle
- Laugh

The best to do … let go, just grin, giggle or laugh.

Practical Heart Tip 16: Let go II - enjoy the pleasant feelings

For now, and with all your heart work as an underpinning attitude, remember to let go every time the heart is at work.

The journey with the heart is in essence a joyful, light and easy one.

There may be other experiences such as cleansing, clearing, or some releasing. Remember 95% or so will be joy and other pleasant feelings, while 5 % or less will be 'the other stuff'. LET GO to the joy and pleasant feelings.

When the joy is opening, let go and experience the fullness of it. There will be small stretches of time where cleansing will happen, too. You may as well fully enjoy the predominantly good and very enjoyable stretches.

Every time you let go, whether some tears flow or you giggle or laugh, remember whatever your heart is holding, including negativities, burdens, blockages or traumas, is all being released and you and your heart will feel freer and lighter. In this way, for your heart there is only one direction.

***Practical Heart Tip 17: Following the heart and feeling III - refresh mind/brain and heart's understanding ***

It is good for your heart and mind/brain to go over the 'following your heart when practising' in section V, as they work together, and a fuller understanding will bring better progress and outcomes.

As you read, both your mind/brain and heart are listening, and your heart understanding will be trained by reading, doing the practices and connecting with the stories and experiences of others.

Most people who have experienced the incredible help from their heart have also enjoyed and appreciated one or more of the feelings listed in 'the good stuff' above. These feelings may happen from the first time you consciously connect to your heart in ways that the book suggests. They may take some time and sometimes they appear underneath some layer of tension or thinking that is still present. These feelings also do not need to be generated, visualised or manifested. The heart will do it, regardless how illogical this may seem.

'The not-so-nice stuff'

What is this 'not-so-nice stuff'? Where does it come from? How should we be with it? What is the best way or attitude for the heart to take care of it? What are these 'deposits'?

The 'not-so-nice-stuff' consists of non-physical burdens that you feel, in the same way you would feel a backpack on your shoulders. It may be subtler than a physical sensation; it may just be a feeling or a physical pressure on or inside your chest.

Where does 'not-so-nice-stuff' come from? The 'not-so-nice-stuff' is deposits made when you had negative thoughts or negative emotions any time in the past - the recent past or the far distant past, as far back as when you were a baby. Your memory of what that was or what happened is not important, the simple fact is that they were there, expressed or not, and they lead to non-physical deposits.

For example, deposits are made when you have negative thoughts about a supervisor, manager, colleague or customer at work. If this occurred 15 years ago most of us will have forgotten these moments, grudges, times of anger or upsets.

Another example can go further back, to your time as a teenager or young adult, even as a child. While we love our parents, we know that they also have the role of setting boundaries. If during one of those boundary-setting times you had negative thoughts or some emotion, a deposit was being made: negative energy was stored in or around your heart.

How you need to be with all this, and the best way for the heart to take care of it, is simple. Start using your heart, follow the practices in this book and the KHHs. Be relaxed, smile, let go of thinking, and let the heart, which will gradually be getting stronger, do the job.

Time to clear out

The moment your heart becomes more active, whatever these deposits are, they will be cleansed, removed or dissolved by the naturally radiating energy of your heart.

The heavier the burdens, the stronger the habit of thinking negatively, having and expressing emotions, the longer it may take.

However, this is not purely logical in the way you believe you know or understand. Firstly, the knowledge of how deep, how old, how far back these events or habits are, is limited by the mind/brain's ability to remember. Secondly, not many people know how well developed their ability to let go is, at the level of the heart and mind/brain. The process of cleansing or clearing may take a long time, or longer than expected. Remember that it is only during rare occasions we can feel the cleansing, and even then, only parts of the negativities we hold are being cleansed. The heart clears much more than we can feel. Given that it was us who made these deposits, it is overall quite a positive arrangement.

Clearing larger chunks

I have not met one person who did not experience some form of cleansing. However, disregarding how large or old the deposits are, or how deeply they sit, they are mainly experienced in two instances. You experience some form of cleansing and related emotion when:

- Larger chunks are being cleansed in one heart session; or
- When you are holding more.

Holding is often expressed in not smiling freely and not being physically relaxed enough.

When larger chunks are being cleansed, it is a good sign. You are letting go, expressed in your free smile and overall relaxation. It is then that your heart and heart connection are working naturally and with gentle, pleasant, enjoyable feelings.

When you are holding more, you experience something like an arm wrestle that is hanging in the balance. Your heart and heart connection are working, yet part of you is holding. In other words, there is an inner struggle going on between the natural cleansing process and a part of you that wants to do something. This is normal and happens frequently.

You just need to have an awareness that you are holding, not why, where or how.

Good responses include just letting go, trusting your heart more, smiling freely, relaxing more, and letting it happen.

My experience over the past ten years has shown me that whatever 'not-so-nice' things you may experience as part of the clearing, if you follow the instructions as best as possible, it will only be 5% or less of what is actually being cleared. In the beginning, very likely this will only happen at times when you sit quietly, do heart strengthening or heart meditation practices. Over time, even the '5% of cleansing' experience will become less.

Try to remember that 95% or more of the time you undertake heart practices, you will increasingly feel wonderful feelings. Being grateful, from the heart, for all that goes will speed up the process.

Heart practices can, however, become challenging at times, when the feelings are less positive, even feelings that we may call 'bad'. Naturally, or more as a habit, there can be an inclination to follow the cleansing and not the heart feeling. Always come back to touching your heart and feel deeper, feel the deeper feelings in your heart. Look back over the helpful heart-hint sections above can also help. Keep going: your heart knows what is best and will do everything that is needed.

How is the 'not-so-nice stuff' experienced?

Every human being has stored the energetic effects of negative thoughts and emotions, and has created a personal collection over the length of his or her life. Is there an exception to this? Is there anyone you know who would not fall into this category? We may project onto certain people that they have achieved a high or near-holy state of being. However, when one gets to know such individuals, it is very likely that negative elements exist in their life, too.

Whether it is hidden emotions, past heavy or traumatic experiences, the heart can help. The mind/brain also has a helpful function here: to be able to forget and not to hold all memory in a more present state. It is a good design feature of the human being that negative events, experiences or traumas are forgotten over time, and there may be others we don't even know, in particular if they have occurred when we were too young to remember.

The heavier clearing

How exactly are these burdens to our heart experienced? When we are cleansing our heart, the most common sensations or emotions that surface are sadness, or less often, anger.

This is the 'heavier clearing'. Compared to the full list of possible negative events or emotions that may have caused this collection, the actual list of 'not-so-nice' experiences experienced during cleansing is much shorter.

Figure 12: Emotional clearing/cleansing process

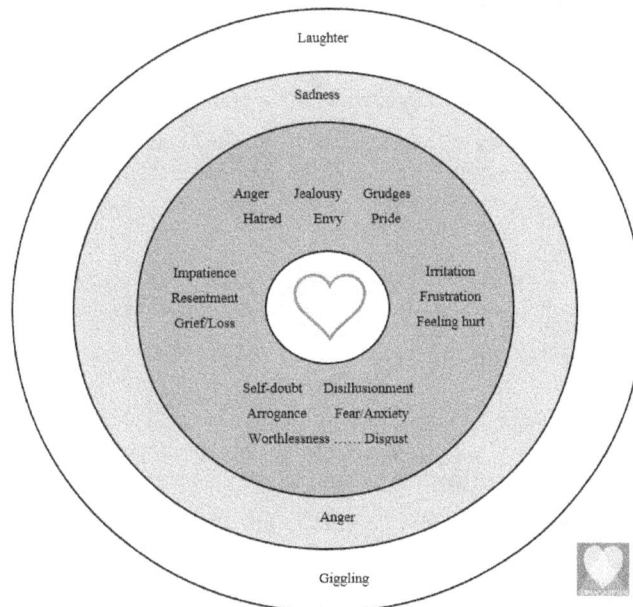

The figure above shows possible negative emotions that cause your heart to be heavy and burdened. These heart-burdens are then possibly feel-able, experienced in daily life as states of heaviness, burdens and everything else opposite to feelings of lightness and joy. Why 'possibly' only? This really depends on your sensitivity. These feelings can also be less present, under a form of cover. This is often expressed by those close who may say 's/he is closed' or 's/he has covered up his or her feelings' or 'such and such activities or busy-ness are a way to cover up his/her feelings'.

The figure also shows that, as the heart (centre circle) starts to become active and is radiating, no matter what the deposits or the cause of the heaviness, your heart will naturally penetrate and dissolve these emotions and bring you to the outer layers of the figure.

The lighter clearing

Observations and experiences of the past have clearly shown that after three to six months of regular heart practices, the occasional feeling of anger or sadness makes room for outbursts of laughter, giggling and related feelings of joy. You may say that this is good. And yes, you can see then that you are clearly progressing. It is important to point out, however, that the 'laughter' or 'giggling' can still have an emotional nature, being either loud or uncontrollable. This means there is still clearing happening, albeit in a much more enjoyable way.

Other negativities may still be cleansed from the deeper layers of your heart too; as the heart's working is like a deeply-reaching tool. This process, however, can be a little bumpy, meaning that you may go 'back and forth' a bit, or 'up and down' in the way you feel.

Similar to when heavier emotions surface, let go, let the expression happen, for a few seconds, then remember the heart, feel more and follow the gentle nicer and deeper feelings from the heart again.

The deepest feelings from the heart have an immense and exquisite depth and your heart will want to bring you all the way there.

There may be a few other, less noticeable and in some way less important experiences or sensations happening. These may be:

- A feeling of pressure in the chest area;
- Contraction in the chest area; or
- Temporary heaviness of your heart, mind or overall mood.

It is important to realise and remember that whatever sensations or experiences you may have, your heart is working, removing significantly more than you can feel in either pleasant or less pleasant ways.

The more you practice and follow the instructions for the heart and the more you follow the heart in a natural, direct way, the more your burdens, blockages and old, deep deposits, are almost instantly removed.

The heart has the ability to remove old or big chunks quickly. Everyone is different, and you may at times experience a period of deeper cleansing. If you find yourself experiencing emotion while using the heart helpers, in particular the KHHs, then always come back to the basic or core steps. In addition, make sure that you are quite relaxed and smiling freely. You can also be aware of the five heart-help reducing interferences below, to improve your approach. In addition, or if the challenges persist, seek out the guidance of a trained heart-based therapy facilitator.

Whatever the heart is removing - you don't want to keep it

Any 'negative' responses are always triggered by something that is holding your heart or forming a layer around your heart. Or it is from something that is in your heart and does not belong there. This process, then, is really not negative. You are, in these instances, feeling something working, something surfacing and being cleansed. Therefore, it is helping you in this moment, in the short, medium and long term.

The heart's intelligence knows what belongs and what does not belong, so the key is to learn to trust the working of the heart. After all, it is not another person, another being or an alien; it is an integral part inside you.

If you feel any kind of release or 'not-so-nice' feeling, as detailed in the previous section, it is best to keep going; keep relying on your heart and keep following it.

This process is a little like weeding your garden. If you pull out the weeds, the garden will look better and have an overall better 'feel' too. As you follow the feeling from your heart, it is as if you do a longer, deeper second weeding, removing the roots, even small ones, and the garden will be cleaner, tidier and in better condition, allowing everything good to flourish.

All this is a way to learn to trust your heart more, to rely on your heart, and to feel your heart and the wonderful feelings it wants to facilitate for you.

During any moments where you feel cleansing or 'not-so-nice' feelings in this process, the best approach is to repeat your exercise, do a full Heart Strengthening (KHH 6) or do the Open Heart Meditation (KHH 13).

You will know when to stop. Be careful however, as there is an inclination in us all to give up, stop too early or have the clever mind/brain 'know' better. It is good to be aware of this inner trickster and attend to the heart, feel and NOT follow good ideas of the mind/brain that can override the gentle heart feelings.

Resistance, cleverness and other things to watch out for

Sell your cleverness and buy bewilderment. Rumi

Let us explore this a little further. You may be familiar with your heart but you may be new to the level and depth of heart awareness and practical heart use offered in this book. In either case, the mind/brain and other parts of you will also still be strong. They have been in charge for some time and now it is more about power-sharing, about finding a new balance that is right for you.

Even though the heart's journey is always an interplay, a working together of parts within you, it is normal to face certain issues and situations where there is interference, which, if you are aware of them, will assist you to find a more suitable balance for you, from the inside out.

Watch out for the five heart-help and happiness reducing interferences that are discussed in the following sections. They are real, inside all of us, and often they reflect the mind/brain's attempt to keep its current employment position: as the manager, the boss, the main part of you in charge.

Remember too that it is never about either-or, about the mind/brain or the heart to be in charge, but for the two of them to work naturally, seamlessly and efficiently together, for the best life for you!

It is, however, good to pay some attention to the heart and to commit to some form of regular heart practice. This will allow you to balance out 15, 20, 30 or more years of paying more attention to the mind/brain development. You can further let the wise heart help the often 'pretending-to-be-logical' mind/brain. Why pretending?

Whatever seems to be the most logical decision or course of action, in many or most instances the information to make these decisions, or take action, is limited in some way.

If you have tried the path of the mind/brain, including the use of visualisations or affirmations, just be aware that they may interfere with your heart path.

The five heart-help and happiness reducing interferences

Resistance

There is a degree of resistance in all of us. You may be aware of situations or times in your life where someone suggests something beneficial to you, and for whatever reason you say 'no'. There can be resistance in us to anything, often out of principle. There is resistance to change or resistance to do or continue something. Therefore we often focus on small challenges, things the mind likes to comment on or be busy with, rather than a long list of clear positives.

Knowledge

With the mind/brain being the main holder of 'all' knowledge and being in the normal superior position, it will give commentary on all of this. The mind/brain, however, has only a very limited ability to know the heart and its full capacity. This reality will not stop the mind/brain from trying to use its existing pool of knowledge to comment on, analyse and categorise what you do in terms of learning, expansion and opening your heart more. Depending on the outcome of this analysis, there may be a decision made to do less of it, to do it in other ways, or to put it aside completely.

Cleverness

Cleverness is related to knowledge. In a very positive way it can mean being mentally bright and having sharp intelligent responses. In terms of the heart there is a less positive aspect to it: a more superficial skilfulness, an attitude of being witty or cynical that is put up in an attempt to guard you from your heart's abilities and your innate ability to grow, learn and have the most wonderful and exquisite life.

Observation

Observation, watching and subsequently holding, is a function of the mind/brain, and it can limit your heart's functioning. Your mind/brain supervising the heart is not an easy one to work with or overcome and it will take time. However, with a stronger heart it will naturally subside. The director of a company does not need to be supervised by the team leader of the factory floor workers. In the same way, the heart does not need supervision by the brain. One effective way to obtain a greater awareness of the heart is to do exercises to become more aware of when you observe and when you feel. KHH 1, PHT 33 and PHT 76 touch on this.

Control

The tendency in most of us to exercise some form of control is more easily explained in our interaction with others. A friend and colleague shared:

I found myself taking over and making sandwiches for my teenage child. There were thoughts in me like 'I know it better, I can do it better or I can do it faster'. This seemed to give me the right to interfere and to take over. Not surprisingly there was no resistance from my child. He stepped out of the way to be helped, served. I then realised that it was not supporting him to become independent, responsible and to learn. I stopped it gradually and yet, at times when needed, still make the occasional sandwich.

As a parent, of course we know that our children need to learn both independence and how to make a nutritious lunch. In the same way there is a tendency to control the heart. Expressions and indications of this are:

- Parts within, other than the heart, are holding;
- The mind/brain is continuously watching;
- Your thoughts are controlling and holding the heart; and
- There is a process of letting go that is triggered by the heart and you don't let it happen; you are holding to stay in charge, stay the same, with an existing dominant mind.

This is sometimes felt by participants and clients. They know and realise their mind/brain is controlling the heart, and they are happy to let go. Other participants or clients do this and are less aware of it. Without awareness it is harder to change.

These five interfering parts in you may function in isolation or at the same time. They are normal and it takes time to be fully aware of what we do in relation to these, and to let them go one by one. To help, have an overall attitude of letting your heart be free.

Micro can reflect macro. Your own relationship with your heart can be a reflection of how you interact with others. Similar to relationship or friendship in your life, when you feel free and easy, trusted and supported, you function well, you are creative, you flourish and you can let go of any guarded-ness and control. So it works with your heart.

The second KHH, introduced below, will help you (both your mind and heart), to become more relaxed and ready to be more involved in your heart/feeling.

This KHH, together with your greater awareness of your heart's functioning, will assist significantly in opening your whole being (mind/brain, body and heart) and will assist you to be in the starting blocks, to really let your heart help you.

Mind/brain and the heart - the need to relax

The first step in making a better connection to your heart is to become more relaxed. It is important to be open to deepening your own levels of relaxation, starting from whatever your current level is. The depth of physical relaxation you can achieve is immense and not dissimilar to the depth of heart feeling or use of your heart. In fact, they are connected.

The mind/brain governs and controls the physical body. To lift an arm, to move a leg, a leg or to speak we need to think about doing so, and then have the ability to move body parts to act in accordance with those thoughts and intentions.

Because of this connection and interplay there is a reverse impact too: when our body is tense there is an inclination to think more and to push the centre of our being from the heart upwards into the spheres of the mind/brain.

Practical Heart Tip 18: Simple heart - head balance self-assessment

Using the picture below. (draw it in your 'Heart Diary', download the free resource or copy it on a piece of paper)

Then rate your personal head (mind/brain) to heart balance.

- *Be spontaneous; and*
- *Feel and draw a circle or 'X' where you feel your current balance between your heart and head lies.*

Figure 13: Mind/brain and heart balance

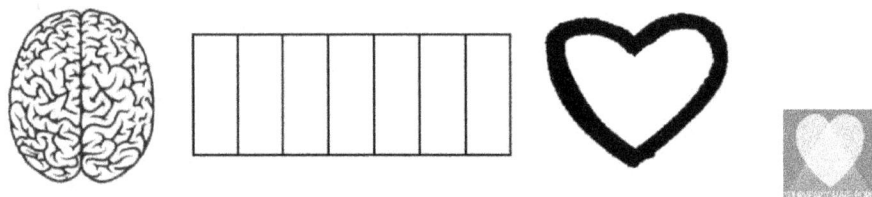

Use the image above or download it as a free resource from www.yourheartcanhelp.org. The online resource is more detailed. Rate yourself, by marking a box closer to the heart or to the mind/brain image. You can do this in three ways: (1) how was your mind/brain balance today, on average throughout your day, (2) how is your balance during times when you attend more to your heart or (3) rate your balance several times, ad hoc, during the day.

Your heart-head balance will not be static or fixed. It will move, even in one minute, hour or day, more towards your head or more towards your heart. However, you can intend to feel with your heart - or for now with your intuition. Ask yourself: where, on an average day, does this balance lie?

Key Heart Help 3: Relax more

The first key heart activity is to relax more. We can do this by intention and by letting the mind and heart feel the response to this intent for a few moments. The short version of this KHH can be just that:

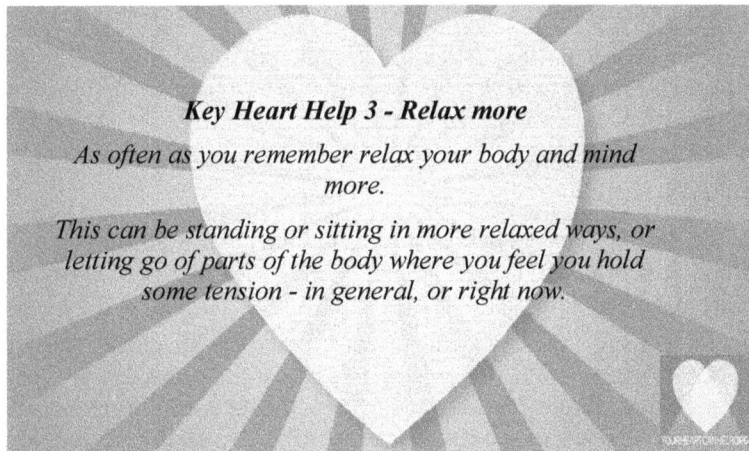

Key Heart Help 3 - Relax more

As often as you remember relax your body and mind more.

This can be standing or sitting in more relaxed ways, or letting go of parts of the body where you feel you hold some tension - in general, or right now.

It will be of great benefit to your heart to include a more in-depth relaxation into your regular daily or weekly routine, and also to use a version of this deeper relaxation as preparation before your more direct heart-connecting practices.

The full KHH 3 - Relax more

In daily life ...

- *Be as relaxed as you can be all the time, in everything you do.*

- *Use any reminders, such as certain daily events, smiley stickers, or activities, such as answering a call or walking, touching a key board or operating a phone/tablet. Use them as 'heart reminders' to feel your heart often and to remind you to relax your body for a few moments or seconds.*

When you do your heart practices, meditations or prayers ...

These supporting basic hints or techniques support a natural sitting position and relaxation:

- *Be comfortable;*

- *Sit as upright as you can but also lean slightly back to reduce any holding in the upper body;*

- *Minimise possible interruptions;*

- *Balance what you 'do' to relax with what your body naturally knows. When you start to trust this natural knowing more, and when you also let your heart help, you can let the body and any tension go; and*

- *A simple breathing technique can assist in physically letting go and relaxing. The below PHT 'heart - breath - intension relaxation' is recommended.*

The way that people know how to, and will be able to, relax can vary a lot. The heart is really the central interest here. It is good to refine your relaxation technique while at the same time progressing your heart's abilities. This will in turn help your relaxation and overall calmness. Here are some additional relaxation tips.

1. Be comfortable

This means you sit where and how feels right for you. There are no rules about how you should sit in order to make you comfortable; at some level of your being you know what is comfortable for you.

2. Sit upright or upright-ish

This can be on a chair or the floor. Upright is good, as a lot of the energy that travels through our body, along meridians, nadis[7] and bio-energy lines, flows the best this way. Perhaps you can already feel this. Also don't sit too straight or rigid. It is good to lean slightly back to reduce any holding in the upper body.

3. Feel your body and ensure you are able to let go everywhere.

Upright-ish can mean that you feel to lean back a bit to let the upper body rest fully against a back support (the back of a chair for example). When you sit too upright, with a rigidly straight back, there can be a tendency to hold the body, which makes you more tense than needed.

4. Minimise all possible interruptions

It is okay for this not to be perfect. We all have a life: family, friends and work. It is, however, very helpful to make a time when you attend to the KHHs and your heart, and to have this time free of distractions, enabling you to be as peaceful as possible. It is also of benefit here, starting with relaxing, not to have the mind/brain in semi-alert, ready to attend to a phone, a person or a door. This semi-alertness creates subtle tension, even if no interruption occurs.

5. Balance what you 'do' to relax with what your body knows

In all the heart learning, there are areas where adjustments can be made. One is in learning to be more relaxed, when you start to practice your heart and in all life situations. Follow the practical tips on how to relax more deeply. Of course, if you know something can work for you, add it to your relaxation phase.

Our bodies naturally know how to relax. When you start to trust this natural knowing more, and when you let your heart help more as it gets stronger, the body's natural ability to let go and be relaxed will kick in. This is a wonderful experience and it will immensely support your heart journey. Know it is there and that it does not need full control or direction from the brain. You can intend for your body's natural relaxation to happen or feel where there is tension in your body and intend to relax those body parts.

Your breath and your relaxation are connected in several ways. The frequency and depth of breath is one 'connection', that is known to yogis, breath workers and therapists. The other connection is the one between intent, breath, and your levels of relaxation.

Intend to let go all burdens … heart help and your breath

You can use the above connection between your heart, your breath and 'intention' combined in a simple breathing technique. While it looks simple, the results can be profound. The very fact that your heart is involved can assist in physical letting go and help burdens to be released, cleansing your heart and improving your overall feeling.

The following PHT 5 is a simple breathing/relaxation technique that will help to demonstrate this. The stronger your heart grows, the more clearly you will be able to feel the positive impact of this preparatory practice. Every time you intend to breathe out deeply, the non-physical matter/things you intend to breathe out will, to some extent, unburden your heart and being.

Simple Heart - Breath - Intention Relaxation:

Practical Heart Tip 19: Heart - breath - intention relaxation (Relaxation I) *

Use the following simple breath - intention technique to deepen your body's relaxation and your body/mind/heart's experience of any of the KHHs or heart practices:

- *Breathe in deeply through your nose, and exhale through your mouth several times to help you relax even more;*

- *Intend to breathe out any negativities, any burdens, all unnecessary thoughts and emotions; intend for these to flow out with every out breath; and with no more further thinking; and*

- *Do 5-10 slow, deep, yet comfortable rounds of breath.*

Breathe deeply but do not use too much effort. Feel that you and your heart may feel lighter, less burdened, just doing this simple exercise. As you intend for negativities, burdens and all unnecessary thoughts and emotions to flow out, a higher/deeper part of you, your heart is assisting.

---

[7] 'Meridians' and 'Nadis' are terms for energy lines in Chinese Medicine, Acupuncture or Indian Ayurvedic Natural Medicine.

This is one of the key, simple preparation/relaxation exercises done in many heart learning centres and workshops, and has been shown to achieve good results, both by itself and as a preparation to further heart strengthening exercises.

Make this simple breathing exercise an important starting point to all your heart practices from here on. Make sure that your body, mind and all of you are as relaxed as possible. It will help your heart, and therefore all of you, significantly.

The magic of a good heart

This is heart-warming.

The above sections explain how your heart works, while others go into detail about how we burden our heart, and how powerful emotions and negative thoughts are.

Equally, with some shift in your behaviour and response, and with the active and practical help your heart has been waiting to offer you, you can start to undo anything that is holding or burdening your heart. The results are present and often able to be felt within minutes, or after a few practice sessions.

The process your heart knows and will naturally apply is much stronger and deeper reaching than anything that may hold, block, burden or limit your natural, given heart ability.

Many sections of this book relating to family, relationship, friendship and work, are all about the quality of relationship we have with the people in these parts of our lives. Because of your heartfulness, your interactions will be heart-warming to them. They will feel in their own hearts how your heart condition and the wonderful feelings from your heart will have grown and are able to radiate in all you say, do and feel with them.

To be more whole-hearted.

When you use your heart more in the way that it is designed, by using more of your whole heart, any regular negative responses or thoughts within will become less. This means that even the subtlest process of burdening your heart will be reduced and can eventually stop. This new whole-heartedness will become clear and able to be felt by and work for you and all around you. The next life-section chapters of the book will all be about this.

What can this being or living more 'whole-heartedly' mean? People have shared:

- They know the other person is present for them;
- They feel loved within and less dependent. In that love is a feeling of knowing and care and there is little doubt about the clarity of this feeling; and
- They are more whole-heartedly committed to their friendship or partnership, or to a project or a piece of work.

These are only a few examples. Your heart will naturally bring all this and more to the surface. Naturally, this means that you don't have to do or say anything to demonstrate your 'whole-heartedness'. Others will feel it within their own being/heart in everything that you do or say; it will be felt or perceived as the genuine and authentic you.

With more whole-heartedness you will naturally become a person who is liked, to whom people will be attracted, to whom love, kindness and help will flow, naturally, magically. It is not a 'like' based on anything that you do or represent. It will be based on a deeper heart to heart connection, on something you and the other person can feel, know and enjoy as you share and walk through life, whether for a shorter or a longer time.

S/he has a good heart.

The heart brings out natural qualities such as patience, care, supportiveness and letting others be more who they are. It will equally help you in being a good friend or family member, a good Mum, Dad, sibling and more. When those or similar qualities are present in us, they are appreciated and recognised by others.

At work you will be an authentically supportive team player, sub-ordinate or supervisor, as these qualities are at the heart of building, maintaining and nurturing good relations at work. This ability to be authentically supportive and caring can easily be overlooked, and yet they are often foundation qualities that many high-performance books and personal development programs focus on.

It is not E. T. the Extra Terrestrial

... phone home ....

Remember you are your heart; the heart is a part of you, such as your mind/brain, your arms, your legs, your whole body and your emotional world. This book is about the complexity and wholeness of who you are and who everyone is.

This book is not a fantasy nor fiction novel. The content is based on over ten years of intensive work, sharing, workshops, one-on-one therapy sessions and uncountable hours of sharing, presenting and assisting others in a volunteer capacities. This is not just myself but many others here in Hobart, Tasmania at the Lotus Centre, visiting and sharing in activities at other heart centres around the world.

The book is also solely in relation to this approach and practice that has worked for many individuals or people in need. Other approaches may look similar and yet they may still rely more on the doer, a therapist, than the profound abilities of your heart being brought to full functioning.

Knowledge about the importance of the heart is hundreds, if not thousands, of years old.

No matter where you are, what you do and what your belief or truth is, your heart is always a building-block within; it is always present.

In this way, this book is about you, offering the help of your heart in a comprehensive, step-by-step manner for your growth and development, as well as help with difficulties or challenges. And to gently remind you, whatever your present or past challenges have been, however heavy or closed your heart may be, it is the very practical and real use of your heart that can and will immediately help you. It is helpful to pay attention to some of your behaviours, attitudes and reactions and make small changes.

Remember that your heart is very special. If we lost an organ or a limb there is a chance that we would be upset or angry. And yet, the part of us that is the key centre of feeling, we hardly use, or we ignore it. Your own heart will first help you personally, and then beautifully, at times in parallel, improve your larger personal and social life. It will further have the ability to become a wonderful and immensely powerful tool in every moment of your life through its readily available help, innate and refined intelligence, and ability to guide.

Why 'phone home?' Because at the core of your heart is your spirit, true self, atman, higher consciousness or whatever other words you are familiar with. A spirit can recognise spirit, the Divine, Source, the Creator. It is your 'phone' also in recognising a much bigger purpose, destination and profound connection. Through your heart you have your spiritual or true home. Your heart can make that call.

Here are some of the key aspects of your heart discussed in more detail in this sixth section, together with some of the first practical heart opening, heart connecting exercises.

Summary - first direct heart steps and practices

The first heart steps can be a 'new' feeling. Practice with commitment and persistence. Your heart knows how it works and the outcome will always improve from the early first steps. To start to let your heart help you, do the following initial and practical heart steps as a foundation:

1. 'Take stock' and track your emotions, emotional reactions and negative thinking patterns, even if they seem insignificant, for several days. Use the PHT 'Negative Emotion and Thought Tracking (NETT)' to do so.

2. The PHT 'A good approach' will help with your first and continuing heart practices, KHHs, PHTs and broader areas of life. It can also be a helpful overall approach to not accumulate worries, burdens or emotions.

3. Perhaps read up on the heart understanding and attitude of 'letting go' and combine it with the first direct heart practices or KHHs. The PHT 'Let go II' is intended as a reminder that the heart's help, and any clearing, is in principal a light and joyful process. Letting go, with relaxing and smiling, will significantly support this.

4. To 'just enjoy' may be a little harder to adopt, especially if you are not in the mood for it or if life is a challenge right now. Be mindful and heartful of it and as soon as it feels 'right' or 'ok' to you, let your whole being, heart and mind/brain be a little joyful. Do this during all practices or KHHs and if you like the positive and direct impact on your heart, expand it into all areas of your life, every day.

5. Any time you experience some form of clearing or not-so-nice-stuff (anger, sadness or any other emotion) being removed, remember the two keys: RELAX and SMILE ... relax a little more and smile a little more freely. This will help your heart and your heart will help you with more strength. Do the same when you feel pressure in your heart or temporary heaviness. These are signs that the heart has started to work, removing some of the burdens or some of the collections or deposits, and you are also feeling more.

6. Do the PHT 'Simple Heart-head balance self-assessment. Take it as a fun exercise, be spontaneous and repeat it several times over the next few weeks.

7. Practise KHH 'Relax more' in combination with the additional PHT 'Heart-breath-intention relaxation'.

8. Whatever your heart will do is in the right direction. Your heart is perhaps the deepest part of you. Everything you read or engage with here is about a deep essential place within you. This is good to recognise, realise, work with and enjoy. Every practical step you take in a more heartful direction will quietly, gently and rapidly have a positive impact on everyone around you. There is no need to do or say anything.

Part B: Your Heart's Help in Areas of Life

Keep reading through the following life sections in Part B of the book that interest you or are relevant to you, your life, your issues, your challenges or joys. The heart will help.

At some point, it will be very helpful to come back to Part A on what your heart is and how it functions. This will deepen your understanding, learning and growth as your mind/brain and heart will want to work together. This will, in turn, support the practical and deeper workings of your heart in the life areas or aspects that you want more help in.

Ideally, practice all Key Heart Helpers (KHHs) in the introductory sections (chapters I to VI) and also those in the life area chapters (1 to 9). Then add the Practical Heart Tips/exercises (PHTs) that feel good to add or appeal to you, even if you don't read the content of a section.

Read the stories or watch some of them on www.yourheartcanhelp.org. You will find that some of powerful shifts, changes and improvements that are shared in these stories inspire and help your mind/brain and heart. Everyone's heart works in similar ways. Changes, shifts and improvements will happen in similar ways to you, your heart and your surroundings.

Chapter 1

Family - Your Heart Set On It

If you begin the day with love in your heart ...
you not only benefit by its presence
but also bring it to others,
to your family and friends. Unknown

For many, family is about love, support and life-long care for each other. Family is often about a place to which we can return, where we can reconnect and let go. If our overall family situation is positive, then family can also be a source of security, support and love from which we go into the world, explore, take risks and crash-land safely should we 'fail'.

However, for some of you the above words may stir or even provoke anger, hurt feelings, sadness or other emotions. Somehow this ideal situation may not be what you have experienced.

There is a further side to this: family members know each other's weaknesses and traits, and at some moment when you, or one of your family members, 'lost it' or felt they had 'the right to do so' then past actions and behaviours towards each other may have caused deep hurt and wounds.

These are powerful realities briefly describing two ends of a spectrum. There is a lot in the middle: where family is okay or pleasant, where not much is happening or some of the special feelings around 'family' have vanished over time.

How your heart will help

To see how your heart can help any family scenario is a starting point from which your family life can improve:

- If your day-to-day, immediate or extended family life is good, even wonderful, your heart-ability will make this even more wonderful. It will create the foundations upon which all the wonderful feelings the heart offers in connection with others can grow and blossom; and
- Should your family life be challenging, rocky, broken or non-existent, then let your heart help in its unique way to make gentle changes in you and through you.

From the heart's perspective we are connected with family members and even beyond family, and time and place do not make any difference. Wherever you are living - with family, close by or on the other side of the planet - your own heart's changes will affect all hearts around you and close to you, regardless of physical distance and time.

This book's main intention is to offer access to the heart's willingness and ability to help. For this reason, in the following sections, there is naturally more focus on family situations which are not so good.

Enjoy exploring the family section, whether you feel you need some heart help in this area or whether you believe it is very good already. Your heart holds a literally endless potential to surprise.

The approaches and natural heart techniques shared over the next 'family' pages are also related to all interpersonal challenges, problems or difficulties. You can apply many of them in relation to children, friends, people at work and your social networks.

Family, the heart of our life

Where the heart is ...

Family is the heart of our life or, at the very least, it is the hub of our heart from the first years of our lives up to teenage or early adulthood. To be part of a family is natural. There is no exception: we are conceived by and born to parents. Even in the case of an adoption, there are physical parents and an adoptive parent or parents. That is a family. To your heart there is no coincidence; whoever was or is around you is in the perfect place. It is also not uncommon for a child to be close to other adults who are important for the child's emotional or mental health - so called 'significant others' in psychological terminology.

Being alive, being on earth and in the human form, our family is the closest and most intimate unit within which we live, experience and grow. This is true whether it is the natural one into which we were born, or one that has adopted us or even one that we 'adopted' and chose at some point in our life. If all goes well then this is the anchor point - the larger heart - of our lives.

And if you like, even go beyond that. Family may also include close friends or neighbours: anyone you hold dear in your heart for the support, love and care they have given. With your heart opening, your sense of family will expand to widening circles of individuals. There will be more love, more support and more inspiration when the notion of 'family' naturally and heartfully expands. This is clearly the experience in the heart community here in Tasmania and other places. From the heart, you will feel a profoundly close connection to others, even non-family members.

You may be familiar with the concept of a soul mate. However, a soul mate only defines one special person. It may be part of your experience already that the depth of some of your relationships with friends or colleagues are of a similar nature: there is a specialness that makes you feel as if these, too, were your siblings or family.

If your family situation has been difficult or even painful, then at some point there is the opportunity to let go from the perspective of the heart, to become free of any emotional entanglement or resentments and to move forward as an adult, to live the full potential and purpose of life's offering. If this 'heart of life', your family situation feels rather heavy and thoughts about family are associated with burdening feelings, then this means that the hearts involved are a little more closed. Also, if there is exclusion, a lack of wanting to meet or be in touch, then it is very likely that at some point one or both parties, did not follow their hearts or did not let the heart help with difficulties, challenges or even hurts that occurred. Fortunately, the heart can help and has the ability to reverse past trends, deal with past events and open doors to renewed connection, joy and love.

Think of family as all the family members around you: your parents, your children, your siblings and the step versions of all these too. Include grandparents, grandchildren, aunts, uncles and cousins.

Family as a beacon of light and love

For some, the family is a shining beacon of light, a source of support, nurturing and love. If that is your experience, then you have felt unconditional love. You may also clearly feel the immense depth of the bond connecting you and your family. In situations like this, we know with all our heart that the family, or key persons in the family unit, will always be there, whatever the situation, challenge or disaster.

> *I have seen this in the clearest way in what is perhaps an extreme end of the social spectrum, during my time working in a prison. For more than four years, I worked with offenders and their families as part of a team of over 40 rehabilitation staff. After some time, especially long-serving inmates, the only visitors who would come were the parents, spouse and close family members.*

This is the bond and ultimate behaviour of the heart, to support those close to us even during the most difficult of times, even when other members of the family or society say the person was 'wrong' or a 'bad' person.

Love and support

Support, connection and care are all expressions of love that bond and give strength to family and all close connections. These are heart-generated qualities. This ultimately means that whatever someone close to you has done or is still doing, there is a deep sense of forgiveness of holding that individual in a space of love rather than emotions.

Love only ever supports, refines, builds and heals

Once we are deeply submerged in the feeling of the purer love that is flowing from within the heart, we are naturally deeply 'in love'. This is felt in the clearest ways with our children: we can do nothing but feel love for them. There is a feeling that this love and care will never cease to exist, even if we do not approve of their behaviour, attitudes or actions, as indicated above in the prison scenario.

Amanda's story is a wonderful account that exemplifies both the help from the heart and how the heart can deepen something that is already quite beautiful or special.

What Amanda does not share below is that her own family background was tough. In her words, it was a rough upbringing in not-the-easiest of family situations in the suburbs of outer London. Various pieces of her childhood that she shared, reveal that there was violence and abuse.

Amanda is a mother of four and is now an incredible beacon of light for a large community of friends and people who visit the meditation and healing centre that she and her husband manage. From her early teens onwards she always had a feeling of wanting to be free - freer and lighter than her quite challenging family situation had shown her was possible.

Amanda's Story:

Amanda sought freedom through experience, by travelling in her early adult life. After ten years of traveling the world trying to realise her goal of freedom, she met her husband-to-be on one of her travels. They arrived in his home country of Australia with all of their belongings in a backpack, with Amanda three months pregnant.

Naturally Amanda wanted to be a good mother and do the best for her child. She read, spoke to friends and attended a wide range of workshops. She added massage and other personal healing sessions. A close circle of friends supported her and the couple looked for a natural birth.

Despite all these amazing preparations, Amanda soon realised that for all we can plan and try, life can be more complex and not go our way. For unforeseen reasons, the birth took place in a hospital, with all the interventions that they hadn't wanted. The first few months were filled with an unhappy baby, who was often quite ill.

Three more children were born. In the meantime, Amanda and her husband had founded two alternative bookshops in different cities, one with a health and meditation centre attached, and the couple were living on a large bush property. In Amanda's view, much, if not all of this, was created to care the best for the family, in particular the children.

Everything seemed perfect but despite all of this, Amanda describes her time as filled with emotional and physical challenges. She says:

'Deeper within me, I was not at peace; I was not connected. I was constantly trying hard to be what I thought I would be, could be, as a good mother and wife but at the centre I felt out of place and even worse, without any knowing of how to change that.'

One typical situation Amanda describes from that time is: 'Communicating with the children and saying what I clearly thought was right, doing what was right and yet I was continuously failing to get the result I was looking for. The result I wanted was for the children to behave in a better way or to help out. At a deeper level it was wanting shared love, connection, deeper understanding of my children and myself and a loving freedom within my family.'

With every one of the four children being a strong character, what this resulted in was upsets, hardened situations, unresolved problems and in Amanda, a painful awareness of disconnection, despite the best intentions and the right words being said.

As Amanda learned about the heart, she clearly felt changes within her. More heart awareness allowed her to communicate more from the heart, not just as an idea or concept, but as a real experience for her. 'I felt my heart responding, taking part in the conversations I had with the children. The children felt the changes too. We started to have heart-to-heart talks; everything was softening, and there was more allowing of the other one to be, to express, to share. There was much less emotional reaction.'

'I recognised that my heart was communicating in a different way than my brain. I recognised when to speak and not to speak. This was new to me; even though the thought was good and I knew I was right, the heart's direction was not to say it, to let it go, to let the heart-to-heart connection dissolve it or resolve it over time. It worked, often better than any words said.'

'The heart empowered me in such a beautiful way in all my relationships at home and at work. I felt clearer and clearer over the months, when I was being loving or when I wanted to control the situation.'

'The children responded to this in the most beautiful way. There is now a sweetness of love flowing between us. Now, after several years of more heart, that sweet feeling is always there.'

'I notice the children also feel more freely within themselves and within our relationship. They do not seem to hide issues, including problems in the relationship they have with us, the parents. They are teenagers and there are problems, but for me the gift of the heart is that the problems are in the open. There is deep love, trust and a freedom to accept and learn.'

'Now when there are problems, they are met with love, compassion and a heartfelt understanding. What is wonderful is we laugh a lot more and we understand and support each other more freely and lovingly.'

'One example of this was when I was recently sitting with my ten-year-old son, who has started to learn the piano. We sat on the bed with his piano song book, talking about his homework. We suddenly started to sing the 'Ode to Joy' together. It was with an almost indescribable feeling of joy and love. It felt like we were connecting deeply as mother and son but also beyond the relationship of mother and son, so deeply that everything was merging into love and joy, whilst at the same time being fully aware of the mother-child relationship we share.'

What Amanda shares is something other parents also frequently experience: a gap, even a chasm between the ideal loving parent-child relationship and what is happening in reality. Frictions and emotions are likely to surface, when concepts, beliefs and even 'knowledge' about what is right or best for the child are not always received as such by the child.

Amanda's story also indicates that the heart softens these beliefs and concepts, showing that the interactions between parent and child and the depth of experiences of heartfulness can be beautified immensely with the help of your heart. It also shows that love is neither a belief nor a 'yes' or 'no' scenario. Love can only ever be felt and has many forms and many layers. With the help of your heart, let the magic of love return to your heart and unfold in its fullest kaleidoscope of feelings.

Shining through Amanda's story is the fact that an overall loving family situation can be beautified and deepened even more. Everyone will naturally blossom in heart and spirit, as the heart will always help and support everyone.

'Family' as deeply challenging, even painful

For some, when hearing the word family or thinking of family, the feeling is not so positive. Now, or sometime in the past, interactions with family members have been difficult, hurtful, even traumatic.

It may have been how you were treated, what was said, even what was done to you or others that left a mark, an imprint in your memory and heart. Because family is so close this can be the biggest challenge in a person's life, something still being grappled with after many years.

Depending on the depth of these experiences, hurts or disappointments, they can significantly limit your ability to journey and grow successfully through life as an adolescent or adult.

Often the missing ingredient was love: genuine, caring, giving and supportive love. In difficult times, or times we were disengaged from our family or parents, it was often this heartful and heart-generated flow that was missing: of love, care, joy, understanding and compassion, that is naturally there when we are 'in love' or sharing love with those close to us.

Of course you want to be 'in love' or in the love, in the heart, ideally in all that you do with or for family members: children, partners, loved ones and those in the widest of family circles. This may not have been the case for you or other people out there. Now you can choose the heart, love and all that it means, to heal and regenerate.

More heart will not only heal, it will intervene: when the heart is strong, there is an inner block that stops us saying or doing things that are hurtful to others.

What is truly wonderful, if not magical, about the heart is that not only will it gradually heal all the hurts from the past, it will also be the best form of inner strength for you, helping you to be on a path of heart, compassion, care and love.

Do not be too concerned if all this sounds too soft or fluffy. Most of us have internalised all the opposing qualities like rationalising, controlling, being firm, holding on to brain-generated concepts and opinions etc. If these qualities have so far failed to help, it is time to try the way of the heart and perhaps discover that what seems esoteric can have very concrete effects.

The feeling has gone

Disconnection from your family, lack of communication, lack of interest in each other may have become obvious or painful.

The heart's work is one of gentleness and softness. Wherever this gentleness and softness of your heart feelings are not present, or overshadowed by emotions or meaningless talk without heart or care, you may not long to be in the presence even of close family members.

Very often, when you look at how your heart works, it is understandable that deep and sweet feelings of love, kindness, care, understanding and more have gone. Sometimes it is only you who feels that they are gone.

Often, too, clients, friends and workshop participants openly share that what were once feelings of sweet love for family members are now tainted with negative emotions like resentment, irritation, anger or jealousy. Making this even harder is the fact that it is nearly impossible to shake this off without assistance from the heart. You may find this heart-help through another approach or by using mainly the suggested KHHs and PHTs. Let this work as directly as possible for you and those dear to you.

Months or years of not looking after the heart, of not being heartful or not following the heart have led to this. If you have followed your emotional responses rather than the love and sweetness in your heart, then the cover over your heart is stronger and heavier.

If you have allowed yourself to be strong in your emotions and reactions to others, for example being irritated and raising your voice, even screaming or shouting in anger, even more heaviness has been placed in and around your heart.

The 'cuts' and hurts can be deep

At one level, the people closest to you know you best: your family members. Under all the rubble and cover-up or pain that may be there now, if you have, or if you are experiencing family challenges, there is a deep and beautiful love connection.

This means there is, programmed into the heart, all the possibility to enjoy closeness, the bond of the family unit, the intimacy of the family home and all the support and joy it can offer. It is very common, however, that only a small part of this program is accessed and experienced - at times none at all - and emotions end up ruling many interactions.

What can this look like? When things do not go so well, or when one family member has a 'bad day', then that knowledge of each other, the closeness and intimacy can be used in arguments or fights. Emotions grow and dominate and are much stronger than any of the softer heart-feelings. These are moments when deeper and deeper hurts, upsets and wounds are made.

It does not take any profound knowledge of the other to hurt anyone close. Emotions may arise or be triggered by events or behaviours and because of the natural closeness of family, the wounds are deep, or immensely hurtful. An expectation that there 'should' be understanding and care causes possible resentment, disappointments or even anger, which fuels other emotions and burdens the heart.

Without the heart, without allowing ourselves to follow this part of us, family can unfold in the opposite direction to what we hope for, and what we understand and know is 'right'. Knowledge is never enough. The use of the heart will start to bring you more onto the side of caring, attentive and loving actions and reactions.

The heart's radiance, if active, will dissolve the past and open the channels to wonderful moments and a wonderful future with everyone close to you or yet to come into your life.

Jamie's open sharing is both an example of how profound hurt and challenge can occur and how the heart, in its natural ways, even from a distance and after some time, can help to heal these wounds.

Jamie's Story:

Jamie grew up in New Zealand. He left the island when he was 21 years old, and now travels the world teaching laughter yoga and meditation. When not teaching this he delights others with healthy gourmet food as a hobby chef.

Jamie has two brothers and one sister. Jamie's parents separated and his mother remarried. Jamie describes his childhood as very difficult.

Jamie shared that his mother was pregnant with his older brother when she met Jamie's father. His parents later separated when Jamie was a small child.

Jamie's half-brother was older, physically stronger and more solidly built than him. He teased, harassed and bullied him over a long period of time. 'My brother was five years older than me. He overpowered me, bullied me at school and manipulated me in ways that disempowered me even further. He tricked me into doing things I did not want to do.'

'I was often left feeling very confused, looking up to him, looking for guidance and love. His behaviour towards me made me feel very upset and withdrawn. I felt violated, powerless and angry. The memory of that time was filled with negative feelings towards him such as deep frustration, hurt and anger. All this continued through all of my childhood and teenage years.'

'In later times, when we were together as a family, I would avoid him. During times we met, I found myself being polite on the outside and inside I would crunch up. I felt trapped being with my brother in one room. I also found myself cutting off, holding back, not being honest with myself and others and I wasn't dealing with anything that had to do with my brother.'

Jamie started learning about the heart in 2007. At the time he was living in Japan. He came across the Open Heart Meditation and started practising.

'I clearly noted that the heart started to help me to be able to let go of the hurt feelings buried inside towards my brother. There was forgiveness, too. The actions, the memories of being hurt and feeling overpowered were still there but some of the feelings of emotional hurt I noticed had vanished.'

'Over time, the forgiving from the heart went deeper and deeper. It was not a mental process at all. It was a real capacity within. It was growing even more, the more I was doing the heart practices. It surprised me as I learned to let the heart do it, doing less myself, and it all just happened.'

'Life brought my brother and me back together again. In the past it was not possible to speak to him. In fact, I avoided him and any moments we could connect, meet and look each other in the eye. This was something I could not do for years.'

'The heart brought me to a point where we could sit down and speak the truth about the time back then, from the heart. The feeling for me was that I could say things to him truthfully, honestly and without emotion, and in particular without blame. There had been many years of pain, hurt and disconnection. Emotions came up and it ended up being half from the heart and half in other, more emotional ways.'

'I was aware that the heart intuitively helped in all this. I was able to see my brother in a new way and he was able to change his views of me.'

'I am so surprised now, really, really surprised, because with this person in my life being like an 'ogre' for years, who gave me so many reasons to complain and hold grudges, now there is an okay-ness, a connection and I see how our relationship is even beautiful in aspects. I can see beauty in him.'

'It is still not perfect, perhaps no relationship ever is, but now we accept each other. I can really feel how he is accepting of me too; we can have eye contact, be together and certainly in me or from me there is no more judgement or resentment.'

'There is still more trust to come back - this is how it feels. Yet there is a sense of closeness, there is also compassion and kindness in me that is beautiful to feel. I can see also that his ways have caused him quite some difficulties in his adult life. I can even say that I love him and look forward to what our future holds.'

It must be an immensely difficult situation where the person giving you a hard time is so close to you in your family unit, in your home and belonging there, as you do.

However, like other stories in the book show, once the heart is starting to work, shifts occur, even without any intention to heal a particular relationship: frozen or uncaring relationships, even where communication is very limited, politely distant or non-existent, all gently and gradually open again.

The cause of this is the blooming of the deeper heart connection, facilitated by the heart. This can be enough to generate the necessary sunlight and fresh air to touch the other heart, which opens up new ways to connect and love again.

For it to work, it needs one heart that opens and understands how important it is. In a family relationship, or any relationship for that matter, when two hearts open, improvements, benefits and the joy of deep love happen much clearer and faster.

The wonderful part of using the heart's help is that however rocky, difficult or even painful a family situation has been, you do not need to be physically close to the family member/s. You also do not need to get close again ever to that family member if the event or situation does not allow this. Naturally, however, you may find that closeness or more intimacy, in the form of trust and sharing part of one's life, will be possible again.

It is important to heal your own heart. The path of the heart means you do not look at the other, you do not wait for the other to improve or make so-called 'positive' steps. A change of one's own heart is the key and only one key is needed to unlock a closed door.

As you attend to your heart it will automatically and naturally help you and those around you. It will start to heal deepest wounds and relationships. The heart's ability and wonderful, healing, opening impacts are not limited by space or time.

The heart never judges or distinguishes between, for example victim or offender, even in small daily events. It will equally help those who may have upset or hurt you and no intention to do so is needed.

This is an aspect some of the past workshop participants or clients in particular situations have not liked. They did not want to help particular persons who had hurt them. At some level, this is okay. However, it is about healing your heart. As the feelings in the heart sweeten and surface, it is a wonderful unfolding toward that love and joy that is wanting to break free from the deeper layers within all hearts: letting go and forgiveness naturally happen, freeing the heart.

Your heart does not judge

One easy trap to fall into when being overly mind/brain focussed, or when there is a lack of balance, is that of analysing and judging, both yourself and others.

What appears logical or a good approach for one to follow, may not be so for the other. A truth for one person is often relevant to a past situation, which today sounds 'right' or feels good. However, for your loved ones it may not have any meaning or could even be the opposite.

This is why wise individuals have said in the past that the mind, brain or thoughts divide. It is easy to have two opposing thoughts or concepts and they both sound 'right'.

The mind/brain easily finds reasons to compare situations or behaviour to others in the past, present or future. These are in some way meaningless efforts, as no situation in its wholeness is the same as a previous one. This is one of the biggest traps in all relationships, when our attitude becomes one of 'I have seen, done or experienced this before and therefore I know or it must be true'.

We can often get by with this, and it can even get trickier: we can find supporters in this mindset. However, no situation is ever exactly the same as before. The circumstances of our own awareness, alertness, emotional stage and heart connectedness can vary. There is more about this in the chapter on work and guidance from the heart.

The heart's important ingredient here is that it can perceive a much greater picture of all surrounding factors not available to the mind/brain. About a person, the heart can consider intentions of others that the mind/brain does not know, or are too subtle and invisible. Similarly, with regard any situation, the moment you judge, there is an iron curtain closing and an openness to split-second decisions can be closed too. The heart will never do that: when you are connected to it and it is active and open, it is always present and will alert and help you in wonderful, practical ways.

Your heart does not expect you to be perfect, not to react to your mother, father, partner or child or be perfectly loving and caring all the time. The heart offers both realisation, learning and healing in one. It will be normal to judge others and yourself until your heart has been opened and cleansed enough and the love and care for others can be greater than any mental ideas or concepts about others.

In moments when your heart is strong, you will find you do not want to judge others or situations. It will feel like a boat that is gently gliding down a river. It will always flow, and there is no effort needed to be within the flow of this river of life that we are all in.

This is a beautiful and special milestone and sign of the direction your heart wants you to take. In those moments you may move the rudders a bit and change course slightly while you are carried by the flow of the heart.

Your heart's openness and lightness will make you strong, resistant to the judgement of others.

There are two levels of heart help. In the first instance your heart will buffer, even block any judgement towards you which won't be able to penetrate the radiance from your strong and active heart. Judgement, while you still hear or notice it, will not affect you.

At the second or deeper level, your heart's radiance will start to dissolve the negative energy that triggers the need to judge you or act in negative ways towards you. Your heart supports an even bigger step toward a gentle, flowing and joyful life.

Past hurts that are 'too' deep

When you know it is very likely you will react with emotion or some sort of outburst to a family member, there is an opportunity, with the help from the heart, to remove some of the deeper triggers and some of the older patterns and related emotions.

This is important as these trigger points are very likely also to flare up when another person, who actually intends well, is somehow triggering that area of your heart and self.

Remaining distant or not being in touch with someone who has hurt you in the past will not be possible if that person is in your family or household. In this instance, follow the heart strengthening path suggested in the book, and with clear commitment and diligent practice you will find noticeable improvements within yourself and very likely in others too.

Even if you seek some distance and choose not to be in touch, then always follow your heart, and be open to when a time may come to reconnect, communicate or meet again.

Your heart is kind, always loving

The nature of your heart is only to feel love: to attend to others with love, to care, to support, to nurture and to help. Sometimes this can mean making decisions that are not liked by another person or even ceasing contact with a person if the heart clearly feels so. To love unconditionally is the very essence of your heart. The clarity of love from your heart also means having the strength to say 'no'.

The nature of love and the quality of your heart is to love and to love and to love.

As your heart awareness and strength grow, this naturally loving quality within will become a part of you, a part of all your exchanges with your dear ones, and depending on how heart-connected others around you are, it will be clearly felt by some, noticed by others and not able to be felt at all by some others. From this place of love and care you can naturally and genuinely offer much support and nurturing to your family and all those around you.

This will be easy when there is an overall positive family environment. It will come to the test when the going gets tough, where it is only the heart and the love coming through you that can support your loved ones. What a beautiful gift to be able to support a loved one through a difficult situation using the heart. Monica's story is an example of such a situation.

When accidents happen and only love can help

Monica offered this powerful story of not judging her own son when others did and it displays her deep love as a mother, to forgive and to trust the heart in standing by her son.

Monica shared that her life and the life of her whole family was rich, easy and blessed until one day, when the police delivered a message to her that her 18-year-old son had had a serious car accident and had to be air-lifted to a nearby hospital.

It turned out that his injuries and those to the passengers of the other car were less serious than initially thought. However, it was later shown that he was under the influence of alcohol, which resulted in four charges and led to a long, expensive and emotionally draining legal journey. Monica had just started to learn about the heart and completed her first workshop weekend.

Monica's family story shows how the heart is always looking for ways to love, forgive and never judge. It helped her personally as well as her husband, whose response was one of support and care but also of emotion, mainly anger.

Monica's Story:

Monica is now in her mid-50s. She describes herself as happily married. Professionally both Monica and her husband were successful too.

With three children, Monica and her husband managed to travel regularly to various countries in world which she describes as: 'our life felt privileged and the children grew up with everything they needed'.

'My son was in college and one night came the call to our home that he was involved in a car accident with suspicion of major neck and spinal injuries. He had been air-lifted by helicopter to the city's hospital.'

'We found out later out that he had been driving under the influence of alcohol and he had injured two girls in the other car involved.'

'Thankfully the injuries to everyone turned out to be much less than initially suspected. What unfolded however, was a long, difficult legal battle, where my son, who could not remember any details of the accident, was being charged with four different offences.'

'I had just started to learn about the heart - my first response was to pray with the help from the heart. Everything was very difficult and I was not very successful in being in my heart, or praying from the heart.'

'All of us were not really equipped to deal with any of this. My husband, who wanted to help and be supportive, and in some way he was, responded also with anger. He simply became angry often and in the end it was his main response. Often it was directed at me, as I was the one talking with him, trying to manage all affairs.'

'What I hid from my family was the fact that I was falling into a deep depression. The whole situation, the legal challenge, my husband's anger, was all coming together. On the surface I am not sure if they noticed. During that time, trying to brush my teeth in the morning was too much of an effort, I was so weak, with no energy, feeling depressed.'

'Thankfully I had just done the first Open Heart Workshops. The teacher was happy to be in touch and when I shared some of the events with him, he was happy to be in contact and kept guiding me again and again into the heart.'

'I still clearly remember that these were moments where, despite all the chaos, there was a calmness, and in this calmness a sense of trust grew. I began to feel at first a gooey, warm feeling in the chest and then it expanded and made me feel like being in a bubble of sweetness and support. I did not feel alone.'

'This was amazing and it got to a point where the anger thrown at me was not reaching me anymore, as if the heart had created a shield around me. I started to smile from my heart to his heart. He felt these changes too and it allowed him to calm down, not to follow the anger. This was a major change and helped us to cope a lot.'

'The time continued to be very difficult and overall it lasted for two years. Lawyers were required and they were costing us $400 per hour. Even though we had enough, this was very difficult financially and in the end the legal costs were over $100,000.'

'My son was very stressed and at times very scared during this whole time. He spent one day locked up, which did not help. Over this process his whole life was shattered.'

'From the calmness within I could tell my son often that 'all will be fine, all will work out' and I encouraged him also to find that peaceful place within. I could do this because I felt the heart's peace so strongly. I was so sure and trusting because of the heart's presence. This allowed him to trust too.'

'He became very accepting of his situation and the overall process. He accepted the main charges and calmly disputed the others. I shared with him often from the heart and also about the heart and how it helped me. He agreed to do a few sessions too.'

'Towards the end of the legal process he was sentenced not to a prison but to an in-residence drug and alcohol rehabilitation centre for two years. Because of his behaviour he was released after 1.5 months with the therapists saying that 'this is not for him'.'

'Before all this my son was a happy-go-lucky guy. He liked partying and he was in many ways tough too. He would avoid me, share almost nothing with me and in many ways excluded me from his life. I realise this now.'

'Now, with the heart keeping me and my family on track, the relationship I have with my son is very warm, loving and there is a lot of trust. This is very special and I had not realised how much I had missed this quality of connection and contact with him.'

'I fully believe that he knew then and knows now that I love him unconditionally and he can always trust this.'

'The heart has helped me immensely through all this, mainly with not judging and not laying blame. He now regularly calls me, we talk about all sorts of things and he has opened to me in a way that he now seeks advice, even in girlfriend matters. This would never have happened before.'

'It is wonderful. I feel the communication now is so beautiful, warm and there is much trust in what will be. He has stopped hiding from me, from the love we share.'

This story clearly shows what is described in the earlier chapters as the potential of the heart's ability to help, in unforeseen and incredible ways.

The heart clearly gave Monica strength to deal with the challenges and emotions that both her son and her husband experienced, and with her feelings of depression. This was in spite of the immense financial and social pressures, legal proceedings and related media exposure.

The importance of forgiveness

Forgiveness is important, not as an idea or concept or something good to do, but as one avenue to free the heart and mind from burdens and unnecessary weight, especially concerning events or past occurrences about which it is difficult or impossible to do anything.

The intention to forgive may be a starting point, yet it will not be enough as your mind/brain can't alone dissolve what the heart is holding or burdened with. In some way, Monica's amazing sharing is also about forgiveness.

Why is forgiveness important? Any negative thought or emotion that is being held in your heart is also limiting your heart's ability to help you, to offer you most wonderful feelings in your daily life and to guide and lead you in your personal and spiritual growth. Anything not being cleared, or being held, will only limit you.

Forgiveness from the heart

For your heart's journey, the lightness of your heart is closely linked to your ability to forgive from the heart.

Starting to use your heart more and doing Heart Strengthening and any of heart practices will start to help in removing burdens or negativities from your heart that are related to forgiving others. More so, they will remove related emotions that are still holding or limiting your heart.

Whatever your challenge, however deep you feel any hurt, pain or emotions, the heart can offer additional help. The first piece of good news is: your heart knows how to forgive. The second is, it just does, even though the mind/brain may still have some discussion or other ideas about it. And thirdly, every time you do the natural strengthening of your heart, and using the KHHs or PHTs introduced up to now, it will automatically strengthen this heart-ability to forgive. Some of the unburdening will happen automatically. Deeper forms of heart-facilitated forgiveness may be needed for deeper burdens or stronger past events. These tools are shared below and later in the book (PHT 20, KHH 10 'Surrendering burdens' and KHH 13 'Open heart meditation').

Only a heart and mind that can forgive can freely support and love others, loved ones, family members or people in wider circles around us.

There can be a tendency to want to forgive more from the mind/brain. It is the heart, however, that has, around it and within it, the storage of everything ever experienced. The more direct way to remove these burdens, negativities, heavy deposits or deep-seated traumas seems to be to let the heart deal with what is around the heart, that the heart knows, feels and can deal with best. The aim is to let the heart help, as it has the in-built capacity to do this.

> **Practical Heart Tip 20: Letting the heart forgive those close to us ***
>
> *Do the core Heart Strengthening (KHH 6). This heart warm-up is important to really let your heart do the forgiving:*
>
> - *Let your heart smile to the person that you feel to forgive;*
>
> - *Do this with all your feeling and let your heart do it, so just let your heart keep smiling to that person for some time, a few minutes;*
>
> - *If you are sensitive, you may feel something from your heart radiating outwards... that is the heart radiance, the wanting to share, the deeper love, the Divine blessing flowing through your heart. It will reach the other person directly, as non-physical matters have no limitation in time or space; and*
>
> - *This is a very healing, freeing and beautiful process; enjoy.*

It sounds very simple and yet often the heart will create a win-win-win situation. What this means is that whatever the challenge or difficulty is, the heart will aim to create a win-win situation. Given the depth and wisdom of the heart it will also often facilitate additional benefits or positives. The more often you do this, the above PHT and use the heart in general, you will connect to your heart and all the positive processes and benefits will unfold. Where greater burdens or trauma exist the Heart Based Therapeutics connected deep 'emotional clearing process' has shown astounding results. It is discussed in wellbeing section 5.

You may feel that the wounds or hurts are so deep that this form of forgiving is not possible. That is okay; move on to the next section and next exercises and allow for your growing heart strength to make the necessary, gentle changes over time. Make a note in your journal to come back to this PHT at the end of the book or in three or six months.

Whatever your heart holds in relation to the one person or several people you choose to let your heart smile to, it will be thoroughly cleansed and cleared. You will be able to approach them and everyone else in your life with a lighter, more attentive, more loving heart. This is very significant.

From another angle, it is important to let the heart do this fuller forgiving. Whatever the deposits or negativities are around or within your heart, they create the potential for future eruptions or emotional reactivity. These deposits function like trigger points, erupting inwardly and making you not feel the best, adding heaviness to the feeling and heart, or erupting outwardly and adding burdens to your relations at home or outside the home.

Your heart being a strong source of help, energy, light and healing, there is a very strong chance, that the wordless communication shared in the PHT above impacts the other person quietly and gently over time.

There will always be some form of limitation in how the other person is impacted by this. If the person is not adding to the 'collection' around his or her heart in daily life very much, there is a higher chance of this working more swiftly.

As the essence of the beautiful radiance from your heart is a deeper flow, a universal love, based on the heart's abilities and its innate connection to the divine. It means that the positive or evoked changes will never be your agenda, doing or influencing at work, but something that always looks for the best outcomes, changes and transformations in you and in others.

These positive heart and forgiveness processes will happen every time you use your heart as described in the tip above. It is a good very beginning. It is also a way to start trusting your heart, to start trusting something other than mind, ideas, hopes or emotions.

For later, if you feel to skip forward, there is the further, deeper and more complete way of forgiving from the heart, also facilitating a deeper cleansing of all heart relationships in the family, through PHT 20, the KHH 13 'Open Heart Meditation'.

Forgiveness and reconnection

It is when you forgive from the heart and when all associated negative emotion, such as resentment or hurt feelings are fully removed, that a beautiful, warm and loving reconnection can occur with family members.

Paula's story below is an amazing example of how the heart opening and the growing love from the heart can reveal the joy of being with our loved ones, our family members, even in situations where it is difficult to imagine.

Paula and her mother had not been in contact for around 30 years. The feelings Paula held were of distrust, disconnection and disrespect. Much of this stemmed from her childhood and her parents' divorce. Now, however, they are the best of friends. They hang out, have fun and do things together with much love. With the help of the heart, Paula has also been able to support her mother during a very difficult time in her life: the passing away of her life-partner.

What is touching to connect with in this story is the unconditional care Paula found in her heart for her mother's partner, who had been in her mum's life for many years. He had the tendency to be violent and abusive towards her mother, much of it based on excessive alcohol use. All of these were additional reasons for Paula keeping her distance and not wanting to be in touch.

Paula's Story:

'As a teenager I suffered during my parents' separation. I felt guilty; there was dishonesty between my parents and I lost the trust I had in my mother. I also felt deeply embarrassed and continuously exposed to lies and hurt.'

'After the divorce I decided to live with my father. During this time, I continued to be filled with disrespect for my mother. This increased when my mother married again only some months later and had further children with her second husband. I also came to disrespect her new partner. He turned out to be an alcoholic and physically violent towards my mother. He regularly and violently hit her. For over 30 years I avoided contact with my mother and did not feel any emotional connection.'

'When I was in my late forties, and over some years, I went to psychotherapy. This somewhat softened the situation and my mother and I started to have irregular contact again.'

'The big breakthrough happened around seven years ago. I learned about the heart and the importance of it in the year 2006. I found the practices very touching and they had an immediate impact. I did the suggested practices regularly with commitment and also enjoyed the Open Heart Meditation very regularly, often daily.'

'The deepest feeling was a gentle feeling of joy spreading from the heart through my whole body. It came together with a gentle feeling of sadness, together with a yearning, of having been so separated from my heart or heartfulness in life. It felt very familiar, like homecoming initially, though often only for brief moments.'

'I felt such a new and deep freedom in my heart and letting go of emotions or resentments which did not clearly serve me any more now. All this happened naturally with more heart awareness. It led to an even deeper and natural reconciliation with my mother, after now over 35 years of almost no contact. A beautiful friendship developed.'

'To my surprise it also came to a peace and reconciliation between her husband and myself. I felt able to forgive him also wholeheartedly and to approach them both, be with them in friendship and love.'

'Only one day after our reconnection he was admitted to hospital and was dying some weeks later. It was special to sit with him for hours at the hospital bed, holding hands, being with him with the help of the heart, praying also with opening hearts as he passed on.'

'All that my heart felt and shared was compassion, love and care for them both, despite the years of disrespect and humiliation that had been exchanged. It was so easy and beautiful to forgive from the heart; no words were needed. And it happened also that my mother was able to forgive her husband too.'

'I was able to be there for my mother as she went through the grief, pain and sadness of losing her partner of many years. Several years have passed since and my mother and I have been the best of friends over these years. Care and support for her feels so natural now and we enjoy being there for each other. There is a lot of love between us. She is now old and frail and I am not too sure how many more days and months we will have.'

'I am grateful beyond words for the heart in opening this special connection again, to my mother and her life - not only opening, but allowing it to bloom, grow and be deeply and quietly joyful. I feel a greater force, energy and love flowing and taking care of me, my heart and all dear ones around me.'

Paula's sharing exemplifies the natural working of the heart in family situations wonderfully. She also shared that she is opposed to any form of violence between people whether this is emotional, physical or verbal. However, in this situation it was important to forgive and to focus on supporting her mum and her partner.

Your heart will dissolve all the emotional baggage from the past, even if you do not intend for this to happen, and it will work in all directions. For example, you may look for heart help for your intimate relationship and find that other, more distant relationships improve.

Unhelpful emotions stored in or around your heart will be 'worked on' and dissolved every moment you use your heart. They will also be of no use to you every moment of your life that they are held within you and holding you back.

Attending to your heart and using the KHHs or heart tips, as in Paula's situation, may or may not lead to reconciliation with close family members. What it will do for you and your heart is to fully open the ability to love freely, to love again, and to experience all the love and care your heart can receive, hold and share.

Everyone has the free will to connect, engage, and make good family choices or not. Ultimately it is about choosing a love response, a heart response. That same free will also offers the choice to you and to family members to go in either direction: to use the heart to love again or not.

It is good to have no expectation to start with. From the mind/brain perspective much can be found or said about 'expectation'.

When you hold any expectation, you also wrap something around the heart, and that wrapping will limit the heart's radiance and positive energy-expansion, including in ways that are impossible to imagine.

When learning more about the heart and letting her heart help her, Paula found it easy to reconnect, to let go, to forgive and to easily find new care in her heart, including offering help and loving attention to her mother's dying partner.

It is very likely, as many of the stories throughout the book show, that either direct positive changes will occur or surprising changes will happen elsewhere or all around.

Love and happiness are the two big headings under which fall many things we look for in all our hopes, actions and aspirations, including in our family life. Paula's story shows more clearly how love can return to your heart and relationships, even if this is quite unexpected. Her story also indicates a joy that is surfacing within her and being shared in this renewed mother/daughter connection.

For the mind/brain and whatever past knowledge and understanding you may have, it may sound strange, yet often the deeper your problems are, the more your heart is able to help you. You can quickly attain wonderful experiences of what we all naturally long for: love and happiness.

How deep is your love?

I love those who can smile in trouble, who can gather strength from distress, and grow brave by reflection.
Tis the business of little minds to shrink, but they whose heart is firm, and whose conscience approves their conduct, will pursue their principles unto death. Leonardo da Vinci

Your heart will also open to other aspects of love that you are already aware of or have experienced. Possible complaints about our family members or family life may be notions of 'I was not loved enough' or similar patterns of thinking and feeling.

From the perspective of your heart, it is much more important to be aware of the heart as the centre of unconditional love, and to take steps in this direction rather than thinking or complaining about anything to do with love, family or the past. To learn to love is more about evolving, growing and changing.

Any love that you give, any love your heart is receiving as an energy, is a greater, universal or Divine love. Any love you share will enrich, broaden and most importantly deepen your experience of love. It will also deepen any understanding and practice about love.

The heart's natural ability is to share the deepest and most abundant form of love. On a journey in this natural heart-direction, any love we may 'want' will at some point dissolve in this greater love, and all wanting, all hurt, all past, all future will dissolve into a wonderful here and now-ness of your heart, an ocean of love you can permanently swim in.

From the perspective of your heart, it is simple:

- If family life has been and currently is 'good', then your heart can help to take you beyond beauty and joy, to where words do not exist anymore to describe the feeling.
- If family life has been a challenge and any feelings of love and care are hidden under some rubble created in the past through not-so-good interactions with family members or loved ones, then let your heart help to make direct, clear and positive steps.

The question is: how deep is your or anyone's love? How much love can you, your heart, hold and feel?

Your heart's ability to love is immense. The analogy some may have heard, 'the heart is deeper than any ocean', is true and also not true because the heart is literally limitless in its ability to help and to feel love.

One key step at the level of your mind/brain and your heart is to let your heart help you to open the heart, to let the heart and the deeper love - that will instantly flow more abundantly - shift you towards loving others more. Be guided by your heart, enjoy the feeling of love and let your heart smile lovingly to others as the main focus. Keep a healthy distance too, if on this wonderful journey you fall in love with everyone you meet or the other way around: everyone you meet falls in love with you.

Feeling love is only one part of this. There is the incredible ability to receive love and the wonderful ability to share love. Love, when flowing freely, has a beautiful healing property. The experience of love is always more like a flow; you are in it, feeling the sweetness of this flow and movement. In return, any attempt to hold on to it will very likely reduce the feeling, or even block it or make it disappear.

Either of the above family scenarios allow your heart to take you on the journey of all journeys: of love, bliss, wonder and sharing. Your heart will take the most direct route to happiness and deep love, especially in relation to those close to you. Your family members will heal, as the heart nurtures and supports, naturally facilitating growth in you and in all those around you.

The heart will help directly and often immediately if you look at your heart as a practical and real part of you; after all it is. Let your heart help you in the natural ways your heart is designed. The following sections are about the practical heart help you can tap into.

Practical help - Your heart is guiding and helping

Where we love is home; home that our feet may leave, but not our hearts.
Oliver Wendell Holmes

Clients, friends and many participants in workshops have shared or realised that even if they are no longer in negative, damaging environments, there can still be significant burdens from the past.

How do you practically let your heart be stronger and help you let go of the past? Here are the suggested steps and heart-supporting options:

1. KHH 4 - Relax and smile (often in your life);
2. Expand KHHs 2 or 6 into short meditations. Smile freely for mind to be calmer and heart to be strengthened;
3. Let your heart help you - relax more, smile more;
4. Set positive reminders to remember about your heart and with the help of these to be connected to it often;
5. Let your heart help you and your family member (use the heart tip above - smiling to family members);
6. 'Clear out the cupboards' - access your own heart more;
7. Remove yourself from the situation to strengthen your heart; and
8. As you practice, be kind to yourself and others. Your practice quality and the emotions you feel will sometimes be 'good' and sometimes tinged with doubt. Be consistent and committed to your heart and persevere.

Key Heart Help 4: Relax and smile

The key heart activity introduced in the Family section is relax more and smile more often.

Key Heart Help 4 - Relax and Smile

As often as you remember or are reminded by prompts, make a gentle attempt to be more relaxed physically, and at the same time gently smile.

> ### The full KHH 4 - Relax and Smile
>
> *We love to relax and we love to smile or receive a smile. Relaxing and smiling works outward and inward.*
>
> *As often as you remember or are reminded by prompts - you can use the next PHT - do this:*
>
> - *Make a gentle attempt to be more relaxed physically;*
>
> - *Gently smile; and*
>
> - *If you have extra moments, or in quiet time, smile to your heart while also touching your heart, especially once you progressed past KHH 6.*
>
> *The further you progress into the book, just relaxing and smiling will bring you into a better mind/brain and heart balance. It will also make your heart help clearer available.*

This may sound too simple or even insignificant. We look for relaxation at the end of the day or in the form of a relaxing holiday. At some level we know that relaxing is important. The following will explain why this invitation to relax and smile often is very important to support your heart and every aspect of your life; regardless of what else is happening.

Why relax?

Your mind/brain executes and guides what your physical body is doing and what it is about to do. Because of this connection, there is a reverse function, too: if you are physically tense, your mind/brain will be more active and pushed to think more.

You may be aware of unnecessary thinking, random thoughts, even thoughts you don't want to have. The amount of thinking any one of us does impacts on how relaxed we are and how much we naturally use our heart. Additionally, within any number of thoughts it is very likely there are burdensome and negative ones. A higher level of relaxation leads to a freer physical body and heart and vice versa. A refreshed mind/brain will also function better if it can have some time out.

Why smile?

> *I want to change the world one smile at a time.*
> *Tommy Franklin - Dancer (Australian X-Factor)*

You know how much a smile from a dear one, even from a random person in the street, can brighten you up, even if only for a fleeting moment. Sometimes the memory or joy from such a smile can last even longer, something inside has been touched or triggered.

The importance of smiling could easily be brushed away as something insignificant, such as 'this is not for serious, busy, or, mature people or what use can a smile have'? There is a belief in a more poker-face approach to life, not to give away feelings, to be less open or readable. However, when you are happy or joyful it is very hard for this not to show as a wide smile. You feel naturally better and often that joy is infectious.

When someone you like or love smiles at you, you know in this moment there is joy, connection, understanding or love and you clearly know it is genuine and from the heart.

Smiling and your heart

From the important perspective of your heart, as you smile, two things happen:

- Your heart will be touched by that smile; it will respond, become freer and start to help you. Smiling naturally strengthens your heart; and
- Every time you smile, your brain will be less active, and any excess thinking will be reduced.

When you smile, there is a connection that is made possible between your smile and your heart; it is naturally there. It is hardly ever used in the way it can be.

The moment you intend to smile to your heart, together with understanding that it is for this very purpose, you directly access and stimulate your heart's functions. From then on, every time you smile, ideally being quite relaxed, your heart will be freer and able to help.

With every intention to smile to your heart, you will increase this natural connection and your heart will be freer, lighter and brighter. You are now ready to explore your heart fully and all it has been waiting to offer you. The next section 'Smiling to your heart' will guide you gently to start exploring and using your heart.

A gentle reminder: all this is very new to most people. You may or may not feel anything for the first few times. Be patient, do not look for any sensation and keep practising regularly. In progressing through your heart learning, the readily available connection between heart and smile becomes clearer.

Do not be concerned, especially if you love your mind/brain and how it has supported you in your life. A stronger, more present heart will lead to a calmer mind/brain. A calmer mind/brain will naturally be sharper and more creative, access the right thoughts more directly and support you even more. Read more about this in the 'work' chapter.

Smiling to your heart

We have all experienced that a well-meaning, joyful or loving smile from a loved one, dear friend or even a stranger can touch your heart. These are moments when the heart likes the interaction with another person. In the same way a smile from another person can make you feel lighter and happier, the smile to your heart can work on your heart.

Your smile and your heart are connected. The moment you intend to smile to you heart, your heart will 'like' this and respond in ways the mind and brain may not know and do not understand.

Make quality time to do this, around 2-5 minutes smiling to your heart. Do it in the following way, using the core heart strengthening steps:

- Relax with the help of KHH 3 [or use either PHT 19, 44 and 45 as a warm up]
- Close your eyes
- Touch your heart [as shown in the figures 2 and 3]
- Smile freely to your heart [KHH 6]
- Feel your heart or all the deeper feelings from your heart. [Keep relaxing, feeling, smiling for some time]

This is in essence KHH 6, the core heart strengthening practice. Practise and enjoy this often. You can do this several times a day, even several times in one hour. Every time you stop, relax, touch your heart and smile, the intention is there to 'smile to your heart' and the process of opening, connecting and using your heart is directly being triggered.

The natural way the heart works the best is if:
- **you don't do anything else;**
- **you have an attitude of 'letting go'; and**
- **you just let this natural heart-process unfold.**

The first feelings from the heart are likely to be a sense of inner calm, lightness, relaxation, feeling less burden/worry and in some instances, a bubbling up of spontaneous feelings of joy.

Sometimes people feel one or several of these from the very beginning. In this instance, let it deepen every time you smile. At other times the feeling is not so clear. In this case, it is good to keep going as underneath any layers of heaviness or collection around the heart, the heart will work, every time.

There is also a likelihood that you are not sure what you feel or you have a sense there is nothing happening. This is perfectly normal. It is very common to have used the mind and brain a lot in the years previously and there is a form of holding, controlling or watching that the mind/brain does for the first days or weeks of heart strengthening practices.

The heart is smart and deep. The moment you start to work with it, it will start to do its part. Feeling and being aware of it, will become clearer over time. However, feeling clearly is not important because the heart will start the clearing, healing, cleansing and opening process underneath, whether you feel it or not.

Your heart will become freer as you smile more and with the practice given, the clarity of feeling will happen, even if not for some time.

Positive reminders

How should we do all of this; how do we change? What are old patterns of behaviours and being: the trained, or habitual overuse of the mind/brain? Sometimes there will be an overall busy-ness, on the outside, on the inside or both, that will slow the heart progress down. Busy-ness can be so strong that new ways of being can be overpowered and forgotten.

An important helper here is to set yourself reminders to relax and smile more often and more freely and to feel your heart at the same time. You will be more connected to your heart and more heartful in your daily life. Initially you may not feel this strongly or clearly. The feelings from the heart are gentle and subtle.

***Practical Heart Tip 21: Heart reminders ***

Set yourself reminders to be more heart connected and to strengthen your heart regularly. Reminders can be in the form of:

- *Stickers around the house, car or office (smileys, hearts or any sticker that you like); and*

- *5-10 times a day set a reminder on your smart phone or e-calendar.*

One major reminder: whatever the situation or challenge that is facing you, choose your heart over any other response: emotion, over-thinking, ignoring something, etc.

Be creative - ensure that on every day's journey you are reminded to:

- *Feel the feeling from the heart more;*

- *Be more relaxed - to actively relax more;*

- *Relax and smile more; and*

- *Add heart strengthening practices/Key Heart Help(ers) from this or any section to your daily program.*

Being grateful and your heart

The gratitude people have expressed in workshops or sessions is immense and immeasurable. When hardness in family relationships softens, the joy and gratitude can run very deep. This is because the deeper spiritual or heart connection we have with those close to us is immensely beautiful.

Gratitude is a feeling from the heart, too, and because of the depth of family relations, the gratitude and wonderful feelings are immense. As soon as you realise or feel that your own heart quality or heart capacity can make these deep and gradual changes, your heart response to any situation becomes an easier choice.

Your heart enjoys the feeling and notion of gratitude. Whatever change you feel, whether in you, others or your family situation, be grateful. Being grateful will support the heart opening and learning and the help your heart will continue to facilitate.

You will notice that, over time, difficult situations can become positive reminders to choose a loving, soft and kind response from the heart.

As a result, your heart will open more and more. It is an amazing upward spiral towards more light, love and being loved.

There is immense gratitude possible to those in your family near and dear to you and those who are further away. At times my children challenge me. Children can be both the love of our lives and the biggest challenge. In situations like these, if there is even the smallest form of emotion in my voice or feeling, there is now very clear pressure in the heart. I pause the interaction, focus on the heart, feel the connection and radiance and often I will naturally feel to apologise to them.

If you are persistent with these simple approaches you will find that control over emotions is achievable and that the damage they can do, or have done in the past, is reduced.

The deeper heart-being

While at times not easy, in family situations, as in relationships, choosing the heart is the most powerful way to let your heart become your strongest ally more often. It is a chance to let your heart fully cleanse emotions that come from the deeper layers of your heart to the surface; from the view of the heart that wants to unburden itself, it carries within an opportunity to learn and to grow.

It is also good to remember that over time any negative responses will become less and less, any trigger points will melt away and what remains is only love, calmness and wonderful feelings towards others, while you are at peace with yourself.

Taking responsibility with the help from your heart

When you know that you are likely to react, there is another strategy available to you in choosing your heart and following the heart strengthening steps. Firstly, you know for yourself that when a family member or other is in emotion, it is not pleasant to be around. Emotion is a burden to this very interaction and over time any emotional reaction will burden the relationship overall.

Secondly, when you react to such a situation you will also place new negativities in and around your heart, burdening your heart and feeling.

Take responsibility and take control of your heart and emotional wellbeing. Take control over your own actions too. The following are your heart's best choices:

1. Before you know that the triggers or overall situation lead to an emotional outburst in you or your family member, let your heart help you! Focus on the Key Heart Practice techniques discussed above or in the following chapters; and
2. Should an outburst/emotional reaction occur or be likely to happen in you or the other, then one good choice is to remove yourself from the situation.

Always choose your heart as you remember to do so. At first this will not be easy or familiar. When we have an emotional response, when we are being triggered, we are 'naturally' in that emotion and it is harder to stop. Use the mind/brain to remind you. Stop whatever you do and attend to your heart. The closer to the event/emotion, the better the healing/clearing effect facilitated by your heart.

In relation to choice (1) you will need to see if this is enough to control the emotion with the help of your growing heart awareness and practice. It will take some practice. Persevere and you will notice changes in yourself and in the responses others have towards you.

You are not perfect; if you find that in most cases it works, great, keep going. Be at peace with yourself, forgive yourself if you have the occasional outburst and if it is not fully working yet. If emotion only knows emotion as a response, where will it end? If you react negatively because you reacted negatively, it will only compound the problem. Regular practice of Heart Strengthening and the Open Heart Meditation will greatly speed up this process by which the heart will help you and by which you will be able to naturally choose a heart response over an emotion response. Long term this is very significant as your heart is your key to feeling wonderful, at peace, loving and joyful.

Clear out the cupboard

As you take more heart responsibility, which is always 'normal' responsibility too, any impurity in your heart triggered by family challenges will be changed, whether you are aware of it or not. Whatever is surfacing in a current situation will very likely surface in future situations and literally make you respond in not the best, most caring or loving ways.

Remember too, even as you attend to other matters with the help of your heart, your heart will cleanse and remove negativities relating to emotions. In most instances, 95% or more, we feel a pleasant feeling and process, not the negative emotions or our disposition to respond negatively.

You may say or believe that it is good to express emotions when you feel them. That is one way to be and respond/react. However, when someone is very angry or very jealous - particularly if you know there is no reason for it, and you feel the quality or rawness of this emotion directed toward you, it does not feel pleasant and rarely feels right.

Your heart offers a unique and effective way to continuously clear out the cupboard of any emotions, as well as any dispositions or habits of responding in any way other than what's best long term, for you and the people close to you.

Let your heart help your family members

Letting your heart help your family members may not sound like a good idea to you; you may not even like it at all, especially if past hurts were very deep.

Remember, the more help is needed, the more your heart will spring into action and radiate, offering you peaceful, even joyful feelings as any mending or healing takes place. Contrary to other approaches, the heart help is a light and burden-free option: you are not required to go over any past hurts or wounds; your heart knows and no conscious (mind/brain conscious) re-experiencing is needed at all.

Practical Heart Tip 22: Using the heart with deep hurts *

Recall a situation where hurt or upset occurred or trust your heart and let it choose past situations.

Then do a thorough heart preparation using KHH 6 or the deeper versions of it, PHTs 57 and 76.

Intend to let the heart radiate and smile to your family members, those you love dearly, as well as those who, now or in the past, have upset, hurt or done some form of wrong to you.

The freer and sweeter your smile, the more love you can feel and add to the smile, the more your heart will spring into action.

Note: initially it may be hard or not possible at all to smile freely and sweetly to these family members. Give it time. As the love grows in your heart, as the burdens dissolve, it will naturally occur. Proper heart preparation (KHH 6) is essential here and also to follow the heart feelings and not any emotions that may still be present. The Open Heart Meditation (KHH 13) is the more complete practice and help.

There may be a resistance within to do this. Particularly to add the people who have hurt you. That is quite normal. Come back to the PHT at another time. The stronger your heart will become the less resistance there will be.

Even though you attend through the heart to another person, you do not need to be with or near that person. However, every negativity, every emotion not released from your heart is limiting your happiness and your ability to love, relate and move forward. This is primarily about your heart.

Before you do the above, it is important that you are a little familiar with your heart, you can feel when you are using it, when it is stronger than usual and perhaps even radiating. There is nothing else needed when you do this so refrain from thinking about others or visualising. These can all connect you more to your mind/brain and emotions.

Logical or not, when you do this you will feel the immense radiation from your heart increase and, over time, become more beautiful and blissful. This is a clear indication that whatever is needed for your heart, and your family member's heart, to heal is being accessed by your heart. Your heart naturally wants to share. This is the process by which it happens with a much greater intensity and impact.

It is normal to have thoughts coming up; let them pass through. It is only if thoughts persist or you struggle to let them pass through that it is best to stop and resume at a later stage.

As you practice a little with your heart becoming freer, you can go to the next step: enjoy with all your heart. Enjoy it, with all your heart, while you maintain a good heart feeling and while not being too distracted by thoughts.

Your heart offers you a new and quite refreshing approach. There is no need to assist this in any form. The idea of this is to 'just let your heart do it'.

If you find yourself in a situation where an emotion surfaces in your being during an interaction with a family member, use it to become more aware of what is feeling and what is 'negative emotion'.

Remove yourself from the situation to strengthen your heart

If you feel that removing yourself from the situation is the better choice at this point in time, you could politely say 'sorry, I need to step out (or into the other room) for a few minutes'. If that will cause friction, then a visit to the bathroom will appear to be more natural.

In the few minutes that you now have, consciously do the Heart Strengthening and if possible combine it with KHH 6 'Letting the heart smile to the other person' should only be started after you can clearly feel your heart. It will then have the strongest effect. It is best not to add any other aspects to this practice, such as visualising. It is very likely that other 'good or helpful ideas' will strengthen your mind/brain and reduce the heart's ability to do the work.

In every difficult or conflictive situation, and from the perspective of the heart, it is always about both people and both hearts. Removing yourself from the situation and ultimately choosing a new way of behaving also means a change to your 'normal' or old responses and reactions.

What is likely to happen? Initially you may feel more emotion or other emotions surfacing. There may be anger or, more likely, sadness rising from the heart. This is good, and a sign that it is working, resolving issues stuck within your heart. Let go and follow the deeper feelings from the heart, not the emotion.

Over a longer period of time, your heart will become freer. At one point you may very likely feel that you are no longer reacting emotionally to the same events or triggers. Any past emotion or reaction will be replaced with love and kindness. Some of these feelings may even be like special moments you remember that you shared with that person in the past.

When to be soft and when to be firm

In an earlier section, it was indicated that the heart can help when it is time to be soft, loving and kind and also when it is important to be firm, tough and unwavering. As a parent, or in relation to your parents, you may have experienced this interplay between soft and firm. It is love and care that is the glue between these two.

In terms of parenting, the notion of being intuitive and following what feels right is easily understood and accepted. Sometimes this means being firm and putting clear boundaries in place.

The clearing of your own pain or any other emotion needs not interfere with this. When your heart is strong it will support clarity around this inner guidance. You will feel from your heart, situation by situation, when to be tough in your love for your child and when to be soft. The foundation, however, is always to be in the heart, that is to be connected to your heart and in the love from your heart, in either situation.

As a parent it is very important to set boundaries and to help children learn these. At the same time, for the child's emotional clarity, 'heart health' and all related processes such as trusting, feeling safe and feeling loved, the heart-to-heart and love-connection is never meant to be broken. You, the parent, are the more mature one, the 'elder'. It is up to you to look after your emotional strength, to look after your heart, and to be the best you can be any moment.

Not everyone will have children of their 'own'. There are always children close to you somehow: in the neighbourhood, in the family or in your circles of friends. Psychology knows that for the healthy growth of a child 'significant others' or 'significant heartful and loving others' are needed in addition to the parents. Why not you, as a family friend, aunt, uncle, teenager or grandparent?

Heart and love are also forgiving. This is one of the foundations in being able to be soft or firm without emotional entanglement.

It is important to know how you can help yourself always to learn, improve and be more heartful. There is already a lot of focus and, at times, pressure on parents. It is best to know the pathway to being loving and from the heart always or most times. It is also important to realise when you are not, to avoid following any emotion for too long and to let the heart be the helping hand that can always be reached for.

Relaxing, smiling and your family

These heart functions or heart-supporting functions of relaxing and smiling are a wonderful tool you can access anytime when you are with your loved ones and your family.

Naturally, if your family life is joyful and light, you will be smiling often, even giggling or laughing. The more you understand about your heart and use your heart, this lightness and joy will deepen continuously and wonderfully.

However, some of you know that in the presence of family members it is also likely that emotions or irritations will surface. These may find expression or not. In either case, your heart feeling and the joy, lightness and love may be less than what is possible to feel and share with your loved ones.

The following heart-supporting reminder is simple, easy to do and offers a first step towards more heart, more lightness and more love:

Practical Heart Tip 23: Relaxing, smiling and upcoming emotions *

If you find emotion or negative thoughts surface in you when you are in a family (or any other) situation:

- *Relax more, smile more and wait;*

- *In addition, feel your heart space and intend to be there; and*

- *Realise that instead of reacting, you have a choice. Make the choice that is guided and helped by your heart.*

Every time you do that, every time you choose 'relax and smile' as a first response - so that the emotion or the negative thought pattern does not get the full grip of your whole being - you are:

- Allowing your heart not to be squeezed and eventually burdened or even closed.
- You allow your heart and all its benefits to help you, your family members and the situation that normally triggers your emotion.

Instead you will feel over time that your heart and feeling become freer, lighter and full of joy and love, and sweet sharing returns or deepens.

Smiling in situations like this can be experienced as 'tricky' or 'hard'. Here is a simple additional tip for how to proceed in this direction.

Practical Heart Tip 24: Stretch your lips *

Again, when you realise and sense an emotional reaction is coming: Relax and smile, smile a little, stretch your lips in the direction of a smile, see and feel what happens.

It is very normal at first that this seems artificial and strange. Yet in the same way as with a free, sweet smile, your heart will be stimulated to be free and become of service to you.

You are allowing your heart to help you, to cleanse every time emotion is surfacing and wants to take over. In time you will find it becomes less of a stretch and the smile will naturally occur.

These are moments when you can remember and quietly do the 'relaxing and smiling' even more: for example, when a family member is distraught or when a family member has much to say and you can hardly fit a word in.

Quite regularly clients, friends and colleagues shared with me how, in some family situations, they struggle to fit a word in or be heard. This is perfect for your heart practice. In these situations you can naturally choose the heart. You will find yourself being fully attentive and present, which ideally you want to be, and the other person will also find you attentive, listening and caring.

All this is continuous help for your relationship and life-long connection with your family members and it can be equally meaningful to practice with others in daily life, or during a phone call with loved ones.

New habits

In many ways, learning about the heart is about using the heart and balancing heart use and a heart-centred life with old and deeply ingrained habits. The following heart tip offers you suggestions about how to change habits that favour a mind/brain dominance and shift towards your own perfect heart and mind/brain balance.

*Practical Heart Tip 25: New 'habits' ***

The first step is to access your heart, to use it and develop a heart routine that works for you. With the aid of a new heart routine, your heart can help you to fully clear out any negative feelings within you or toward others, however deep and old they are.

Here are some helpful approaches:

- *Practice the KHHs and progress to KHH 15 as soon as you feel to, to have the full strength of your heart available;*

- *Include the Heart Strengthening several times a day (KHH 6) and the Open Heart Meditation (KHH 13) in your daily practice;*

- *Use the above PHT 'Heart reminders' and be creative as to how and when to be reminded to use your heart in action;*

- *You will need various levels of heart reminders or approaches: (1) throughout your day and (2) when difficult situations arise. (It is when difficult things happen that our normal, old or less-heartful responses surface or are triggered most strongly);*

- *Develop a program, timetable and use your Heart Diary to keep you on track; and*

- *Be creative and find ways that suit you in integrating these new or additional heart habits into your life.*

Developing new habits will allow you to experience the help from your heart consistently over some time. It will be immensely valuable and with growing heart experiences, you will find equally growing trust in this 'heart stuff', 'heart being' or in using your heart more every moment of your life.

Some of the suggested practices and heart tips throughout the book will very likely seem strange to you at first.

It is important to realise that anything and everything your heart will facilitate or change, will be a positive change from within the core of who you are.

Your heart offers safe new behaviours and responses to what are otherwise difficult situations or where you want to enhance what is already being shared.

Practical Heart Tip 26: Unlearn the old

In all this awareness, in the key heart activities throughout the book, are new behaviours, new responses you can learn. You will re-condition yourself over time to let your heart be the first response in challenging or difficult situations.

You will access the full capacity of this sleeping gentle giant within. This is an endless source of bliss, love, joy and more. As you start to experiment with these activities, you will clearly experience your own heart taking you in this direction.

A dear friend shared recently how the heart has helped her.

Initially I did not feel much. However, I continued to practice it every day. Then one day the feeling became clearer and clearer and now the help I have from my heart is very 'feelable' almost every moment.

I now say to my family members and friends that learning about the heart is like going on a diet or changing your eating habit. For instance, if you are 110kg and you want to lose weight, to eat one fruit salad instead of one meal is not enough to lose weight. You will need to replace many old-habit meals with salad-like light meals if you are to succeed in losing weight.

This sharing from a friend is a nice example of how heart learning can be approached. We also understand that no one would be able to play tennis in Wimbledon after one week of tennis lessons and one month of practice. It takes practice and time.

Practical Heart Tip 27: Start a 'Heart Diary' *

Start and maintain a Heart Diary. As you start being more aware of your heart and using it more consciously, give yourself time to develop a practice program. Write your intended program into the diary and alter it if needed as you progress through the book or online course. Then, on a daily basis, write in the diary:

- *Your actual practice and practice duration/times;*

- *What you feel from your heart or overall when practice;*

- *What you feel in the time afterwards;*

- *Any challenges external to you or challenges where you fell into old patterns of behaviour or attitude; and*

- *Any successes or 'good news' stories.*

You can do this as you go along or at the end of every day. Over time you will notice subtle yet continuous changes. Practice regularly - be kind and patient with yourself when you forget to practice.

Let the diary remind you, keep you heart-focussed and bring you back after a busy stretch or distraction away from the heart.

In the same diary you can also make brief comments about the quality of relationship with your family members, in particular if there is difficulty. Subtle changes are likely to happen in short to medium time frames. However, it is best to look out for changes in your family relationships or any other relationships over a longer period. Practice diligently and consistently, including the use of a simple, basic diary habit.

Family and the heart purpose

At a deeper heart and spiritual level, the learning we are 'supposed' to experience with family and loved ones is often deeper than in other life situations. This means there is a likelihood of deeper love and joy but also of deeper 'stuff' coming up: deeper-reaching challenges. None of these need to be issues once we understand the function of the heart. Not only can the heart help, it can also remove deeper disharmonies and disconnectedness from love, growth and all that the wonder of family closeness can offer.

In what way does the heart help here? Any experiences with family and loved ones can help you, and they often do, in bringing weaknesses, especially emotions to the surface. Then these situations offer you the chance to choose the better, more attentive, compassionate and loving response, every time they occur. This is the choice everyone has every moment, including moments when the interactions are not so positive. It is this choice that will make the heart and love grow, while healing everything else.

You will find whatever your heart shows you is quite logical and offers the best outcome for all concerned. If you choose your heart every time a difficult situation in your family arises, and respond heartfully, then you will keep your heart clean, it will keep opening and it will also help the other person.

This is important to do, for your heart and those close to you. The healing of relationships and all that has happened in the past is something wonderful, too. Again, it does not mean you need to be actively in touch with anyone that has hurt you in the past. This may not be possible or the best option.

Sometimes your heart and feeling will show you it is good to heal the heart, but to keep a distance physically or otherwise, for example, not to be in touch by phone, mail, e-mail or in person.

Practical Heart Tip 28: In every challenge, in thought or emotion, let your heart be present *

How your heart can start to help is in the next section 'relax and smile'. In relaxing and smiling you naturally allow your heart to be present, which allows you to respond in new ways when you are challenged.

When the challenge from a family member or other person is in the past and there is no current emotion or hurt, general Heart Strengthening (KHH 6) is the best way forward. Then select from some of the other supporting practices: KHH 7, PHT 20 or KHH 13.

At the core of any alternative to choosing your heart, is the risk that you follow your emotions or you trigger more emotions within you, your family member or both. Should you react with emotion, and very likely you know the kind of situations where you are inclined to do so, it will be like pouring fuel on a fire, unless it is with a loved one who has a strong and loving heart that does not react and is able to help you.

Remember that any (negative) emotions, whether you show them or not, will add to the burdens and negativities that will limit, hold and potentially close your heart.

You may not find this easy at first. However, your family challenges can help you, and your family members too, to be more heart-reliant, heart-focussed and to actively let the heart help you.

As you practice - be kind to yourself and others

Be kind to yourself and to others as you start to use your heart more and to apply some of the suggestions and practices. The process will take some time. The more diligent and rigorous you are in following this 'regime', the faster you will no longer feel and display these hurtful emotions. If you find yourself still reacting or being overwhelmed by your emotional reactions and responses, be at peace, and start the practice. Over time there will be a newly felt kindness radiating from your heart. It is a sign of strength and courage within to acknowledge to your family member and to yourself that you are learning and improving. Apologise to the other person when you can do so sincerely and from the heart. This is another sign of strength and will help your heart on its journey to lightness and a burden-free existence.

For a strong, open and healthy heart, it is important to forgive yourself and others, and in relation to others, it is also best to say it to them from the heart.

> *There is a courtesy of the heart; it is allied to love.*
> *From it springs the purest courtesy in the outward behaviour.*
> *Johann Wolfgang von Goethe*

All your family members, some closer to your heart than others, are dear to the heart. Just as Goethe inspires our hearts to be allied to love and courtesy, your heart will, at the very least, bring that courtesy, deeply-felt respect and love back into your family relationships.

Family life is already beautiful

Starting out in the family section, there was a mention that most of this section would be focussing on difficult family situations. In many families there is a lot of love and care and the overall family life, the interactions and conversations are beautiful in many ways.

What if you already live in a wonderful and perfect family situation? If this is you, then let your heart help you in two ways:

- Prevention: Let a heartful life, every day, every moment, help you keep and nurture the love you feel now in your heart, helping you never to be in a situation where you explode or hurt your family members.
- Exploring every corner of heartfulness and love: the heart, like the love you can feel and share with your family, is limitless. Let the positive foundation of more and more heart, more and more love, help you to go to even deeper levels. And in realising more and more that the heart always shares and connects with others, your commitment to your heart will gently pull those dearest to you in the same direction.

The sharing from Paula above illustrates this in a beautiful way. Living with more heart has been the greatest gift to my family, despite separation, differences or divorce. It can be a profound addition to any family to realise how important it is to choose 'love' and the heart in daily togetherness, and how beautiful and unexpected changes can unfold.

The magic of love unfolding

More than courtesy, the heart will open the doors to that 'island of love' feeling that we know in our heart is the 'right' one: being at home and in our heart, with close family members in a bubble of love, support and joy that carries us forward, that heals and propels us gently and wonderfully through life.

It is never too late for more heart and love

> *The heart gave me my daughter back.*
> *Workshop participant*

The importance of the heart in our family relationships was recently revealed to me at the end of a weekend of teaching heart workshops in the community here in Hobart.

At the end of the second day, a 70-year-old father walked up to the front of the class. He was obviously deeply moved and had tears in his eyes. First, he shared how deeply he was touched by everyone's care and love during his first heart workshop day and how everyone was very willing, in particular the repeating participants, to help him with hearing difficulties through the day.

Then he shared how he had been encouraged to join in the workshop weekend by his daughter, who had started a few years before him. It became clear in our brief exchange that there had been a long time when they had not been in touch and for him it was deeper than that. He said that he 'had lost his daughter'.

I could only guess it was due to some falling out, challenge or upset. He first expressed his gratitude for his own learning and heart opening and then for that of his daughter, saying in the end 'the heart gave me my daughter back'.

Summary - more heart at home and with your family

Family and heartful interactions and sharing are often associated. Loving is what families naturally do. It is a family's love that nurtures and brings up children. However, not all families are like that all the time. The family situation can bear challenges, trauma and difficulties.

Through the specialness of your heart, family issues can be resolved, traumas can be healed and a wonderful love, peace or moving on can result from it.

To let your heart help you with your family situation, the following practical heart-steps will move you in the right direction and, over time, your family member(s) too:

1. Use the KHH 'Relax and smile' often. Combine it with PHT 'Heart reminders'. Set yourself reminders to connect to your heart, to be heart-connected, through smiley-face-stickers or whatever works for you, around the house, car, garden, shed, boat, bike or office.

2. Ideally, you also start a Heart Diary at this point in time (PHT 27). This will allow you to follow your progress and remind you. As the feelings from the heart are subtler, it will also help to point out changes and progress. A diary will likewise prompt you to do some heart activity or KHH regularly, as you can write an entry daily or as you complete a practice. It will function as a motivational tool: as you read through positive heart-guided experiences you have had, understanding and realisation of these can motivate you to do more.

3. Read up on how, from your heart's perspective, to best deal with trigger situations that cause emotional reaction. Then, let your heart help you by attending in a practical way to your heart, strengthening it in those situations, or at least afterwards or at the end of the day.

4. Plan and then establish new ways and new habits of choosing the heart in all difficult family situations. Be kind; make notes in a Heart Diary about ups and downs, when you follow the new or old habits. You will make progress if you use the heart in practice. The diary will allow you to see progress and positive changes more clearly. When emotions rise, at times they can appear much stronger than the progress of a strong heart maintained well over weeks.

5. If you feel or know there is emotional hurt from the past, PHT 'Using the heart with deep hurts', establish a routine for a few weeks or months to let the heart help you. Do this in two ways:
   - Practice regularly to have a stronger and lighter heart overall; and
   - Attend to and strengthen your heart every time memories from the past rise.
   Let your heart help you to remove deep or painful past hurt, or if these events are occurring now, then include these too.

6. Family relations need healing and forgiveness. The best way is to let the heart do this. To forgive wholeheartedly, use the above PHT 'Letting the heart forgive those close to us' and the KHH 13 'Open Heart Meditation'. KHH 13 is the natural progression to truly forgiving whole-heartedly. These practices will help and 'heal your heart' directly and steadily over time. Everyone close is connected to your heart and healing your heart will always be a wonderful support and help to others.

7. The PHT 'Using the heart with deep hurts' is another way to let the heart help with past hurtful events. Proper heart preparation is essential and also to follow the heart feelings and not any emotions that may still be present.

8. Use the PHT 'Relaxing, smiling and upcoming emotions' as a first response to letting your heart be stronger, more present and in a position to help. Then, after you start to feel your heart, smile from the heart to your family member(s) (KHH 7).

9. Establish a new response when you are stressed or triggered negatively in a family situation, whether in person or over the phone. Letting go, relaxing and smiling (to your own heart) ideally becomes a first response.

10. Removing yourself from difficult situations can also be very helpful, in order to gather yourself in your heart first, then re-enter the situation, not responding emotionally but more from a heart space.

11. Even if there is no problem or challenge, this is a wonderful and simple practice of kindness, connection and sharing love: smile often from the heart to those close to you, and a little further, too.

12. The PHT 'Stretch your lips' is solely another reminder of this different or new choice. When you are challenged or your own emotions rise ... instead of going there, smile a little, stretch your lips in the direction of a smile, feel your heart and see what happens over time.

13. The PHTs 'Unlearn the old' and 'New habits' invite you to establish new, more heart-centred habits in life and in particular in your interactions with others around you.

14. The PHT 'In every challenge, in thought or emotion, let your heart be present' summarises and reinforces that the heart has a powerful role to play in all family relations. Allow your heart to be present, when things are good, when you are challenged or experience emotion, to make the shift towards heart-helped presence and change.

Important note: the 'family section' is at the beginning of the second, 'life area' part of the book. The heart practices shared go deeper and work more deeply with every chapter. One way to have more assistance and depth is to read the whole book, do all the KHHs and then come back to life areas, life aspects, events or issues where you want the heart's help.

Chapter 2

Children - So Dear To Our Heart

If my heart can become pure and simple, like that of a child,
I think there probably can be no greater happiness than this.
Kitaro Nishida (prominent Japanese philosopher)

The heading 'children' can be read and meant as your children or as 'children, teenagers and young people' in the community. It could also stand for 'the child in all of us' and is hopefully interesting to you in this light whether you have children or not.

While this section is in many ways about the relationship children or young people have with their parents and parents with their children, it is also about healing parts in us, in our hearts, from our own childhood, which are still holding pain, unresolved issues or emotion. With your heart's more complete help, the inquisitive, beautiful, loving, spontaneous child-nature in you will be freed again and you will find the perfect expression tailored to your needs and possibilities for growth, love and joy.

If you are a child or a teenager, then this section is for you too. You will find, contrary to many books offering mainly the perspectives of adults, children and young people actively contributing to and sharing in this section. You will hear some of their points of view, stories and voices.

Young people freely and generously offered their heart's insights or wisdom, and shared how the heart has helped them, in a beautiful and deep way.

Looking at life in a simplistic way shows that the world is made up of children and grown-ups. This view is not intended as a 'divide'; it is more so an acknowledgement of the different phases of growth, learning or heart learning someone has reached.

From a heart's perspective, at the core of who we all are there is more similarity, one-ness, brother and sisterhood, than all the other 'stuff' that can divide us. This is the same with children.–Whether you have children or not, you may find that opening your heart will not only bring abundant child-like joy into your life, it may also bring wonderfully enhanced and loving relationships with children into your life, whoever those children or their parents are, or it will magically deepen the relationships that are there now.

In turn, renewed, deepened and lighter heartfulness will offer children around you even more love and support. It will also nurture the relationship and add clarity and joy that both you and the child will experience as the most wonderful, natural 'fertiliser' for growth, even more heart opening and a deep opening to love, which can overflow into everyone's life. Naturally it will also extend to others from these sweet and wonderful child-adult friendships or relationships.

Children and young people around us

It is natural and important for children and young people to have a voice that expresses their views, perspectives and stories; it is important that they are heard.

In the same way that adults can have issues and difficulties with other adults, children and young people have these too, with each other or with adults, including their parents. The sharing about children and young people and the heart will feature:

- The perspective from our adult point of view; and
- The stories and perspectives from young people who, with experiences of using their heart more, look at the adult world and their parents.

The heart loves children and youth. There are several sayings in the Bible that children are pure in heart, and in a spiritual analogy Jesus said:

Let the little children come to me, and do not hinder them,
for the kingdom of God belongs to such as these.

From the perspective of your heart, is it not really important whether you have children of your own and if you do, what age they are. It is much more about opening your heart, finding that deeper, greater love within and gently being shifted, by your heart's doing, to the sweetness and gentleness in all your relationships; and especially where children are around.

The agelessness of the heart is equally in you as a child or adult. As we are essentially of the same inner or spiritual age, learning about the heart offers an insight into this reality where it is appropriate. When this realisation arises, together with the heart's practical daily help, it shifts relationships, softens them, gives clarity and, where needed, can ultimately resolve hardened situations.

The love for our children is special

There is no love that is more magical, more beautifully described and more enduring than the love parents, other siblings, other children and other grown-ups feel for children.

Regardless of what your child does or the choices s/he makes, at the core of your being, your existence, your heart, you will very likely always love and feel this special love connection with him or her.

What your heart naturally wants to facilitate for you, and for the children around you, is at the very least to maintain these special moments, special feelings.

One of the functions of this infinite and beautiful love through the heart is that you can offer structure and guidance to your child, even if that causes resistance, reaction or disapproval. Deep within, you and your child will always know and feel that this love is real, and that structure and guidance is equally natural and normal in raising and educating a child. This heart-supported dynamic enables child and parent alike to move freely and respectfully within the norms of society and also challenge them where needed.

The love we feel for others, often highlighted in love for children, is really only a reference point for what it is possible to feel, experience and share. The love from our hearts can grow infinitely the more and the deeper we are within our heart.

Growth in connection with your heart will always be something you will feel, experience and enjoy, and in turn that joy, sweet love and care will be felt by others around you.

All love flows through your heart

All the love for your children flows through your heart. It is a wonderful feeling. Recall, as a child, how it felt when you were 'in love' with your mum or dad. These sweet, enjoyable moments when you are truly connected heart-to-heart with your child, the love just is and flows; it is magical.

This special love is not only meant for some moments with more heart. We are all meant to be deeply in this love, always.

In these moments the heart is very present naturally. It is more present than the mind/brain consciousness that so often 'rules' will ever be. It is then that the heart offers these wonderful feelings, while you are not doing anything, just pausing for a while. These timeless moments that nurture your heart naturally can support you and the connection with your child; they will also heal and open your heart.

Relating with more heart

These magical and treasured moments can perhaps be easily illustrated in the special relationships parents, grandparents and other adults can have with children. Your heart will take you on a new journey of defining, and more so living, these relationships with more and more sweetness and love. The greater knowing and truth from the heart will ultimately guide you every moment in life fully, to be present in these relationships and all relationships you have.

It can be somewhat new to interact as a parent with a child or as a child with adults or parents, once heart awareness and heart strength is learned.

The interplay that constantly happens between structure/guidelines and love/care is not an easy one to navigate.

Parents provide all kinds of support for their children, give structure, provide norms and behavioural guidelines and this includes some form of discipline. It is not easy; if it is solely from the perspective of the brain, it can be heartless: too hard, too soft or not understandable and this can create friction.

The guidance from the heart, together with the help, the 'en-lightening' ability and purer love will naturally lead to a growing relationship.

It will also be a relationship that evolves when children mature and circumstances change, for example, the relationship a toddler has with an adult is naturally different from the relationship between a 5-year old and an adult.

Something quite special is added as soon as a parent or a child starts to use the heart more consciously and more practically in daily interactions: whatever is being said, suggested, required or demanded of the other will not only be heard by the mind/brain and the emotional world, but also by the heart. This can immensely soften the response or reaction.

It is good to be patient here, to rely on the heart and to work with it more and more. The softening of response and reaction may 'only' be seen and felt over time.

I recall an interaction with my son once when he was around 12 years old. He had done something naughty and as a responsible parent I initiated a discussion. There is no memory of what his actions were and yet there is clear memory of his initial response: 'Daddy are you in your heart'? I paused and with his already quite strong heart awareness, he felt that there was an emotion on my side, which would have been irritation, anger or upset. Even if it was small, he detected it and kindly, calmly pointed it out. After a pause and with now more active heart presence we continued the discussion. He easily agreed to the consequence we discussed and it was an emotion-free, light, even beautiful interaction.

There can be a lot of pain and heart-ache, on both sides when the child reaches late teenage or adulthood. With a teenager there is often an urge to be free that grows stronger. It is also a longing for expression and learning in the physical and broader world. It also means that children gradually move away from the parents. It may also be expressed by children in other ways that show his/her need to be mentally, emotionally and spiritually free.

Your heart will offer help with loving, caring feelings to support either the child or the parent and will gently guide each, if that is what is supposed to unfold, to make the shift from a child-parent relationship to one of friendship, companionship and one that has mutual support, guidance and mentoring.

The child-parent relationship is 'stretched'

These moments and their qualities do not stay forever. The child-parent relationship is frequently stretched, emotions surface and the mind/brain becomes more dominant in an attempt to manage the situation. Most parents experience how this wonderful, purer love is regularly challenged and stretched.

Within this lies one of the root causes of the child-parent difficulty dilemma. During times of stress, hurt, grief or disagreement both parties often long for that past experience of love: understanding, support, care, and attentive listening to what is really going on, or just to be held, either physically or in heart-space. Yet there can be a tendency to want to solve the issue with reasoning. This is a logical approach and may work, yet, without feeling, and without the authentic and genuine care that runs through the heart, there is a chance that any attempt, even a good one, to resolve, help and support, will meet an emotional reaction or other form of block.

What is often needed in this heart or love foundation, this ocean of love, is for everything to be held 'in love' so that everything is said and done with love.

The adult or parent-child 'stretches' can have endless causes. These causes may in essence be based on:

- The nature of the interactions between the child and the parent;
- Interactions and stress experienced by the child or adult that flow into the parent/other adult and child relationship;
- Other external causes; and
- The nature, characteristics, related qualities and attitudes of the parent and the child.

Yvonne's story is a very open and deep sharing that exemplifies the second point. This circumstance the potential to touch really deeply, especially if there is a memory and range of related emotions from similar experiences in the past.

The story also shows how in times when you are not 'in love' and not deeply enough in your heart, there is a high likelihood that emotions can be stronger than anything else. What can then happen is they 'rule' and the natural sweetness of the child-parent relationship is stretched. It also shows how, gently and instantly, your heart can help.

Yvonne's Story:

'Prior to becoming more familiar with the topic 'heart', I thought that I was a content and happy person. Today I know that a much deeper and more beautiful contentment is possible which resides deep within and which is incomparable to anything else.'

'There were different kind of challenges in my life that had to do with family, my relationship to my husband and also to our daughter. I would like to share in more details about the challenges that had to do with our daughter Sophie. As a small child Sophie had immense difficulties in filtering out external stimulations such as noises, voices and other sounds. It clearly seemed she received them as much louder than any other person would. This became clear to us one day talking in the kitchen, very far from her room in quiet voices when she all of a sudden replied from her room to questions that were in our discussion.'

'It was unfortunately normal for her to return home from kindergarten very stressed and agitated. It required all my effort to calm her down. In these situations, we often argued. As a mother I wanted to help her and wished for her to better be able to cope with her over-sensitivity and her life. However, I reached my limits almost every time, became exhausted and sad for not being able to help.'

'Thankfully I had already become familiar with the technique of strengthening my heart and I practiced the Open Heart Meditation often. I had never imagined that both would be able to help me so much in this despair and situation. At one point I remembered and simply used the heart. In one of those situations, when my daughter was agitated, I went into my heart using the technique and steps.'

'Surprisingly it instantly calmed her and of course me too. What was nice, it allowed me to not do anything, just to be there for her ... It worked: I just had to go the heart, to the familiar feeling of being held by my own heart and to let the energy of the heart flow to her.'

> *'It was exceptionally beautiful to feel the healing that was taking place in that very moment. The only way I can express it is that in that moment, when I turned to my own heart, a deeper love could work within me and her.'*
>
> *'I later realised that this daily event and the process of the heart working did not only help my daughter. Over time an immensely deep, close, loving and trusting relationship developed with my daughter, more than before and more than I ever imagined possible.'*
>
> *'At some point I felt that it was not about the problem but about the learning. I learned to choose the heart, love and not my emotions in relation to a specific problem and the difficulties Sophie was experiencing, or the difficulties that Sophie and I had between us. The more I chose the loving feelings from the heart, the less there was a problem. At certain times through all this, I did not know whether everything had improved or whether it was my perception and response to what was happening.'*

This very personal and initially heart-wrenching experience between mother and daughter, beautifully describes a different kind of relationship that starts to flourish when the heart, and naturally or automatically both hearts, become more and more involved.

It is here that the guidance from your heart can help you to make right choices, be attentive to your child, and not give in to negative reactions but stay in a feeling of love while being firm, assertive and directive when needed.

This and other experiences has encouraged Yvonne and her husband even more to share their own experiences and to offer the same help to others. They have been offering heart learning and a regular Heart Meditation session at their home to friends and family for a number of years now. This circle has now widened and other members of the community join regularly.

Paula's story in the previous section is one particular situation where a parent and child can drift very far apart. In her case, the relationship was not only difficult or strained, Paula, as the now grown-up child, had made the decision to cut all 'emotional' ties, including those the heart will always feel, the deep love that is often there in family connections. Without the heart's help it will be hard to come together 'in love' again.

Parents too make these decisions, and without the assistance from the heart's practical help and wisdom, unnecessary separation may seem purposeful.

The story of a neighbour comes to mind: a mother found her daughter too difficult to be with. They were continuously arguing, often over trivial matters, and the energy was so strong that it became unbearable. With the mother questionably 'in charge' and self-righteously stating her ownership of the home, she asked the 22-year-old child to move out even though she had only just returned from a year-long overseas trip.

This may have been the best decision in terms of the heart, too. It is hoped that Your Heart Can Help offers for both parents and children a broader and deeper foundation to make these important decisions.

The fine line

There is a very fine line between your role as a parent to provide clear, consistent and firm boundaries of behaviour so the child can grow, learn and blossom. The adult world tends to want to over-control children, to tell them what to do or what is right or wrong. The emphasis is on 'tends to', as our culture somewhat supports this. Just because someone is older and has more experience of the world than a child, does not mean he also has wisdom, insight and natural ability to guide.

Without the greater love and knowing of the heart, there is a risk of imposing truths and guidelines or rules onto our children that are based on our own experiences, our limited or temporary truths that our minds/brains hold. It will create friction with our children, or anyone, as the child/other person feels that it is not truthful.

When issues arise, the feeling from your heart and intuition about a particular response is immensely helpful and the right direction. Tapping into this deeper knowing, and connecting to the heart is good and you may want to have a strong heart, all the time, to offer the best guidance to your child, or any child, as often as possible.

There is no one complete book or parent-guide and equally no guide for children on how to live, work, support and be with each other. Every piece of information, every book, every thought is ideally supported by a present, light and loving heart. With more heart you will be 'in love' as often as possible and all decisions you make, whether daily ones or bigger ones, will be guided by your heart.

The parent's emotions interfere

A torn jacket is soon mended, but hard words bruise the heart of a child.
Henry Wadsworth Longfellow

Children can be emotional or emotionally reactive at times. Yet, emotions can surface in both children and parents. Becoming adults also means we need to manage our emotions, which means that they are kept at bay as much as possible, and not let loose, expressed the way children do at times.

This more adult ability to consider and follow emotions less, gives us time to respond more appropriately and more heart-fully. As an adult you may be at risk of losing a job or a partner. The mind/brain does not override a possible emotional response. However, it can also help you to remember to be in the heart or to follow it more.

It is very common that emotions surface between parents and children. Rose's story below is a good example of this. There is a knowing that something is not right, when it is triggered by a certain situation, such as when a child is behaving in an unacceptable way. In other situations, as in Rose's story, it is sometimes hard to understand where emotions come from, and why they are there.

Unfortunately, in both situations, the emotions will not serve the child-parent relationship well and it will not serve you and your heart well over the years, unless you see past the pattern and you let your heart help you to break through it.

You will find that the relationship with your child will gradually, yet clearly, improve over time. And the wonderful part is that you can do something about this now, quite regularly and with no extra resources, expenses or help from others.

The heart does not judge. Whatever the situation is, and whatever the challenge, problem or lack of connection or warmth may be in a child-parent relationship, the heart will want to assist.

Rose is in her early 60s now. She is divorced and has several adult children and grandchildren. At several times during the meetings with Rose, she described herself as being 'emotional', with perhaps the main emotion being anger. There have been difficulties with one of her daughters, where emotions got in the way and this has led to dis-connection and almost full separation from her child.

Rose's Story:

'I remember myself being deeply unhappy and a very angry person. I also had no understanding of what the dynamic was or why it was coming up, or from where.'

'What happened was, when one of my daughters and I interacted, there was often a feeling that I knew better and this made me behave in such a way that I acted 'to fix her life'. All this would make me tense. I thought she should do things differently. Along with all this was rising anger and rising silent criticism and judgement of her.'

'I now know that my children would have felt this and become very uncomfortable. They would have felt unsupported and unloved in these situations.'

'As my children became adults, they stayed away; they did not contact me and they hardly ever came to visit. I was suffering, feeling the deep longing within to be close, to have contact, to love and to be loved.'

'I became more aware over time of what I was doing and there was more awareness too of the inappropriateness of my actions towards my daughters. I started to do personal development programs, workshops, and joined groups to find some help. The first stage was ... that I kept my mouth shut. The emotions and feelings towards them stayed the same though.'

'After I had learned about the heart, I joined heart meditation sessions, did workshops and regularly repeated the workshops. The heart helped me to be able to let go of the need to control my daughter and to advise her with such intensity and at times with anger.'

In the beginning also I still did not know how to be with my daughter. I would start to sit with her, in her presence, be quiet and focus on the heart. Being quiet made it easy to let my heart be stronger and to smile from the heart to her, often just listening. My daughter would stay and tolerate my presence better.'

'I realise now that the anger was a strong undercurrent and seemed to frighten my children. At an unconscious level, I seemed to blame my children for unhappiness in me, which of course was not their doing, their fault at all.'

'I am very grateful for the help that the heart has offered and accomplished. It is much easier between us now, and I see her once a week. And when we meet it is easy and light. She is starting to enjoy my company and I can feel she is starting to trust me again. It feels nice and at times we sit shoulder to shoulder and snuggle a bit.'

'It feels really nice that we can be together again. I have an eight-month-old grandson now and the trust is extended to us spending time together too. I am so joyful that this can be.'

Rose started to learn about the heart approximately 10 years ago and has since committed to being in her heart more to help herself and the relationships with all those around her, in particular with her two children. Rose's children, in their responses or reactions to their mother, are actually, and perfectly, teaching Rose about herself.

Rose, in choosing the heart and letting the heart help her, managed to stop a damaging spiral downwards. Emotions grow over time and any heavy use of the mind/brain brings unpleasant aspects with it like judging others, being clever or being taken away from the deeper, truer heart feelings. The growing impacts of this on others around us, including close and dear ones, are disconnection or disengagement, especially when little or no heart is present.

In Rose's case the children were aware of this. Closeness, even to the parent, fades. In situations like this there is often less inclination to go and visit 'Mum' or 'Dad'. This unfortunately is the case for some older persons who over the years have had too much mind/brain domination and accumulation of emotion-related burdens. These have made the heart heavier or even closed.

If this is the case, there is little love, joy or lightness radiating from them and the heart in this state grows weaker in its ability to naturally radiate love or joy. This manifests in conversations and relatives or friends may find it hard or unpleasant to be in the presence of such energy despite the love they feel for the person.

It is never too late to let the heart help. Remember, whatever your age, however heavy your heart may be, in a comparatively short time it will shine again and others will feel the love, joy and special connection that is under all the rubble and heaviness around the heart, and the heart can begin to heal.

The child - in the heart - knows

Children are naturally connected to their hearts. In this state, they will respond to you in a heartful, loving, kind and gentle way.

Although you have read, studied and consider yourself wiser and more experienced than the child, at the heart level the child knows, as you do, that the difference between you in spirit - your real selves - is much less than your physical age difference. It is even very likely you are spiritually of a similar age, or, as the adult, perhaps even younger, or less mature, less wise than the child.

In some way, because of the lightness and free-spiritedness of children, to be around them is often an indescribable joy or bliss.

Equally the challenges can be huge, when the child is experiencing a 'tantrum' or when that natural flow is interrupted. Children are complex; they are a complete human being with the full capacity of all the heartfulness, mindfulness and the full world of emotions.

The discussions in the first two chapters of the book apply as equally to children as they do to adults, in almost all instances. The main difference is that children have had less time to accumulate burdens, negativities and heaviness around the heart.

Very similar to adults around us, when we are in the heart, there is a natural and sweet connection of spirit, love and deep friendship. When you are not in that connection, you may find that the children of your friends or family members are less interested in you or even react negatively to you wanting to connect with them.

Following or not following emotions

As a parent or friend of the child, without the connection to your own heart and from your heart to the child, you may find yourself spiralling downwards into the emotions because you are upset with the child's behaviour. Both Yvonne's and Rose's stories illustrate that. Children too have emotions and can follow them.

Your own heartfulness can be the direct guidance for your child or a child around you to also be more heartful.

Heart to heart you can help your child, and a child can help an adult, to learn about the heart so the heart can be more active and helpful. As the guiding adult, it is even better for you to share some of the direct heart-helping practices, like the Heart Strengthening (KHH 6), with your child.

When a child is in an emotional state and an adult's or parent's own emotional reaction is triggered, it is very likely the situation will escalate, making a return to calm or a solution to the problem difficult.

Parents and adults are also triggered by the actions of children. Rightly or wrongly, when emotions or negative responses surface, the heart will be covered and in this state cannot assist. Parents who rely heavily on logic or reason (mind and brain) or who are self-righteous will not let the heart be present to help and guide them. The result is often a form of disconnection or disengagement, as the child can't fully understand this perspective.

Showing feelings

It is important to point out that the 'full understanding' means that the child's heart understands and knows, including when she or he has done something wrong. When this is addressed or dealt with from the heart as well as the mind/brain, there is understanding, care and love. Parents or adults who are not heart-connected, especially when they are in emotion, will not only find it hard to engage the child, but will also stifle the important assurance that the child is supported and loved.

It is important, for us as adults or parents and equally for the children around us, to find a practical way of being open and honest in acknowledging that in some or many things we truly lack the full picture. We may be guided by what we think, believe or have experienced at some time as 'the best' for our child or children around us and yet it may not be the full truth or it may even be the wrong action in certain situations.

The solution is to be increasingly more aware of how you feel and what feelings you share when interacting with your child. When the heart is strong, the sweet and loving bond between child and parent stays intact, no matter what the topic of the conversation is.

The sharing of feelings can also mean that you, as a parent or a child, find the heart-strength to share with the other when you have emotion, or when you are emotionally affected by the others' behaviours or words. Saying this of course, 'ideally' comes when you have calmed a little, are in the heart more and can speak with kindness, softness and feeling from the heart.

This is not a sign of weakness or loss of control. Especially as children grow older they will learn to respect and trust you more and equally learn a more comprehensive way of relating, acknowledging and living openly and honestly with the fact that we get things wrong. In any case, your heart, as an adult, and the heart of the child will always know or have the feeling of what the truth is to some extent; there is no point hiding anything from your child, or in the child hiding from the parent.

The ideal is, and your heart will want to take you there, a place of inner heart-strength, where only beautiful feelings and clarity of mind exist.

This may sound like an unreal goal or expectation. Read Verne's story in the section below, and if you find the time, watch her video clip on the book's website. Verne shares about deep challenges experienced at home. You might be able to recognise and feel the peace, calmness, clarity and love with which she shares, from the perspective of a child.

As a parent, perhaps imagine yourself ten, twenty or thirty years from now. The love foundation, the love interaction with your child, is what will remain.

From the child's perspective

This section is about children, and it is important and natural to let children have a voice too and share their wisdom, perspectives and stories.

Verne's story is unique in that her challenge with her family started as she joined some of her peers in going to Open Heart Meditations and started to learn about the heart.

'I know they love me and care for me, and want the best. I also feel that some of their love has controlling parts in it that do not feel nice, not right. I know I will be an adult soon and have to know how to make good decisions.' Verne

Verne become so interested in the heart that she also started to join workshops. This is where some challenges started; some of the adults around her did not want her to attend.

Verne, now approaching adulthood, started to learn about the heart when she was around 14 years old. She describes how her heart helped her not only to keep her calm during her teenage years, it also helped her working with the challenges she experienced in her parent relations.

Verne's Story:

Verne lives at home with other siblings, her mother and her step-father. She is well known in the Tasmanian heart learning community for her kind and gentle nature. Other parents enjoy her work as a baby-sitter and trust her with their children.

In talking to Verne it became evident that she lacked some support from her parents to meditate and to continue her journey of opening and following her heart. Often in situations such as this the challenge or difficulty at home or in a relationship/friendship is a symptom of deeper, more 'core' issues that arise when they are triggered and cause the heart energy to be blocked. This reduces heartful communication. Like in Verne's situation, our hearts tend to show or highlight these aspects.

Verne shares about her beginnings: 'When I started with heart meditation I remember I was quite unhappy; there was something missing. I often find myself caught in emotion, like being upset or angry. Often this would happen inside of me, not showing much on the outside.'

'This unfortunately came up in my relationship with my parents. I wanted to find out who I was and what my place was in this world. I felt trapped at home and controlled in a way that was often more than I could handle. For example, I wanted to spend more time with my friends but was not allowed to. Then if I stayed out longer, even a bit longer, I got into trouble.'

'I got angry and upset, and didn't want this to happen. I tried to hide these feelings but that did not work. A couple of my friends had started to go to Heart Meditation at the Lotus Centre and invited me to try it, to go along.'

'Before that, I had noticed that one of my friend's parents had changed a lot over the past year or so. I clearly noticed that they were much calmer now, very kind, nice and they laughed very often now, something I had not seen at my home for some time.'

'My first experience at the meditation was nothing special. It made me feel very relaxed, but my mind kept being very busy with everything. I really did not understand why my friends would go to these meditations again and again.'

'Not really knowing why, I kept going. Later I heard this happens a lot. I went regularly for over a year. Somewhere during this time, I started to feel my heart opening more, becoming much lighter. The feeling of calmness deepened much more and my mind became much calmer too. I also started to feel free, much freer, on the inside.'

'At home my parents kept being quite strict. In addition, I was being questioned in my choice to go to a meditation session each week with my friends. This led to regular clashes and conflict. It made me feel hurt, not heard and upset. I did not want my parents to agree with my choice, but wanted them at least to give me some support. It was strange in some way too, as my friends struggled with their parents encouraging them too much to go to the meditations.'

'The feelings and the help I have experienced from my heart have helped me hugely to be at peace with my choice to go to these meditations and do other things too. I understand and feel where my parents come from now with more freedom and love.'

'I know they love me and care for me, and want the best. I also feel that some of their love has controlling parts in it that do not feel nice, not right. I know I will be an adult soon and have to know how to make good decisions.'

'Before the heart meditations I would quite easily be swayed by others, my mates and friends, and I was not confident enough even to say something. I was even further from saying what I truly felt. I could not stand up for myself. This often left me crushed, doing things I did not want to do.'

Now, with a more open and light heart, I feel a deep inner strength and calmness. From here I feel the strength to decide, not feel as though I have to agree with others, and to make decisions that feel right. Somehow I know that if my heart decides, it will also help others too.'

'My heart can almost instantly now bring me into a very calm state, even when in the past a similar situation made me angry or upset. I feel much more confident too, and somehow clearer in who I am. I look forward to every day and to what the future will bring.'

It was a particularly special session when Verne shared her story and experience. At no time did she show any of the negative emotions discussed in the earlier sections of the book. Radiating from her heart and voice was calmness, deep respect and compassion for her situation and her family.

Verne, at the time living with her mother and step-father, also brought her biological father several times to heart meditation. After sometime he was drawn to attend workshops too. Perhaps there was some form of support and encouragement from him that she experienced that allowed her to have faith in following her heart.

Whether Verne or her parents were right or wrong is a mind's decision or assessment. What the heart does is to offer a deeper understanding and wisdom. In moments when you allow it to be present situations can be helped. What Verne's story clearly tells is that she realised she had emotions even before heart meditation or the issues about her commitment to her heart learning surfaced. The key to this or any stories, hopefully, is that the heart offers help with how to clear out emotions, emotional disposition and any other negativities that exist within us. It opens us up to be lighter, more joyful, more functioning and have loving relationships in all directions now and in the future.

It is not uncommon for children, parents or clients to share this in sessions. The once-felt sweet feelings of 'pure love' for the other family member, are still present at a deeper level, but during emotional times they disappear or are only rarely felt.

The many challenges that naturally happen in child-parent or child-adult relationships, coupled with over-representation of the mind/brain or emotional behaviours over the many years spent closely together, can easily lead, to complex and problematic relationships. In this case, the longed-for pleasant feelings and possible sharings between parent and child become less frequent.

Without the heart's help this can trigger even more emotions in parents or children alike; guilt, pain, hurt or frustration can surface.

With the help of the heart, the important structures that parents need to set in place are clearly recognised by both parent and child. The ultimate foundation of a wonderful and nurturing adult-child relationship is love, the deeply held understanding that 'I am a loving parent', 'I am a loving, caring adult' or 'I am a loving, caring and responsive child'.

Young persons' heart group

Verne became one of a few teenagers who decided to set up a new Heart Meditation session at the Lotus Centre in Hobart. A small group of 12 to 17 year olds requested from the centre owners the establishment of a session for their age group.

Initially only a few in number, the group grew fast, filling the whole room, and now 10 to 15 or more attend. Something unusual also happened and the 'young ones' seem to be quite open and at peace with this: some of the adult meditators asked to join and were welcomed to the group. Their reason for joining was there was more noticeable lightness and joy and an infectious energy which was clearly helping their hearts and generating pleasant feelings.

The deepest, heart-wrenching challenges

There is an additional section on the deepest challenges related to being with or raising children. Many clients and friends have shared openly how their children are not only the greatest joy in their lives, they can also be their greatest challenge.

Some of the above stories imply that a child, in teenage years or later life, may decide not to be in contact; to temporarily or permanently cut the ties with the family or parents. This is a profound emotional and mental challenge, for the heart and for all of who we are.

Some situations that have cut deep wounds or posed the deepest challenges, were when either a parent or a child went through mental health difficulties. Hurtful situations arise from irrational behaviours, un-kind things said and, at times, lack of understanding of what is really going on. Emotional states described by clients or friends include:

- Feeling left bare;
- Feeling helpless;
- Being in despair;
- Feeling angry or resentful towards the loved one; and
- Feeling annoyed, irritated or frustrated.

Adults also expressed a sense of feeling torn, at an inner level, between the huge love for the child and the deep, disruptive emotions surfacing.

It is important to realise, relating to the first few chapters in the book, that there are negativities in and around the heart of everyone to some degree or other and these emotions can be triggered in any situation and by anyone, including an infant, child, teenager or adult.

This is normal. It means, having studied the essence of the function of the heart in chapters 1 to 5, that the best solution is to be aware that an emotion has been triggered and to let it be removed from the heart rather than let it take control.

Negative emotional reactions are 'normal' as they stem from deeply rooted negativities, whether related or not to the other person. They can be strongly felt and can cause strong reactions if not in balance with other, more heart-centred, qualities.

The pressure on a parent-child relationship can be immense. As we know, our society suggests that the relationship between child and parent 'ought' to be good, loving and even joyful. When the true feelings from the heart are not there, and deep emotions arise when there 'ought' to be other feeling, deep inner conflict can occur. It can be hard to overcome the reality of this conflict through rational thought or positive thinking.

> **Practical Heart Tip 29: Centre yourself in your heart ***
>
> *In moments of deep challenges in a relationship, remember the key steps (KHH 2 and KHH 6) that will gradually bring in your heart's help, as it suits your needs and situation:*
>
> - *Acknowledge to yourself that you are experiencing the emotions and that, for now, this is normal;*
>
> - *Use the KHH 5 'Do everything with love' from this chapter as one clear step towards more heart and love towards self and others and start to let the heart dissolve everything that is not a positive, helpful or supportive feeling;*
>
> - *Use the KHHs from other chapters - best is in sequence - to strengthen your heart gradually and consistently;*
>
> - *Do KHH 6, the complete Heart Strengthening, regularly to maximise benefits for your heart;*
>
> - *Do KHH 7 'Smile from the heart to others', to your child, as an additional and direct heart-help tool; and*
>
> - *Do KHH 13 'Open Heart Meditation' for all past hurts, burdens and emotions to be cleansed for the true nature of the relationship to bloom again over time.*

If you are really challenged by your child's behaviour - even if your child is now an adult - your heart can offer help. The following sections outline additional approaches and practical steps to access the full heart help, improving your relationship:

- Model heart behaviour to your child;
- Model heart behaviour to your parent; and
- Open, access, clear, cleanse and use your heart more.
- Model heart behaviour to your child;
- Model heart behaviour to your parent; and
- Open, access, clear, cleanse and use your heart more.

Model heart behaviour to your child (or parent)

Understanding about your heart is not something fluffy, mushy or sentimental. Your heart is an integral part of you that, like your arms, legs and ability to speak, touch or hug your child, ought to be used in the right way and at the right time.

Reflect on the qualities and feelings your heart supports and brings to the surface in support of your relationship. Reflect with kindness, and yet with honesty and rigour, on the parts of you, the behaviours which are not connected to your heart, or which are not connecting you from your heart to your child or your mum or dad.

Natural heartfulness in reality, not as an idea or concept, will improve your relationship, even if no words are being said.

This is really something magical and immensely helpful. Additionally, as you speak in regular interactions from the heart as well as from the mind/brain, deep healing will occur, as the love flows and nurtures others when you connect and share.

When you get things wrong, even when you know a better way to communicate, it is best to sincerely apologise, from the heart, just as one of the essential features of the Open Heart Meditation suggests.

As you do this, the emotions held around your heart and around the heart of the other, the child or the parent, can be dissolved within the naturally stronger radiance from the heart. A deeper healing for both can occur if one or both parties do regular heart strengthening or, even better, the full Open Heart Meditation, over a period of time.

When looking at the foundation need/wants underneath what we think, hope or say we need, those for parents/adults and children may look very similar.

Figure 14: What a child wants-what adults want

Child wants	Adults want
Love	Love
Attention and support	Support and attention
Care, affection	Care, affection
Quality time from parents and others close to him/her	Quality time from people close to us
Someone to listen to their feelings, concerns or fears.	Someone to listen to their feelings, concerns or fears.

You will find as you allow these feelings to grow naturally with a lighter, more open heart, others will often miraculously connect, even mirror these feelings back to you.

Read the section at the end of this chapter about how to use your heart practically in your relationships with your children and vice versa. Use the suggested more advanced heart strengthening practices so your own heart qualities surface more, help you more, and with or without words, help your child too.

Modelling heart behaviour to others involves practical heart understanding. You will reach a sufficient depth by studying the book and by carefully and attentively going through the KHHs and PHTs and following some of the other suggested heart practices too.

This behaviour is naturally not limited to an adult modelling it to a child. In some cases adults are stuck, rigid, or busy with concepts or models that do not work in certain situations. Some of us are less wise, less developed than the children we spend time with. All this invites humbleness, openness and more heart into these precious relationships. At its core the heart does not know of any of these differences; it will only ever want to offer the best and fulfil the heart's fullest potential - deepening calmness, love, joy and purpose. This also means looking for the best heart-felt ways to engage in every moment, with full recognition of the various roles we naturally have: as a child, niece, nephew, as parents, uncles, aunts or as close friends in the lives of others, offering heartfelt care, support, love and guidance, not only to younger ones as they grow up, but really to everyone.

Your heart and your child

At the core of your relationship, like every close relationship we have, is a unique heart-to-heart connection. Opening, accessing and using your heart in its more complete capacity offers a direct route to unique feelings of love, wonder and joy that naturally exist; and from here the heart/the feelings/the heart's capacity/the relationship can grow infinitely. How can any thinking, concepts or elaborate techniques directly encourage 'heartful feelings' and this direct connection that can really only be felt inside, by the heart?

If the relationship is with your own child, the recognition and familiarity, the depth of feeling, is very strong. Increasing our capacity to love is one of the greater purposes. Naturally, you feel love for each other and for certain with an opening heart it can also grow. This is meant to be so; despite the challenges, problems and even negativities presented to you, healing at a very deep level can occur.

A dear friend once said wisely when referring to all relationships we have with those close to us, such as children, parents, other family members, partners and dear friends:

> 'I realise and feel that everyone close to us in our lives is there so the love from our hearts - the purer, greater love - can help and heal our hearts.'

It is in the child-parent relationship that the love can be the easiest to recognise. When a child is in pain of any kind, naturally you sit with the child, hold, hug or console them from the heart. It is this direct and deep love that can heal and reduce pain or sorrow.

Healing in this sense means that the finer radiance and love from your heart can heal whatever burdens or limitations are in your heart as well as in the heart of the other.

This is one simple example. From here on your heart can assist with your own issues or those concerning your relationship. Either a child or a parent may point out a weakness, a tendency to be impatient, easily irritated or unkind. It is in heartful moments, and when you have the courage to admit these, that your heart helps you with all of these. The book's heart practices will naturally facilitate this. It is in moments when weaknesses or emotions surface, when we admit them to the greater love within the heart, to the source of love, or Divine, that profound healing can occur.

Your heart will be freer, there will be more love - sweet and gentle love. When you and your child are in your hearts you can become beautiful teachers to each other.

This is a teacher-student role with no hierarchy and one that can change moment to moment as to who is teaching and who is learning.

Every time you interact you have a chance to use your heart, and let the heart help. This is one way to open your heart, as every time you use it, it will open more.

Use every situation as an opportunity to use the heart more
I love you with all my heart.

What is amazing about the heart is that either of the two situations can help:

- When things are wonderful and beautiful in sharing or being with your parent or child; or
- When things don't go so well and you are quite 'stuck'.

In moments, or during times or days when things between you are wonderful and beautiful and you really enjoy and feel it, you can use these gifts as reminders to be in the heart more, to smile to your heart more (KHH 6) and to let the heart smile to others (KHH 7). Let these times be an opportunity to deepen your own heart connection, and for there to be more heart in the connection with your loved ones.

There may also be moments, even days, when you feel subtle or strong emotions, such as irritation or annoyance, sometimes for no apparent reason. Sometimes this is even directed at the family member whom you dearly love. You can let these moments be a reminder to be more heartful, at least as soon as it is possible to do so. Just be in the heart more, smile to your heart, let the heart smile to the other person or persons and let these times be an opportunity to deepen your own heart connection, by letting the heart start to dissolve whatever has surfaced in you. This will become easier and easier and words, even ones that 'really need to be said' will seem less and less important.

Learn from your child

The next story is an example of how the heart and more heart presence can facilitate shared learning and lead to a better result too. I fondly recall one exchange with my son Alex who would have been around twelve years old. He had broken an agreement of allowed electronic game time on his iPod.

Alex's Story:

Like many children of that age, boys perhaps more so, Alex loved his electronic items/gadgets. One day I caught him having ignored our arrangement of one hour playtime on a device unless there was extra permission to do so. He had secretly played long into the night, even disguising it under his doona. He woke sleep deprived and irritated.

It felt best not to let it go, to talk to him and to remind him of the 'deal' we had and, as a parent, to challenge him as to why he broke it. There was an element of anger rising in me, subtle, yet it was present during the talk.

As I was doing so, he patiently looked at me, waited for a pause and then said: 'Daddy are you in your heart?'

What was surprising was that he had realised that I wasn't in my heart or deep enough in my heart not to feel and express emotion. I also realised that at that time he was in his heart.

I had clearly followed that rising anger that had surfaced which I now notice as a pattern from the past: a need to be excited or slightly emotional in order to make an important point. Alex obviously felt a 'not-so-nice' feeling and thankfully felt empowered enough to say so.

I stopped and sincerely thanked him and paused for a few moments, to re-connect more deeply with the heart and with the deep love for both of my children.

Then, with the help of the heart and more 'in the love', we discussed the matter further. He was clearly more at ease now, and felt the 'love' helping with the issue.

We discussed that there should be a consequence and he agreed. It was a beautiful situation and when I asked him what the consequence should be, he said 'one week no iPod'.

> *I found it easy to agree to only two days and he was very pleased with the outcome, while at the same time acknowledging the issue and the breach of confidence that had occurred.*
>
> *The conversation ended up with a very gentle and loving father-son hug, smiles and a wonderful day spent partly together and individually following our own weekend interests and activities.*

One key aspect in the adult-child relationship, and in all relationships, is trust. As parents we have always offered trust to our children and given them opportunities to feel that trust, which they use or sometimes 'abuse'.

Perhaps 'abuse' is too strong a word here. As parents we may have had many situations where this trust was honoured and sometimes when it was broken. When we learn more about the heart and how to respond more heart-fully, then the exchange becomes less about the instance, the broken trust, and more about opportunities to share the love. We can interact with love from the heart, which engenders kindness and understanding, while learning the values that are felt by the heart.

Offering trust to give a child an opportunity to use, respect or abuse trust is very much a concept and can be valid and important. For us as parents this describes more than one of our initial approaches to parenting.

Now, with the clear presence and help from the heart, the heart feels what is right in terms of offering trust, freedom and responsibilities to the children and this seems to be more successful.

All this will make sense to the children around us too, as they can see and feel our use and abuse of trust given to us. Educating, raising and nurturing children can then include an awareness of the need for real mind/brain-heart balance. This will lessen inner conflict in them, as many things are asked of them - especially in terms of how to behave - and they see adults or the adult world as not always as following these values.

Your child is learning too - stages of (heart) learning

Every child is an individual, with their own personal characteristics, attributes and attitudes, including emotional tendencies and dispositions. These will be expressed in different ways as the child grows and matures. One way that will create more emotion and challenge is when we, as parents or adults, believe we are solely responsible for our children's wellbeing, correct upbringing and learning.

From the perspective of the heart, there are two aspects that need to work together: the abilities of the mind/brain and the abilities of the heart. The heart's being and doing is the foundation of all interactions: to always have the attitude and feeling of love and care in the heart, as well as seeing the child through the heart, and guiding the child.

When this togetherness of heart and guidance is present, there will be moments of enjoyment, deep love and connection. These moments when you are in the feeling of love, care and connection are perfect for giving guidance or structure to your child. It is also the best, if not the only, time to discipline, to discuss and implement consequences of behaviours.

When your own opening and expanding heart helps in this way, then the child's learning, including emotional learning and maturity, or 'emotional intelligence' develops naturally. The child and the child's heart are learning from your heart and also from everything else too.

Our hearts are comparatively pure when we are born. 'Comparatively' as a baby's heart in utero can pick up on how the mother or parents are feeling or behaving. As a consequence, the first burdens may be placed in the heart even before the baby is born.

Having read about the heart and having had your first experiences of it, you may now know that when there is emotion, you feel pressure in your heart. In relation to the mother-child example, when a mother experiences emotion or her heart is under pressure, the heart of the child will feel this too. A child growing in the womb also has a heart. It will feel these emotions with its own fully present spiritual heart and realise them to some extent as pressure, given that mother and child are emotionally, physically and spiritually quite close during this time.

Children go through different stages of how they respond to adults as they grow older. During these phases every child responds slightly differently to being shown affection and to being given instructions and guidance. They also respond differently when faced with the emotions from their siblings, friends, parents or grown-ups around them. Using the heart will help them develop greater emotional and mind/brain intelligence, including being at peace within themselves.

You may notice as an adult, teenager or child reading these lines or looking at your life in general, that there is a part in you that is naughty, rebellious, strongly strives for independence, or wants to do it your way. An example of this is teenagers or adults who, once free from outside guidance and control, may do the opposite to what someone asked them to do, even if they agreed to do it. At work, staff might freely 'play' by doing less or no work when the supervisor is away. Or there might be other behaviours, that when in the heart you know (even your mind/brain logic knows) they are not right and you go outside the rules of accepted, 'good' behaviour.

As an adult you may have learned to hide these responses. These qualities remain in most adults. Yet, as adults, there is a trickiness or even cunningness as to how these parts may show. Children are often more spontaneous and find hiding their 'naughtiness' more difficult.

Amber's frank and open story shows not only how she has had such reactions, but still continues to have them. It shows, that as she became stronger, she was more aware of a clear alternative behaviour that she, as a child, could choose to have.

Amber's Story:

Amber began her journey learning about the heart at the age of nine. Her parents started together with a few workshops and became quite enthused about the changes that were facilitated in them.

Amber shared that she noticed changes in her parents, a softening, a greater kindness and gentleness. She also noticed that these changes lasted longer than they had through other workshops or healing modalities her parents had explored over many years.

When these positive changes had faded in the past, there was more impatience, irritation and even anger in the parents' responses to her and other siblings, in particular when they were not doing what they were asked, such as tidying the room or doing a chore to help.

Amber further mentioned, very calmly, that her parents always had good intentions and kept on telling her and the others what they thought was good for them but it somehow did not work, and often she would resist it.

Amber has a strong sense of both independence and awareness. She remembers her early curiosity and how she approached her mum asking her: 'how do you know this (the heart) is working?'

She shares:

'Interestingly, mum left it open. She did not tell me to do it too, as she had on other occasions. This just made me more curious, together with the changes I felt in her.'

'I went to a few heart meditation sessions, felt nice afterwards, but nothing major happened.'

'Particularly, I did not understand how all the heart focus and working with the heart would help.'

Because of the continued involvement of her parents, the gentle encouragement and feeling drawn to it, Amber, as a nine-year-old, did her first workshops.

She still vividly recalls those days and shared: 'What would happen when my parents wanted me to do something, was that a part in me would rebel, only agree in parts and then react with strong emotions and resistance, like anger and resentment, and I was feeling quite self-righteous.'

'Often in those situations I would storm off, and also be shut off internally from everyone, separated in particular from Mum and Dad, and I could stay in this mood for days, or weeks.'

'Leaning more about my heart and how the heart can help me in my relationships with my family, now there is not so much of this black-and-white and separation I experience. We still disagree on matters.'

'I noticed that now I am much more relaxed and I can feel my heart. It guides me and helps me to respond differently.'

'I also feel that there is less heaviness inside me, more lightness, and it also helps me not to react or respond emotionally, as I did when I was younger.'

'I am almost 18 now and we still disagree here and there. Now it is not an issue anymore at all and there is much more understanding and love. It actually now feels like a deep friendship that I have with both my parents. When we disagree, and at times argue - which is less than before - normally this only lasts a very short time, a few minutes. Afterwards we find ourselves laughing, joking and just getting on with life. We always find agreement somehow and the emotions are no longer overpowering.'

'Through the heart I am really aware of this 'other choice'. I can be calmer, more relaxed and softer. I am aware how I can follow my heart, not just in words or as an idea. I find it much easier to let go of the argument, my point and any emotion that comes up.'

Amber's story highlights the natural tension that exists between parents, or adults, and children. It also shows that the heart needs time and attention, and with some perseverance, the heart will support not only adults in their heartfulness and life aspects, but also the child's learning, heartfulness and interactions with the world around them.

Amber's story also shows that because of the heart's role and function, it will naturally move anyone, child or parent, towards an even more joyful, light and loving life.

This is something very significant. As the heart learns and assists in living a joyful and loving life, the core longings of the heart are opened and fulfilled at a deeper level. This will directly impact on other areas of life.

Choosing the heart in moments when the challenging, naughty or difficult/emotional situations occur is quite important for long-term heart health. Realising that we all, children and adults, have choices, it is immensely important not to burden your heart, feeling and relationships with others, which would reduce the immensely wonderful moments that children and adults can share.

The story is a wonderful example of how indirectly a child's heartfulness, can have a positive influence on the relationship with her parents and on how the parents respond to a calmer, more heartful child - more about this in the section 'doing everything with love'.

The heart's natural guidance

The love that our hearts can hold share, feel and access is immensely beautiful. It is often hard to describe its levels of depth or beauty. This love will always flow through you, open and beautify your heart, then your heart will increasingly share it with others. Naturally this will often feel the deepest and sweetest with those closest to you.

There is an almost endless number of books and resources available on parenting and giving children advice and support. It would be impossible for anyone to access and read all of these. There are parents and children out there for whom the reading or absorption of resources is not their interest or strength. What the heart offers in addition is something like an 'automatic pilot' for parenting, and for children interacting with parents. The heart is intelligent. It knows and will guide you to do new things, be more courageous, try new approaches and most importantly, just be softer, gentler and more loving in everything you do. This includes when, as a parent or adult, you need to offer structure and some form of discipline to help the child understand what is 'right and wrong' or what are more appropriate ways of behaving.

One way your heart will be more present and offer its help will be in practicing the next KHH 'Doing everything with love'. This will work even better as the heart gets stronger. Doing things with love will only work as long as there is a feeling of love in your heart that you can access and feel. The moment you do, it will also be felt by others and will start to work.

The heart's universal and all-integrating qualities, as well as doing things with more love and feeling, will support the relationship that you have with your child or children around you. It will also nurture the quality of your own heart and allow your heart itself to expand.

Saying 'no' or being assertive from your heart with another person or your child with feelings of care and love will align your heart and the other person's. It will naturally be more acceptable to him or her. Less friction and less emotion will surface and over time emotional reactions will clearly reduce, if not disappear.

You may not be using your heart now with clarity, feeling or in all your interactions. If you and your child are adults, you may even have moved quite far from it. In your heart you once felt and perhaps you 'know' or still feel how deep that love is. With all your heart, enjoy and reclaim all parts of your heart and all the love for everyone close to you and beyond.

All this will support a gradual moving away from a more 'hierarchical' parent or adult to child relationship towards a more equal relationship and, over time, towards friendship. This can start while a child is quite young in certain aspects of the relationship or at certain times. It will ultimately assist the full transition to an equally and mutually caring and supporting friendship between all involved.

Key Heart Help 5: Do everything with love

The key heart helper and activity introduced in the Children section is 'do everything with love'. More correctly it should be, 'do everything with love and feeling from the heart'.

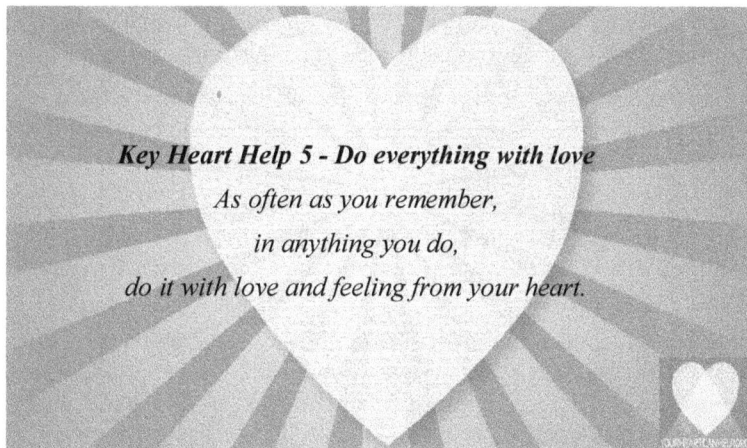

Key Heart Help 5 - Do everything with love
As often as you remember,
in anything you do,
do it with love and feeling from your heart.

The full KHH 5 - Do everything with love

You know how to love and how love feels. This KHH is about connecting 'in love' with someone else, a dear and loved child or family member.

Helpful reminders or additional prompts may be:

- *Have the intention to interact with love;*

- *Really feel the feeling of love and care in your heart; and also*

- *Feel your heart and any pleasant feelings there.*

The more you become aware of your heart's presence and radiance, you may smile a little, even follow any of the growing and pleasant feelings in your heart that are beginning to develop.

In practicing and using this KHH, your heart will naturally be involved in greater, deeper ways in all your interactions. As you use it, it will become a habit to be connected to your heart, and have its growing help available to you and to the people you interact with.

The deep nature of the relationship between child and a parent even extending to how most adults feel when they are around children, makes it easy to understand that love is close to this natural relationship. It is perhaps the most natural relationship we have where heart, love, care, support, nurturing, embracing and warmth are easily present.

For the same reason, doing everything with love, letting this deeper and purer love be present in our interactions, is something quite wonderful. It will have connecting, sustaining and challenge-resolving qualities to it. The heart will naturally resolve these: within, you and within the connection both of you have, as child and adult. This dissolving quality will function more with the persons you directly interact with. It will, hopefully, be easy for you to be reminded of this KHH in your child-adult relations.

Practical Heart Tip 30: Setting 'do things with love' targets

Setting yourself 'do everything or do things with love targets' can look like this:

- *In the relationship where you experience issues or challenges, do things with love as often as you can and let the issues be the reminder and trigger you to do so; and*

- *On any day, at home or at work, set a target as to when or how often you feel to practice, and use this KHH.*

In both instances it will be helpful to diarise your experiences (the feelings you feel and perhaps how relationships are subtly changing) and how you are tracking (when you do it, how often, etc.)

It is more beneficial to practice over a period of time. Set targets, say, to practise one day a week, over one week, one month or more. Practise until you see the benefits, within yourself and in your relationships, or until you find it nicer or more natural to be in the 'doing things with love' state than any other way.

Remember that doing things with love will naturally bring more of you into the interaction or communication. It engages the heart and its loving, caring and attention-giving function. It also engages all that your heart stands for and can help with. It is often surprising what new paths open or what new outcomes, feelings, realisations and qualities are added to life.

It is when we do things with love and feeling that the heart is automatically involved, present and helping, and all the qualities as well as the healing and nurturing abilities of your heart described throughout the book will 'kick in'.

Help in difficult or challenging relations

The moment you start to bring the two together, your commitment to your heart and doing things with love, a wonderful foundation is laid. This will gradually deepen as you include more heart into daily life, and it will ultimately help with difficult child-parent issues.

As your heart becomes lighter and more open, it will also become significantly less tainted by emotions or emotional reactions. This will allow you to make clearer decisions, including when you as the 'parent' are guiding, teaching or setting boundaries for your child. In turn, whatever decisions are made by the parent or child will be felt by the other person's heart. They will be easier to understand and accept, even if it takes a while for them to surface. This is particularly important when things are challenging or even stuck.

If a decision is truly made by the heart, then at the level of their heart, the other person will instantly understand and accept its truth, even if on the outside other things are said or there is an emotional response. Over time things can shift so this acceptance manifests more quickly on the surface, with fewer emotions present.

As indicated above, if there are challenging or very difficult behaviours at home, having an open, loving heart towards the child, or the parent, will help with less emotional response or reaction.

Helpful approaches in difficult times can be:

- Be patient;
- Feel and act from the heart;
- Be aware of your own emotional reactions - expressed or not;
- Choose the heart as often as possible and commit to opening and en-lightening your heart; and
- Be aware of unhelpful mind/brain-driven aspects, like judging or being self-righteous (because of age or status).

To judge anyone's behaviour is not the nature of the heart, neither is the natural response to react with emotion. However, a heavy or burdened heart may make anyone lean towards these reactions. A lighter, purer and more open heart is a powerful way to remove uncaring actions or anything not loving or kind that is driven by the collection of negativities in the heart.

Patience is a quality of the heart that is timeless and unlimited. Impatience can easily fall into the 'emotions' category. While the heart's help is immense and often instant, deeper changes in difficult situations may take some time, a few days or weeks, even months. Some if this will always depend on:

- How much commitment you make to your heart and practical heart-opening;
- How the child connects to the heart learning, if this is at all possible, and how s/he follows practical heart learning methods and ways; and
- How long and with how much emotion other behavioural patterns have dominated past interactions.

In an amazing and special way, the heart teaches us about love. This will always be practical, in its presence being felt by others, and will want to be shared in caring, attentive and loving ways. In this connection with children and also with other adults around you, it shows new or refined ways of being and approaches. This is particularly helpful in challenging parent-child situations or when things are stuck.

The special child-parent love and its radiant quality will be activated and deepened and grow beyond whatever you have ever felt. It will gently, and yet in most profound ways, touch and transform your heart while working on the heart and the relationship of your child or your Mum/Dad or other adults around you. At the very least there will be more peace and calm in you. On the outer level, it may help the other to let go, to feel more calm and heartful. Over time the relationship will naturally either heal or blossom into purer forms of joy, bliss and love.

The child can help you too

Children are amazing in many ways. Some can have a wisdom that's beyond their time and at times beyond words.

It can shine through in their actions, attitudes or words. They can remind us of the deep potential slumbering in all our hearts. Children's presence can remind us powerfully of this and make life so enriching, joy-giving and filled with love.

Children can also help adults in another way, in relation to what the heart is and how the heart works. Children have had less time to accumulate heart-limiting negativities within and around their heart. In that sense, their hearts are lighter and purer. This is one reason why we love being around children or seeing a young child or baby - just looking at them can bring joy and peace in our hearts.

Amanda's story above in the Family section also refers to this. She shares about her children and her best intentions to be a good mother. In learning more about the heart, in using it more in daily interactions, she realised that naturally some of her own learning could come through the heart of a child.

The child's heart quality can assist parents passively by reminding them of that purer feeling that lives inside everyone's heart, reminding them to follow the heart more and, as several sections in the book share, to practically choose heartfulness over emotion. This will also support a clearer mind or greater mindfulness.

You can take care of your own heart; let it open, let it shine and it will take care of you and everyone around you, naturally, gently and unseen.

The above story, where my son paused our interaction, is one example where the child helps the parent. The child's heart can also help others around them more directly. This will require learning about the heart and having a clear understanding about the workings of the heart. This more direct help can take these two forms:

- Letting the greater heart/mind balance be present in what you, as a child, 'do' with adults. This can be in talking, working together or in shared play or time; and
- Smiling from the heart to the adults around. This is the speechless and yet direct heart-to-heart sharing and helping (see KHH 7 'Smiling from the heart to others').

It is good to work as a team, too. At the heart of who we are, no matter what age, we are all the same essence. Both of you know about the heart and have now experienced the function of the heart. You can remind each other in daily life or when the going between you gets rocky or less loving, to be more heartful and heart-connected, with the heart helping constantly in growing ways.

Let the child or children come to your heart

One of the well-known quotes from the Bible is the words said by Jesus 'let the children come to me'. With the help of this metaphor the meaning of the heart can further be illustrated:

- As adults, let your heart help to regain that purity of heart that offers joy, love, wonder and freedom - perhaps an ultimate freedom - in accordance with your faith; or
- As a child, recognise that the purity or lightness of heart is precious. Despite the different roles now (you are a child amongst other children and adults), your heart can help - you and all others around you.

Many adults adore children. The quality of your adult heart will somewhat impact on how children are drawn to you. Children will recognise with their own inner radar, their hearts, how heavy or light, open, loving and joyful you really are and they will be attracted to the latter qualities. More heart is likely to enrich your adult life by lighter, joyful, spontaneous moments of sharing with those who are 'young at heart', children and really anyone.

There are so many constellations in a seemingly freer and freer world of behaviours, adult relationships, travels and world-connectedness. One aspect of this maybe that you are not be in the natural family, the 'ideal' Mum, Dad and children. There may be other parent-child relationships such as one parent, a step parent, three parents, same-gender parents or child-parent relationships over longer distances. Here the heart can be a wonderful facility.

Whatever your situation is, where and how you live, whether you are rich or poor, whether you are in a relationship or a single parent, your heart can always shine and you can really enjoy being with your children in every way. An ever-deepening and wonderful love can grow beyond words, hopes and dreams, even when things get difficult. This will be facilitated by your heart's natural qualities and abilities that are waiting to be fully uncovered.

A greater heart/mind balance and a stronger heart means that the heart will be active, radiant and more able to facilitate beautiful feelings and healing potential in this special relationship you have. Utilising the heart more at home, choosing the heart more in beautiful or challenging situations alike, will have a natural flow-on effect to your world outside the family haven. Especially if, as a parent, you support your relationship with your child in this way, the heart will facilitate smoother relationships in the child's wider connections: in the family, at school, in the community, at a first job or at any sporting, social or hobby activities.

Following the practices in this section of the book step by step, your heart will gradually become freer and lighter, and the love that is already there will be felt deeper in your heart. Even if you are mainly interested in this Children section, study and engage with the KHHs in the other sections as a minimum practice in support of your heart. You may find some of the PHTs are also relevant to your situation or in general, and of further help to you, your heart and family.

Summary - Having your children at heart

Children are amazing and wonderful beings and an incredible joy in life. At the same time, they can be an immense challenge to the world of adults, parents and even the wider community.

In reverse, parents too can be a challenge to a child or teenager. The clear functions of the heart offer additional strategies and new avenues of direct help, or ways to make something that is special and beautiful even more so. Here is the practical heart help summarised:

1. It is important to use other parts of who you are as well as your heart. For example, it is good to reflect on your own and your child's behaviour and to work out what is workable, acceptable and truthful, or in line with what your community or society accepts.

2. Let your growing, active heart balance itself with your mind/brain and help you in all you plan or do. Care, love, attention, respect and other positive, natural human interactions are qualities that most humans find easy to value and appreciate.

3. While no one is perfect or expected to be so, emotions as defined here are destructive or at the very least do not help the parent-child relationship. Realise that any emotional reaction has a connection to negativities or past emotions that were placed in your heart. Attend to your own heart's health and strength as much as, if not more than, to the situation.

4. There are most likely many guidelines, concepts and approaches to 'parenting' available. In addition, there are the past experiences and 'good ideas' of those close to you: your own parents, family, friends or doctor. Let your heart guide whatever you do; strengthen your heart and pro-actively have it growing, strong, active and working, so that current or future challenging situations are helped by all facilities and 'tools' you have available.

5. In the heart you and your child know what is right and when particular behaviours are suitable or supportive. Whether this is in challenging or mutually supporting each other, there will be clearly discernible respect and care. With practice you can ultimately let your heart be present in every moment and in all interactions or being together.

6. In moments of deep challenges in your relationship use the PHT 'Centre yourself in your heart' and the following key steps:
   - Acknowledge you experience a challenge and/or emotion;
   - Use the KHH from this chapter or other chapters to strengthen your heart;
   - Do KHH 6 the complete 'Heart Strengthening' in a regular pattern;
   - Do KHH 7 'Smile from the heart to others' as an additional and direct heart help tool; and
   - Do KHH 13 'Open Heart Meditation' for all past hurts, burdens and emotions to be cleansed and for the true nature of the relationship to bloom again over time.

7. The KHH of this section 'Do everything with love' will help to will help you to be in the heart or will help you to have to the kind of loving relationship you envision. Combine it with setting reminders around the house and keeping a daily journal or diary as to how often and with what depth or 'quality' you were interacting with your child from this place of love, your heart.

8. While being with children or your Mum/Dad can be magical, it can also bring to the surface the biggest challenges. In attending to this deep relationship with more heart, be patient, kind and loving to yourself too. You will have good days and not-so-good days in doing everything with more love, and there will be days when you forget or when emotions are a bit more at the surface.

9. Let the KHH 'Do everything with love' be a practical reminder when you realise that you can bring more heart into the relationship and when you had not-so-good moments or days. Equally 'do everything with love' when you have moments of deep joy and bliss. Continue, feel and practise it when you cuddle each other, when you read a story, when you play a game, when you talk about computer games or when you share the favourite thing you do together.

10. Use the PHT 'Setting do things with love targets' to stay on track and to feel more and more often within, your heart. This means that you will use your heart even more frequently. Diarise your experiences.

11. Model heart-behaviour to your child/teenager or to your parent/adults around you. There is always learning through mind/brain understanding, which we are more familiar with. However, in everything you do or see, your heart is participating, learning and helping.

12. In the medium to long-term a thorough facilitator of positive, growing relationships is an open, clear and cleansed heart that is present, guiding and helping in ways it is designed to do.

Chapter 3

Relationship - Loving with All Your Heart

All I know is love and I find my heart infinite & everywhere. Hafiz

In cultures around the world there is a clear association between fulfilment in love and the heart. On Valentine's Day, the day of romantic love, you can see hearts everywhere as symbols of true love or a special bond between two hearts.

To be loved and to love is one of the most wonderful experiences in life. There is much opportunity to share love with family, friends and widening groups of people as your heart opens. However, it is deeply engrained in our being, psyche, heart and mind that there is one special person to find and to love in this life. We hold it immensely dear to the heart that loving that someone special and being in a loving romantic relationship is a treasure or something deeply longed for, offering deep fulfilment, joy and purpose.

Many people also know or have experienced that a relationship of 'true love' or 'endless love' is an ideal, a vision or a hope. You may have experienced in your own past, or in the lives of people you know, that this very relationship has been the cause of deep challenge or hurt in the form of a painful separation, the loss of a loved one, love lost or feelings of insecurity, of 'is s/he the right one, the right partner'?

What is the role of the heart in relationship and how can it help in your relationship? The following sections cover how the heart can offer unique help in the search for a lover/partner and during an in-between time 'alone'. There are further sections and stories on how the heart assists with challenge, 'heart-ache', or when love is reduced or lost. You will find what is happening from the perspective of the heart when 'the heart is broken' and how to let go and love again. You will also learn how to support and nurture your special relationship now to ensure, with all the heart's help, that it stays special and even grows in depth, purpose, beauty and expanding feelings of purer love.

One of the key qualities of the heart that is highlighted in this chapter is the letting-go ability of the heart. Mind, thoughts and emotions are naturally more inclined to create attachment and to be busy with it, taking you away from love and loving. A typical relationship example is when one is upset or busy in the mind or with emotion, feeling and expressing some form of disappointment or dissatisfaction like 'you never do this' or 'you always do things this way'.

One unique aspect not only limited to relationship help, is the heart's direct and immediate ability to help in times when it is important to 'let go', when things are stuck, heavy or feeling burdened. The deeper version of this, explained in this chapter, is the heart's next level of letting go, to assist with older, deeper issues, challenges or heart-aches: the heart's ability to surrender unwanted, unneeded and unhelpful matters.

This chapter may also offer you insights as to how greater heart understanding and practice, and a greater, deeper love, can prepare you for relationship, offer a deeper form of being within relationship and even heal past relationships.

The essence of the heart's help

*Heart warmth is the magic ingredient
in our healing intentions for ourselves
and all life that it touches.
Doc Childre*

The essence of the heart's help is through love. The heart is the centre of love. This means it is the centre of all the love that is in your heart and all the love that can flow through and grow in your heart. It is also where all the love can radiate from your heart and can envelop your heart and, with a growing heart, can envelop everyone and everything around you.

In more specific terms, the more you learn to be heartful and use your heart in real, practical ways, you will find and clearly feel that your heart can assist you and those dearest to you immensely, in a range of ways, for example:

- How to truly follow the heart and to use the heart's guidance in who to be with;
- What heart's role and function is in the 'falling in love' time;
- How you can be 'in love' when things get difficult;
- How to let the heart work … as opposed to 'working hard' to ensure love continues to stay in your relationship;
- How to be guided moment by moment and in 'big' decisions, for example to stay or not to stay in a relationship;
- How the heart helps to envelop you, others and your dear ones and how the heart can radiate and quietly assist and transform all around you;
- How the heart helps in moving on, letting go and letting the heart heal any wounds when a relationship has ended;
- How the heart will naturally help in gaining all the freedom and openness, or more, to love again; and
- How to discover, through your own heart, the deeper purpose of relationship.

Your heart is unique in how it can help you. Relationship is about love. The more love there is, the less room there is for other aspects to creep into relationships and make them a challenge.

In its essence, the heart will remove everything negative from within you, such as any feelings or emotions that are not love.

Romantic relationship, 'one love' and your heart
You are always in my heart.

Perhaps you have heard the expression or you've said to someone, 'you are always in my heart' or a similar beautiful and heart-related expression. Depending on the age of your relationship there may have been, or still be, a clear hope for the relationship to be this way. The entire relationship chapter will cover how there is permanent and growing heart room for one other special person. The 'room' analogy is perhaps how you walk into the space of love, meet and spend time. Greater heart awareness and deeper heart help will offer new directions and practical assistance on how to purposefully, joyfully and lovingly be in this love space together.

Your 'relationship' theme may also be that you are looking for someone, actively or less so, or that you are happily, by-choice, living on your own. In our society there are also more people who are single or are choosing to be so. This chapter will also have a section on this. The highlight perhaps is how Karli, in her beautiful story, shares how her heart guided, helped and offered her clarity in her situation as a single person.

Love in a romantic relationship is about the special love and deep love we feel for someone else and the fulfilment of this love in an intimate connection. The heart's role is no less than to support you at the beginning of your relationship, even before it starts and in completing the full cycle of it within your life. The heart helps at all stages: with recognising the 'correct' or deeper feeling of love for another person at the start; being within the relationship with love; and in helping love to grow continuously. It also helps in learning important life and love lessons and in letting go when the relationship ends or when the life of one partner ends.

What 'you are always in my heart' means is the deeper understanding, that your heart can open beyond the physical body, beyond imaginable size and depth, and when your heart is that open, then wherever that person is, they will always be in your heart.

When the heart is growing, opening and expanding, there will be a point, too, when so much love will fill the heart, that whatever someone else does, there will only be love. All irritation, emotion and everything that is not love will be cleansed, removed and will cease to exist. It will take time; however, your heart's journey is to be there.

What the heart knows as 'true love' may need small, subtle and gentle adjustment. Your heart will facilitate this. When your heart is burden-free, there is only love. You will once and forever only feel deep love for your partner, other loved ones, and everyone.

On the journeying with more heart there is a growing love that will fulfil all your needs, hopes and deepest inner longings for love. It is in this greater, all-embracing love that all love, including the 'one love' that we hope to find and maintain, can be nurtured. Your heart is the most wonderful help you have available all the time, to bring improvements to you and your relationship and to guide you in your decisions - for your relationship future and every moment.

Following the heart to find love, romantic love
As you live deeper in the heart,
the mirror gets clearer and cleaner. Rumi

Following the heart to find love is one of the functions of the heart. The above quote implies that as one mirror, your heart, gets clearer and cleaner, it will look for a similar mirror and heart. The saying stems from understanding that when you truly follow the heart, the best outcome for you and all around you will be facilitated, including in aspects of fulfilment in romantic love.

Taking guidance from the heart, directly, correctly and deeply is important, especially in making the right choice, and brings you closer to finding 'one love'.

Following your heart may start with finding the right partner. What attracts you initially to your partner? It can be something visible or spontaneously likeable such as appearance, facial features or an attractive sense of humour. Naturally it may also be inner qualities such as their kind nature, care or love for you and others. It can also be a combination of inner and outer qualities.

This 'liking' or loving can become deeper and deeper after days, weeks, months or years. Sometimes, as your connection deepens, especially in relationships where there is more love than emotion or mind/brain domination, you start loving your partner because of his or her heart qualities. When or if you get to this 'phase', your love is far more beautiful, deeper and more expansive. Outer appearance becomes secondary as the heart becomes primary, and what you really start to 'see' and value is real.

Some couples who have been together for a long time experience this. Often these couples stayed 'in love' longer. This actually means they stayed in the heart more, used the heart's help more often and naturally dwell in a greater love that two hearts generate for each other and their environment.

Interestingly, even if the initial attraction is clearly physical, based on a particular look or character trait, the heart is always present whether you are aware of it or not. It encourages you to meet, connect and possibly get involved with this person.

Within your heart there is a deep love for many people around you and at the core of your heart, and everyone's heart, there is love for everyone. These circles of love will expand as your heart opens more. From here it is quite heart- and mind-logical that not everyone you feel deep love for is destined for a relationship with you. It is quite common to feel deep, even exquisitely beautiful love for someone and not to pursue relationship.

Some people call the 'perfect' partner a 'soul mate'. This implies that there is recognition of another person through a deeper inner part. While 'soul' means higher consciousness, it can be your heart, inner heart or true self that is used. However, it can also be the soul and the level of clarity in choosing wisely from your soul is not as accurate as from your heart. Your heart recognises the possible partner at a deeper level. It knows who to enjoy friendship with and who to be in a close, romantic relationship with.

Your heart is the key for you to make a romantic decision deep enough to ensure the love you and your partner share will support both of you in your heart connection and growth.

The heart is deep, and depending on how far you have allowed the layers of your heart to open, you will find there is love for many people you meet. Often this love is surprisingly deep, sweet and wonderful to feel.

Guidance on-the-go

What follows is the first 'on-the-go' method of using your heart more in making an early decision or commitment to be with someone. Love for others always flows through your heart and through you. So in many ways, whether you enter into a romantic relationship or not, it is something special to be grateful for.

Your heart knows how deep your love for the special other is and will be. This is not easy to feel and recognise at once or in a brief encounter. On a practical level we know this and that it is good to meet with the possible partner a few times socially, staying clear of everything that is not just friendship. It may not be easy to be strong and enjoy this getting to know the other person. If you are already good friends, lovely - you will be able to enjoy this time while feeling deeper.

This is very helpful as the heart is still opening or being cleansed, becoming more present and clear. When you meet several times, it is not so much about checking the other person out, it is how deep, sweet, gentle and expansive your feeling of love for the other person is.

Guidance with intent

To deepen awareness, understanding and ability to feel with your heart, use the KHHs and other practices in the suggested step-by-step guidelines with some commitment. When you start to feel with more clarity and your heart is responding to these practices, you will be able to be more specific.

You can then ask your heart with the intent to show you, as a feeling, what choice to make: ask your heart how a relationship with the person you like feels. Then really feel your heart's response, the feeling from your heart, as you feel the question.

Practical Heart Tip 31: Following your heart III - starting to get answers from the heart *

'Follow your heart' is much more than a common or casual saying. You can follow your heart to obtain answers that are supported by the wisdom of your heart and by your heart's deep intelligence.

This can be in two ways: casually yet with awareness, 'on-the-go', or with more intent. If you look for more intentional guidance or answers from your heart, you can follow these steps:

- *To get a clearer answer, it is good to ask 'how would a relationship with this person be', or 'how would it be not to be in a relationship with this person, or just to be friends? If there are two people in your life as possible relationship choices, then let your heart feel how Person A and how person B feels as a relationship.*

- *Feel the difference in your heart as you give time after each question for the heart and heart-feeling to respond. Give each question or sub-question time, as the feeling from your heart is deep and can take you on a journey, showing you 'yes' or 'no' and also showing you the feeling over the course of being together.*

- *It is important to be aware that the head is quite strong and may override the heart's response. This may happen with a choice you already think about or even favour.*

- *It may also help to ask - silently or out loud - 'how does it feel to be in a relationship with the person my heart considers to be a good relationship'?*

Your heart will only ever answer in the language of the heart by showing you a feeling. Read more about this in the following paragraphs.

It may be helpful to add an additional, open question. For example, not related to the obvious yes/no way of asking. Such a question could be 'what does the best relationship feel like' or, 'how does my heart feel to be with the person, whoever that is, that is the best for me?' You will receive an answer from your heart in the form of a feeling. If, the feeling from the heart for the person you are 'considering' now is very strong, radiant and gentle, more so than for a possible other person 'who is the best for me' then that would be clear yes. If it is the other way around, then there is a better choice, a better-suited person out there, who you may not have met as yet.

To seek guidance from the heart in this way, to follow the heart in relation to romantic love questions, will be new for most people. This is what the casual saying 'follow your heart' really means, to truly follow the heart by using the heart. For some this seems natural; there is already clarity that it is good to use and trust intuition or gut feeling to influence a decision.

Directly using the heart and feeling its answer is not about 'good' or 'bad' or 'right' or 'wrong'. It is about 'feeling out', with the heart, what the potential is, or what is more in accordance with the greater knowing of the heart.

Before entering a relationship, it is really helpful and important to feel deeply how much love is in both hearts, how the deeper heart connection is, in order to later maintain this special connection.

It is about finding out how strong the shared love foundation, upon which you build a relationship, really is. We know, from others or our own experiences, that once the initial 'falling in love' time comes to an end, it is this deeper love that carries a relationship though its ups and downs. It can also happen that after the falling in love time there can be surprises as to who the person 'really' is and how the person really behaves, which are often love or heart issues that the heart can help with.

Your heart knows, has a much better and bigger picture as to how suited you are to each other long term: what you like and will like in the future, your lifestyle choices in the future, developments or growth directions.

A relationship needs this greater amount of love or love-potential. The time of 'being-so-in-love' or 'falling in love' will come to an end and no one wants to be in situations, going out or living together, of being irritated by behaviours or simply being in the other's presence. Painful separation may follow, or difficult times together, trying to find again what you once shared in the beginning.

Your heart will help you to make the deeper, more correct choice, for the short, medium and longer term. When feeling how it feels to be with person A or B who both like you, look for the feeling of gentleness, calmness and depth.

There is no need to be concerned if you entered a relationship and you have followed other ideas, feelings or emotions. While the heart is a fantastic guide, and no doubt has done some guiding in most cases, it is also an in-depth tool to 'rectify' and beautify any relationship.

Passion, heart and deep love

Passion and love, with the help of feelings and insights from your heart, offer a much clearer and more refined view of romance, love and relationship. With the clearer help from your heart you can learn to distinguish between two types of romantic love: passion and love. For the choice as who to be with, this is significant.

There is a fine line between experiencing a form of 'passion and love' that supports your relationship, including long term, and a 'passion and love' that will give rise to many challenges and emotional difficulties.

On the one side, if strong excitement, rush, passion and desire are how you feel about someone, there are indications there could be more emotion than love involved, now or in the future.

You may already know this by experience. There is a high likelihood that later in your relationship, that you will find it hard to find the calm, joyful and deeply growing love your heart longs for. If you are in a relationship, indicators of this can be feelings/emotions like 'I can't be without you, not even a few hours', deep and painful missing the other person, not being able to live without the other person, as well as passionate and wild love-making. To understand and choose differently from the heart in this situation is potentially a huge shift in perception, understanding or approach. If you are already in a committed relationship, let your heart help you to be more and more on the side of love and the pleasant, wonderful, enjoyable feelings, like missing the other person but with joy, peace and wonderful feelings of love.

On the other side is the more gentle feeling of love in your heart.

One example may help to make this clearer. If you see a dear friend, partner or family member after some time of separation and there is a lot of care, appreciation or love for each other, you would usually greet each other with a hug. If this person were to grab you, squeeze you very tight, shake you quite strongly and loudly say 'I love you' then this would seem over the top, even too much. It is often more natural when we feel love to let the heart express this and show these tender feelings through the body in a gentler embrace and in quietly spoken words.

These lighter and gentler feelings are indicators that as a heart-to-heart connection there is more lightness and more love than can easily unfold. While such a love connection is gentler, less 'outrageous', less extraordinary, the love that can unfold through your heart when there is more calmness is fuller, richer and deeper. It is more like an ocean of love within and around and it will start to feel limitless and at times beyond words.

In the same way that you will find it very hard to enjoy a special, gentle piece of music in a public place when there is so much noise around, love will grow more easily on this innermost peaceful ground, where there is less passion and more heart. You very likely know these gentler feelings of deeper love in your heart when sharing them with someone close.

In your heart you know, and perhaps in friendships around you can see some of it. You may have fewer friends around in the longer term that you shared extreme or outrageous adventures with. It is often the quieter ones, where the heart-to-heart connection is a deeper and calmer one, that support you, love you and are there when things don't go so well, that are really important.

This is not represented well in the media or movies. In movies in particular there are only one and a half or two hours to quickly get everything done ... the 'passionate' kiss the wild sex and similar displays, teaching us in some way to be aware of these shallower connections. In moments when you use your heart and the deeper feeling within, the simple intention is enough for your heart to guide you quietly, to facilitate more and more love, to make more heartful decisions in relation to everything you do with a potential or current partner.

Whether you hope, dream or long for passion or whether you are in such a relationship now, all your heart work, heart opening and greater heart connection will gradually and gently take you to a deeper, more blissful and more lasting form of love-relationship.

Falling into love

Fall deeply, into your heart, into love.

Falling in love is something beautiful and enjoyable. It is a time where people in love let go and trust. It is a time of special moments and pure love, untainted and unspoiled. Everything seems, everything is experienced as perfect, beautiful, wonderful.

From the perspective of your heart, 'falling in love' is something your heart is showing you. It can be something very deep and can only be experienced when you let go control of the mind/brain.

For those who have been there, there is a clear knowing how real, how special this experience is. These are moments when there is deep and seemingly endless love within you and the only way life can be fulfilled is in sharing this love. In these special moments you are naturally, by default, much more heartful than mindful.

One of the dilemmas in modern times is that we long for this feeling of deep or pure love and we have the freedom, or believe we have the freedom to follow it, to fall in love again and again, in the hope to find it. Wanting to fall in love again and again, looking for another person to fulfil this need has led to difficulties or the destruction of relationships or marriages. It can be a path to more trauma, pain and hardship rather than pure love found.

The truer, deeper and purer feeling of love - including falling in love again and again including with the same partner - will only ever be an interplay between that other beautiful and special person in our lives and the functioning or 'condition' of the heart.

If you always want to be in love, find love again or deepen the love relationships around you, use your heart more, then look at what 'falling in love' really is: moments when you surrender more to your heart, when you are more heart-centred than guided by logic and reason. If your relationship is 'right' for you, if you once fell in love deeply, it is highly likely that with an expanding heart, more love than you ever felt before can grow.

Contrary however to 'falling in love', when you fall more into your heart and connect with it more, you will not put salt in the coffee instead of sugar or dream all day or do other 'up in the clouds' things. Your heart will offer beautiful feelings, while helping you to let go of an over-active mind, at the same time sharpening your mind/brain processes. You can have both.

Letting go of the mind/brain when it is time to do so, in romantic life and in daily life, is the challenge or 'problem'.

You know that you can't 'fall in love' when you want to or when you ask for it. It happens ... and as an inner experience, it only will happen when you let go, 'fall' into the deeper love in your heart and surrender some of the parts that hold you back from these most blissful moments.

So why is there this 'falling in love'? 'Falling in love' first reminds us that letting to go into love, into the heart is wonderful. The purpose of course is to recognise another human being whom your heart and all of you can deeply love and where relationship is possible. It is a gift of love to recognise too, that the deep longing for a greater love in us all is real and heart-related and has a spiritual, all-of-life-embracing meaning when we follow and realise it.

The answer is not so much in who to find and fall in love with, but more so how to open and purify the heart and how to access its deeper layers to realise the same love as a feeling within - the feeling your heart recognises.

When friends or clients, often disenchanted about romantic love, ask about falling in love, the answer is not 'be more careful' or 'don't ever let love happen again', but 'use your heart', 'open your heart and fall deeply into a greater, purer and all-embracing love'. The real wonder is that you can do this with or without a partner. And either to eventually choose a partner with a more available heart wisdom or to let the love grow within the relationship you are already in. In both instances, the answer is within.

Being 'in love'

Love has no desire but to fulfil itself...
To melt and be like a running brook
that sings its melody to the night.
To wake at dawn with a winged heart
and give thanks for another day of loving.
Kahlil Gibran

Being in love does not require you to fall in love again and again. It is easier to look at the 'falling in love' as a special gift, as a blessing given for us to recognise that other special person. Together with this recognition is an opportunity to be grateful, to be reminded of a deep and growing love that can be accessed and the joy associated with being in love. From there onwards, we can build something even more precious starting from this unique platform.

This special dose of love is available for two purposes: to recognise a special heart-to-heart connection with another being and as a starting-bonus to cleanse, heal and prepare for what any relationship will bring with it: challenges, heart-aches, difficulties and within all this, opportunities to choose the source of love and the greater love through your heart.

You may know or have experienced that this early or 'young' love does not last. Some say a lot of work is needed and there are many other helpful ideas around how you can maintain or re-kindle relationship love. What you may not yet have tried is to access and work with the very source of love and let your heart do the work for you.

Perhaps now is the time to use this gift of love, together with the gifts your heart is holding and offering to you. You have the chance now to work continuously with this gift that was given a long time back. You have access to all the core steps and first level practices, meditations and prayers that will assist you to take care of your heart, the centre of infinite and unconditional love.

Remember there is no effort needed to be 'in love', to venture into the deeper layers of your heart. As you attend to it, it will happen naturally; you will gradually be more and more 'in love'. And this love, even if fulfilled in one relationship, will also spread to people around you, your family, social circles, everyone at work and people you meet by chance.

The simplicity of the key heart strengthening 'relax' and 'smile' is the very expression of this - less doing and more being, including being in the heart and in love more.

Being 'in love' does not necessarily need an expression or action. It is important to realise this and learn from it every so often, every day, or every moment. In some way we accept this if we 'fall in love' with someone who is with someone else. Here the heart can uniquely help you to surrender, let go, wish the other well and to enjoy the beautiful feelings you feel for him or her, without necessarily acting upon those feelings.

The heart's work for you is not linear or sequential. For example, in a comparatively short time, it can bring back feelings that were deeply buried or seemingly no longer present and raise them to heights never felt before. It can bring feelings to the surface where they are felt again clearly and strongly.

There is one trick or heart-quality that requires understanding: not to follow what you once had, or what you want or know. What you once had may not be available within a current set of internal or external circumstances. It is more likely that the mind/brain connection to some emotions wants to create something here.

The brain can only do so in a limited way. All feeling is connected to, even stems from, the heart. The heart will take you there. As your heart opens more, what you knew or remember about love is only the beginning. An opening heart feels love in infinite and growing ways and will always take you deeper into this ocean of love for your partner and for others.

During both periods of 'falling in love' and 'being in love', it is important to reflect, observe social norms and not force, push or want when it is not appropriate to do so. For example, if you feel love or 'fall in love' with someone who is in an existing relationship, it is best for the purity and opening of your heart, and everyone else's too, to enjoy the feeling of love and be less inclined to act on it.

The more you are at peace in your current situation, the more you are in the heart and enjoy the bliss, peace, calmness and love in your heart, the more others will be drawn to you and share with you. Friendships form easily and when both parties feel in the heart that it is right to take the next step, to let it happen and be more whole-hearted within, a new relationship can blossom.

When it is only one, for example friendship that feels right, then enjoy the feeling, be grateful, be open to what a friendship can offer and be aware too, that love, friendship and the heart are wonderful gifts.

The greater love that is gradually facilitated through your heart's help, or is naturally presented to some extent already, will never want, force, seek or push. Love naturally happens. Love only knows love and your heart's deeper desire is solely to love, to be in a deep flow of love.

If you are unsure, upset or even 'lost in love', including being disenchanted or disheartened, then to attend to the heart is a wonderful choice in moving forward, as neither of these are good 'places' to be. Equally, if you are not happy with what you are experiencing right now, or think it should be different, the best choice is to keep opening your heart. Keep looking after your heart to allow all your heart's potential to help you and others around you, not only to be 'in love' but to be in love more unconditionally. Being in love is how your heart naturally wants and will help you to be.

You are single

It is perfectly normal and 'ok' to be single. Yet for many it is a burden not to be in a relationship and their hope and wish is to find someone to share life with.

Being in a romantic relationship may not be the only or ultimate purpose of life for you, or for any one of us. People like the Dalai Lama, the Pope and people who do not choose or want a partner would otherwise be hopelessly lost.

Some time ago, an article stated that in Western cities there are growing numbers of single households. Is this due to growing numbers of people choosing not to be in a relationship, is it an expression of how people now want to live, or does it just happen to be?

What you may want at a period or moment in your life, including partnership, relationship or marriage, may not be the best fit or what is supposed to occur according to a bigger picture of learning, growing and loving. It is ultimately this bigger picture of growing and loving that will fulfil the deeper yearning within for your individual life purpose. And whatever this life purpose is, it is only able to be lived by you, with the guidance from your heart. I t will be in your heart that you find fulfilment, clarity and happiness.

Karli's story is a wonderful example and a very open and courageous sharing. Karli came to Hobart in 2011. She came to visit a friend in whom she had a romantic interest and, in her words, she hoped 'he would be the one' and it would turn into 'a serious relationship.'

After a brief period of being together, it became clear to Karli that he was not the 'one' and they continued on different paths forward. It was around that time that Karli first found out about the heart. She started regular Heart Strengthening and attended regular Heart Meditation sessions.

Karli's Story:

'When I arrived in Hobart, I was looking for a man in my life, a partner. I had been married for seven years. Now, having learned about the heart, I can see, having lived apart from my first husband, that we were not suited for each other in the first place. We fell in love, of course, but over time too many significant differences surfaced. I am now determined to get it right.'

In the following months Karli, who is now in her mid-30s, got to know two more men she liked. 'I was always interested in developing a friendship first'. Karli however, soon found in both instances that neither of them were suited to her and to what her heart wanted and knew was right for her.

Karli enjoyed all the heart opening activities immensely and followed her passion and enjoyment with participating in the Heart Workshops.

With the help of her heart's realisations and more defined feelings, Karli became more and more aware of her own actions in past relationships that were present now in her friendships with men.

In past relationships, 'falling in love' and 'being in love', in what she now describes as the old way, she would lose herself, be absorbed by the relationship and lose her sense of freedom. She also described it as not being in balance and realized that she could not be this way with someone anymore.

> *She realised more and more the depth of feeling of a purer love and how only that depth of feeling, from her heart, would be the one that would carry her and a partner-to-be through a relationship.*
>
> *Karli and I became very good friends. Our early meetings were often characterised by sighs of 'I want a partner'. This shifted in later get-togethers to conversations where joy and feelings of contentment were present. Karli said 'I feel love in my heart...and peace. I am open to being in relationship or not; I also trust more.' In fact, for quite some time now, perhaps even one year, we have not spoken about men. Any painful emotional longing and sighs have completely disappeared, which she clearly and directly attributes to the work of her heart. The urgency and painful longing of 'I want/need to be with someone' is no longer there.*
>
> *Karli, an attractive woman, with a light, bubby and communicative nature has since been on her own. While the relationship she sought has not happened, other areas of her life where she was a bit stuck, like her work situation, have blossomed and given her more freedom.*
>
> *Karli relies on the heart a lot now: 'very often throughout the day I experience the heart's help and guidance'. She describes her feeling as: 'I feel free, lighter and much happier at a deep inner place. I am on my own surrounded by loving and wonderful friends and much freer to enter into friendship and relationship than ever before.'*
>
> *'I connect with people at work and socially now from a deep and beautiful place in my heart, not looking for fulfilment anymore through someone else. The heart has also allowed me to learn to share with others, to speak and feel together from a heart place, in equal relationships, at work or in my private life.'*
>
> *'I am very happy now; I have found a deep-rooted calmness and happiness and a trust that through my heart I will be guided in all aspects of life.'*

Karli felt, almost from the very beginning, a strong and clear sense that connecting to her heart and strengthening it 'was something very familiar'.

Her commitment to the heart was incredible. She was very dedicated to go deep, quickly, with a zest and drive not often seen. She also realised that in order for her life, including her relationship life to be free, that an open, pure heart was very important.

Her heart feeling developed fast. She could feel clearly the occasional times when there was cleansing, removal of negativities or heaviness and the very frequent times when there were feelings of happiness and calmness expanding together with her heart.

You may or may not have noticed the quite significant shift in Karli where she went from 'I want a partner' to just being happy, content and no longer wanting.

Do you have similar experiences where the more you have wanted something in the past and the more you have excluded your heart in the decision-making processes, the less likely you were to get it?

In fact, when you are very keen to want something, or are even emotional, like 'I am angry and I want this' or similar, what happens is that you cover your heart and you disallow your heart to support you, guide you and facilitate the decision-making processes. Not only are you excluding your heart and its wisdom, you are also burdening it, going against the heart.

On the other hand, you may have experienced, as you let go, surrendered, or gave up, 'miraculously' events happened, people came into your life, doors opened.

From the perspective of the heart, the label on the thing we want is not so important. By letting go more of us, our ideas, and what we want, a greater Divine or universal plan can unfold.

You know this when you are the opposite: when you are relaxed, happy, at peace or already happy in a relationship. It is often then that we find it very easy to engage, meet new people, including of the other gender or of our romantic choice. We are naturally in a more relaxed, letting go state. You may say, this is because you already have a partner. So, with a small shift inside, the heart helping, make the shift now; if you are looking for a partner, you can be in this same heart frame-of-mind or heart-facilitated attitude: relaxed, at peace, joyful and emotionally light and open.

Your heart will always naturally bring you more into this second stage, and, more importantly, to all the wonderful sharing and experiencing that is opening with it.

In Karli's situation there has been no 'happy ending' as yet, nor a happy beginning of a relationship. At the same time, due to her incredible commitment to her heart, Karli has found peace, love and joy. She has found ways to share, opening herself to new aspects of life, including a much longed for spiritual journeying, which is deeply fulfilling for her.

Emotions and your relationship

Keep love in your heart. A life without it is like a sunless garden when the flowers are dead.
Oscar Wilde

When love is in your heart there is supposed to be only love. This is the ideal scenario. In reality you may have experienced that after a period of falling in love, being 'head over heels' and only seeing your partner in a blissful light, emotions and irritations can surface.

In romantic relationships there is a love expectation. We look for love, we long for it, we want it. One source of irritation or unhappiness may be that you want more love from your partner or more love to flow between the two of you. There can be a fine line between being loving, sharing love and feeling emotions caused by a degree of unmet expectation or dissatisfaction.

If you face a difficult situation in your relationship, it is often caused by emotions that have arisen and come between you and your partner. These emotions may be subtle or at the surface, nagging you or your partner. They may find expression in 'looks', exchanged words, a raised voice or at the rougher end in shouting.

Emotions between partners can be anything from small irritations to jealousy, envy, distrust, hurt feelings, disappointment, anger and even the more powerful hatred and rage.

Emotions can be either from the inside or focused outside, on what the other person has or hasn't done. They can also be about the other's normal behaviours or who the other person is. They can present as a subtle arrogance over what one feels they are better at. The list is longer than these examples. Emotions will always pull you and your relationship backwards.

Emotions are tricky in relationships in two ways. On the one hand they cover the truer feelings your hearts hold and feel for each other: deepest caring and sweet love.

On the other hand, if you keep following any single emotion or a range of them that has surfaced, you will keep adding to the burdens in your heart. This behaviour and response will, gradually, slowly but surely burden the heart and any love-feeling.

This is a huge challenge. We long for love and to be loved yet over time we add burdens to the heart, make the heart heavier. The heart can even close depending on the intensity and frequency of the emotions followed. A closed or very heavy heart will find it hard to love and to find love.

There is a third scenario too: your partner upsets you and it is up to you to choose, either to keep loving or to follow the emotion. You love your partner but your partner has upset you, hurt you or even decided to leave you. This is an even harder situation in which to choose your heart and to keep loving.

All too often, as a therapist or in friendship circles, this has surfaced as a theme. I recall a client who came to sessions and shared the following story:

Annette's Story - Part I:

Annette was in a relationship with her partner who was quite angry, especially when he drank alcohol. Over time, despite their expressed love for each other, Annette found it draining and decided to leave the family home. Two children were involved, too.

It became clear that Annette was open for the relationship to be healed and to return. She committed to therapy, sought help from several sources and also found the heart learning and heart strengthening a significant assistance during a very difficult time for her. She often expressed her love for her partner.

I met her partner outside these sessions. He was very much in love with Annette and yet declarations and actions did not match. He started to learn about the heart, too. He learned to recognise the difference between feeling from the heart, and the gradual help it offered, and emotions, like anger and sadness over his partner deciding to leave.

He chose anger and, once the physical separation had occurred, also chose to fall in love with other women. It was made clear to Annette, that words are not sufficient and that her partner did not show the strength of heart to follow the deep love he expressed for her. Following emotions and attraction to other women was strong and competed with the love for his partner. One could also say that the heart was not yet strong enough, not giving enough clarity of feeling that would guide behaviours or actions.

It is not easy to keep choosing your heart, which means choosing compassion, love and care. Choosing the heart does not mean giving in or putting up with unacceptable behaviour. The observation from many clients and workshop participants, often in difficult situations, is that more heart equals more clarity to make the right decisions.

In some way emotions are normal, as it is normal to be human and be exposed to them or feel them. The key is not so much to analyse or to be critical of your own behaviours that are 'emotional' or lead you towards more emotions. The key is to choose the heart, to let the heart help to clear and transform them. In this way, you always also choose love and make a choice towards a growing loving relationship.

Always choose love

This makes my heart sing.

Choosing compassion, love and care in a relationship can mean that you only follow these gentle feelings that are always in the heart and you do not act. Or it can mean you follow these feelings and act, holding these feelings in your heart as you interact with your partner. This is the more mature and relationship-supporting choice and attitude.

This means that you will keep your heart clean and the radiance of your heart will help your situation. All opportunities to love again and again will remain open, even blossoming as you remain true to your heart.

At times you may feel so upset and know in your heart that any action or words will only inflame the situation. Holding the gentle feelings in your heart, being in your heart, is then the wisest, or even the only choice.

Depending on the level of difficulty you experience, or on the depth of hurt that may have occurred, you may find it hard or nearly impossible to choose your heart in the beginning. This changes over time. When you choose all the feelings your heart is offering you: love, compassion, understanding and forgiveness, and you let go of everything that is not love or a or sub-category of love, you move in a more loving direction. After all this is what many long or hope for, both in relationship and beyond.

Any time you follow your emotions, those you have towards someone else or those you feel you have the right to have, because you were upset or hurt, this will envelop and squeeze out the love you have in your heart.

Following emotions will reduce or limit the ability to love or be in love with your partner. Maintaining, following or nurturing emotions, will reduce all love for all those dear to you.

You need to be careful too, not to be too clever or righteous. It is always the best to attend to your heart, to let your heart work for you. You may feel you have the right to be upset or disappointed or angry in your situation, and perhaps this is supported by the views of friends or others around you. Every emotion you have, even as a reaction to wrongs done to you, reduces feelings of love, now and in the future. Love flows through the heart; emotions will block this flow of love.

On the positive, even if up to now you have followed emotions more or attended little to your heart, in a comparatively short time you can un-burden and free your heart.

Annette's Story - Part II:

In Annette's situation, her life wonderfully unfolded. She is now very happy, as an almost permanent state of being. She is so grateful to have had the help from her heart that she is now offering regular heart learning and heart meditation sessions as a volunteer every week. Her ex-partner did not go so well. A lovely man in many ways, he continued to face relationship and business difficulties, lost his driver's licence and according to his own admission often feels burdened and unhappy.

Relationship, heart and love are one

Relationship is one of the main areas where people can struggle. Challenges in relationship almost invariably increase if other parts of us or other motivators dominate the heart and the natural sharing of love.

Relationship is formed around love and yet it is not always about love, especially as you and the relationship grow older. It does not have to be this way. Relationship, heart and love are one and, as one, support each other. This trilogy can be a reminder and an opportunity to let the heart be stronger and facilitate deeper, sweeter love. Despite all the challenges and emotions there may be or have been, the love you share can grow and blossom continuously and wonderfully in your heart's garden.

The essence is that the heart is the main, if not the only facilitator of love. The invitation is for you to go on a path with more heart and find out.

Relationship can turn to companionship or friendship. Some couples become more gentle and loving as a result of more heart and tapping into the heart's greater love. Equally a relationship can turn into a practical, economic union where little feeling, warmth and love is present.

In some way all combinations are okay as long as there is no suffering. When hardship or pain, visible or invisible, burdens those in the relationship or others close to the couple the feeling is 'something is not quite right'.

The role of the heart is to turn any relationship, whatever its current form or expression, into a deeply and sweetly felt experience of gentle and blissful love.

The difficulties, some of which are discussed in this chapter or across the whole book, can be many. It is timely now to share with you how you can strengthen your heart. How much the heart is able to help you is directly related to the strength of your heart.

All the help from the heart discussed in the book will rely on a stronger, more open, more radiant heart. The next KHH is the essence or nature of how your heart works and how it responds to this natural heart activation method.

Key Heart Help 6: Heart Strengthening

In the Relationship Section, two key heart activities are introduced. This activity is the foundation of direct heart strengthening often with immediate impact.

These are the core steps to let your heart become naturally stronger and to assist you not only in relationship matters but in other aspects of your life as your heart is always present and ready to assist in its unique way.

> ### *Key Heart Help 6 - Heart Strengthening*
> *The five core steps for your heart are:*
> 1. *Relax*
> 2. *Close your eyes*
> 3. *Touch your heart*
> 4. *Smile to your heart*
> 5. *Feel*

Note: in order to know where and how to touch your heart, place one or two fingers gently on the armpit line. You can see this in figures 2 and 3 in section III. To focus more on your heart and heart feeling, relax your arm/fingers and do not move or massage this area.

Here is the complete, more detailed version of the core steps to strengthen your heart:[8]

The full KHH 6 - Heart Strengthening or direct heart strengthening

1. *Close your eyes to decrease the activities of your brain;*

2. *Completely relax your body and mind;*

3. *Breathe in deeply through your nose, and exhale though your mouth several times to help you relax even more (see KHH 3 'Relax more');*

4. *Touch your heart with one or more fingers;*

5. *Smile freely to your heart without thinking how;*

6. *With your eyes still closed and staying relaxed, smile to your heart for about one minute. When you find yourself thinking, don't follow your thoughts; just relax and allow them to pass easily through your head;*

7. *Gradually, you should start experiencing an expansion in your chest area, along with feelings of calmness, peace, lightness and joy;*

8. *When you feel any of these nice feelings, it is a wonderful indication that your heart is starting to work. Just follow the pleasant feeling to let your heart and feeling become even stronger;*

9. *If you are not feeling anything yet, don't put in any effort whatsoever, stay relaxed and keep on smiling. The moment your brain stops trying and looking for sensations, you will be able to feel one or more of the pleasant feelings;*

10. *Relax even more now and smile more freely; and*

11. *Once you start experiencing calmness, lightness or joy, follow your feeling while continuing to relax and smile (two minutes or more).*

You can find a printed version and audio/recorded copy of this on www.yourheartcanhelp.org. You will need a copy of it readily available as KHH 6 is the 'heart-warming-up' for most following practices.

---

[8] The core heart strengthening practice is shown here with the kind permission of Irmansyah Effendi, author of Smiling to the Heart Meditations and other heart related, spiritual intelligence books.

You will also find video clips on Heart Strengthening on the website. In several clips you will find Heart Strengthening explained, common mistakes highlighted and corrected, with tips on how to improve and progress in best ways.

You can practise these basic steps daily or every now and then. For the first few weeks it is good to do this in a quiet environment and ideally with no interruptions. This is important, as you may only start to feel your heart, and any distractions in the beginning will trigger and strengthen the mind/brain functions.

This is the core of your heart strengthening practice. It looks long and involved and yet, after you do it for some time, you will learn it by heart, your mind and heart will know what it feels like and it will become natural and less 'wordy' or involved.

You ideally approach it like learning a game such as chess or a sport like tennis, snow-boarding, or skiing. In the beginning you need to attend carefully to each move but after some time of practice, you just enjoy what you are doing and the feeling of it.

It is also good to know that the exact words do not matter as long as you roughly follow the program. What is written here is a guide and once you have done this 20, 30 or 50 times, you will remember it well enough to use your words with confidence. Later on, with a strong and radiant heart, even the five steps in the above KHH 6 will be shorter. For example, you will be able to smile to the heart with eyes open and won't need to touch each time either. You will feel in every situation what will be the best support for your heart.

The first few times you may need to hold the book in front of you, open your eyes, read one or two lines, close your eyes for a few moments and feel with your heart and feeling.

Following your strong heart

Looking at any relationship challenge, from the perspective of your heart, you have two ways in which you can respond to a challenge:

- Following more the emotions; or
- Following the heart and choosing love, understanding and compassion.

Truly following the heart is the opposite of making blurred decisions based on emotional confusion. The clarity the heart gives you will support you and your partner in the best possible ways.

Following the heart will always benefit you and others. However, the way you follow your heart now may need to be fine-tuned. Saying 'I follow the heart' is not the same as really feeling and following it. Every time you attend to your heart or you really follow it means it will work naturally for you, and in lesser ways, for others. It will automatically work in a healing and clearing manner.

This can be a new approach that engages your heart more - in action. Every moment you are challenged, use the steps introduced above. You will strengthen your heart, which gives you the inner strength to face your challenge and to choose love. The love from your heart is always there once all else, or at least any heavier covering parts, are removed.

Ideally you do this internally, or you strengthen your heart once you have removed yourself from a difficult situation. While in the situation, do the heart-connecting as best as possible and as you listen, respond or react, let the heart be involved.

The further you use your stronger heart, along with opening your heart more, you will feel a growing guidance that your heart will open up to you. It will feel clear how you are supposed to be in an individual situation or in this one relationship that is causing challenges, in all relationships at home, at work, and in your wider social or family circles.

This will also create a shift. It will move you further away from looking outside of yourself for solutions, answers or love. It will also make you more responsible for your input into situations, for example asking yourself is it emotion or is it love? Other tendencies such as laying blame, will also be naturally limited by a stronger heart.

In this way KHH 6 is essential to become familiar with, to practice and at some point to know off by heart. It will then work more easily during life challenges where the mind/brain or emotions will be at their peak and will want to take you away from the heart.

Practical Heart Tip 32: Is the heart working or not?

When you start to work with your heart, there will be a range of possible experiences, questions and doubts that pop up. KHH 6, above, is the main KHH to get things moving.

The moment you directly strengthen your heart with this natural heart-helping technique, you may have any of these sensations or experiences:

- *You don't feel anything at all; and*
- *You feel uncomfortable feelings of pressure, heaviness and even sweating.*

- *The mind/brain that has been dominating and 'in charge' for years, if not most of your life, may also have a lot to say:*

- *'This is auto-suggestion';*

- *'This will never work';*

- *'This is just my imagination';*

- *'This is stupid';*

- *'How can this work? It is not even physically there'; or*

- *Any other comments that may discourage you for using your heart.*

These are common first responses and it is good to persevere; read on, do the additional KHHs or PHTs to continually strengthen heart understanding and use the heart practically.

Keep going, keep trying, find a slightly more experienced heart practitioner or open heart group in your area or online and you will progress. Understanding your heart and how heart and mind/brain work together can assist to deeper your early practice. If you haven't fully read the introduction chapters I to VI, perhaps make time to do so.

A key area where you need the help from your heart, where only the growing feelings that clearly come from your heart will assist, is in overcoming doubtful thoughts or emotions generated from within.

Remember that the heart is your centre of feeling and feelings like love or joy cannot been seen, touched or measured ... they can, like the heart, only be felt.

There is no one in my experience that has ever come for help or out of curiosity or spiritual interest that has not found the heart to work and eventually offer significant help. Gentle perseverance and regular attendance to the heart did the job.

All this looks very simple and, for some minds/brains, too simple. And yet this is the direct, natural and working technique that will connect you to your heart. In fact, this connection can continuously deepen, helping you more, and offering feelings beyond imagination and hope. There are a few additional aspects and related practical tips that will help your heart to become stronger in easier, faster ways, offering you more immediate help:

Practical Heart Tip 33: How to do heart strengthening the best way *

These are additional heart-helping observations. They are additional techniques that support the above core steps detailed in KHH 6. They will also make sure that the full potential of your heart is available as soon as possible:

- *Do not try or help the process. The urge to do something extra may surface. Apart from the core steps shared above, the heart does not need more help or additional ideas;*

- *Do not observe. Observation is a function of the mind/brain. You may gain a little clarity about the heart's function in observing it, creating a mind-to-heart connection. However, the further impact of this observing will be that the mind will limit your heart's much greater urge to open, expand and help;*

- *Maintain the right head position - natural, not looking downwards or too much upward. The head is in the ideal position if there is no pressure in the neck/shoulder area and if there is not muscular tension needed to hold it in position;*

- *Be natural.*

Remember always the key is to relax and smile ... relax more and smile more freely ... the more you relax the more your heart will be helped to open.

This PHT will help you with all the mind/brain attempts to interfere or will reduce the learned dominance of the mind/brain. In this way you will have a little more peace and quietness of mind and the feelings from the heart can become much clearer over time.

The flow-on effects of a stronger heart on your relationship can be immense. For the mind/brain it may appear as a small matter. Love is not a matter of logic or for the mind/brain only. Less dominance or over-thinking of your relationship issues, replaced with more heart energy, heart quality and feeling from your heart in everything you say and do, is the natural transforming power to bring more love into everything.

The next sections are about different situations where our love relationship is more of a falling-out-of-love, where love is gradually leaving a relationship or there is a sense that love has left or where broken-heartedness has occurred.

Falling out of love
This is heart-wrenching ...

When you fall out of love, you can be in a neutral state or you can flip to the other side, to emotion. Naturally, you are very close to the person you love. You know each other well and you know the other's weaknesses and vulnerabilities. This is natural and it is of course a very 'okay' knowledge to have. It is about intimacy and knowing someone intimately; it is not good knowledge to use in combination with emotion. Let us look at the emotional part first.

This closeness can be used to create even greater relationship challenges if the intimate knowledge you have gained over the time of your being close is used in a state of emotion. It can cause deep hurt and resentment and lead to lasting damage to the love relationship you share.

You may do this carelessly, in a state of emotion or in a state where you lack clarity or composure - in other words strength of heart. The hurt and pain can be even worse if this knowledge is pulled out and used with intention to wound or get back at the other.

This is the 'harder' end of the spectrum, where the deeper hurt occurs. Your heart can help. It will take time and a clear commitment to your heart to break these deeper habits of following emotions. If hurt has occurred, your heart will clear any deeper storages related.

At the softer end of an emotional response is gradual irritation that can surface as you and your partner go through life. You may be very sensitive to this and even a subtle level of emotion may affect you and be in contrast to the truth you feel and long for in your heart.

It is important to realise that whether you are the one doing it or you are at the receiving end of it, it looks different from the perspective of your heart. Let us talk about this in terms of the 'emotional person' and the 'receiving person'. Commonly there may be a perception that the one who is the 'receiving person' is the only one suffering. The 'emotional person' is having a difficult or emotional time.

Whatever your challenges are, let your heart work for you. You can only ever attend to your own heart, open and purify your own heart. Lead by example.

The heart is your emotional/love book-keeping account:

In the situation where you may be the 'emotional person', every emotion, expressed or not, that you feel and follow will be in your heart's memory. As it is emotion and often carries negative thinking with it, you will burden your heart and eventually even close it.

In the situation where you may be the 'receiving person', what happens you will largely depend on the strength of your own heart. If you heart is very strong, then all you will feel, even when strong emotions are expressed towards you, will be care, compassion, understanding, love and calmness. This is where you want to be.

However, it is not easy, as long as your heart is with its own burdens and disposition, not to respond with emotion. If you respond with emotion then your heart will also be burdened, depending on the strength and duration and for how long you hold to emotion after the event. In this instance emotions may be anger, disgust, resentment or from the other end of the spectrum, more directed at yourself: self-pity, self-doubt, sadness or other hurt feelings.

Love gradually leaves

You are very close to your partner and after some years you tune in and realise that the love between you has faded a lot, or even vanished. You may have both fallen out of love quietly and steadily. There is often no more feeling of love left.

The way your heart works requires you to have a close look at how heart-aware you are every day, not just in your relationship with your partner but in all areas of life. With all the understanding you have gained about your heart, you will very likely realise how you have taken care of your heart and love-centre, or how you can take better care from now on.

Unfortunately it is common as emotions surface in relationship or other areas of life, that there is some tendency to give them strength and to follow them, even if only in small ways. There is a negative reaction that follows too, meaning there is an inner generation of negative emotions or negative thoughts as a result of a situation. The moment there is a negative emotion, with its unavoidable negative thoughts, burdens are being put into the heart and these accumulate over the years.

Relationship is not easy, some would say. After falling in love, perhaps living with your partner, your relationship may even be one of the triggers for emotion or negative thoughts to surface. A classic example may be where the toothpaste is pressed out the 'wrong' way, the way one person does not like, or similar things are done in ways that cause irritation.

A loving relationship, after some time, can all too easily slip into being together, living together, sharing a space, sharing income, time, hobbies and interests with little or even no love flowing through or being shared in this special togetherness. The deposits of burdens or negativities in the heart that accumulate over time will make it very hard to feel love.

'I don't feel it anymore'

This is perhaps one of the most commonly expressed concerns that friends share or that relationship counsellors hear. The heart is your centre of love and compassion and therefore the energy plant of love. Not feeling it anymore may have to do with your relationship status as much as it has to do with the condition of your heart - how much your heart is still able to feel the passion and deeper love you once felt for your dear one.

As much as a burdened or even closed heart will struggle to feel love and to freely share it, an opening heart, using the natural techniques suggested in this book, can turn things around immensely fast.

If this 'not feeling it anymore' is occurring and it happens to you or someone close to you then it can have dramatic consequences when the couple does not know what to do and perhaps 'naturally' thinks of separation. It is more dramatic, sad and difficult, when children are involved.

It is very unfortunate that we don't often allow our hearts to help. When the layers that cover the heart over the years are removed and cleansed, the love that our heart contains resurfaces and it is a joy to be in the relationship we once chose to be in.

Love has left

It is amazing how someone can break your heart
and you can still love them
with all the pieces. Unknown

The loss of feeling love for our partner deeply affects how we feel, not only about our partner, but about every person in our life, even about life itself. The fulfilment of being 'in love', loving someone and feeling that love radiating through our being and body seems essential to all that love means.

Understanding the nature of your heart will make it more understandable how love can be 'lost'. In fact, what happens is that the connection that is natural for you to have with your heart gradually 'disconnects'. The heart is being burdened over months and years and feelings you are supposed to, or long to feel, are covered under a growing pile of rubble, a collection of burdens and negativities around and within the heart.

This situation can clearly seem desperate or unresolvable. Perhaps this is so for the mind. It is not so for the heart. The very solution for a heart that does not feel love anymore is the heart's ability to help. Even after years of being with your partner, in what may be a hardened relationship, your heart is so special that it can offer direct help in your love life. It is magical what can happen. Helen's story below, even with compounding mental health issues in her relationship, is a beautiful example of this.

Helen is approaching retirement age. She has been married over 25 years and is living in Hobart. Her children are grown up and no longer living at home. Helen is a lively, outgoing, very pleasant and much liked person. Like many Tasmanians she has a love for bushwalking and nature.

Helen's Story:

'For many decades I felt that there was something missing from our marital relationship. On one level there was always a deep respect for my husband. Our philosophy of life, love of nature and our love for our children was very similar. On the other, our relationship was never a really close, free and trusting one.

Throughout our marriage, a subtle level of competition or one-upmanship between us seemed to pervade our communications, a need to 'beat' each other with words, which rarely, if ever, came out right. We'd both feel disgruntled and resentful and wouldn't speak to each other for a while. We also found it difficult to hear each other. I didn't understand what was happening between us and our 'important communications' were actually very often miscommunications; they always left me feeling very despondent, disillusioned, a failure and separate from my husband, myself and the world. Over the years, I read many books hoping for understanding and wanting to find a solution to my problems. I found the words and related ideas, suggestions, but the words and suggestions changed nothing. All I could see was that my husband needed to change.

I realised our marriage was less than healthy, loving and trusting and was certainly not the one I had dreamt of. I had no idea what was wrong and how it was going to be 'fixed'. As nothing I did seemed to make a difference, I gave up trying.

My husband started to suffer from depression. I felt compassion and sympathy for him over his long and often regular bouts of depression, but instead of this drawing us closer, my resentment grew. I was continually 'treading on eggshells', I wasn't being heard and as a result my self-confidence dwindled. I often felt very separate, alone in our relationship and a very strong sense of loss within myself became evident; I was on my own and I was lonely.

Although our relationship didn't really change over the years, I never wished to sever it; I felt there was something to 'get over', something to understand, something that needed to be realised and released.

Our various misunderstandings and missing each other time-wise and place-wise led me to finally realise that we were out of synch with each other. That was an eye-opening moment. It seemed that we were travelling along two different pathways that occasionally met and then diverged again, but I didn't know then how to walk on the same pathway.

Around seven years ago, I discovered the incredible and life-changing heart meditation which, through deep relaxation and its simple techniques, helped me to open my heart. I regularly attended the meditation sessions and then started to do the courses offered over this

---

> *time. I came to realise how heavy my heart had become; there was negativity and holding too. It made me also realise how stubborn I could be and that all this was impacting on my life and affecting my relationship; I hoped the meditation would help me to change ... somehow!*
>
> *Over the seven years many beautiful changes have happened: the heavy heart became much lighter and freer.*
>
> *A half-hearted realisation of how much I had changed occurred a couple of years ago when my husband, who was going through another bout of deep depression, agreed to come to meditation with me. This was amazing to me as he, being a scientist, had never before shown any interest in meditation. With both our hearts opening, an amazing freeness, openness and trust in our lives was occurring that was so seamless and smooth. I still can't quite believe it has happened, but I do believe it has happened as there is so much more peace and feeling of togetherness in our lives again.*
>
> *Although we still have our misunderstandings and reactions, they are shorter and less intense than previously. I am so eternally grateful to have discovered the immense and gentle abilities our hearts have to remove long-term negativities and bring us closer. The heart meditations we attended helped trigger the changes. I am strongly committed to continuing the meditation practice as the benefits, realisations and understandings are continuous, very real and very deep.*

Love is something beautiful and wonderful to experience and share. Your heart, as in Helen's story, will make gentle, sweet and deep changes over time.

Love never forces, never wants. Love flows as a river through your heart and ever only longs to be shared. As you experience this, it will flow continuously and abundantly in every interaction you have with your partner and extend to others naturally and with ease.

Before we look in more detail how exactly the heart can and will help, there is one more topic that requires exploration - when a heart is 'broken'.

Feeling 'it' again

The burdening or over-whelming sense of 'I don't feel it anymore' can be turned into 'I am starting to feel it again' when the unique capacity of the heart starts to work again for you and your relationship. Jasmine's sharing is a wonderful example of this.

I met Jasmine and her husband several years ago at one of the intermediate to advanced heart workshops overseas.

Jasmine and her husband came very close to a story that exemplifies the working of the heart, in this way. Jasmine's friends were about to separate with two small children involved and it was very touching that the heart could help their hearts to find love again.

> **Jasmine's Story:**
>
> *'A couple who were friends with us were going through a heavy marriage crisis and they were close to separation. The woman in particular was a good friend of mine. At the time she was very agitated and did not know if separation would be the right decision as there were also two young children under the age of five in the marriage; the decision was not easy for that reason. During that time we talked often and, as there was a lot of trust, I asked her if she would be okay to try a few heart practices, to help her personally cope better. She was very open and she wanted to try it.'*
>
> *'I then guided her into the heart (using the Heart Strengthening steps) where she found, in her words, beautiful peace, a peace she had longed for. The heart led her there in a very short time. With the help of a meditation and a prayer, similar to the Open Heart Meditation, she was able to let the heart help in releasing stored negative emotions that had accumulated and were directed toward her partner. This meant a lot of letting go and becoming lighter and less burdened, which she could feel clearly.'*
>
> *'A short time after, we repeated a similar session with her partner. He too, with the help of his heart, could let go of accumulated negative emotions. He was, even after the first session, in his attitude and feelings towards his wife, totally changed.'*
>
> *'It was afterwards that my girlfriend told me that the heart practices with both of them created an opening for each other and it allowed them to openly talk to each other again and to work towards solving their problems in a new way.'*
>
> *'They started a couple therapy with a very sensitive and intuitive therapist and today are a very happy couple again. Both are immensely grateful that they could find a way back then, to release negative emotions that had grown between them and to find a way to feel the heart and the deeper feelings for each other.'*
>
> *Jasmine continued to share. 'What is a beautiful gift for us now, when we face difficulties in our relationship, is those two dear friends who are there for us, who give us so many gifts of joy and love from their hearts that it is very difficult to follow our old patterns. I am very grateful to them for that. Love, the heart, works on so many levels and in so many ways, it is simply wonderful.'*

This is the story of someone with a big heart, concerned about someone else, a young family. While it is not a direct sharing by the couple themselves, it exemplifies beautifully the working of the heart. Love is all about the heart. In the fast-paced world we live in now, relationships can be changed a fraction too fast, which becomes difficult and painful when a relationship has grown into a family. If the heart can help, and it may not be able to, then this is wonderful of course.

If the heart can't help to 'save' a relationship, with or without children involved, then let your heart help you to heal all the wounds, to move on, to be grateful for any learning, good or not so good, and not to be burdened with a heavy or broken heart for a prolonged time. You will find more about healing the wounds in the following sections.

Jasmine's own heart journey has so deeply touched her that she and her husband have started to offer heart meditations, weekly heart sessions and regular workshops in their home town. Jasmine is also offering one-on-one, heart-centred treatments from her home, to share what she has learned and to help others.

In addition to the burdening occasional sense of 'I don't feel it anymore', can be a deep feeling that the love that once attracted you to your partner, that once sparked excitement, joy and deep levels of care, has left completely.

A broken heart or loss of a loved one

I can heal a broken heart with a smile. Rumi

It is in romantic relationship and other deep relationships where our hearts can be broken. You have already read above that in your love relationship it is easy to be hurt or upset by your partner and for deep wounds to occur.

What is a broken heart? Hearts are broken when our partner leaves us and another deep hurt or upset occurs. Hearts can also be broken when there is hope for relationship and love and one person is not interested. Perhaps ultimately a broken heart can occur in any situation where one partner can't find expression or the love is not flowing. The end of love may be the end of feeling it, as in the section above, or the end of a relationship. This includes loss of a loved one in a relationship and is perhaps similar to the loss of a dear one through death. It is one of the few, yet immensely deep, experiences of hardship, suffering and for some inexplicable pain.

The 'heart-ache' can be so strong that the expression 'my heart is broken' seems the most appropriate one to describe this deeply felt pain.

Learning practically about your heart will offer a new perspective on this. Any pain you feel is actually not from your heart. Whatever others do to us, whatever we experience as a subsequence of any 'broken heart' experience is much more connected to and therefore stemming from our centre of self, not the heart. This is the storage area and centre of our ambition and self-focus.

While both parts, the centre of self and the heart, are real and integral parts of us, this understanding of what a broken heart really means can help. It can help to shift the focus from the heart as the centre or even cause of pain to an actual source of help. The heart is the very resource and tool that can help. This cognitive shift can really be significant. It is human and in some way normal to turn away from what causes us pain, while in fact the heart is not the pain-giver but the very part of you that offers key help.

Your heart can help. Every time you feel pain or connect with your broken-heartedness, choose your heart's help. It will help with how long your broken-heartedness lasts. It will also reach into the depth of your pain and begin to heal it.

Your heart will offer you one more incredible benefit: as you allow your heart to help you, as you strengthen your heart, not in words but with the practices suggested, your disposition to feel this deep hurt, to be in turmoil or suffering will disappear with this new strength of heart. At the same time your ability to experience, share and enjoy love will increase beyond expectation, dreams and visions.

The time it will take to heal your heart will depend on the depth of love you have shared, the openness of your heart and your heart's ability to experience and share love.

Another layer of who you are, in relation to your heart, is able to open here. It may not be the right decision, your partner may not follow the greater truth from his or her heart, in 'breaking your heart'. This at times may be an easy thought or conclusion. However, it may be that he or she is following the deeper truth. In this instance knowing is no consolation, as there is still a response of loss that is causing deep pain.

There may be no answer to this 'right' and 'wrong' question. Who did or does the right thing when it comes to heart-brokenness? If anything is happening at all, then it is the mulling over of this question or just 'why', 'why', 'why' … why does this happen to me, why can't it be how I want it?

The heart does not seek to find an answer in the way the mind/brain does. It just looks for love, to find it within, to share with others and to see in everyone, everything and every action a chance to love.

Your heart is designed to help you in the best and most natural way, including healing your broken heart. Your heart will also move you onwards in the gentlest of ways, often hardly noticeable as you open your heart more, towards this pure love waiting within the deeper layers of your heart.

It is this purer love that will readily surface the more that help is needed. It will also become purer and more present for your loved ones, your partner with whom you struggle, and others in your life or yet to come into your life. It is the same love that will grow all around you, your family, your social circles, colleagues, clients, customers, everyone.

You can see a pattern in how your heart is able to help you. Intuitively you may know or have realised that love is not something we can ever possess or even have, but something greater than ourselves that we can only share.

The path of the heart is very logical too. There were quite regular instances in and around the heart learning, or heart-guided therapy where participants were inclined to get really angry or upset about their 'broken heart'. There is another person involved and whatever the circumstance, if that other person is challenged and confronted by anger and other strong emotion, how likely is the person to look at their decisions and to see or find the love they could not see before? It is much more likely that love, kindness and choosing your heart will also be answered with more heart.

There is something natural in how life is designed or how life naturally happens, including the loss of loved ones. We are born, have parents, and at some time, as we grow older, we lose our beloved parents. We have children whom we love and when we die, they will need to let go of us too, in some positive way. These bonds, realised or not, are immensely deep and special. Yet, in time, we need to let go and learn to love with no want, no aim, no desire, just for pure love's sake, the purest sharing our hearts are capable of. Good!

Your heart as the centre, hub and generator of love

What is the heart's role here and how will it help? Whether love has gradually and quietly left or whether there has been deeply felt loss or heart break, the heart can help as the centre of all love: the love you feel within, the love in every cell of your body and the love you share with others.

It is ideal if both of you follow this path of letting the heart help, that is, if there is still togetherness. If there has been loss or separation, even temporary, or 'a break' to work things out, do not wait for someone else to be more loving, attentive, heartful or free in showing their love.

The only direct way to help you, your heart and your love connections is by clearing, cleansing and opening your heart more.

In many relationship difficulties, one partner feels to seek help but the other person may be less inclined to do so. To be okay with this, one option is to find the peace within your heart. In fact, here is where the heart offers something extra. As you commit to your heart and gradually open your heart more, your burdens, heaviness and anything limiting the flow are dissolved. Your heart will naturally start to radiate the heart's wonderful vibrancy and love, the strongest to the people closest to you. This will help and start to soften whatever your challenge is and the very relationship too.

A few words of caution in relation to this: you may have the urge to help the other person, your partner. It is important, though, to be free of any anticipated outcomes or expectations. Any time another human being is involved, with their full range of heart, mind/brain or emotional choices, there is hardly ever a clear line of decisions ahead. Ideally, the opening of your own heart is a higher priority than what will happen to your partner, husband, lover or dear friend. A gradually stronger heart will help this process towards more inner freedom. Ultimately, your heart's greater joy is to share love, freely, unconditionally, no strings attached.

The journey within your relationship will be much easier when you add more heart awareness and real heart-FULL-ness, a heart filled with love, to it. As you will see in the next paragraphs, the heart naturally forgives others, including all dear ones. It will naturally unburden your heart, of things you may have done that have hurt others, intentionally or not.

It is normal for individuals, couples, therapists and workshop facilitators to say 'you must work hard on your relationship to ensure that love stays in your relationship.'

The heart adds a new perspective to this. Enjoy the heart, enjoy the wonderful feelings that naturally want to surface in your heart as it also helps every aspect of your relationship with those dearest to you. The lightness you can feel in an expanding heart will assist whatever is happening.

Imagine someone wanting a break and temporarily separating from their partner. During this time the partner, with the help of the heart, becomes more and more joyful, light and free. There will be an automatic attraction-response in the other partner. It is the nature of things. If that is not the case, then something other than the heart and love are being followed or a longer break may be needed.

The other scenario would be for the person to become increasingly angry, irritated or annoyed. What would be your response, if your partner showed these emotions in a difficult or temporary break situation?

Every moment you give attention to your heart, every time you practise the natural techniques, including the KHHs in this chapter, your heart will grow in its ability to help. It will naturally support you and your heart and inner strength will grow. Every heart, when active, naturally generates infinite, ever expanding love.

Love is the most transforming power between two humans and your heart is the connector. No thought, visualisation, piece of advice, or therapeutic intervention will help you or your relationship unless it also touches the heart and opens it more to improve that natural flow.

Like a river, this love will touch everything in its way - within you and in a lesser but equally beautiful way in your partner - without words needed to be said. It touches and gradually transforms all that is yucky, sticky and negatively affecting your relationship.

We are not perfect when we love. We are within the limitation of who we are, in a complex, unique and yet incomplete existence. Commitment to a partner can support shared growth, particularly if both hold each other in love, non-judgment, non-blame and a deepening level of understanding that the heart naturally generates and always looks to facilitate.

This imperfection is normal and it means that love and heart are not fully free yet. It also means there is conditional love, expectation and a sense of loss and grief in a difficult relationship situation. This is all very normal. Deep emotional challenge or loss often comes with strong emotions such as anger, betrayal, jealousy or deep sadness. These are not pleasant to feel. It is here where you want your heart to help you. The best response is to strengthen your heart with even greater resolve.

You may be at the other end of the spectrum and have realised that love is beautiful for love's sake. Love has a clear unconditional, non-wanting feel to it and you are at peace with this. If your purpose in loving is more for the sake of loving, then the pain and experience of loss and hurt may be even deeper, as your heart feels more deeply and clearly. At the same time, your heart can help you earlier and more directly, if you choose your heart's potential. Everything that is not pleasant or wonderful within will be removed by the heart's radiance and love.

Often those with a broken heart will experience loss, sadness, anger and the spiritual loss of a close heart and soul. Whatever your challenge, your heart's present condition and innate ability can help you the best - now.

Always choose to love

My friends, do not lose heart. Clarissa Pinkola Estes

Your relationship may be perfect now, it may be 'ok', or you may be in the midst of a break up or recovering from relationship-related pain, or even trauma. To choose the heart and all it represents is perhaps the most important choice in any relationship.

It is not for your heart and the heart ability shared in this book to replace what you would normally do. It is for your heart, so special in its essence, to support and help you to be free of everything that is not joy, calmness, love for others and a wonderful zest for life. Whatever else you do or try, have done or have tried, it is the real condition of your heart that will always be the foundation upon which all relationships are built. With the heart involved, you will find calmness, nurturing, strength-giving and stable ground.

If you need help, talking to a friend or someone professional, like your doctor, psychologist or other therapist can be an important step. There is a likelihood you are already being guided in some way by your heart and your higher self in making supportive choices. Let your heart assist you to move forward and be moved to a greater love.

Relationship is all about love: sharing love and lovingly interacting as you go through life in togetherness.

Choosing love is the best choice of your heart and perhaps all of your life. Choosing love is not something mushy, fluffy or weak. In looking after your heart, you open the prospect of a wonderful friendship sometime in the future, should you not continue your connection.

Whatever the depth of difficulty, as you choose your heart's help during your relationship challenges, your heart will also become free, of hurt, burdens and even limitations in loving freely.

Choosing love and forgiving

How does your heart help in relation to forgiving dear ones, loved ones who are in your life or have left your life? Your heart has a programmed ability to unburden you from everything that is not a pleasant or positive feeling.

Your heart can easily forgive, much more easily than your mind. This is important in several ways. Whatever has happened to you, whatever someone has done to you, it is important to forgive, wholeheartedly. Only with forgiveness that is from your mind and from the heart can it be complete.

Remember, this is forgiving from your heart and you may forgive and yet never see the person again, or whatever the right action is for you, as a couple or as friends. Every situation is different, every day, every moment.

In order to choose love wholeheartedly you must forgive others and yourself to lighten your heart and whole being, to unburden all deposits made in your heart, to love freely again, whether in your current or your next relationship.

Forgive wholeheartedly

At the core of our heart there is love for everyone ...

You must forgive everyone who has hurt you, upset you or done wrong to you in any way. This is not easy to warm to. When someone has hurt us, there can be a sense of right and wrong. In the case of needing to forgive, the other person was/is wrong and 'I' am right. There may be a tendency to hold on and 'cement' this status. The reality, however, is that this holding on is of no benefit. Emotion that we keep also means a pattern is running at a deeper level that will create an emotional reaction when triggered. This is likely to limit the joy, warmth and function of future friendships or relationships. If stronger, it may even significantly interfere or disable the chance for the relationship to work.

The invitation here is for you to use the following simple technique to let your heart naturally forgive others. It is not that you need to agree to do so; it is not your brain doing it. It is the burdens your heart keeps holding onto that will make you stuck and ultimately less able to love again.

Practical Heart Tip 34: Forgiving from the heart I - forgiving a loved one *

This is one of the immediate ways in which you can let your heart do the forgiving:

- *Familiarise yourself with Heart Strengthening (KHH 6);*
- *At the end of your heart strengthening session and once you feel your heart feeling; then*
- *Let your heart smile to whatever part of you is hurting or holding pain;*
- *Stay in the feeling from your heart;*
- *Have an attitude of forgiving whole-heartedly and of letting go; and*
- *Keep smiling freely to your heart for several minutes.*

Make sure you follow mainly the gentle heart feelings. Moments you find yourself following any emotion or thought, which is normal, relax more, smile more freely and make the choice to follow the feeling from your heart more than anything else.

You can also let your heart help you, using the following variation (instead of point 3): let your heart smile to the person or persons who have hurt or upset you or that you feel emotional disturbance with.

Forgiving from the heart and brain are two slightly different matters. From the mind/brain it is a thought process and can be useful. However, when you use the heart in any forgiving process, any deposits or collections you may or may not be aware of can be removed. Your heart, feeling, actions and how you interact with everyone from then on will have different qualities to them.

Letting your heart help in this way to clear what is between you and your partner is a gentle and easy way you can 'work on the relationship' without having to engage the other person: no discussions or arguments are needed. There is no need to find words or approaches. It is one additional avenue of help available.

It will be comparatively easy to smile to a loved one when the feeling of love is still somewhere in your heart, whether this is a clear or somewhat tainted feeling.

You may feel to use this technique with someone who is or was in your life, where the feeling of love and sweetness has been greatly reduced or is not there at all. You feel however to 'clear the deck', to clear the heart and any burdens connected to a situation or person. It will still work and it is good to use the technique. There is a likelihood in some instances that, because of a chance for there to be more burdens, some of the emotions still held will make the mind/brain busier during this process. Simply relax more and smile more freely and follow the heart and the feelings from the heart more than anything else.

Deeper, additional and more comprehensive forgiveness elements are worked into the Open Heart Meditations (KHH 13). You can skip ahead to this section if you feel you want all the possible heart-help for your situation now.

Being guided, making the right decision to stay or to separate

Your hearts know in silence the secrets of the days and the nights. Kahlil Gibran

To stay in a relationship or to leave is one of most difficult decisions to make. A couple of more heart-related reasons are:

- You love the person deeply and whatever has happened between you does not affect this love; or
- Whenever there is love, there is also attachment and comfort. Unless your heart is fully open and you have only pure, unconditional love for others, this will be the case to some extent.

There may be a long list of reasons and non-heart matters that guide you to think about this decision. Of course, some of them will be very valid reasons.

You will find your heart's help here similar to that in the above 'guidance from the heart' section.

Before sharing about the heart's help in relation to the two points above, apart from situations where there is abuse, violence or other unacceptable behaviour or danger, let your heart help in the ways summarised at the end of the relationship chapter. The heart naturally wants to put a lot of attention, care and love into matters related to other human beings, especially those close to our heart or who were once very close to our heart.

If you open your heart more, the focus moves away from the issues, relationship challenges or drama. It also shifts away from the other person and back to you. This empowers you, giving you something to act on, and places you, your question or decision more strongly into a sphere where you can act, change, improve and learn.

It is also wonderful that through your heart's insights and realisations, you may learn something about yourself and what part you may have played in creating or adding to any drama or difficulties within the relationship.

Your heart's ability to promote a greater and deeper calmness will also assist you not to rush into decisions that you may later regret or that may, at the core of your heart, not be the right ones according to the greater truth your heart knows.

Direct guidance

At the other end of the spectrum, greater calmness and other benefits your heart facilitates may bring the clarity you need to make a decision earlier rather than later.

> **Practical Heart Tip 35: Getting answers from your heart ***
>
> *Your heart can help you with your decisions. To be in a relationship is precious and another person is often a gift for us. Sometimes this is hard to see. In addition to PHT 29 here are a couple of extra considerations:*
>
> - *Give this activity, and your decision, time and ensure you have a strong heart when you ask relationship questions;*
>
> - *The limiting factor is not the ability of your heart, it is how free your heart is. How light is it, how much clarity is within your heart already and are you able to be helped, by a strong heart and calm mind, to detach from emotion and strong thoughts associated with the issue; and*
>
> - *Also, be aware that the questions that are being asked may not exactly reflect all the options available.*
>
> *In relation to the last point, whatever questions you ask, you may ask a third question along the lines of:*
>
> - *Is there another option that I can't think of or see yet? ... and let the heart respond. If you receive a 'yes' or clear 'yes' in the form of a light, gentle or opening feeling, then it can be good to wait, to be open to either realise what this question is or to wait for changes that will naturally happen.*

What does it mean to 'have a strong heart' when asking these questions? It means that you have practised using your heart and can feel beautiful feelings emanating from it with some confidence during Heart Strengthening.

How does the heart answer when feeling 'how does my heart feel' or 'what is my heart's comment'? The answers will be feelings from the following possibilities: (1) gentleness, calmness and expansion, (2) contraction of the heart or (3) a neutral feeling, no reaction or response from your heart that you notice. The first one is your heart's 'yes', the second one 'no' or not so good and the third is a 'neutral' which means both options are okay to follow.

Indirect guidance

It is important not to rush here, so read on for some additional sharing and advice:

- Take your time, be deeply connected to your heart;
- Repeat your questions over a longer period; and
- Fill this period of time with dedicated, regular and good-quality heart practices.

Take your time to prepare your heart with either Heart Strengthening or with Heart Strengthening and Open Heart Meditation. You want to be deeply connected to your heart with all other parts of you less dominant. Do not do this when you are rushed or experiencing some form of emotion such as upset, hurt, anger or jealousy. Here the focus is on getting to a depth where you feel only your heart's response and the quality of that feeling. Everything else, thoughts, ideas, even tension or pain, is not the feeling from your heart.

Your heart will support you and give you confidence to make the clearer, wiser and much more long-term decision. It will support you and your partner's happiness and fulfilment, as well as those of others around you. Repeat your questions over a period of time. Your heart is very deep and when you want the answer, the wanting is stronger than the connection to the heart. It is good to do this maybe once or twice a week over a longer period.

When you go through this period of working and feeling things out, commit to your heart and heart opening. A greater heart depth and a greater feeling of what is the right thing to do, and what the next steps are, may naturally happen. In the meantime, until any bigger decisions are made, the transformative quality of the heart will work on you and all those around you. You will be indirectly guided by your heart in this way.

In relation to being directly or indirectly guided by your heart, your emotions, any attachments, any strong thoughts or pre-conceived ideas of what should be or what you want are likely to limit your heart's knowing and guidance. It is good to let these go a bit when seeking guidance and help from the heart.

Consider a wider environment, feel broadly

As most of our hearts are not fully open yet or our experience with the heart is limited, it is very important you also look at all of your other life circumstances and the guidance from your -hopefully clear - mind/brain. The most practical and important considerations may need to be are children involved, and also are others involved and how will this affect your partner and/or others close to you both?

While it is always about you and the union you share, looking wider may offer new realisations that help you to make clear and heartful decisions. Remember, when you realise, feel something, feel into a situation, it is very likely that your heart and your heart's guidance are involved. This will help you to make a better decision giving consideration - including feeling with the heart - to all involved and the flow-on effects.

Reflect on why you consider separation. What are the aspects that are related to integrity, wisdom and greater good? What are other aspects of a more self-centred nature that are more about you and may have emotions attached, such as dissatisfaction, accumulated irritation or annoyance or still-held hurts from past events or exchanges?

The question to stay or to leave is in most cases entangled with emotions. You will need to make a stronger and clearer commitment to your heart to get clearer answers and guidance.

You will also be more prepared to look at the two tendencies in most human beings described in the previous paragraph.

It is not uncommon at all that in your heart you already know what the right decision is. However, be sure that you are feeling and using your heart. For this, be aware that you are within the deeper state of calmness from your heart. This is important, as relationship decisions are often connected to emotion and ideas, plans or concepts, all of which influence the deeper heart wisdom and choice. If you are not sure, commit to your heart's opening and purification for a period of time and then re-evaluate, or better re-feel, your heart's 'comments' in the form of feelings. It will help you and it will help your partner indirectly. After some time, and this may be a few weeks or months, even years, your initial insight may still be the same. Alternatively, it has changed and very likely your relationship has improved.

This can be very meaningful. If the relationship in question has improved, perhaps there is enough heart reason to continue. If the relationship has improved but you are still not sure, maybe you commit to another time of feeling what is ultimately right, on your own or together. If the relationship has improved but there is separation in your hearts and in real life too, you can become or stay wonderful friends.

This is, of course, if there is meaning for you both in doing so. This is very helpful and purposeful if there are children involved. The children will be in this greater peace, harmony and a continuation of love and loving interaction. It will make a lot of sense to them and their hearts.

Setting your heart care as a high priority will help no matter what. You may continue in togetherness and love or you may walk different paths as precious friends and companions with equal or more love than ever before.

All this or more may happen. With more practical, real heart involvement there is always going to be a different outcome, short and long-term. It would be wonderful if you and your partner together commit to a time of heart connection, strengthening both of your heart's abilities to assist, to be in greater, deeper love … whatever the future may bring.

Moving on, letting go

Letting go gives us freedom, and freedom is the only condition for happiness.
If, in our heart, we still cling to anything - anger, anxiety, or possessions - we cannot be free. Thich Nhat Hanh

There are parts within that may either struggle, or at a less aware level, are prepared to let go. Moving on, letting go and letting the heart heal any wounds when a relationship has ended is important. It will let you be free, feel free within and approach all other relations with renewed spirit and love, including another romantic relationship.

You may have felt in the past that some people are willing to engage in a new relationship and yet they are not free, they are still attached to the past, to others or to past events.

The heart can be of immense help here if this is a current or recent situation. If there has been a separation in the past, even years back, then within or around your heart you may still carry some of the burdens that the separation caused back then. Your opening and radiating heart's ability may be very relevant here.

What are some of the situations when it is helpful to move on, let go?

1. You have recently separated from your partner;
2. You separated some time ago but you are still feeling a sense of hurt;
3. You separated some time ago yet there seems to be a lack of ability to love again;
4. You feel strong love for another person and yet that person is not available; or
5. You are in an in-out/on-off relationship situation.

The heart and love connection you have with your partner is deep whether you feel it clearly or not. It includes emotional connection or entanglement. This may or may not be related to the length of time you have been together. Your experience may be as deep in a short-term relationship as it can be in a longer one.

Separation opens the door to even deeper emotions and may lead you away from what your heart wants to facilitate for you.

When you have already separated or when separation is clearly happening, then it is time to let go. Letting go at the level of the heart never means letting go of loving the other person, it means letting go of everything that is not pure, unconditional and eternal love.

No one really knows what the future holds. When you let go, you open a gate that could be called the 'miracle gate'. As your heart is gradually dissolving all that is not real, unconditional love, a truly wonderful world of love, joy and more can open.

1.   *You have recently separated from your partner*

This may mean that there is grief, sadness, anger, hurt, or disappointment closer to the surface of your awareness and experience. You may even feel there is no present emotion or negative feeling towards your partner or ex-partner. Emotions may also rise to the surface more as time goes by.

If you want to be pro-active, whatever you experience right now in terms of emotions, this is a chance to choose love. Choose your heart as an alternative, even as an alternative to advice you may get from friends or others. If you feel that advice would help, then follow that. Your heart's help can be added to other forms of assistance, working alongside advice from a counsellor, for example. While it can be normal to experience strong emotion, you may have had sufficient heart experience up to now and prefer to follow and strengthen your heart. Emotions will be kept at bay and will not burden your heart. Your present and future ability to love with not only stay intact, it can even grow.

2.   *You separated some time ago but you are still feeling a sense of hurt*

There may be other forms of limiting, burdening emotions such as feeling disappointed in yourself or the other person, feeling let down or angry. Let your heart help you. As often as you can, do the core heart strengthening steps shared in KHH 6, followed by KHH 7 below.

The use of KHH 7 is optional and initially may be hard for you. If this is so, then this means that a part of you is still attached, not letting go enough yet, or the emotions are stronger than a feeling of care, love and concern for the other.

The ties that bind, the deeper, heavier emotional ties that hold your heart and hold you back, are often not directly related to your issue, your separation, even your partner or ex-partner. They are deeper patterns that run within you that any relationship, often the one close relationship you have, will naturally bring to the surface. This is a huge chance to have un-helpful, interruptive or even destructive patterns and deposits cleared.

These heavier emotions come from a deeper place and are something like a systemic issue. In this way, whatever is or has surfaced, particularly in the form of emotions or attachments, it is a unique chance to have them cleansed. It is a gift that will offer freer love and connections to others in all love relationships you have, right now to your children and wider family, and to any future partners.

As you gradually do this letting go exercise, with an increasingly free smile, the ties that are still holding you, and all associated emotions, will be dissolved by the power of your heart. 'It is time to let go', you may say and you may plan to. However the mind/brain does not know how to let go. Your heart does! The mind/brain can understand the meaning and purpose of the heart's role and invite, engage and facilitate the help of your heart.

3.   *You separated some time ago yet there seems to be a lack of ability to love again*

Your heart's remedy and the steps to take are identical to the above. Do not rush or try to do anything. The heart's help for us to love again will be very limited if we use intention or will power.

It is commonly understood that love is a matter of the heart. In an equally common and simple way, as you attend to your heart, it will naturally and in ever increasing ways, step-by-step, let you feel love again.

When the love connections from your heart remove any burden from around and within your heart and the love connection and radiance from your heart reaches outward again, love will come into your life in surprising, new and unexpected ways.

Your heart will pull you forward and you will find your understanding and feeling of love shift. It will bring you, gradually and naturally, into a sweet and even deepening ability to love again. The heart will always cleanse more than what we know needs cleansing, clearing or healing. As this process happens, and as you let go of whatever has been kept within or around your heart, love will enter your heart again. From there, naturally, you will be able to love again.

4. *You feel strong love for another person and yet that person is not available*

Love can never be forced or hurried. Life, love, friendship, relationship only ever can be a dance between the two hearts of two human beings. As such this sweet and from-the-heart invitation to dance needs a 'yes' from the other to allow the dance to start, to continue and to unfold and blossom.

If the invitation from you for an intimate dance, however, 'only' receives a 'yes' for a friendship dance from the other, then it is best to let go, to be grateful and to trust that there is a rightness to it now and in the longer-term.

Let your heart help you to enjoy the curious nature of what a connection with this dear heart and friend of yours will bring. The heart's chambers have no room for anything but love when you feel the closeness of a friend, lover or someone you hope to love.

When this love can find expression in friendship or being on a work or sports team with that person, then there is a good reason to be grateful. If for some reason there is no contact or you can't be in contact with this person then it is time to let go with a strong heart.

5. *You are in an in-out/on-off relationship situation*

In sessions clients often share that they struggle with letting go when it comes to relationship, in particular if there is still love or hope for love. 'Letting go' how the mind/brain understands it can have a plus and minus side. In that context, 'letting go' means no longer caring, dropping someone or not attending with love and care to that person, whatever the challenges or difficulties. 'Letting go' can mean to ignore, to forget, to not do the best in trying to solve any challenges or obstacles.

Letting go from the heart is good because as you let go at the level of the heart, all that is not love within you will become freer and a clearer and stronger expression will result. This can also be directly felt by others or by a partner.

Letting go at the heart level will help in a wonderful way. Letting go in this case also means physically and mentally, with mind/brain's full intentions. Focus on doing the best, attending to the other, being polite, courteous, and inclusive and focus on listening with your heart and mind.

The heart's letting go of the other, the partner means that she or he will feel the greater freedom to be and to love, too. Sometimes this lack of freedom can be the very reason for relationship problems in the first place, or a desired separation. One outcome may be that, in that freedom felt by your partner, a door opens and she or he feels to return. If one possible result is that you lose your partner, then there is a greater purpose, another purpose for your life right now or a deeper love is meant to enter it.

As you learn to trust your heart more, to open it more, you will find greater trust in life's events, too. You will learn to let go more and more easily and to surrender.

Your heart will help this positive heart-letting-go process. It will lead you continuously to deeper, more wonderful layers of love that you will always feel at the same time you are sharing these with others, with your partner. You will only ever gain in the heart's letting go, letting go to the greater healing ability, the greater love your heart is connected to and always longs to express and share.

This is very significant in other ways too. You could say in 'spiritual' ways. Life and love are matters of living and enjoying life with a growing purpose and ease. When guided by that deeper part within, your heart, whatever you 'let go of', is no longer occupying your mind or emotions. You will be more present, more able to enjoy each moment and life overall. The full potential of life has the chance to unfold, including in a romantic way.

The very question may surface that scholars, wise people or people from any walk of life have asked: is it right to stay in a relationship or marriage, or can it be a right decision to move on too?

While others can help or give advice or counsel you, ultimately you will have to live with the decisions you make. It is in these moments that counsel from a deeper place within is also wise. You are in union with another wonderful human person. All necessary care and love are required to solve issues, including the possible issue of separation and moving on. Sometimes to move on is the best and right decision. Allow your answer your decision be helped and given clarity by your heart.

Sometimes the hope of getting back together, finding love again, is so strong that even after separation there is still a lack of willingness to let go. Your mind/brain, heart and higher self or deeper knowing can help you to grow, to become more loving, to let go more easily, to be a free spirit with an equal amount of clarity around commitment and to know what love and relationship means. The help from your heart, letting go of all that is not love that you carry in your heart, is a magical blessing beyond words.

Surrendering from the heart

Sweet surrender. John Denver

There is a deeper level of letting go that the heart can facilitate and help you with. You know that getting into the deeper levels of sharing love with a dear one can only be in the form of 'surrender'. Making love, the deepest feeling, experiencing the highest joy and union, in French is commonly referred to as 'le petit mort', the 'little death', the ultimate letting go and surrender.

To access this deeper level of heart help it is good to remember that love, heart and surrender are natural to you and your heart. Memory of past experiences of surrender into love can be a guide to let the heart help with surrendering everything at the other end of the spectrum: everything burdensome, difficult or worrying in your relationships.

When is this a helpful thing to do? You will have experienced in your relationships, that there are times when any discussion about a difficult matter or disagreement does not progress the situation, does not help anymore. In fact, emotions may surface and make things worse.

On your own, you may struggle to work out something that has happened to you. For example, someone close to you has upset or hurt you or you try to work out a difficult situation. Despite all thinking efforts there appears to be no obvious or easy solution, or if there is one, it will cause another string of difficulties.

Especially in relationships there are situations where one hopes for something from the partner. It can happen that the partner does not feel to do this, or to do it exactly the way it is hoped for. He or she can also try to meet this hope and still fall short of what was hoped for.

There is no perfect human being or partner, who can meet all the needs, wants and hopes of another human being.

Here it is advisable and helpful to let your heart surrender any unresolvable or burdensome matters. When you surrender, let go in a deeper way, from your heart. Then the deeper intelligence from the heart can help to find solutions or paths forward that the mind will struggle to find. The deeper, unconditional love that is flowing through your heart will be able to transform all that is not real, deep or unconditional love into love and being together, however the deeper part within feels to, beyond any conditioned hopes or other drivers.

What are examples of worries, burdens or challenges that you can surrender from your heart? A 'worry' maybe that you are not sure if a certain behaviour of yours - or your partner's - is supporting your relationship. You raise an issue, such as asking how to behave in a certain situation and there is some irritation in your partner. You feel that raising it again may trigger more irritation or other emotions. An alternative is to surrender it from your heart.

A 'burden' is something that happened in a prior relationship that still 'hangs around'. This means you still think about it and when those thoughts come up, it feels heavy, your heart races, tension increases in body areas; or other unpleasant physical or energetic sensations come up. You may or may not even know exactly what it stems from. The situation of that burden may be of such a nature that raising it will not help, will alienate your partner or bring to life again a memory that is more burdensome. Let your heart help to surrender this burden, and all related to it, from your heart.

A 'challenge' may or may not have aspects of a 'worry' or a 'burden' in it. It is often solely a past, current or future situation that presents a challenge to you personally. In addition to, or instead of, planning for it, or working things out in your mind, you can surrender the challenge from your heart. You invite the heart into the situation and you let your heart help you to dissolve aspects that may block you or side-effects such as excessive nervousness, anxiety or worry.

Practical Heart Tip 36: Surrendering from the heart *

Surrendering from your heart will always be additional to what you know or have experienced in the past, in dealing with relationship issues or challenges. In doing so, you will allow the heart's innate intelligence and radiance to support you, to shift inner blocks and to bring more heart into the 'now' as well as the path ahead.

- *Write a short list of three to five worries, burdens or challenges that fall into the above categories;*

- *Do Heart Strengthening (KHH 6) for a few minutes until you can feel more peace, lightness or until you can feel the heart become more active, stronger, radiating;*

- *Then, from your heart (only one intention is needed) let your heart surrender item number one on your list;*

- *Look at the item, close your eyes and just keep relaxing and smiling to your heart; your heart will do it. If there is a response or feeling from your heart, follow the feeling; then*

- *Follow the same process for the remaining items on your list.*

Do this daily or a couple of times a day. If you do it more than two or three times a day then you might get busier again with thoughts and emotions, especially if the burdens are of a heavier nature. In those cases it is better to add more general Heart Strengthening or Open Heart Meditation.

This is also a very helpful daily practice, even if the burdens, worries or challenges in your life are only of a small nature. Your heart will be daily 'en-lightened' and a positive process of continuous opening will be supported.

Depending on your spiritual or religious belief you can add 'Let my heart surrender burden number (one) to Divine, Source, God (of your belief) or the highest Being my heart recognises'. If you feel comfortable doing this and your feeling is deeper, then continue this way.

At a deeper level, your heart and the core of your heart is recognising this connection to its own 'Divine Source'. Instantly or after some time, a deeper feeling and deeper help is likely to be facilitated through this natural heart connection.

This PHT is immensely important and of essential help to your heart. Surrendering from the heart is often a totally additional tool to someone's abilities in dealing with difficulties, in romantic relationship, any other relationship and many other matters that challenge or cause us burdens.

Why is the heart's help here so important? Your heart knows firstly what your challenges are and also what is in your heart, or around it, that is reducing your ability to love freely, to be and to grow. Every time you surrender one matter, your heart is getting this as a 'yes' from you, that you give your heart permission to help, and it will do just that.

 A deeper form of the above exercise would be to 'let my heart surrender burden number (one) and all related matters and causes'. In this way you give your heart a more complete permission to facilitate its, opening, healing and transformation.

Depending on your challenge, difficulty, burden or worry, you may feel that you don't want to let go. You don't want to surrender it because a part of you may feel that you will lose something or that something good will go, almost by accident, in surrendering the not-so-good parts.

There may also be a self-righteous part that says something like, 'I have a right to have this emotion. I am justified in being angry or upset. Until you realise that it is not true, not part of the truer and deeper feeling within, it will be hard to let go of such love-reducing or even damaging emotions.

This is a very normal and natural concern for some. It is connected with the level of trust in your heart that you already have or that you have gained by now in following some of the KHHs and practices. After all, it is your heart; it is not a stranger or an alien or a part of you that wants to cause you trouble.

In the same way you trust your heart, it loves person A, your child, or person B, a close family member, or person C, your partner or dearest friend. You can trust your heart even beyond this love for others in terms of surrendering burdens. Why 'beyond'? Your heart, in essence, is pure in its ability to know, love, share and feel. As soon as another person is involved, there is a history, there can be wanting, past hurts, and other emotions and therefore a blurring of this purer heart ability.

In moments when you use this PHT, because the heart is intelligent, whatever your heart surrenders will only ever be parts that limit you. Your heart will then be free to do what it does best - to be in a state of deep love and care for others.

There will be no loss when you have surrendered something not-so-good or burdensome from your heart. Whatever the burdensome aspects are, they will be replaced with more of the wonderful feelings your heart has been waiting to help you to feel, in your relationship with your partner and all your loved ones.

'Wanting', your heart and love

If you feel that there is a want in you that is strong and can also be lessened, then it is good to add this 'wanting' or 'desiring' to the list of items to be surrendered. With regard to surrendering any wanting, this is your call and a case-by-case decision. There is a fine line between what is okay to want and what is desire, an over-hungry or thirsty need for something, which doesn't come from a place of love, care or balance.

When wanting is desire, more than natural appetite or what is needed, then the person or object of that desire will become the object of negative energy generated by the non-fulfilment of this. It will not support the growth or even existence of your love relationship.

Only you will know in your heart and being truthful to yourself and all those around you, when this is the case. If in doubt, surrender it anyway from your heart, only good or adjusted feelings, needs and longing will be generated. The heart's role is to adjust, refine or change whatever is not in line with purer, deeper and more blissful love.

'Emotionally' available again

How deep is your love? Bee Gees

One possible feeling around relationship is commonly described as being 'emotionally' available.

In the way that the book defines emotion and feeling, in relation to the heart, the deeper situation is that the heart is burdened with past issues, and has reduced freedom to relate to others or to love. How deep your love is, or the love needed to make you happy and fulfilled in relationship, will differ from others. It is the lightness of the heart and how the hearts connect, that free love and make it available. It is the amount of emotional memory or burdens that are still in or around the heart that leave a feeling of 'emotional unavailability'. The heart can help in freeing those memories and limiting energetic deposits.

What is needed is individual and will be facilitated by your heart perfectly in accordance to your needs. Viewed through the heart, for you to have moved on means that it will not only be a matter of physical separation, such as no longer living together or no longer seeing each other. It will equally be about non-physical separation: to have all burdensome, attaching and unhelpful emotional ties cleared.

When these binding ties, these burdens in and around the heart are dissolved, you will be able to freely and whole-heartedly love again. You will be, as commonly said, 'emotionally available'. This is mainly a feeling you will have. It may also be felt by others depending on their sensitivity or ability to feel, that is, their own freeness of heart.

The freedom in your heart can also be felt by other hearts. True emotional freedom will attract another form of energy into your life: of an equally free and mature heart that has a lot of love to share.

It is also of benefit to your whole life. This feeling of freedom will naturally spill over to all your love relations: family, dear friends and possibly dear colleagues. You can enjoy emotional availability, emotional freedom and a light heart and not yearn for a relationship. That is perfectly normal too.

If you feel that a partner or partner-to-be is emotionally not fully available, you can only encourage them to learn about the heart and to also use the heart's abilities and qualities. If you feel that there is still a degree of heaviness or attachment in or around your heart, then KHHs 6 and 7 introduced in this chapter are fantastic tools to help.

Even if you are no longer with a partner, and even if that partnership or relationship was a long time ago, you can still use KHH 7 and let your heart smile to that person.

It will gradually dissolve all that is not the purer love that your heart holds for everyone. Naturally, a greater, sweeter and more blissful freedom to love again will become your heart's natural state.

Whatever the issue or problem - let your heart help

Whatever the issue or problem in your relationship, after you have practised the basic strengthening of your heart, you can further let your heart help you and your partner in letting your heart radiate and smile to the other.

Key Heart Help 7: Let your heart smile and radiate to your partner/others

The second key heart activity introduced in the relationship section is to let your heart smile and radiate to your partner.

For the mind/brain and perhaps common understanding this looks simple and even like a small matter. However, with all the learning, deeper understanding and, even more so, your experiences up to now, it is anything but a small matter. Whatever your heart does for you will have a profound impact, in that moment and over time.

Your heart is special and at the core of your heart is a profound and strong part of you, your spirit. In moments where you activate this part through Heart Strengthening and where you then let your heart smile to your partner, triggered and facilitated by your smile, it will free the relationship. It will further free your heart and have a similarly freeing effect on your partner. It is in that freedom, or greater heartfulness, that love can grow and find expression.

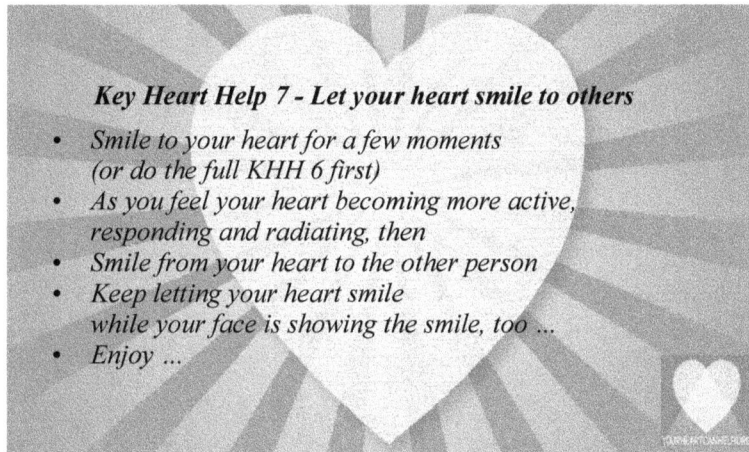

Key Heart Help 7 - Let your heart smile to others

- *Smile to your heart for a few moments (or do the full KHH 6 first)*
- *As you feel your heart becoming more active, responding and radiating, then*
- *Smile from your heart to the other person*
- *Keep letting your heart smile while your face is showing the smile, too ...*
- *Enjoy ...*

The KHHs build on each other. Practise the earlier one, in particular the full Heart Strengthening introduced as KHH 6. A more active, glowing and radiating heart is then sharing all that your heart can naturally share, directly heart to heart, with your partner or any other person with whom you feel to share in this way.

Smiling from your heart to one or several others when there are difficulties, challenges or times of high-intensity emotions, becomes even more important. It help you to be more in the heart, not affected by these challenges, not falling into reacting or becoming emotional. It will strengthen your heart and offer direct heart-to-heart help in resolving issues especially in times when words do not help.

You can use this technique with all your loved ones. You can use this when you feel wonderful and that there is love, a flow, or during moments of joyful sharing, being together, being creative or productive. It can be the beginning of feeling how beautiful it is to share love freely with those dear to you, without any expectations.

The full KHH 7 - Let your heart smile and radiate to your partner/others

Here is the complete and more detailed version of the full KHH 'Let your heart smile to others': Close your eyes to decrease the activities of your brain:

Smile to your heart for a few moments (1-3 minutes, or even better, do the full Heart Strengthening - KHH 6);

- *After that time and as you feel your heart becoming more active, responding and radiating, then with one intention;*

- *Smile from your heart to your partner or to others;*

- *Keep on smiling freely and with feeling for some time;*

- *As long as you stay in the feeling from your heart, heart-connected, it will work and help your heart, the relationship and the other person;*

- *You can end this practice when you feel to, or keep going until you get distracted or pulled away by other things, events or people; and*

- *Do this often and regularly, several times a day.*

Note that ...

- For this to work, for your heart to share love, warmth and kindness in a non-physical and non-verbal way to others, only one intention is needed. Your heart will note this intention and it will happen. This may take a while for you to feel or trust;
- For your trust and feeling of the reality of this happening, switch a few times between 'smiling to my heart only' and 'let my heart smile to person A'. After some time, you will feel that smiling to others (after doing some heart strengthening beforehand) will be a sweeter, deeper and more heart-opening feeling;
- The heart sharing and heart help facilitated in this way will keep working for as long as you smile. While you smile and feel your heart or any pleasant, nice feelings, you will be heart-connected, the heart will be active. In moments while you are enjoying what you do, being grateful for the heart, it can continuously deepen and last longer;
- The person does not need to be near you. Your heart will bypass everything irrelevant including time and space;

- You may create reminders on your wall or phone calendar. You have certain reminder situations, such as hearing from the person or being near the person during a particular time. For example, the person dear to you watches TV or talks on social media to friends;
- Be free from expectation. As you are the one doing this practice, it will clearly help your heart and the relationship. However, as others have the every-moment-choice to follow the heart more or their emotions/thinking, the impact on the other person will depend on their choice, state of overall relaxation and their relative openness at the level of their heart; and
- One person committing to the practice of this KHH is all that is needed. It offers an additional choice and the heart can help.

The best results are achieved when both of you practise Heart Strengthening, Open Heart Meditation or other KHHs or PHTs and then smile from the heart to each other simultaneously. In these moments, not only the full capacity of both hearts is present, but the hearts will be in synergy and a slightly enhanced effect will be felt.

Sometimes it is not certain where the relationship path will lead. From the perspective of your heart, and the deeper being within, uncertainty is okay. The heart does not judge, plan, want or do anything that is not related to being kind or loving. In particular, it does not judge others. If your relationship is experiencing any form of difficulty, it is important to let every part of you help. Use all the resources and innate abilities you have to do the best. One of the aims ought to be to stay in a loving or kind feeling, in your heart. The outcome will always depend on both partners' decisions and their ways of being in this greater love from the heart.

Your heart will guide you, help you and support your relationship. It requires trust in your heart that you will gain with time as you go through the practical heart helpers. The heart way to be is not just 'either/or', what is right or wrong. It is to use the heart more and in some way disregard what the outcome may be. Choosing the heart always means choosing love, even though how that love unfolds may not be fully understood yet.

In using the KHH above, your heart will help your partner to be a little more relaxed, to be touched by the radiance and pure energy of the heart while at the same time you, through your heart, will be helped, too.

A little letting go, as discussed in section V, can assist immensely when emotions have surfaced or when you are stuck in an argument or holding to a particular position. Your heart has an ever-growing and in some way limitless ability to share the purer love and healing qualities from your heart with others. In this way, you can smile from the heart, not only to one person but to several at the same time. This is a deeply heart-opening, heart-clearing practice.

Practical Heart Tip 37: Let your heart smile to all around you *

You can let your heart smile not only to your romantic partner. Use this heart helper in all your relationships, at home, at work, in your social settings, as often as you feel to. It will work if the person is next to you or near you, it will work over any distance, over the phone, via Skype, via text message, through internet chat and even just heart to heart, with no internet or phone connection.

To joyfully love again - your heart's only 'program'

Goodbyes are only for those who love with their eyes.
Because for those who love with heart there is no such thing as separation. Rumi

Your heart can play a significant role in loving again. The previous sections covered different aspects as to how your heart can help. For example, how you can choose 'love', how to seek guidance, how to let go of past 'love', how to deepen your love and how to forgive and heal relationship past.

To simplify, romantic love can have two parts to it. There are those parts that are heavy, mixed with emotions or attachment. And there is the deeper, more unconditional or purer love flowing through an active, light and present heart. Whatever you feel is your current situation, the status of your heart or the status of your relationship, the heart will naturally improve what is already there.

The more you attend to your heart, and ensure it stays or becomes light, the more likely it is you will feel greater feelings of love. This finer form of love will always look for ways to express itself, within relationship or in every moment of your life. It will be an energy, an aura you carry that will gently touch others and beautify their lives. You can describe these feelings of love, or your heart, like an endlessly opening flower whose beauty can be felt by a widening circle of people.

It is the very essence of your heart, of every heart, to know love, to feel love and to share it in all actions, words and silence, as well as in your intimate relationship.

Is it interesting, or perhaps only logical, that it is that very same heart that can help you to be free and ready to love again with an open heart when love has left your life or your relationship.

This is very significant, given how deep or difficult relationship issues can be, or how deep the wounds can be when relationships struggle or end. As you use your heart during the important letting go process, it will be filled with sweeter and sweeter love. From the first moment onwards you start to rely on your heart.

Any time anything other than peace, calmness and love rises to the surface of your feeling, let the heart take you deeper into your heart. It is from these layers, and ultimately from the core of your heart, where the purest love, light, and blissful, joyful feelings exist. That part of the heart does not know 'too hard' or 'too painful'. You will find from the very beginning, or within a comparatively short time, you will experience some of these feelings of calm, joy and love. It will then be your preparedness and degrees of 'letting go', that will bring you into love again, along with others around you.

The journey, this life, is meant to be joyful, light, easy and filled with love. Every moment that you still experience emotions, that you suffer, or the opening to love and being loved again is rocky or hard, is essentially a reminder that in the past, the heart was not used to enough depth. There is a choice now to use it. Situations or times like these assist us, and taking a new approach, with the heart actively helping, can create the necessary shift.

Interestingly, it is also your heart helping you to be free and ready, with an open heart, to love again.

The story Francesca shared was sent in an e-mail after a couple of sessions. She is a successful manager in a health service and an attractive woman. She had been single for over ten years at the time of telling her story. Her experience is a wonderful example of how, in a comparatively short time, and often unexpectedly, love can return to your life. The below lines are from an email she felt to send, feeling overwhelmed by the feelings of love within. She had previously shown a silent acceptance of the ability to feel and share love again.

Francesca's Story:

'Hi, I was struck that you wrote ...' and as you say it, the heart intensifies the deeper, gentler feeling and perception of all.'

'I didn't think that I had said that to you in so many words. Yet I wrote in my diary that through the power of the heart, my world has become softer, more tender and filled with compassion and understanding. It has also become richer, infinitely richer.'

'My anxiety aside, this is the best thing that has ever happened to me. Apologies if this sounds enlarged beyond truth or words. It is sincere and it is my truth as far as I can tell.

I was walking through sections of my workplace the other day. I have been there many times before, but this time one of the panels of a large word-collage that is in the main lobby space caught my eye. Two words that were fragments of the whole stood out- 'heart' and 'meet' - reminders of my new state.'

'It brought tears to my eyes. The feelings are not pure or absolute - I'm still terrified and feeling about to topple over a lot of the time in this new state, but I wouldn't give it up for the world.'

'Deep gratitude for the opportunity to love again. It makes me know I'm alive, so alive.'

'And still find myself wearing that ultimate fashion accessory - the grin.'

Shortly after this note, Francesca found a partner again and they seem very happy together and in love with each other. She introduced him to her heart practice and it became clear very quickly to the new partner why Francesca is so happy, radiant and light. She had been relying on her heart for some time. They both now have a heart practice at home and have in the recent past also attended centre-based heart meditation sessions and workshops.

To love and to be loved means that there are feelings of joy at the same time. The heart's nature and functions will naturally bring about a heart that can love again. Being able to love again is only one of the qualities needed to re-enter a romantic relationship. Another key quality is the freedom from burdens, held traumas and even hesitation, doubt or fear, as well as the freedom from being emotionally busy with a past partner or experience. If you are preoccupied in this way, your heart will still be attending to these matters, and not be free to love fully. In contrast, any heart help will allow for your love, including in new togetherness, to flow freely, lightly and joyfully.

'Always in my heart' ... the greater love flowing through your heart

I want to know what love is. Foreigner

When we are deeply in love, we often say 'you are always in my heart' and we know that the greater, deeper meaning of this is for love to last forever.

Unfortunately, the reality is often different. Tender feelings of love or that sweet loving connection when first in love can fade after time. Irritating emotions or distracting matters can also burden the heart and lessen feelings of love. There is a tendency for this to happen especially in relationships that have been going for a longer time.

The heart always looks for ways to love and to find the love within you that lasts, that longs for sharing and longs to seek expression. It is that greater love that the heart can receive, and in some way generate, that will move you to a place of feeling where you can truly say and feel 'you are always in my heart'.

When your heart truly and more fully opens, you will have a greater heart awareness, heart feeling and a better heart quality. A gentle, subtle, yet immensely beautiful feeling of love will always flow and radiate through and from you. The love that flows to your heart, the love that flows through and from your heart, as your heart opens, becomes purer and knows no condition or limitation.

Whatever your relationship situation or challenge is, you will simply and solely feel this way. There will be a clarity too, that will make any words said, any movement made and any feelings shared, of assistance to your partner or loved one.

If you are in a relationship or you long to be in one, let your heart guide you and help you at every point along the way. A heart or love question may be:

- How can love come into my life?
- How can love return?
- How can love stay?
- How can love grow?

And the answer is always very similar: love is always connected to your heart and your heart's condition. While these are all valid questions, in some way your question is much less important than the answer.

Love will always flow and be generated through your heart. Whether you are alone, lonely or in a relationship, you will always perceive and feel love in your heart first.

The following story is a simple, wonderful, yet 'normal heart example' of how your own heart focus and the heart's help, can support, heal and deepen your relationship.

Growing love

Matters of the heart are best left to the heart.

Alistair and Amy's sharing below is a wonderful example of how the heart can help you to maintain and grow a deeply loving relationship. Their sharing shows a quite rocky relationship at first, much in love and yet with quite some emotion and challenges. It also shows how the heart can directly help you to work through issues that tend to come up in relationship. These may be issues that arise between you or ones that you or your partner carry from past relationships.

Both Amy and Alistair had been good friends for several years before they started to feel more for each other. In the time before they became a couple, both of them had been through separations. Alistair had been through a difficult divorce and Amy had been through what she said was a 'big' separation.

It started during her separation time, when Amy felt to talk to Alistair. He had just been through separation. There was a shared experience and on both sides a bit of heart, too, as they had both been through some of the heart workshops available in the community.

As they kept talking and connecting, they felt a strong attraction. They also found a deep friendship developing. For example, they shared that they, loved talking on the phone for hours and enjoyed each other's company a lot. Perhaps in their hearts they knew that the attraction was deeper than just their physical selves. Despite sincere advice from their friends not to, they entered into a romantic relationship.

Alistair and Amy's Story:

Amy shared about when and how they met:

'I was needed to talk to someone about what I was going through, my separation. I was very angry at the time. One time, meeting Alistair again, he offered 'If you ever need to talk ...'. I felt grateful for this offer and how genuine it was. It also sparked my interest: 'who the hell is this guy?''

'We quickly became inseparable, talking all night, becoming very close. We moved in together only several months later.'

Alistair and Amy had met just before heart learning came into their lives. Alistair offered a description of the early days of their relationship: 'Our initial relationship was based on a change. We wanted to change together and we tried a number of things, workshops and spiritual things. We were bouncing off each other a lot.'

'Things got stirred up and there were a lot of emotions between us. Stuff would come up all the time, leading us to blame each other, to argue, to get angry and we wouldn't want to support each other because of it. What made it harder was that things would come up between us that were from the past, older relationships we had. It was hard to be with that.'

'It got to a point where there was so much emotion that Amy would also cry often, where I simply did not want to hear her voice anymore.'

'*Roles would flip between us and we couldn't help but blame each other.*'

'*When all got quieter again, we realised this and felt quite limited. We often ended up 'being there', in emotional states, and blaming each other again. In hindsight, it was difficult, despite the fact that we were newly in love.*'

Amy:

'*Blaming each other, upsetting the other, was something we did not want to do and yet it happened. We wanted to be sorry and to say, 'I am sorry' genuinely and this became so easy and genuine from the heart.*'

Amy then described some of the early changes, as they both started to learn about the heart and began to use the Open Heart Meditation as a regular way to strengthen their awareness, feeling and overall heart capacity.

'*We would choose to do the Open Heart Meditation when a trigger event happened and when emotions between us surfaced. Then, afterwards, we came back to the issue and talked more.*'

'*It was at first not easy to do. To stop what was going on, to stop talking, to sit and to do a meditation.*'

'*We soon realised that it was something we could do to calm us down and to talk to each other from another place that was more from the heart and less from our emotions. This was huge.*'

Alistair:

'*When we started to learn about the heart, it was quite liberating, freeing in a way. It was like suddenly having a tool to help you through hard times.*'

Amy:

'*I am a woman; I was looking for some form of 'validation' or signs that would show the status of our relationship and love, like 'he brought me flowers'. As my heart opened more, instead of looking to Alistair for this validation, it was the love in my heart that was helping and healing my own insecurity and dependency. I realised that I was healing through my own heart.*'

'*Together with this shift, I noticed that things that would trigger some form of emotion, or make me upset, started not to do that anymore.*'

'*There is much more harmony in our relationship now that I am more in touch with my heart, more loving, more giving. All feels more whole and wonderful.*'

Alistair:

'*It is very similar for me. With more heart, there is more peacefulness, more joy ... and I can feel more love more often between us, in a light and quite natural way. This is after we have been together now for over five years.*'

'*There is a deep, genuine gratitude that I feel for Amy and for us being together now.*'

Amy and Alistair share about the shift that occurred when their hearts became stronger and more open. This is very significant, as it is a shift that the heart facilitated, where the heart was clearly helping. The challenges Alistair and Amy experienced are some of the major issues in romantic relationships.

In a romantic relationship there is often a hope that something 'magical' will happen; someone 'magical' will enter our lives; problems will magically be resolved; a few counselling sessions will bring the magic back, or the old 'magic' will return in other ways.

You may know people who have tried this again and again, either within one relationship or again and again with new partners. This hope is deeply engrained in us. It can be coupled with trying or other mind/brain efforts in the hope that somehow the heart's deep longing for love will be fulfilled in a magical or mind/brain way.

Amy and Alistair's sharing summarises what I hope this entire chapter will bring more to the surface: that matters of the heart are best left to the heart. In saying so, however, the heart's active role is much more than a saying or nice words that ring true. Your heart has an in-built program, an in-built capacity that is not simply 'there'; it is dynamic and expanding, in helping you and all loved ones around you.

The beginning steps are easy, too easy for a clever mind to want to believe that the full potential of the heart can be launched and accessed in this way.

It is a beginning, yet for some experiencing hardship or pain, these first steps will offer all the help that is needed initially.

Your heart and deep love are one

Go deeper, past thoughts into silence, past silence into stillness.
Past stillness into the heart. Let love consume all that is left of you. Kabir

When you start to open your heart, you will recognise that love needs only love to fulfil itself. 'True love' or the purer love that your heart carries deeper down, is enough in itself. For an opening heart there are endless moments every day where you heart naturally longs to share and is sharing love, with strangers in the street, when shopping, at work and of course in deeper ways with those close to you. When you feel naturally connected to these blissful moments, this natural way of being, it is more than normal to smile.

In these moments, smile to your heart, or let the memory of these moments help you when you sit down to do your heart strengthening or heart meditations.

There is one aspect your heart will help you with that is essential to making a relationship work: your heart knows how to surrender, let go, release.

These are the two heart-related qualities essential to remember in a relationship:

- Smile often and strengthen your heart; and
- Use KHH 6 often to let your heart help you to heal and to let go, surrender, release the issue that blocks or limits love and everything that is energetically related.

Not all difficulties can be resolved with words and conversation, including counselling. This allows room for another avenue of help. In this way you will take care of your heart, and your ability to love and be in a loving relationship will be nurtured. Whether you have a partner or not, being in a relationship is ultimately only one way to share the purer, finer and blissful love from your heart.

Your heart and deep love are one and it will be you who lives and loves more wholeheartedly.

Your partner will love you, offer love, share love, but you know that he or she will also challenge you, not love you at times and be busy with other things. Like Alistair and Amy shared, sometimes emotions fly and all loving is on hold. Despite the hurt, deeper challenges or upsets that relationships can cause, your heart has an innate ability to surrender these accumulations and negative emotions, without the need to talk it through. The heart offers another way. Sometimes, it is the only way.

Romantic relationship and love is always a connection to another dear human being. There are moments, big or small, where this becomes clear. These may be moments when you feel less love or simply emotion from the other person over a period of time, despite your heart commitment and deepening heart journey. Then you need all the help from your heart to surrender and let go. You can open and attend to your own heart and all qualities related. The other person will always have this free will and choice too. Here you can only encourage the other very gently, motivate and be a wonderful example.

Love never forces.

You can love your partner, share love and be loving and kind, yet you will perhaps be able to recall times when you were not in that space either, or when you felt disturbed by the other's emotions or inattentiveness. Let this be an invitation to let your heart help you first. Be firmly on a journey to being in love, in feelings of love always, whatever the nature of your current connection or relationship. This will always invite kinder reactions, love and beauty.

Your heart's direct help for your special relationships will be a wonderful journey for you and for all those around you. It will change you from the inside out, too. Perhaps we know that true love is somewhere 'programmed' into our hearts. Your heart may just be that key to unlock it all. It will if you start to truly and in action follow your heart. Alistair's and Amy's story show this in their open sharing.

The moment you start to attend to your heart, start to use it and choose it, wonderful feelings of love and tenderness will surface. A wonderful energy will spread and both your hearts will open and flourish with all the heart help unfolding step-by-step for all areas of your lives.

All the love in your heart, all your interactions, all relationships at home and at work will become increasingly love-filled and immensely enjoyable. This is the nature of everyone's heart.

Summary - be within love and love with all your heart

All the heart wants is to facilitate, step-by-step, for you to be in love, deeply and always. To access the deeper and more continuous love potential within your heart and to let your heart help you, the following practical steps will help:

1. The key heart supporting practice, KHH 'Heart Strengthening', is introduced in this chapter. Every direct or indirect level of help from your heart will depend on this practice and the quality, commitment and regularity you bring to this. You will begin to live and interact naturally from the place of a stronger heart. What will surface over time is how deep, sweet, gentle and expansive your feeling of love can grow, including for your partner, wife or husband.

2. To deeply love, you and your heart need to master the ability to let go all that is not love. Living with someone and being close to them will make it easier for emotions to surface and for hurtful interactions to occur. The more you strengthen your heart, the more you will be able to let go. There is also the heart's work, where 'you' are less involved or active; your heart will do it. This letting go is of things that bother, burden or nag in relation to your partner and any past hurt or upset that occurred, intentionally or not. Every time you think about it, possibly with emotions arising, you risk continuing attachment to the issue or burden. Use KHH 6 and 7, and combine them with KHH 10 'Surrendering burdens' (in section six) to deeply let go, to surrender burdens, unnecessary or excessive thoughts and everything else negative or not needed by you or your heart.

3. To follow your heart into and within relationships is more natural for some than for others. Making 'following the heart' and following the love that you share a real practice, a truly heart-felt exchange, is one of the foundations for love to remain, grow and blossom. You ideally want to follow your heart, not only for anything directly relating to your partner, but in every interaction, every moment of your relationship. PHT 'Following your heart III' offers a how-to practice. As your heart and the heart feelings get stronger when you are more connected and when your heart responds to situations and events, you have a choice to follow the feeling and responses from your heart, or you can do it in a more structured, more attentive way, with focus. Both ways of following the heart are important - the 'on-the-go' version or with more intent.

4. There is a great deal of confusion caused by common, media or movie-like interpretations of 'real' or deep love. Often, when representing real and deep love, unfortunately the shallower and overly passionate way of loving is highlighted. When choosing or being with a partner, use your heart to feel, the deeper feeling within you, the gentler feelings of love you have for each other. The heart is essential for this. If you are in a relationship now and you find some of this rougher end of passion to be present too often, let your heart help. Do KHH 6 and KHH 7 regularly, and ideally one or both of you go on a heart program for some time.

5. 'Relationship' is also a topic for people who are single. The real, practical help your heart is offering you and - starting now - a possible future partner, is two-fold: (1) to be happy as an individual, on your own and single and (2) to be emotionally free, not burdened or still in thoughts of old situations, partners or lovers. You can use general heart strengthening exercises from throughout the book or specifically in KHH 6, Open Heart Meditation (KHH 13), or join a workshop, and surrender everything that you feel is excess thought or burden from your heart, to be happier and freer now and in the future (KHH 10).

6. Being single or not being with a partner for some is a burden. Karli's sharing is a wonderful example of how there can be a rightness to a situation and how the heart can assist to find happiness, peace and even blissful love in other aspects of life: with dear friends, family and a wider social network. Why things happen or don't happen for us is not always easy to understand and, especially in hindsight, can appear a mystery. The heart does not analyse or seek for answers. It is always willing and ready to help, in every moment, to facilitate the next step towards a loving, wonderful and purposeful life.

7. The heart longs for love. It seems then logical for one of the key steps or approaches to life to be to always choose the most loving response. In this way you choose the heart and you choose the chance to always let love grow. Depending on the level of difficulty you experience or the depth of hurt that may have occurred, you may find this hard or nearly impossible to do. This is where general Heart Strengthening will help (KHH 6 and KHH 7). In particular, the Open Heart Meditation (KHH 13) will pave the way to a more loving connection with your partner and those close to your heart. Choosing the most loving response all the time is an ideal. It will take time to get even close to this. Yet, your very heart will take you there, day by day with some heart practices, heart moments and smiling more often.

8. When you start to practise and use your heart more, there will be some doubt surfacing either during your practice or afterwards. Review PHT 'Is the heart working or not' to be aware of what may be happening for you and how to overcome reasonable, unreasonable or unnecessary doubt.

9. Then also look at PHT 'How to do heart strengthening the best way' which outlines the best way with which to approach your heart practice. This PHT offers a list of pointers which give the heart the respite it needs and deserves, during your early days, weeks or months of heart practice. This will help the heart grow stronger without too much overshadowing or supervision from the mind/brain. In all your heart practice or moments when you enjoy being in your heart more, be aware of the key mind/brain-driven interfering habits or activities. The main obstacles are: 'wanting to try more', 'trying to help your heart' or 'observing or watching'. Instead of following these tendencies or habits, remind yourself, using the helpful part of your mind/brain, to feel more with the feeling from your heart.

10. The flow-on effect on your relationship of you choosing a more loving response more often can be immense. For the mind/brain it may appear as a small matter. In a loving feeling, supported by your heart, you can be firm, clear, strong as well as kind, caring and attentive. The KHHs in this chapter, together with the PHTs, will balance heart and mind for you to be naturally in this loving feeling more, all the time you interact with each other. Actively strengthening and then using the heart more and more means that the trained or conditioned mind/brain dominance can take a back seat. This will bring a transforming power and love quality to your relationship. Any habitual over-thinking of your relationship issues will be gently replaced with more heart energy, heart quality and feeling from your heart in everything you say and do.

11. When in a relationship, there are also the heart-wrenching times when you are not sure anymore. 'I don't feel it anymore' is unfortunately a common statement shared by friends, clients or colleagues. The love feeling stems from the heart and any clear attention to your heart will assist. Every love connection that you have, every love relationship, is unique and precious. Yet, it may be the best choice in some situations to consider whether not being together is a better option. You will find that there is no essential advice other than to follow your heart and the deeper feelings within, in the most attentive and careful manner, to support such decision-making in the best way. Often however, your burdened heart is part of the reason you don't feel it anymore. 'Have you done enough to unburden and open your heart?' is an honest and important question to ask.

12. Unless there is an emergency, such as domestic violence or other similar event, the heart will always move slowly and with consideration - meaning feeling into all areas and aspects, including giving it time. You may find as you attend more to your heart that love can grow again. Love may grow and you may still feel to separate. Your commitment to your heart, ideally before you consider separation, or at least when you go through this decision-making time, will help you to have a growing clarity in any 'bigger' relationship decisions. When your decision to stay together or not to stay together is from this deeper place of feeling and realising, there will be peace, calm, and no regret. This also means that the precious love once shared can find new expressions within relationship or friendship. Friendship is another wonderful way to share, love and help each other.

13. Relationship is the source of some of our deepest and most wonderful experiences. It can equally be a source of the deepest anguish, emotion and hurt we are able to feel. It is immensely helpful here to refresh your understanding of what emotions are and what feelings from the heart are (sections II and IV). It is then in harmony with the heart to realise that there is a choice, when you feel you want to make that more heart-centred, heart-guided and heart-supporting assessment: 'when do I tend to follow my emotions?' and 'when do I follow the heart more?'. This honesty is for you and your heart. The Heart Diary (PHT 27, section 1 'family') can be helpful here. Make regular entries every day to see what these emotions are, when they surface and then also note when you choose to follow the heart. Analysis is much less important than realising when emotions happen and responding with some form of heart strengthening as often as possible. There is a unique opportunity when emotions surface to let the heart assist in their gradual removal, including deeper drivers or causes. Following the heart here means attending to the heart in moments when you are experiencing emotion, letting the heart work and dissolve negative, relationship-limiting tendencies or dispositions entirely.

14. The heart's gentle, deep ability to help can be unlocked with the beautiful KHH 7 'Let your heart smile to others'. Every moment you smile from your heart to your partner, love will deepen. Your heart will release even more burdens, heaviness and everything that is not love. That radiance from a lighter and lighter heart will reach your partner's heart, too. The blissful and gentle energy from the heart will allow the other to 'let go' a bit more of emotion, for example anger, resentment or irritation. It will help his or her heart to remember about the heart, to start to feel it more and for their own heart to start to be more present. It will have a clearing effect on the relationship of the heavy ties that can exist, and the lightness within your connection and the freedom your hearts long for can surface more.

15. Forgiveness in relationship is important and helpful. In closeness, with or without intention, upsets, mistakes or hurt happen. It is almost unavoidable when you are close to someone, when you live with someone. Forgiveness in a more complete form is from both your heart and mind. Really looking after the heart, and all it facilitates in forgiving for small daily matters, is as important as letting the heart clear out everything remaining from any old hurts. The mind/brain's best contribution is the willingness to help this process and to commit to a heart practice of forgiving. It is important to remember that negativities are stored in or become attached to the heart. Logically, the heart needs to be looked after or cleansed and your heart can do this the best. The PHT 'Forgiving from the heart' is the direct way to let the heart do this deeper form of letting go. The heart knows the best for you, your heart and the relationship. It also knows what needs to be let go of and how to do it. Forgiving

from the heart is a 'package deal'. Depending on how deep a hurtful experience has been, how old it is and how many other events connect or compound it, the process may take some time.

16. The PHT 'Getting answers from your heart' offers a few more pointers and things to be aware of as you begin to use your heart for relationship or other questions in your life. It is an extension of the earlier PHT 'Following your heart III - starting to get answers from the heart'

17. The PHT 'Surrendering from the heart' is introduced to offer another possibility to the things you can do when relationship issues or challenges occur. In moments when there is nothing you can do, or when, in addition to doing something, you feel to also surrender the issue or challenged. The benefits will always be a clearer and lighter heart. You will be able to be lighter in this relationship too. In surrendering can also be an invitation to the Divine, to God, to assist in ways that are not clear to you or that don't seem possible.

18. PHT 'Let your heart smile to all around you' is the invitation to you and your heart to expand and to allow love beyond a more focussed 'romantic love' to fill your heart and to flow to wider circles of people around you. After some Heart Strengthening let your heart smile to your romantic partner and to a group of 5, 10, 20 or more people around you. More flow of love will always be more love for everyone around you, including for your partner.

It is natural that most, if not all, humans have an unfortunate and unwanted collection of burdens or negative deposits around and within the heart. These are the seed-blockages and causes that move us away from love, compassion, understanding, care and everything that supports a loving relationship and all close relationships.

If you truly attend to your heart, there is no other way than for more love to grow within and to be in radiant energy beaming from your heart and through you, felt by you, your partner and others.

This is something truly magical and wonderful. It is in those moments that you will be 'in love', the truer, deeper love, and others will feel, respond and engage in new ways with you. Love will always flow through an open and light heart. Whether you aren't in a relationship, whether you enjoy what you share with your partner or long for more depth and feeling, or whether you experience difficulties or hardship in your relationship or marriage, the direct route to more love will be through the heart.

Your heart will always facilitate more love. It is a process that lies outside the domain of the mind/brain. While mind/brain and thoughts can always help, it has been known for a long time that all matters of love belong to the heart. It is up to you now to reclaim the complete love territory that the heart opens to you and all the heart wants to give to you, and give through you to your loved ones and to everyone.

Chapter 4

Friends - Rich at Heart

Friendship is the golden thread that ties the hearts of all the world.
John Evelyn

There is something very special to friendship. Some of the most precious and enjoyable moments in life can be with a dear friend. Often this specialness comes simply from being able to share these moments with somebody close, a dear friend. When your life is filled with trusting, caring and joy-giving friends, you truly are 'rich at heart'.

Very likely you have experienced that friendship can incredibly enhance many aspects of your life. However, like all other relationship, in friendship also lies the potential for challenge, hardship and pain.

The following section will explore some of the aspects of friendship, through the lens of the heart, including the positive, the very positive, and the challenging ones. You will also find examples, stories and discussions about how more heart can enhance current friendships as well as help you develop new ones.

When things flow

When things flow, friendship is often associated with support, advice, emotional or practical help, companionship, care and even positive challenge. There are many forms of friendship. There may also be a wide range of very different friendships that you may have with a wide range of individual friends. Some are similar in character, some very different. Some people have similar kinds of friendships, others have a wide range of them. There is no easy formula.

When things flow, friends help you to experience life with more joy, ease and wonder. Sometimes just having company adds specialness. Often there is connection or deep and gentle care for each other. Some people feel this as a kind of love, like the love between siblings.

Friendship as foundation for connection

The positive aspects of friendship are often a vital foundation for romantic love. Therefore, for many people, friendship is an important part of the relationship with their partner.

There is a lightness, ease and joyfulness in being friends with someone. This gives 'friendship' a unique role in life.

It can equally be a foundation for the changing relationship that children have with their parents and vice-versa, and also for the often talked about team spirit at work or in sporting and social activities.

Friendship can also strongly underpin and support relationships with family members, adding that special 'extra' to an already deep and loving connection. In the children section are stories by children who talk about this growing friendship with parents and who describe it as something very positive. However, when the family connections and love-sharing within the family have not been so positive or have ended completely, then friendship can offer another unique and wonderful avenue to live these wonderful qualities. As shared by one of the heart friends in Hobart, what you will find, with an opening heart, is that any friendship, or any connection with another, can reach an immensely special and wonderful depth:

The help I have had is that I feel I can rely on my heart to find love and strength. It is always there even when other sources of love are elusive.

Timelessness of heart connections

The depth of a friendship does not necessarily depend on how long someone has been in your life. Deep friendships can form quickly, and in some aspect friendships are not bound by time. This may be also related to the ability of your heart - whose nature is unlimited - to instantly feel and enjoy a deep connection.

Of course, growth of friendship requires time. Getting to know each other and forming trust are two examples. However, ultimately it is how you feel, how connected you are, and how mutual and mature your friendship is that will be the measure of its depth, rather than how long you have known each other.

The part that feels this depth is your heart. It may also feel, in a non-logical, non-brain way, that there is a deeper connection with friends you may have known for a shorter amount of time than others. This is normal, as every connection you have, both within and outside your family, is unique and has its own character, depth of connection, and depth of feeling and love.

It is good to know this and to accept that every friendship is unique and special.

The logic of our mind/brain may believe that friendships with similar length, characteristics and quality should be similar, if not identical. This may create tension within you and within a friendship. You can gradually realise, with more heart-awareness, that in every single friend connection is uniqueness and depth and quality of friendship are not necessarily bound by time. You can feel closer to some friends in a shorten time than it took you to befriend someone else in the same way, and yet both can be dear to you, your heart.

You can learn different things from different friends. Friendship, like everything else in life, also contains many lessons to learn. With the help of an opening, fully active heart, this learning will hopefully be a growing experience of joyful, wonderful and loving sharing and being together as your heart is helping the friendship and guiding you.

Your heart's role in friendship

A friend is someone who goes to take your hand ...
but touches your heart. Anonymous

The heart plays a key role in whatever kind of friendships you have. If you have been with one or several friends for some time you are very likely to have experienced times of upset, hurt or other experiences that may still hang around and burden you in some way. Very likely, you will want to remove any of these underlying emotions, resentments or hurt feelings.

Your heart can help you to find new friends, deepen existing friendships and find the right way to be with friends for it to be just right for both of you. This includes helping you to feel how to interact with the friend and how close to become to the friend.

With a glowing and opening heart existing, new friends will be attracted to you and deeply enjoy your company. You may have experienced that at parties the people who are the lightest, who are genuinely joyful and radiate calmness, happiness and love, are those we are attracted to. Their hearts are light, beautiful, open. You may know or find out that these people are often genuinely good people too, and in this way they are looking after their heart.

There is the other end of the spectrum too, which is when your own heart is heavy, burdened or even closed. With limiting layers of 'collection' accumulated around the heart, it will likely be harder in social situations to engage and connect meaningfully with people. Without being light, joyful and free, you may find it almost impossible to make new friends, or even to connect with old friends.

In relation to your friends, opening your heart and growing heartfulness will naturally, gradually and gently make you:

- A more supportive friend;
- A gentler person to be with; and
- A kinder person to talk to, hang out with, to interact with.

More heart will also naturally allow you to:

- Listen with genuine, heartfelt intent, care and patience;
- Be a friend to others with more authentic interest in them and who they are; and
- Offer more understanding, love and genuine support.

As your heart brings these qualities to the surface more and more, your friends will, over time, begin to immensely value you and your presence and support. In turn, these friends will grow to become wonderful supports and companions for you.

As your heart becomes lighter and brighter it will also allow the aspects of friendship that you and your friends appreciate the most to come to the surface and shine even more. These may include a light, joyful connection, laugher and joy together, and genuinely deep and supportive conversations. Or it may simply be just being in each other's space - whether in person or by phone - while showing love, care and attention to each other's issues or problems.

The connector in friendship

Rich at heart.

There are qualities that support friendship and help it to grow. They are also often the ones that make friendship stagnate, pull it backwards, make it a challenge and make you feel stuck.

There is the nature of friendship you have with every one of your friends. This quality is about the depth, trust, care, enjoyment you share and about things you have common and more. This between you and your friend.

There is also your ability, your qualities within that support your friendship. This is similar, it is about the depth of connection you feel and the depth and clarity of trust, care and enjoyment you feel. There are the things you have common that you connect with and enjoy or like sharing or discussing. There are also the things you don't share, don't appreciated so much or you don't like. It is here, that the ability to let be, tolerance, and unconditional positive regard of the other within you are at play. To illustrate the heart's help easier, this is within you, these qualities and abilities within you support your friendships.

These in between and within qualities are of course connected. The heart plays a direct connecting role in both instances.

The 'in between' qualities are directly influence by your heart. The lighter and freer your own heart is, the more you will feel the full breath of qualities that uniquely connect you with every one of your friends. That joy will naturally flow into every interaction you have. All that you feel within this clarify of your heart, will not only flow into the relationship, it will also be feel-able, even if in lesser intensity and clarity, by your friend.

The 'within' qualities are what really makes friendship such a treasure and joy. The more you already use your heart, the more you have used the suggested exercises in this book, or the online program, the more you will feel the full depth, nature, joy and companionship you share.

The connector between you and your friend or friends is both: your mind/brain and heart. You will also enjoy friendship, where the mind and brain are engaged or stimulated. You many also select friends from certain groups, location, social or interest-groups. The mind/brain is then often a dominant player. By now you know, or equally feel, that the heart qualities are

I hope that the examples, stories and details of how you can let your heart help you with your friendships will benefits you as a person and all your friendships.

The explorations in the next sections may also bring to the surface things within you that limited you being a good friend, including attitudes, behaviours, personality or character traits. This is hopefully a good thing, as we all learn, realise and growth, also in friendship.

If you find yourself in a difficult friendship situation, for example having been hurt or been used with few or no friends, your heart will offer its unique and often instantly change-creating assistance.

You may even recognise some of these not-so-nice friendship aspects or challenges from your past. Whatever the joy or difficulty in your friendship situation is, in letting your heart help you, in using your heart, you can make a step forward.

Strengthening your heart over time, you will build a deep and very solid foundation within for all existing friendships. The degree of beautiful, joy and care then become limitless.

Improved connection ability also means that a strong and clear heart can help to bring new friends into your life. It is often equally an energy, attraction, a feeling or inner knowing that determines who you become friends.

Whatever your friendship situation is, ultimately even one strong and clear heart in the connection, will be an asset to 'stand' on, to rely on and to help in any of your friendship matters.

Friendship characteristics

What friendship may offer ...

What do most of us appreciated about friendship? Some of these positive or wonderful qualities are:

- Companionship - being able to share and enjoy experiences with someone close;
- Choice - there is a sense of choice, and we choose people we like to spend time with;
- Care - friends want to there, chose to be there, and care; they feel with us, they show compassion, they care;
- Warmth and love - friends are just there, in person, in thought or in spirit. Their friendship can include heart-warming hugs, care, love and assurance;
- Freedom - you can be ourselves around them;
- Stimulation - friends help us to grow, help our self-esteem, can help us to be more healthy, and can support us with daring new choices or steps;
- Challenge - friends help us to grow in challenging choices, positions, plans or actions;
- Support - friends can be generous in their support, have our best interest at heart;
- Light - when things seem or are the worst, they are there, be a guiding light, or motivate;
- Listen - they ask 'how are you?' and give their time to listen;
- Patience - friends can be patient, giving us the time we need to work things out, plan or do; and
- Trust, faith - in trusting or having faith in us, another level of support, care and unconditional positive regard can grow. This can be a wonderful, helpful and life-assuring foundation - overall or in times of crisis.

The list is longer. The positive aspects or depth of friendship naturally varies. For some, friendship can be deeper at times than the bonds of family, and the level of support felt from friends even more than that of their romantic partner. In any case, friendship is another gift available instead of family, romance or in addition too, to make life a special journey.

A very close friend

Friends already see you as the person you long in your heart to be.
Anonymous

There is a level of depth and love that friends, clients and family have shared with myself or my family. One of the most magical aspects of my own heart journey and learning has been the growth in terms of breath and depth of friendships; including the development of close, very close and immensely valued friendships. What the qualities that can friendship and even greater depth?

There are perhaps some key characteristics of friendship that stand out from the above discussion. These are that a good, supportive, nurturing friendship …

- Is more positive than any other human connection experienced;
- Is supportive of whatever your needs, issues or challenges are;
- Is full of care and love;
- Is characterised by helping each other, giving and sharing;
- Has a nurturing lightness or ease about it;
- Involves interactions that flow freely; and
- Makes you feel confirmed, supported and nurtured for who you feel you really are.

All these positive qualities are supported by your heart's very nature. The more you connect to your heart, learn and understand about it, and as you live with more heart in your daily life, the heart will naturally support these qualities in your friendships.

The highs and lows of friendship

As in all connections or relationships there are challenges and there is the possibility of intentionally or unintentionally hurting or upsetting the other.

Not all friendships flow well or are supportive or enjoyable all of the time. It is just as normal in friendships as it is in all other relationships that doubts, challenges, and feelings of lack of enjoyment or support surface. Friendship, what we believe friendship is or should be, becomes out of balance. It becomes an obligation or is even experienced as one of the hardships, challenges or pains experienced at some time in one's life.

When all is 'good' with your best buddies or dearest friends, then you know you are deeply at peace and it feels right. When things are not so good, then friends can be the cause of hurt, emotions and painful exchanges, and of hardship, challenge and at times even deeply upsetting experiences.

What are some of these other experiences or qualities that friendships can bring about? The next sections discuss some of these and how the heart, both generally and specifically, can assist, support, gently change and improve these wonderful connections.

Emotions and friends

It is normal that in friendship you will be exposed to two kinds of emotions: your own and those of your friend. When emotions surface in a friendship they can strain it and cause feelings of pressure around your heart. Like in all other aspects of your life, it is important to first be mindful and heartful as to how emotions influence your friendships. Then, as a further step, you should let the heart do its natural function in helping, clearing, supporting and beautifying your friendship.

In friendship emotions can be hidden in behaviours that may appear common or normal. For example, if an aspect of your friendship, like competitive play, is taken too far, emotions can surface. Over time, these will negatively impact on your friendships.

Whatever the individual situation or case is, you or your friends will not be happy or at peace with experiences of emotion in your connection and sharing that are 'too much' or 'too frequent'.

The interference of emotion in your friendship may be at the level of conscious awareness or may be happening at less aware levels. At one level, your growing attention to your heart and regular heart strengthening and heart exercise will dissolve some of these emotion-patterns. At another level, it is good to be aware of what is happening. This will help you work actively with any emotional patterns, in particular your own, as well as use your heart to improve your friendships and find growing help and growing joy in your close and wider circles of friends.

For example, imagine you are aware that you are holding some resentment towards a friend. If this is not resolved then it may lead to more or less conscious exclusion, pulling back, or withdrawing from the friendship. It may also lead to you reacting and acting with the emotion still stuck inside around your heart, which again is not helping the positive growth of your friendship.

In this instance, as you know, your heart offers another avenue to help. This is something you can do non-verbally without necessarily having to 'raise an issue' with your friend or discussing a part of you that is upset or hurt, if that does not feel right to do. If the emotions are cleared through the heart, properly, they should be completely cleansed. This means that they will not linger, lie under some surface cover, or rise again to cause more hurt or damage in the future.

Any learned communication and non-verbal abilities in your friendship - including abilities that are heart based - will 'energetically' support all your interactions. Without having to raise issues, past and recent disturbances will be resolved gently. As more and more heart enters your life and your friendships it will simply deepen the specialness of what you share already.

The emotions in friendship can somewhat differ from your other relationships. While there is a certain range of negative emotions, some surface more in friendship than others. You may have experienced some of these or slight variations of them. You may have also experienced how it does not feel so nice when they dominate aspects of your friendship or when they are more important than the gentler, more connecting and supporting qualities.

Emotional awareness

In friendship there is an almost infinite range of ways of sharing and activities that you can enjoy. Equally these things can also trigger or produce emotions that, instantly or over time, will limit this special sharing.

Here are some examples of some more friendship specific activity patterns that may assist you to be aware of emotions, and to let the heart help you to become more and more emotionally 'mature' and free. The examples also point to possible emotion-triggering situations and emotional traps in the wider range of activities that you share with your friends.

Competition

Competition is a little unusual. You may say 'what is good about competition' or 'what is not good about competitiveness' or 'a bit of competition will be helpful' or similar statements. Yes, in some ways, for example when focussed on a game of tennis or chess, some competition can be good, even enjoyable. If in games, sport or any part your life the bond you share as friends is not equally nurtured by heart qualities, such as enjoyment, then the harder edge of competitiveness will likely trigger emotions such as jealousy, envy or anger. This will impact negatively on your friendship.

Therefore, the quality of a friendship and nice feelings that result are reduced when there is a high level of competition between you and your friend.

While the source of this competitiveness may be just one or both of you wanting to be better at something, when this competitiveness is stronger than the bond of sharing, joy and love then the friendship tends to not feel so nice anymore.

The moment your heart becomes clearly present in your life, any competitiveness will be balanced and will not exceed something that is enjoyable, playful and helpful.

The mind and brain are also helpful here. They can help you be aware of your competitive behaviours and where they are supporting you and others around you, and where not. They can also help you make conscious changes in the direction of new behaviours.

Jealousy or envy

Jealously and envy are two emotions that can easily surface in friendship.

A simple example may be that your friend is doing better at something such as work, sport or even at socialising. In this instance, jealousy or envy is easier to detect and to be aware of and you can do something about it.

Another example is when your friend has another friend and seems to like that person more, spends more time with them, or is simply closer, more joyful, lighter with that other friend.

The trickier situations in which jealousy or envy can surface are when the other person does something that may be seen by some as 'ok' or 'natural'. For example, you and your friend go out together, with the intention of having a good time. Your friend meets some of your other friends and flirts quite a bit. Some of this flirting may be with the current, a former partner of yours or someone close to you. It may be seen by many as 'ok' or 'normal' to react, and to be jealous, upset or even angry. When from the perspective of the heart it is solely a negative emotion, that will burden your own heart and will burden the friendship too.

What is happening in this instance is two-fold. First, any kind of negative emotion you react with will never be pleasantly experienced by a friend, and so reacting in jealously or anger may cause the friend to distance him or herself more. Second, the surfacing of jealousy or envy will place negativities around or in your heart. The damage will be deeper and more long-term if you follow the emotion.

The better choice when you feel jealousy or envy surfacing is to attend to your heart. You can begin by feeling your heart, and then do heart strengthening in whatever way it is possible - even in the actual situation - to let the heart help you to let it go. You should also follow your heart in whether you should talk to your friend about the matter later. However, bear in mind that it is often not the best to talk to someone while you are experiencing emotion, that is, when you are 'in' the emotion. An 'ok' choice also is to spend less time with any friends who behave in ways that do not feel so nice to you opening and being increasingly 'aware' of or feeling your heart.

Anger

Anything relating to anger can be looked at in the same way as jealousy and envy. In relation to the heart anger can be experienced strong or stronger than other emotions. In other situations anger is more common, more at the surface, and therefore can be triggered easily.

Again, from the perspective of the heart, and in terms of becoming a 'heart-grown up individual', anger is also easy to look at and to reflect upon. You can be angry about someone, something, or your friend. Yet, with anger, it seems often also easier to see than with other emotions, that it is the 'emotion that I have'. If you can view anger, and any other negative emotion, in this light, then the next logical step is to take responsibility for it too. You can realise that any emotion that you experience is somehow finding an anchor-ground within. With this realisation, together with knowledge and experience that the heart can help to clear whatever externally thrown anchors touch, you can be on your way and let your heart clear all that is not joyful sharing or being together.

When, in your inactions with your friends, competition is only one small flower that grows in the garden of a pure, opening and glowing heart, then no matter how competitive you are, it is truly then only a game, a joy you share. Whether you win or lose brings equal joy to what you share.

The critical friend

Being critical, assessing, and judging others is largely - if not solely - the functions of our mind/brain. Criticism and judgment are usually based on our ideas and concepts of friendship and the past experiences we hold. The 'critical friend' may be someone that has as a life principle something similar to 'let me be critical of everything and see how the world and others respond'.

Why is someone overly critical? There may be a wide range of reasons, such as wanting to help or give advice. However, at some level it seems to be a form of taking comfort in, or retreating into, the world of the mind/brain. Linked with this appears to be an illusion, or partial experience, that being in the mind/brain is safer than to be in, to feel, and to be open at the level of the heart.

In some way, if it is your friend, this is not too important. The more you realise about your own heart quality and ability, the more you will use it and live with more heart. This in turn will cause others around you to be more relaxed and at peace, and within this process their mind/brain will naturally become more calm. This is also a chance for the friend to feel more and to let go of some of the mind/brain's over-activity and need for control.

Be careful not to judge your friendship or your friend too quickly. Whether it is your friendship or the friendship between people you know, there may be a 'perfect balance' for them but not for you looking inside from outside. Life is about learning and often in friendship the reasons for being together exist at deeper levels, with learning occurring at a range of levels not visible to the eye and not perceivable by rational thought.

Whatever the situation, if you are being a bit too critical at times of your friend, you will find the next PHT offers an enjoyable exercise to change your own approach towards others. While you may explore and do this in a friendship, it can also work really well at work or in other life situations.

Practical Heart Tip 38: Whole-hearted support team

The 'whole-hearted support team' exercise is you just being heartful and supportive for a set period of time in your friendship or connection with others.

Decide who is part of your 'whole-hearted support team'. It may be just you and one friend, or you and several friends. You can also do this just on your own, not sharing it with your friend(s), or you can discuss it with your friend and agree to do it. How to 'do' it:

- *Every time you have contact or you are together, commit to being in your heart, feeling your heart and be only supportive, encouraging, helpful, kind, caring and loving. Everyone on the team must commit to this; and*

- *If you feel to, enter a few lines in your Heart Diary to monitor how you feel, how you respond, learn and experience the friendship in a new way. Make lesser note of how the other responds.*

You may notice or realise as you embark on this that it is really more about 'being' it than 'doing' it. The doing parts are getting less. They are also less important in friendship. What matters more are the heart-qualities such as care, love, joyful sharing and support that is being felt.

Note: when you are in your heart, your mind/brain naturally being present too, you will of course feel and know when the whole-hearted support is less or not appropriate. Consider stopping this PHT if you feel uncomfortable or feel pressure in your heart.

It is normal to fall back into non-supportive patterns. This is okay, just acknowledge it - with a smile - and return to the exercise.

You can also do this exercise with a family member, your partner or someone at work. Also, if you have realised that the critical, less supportive patterns are strong in you - which could be in relation to one particular person or a group of persons - then you can do this on your own for a set period of time.

Combine this PHT with regular Heart Strengthening (KHH 6) or other direct heart strengthening exercises to give depth to your interactions, to your times when you are with someone.

Your heart will always invite you to find and remain within a place where others' critical comments or actions are of little or no influence on how you feel. This applies both in general and in being with particular friends.

Even if a friend of yours is more critical at times than is comfortable or helpful, the friendship is still there, purposeful, and has other special qualities.

With growing self-reflection and heart awareness you will also find that the above PHT is not always right to do or to continue in all situations. At times you will be in a situation with your friend where you need to be 'critical'. This may be more so a time of sharing what you feel to share, speaking your truth and speaking it from the heart.

An example may be where an employee or colleague of yours has stepped out of line, does not follow the correct procedures or does not do the right thing by a customer or client. Timely interventions and discussion is needed, not whole-hearted support. In fact, you want to whole-heartedly support this person still, while discussing the right actions or behaviours.

The above PHT will certainly offer you one way not only to know it is good to be supportive in friendship, but also to trial it more, with more vigour and with more heart.

Past regrets

Clients and friends have often shared that in relationship to friends, they wish 'they would have', meaning that they did things they now regret with the benefit of looking back or having grown more in heart awareness and in general.

Some of the regrets that can surface around friends have been:

- I hurt someone or I was hurt, despite the love and care felt;
- I lost a friend, maybe by being slack in staying in touch, and now miss them;
- I should have stayed in touch but lost sight of how important that friend really was;
- I acted in ways towards a friend, often in an emotional way, and it made the friend pull back or not want to be in touch anymore; or
- I walked away from a friendship and regret that I did.

Walking away

Walking away from a friend is often one of the biggest regrets as life goes on. Walking away can be active or passive.

In some situations, you may walk away from a friend because of actions by that person that clearly were unacceptable or hurtful. In these cases the choice to walk away was more active.

Walking away may also be less conscious and more passive. During some phases of our life, we become busy with work, family or other friends and staying in contact with friends is not so easy. Time and people slip away and sometimes good friendships do, too.

When our behaviour or that of a friend's creates distances, it does not feel nice, as there will be qualities to this behaviour that undermine the wonderful and positive aspects and qualities of an overall positive friendship discussed earlier.

Practical Heart Tip 39: Healing friendships through your heart *

To heal past regrets and to avoid new ones, try the following:

When you are with your friend or when you interact - whether on the phone, by sms, e-mail or on social media - allow yourself to follow your heart and be in your heart all the time. Add KHH 7 to this PHT to make it more effective.

In this way you and your heart will naturally enrich your experience and to a lesser extent that of your friend(s). As times goes on friendships will automatically become lighter and freer, and all the positive qualities of friendship will be brought to the surface.

In friendship, as in all relationships that you have, when you follow emotions and not your heart, it will challenge and stretch the friendship you share and over time erode this connection. It is important to look at some of these emotions first before the heart help is illustrated more.

Royal Treatment

Friends are special, very special. Treating your friend like royalty is an approach or concept that can be helpful in some way. It is particularly helpful when you combine it with clarity from the heart and the wonderful, free and guiding feelings from your heart.

The 'royal treatment' then means that in your heart you hold the highest respect and purest feelings for your friends, while emotions are also less likely being followed. In real life action you feel what is the right way of being in touch, seeing each other, doing things together etc. By following this approach, you may see much less of some friends, 'temporarily pause' seeing other friends to see more of other friends etc. However, the process is natural and directed from your heart.

Treating your friends as special also means that you take care of your emotions. The deep respect, love, care and positivity with which you may want to meet and encounter your friends will be directly connected and dependent on your own heart clarity and openness.

The heart or royal treatment does not mean that you always obey or do what your friend wants you to do. At the very least it will balance situations and interactions where 'familiarity breeds contempt'. Critical reflection and heart feeling are supposed to work together. One way is to see yourself as a personal, close or intimate advisor and friend; and at a deepest inner, heart level you know or feel that you are equal to your friend, and perhaps to anyone.

Stepping out of line

What does stepping out of line in friendship mean? You are close and you trust each other, which really means that your friend trusts you and, even without intending to do so, you or your friend may step out of line by saying or doing the wrong thing to you or others. This can also be in the form of not doing something that is normal or that you or your friend 'rightly' or 'wrongly' expects. Of course, it is good or ideal to have no expectations in friendships. In reality, however, it seems that this is simply an 'ideal' and that expectations are real and present in most relationships.

Stepping out of line can also occur at a subtler level. You or a friend feel that the way you were approached, treated, spoken too, etc. was not with the more heart-governed qualities such as genuine or felt kindness, respect or care.

Stepping out of line may be small or major, and has the potential to cause some surprises, disturbances, upset or hurt to you or the friend.

Stepping out of line may be just between you and one of your friends. Stepping out of line may also be that you or your friend treat a third person, close to you or not known to you at all, in ways that do not seem to be acceptable, 'right' or heartful.

A step out of line can lead to a sense or feeling that the friendship is out of balance, perhaps in the way that this interaction or something 'is not right'. There can also be a range of more or less clear emotion surfacing such as disappointment, embarrassment, sadness or anger.

If the stepping out of line was by your friend, then there perhaps also was an expectation that this should not happen or should not happen with this particular friend. If it is you who overstepped the line, then you may be disappointed in yourself or embarrassed and you may have subsequent burdensome thoughts. In either case there can be emotion, heaviness and a burdensome feeling when you think of that friend or when you are in the presence of each other.

From the perspective of the heart none of these negative thoughts or emotions are helpful in any way. You may choose, in either case, to discuss this with your friend or, with the help of your heart, to let it go and surrender it. In the same way as in the earlier example, the better choice would be to attend to your heart, to use your heart in the situation, or as soon as you can afterwards, and to do some form of heart strengthening.

Using or being used

Using a friend or being used by a friend can be subtle or more obvious in nature. The initial impulse or reason for you to be friends can be as varied as the reason for meeting, getting together and staying together as friends.

Within these reasons can be unhealthy aspects of a friendship, such as your friend having a status you do not have and you wanting to borrow or be attached to this 'status', or vice versa.

Using may also occur as part of the inner wish for flattery. The part of us that is less confident or has lower self-esteem may steer or set up a conversation with a friend in such a way that it is giving us the comments that we need to function as some form of compensation or uplifting. One is used to fill an emptiness in the other.

Being used, from the perspective of the heart is, when logic mind-driven interactions, and the desire for some kind of transaction or exchange, have more room or dominate in friendship compared to all the qualities that the heart feels, nurtures and longs for.

This lack of heart connection is often more obvious when being used by a friend, because it never feels nice nor 'right'. The clearer this becomes, the more emotions are likely to surface similar to in the above examples: disappointment, disillusionment, upset, sadness or anger.

Any of these behaviours do not feel so nice when we are within such patterns. What is interesting is that the more you are heart-strong and heart-aware, it will not feel right to your heart whether you are the one being such a friend or whether a friend is using you in this way. The moment you are more heart-aware and use your heart more, those friendship-draining qualities - often based on unfulfilled needs or emotional reactivity - will be naturally reduced in you.

The further wonderful aspect of the heart is that you will also feel this with more clarity as you use your heart more. If you have such tendencies in you, the very heart-strength and clarity you gain, following the KHHs or heart practices, will make you less needy or wanting such forms of attention as they are not naturally existing and the beautiful feelings from your heart will tend to override them.

Friendship out of balance

The heart wants to share and in sharing there is always a level of care and balance. Each of these balances are unique. In some way it should never be up to any of us to judge the friendship of others, even our own. As long as it feels right and there is overall a positive attitude by all involved and equally positive behaviours the friendship is okay. In some cases, it may feel nice to be friends and to meet or hang out often, whereas in other cases it may feel nice or just right to meet only occasionally or even to just be friends but not to meet up.

However, as in all relationships, sometimes between friends a degree of imbalance can occur when the times you spend together - or the whole friendship - does not seem or feel right anymore. What are some of these situations where there is a more than comfortable sense of imbalance?

- One situation is where one of the friends feels less pull, less inclination, to have an active friendship.

- Another situation is when there have been past events in which emotion was acted out in the friendship. This could be anger, jealousy, irritation, or any other emotion. In particular, if one or both of you have a tendency to let emotions surface and to act them out, then the friendship can become burdened over time. This also means that the heart gets burdened and the love, care and enjoyment you feel in each other's company is significantly less. Those nice feelings will always be the same or even deepens, however, under a lot of rubble of emotions and deposited negativities. It will be hard to feel them.

- A further example is that one or some of your friends may ask too much, have a high degree of neediness, or want help or support from you often or too often. This may leave you drained, exhausted or even feeling used.

- On a flip-side to the above example, if you are a 'giver' (someone who feels they give too much all of the time) then the friendship may also feel draining or burdensome. Your giving may be in the way of time, listening, being caring or caring in action by helping your friend with projects or emotional difficulties. It may also be giving in a material way, such as giving gifts, money, items, etc.

- Yet another situation may occur, in particular as you start to attend to your heart and your heart becomes lighter, more open and you start to feel more. You will then enjoy more the feeling of being together, the non-verbal communication, interaction and sharing that will surface more and more in you. In the same way you will also feel the hardness, heaviness and even harshness when there is too much exchange or sharing that is dominated by the mind/brain. In some way you may feel less attracted to be in that energy. Over-active minds/brains are never associated with relaxation, joy and joyful being together, and even less with inner peace, compassion and love, all of which are vital ingredients in supporting connection with friends and dear ones.

It is natural that new people come into our lives and for us to spend more time with them and spend less time with others who had a larger role to play in the past. Some of this may also happen naturally as you move to other town, state or even country.

However natural or less natural any of the above 'imbalances' may be in any of your friendships, you are likely to find two energies or qualities within: one of holding on and one of letting go.

The quality that wants to hold on has the tendency to attach to a friend or a friendship situation, even if it feels unnatural or hard to do. For example, you may try and maintain the friendship even when it has grown apart, become out of balance, or despite there being more and more emotion or un-relaxing mind/brain dominance.

The other quality of letting go is about being in your heart, being at peace and knowing that either this one friendship will be 'ok', live on, or even grow or that new friends will always come into your life.

All this will become more evident, clear and feelable as your heart is growing lighter and stronger. The heart does not know 'concern', 'attachment' or concepts of how to 'do' friendship. It will simply and immediately support you, give you clarity and give you freedom to act in ways so that you can be in an immediate and active friendship, even if you rarely meet with the friend. It can also give you the freedom to let go of a friendship where the time of purposeful and joyful sharing naturally has come to an end.

Feeling excluded

A sense of not being included to the extent that it feels or seems 'right' may also be an aspect of one of your friendships. It is natural that other people are involved in your life or in the life of your friend. New friends also enter the scene and the friendship you share.

Some form of 'feeling excluded' may also just happen naturally, as you grow apart by distance, or in your interests, and one of you perceives or experiences this as unnatural or hurtful. Whether you seem to have less to share, less to talk about or whether there is less of a pull to spend time together, when someone feels excluded there is something else at play. Often one person feels the pull to spend time together or be in the friendship more than the other. When you are the one who feels less urge to be in touch and maintain the friendship, then this drifting apart tends to be easier. However, when you value or want to maintain the friendship more than your friend does, then it can be more hurtful or upsetting.

In any case, there may be a feeling, in some situations, that you feel excluded. In fact, you know by now that this is not a 'feeling', but rather it is an 'emotion'. When in the natural flow of the heart and your heart is strong, there is just joy for the time you share, as well as joy in many other moments in your life with or without this friend.

It is time to let the heart help you to let go, be free at a deeper, inner heart-level and to enjoy every moment of your life more.

Every moment that you include your heart, strengthen your heart more and invest more into your heart you will be taken there, step by step, and without a doubt.

In the case of feeling excluded, the heart's helping hand in achieving greater inner freedom is easy to illustrate. Having an emotional response to a sense of being excluded is only possible when there is a connecting part in you in your heart - such as an 'impurity', a receptor, or part of the collection of emotion-related burdens or negativities - that respond to this sense. If the heart is open, clear, light and therefore free, all you feel is the wonder and joy of the friendships you are in now and whatever shape and form they take. It is magically wonderful how, in particular in friendship, the joy of being alive and to be able to share this aliveness in free and unconditional ways with others is a gift beyond gifts.

Few or no friends

Beauty is not in the face; beauty is a light in the heart. Kahlil Gibran

You may not be in the situation of having to decide which friendships to nurture and which to seek some distance from or even stop. You may feel that you have very few friends or no friends at all. This aspect may also find expression in your life in feeling that you have the 'wrong' friends. There is, of course, no one wrong in our lives.

It is more likely that the situation that the choice of your heart, and how close a friend naturally ought to be in your life, is very different from that of logic or your mind/brain's calculations or ideas.

Friends, like family members or a partner, come naturally in our lives or through some form of effort. However, at the moment you might not have many friends. You can try to go out more, be more outgoing and even try make others like you. There are different levels of effort, and the right amount of effort is certainly okay and even helpful. Effort may include not sitting at home but going out, including to places where you are not entirely comfortable. For example, you might go to a social get together where you know few or no people there, and have few or no friends to lean on. These and many more can be situations where a gentle effort is helpful and very likely to be supportive of the development of more friendships.

Effort alone, however, will not directly lead to warm, joyful and nurturing friendships. If your social contacts are purely based on effort then the logical next question is how real, authentic, how genuine and truthful will that friendship be? In contrast, when you also use your heart, those qualities, as well as enjoyment and meaning, will be naturally present.

In your heart you perhaps already feel that making others do something they do not want or feel to do is not the best. Let this book and the sharing from others in the book be an invitation to use your heart more, in everything that you do. By doing the simple and natural heart practices suggested you will - like many others - feel the gentle changes. You will also progress to a strong and clear heart.

When you are in a low or no friend situation your mind and emotions will only ever feed you one set of information. For example, the mind/brain will say 'I have no friends' and your emotions 'no one likes me',.

Your heart has a much bigger picture: in some way your heart already recognises 'friendship' in people around you with whom you are not friends; however, this friendship has not yet manifested because either one or both of you don't feel it.

To be friends with someone you and your friend need to feel it; then it will be true friendship, not the pragmatic version of it. The truer friendship is the one that will help you through thick and thin, the good and the challenging bits of life. Life will be easier and more enjoyable, which is one of the goals of many people in life.

Attend to your heart and, as your heart opens and shines more, you, at the core of who you are, will become more beautiful and attractive. When this happens it is very common that equally beautiful friends come into your life. Often this happens miraculously and effortlessly.

Lack of support and love

Friendship is essentially about love. You like, adore or love your friends. You enjoy time together or you just enjoy knowing that your friend is there if needed. There is also mutual support and encouragement that can be given and received with or without words.

Things can happen or be said in a friendship that is unpleasant, even hurtful at times. When this happens regularly or when there is more negative energy or heavy sharing than you, your heart, mind or emotional world are comfortable with, you will naturally seek distance. This may happen to you as the receiver of the negative behaviour, or equally you may the person who, in reflection, is behaving in this way towards a friend. This behaviour may involve too much arguing, disputing or too many differences in opinion. These are all children of the mind and brain and they tend to stretch the bond of friendship and love. They lead to a gradual drifting apart.

Breach of trust

At the other end of the friendship continuum are perhaps a breach of trust. The list of above challenges or any other friendship-related issues may lead to a sense that the trust you shared has been damaged or broken. These experiences may have a wide range of intensity or heaviness.

Breach of trust usually occurs when behaviours towards oneself of others are not really acceptable or when displays or expressions of the not-so-nice, not-so-helpful emotions happen. Often these are related to unkind, uncaring, unfriendly words, gestures or actions and the misuse of trusted, confidential information or secrets.

Any of these can deeply rock the foundation of a friendship. A strong heart is able to weather these kind of storms. It is also essential here to help you to make heartfelt and clear decisions. Sometimes stepping away from the friendship and gaining this heart clarity is important.

The heart always keeps a door open or a special place for friends like these within for healing, growth and re-connection at a new level of understanding.

Even heavier for you are when friends talk behind your back or gossip, rumours, or lies about you. When a friend intentionally or carelessly hurts you, bullies you or puts you down, then the wounds left can be deep, trust is broken, and it can take long to heal and for trust to be strong again.

The pain can be very deep and also deeply felt when there has been a breach of trust. The instant reaction may be to cut ties, to break it all off. These instant reactions are rarely heart-decisions. Regardless what the situation may be, no one is perfect and almost everyone has breached someone's trust before, perhaps even you?

If there has been a 'breach of trust' then your heart will help you to heal any wounds that were created or it will help you to make better choices; or both. It will further help you to freely and joyfully be in the friendship again if that is the heart's or mind's choice or to move on. In fact, if you choose your heart and its abilities, then any existing or future friendships have the potential to be even deeper and sweeter.

To end or not to end a friendship

If you are looking for a friend who is faultless, you will be friendless. Rumi

Reading over the possible challenges that a friendship may bring, there are many situations where you may think about the decision to walk away from a friend and to end a friendship. Perhaps you were in the past, or are now, in a position where these thoughts come up.

Yes, at times these are the right turns and it is natural to move on with life, to move forward, and to form new friendships. This moving may happen naturally; time, space, and making other friends naturally lead to a phasing out of a friendship. There may also be the thoughts, concerns and challenges of actively deciding to do so, including whether or not to tell your friend.

All too often in life our heart's ability to connect, to love a wider circle of family and friends, is not acknowledged. We are swept off our feet by life's fullness, busyness and distractions. A friendship which we treasure or enjoy can disappear if we hastily decide to end it.

It is easy to be so caught up in your own life, over-looking your key heart connections, and most importantly not feeling deeply enough and letting go of golden, valuable and dear friendships over the years. Without the heart, or with a life full of mind/brain moments, you may not realise deeply enough the full enjoyments, benefits and value of a dear friend.

Every friend, every heart connection, offers a deep and unique opportunity to learn and share together. This, in some way, can been seen reflected in many internet sites popping that help people to look for old friends. This seems to be because hearts want to reconnect. Getting older, approaching the end of life, often it is easier to let go of all physical things; the heart however misses dear family members and dear friends.

Coming back to the question of whether to end a friendship or not, let us look at the heart's function and role in this context. Firstly, there may be an urge to decide, to do something. You can start by feeling your heart and ask 'is there a need to act now'? Let your decide or help. There is a risk, even a tendency, especially when not-so-pleasant things have happened, that any decision is not from your heart. This also means there is a lesser long-term perspective. Your heart is more inclined to show you how close you are supposed to be with which friend, as well as how often and where and how to see each other.

There are friends that nurture you and support you but also those that occasionally (or more than occasionally) challenge or even hurt you. Let your strong heart guide you as to how often you feel to meet, when to meet, where and if at all.

Here are some examples: if you have less interest in a friend now, naturally, following your heart, you may feel to meet less frequently. This may change in the future. If you feel there is lightness, joy and purposeful sharing with a friend, your heart may feel to see and meet them more often and also in more private settings, for example at your or your friend's home. If there has been a lot of emotion in your exchanges with a friend, then feel where and how you want to meet; and if at all. You may not feel to meet for some time. Naturally you wellbeing and safety and the wellbeing, growth of your heart are very important. Always feel deep to look after yourself in the best ways.

Let your heart help in deciding where to meet. If a friendship doesn't feel particularly light or if a friend is inclined to challenge, tease, upset or hurt you, the choose a venue that is public or where you can both end the get together in a light or positive way - or just walk away. Feeling with your heart where, also when, how often, will support all the different friendships you have or can have in a light and yet direct and helpful way.

For the heart, friendship is much more a continuum of closeness. This closeness and love may become less, more again, less again, more again. In a pure or light heart there is only love and care no matter what kind of friendship is unfolding.

If a friendship is really challenging or draining, then you may want to 'end the friendship', meaning you actively tell your friend it is over. This can be tricky. It is of course okay to do so. In some situations you may want to make a very clear statement of not wanting to be in contact anymore. The nature of the interactions, in particular abuse, verbal, emotional, psychological or physical violence, clearly point in this direction.

Why is it tricky? Once you end something there may be a door closing in the other person too. They may detach, at a deeper, inner level, not so much let go, but rather give up. Even though it is still possible it can be harder to reconnect. Personally, I do not end friendships any more. A friendship may end up on ice, being paused or being put 'on hold'.

In situations like this, I may say something like 'I am really not sure when there will be a chance to connect again or to spend time together' or 'I feel to give other things priority and I am not too sure when there is time and space again to meet'. Sometime I add 'I would however like to loosely stay in touch and see how things develop or change'.

This then leaves an openness in oneself and in the other for whatever to surface or re-start to be able to do so. This keeps an openness, hopefully by both hearts and minds, so that if the time comes, and the heart-feeling or friendship feeling changes, the foundation is there to connect and meet again.

For this reason, unless there is no feeling any more at all for the friend, if you somehow can, never announce a full and ultimate closure.

For your heart to sever all ties and to announce the end of a friendship is not natural. At the core of your heart, and in a clear and opening heart, there is always growing love. Your mind/brain does not know yet, or if so in quite limited ways, in what friendships and with whom you will grow, learn and profoundly enjoy life in the future.

All this talk about letting your heart help can appear in some way blurry too. To really feel with the heart and to follow the heart will take time. Until your heart awareness and the trust in your heart has developed, the following friend inventory offers a heartful living supporting tool that brings mind/brain and heart together. It also nurtures a positive and appreciative attitude towards your friends.

Practical Heart Tip 40: The friend inventory

The friend inventory will help you, together with an opening heart, to connect with all your friends and to make steps to re-connect if you, in your heart, feel to. There are two stages to it, with the first stage covering existing active friends and the second stage less active, past, lost or forgotten friends. Draw a simple table with three columns headed: 'list of friends', 'now', 'feel to/heart feels to'.

Active friends:

- *Make one list of friends that you value and who are currently in your life;*

- *In next column note down in '1-5' how much (time and quality of time) you see this person right now, regularly (rate 1-5; 1 being rarely and 5 being very regularly)*

- *In the 3rd column rate, as you feel with your heart, or simply feel and trust what you feel, how would you like to be in contact (rate 1-5; 1 being 'less than now', 2-3 'ok as is' and 4-5 'would be lovely to see more of each other/this friend')*

Passive, less active, past, lost or 'forgotten' friends:

- *Make another list of friends that come to mind who you value, may value more and who are currently not really or hardly present in your life;*

- *In the next column rate, as you feel with your heart, or simply feel and trust what you feel, how would you like to be in contact (1 being 'less than now', 2-3 'ok as is' and 4-5 'would be lovely to see more of each other/this friend')*

- *In the 3rd column rate how natural or beautiful does it feel to make an effort, to at least make contact, to re-connect again, opening the chance for a renewed friendship and seeing that person again a bit more? (1 being 'ok as is', 2-3 'a gentle effort' and 4-5 'more effort on my behalf - would be lovely to see more of each other/this friend')*

You may add a 4th column on both of these table. In this column you can make a brief note of any additional thoughts, planned actions, or actions taken in your resolve to connect more, reconnect or leave things as they are.

Find the place in your heart where you do this to open your life, your heart to the wealth of friendship and to use this 'positive' inventory to grow and strengthen your existing friendship, to renew old, slipped away or 'forgotten' friendships and to make space for new friends, too.

The friend inventory is a wonderful tool to also be grateful for the gift of friendship given and experienced. It is also brings a focus back to you, to your heart, on that inner centre where friendship is felt. The more active your heart becomes, the field of friendship naturally widen, deepens and becomes more beautiful. Any difficulties, natural in any close connection, will be short-lived, dissolved and let go of easier.

Your heart will only ever want the quality of the feeling and connection you share at heart level with every single person and friend to be fully realised and expressed in your everyday life.

Whatever effort you make to re-connect or connect more, let it be from your heart. Past or old friends may need time and many reminders such as gentle notes, SMS, emails or phone calls before they feel it in their heart too. Sometimes, your efforts will not find a fertile ground for growth in the other. When this happens, you need to let the heart help you to let go.

This is in some way one difference between friendship and relationship. When it really does not work anymore, then in a relationship you are more likely to need to decide and to make a decision to continue or end it at some point. Friendships however are more fluid, flexible and light.

Be honest with your friend, too. If you want to see less of him or her at this present time, as indicated above, with love, care and genuinely speaking the truth, say so, perhaps in ways like 'at this point in time I feel to see a little less of you', or something similar in your own words. Gentleness, softness, flexibility, kindness and openness always supports friendships and relationships. If you pull back a little, less with words and more with heart, sometimes two things are likely to happen. This is you either feel that you really miss seeing that friend, or you don't miss the person and you naturally drift apart.

When drifting naturally apart, helped by the heart, it occurs without the drama of actively ending it, without emotions burdening your or your friend's heart.

Pausing friends - friendship

The term 'temporarily pause' seeing a friend may appear a bit unusual. The relationship between your own heart and the heart of your friend is always interlinked. Pausing a friendship may be a gentler and softer alternative in comparison to ending one. The more your own heart is clearing, freeing, the more you feel the deeper and more blissful, special feelings in their truest form for everyone close around you. This includes your friends.

With an open heart you will find it near impossible to take such 'big' and 'dramatic' steps like ending a friendship. There is a high likelihood when doing this that there is a degree or even high degree of emotion and less or no heart-feeling or heart-clarity involved. Pausing a friendship will allow both of you to re-feel and to re-start your friendship at any time in the future and it will take away the risk of ever losing a friend by making dramatic and ultimate decisions.

Friendship and the ex-partner

How can friendship and an ex-partner, wife or husband work, and what is the possible role of your heart in this? I was once listening to a morning radio program and the presenters, both a male and female, were engaged in vivid discussion about should you or should you not stay friends with your ex-partner? They came to the conclusion that one should not stay in touch, but that it is better to walk away and simply get on with life. This conclusion came across as very strong, like a profound truth; perhaps this was because two people reached the same conclusion and there was a feeling, as radio presenters, that they had some kind of authority.

Perhaps this is the truth for some. The heart does not have universal truth in this way. In relation to people the book is always open, there is always the possibility for change. For example: you may not be friends with your ex-partner now, and yet in the future a beautiful friendship develops. After all, you were 'lovers' once. Lovers in the deeper sense of the word, sharing a deeply felt love for each other.

There are no doubt almost endless ideas, concepts and approaches around this topic. Following your heart here may simply mean following what feels right in every single instance and situation. Everybody's situation is different, too. One scenario may be that perhaps a deep friendship was all that was meant to be, and after you had it 'wrong' for some time you can now live this wonderful part.

When children are involved the whole scenario is instantly very different. For the young and forthright radio people, no thought was wasted on the endless range of situations and on what ultimately is needed: support, love, care and deep respect, whether you are together or not. When children are involved, there is certainly a hope that the emotional wounds cut were not too deep leading up to or during separation. Separation is often a time when emotions are more at the surface. It should, however, never be an excuse for emotion or even more damaging behaviours to self and other, such as becoming physically or verbally violent.

With the help from your heart, let whatever residue or rubble that is still around be cleansed. Your freedom from these burdensome sentiments allow you to be naturally open. You can feely and lovingly interact, for the sake of the peace, growth and joy with any children, everyone. You are a wonderful role model then, too. No matter what behaviours the other person is displaying, be that heartful role model.

Every situation is unique. From a purely heart-focused perspective, once you are with someone close as a friend, lover, or partner, at the core of your heart there is always a beautiful and deep love for that person. In some way it is natural for this connection to continue. You may, on the one hand, hold this love in the heart and let go, not be in touch, even decide to discontinue an active friendship. Or, you may be in a situation where it is not possible or not wanted by you, the other or a third person to still be active friends. On the other hand, there may be the possibility to be friends and to live an active friendship. You may not feel this now, which may be because the mind/body/heart and soul are still not clear or even confused. However, once the heart is clearer and stronger - even with the mind/brain not knowing or experiencing this yet - a growing friendship may unfold.

An additional challenge or issue may be if your partner, or you, have a new partner. Another layer of emotions may surface. Some of these are closely related to this fact, such as envy or jealousy; others may be more 'general' such as anger, or hurt feelings that are still attached to the heart.

These emotions are simply and ideally a reminder that anything other than love and joy for someone whom we love or once loved is limiting our ability to joy and love. With a strong heart, you feel growing and sweet love for anyone. We find joy in relationship, overall, including for your ex-partner and to continue, if possible, some form of friendship. Especially with children involved, to genuinely feel this way, is very beneficial.

At some level it is normal to feel this way. If it is the case that emotions are still there, even at a subtle level, then it is best to choose your heart and not any emotions that surface. Many would consider it normal to have these kinds of emotion or to be challenged. Yet from the perspective of guarding your own heart from your own emotions - opening it more, purifying it more - there is no benefit in harbouring or following any of these. Following the heart and your heart's help is the better choice.

Our hearts are not fully pure, and being newly separated or in any post-separation time there is a stronger tendency to have and to hold on to strong negative emotions such as resentment and disappointment, for long periods of time in some cases. None of these emotions serve you or your ex-partner. Over time they will make your heart very heavy and, depending on the severity, may even lead to a closing of the heart.

You have let your heart help you; if you do this before, during, and after the separation you will find that any negative emotions will gradually but clearly get less, and even disappear completely. In some way the opportunity here is to look after your own heart; if needed, this may involve seeking some distance and space, to strengthen your heart.

If you can stay in touch you can use your heart's natural ability when you are talk with, interact with, spend time with or even when you are thinking of your ex-partner. What can be a very deep healing experience is to share about the heart, do some of the exercises or KHHs from this book together, or even do a Heart Meditation together.

In the togetherness of hearts both Heart Strengthening and Heart Meditation can remove a lot of rubble and free up a possible path forward in friendship and non-romantic love with your ex-partner.

While it is possible to love in your heart and from it, without the need to see someone or be in contact, you may still feel a feeling of love and friendship of this person.

Every one of these situations, is unique and requires heart-clarity and heart-strength. When your heart is really strong and light, then whatever 'can be' or 'is best to be' - for everybody involved - will generate or be a peaceful feeling for you. Living the present life and every moment with your new partner, if there is one, is more important than to hope for continuation of friendship with an ex-partner if that is not easy to realise and do. Until all hearts involved are free, light and full of love, your emotions and those of your ex-partner and new partner will be mixed with emotions, ideas and concepts, some of which will be heart-felt, while some will be quite far from it.

Family violence heart help

To be friends with an ex-partner, an ex-husband or wife is not easy. A much more significant and sad topic is the wide-spread issue and tragedy of family violence. The vastness of this problem has risen more to the surface. Programs and services are growing and, from welfare to policing services, new approaches are needed.

When there is a dangerous situation, for you and any child, then naturally keeping everyone safe is the most important immediate response. With the understanding shared in this book it is hoped that heart-learning and heart-therapeutic work can become a growing part in the work with the victims and perpetrators of family violence.

The heart can help to heal and dissolve the stifling trauma caused in such situations to, mainly, women and children in our communities. It can also help to facilitate a change within, in the offender so that a structural change, the reduction in the negative energy and drive - the negative emotion - can be changed to such an extent, that the impulsiveness and other causes, over time, cease to exist.

Friendship help from your heart

When you look at the issues raised in previous sections you will already have learned and possibly experienced that in all of these friendship 'imbalances' your heart can and will play an active role.

Your heart will always lead you to a place of joy and giving. Your mind may have some ideas or concepts about what is right and wrong and sometimes you may have a third person give you advice, for example, 'don't give so much' or something similar.

You will only ever find the right answer in every situation and for every individual friend in your heart, by feeling what feels truly and absolutely right to you. Every moment in itself is a gift, as is every one of your friendships. When your heart and feeling say give, then 'just do it'; there is no second chance to share in this giving with the same friend, to share the joy and love and wonder in that moment.

Some people say that there is abundance, and in giving you are also receiving, and everything you give will return two or threefold to you. In a way the law or a law of the universe may work like this, however, this may be a hopeful concept. When a friendship is out of balance then there is not much point to go there, to invest, to do. At times the best is to be in the heart, find peace within and to see what unfolds over time in a more passive way.

In friendship, choose the heart more often: be, wait, feel and commit to your heart. If there are issues in the friendship, never do anything too quick or too drastic unless you really need to. Sometimes there is little or no need to do anything.

The friendship door you may shut today, may just naturally open again in weeks, months or years from now and lead to the most wonderful, joyful and blissful friendship with the same old friend that you feel nothing in common with now.

As your heart becomes stronger you will also be able to feel clearer about where and with whom you feel to spend time. When issues are there that bother you, you may want to 'listen to your heart', 'speak from the heart' or just be present with more heart.

Bringing things up

One avenue of help from your heart, in a more indirect way, is to bring up with your friend things that bother you. 'Things' are issues or not-so-nice things that have happened between you. However, the experiences, when using the heart for some time and with confidence, that to let go and surrender issues is often the advice from the heart. The climate can change very easily and fast in a friendship and something 'big' may only seem very small a little way down the track. Any upset caused by bringing stuff up may linger much longer in your own heart and that of your friend.

If you raise some of these issues with your friend, take your time to find a genuine and caring place in your heart first from which you can talk, ask, and seek to understand or share how you feel. Let your heart be present, too. It will keep you stable and prevent you from slipping into even subtle emotions. Your heart will encourage you to listen, be loving, kind, understanding, flexible and simply a good friend at all times. In times when friendship challenges, or changes occur, your heart will also guide you, indirectly or with direct intention or skill, whether or not to address an issue or challenge with a friend. There is often a part in us that wants to solve things and solve them 'now'. When you have an issue with a friend, bringing it up and go in both directions: you may solve, help or improve it by talking about it; however, or you may also make it worse. Bringing up triggers old or further emotions in you, in your friend or in both of you.

From the perspective of the heart this is very interesting. You discuss a difficult, potentially emotionally challenging issue with a friend. Afterwards there is a verbal statement made by your friend or both of you that 'it was good to talk through'. If the emotional challenge of this conversation was too deep, then the friendship may be more burdened than before. Ultimately it is the before and after the feeling in the heart that will make things feel lighter or heavier between you.

You really want to tune in and listen to your heart: how does it feel to raise an issue, how does it feel to let it go and to surrender it from the heart? This is a key question to ask. It is best to ask this question when you are free from the emotion or emotional issue that you are thinking about bringing up, and then follow the advice from your heart.

Smile often as one heart-helping choice

The KHH introduced in this chapter is intended to help you and your heart all the time and throughout every day and every situation or challenge. It seems far too simple to just smile when there are other important choices to make. By now you know that any help from the heart is meaningful, purposeful and brings into the equation not only another helper but also a bigger picture.

Key Heart Help 8: Smile often

Hopefully by now you have experienced the gentle, yet clear and at times miraculous feelings and help from your heart. Smiling often as a KHH is introduced here as a general heart strengthening and heart-capacity building exercise.

Smiling often, at any time of the day, every time you remember that you can smile 'right now' and for no reason will help your heart. The clearer your awareness and experience has grown to realise the connection between any smile or the intentional smile to your heart and the impact of that smile, your random and frequent smiles will have an even greater impact.

It is time to get more serious now by inviting you to smile more, randomly, as often as you can.

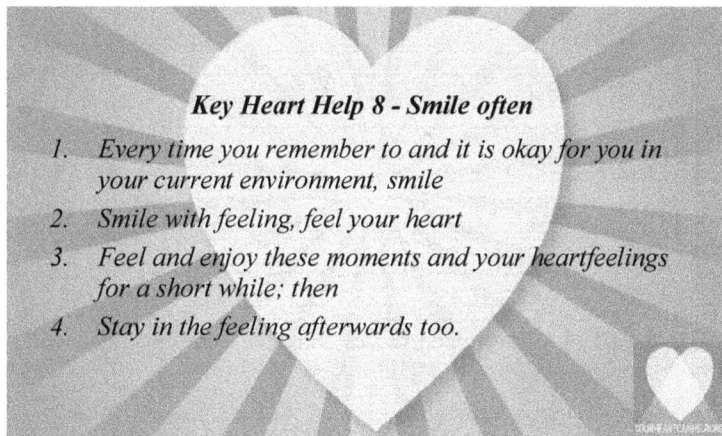

Key Heart Help 8 - Smile often

1. *Every time you remember to and it is okay for you in your current environment, smile*
2. *Smile with feeling, feel your heart*
3. *Feel and enjoy these moments and your heartfeelings for a short while; then*
4. *Stay in the feeling afterwards too.*

This is unusual for many and at times people feel resistance and think 'why should I smile for no reason?' True. Normally speaking, this is a normal response or resistance. However, this is all about you and your heart and once you realise how your heart works, then do more of it. In this way, be logical and rational.

Why is there an impact or an even stronger impact when you are more heart-aware? With earlier heart strengthening practices you have experienced the clear connection between your smile, the intention to smile to your heart and the heart's positive response. Your heart can start to help. In some way, all of our being is connected and working together, whether this is with or without intention. A heightened awareness of your heart, which is really your experience of the heart, will naturally and directly then improve any heart supporting thing you do, like this casual KHH.

However, do not force this KHH or any of the other heart practices. You can also skip it if it is too casual or random. Randomly smiling may just mean doing whatever feels right to you. Just smile more often, more freely, with feeling and EVERY TIME you smile, ideally remember your heart for a few moments and feel or enjoy the feeling.

Time will heal

Time heals a heavy heart.

One approach in difficult friendship situations maybe 'time will heal'. You may have heard this common phrase or someone may have given you this piece of advice. From the perspective of your heart this is true as more and more layers will be covered within and around your heart unless you attend to your heart and keep it clean. In this way your daily remembering or experience of any pain or emotion will become less and less. At a first glance there seem to be two equal options:

- Wait and hope one day your upset in your friendship is no longer burdening you or affecting your life or other friendships; and
- Let your heart help you in unburdening, removing whatever emotional reaction has been there, and keeping your heart unaffected by a specific interaction and keeping all other layers in good condition at the same time.

These options only appear equal. What is really happening is that in one situation the emotional memory or trauma is only covered, it is not removed. What is also very likely is that this memory will surface again in similar situations, as you have this emotional negative deposit, and it will limit or even block you from making helpful and good friendship decisions. At the very least it will influence you.

The second option is the heart choice. It is one that is in tune with your existence as a complete human being, mind and heart. Using the heart as a new or additional, if not key 'building block', it will remove not only the deposits made in one event or one not-so-nice friendship experience, the heart's radiance in action will also cleanse other related deposits from experiences even longer back; including forgotten ones.

Direct friendship help

Let your heart prevent …

Actively attending to your heart will bring about preventative effects and qualities. There are no doubt endless more scenarios, challenges, difficulties and even reasons why or why not you may move closer towards or further away from a friend.

Whatever any of the past emotional outbursts or challenges have been or whatever undercurrents or subtle emotions linger, do not wait or hold back what your heart can do now. Otherwise the risk will be that one day when the friendship is challenged all that has been hidden or placed in or around the heart can be triggered and surface in a tidal wave of emotion, seriously threatening the deep bond of friendship.

As in all relations, and in all the above scenarios, there are emotions that interfere, pull, force or lead us apart. There are times when this is not the right time for the friendship to end, when more can come of the friendship, yet emotions take over. There are also times when the shared learning and fruitful time of a friendship has naturally come to an end. If that is the case, then all your 'heart and soul' felt to learn has been learned and you may or may not continue on your friendship path.

A word of caution - and something that you may already know - is not to jump too quickly to solutions and make decisions about friends. The deeper method of prevention is for you to choose the heart in times of challenges. You may discuss difficult things with your friend or you may choose not to; in the end, this is the smaller matter. What the heart offers is a non-cognitive, non-talking solution and also one where you do not need to act, unless it is important and urgent that you do, for example when there is abuse, unlawful behaviour or simply too much emotion.

Attend to your own heart and use the KHH 7 introduced in this chapter. You have learned enough about the heart to use your heart properly and to do the full Heart Strengthening (KHH 6) regularly.

With the heart awareness and practice you have already completed, in moments when you smile the heart will naturally spring into action, work and help you and your friendship or friendship issues.

When, heart assisted, the real value and immense joy of our friend-connections are revealed, you see the real person, the person your heart values - even after years of knowing or after years of little or no contact.

This revelation may help in being slow or cautious in making any hasty friendship decisions.

Letting the heart help

> *Search your heart.*
> *Bruce Springsteen*

The heart wants to help and heal. Attend to your heart, focus on your heart more than on the event or your reaction and hurt feelings. Letting the heart help is a willingness to give credit, time and commitment to your heart. This may sound like a marketing line. However, this should not be too difficult as the very moment you use the natural heart-supporting and heart strengthening techniques introduced, your heart experiences become real. The heart will guide you to how close you want to be with a friend or how much distance is helpful for the coming time.

When you let your heart help more directly, for example in situations or issues discussed earlier such as 'being used' or 'feeling excluded', then these issues will grow smaller and your heart will become stronger and clearer.

While this may or may not help the one friend or situation you are in right now, it will prepare a direct path towards more joy, wonder and mutually beautiful friendship experiences.

A stronger heart will also help you to be guided, to make clearer and better situation, like a device detecting 'difficulty' or 'trouble' such as a weather predicting tool. It will help you to avoid situations and encounters with your friends where there is a likelihood to be hurt, to experience friendship challenges, like 'a breach of trust' or 'being used'.

When you give in friendship then give with heart. This can be with a feeling of love in your heart or by learning to feel your heart more; be in your heart and act in friendship from that place - your heart.

When you give from your heart there is more meaning in the way that your heart is being involved. This means that whatever the nature of your connection, be it distant friend, acquaintance or a close friend, any act of giving will be one of heart opening and heart healing for both you and your friend.

The impact of the heart's help is shared by Thomas in the story below. Thomas' story was surprising. He attended heart sessions, heart workshops, for many years. Early during this time he came across as a balanced and confident young man. He also appeared clearly as someone who had a group of friends and positive relationships all-round.

Thomas' Story:

Thomas lives in Hobart, Tasmania. He is 25 years old and started learning about the heart about two years ago. Thomas shared: 'Before I opened my heart more, started to use my heart, I was quite happy, happy enough. But now, looking back, I would say it was happy in a very small way.'

'For me friendship, being with my friends, was the clearest measure of the happiness felt. My friendships were nice. But there was always a distance, too. I kept my friends at arms-length. This was not necessarily a conscious and aware process. It simply happened; there was distance and I did not have the inner strength, feeling or clarity to be closer, more 'friendly'.'

'Being like this, doing this, I always had a sense that I was never really a part of any group of friends either. With individual friends there was a connection, but it never felt very close or deep.'

'It seemed to come from a deep sense of loneliness and disconnect that I was feeling inside at the time.'

'When I first did heart strengthening and the meditation shortly after, too, I noticed that I was having more and more interactions with my friends which felt more real, genuine. It was like I was really able to relate, connect to them in a new way.'

'It seemed that my friends felt this too. Without me being any different, acting in any different ways, they started to share much more personal matters with me. Friendship deepened and became more beautiful and special. Some friends have shared with me that they feel a certain trust and safety.'

'I feel a real sense of gratitude and compassion ... a beautiful feeling of love for them inside, in my heart. I can relate to many of the things and problems they talk to me about.'

'For me the most beautiful thing that has changed is that I can freely relate to others now. I feel deep love and it seems this has allowed me to be with people who are not going through such an easy part of their life. I feel that I can be there for them, help them, be in my heart and at the same time their problems are not pulling me in. It is a beautiful, gentle joy to feel that depth of care for others.'

When you give without using the heart there is a risk you give as a transaction. As discussed earlier there is a risk that friendship becomes unauthentic, an obligation or an idea. Giving that is not from a place of deep connection and love is also much more likely to leave you feeling empty and potentially disappointed. This, in some way, also comes through in Thomas's story.

In friendship it can be easy to feel and enjoy a lightness and not be too serious. There is a chance to really practice 'heart'; to have a heartfelt presence and exchanging time, sharing material events or things from the heart.

Every action, every interaction, every thought and every feeling from your heart in friendship or companionship will be a moment of bliss, of instantly receiving of all there is: all the joy, love, wonder and purpose. Friendship becomes a special avenue for growth, learning and moment-by-moment joy. Your heart only knows the perfection of 'here and now' - and is leading you there.

With more and more heart, the giving and living from the heart will gradually and naturally bring about profound fulfilment, joy and experiences that will assist you in realising that in sharing from the heart with others, all is supported and growing immensely.

Friendship, your heart and love

I practiced to make my heart wider and wider and to feel friendship and kinship with all beings.
The Buddha - in Detlef Kantowsky

What you feel for a friend is ultimately love, such as the love for a sister or brother. There are friends who do love you more unconditionally than others. Unconditional should be just that - unconditional. Yet it is good to be realistic, to be aware of our human nature. Unconditional love in friendship, romantic relationships and in other relationships may have its limitations. Your love for a friend may feel at times unconditional, at times not, and it may also depend on the circumstances.

Our capacity and depth of loving and caring for someone unconditionally is deep. You may believe you experience this unconditional love in friendship already. What is wonderful about the heart's help is that it is very likely that an even greater depth of love, a sweet love and something more exquisite, can unfold.

The only experience that it is possible to have as your heart connection strengthens and your own heart becomes lighter, clearer and more open is the deepening of your friend-connection, friend-experience and love.

At this point of learning about and using your heart, you may know this already to some extent. You may have clearly experienced that as you feel more at peace, closer to who you are and closer to your friends, your friends can also be more who they are, be more natural and freer in their approach to you.

The heart's transformative quality

In friendship, as in most deep relationships that you have, the wonderful quality of the heart easily bears special fruit. When in friendship you 'learn' to love more freely, naturally and unconditionally, then that feeling and that love is automatically transmitted to your close ones. Naturally, they can also love you back more, letting you in turn be even freer.

This process may not necessarily happen at a conscious or thought level. It may simply unfold and find its own unique form and expression in you and in all your friendships.

Cheynie's story is a fitting example of this kind of heart-help or heart-facilitation. Cheynie is a massage therapist, yoga teacher and a mother of two children. Her story beautifully describes the rocky road of friendship in her past, indicating some of the challenges that can happen between friends when coupled with her own self-doubt - and how this was gently transformed by the abilities of the heart.

Cheynie' Story:

My story is about friendships and how beautiful they have become since opening my heart more and more. I started opening my heart around eight years ago.

I was a shy child, quite unsure of myself and lacking in confidence. This affected my ability to make and retain friends. Friends would come into my life, but ultimately they would move on. I never quite understood why and lost more confidence with each friendship.

Upon reflection, I realise that I felt that I didn't have much to offer people in my life. I was insecure and lacking in confidence - why would anyone want to hang out with me? Basically I was a drain. This continued into my adult life and caused me a lot of grief and loneliness.

It wasn't until I began opening my heart that I discovered the endless well of beauty that was shared quite naturally from my heart. I started to feel more and more that the deep clearing and cleansing through the heart and feeling with the heart that the depth was through the feelings and blessings that came from a higher place or source.

Negativities stored around my spiritual heart melted and I began to feel lighter, happier and abundant in so many areas of my life. Where once before I was seeking to gain some kind of strength through others, I more and more often found myself in the position of giving and sharing and helping others. The cup that I was constantly trying to fill was all of a sudden full to overflowing-continuously! It was so natural and beautiful to share around.

I simply found that I wasn't needy anymore. I felt rich and full and fun and it didn't really matter what I thought of myself anymore. I became happy. And yes, my life filled up with friends! Deep, rich and lasting connections of mutual support and love have been built effortlessly. Any corner I turn now in life has a dear friend walking beside me. It is all so joyful.

There have been setbacks along the way, for sure. But each one has helped me to realise that I don't need to go down the old path of closed-mindedness, of following my emotions and closing my heart. The choice is easy, and I know I can help others and be a beautiful friend. Every area of my life in fact has been blessed in this way. I feel like a different person, completely.

Any transformation often begins with oneself. What Cheynie's story shows is the direct, immediate and wonderfully gentle yet strong ability your heart has to assist, to change, to transform you first.

The heart in friendship is uniquely empowering. It is empowering because any change comes from within you and your heart's unique abilities and wisdom. When using the heart, any change or help may also come from an outside influence, such as another advice-giving friend, family member, counsellor or psychologist. It will also always be steered and helped from within.

This process is even more empowering as it is giving you the choice to make a change, to take a first step in times when one of your friendships is facing difficulties.

Freedom from all the past

One of the natural things that your heart will facilitate that will be clearer and clearer as time goes by is freedom from the past. At times you may find that either you, your ex-partner or even an ex-friend are not choosing the heart's help or are simply not prepared - with mind and emotion - to let go and to accept what is. When this happens you can let your heart help you to let go of whatever is there for you, to let go of any of your ideas of continued friendship and the related hopes, wishes and ideals.

As you surrender these from your heart, you will find that - without intention or the involvement of the other - it will make your heart and feeling lighter and indirectly prepared for freedom in that friendship at a later stage. In fact, the very moment you start you will become freer to share, to be with others and to love deeply.

The harder the heart, the longer this process may take. If you keep adding to the rubble, it may take a long time.

At the other side of the spectrum is a generally light heart that will always see friendship and love, will always find it easy to experience these and other beautiful, wonderful qualities in many moments and situations every day.

Remember the heart is offering the easy, fast and joyful path to surrender - which is letting go of everything - that is not a wonderful, sweet and blissful feeling. As you surrender and let go from your heart, the love that you feel - which your heart will always feel for the other one - will become purer and deeper. And yes, sometimes the person, ex-partner or ex-friend will once again be in your life as a friend or as someone you need to see, although this is not always the case.

Whatever the situation is for you, the heart only knows one choice: being present, to facilitate the balance of heart and mind and to let the heart do its work; to help you to find peace, calmness, deep joyfulness and deepening love for everyone in your life, in your heart.

A heart-to-heart

The best way to mend a broken heart is time and girlfriends.
Gwyneth Paltrow

In a light way, having a heart-to-heart between 'girlfriends' in the way Gwyneth share is simply a way to talk about your problems and friendship issues with your girlfriend. This may be of some use only, or make the feeling worse, as discussed earlier. It is however an often-held belief.

Experiences where talking about something can help are common. To talk to a girlfriend or male friend, anyone, may be of use. This is, if the conversation is reminding you, or you remind each other, of the deeper heart-to-heart nature. The real presence of the heart is needed, in particular when things are difficult, emotionally challenging or don't go our way. The heart offers an alternative way or something you can try in addition to 'girlfriends'.

There is one certainty in using your heart's help. After you strengthen your heart, you let your heart naturally remove burdens, then whatever has been affecting you and your friend - any burdening emotions or thoughts - will not, contrary to re-living them in a conversation, burden your heart more.

A true heart-to-heart is about two things: how the heart can help when there are issues or challenges. And how everything related to the heart, like friendship, is experienced deeper and with more joy and wonder.

Getting the heart's help with any friendship issues, challenges or irritating matters is just the first step needed to get to the deeper lying feelings.

Whenever you are challenged or hurt, try to delay any response for a while to minimise emotion. You can, instead, smile while feeling your heart as your first response (see KHH 2, 6 or the PHTs 7, 23, 28, 47, 53, 61 or 72). In talking with someone about an issue, be aware of the fine line that is between having a helpful conversation, a true heart-to-heart - with your heart present - and having a conversation where you re-experience, re-live emotions or negative thoughts of the challenge.

Have a heart-to-heart talk with my friend.

You may of course, also with more heart understanding and with a growing heart, be that friend that is directing the conversation, gently steering it in that way, where the heart qualities naturally help and offer a deep level of support. Having a heart-to-heart is the expression of this kind of conversation that we are perhaps 'meant to have' in difficult situations and with a dear friend, sibling or close one.

Following on from what you read above, you will need to keep a close eye on when you share with your friend. You have likely experienced that when you share about your pain, hurt or emotions with others it may only sometimes help. Other times, you may have found that when you recalled the event, that you re-experienced the pain, emotion or trauma all over again.

How the heart works is that when you re-experience any of the emotions you felt during the event you share about, for example when you were hurt by someone else, you will add more burdens and make more deposits in and around your heart.

It can be common belief that when you complain about the other person you 'hurt' them back. The reality, however, is that you will burden your own heart. Further, complaining will not help that relationship and it will not help your ability to feel and enjoy the deep joy, wonder and shared growth you know or have experienced in friendship.

When you have a heart-to-heart, be aware of this. When you find your friend going there, becoming 'negative', complaining or re-experiencing emotion, there is not much you can do unless they are familiar with the heart and committed to keeping it clean and open. You can, however, let your heart smile to them to balance some of this and help their heart to become lighter even though there are complaints and burdens added. Your heart, if strong and present, has this ability.

When you find yourself going there, bring yourself back, feel the presence of your heart more, find a gentle smile and feel your heart more continuously. Naturally your heart will help you to be in a greater balance of truly sharing from the heart, as compared to spiralling into emotion and not feeling so great after some time.

This is the real meaning of having a heart-to-heart. Can all interaction, sharing and talking be from the heart? If by now you feel so, then let it guide you in what to feel, say and do.

Using the heart in this way you will be more likely to express, in gestures and words, what needs to be said and what the heart feels to say. Heart and mind in tandem will bring to the surface the specialness of what friendship can be all about and lead you to deeper layers of learning and realisations that can benefit all of your life.

A true or truer heart-to-heart with your friend makes every moment together more enjoyable and wonderful. The friendship will naturally deepen too while at the same time, just by using it more, the quality of your heart will change, deepen and improve. Naturally, the often light, helpful and enjoyable value of friendship - experienced through the heart - will spill over into all aspects of your life.

The very practical help

In the sweetness of friendship let there be laughter, and sharing of pleasures.
For in the dew of little things, does the heart find its morning and is refreshed. Kahlil Gibran

Friendship can be all this sweetness, laughter, sharing of pleasures. And yet at times things just don't flow or happen or feel as they used to for no apparent reason. How can your heart help you in practical and direct ways in all your friendships and with friendship-related issues? The following will set out some of the general and very practical ways of how more heart can help your friendships when things don't go so well, or simply in enhancing what already is.

In your friends' presence

Whenever you are with your friends, be in your heart, both when the times are joyful and light and when you find it not so easy. The KHHs up to now would have helped you know the steps to go and be in your heart and to perhaps also feel when you are in your heart or at least connected to it.

It is mainly when you feel your heart that your heart can help you in the best possible way. If you are in the physical presence of your friend, it will help you to respond to any challenge with calmness, kindness and love.

In these moments when you feel your heart, your friend's heart will also be more present and your own heart will heal and become lighter. In this process both your hearts will open more and there will be more room for kindness, joy, sharing, love and a deeper form of friendship.

If your friend is not present

If your friend is not present and something happens in your friendship that is of concern to you then the following PHT can be helpful. This may be in a situation when you hear about something upsetting, you feel a reaction or when you feel an emotion rising. In these moments the encouragement here is to respond first by giving attention to your heart, to act inward first, then with a more present heart, to act on the outside. Sometimes this outward action is not needed. If it is needed, wanted or appropriate to the situation then you will be coming from a greater heart - mind balance.

Nowadays, these friendships are even more likely. It is easy to travel, live in other locations, countries and a mobile, internet directed world has opened new ways of being in contact. Possible upsets may have happened via e-mail, social media, like a tweet or a Facebook exchange, a sms or message left on the phone. There are more channels to communicate and this, unfortunately, also means more channels or chances to hurt others and to be hurt. Also here the heart can help. It will help you and also indirectly help our friend in exactly the same as you would use the heart in face-to-face get-togethers and communication.

Firstly, the heart can help you by communicating more from the heart, with a greater and real heart to mind balance and by avoiding the trap of being in emotion when communicating. Secondly, when damage has been done, the heart can help you to shift, let go and attend more heartful to others.

> **Practical Heart Tip 41: Long-distance heart-to-heart ***
>
> *This Long-distance heart-to-heart exercise can be done anytime. It is particularly helpful when you can't be in contact or when the contact has broken down and either your friend or you don't feel to talk or be in touch:*
>
> - *Prepare and warm-up your heart (KHH 2 or 6);*
>
> - *Then, after a good quality warm-up, let your heart smile to your friend for some time (good is for several minutes);*
>
> - *If the quality is good (this means if you are in your heart, not following emotions or thoughts too much and too often and if you feel the nice feelings in your heart clearly or even growing), then continue for longer; then*
>
> - *End the practice by letting your heart be grateful for a few moments.*

You can do this exercise for one friend or for a group of friends. You can also do it for a person who used to be your friend or who you had a falling out with.

This PHT, similar to KHH 7, is quite wonderful when your friend is going through a hard time. You may do this with letting your friend know or not. Without heart experience or reading this book, it may be too 'esoteric' or 'out there' for some and it could be better, in some situations, not to share.

Remember, it is best to not let any emotions interfere. To some extent you have this choice. It is also normal that emotions surface. In this case, be diligent with the heart-supporting KHHs and let these emotions be cleared, either just before you do this PHT or for a few days before. If you sincerely feel to live a more heart-centred life, use all the KHHs step-by-step and the PHTs 7, 47, and others, to let the heart remove burdens or stop emotions surfacing or becoming stronger in instances such as this.

Your heart's profound role

Whatever positive or negative experiences that you have had in friendship, your heart and its connection to a deepest and sweetest care and love will gradually shift everything to a new paradigm of closeness, being and sharing.

Figure 15: 'Old friendship model/paradigm' - heart less strong

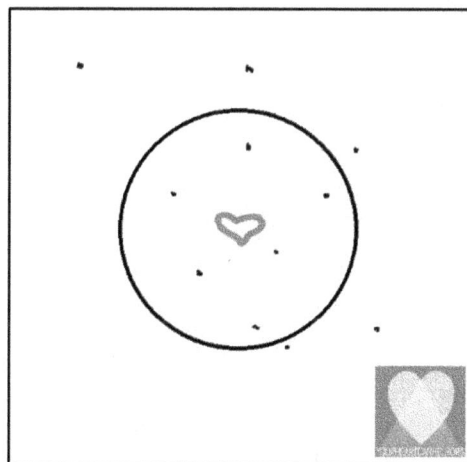

What the image shows is a person in the centre, represented as a heart, and his or her friends around. Some friends are close, some are very close and some are further away. Also, some are in the 'circle of friends' and some are out. Because there is a circle there is also less movement from the outside and in or the other way around. At some point, a decision was made to consider someone a friend or not. With a strong mind/brain there can be a tendency for individuals to be 'in' or 'out' of a current circle of friends.

Figure 16: 'Heart-supported' friendship

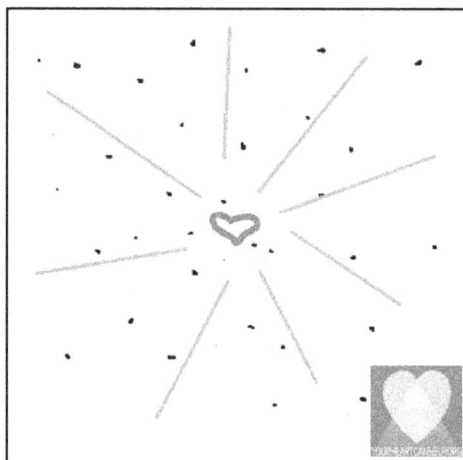

This second image shows an open and more limitless reach towards others by the quality, ability and radiance of your heart. Friendship here is the possibility of an ever-moving, growing and expanding circle of sharing in deep, purposeful heart-centred learning and growth.

Friends, family members, colleagues still grow in closeness or move further away in a constant dynamic interplay of life and heart-to-heart connection. Within this is the reality of deep and joyful heart connection. As your your heart moves you toward this reality joyful and purposeful friendships unfold.

There is no 'in' or 'out', as your heart only knows care and love and qualities associated with these, even though you may decide or feel not to see a particular friend. 'In or out' thoughts and realities produce feelings such as separation or exclusiveness which never feel nice or right.

Friendships and the heart

You know we're two hearts believing in just one mind. Phil Collins

The heart and heart learning is something still new. With a heart of an infinite depth, there is still 'room to move' and to improve. If you don't feel gentle responses while you do this PHT or any practices, give it some credit. Do your personal 'exercise program' and over time re-evaluate and see how the feeling in your heart, your friendships and your feeling within about a friend has unfolded or changed.

There are two general possibilities as to how things tend to go with friendship challenges. The experiences in heart community have shown these two broad possibilities to be:

- Your friendship will not change or will change only marginally, and if there have been challenges it may even get worse in two ways: firstly, there may be even more emotions that surface and interfere with the good things and wonderful friendship feelings, or secondly, you simply lose contact and the connection fades away. There is a naturalness to this. Friends come and go and often old friends move on, we move on - especially with some of the stuck material, collection and emotion being removed.

- The friendship issue, even the friendship itself, becomes less of a focus and therefore less of a 'problem'. People start to open to more of what the heart offers. In some way they focus a little less on what happens in the friendship.

In any friendship, like in all other relationships are 'lows' and 'highs'. In times of challenge, especially with more heart, the connection and feeling within a friendship invariably will become gentle, light or positive again. If you smile through any challenges by letting your heart smile to your friend, or all of your friends, with no particular outcome in mind, you will feel flowing love, lightness, joy and connection. (Adapt KHH 7 'Let your heart smile to others') This will always also expand and help your own heart. Growing feelings of happiness, peace, care, love and connection are the 'side-effects' for you.

Every time you smile with intent and feeling to a friend, whether they know it or not, your friend will receive the gift of your radiant heart-energy and all that this means.

Very often when this happens friendships wonderfully improve, deepen and become immensely beautiful and supportive.

The preciousness of friendship

Where would any of us be without our friends and family? Kobi Yamanda

Friendship is or has the immense possibility to be something very special, very beautiful and very helpful to us all. To become friends, to meet someone, there are two hearts which are needed: two hearts open enough to meet, to recognise the other and to start a journey of sharing and growth.

However, to heal a broken heart in a friendship, to heal whatever is burdening your friendship, one heart is enough. Your heart is very special and so just one heart that is lighter and freer will positively influence all friendships around it, including the one you are perhaps a little concerned about now and all future friendships.

Investment in the heart is investment in friendship and more.

It is natural for one heart or person in a friendship or relationship to be a step ahead, wiser, more mature or more heartful. You will find that this can change easily and today you may be the wiser one while tomorrow it is your friend. Your heart, or you with a clearer heart, know no competition - at least no competition that stirs emotion or discontent.

Your heart's wise call - to you - will always be to want to help, support, or just be there, with a gentle, smiling and radiating heart. This seems simple, and yet this is a very profound step in attitude or approach to make. One tendency can be to over-think problems. If there is, or has been, a difficulty or upsetting event then emotions will also be present and drive behaviour and feelings towards a friend.

Friendship is not all rosy and beautiful. Similar to other relationships at home, socially or at work, emotions can enter friendship and burden our connection to dear friends.

Let your heart help you to be with your friend more often in a 'heart-space' and to support all your friendships, as well as at work and in your social life. Emotions that are naturally cleared will also no longer be present in or burden your friendships and relationships. With your heart, you can always feel the deeper and more connecting - even joyful - heart-to-heart connection that you have. This may just be enough to re-invest in a friendship or just to stay present to what may unfold.

Friendship is not just about the friend, their behaviours, or their feeling towards us. It clearly is about our feelings towards them, too, and equally perhaps our issues, what we struggle or wrestle with, our current challenges. There are also certain behavioural or emotional patterns that do and don't support our friendships. All this creates or feeds a form of entanglement between us and the outside world, including with our friends. The more the heart's unique abilities, radiance and work untangle us and help us with the inner struggles, then everything, including all of our friendships, will be gently and positively affected by the heart.

In this way, your heart can be utilised in friendship with some lightness, ease and without perhaps the seriousness or importance you may look at with relationship or family issues. You can practise being heartful in friendship at times when you are with your friend or over long-distance, as in the PHT 'Long-distance heart-to-heart' above.

Ideally, you should let there be a lightness to your heart-practices and heart-joys. This will have a positive flow-on effect across three areas: first for your heart, as a lightness in practice will always bring the heart's qualities more to the surface; second for the particular friendship you are focusing on; third for all aspects of life, as any heart improvement will always spill over and impact on all that you are and do in all of your life.

Thomas describes in his story that friendship with more heart offers genuineness and clarity. More heart will naturally take you and your friends to new levels of experiencing friendship. Whatever the heart facilitates, like in other areas of life, will be positive. It will take you in good, better, if not magical, directions.

My heart, sit only with those who know and understand you.
Sit only under a tree that is full of blossoms. Rumi

Summary - sharing & enjoying in friendship with all your heart

Friendship is something very special and has a wonderful quality of adding immense joy and wonder to one's life. Experiencing heart-to-heart time is often what friendship is about. The heart enjoys friendship. It wants to help and gently lead you and your friendships to the fullest of experiences that are possible to have in this free way of sharing with another human being.

Here are the summary points to remember in relation to how your heart will assist, grow, strengthen and beautify any of your friendships:

1. The first level of help from your heart is to remember that whatever the nature or depth of your past or current friendship challenge your heart can offer additional, and as shown also, profound help for all existing friendships.

2. This is particularly important when challenges, issues and difficulties arise. With a strong and clear, cleaner heart you will feel clearer about what and when to do. You will be able to listen with your heart in any conversations in person or otherwise.

3. Your more present heart will help you even in conventional ways of dealing with a nagging friendship issue when you want to 'bring things up' and have a discussion around something that is bothering you. It will help you in the same way as above.

4. Use the PHT 'Whole-hearted support team' to be a heartful, supporting and caring as a friend. You can do it for a period of time, in specific friendships and gradually extend it to all your friendships.

5. The PHT 'Healing friendships through your heart' is helpful where things are difficult or where there have been past hurts or upsets. It combines well with KHH 7 'Let your heart smile to others' and will make it more effective.

6. The PHT 'Friend inventory' is designed to bring you back to your heart and to be heartful in all your friendships. In tuning in or feeling which friends are around and good for your heart you can spend more time, more often, at the right places, with friends that support your heart opening.

7. Additionally, you can actively use the KHH 'Smile often' introduced in this section and every time you are together, think of your friend or your challenge, then smile often and freely to bring your heart in more fully. Let this smiling practice always be with and from your heart.

8. 'Smiling often' looks so simple. By now you have learned enough about the heart, together with first and clear heart experiences. Smiling is often easy with a friend. This KHH can help you to make the smile more natural and more to your heart. A stronger heart - and all the abilities and qualities of the heart - will unfold, for all your friendships and all of your life.

9. Your heart can help you by communicating more from the heart in friendship. Use the PHT 'Long-distance heart-to-heart' when you feel to be touch, when you miss a friend, and when you can't connect in person or by phone.

10. You start to move into the more direct abilities of your heart to help your friendships when you recognise that all friendship issues, nagging things and challenging problems can function as a reminder to attend to your heart. In turn the heart helps you and your friendships. You will find that it is either negative thoughts, unhelpful or excessive thinking or one or several of the vast range of emotions, that interfere with a gentle, joyful and light connection.

11. Some of the friend challenges described, and there are more, such as 'breach of trust', 'being used', invite some form of analysis. In life it can feel wonderful to give to someone. Whatever the nature of your connection, any act of heartful giving will be one of heart opening, heart healing: yours and your friends.

12. In friendship, where time spent together is less and less intense as closer relations, it is easier to enjoy, feel a lightness and not be too serious. There is a chance to really practice the heart. Let every action, every interaction, every thought and every feeling be one from your heart. Gradually all your friendships, and from there other relations or connections, will become moments of deeply joyful giving, receiving and close sharing.

13. Your heart will also gently, gradually and naturally facilitate a freedom from all the past experiences. This means that all the KHHs and suggested heart practices will gradually remove all past hurts, heart burdening 'rubble', emotional baggage and more. All friendships will become freer, less emotional and even more enjoyable. It will bring the preciousness that lies within every friendship to the surface clearer or will refine it to profound degrees of joy and wonder. Whatever is cleansed by the heart is, guaranteed, not helpful for the 'now' and the future.

14. How can there be a heart-to-heart with a friend when the knowledge, understanding and practice around the heart is just a hope or idea? The section about having a heart-to-heart is detailing about how the heart can help when there are issue or challenges but equally also how everything heart is about experiencing the joy of life, friendship and more. Take the plunge into the heart and, maybe for a set period of time, use the heart more intently.

15. Whether a continuing friendship with your ex-partner is possible or not is less important than the use of your heart in any interactions, contacts or thoughts that you may have. Because of past closeness there is often a deeper heart-healing necessary. This may not benefit this relationship, it may however be immensely important for your heart and all that the heart means. It will free the heart's help in friendship, all of life and in relation to a possible new partner. If a heartfelt friendship with is possible with an ex-partner, that something wonderful of course, especially if children are involved. Go to relevant sections and practice heart-facilitated forgiving (sections 1, 3, PHT 34 and KHH 13).

16. The real practical help in friendship is the use of KHH 7 'Smiling from the heart to others' and KHH 6 'Heart Strengthening'. For an overall good and improving heart condition KHH 13 'Open Heart Meditation' is important to let the heart play its role in clearing deeper lying emotions, burdens and hurt feelings. These will also help to take any good or wonderful friendship to the special heights and qualities that true friendship can be all about.

17. Let your heart help you to be in a 'heart-space' with all your friends to clear, over time, anything that is not clarity, care, support or joyful sharing. Your heart's wise call is to choose your heart's help in good times and equally, or more so in challenging or rocky friendship moments. There seems to be a simplicity to this that may or may not find the mind/brain full support. However, this is a very profound step in attitude or approach to make. Remember, some of our conditioning is to think or over-think any issues or problems. Choosing the heart in friendship is something profound and meaningful, and every time you do so, the foundations and opportunities will grow to enjoy something as special as a good friend.

Chapter 5

Wellbeing, Health and Healing Through Your Heart

I can cope better now, accept it a lot more;
and the program helped a lot.

Perhaps the greatest number of people - community members, clients, friends and colleagues - who come to heart or heart meditation sessions are those who are there because of health issues whether they be physical, emotional or mental. For some there is a longing to be healed at a deep level, but for most, to be well and healthy again, and to be happy as part of the wider definition of being healthy and well, is their motivation.

Your wellbeing, health and healing are of immense importance. If you are well, then the right life-style choice will be important to ensure that illness is either reduced or prevented. Good health and wellbeing is more likely to continue. If you have been unwell, then you know that everything stops, and with it many other aspects of life that appear hugely important, until wellbeing or health are restored. Everyone who is unwell deserves the best - the best treatment, the best resources and the best love and care from experts and close ones. One essential resource that you always have is your heart.

Yet, in many instances people who are ill or those wanting to maintain good health don't usually seek help from their heart.

Your heart is always available and is always ready to help. The following section will make it clearer that the heart is not only one ingredient, one resource but also the central hub around or through which healing occurs or occurs better. You will also see in the discussions and stories that it can help in two significant ways:

- to decide what the best options are, treatments and life-style choices included, that will support your health, healing and wellbeing; and
- with direct assistance in promoting and facilitating health or healing as a 'one-stop' shop or focus or as an additional treatment option.

Your heart is unique in that it can do something that no one person or healthcare treatment can do; it is intelligent and knows and works with the root causes of illness. In this sense is it always of importance as an additional health or treatment choice.

Given the important role of the heart in promoting wellbeing you will find in the following section discussions around the genesis of illness and the way the heart can help. It will be easier for you to follow the direct connection that an open and radiant heart has on your health, healing and wellbeing.

Have you tried the heart?

Significant illness or smaller, niggling health issues can be helped by your heart. The heart can also be of help with any serious health issues or major health challenges. It works as one key tool in facilitating help with past injury, accidents or on-going health issues.

When it comes to your health and what the heart can do to support, help and play a role in healing, practical heart knowledge is needed. Even more than this, let the heart work in action for you to help or to prevent onset of illness or un-wellbeing. It is not uncommon, for some clients and certain conditions who have treatments, to hear that 'everything else' has been tried to prevent or to cure illness except the heart. The heart needs to be able to become and be a key element in support of any of your current, past or even future not-yet-known health issues.

In some of the stories, such as David's or Jonathon's described below, you will find that the heart played a major role in achieving a breakthrough in the illness and improved their health markedly. So does one need to heal one's heart first, or attend to the health issues first or attend to both at the same time? The stories and experiences help you to realise the importance your heart has for your health, wellbeing, for healing and prevention of illness, spanning from short term, now, to medium and long-term wellbeing.

It is also often older people, who after having tried many other health modalities, finally discover the heart. These heart experiences included profound changes and healing on all levels of their health, wellbeing and happiness. Feeling well after all is a feeling and when your heart, or centre of feeling is engaged, the feeling of wellbeing alters.

The function of your heart is not related to age, as more and more young people also look to the heart for healing or to gain a greater sense of wellbeing. Young people who might have nagging or serious health issues that seem to resist common treatments are looking for alternatives as well as a deep form of guidance that includes making the right choices within a vast array of health modalities. It seems that anecdotally more young people than ever suffer from a variety of health issues, such as dietary intolerances, emotional, mental health and physical problems; and some of them have very serious conditions given their age. There has been a regular attendance at therapeutic sessions, workshops and heart meditations by young people ranging in age from 13 to 25 years who have one or several health issues. Before sharing more about how exactly the heart is helping and how is has helped in many situations, let us look first at the common understanding about health and wellbeing and some of the obvious avenues of available help.

Direct heart-supporting modalities and learning

By now, following some of the exercises, you would have some experiences with your own heart. Even before reaching the health section of the book, you will have realised that the heart has already facilitated some positive changes in its gentle and yet profound ways.

Perhaps there is more calmness, confidence, clarity or hope within all stemming from a better heart connection and a lighter heart.

Greater calmness or deeper relaxation are a proven and significant contributor to greater wellbeing and health. It moves you to the other end of the stress - relaxation spectrum.

As this book is about the heart and how the heart can help you the best, you will find chapter sections on Heart-Based Therapeutics and also the heart-learning related practices of Reiki Tummo and Secrets of Natural Walking. These health, wellbeing and complementary therapy modalities, are offered by the US Heart Based Institute, the Padmacahaya Foundation and Secrets of Natural Walking. These are all not-for-profit organisations. Their programs have helped myself and many others to learn about the heart and to fast-track living a more heart-centred life, as well as having the heart available for often deep-lying health or personal issues or challenges.

Health - wellbeing - choices

Health is often understood as the absence of illness or dis-ability that allows you to fully experience and live your life.

The World Health Organisation already indicates a broader understanding of 'health'. It defines it as 'a state of complete physical, mental and social wellbeing and not merely the absence of disease or infirmity.'

Wellbeing is often understood as a wide range of qualities in your life that help you to be healthy, prevent illness, cope with illness, dis-ability or your health-related challenges.

The measure of your wellbeing, depending which approach or model you use, often includes quality of life aspects such as level of happiness, social engagement, positive or supportive relationships and positive emotional qualities or expression.

Your ability to cope with stress, and the depth and length of your sleep, are also reflections of your wellbeing. Wellbeing can also be how safe and at peace you feel with the state of the environment, conflicts around you, in your community, country or the world and how you cope with these broader challenges.

Wellbeing definitions at times include terms like 'positive affect' that link wellbeing to a more refined, developed and positive emotional state. It is the balance of this state that determines, through your all relations, how happy, engaged or positive you are and how purposefully your life unfolds.

There are literature and definitions available, too, that connect wellbeing with a perceived or real 'quality of life'. Without going too much into what was a whole new direction of welfare, health and personal development school of thought 'Quality of Life' in summary can be defined as the positive satisfaction of your individual needs, values and goals.

To improve your health or wellbeing you have a few broad options. The list below is clearly not the full range of options. Some of you may add to these broad options a healthy or wholesome diet, meditation, exercise and your choice of energy-focussed exercise such as Yoga, Tai Chi, Aikido or Chi Gong.

Option 1: Modern medicine and your health and wellbeing

Modern medicine is a wonderful addition to the spectrum of health modalities. It can be criticised for its lack of broad perspective and yet how many of us would want to not have it as a choice when a broken bone, damaged body part, particular organs or a particular illness occurs. It is in many ways an amazing blessing to have been added to our choices. With the help of modern medicine some of the tricky and previously incurable illnesses can now easily and safely be healed. Criticisms, however, are that it is often costly, not available to all, or not in all countries of the world.

Modern medicine is effective in some areas and less effective in others. Often with the same intervention results and outcomes of treatments can still vary significantly.

Perhaps another aspect of criticism is the perceived and sometimes arrogance of the machinery of modern medicine. The pretence that it has the answers now, or will have in the future, for all problems in the world. This clearly is not the case as alternative treatment options are also chosen by people in need.

At the opposite end of this arrogance, which we now know is an emotion and not so helpful or well-perceived by other people and their hearts, is the work of one medical professional. At an international conference a doctor, working with terminally ill children, shared in an opening address:

> *Family members and parents always look at us (doctors) for advice and for assurance and for a guarantee of some sort that everything will work out fine for their child. We don't know and we can't give these guarantees. We do our best according to what we know and we are there for the child and the parents.*

What is the difference here? There is a modesty, humility and honesty present that is refreshing. What the person says may not be what a parent with a seriously ill child prefers to hear and yet it is closer to the truth and will always be the better approach and response to a parent or child. It is a more heartful response: it is clear and closer to the truth than any promises that are made, as every individual's journey of wellbeing and healing is uniquely personal and unpredictable.

A message or response from the heart in its true meaning is travelling with feel-able love and compassion, the person receiving the answer will also be able to hear it differently, work and be with it in a different way.

The heart quality here will also allow the other, the patient, client or family member to respond with more heart, being helped to understanding what is happening at a deeper level, to accept the message, options and opportunities. At the same time the heart will start to kick in, help, offer answers and radiates calmness. Paul's sharing, the perspective of another doctor, an anaesthetist, who also practices and uses the heart in his work, illustrates this clearly:

> *There is a deep peace within ... and it is not uncommon for patients to say to me 'I feel peaceful'. It seems they connect to the quality of the heart, the calmness and peace it has given me. For my patients this means something special, in a way that there is a peace within them, despite their situation, which can be serious and stressful. The day before an operation, especially for major surgery, can be extremely stressful.*

Modern medicine and the heart are very compatible. Paul came to attend heart sessions, meditations and the related workshops several years ago while working on secondment at a hospital in Australia. Paul had his own health issues and sought help from a range of sources and modalities. However, the story he felt to share in this book was equally if not more so about the work relationship he had with his colleagues. He has now returned to his home country in Ireland, works as a medical doctor and in addition, he organises, coordinates and teaches heart workshops where he lives. Paul's complete story and sharing is in the work section of the book.

Option 2: Alternative medicine or therapies and your health and wellbeing

Many years ago I saw research that found that 40% of people with health issues seek alternative treatments, either as their sole choice or in addition to their more conventional, medical help sought. Anecdotally I have since heard that this has gone to an even higher percentage of 50%. This is certainly one indicator that people want more choice in relation to the direction of their health, wellbeing or medical treatment; more than what is offered by 'modern medicine' or government supported choices.

This is now also supported by many of the private health funds in Australian and around the world who fund some of the more established or reputable choices.

Alternative therapies span across a huge range of treatment options and interventions. Some are old, well established and well researched, others are of much less clear as to what they do, what they offer and how they work. It is always advisable to do your own research too.

The heart, our non-physical heart, takes you on a similar journey only in so far as some of the alternative therapies are also working on an energy or non-physical phenomena. There is an almost endless list of energy balancing therapies available. Acupuncture, Homeopathy, Bioenergetics, Kinesiology and Shiatsu are some of the more established examples. These are acknowledged modalities and are covered by health funds in Australia and other countries of the world. Some of the alternative modalities are questionable, not fully researched or researched with enough depth, promise more than what they can achieve or even have potential side-effects; in a way the results are very similar to those of modern medicine.

The one advantage that any heart input, any heart help clearly has, is that there are no negative impacts, side effects or any future difficulties that can arise as part of the (heart) treatment.

The role of your heart is more aligned with the broader understanding or definitions about health or wellbeing briefly indicated above. The first input you heart can have is to help you choose the intervention that is best suited to you, or the best preventative program, regardless of any expert, professional or personal advice you may get.

Whatever you choose, consider adding your heart to it. It will always support whatever you have chosen. As you will see further down in this section, some of the stories clearly relate to healing, greater health or improved wellbeing directly to the help from the heart.

In the same way as you would choose the best option for your health or wellbeing issues, for example a combination of modern medicine and supporting alternative interventions or alternative medicine with supporting modern medicine interventions, at times it is heart-wise and brain-wise to really tune in, feel what the best combination of interventions for you will be.

Up to now there have been discussions and at times fierce arguments around the benefits of modern versus alternative or traditional medicine. It is perhaps times to acknowledge that both can offer something important in certain circumstances and in both there are weak or strong skills, insights, wisdom and experience of the actual practitioner.

There is also your and your practitioner's innate heart intelligence: the ability to understand and to work with illness, causes of illness and the deeper physical, non-physical, meta-physical and spiritual understanding around life, illness, wellbeing.

The question are, how much innate heart intelligence is being used, and, is any diagnosis and treatment plan able to be complete without a deeper understanding the whole person? There is one more option.

Option 3: Your heart and heart radiance

Few are those who see with their own eyes and feel with their own hearts.
Albert Einstein

Your heart is immensely important in helping you with both your health and wellbeing, now and in the longer term. Your heart has the inbuilt and direct ability to positively affect your wellbeing and health. Many natural health practices are concerned with the re-balancing of the energy flows that exist within your body-mind-heart being. A greater and more natural balance in turn then triggers the body's given functions to restore health and wellbeing.

Other groups of therapies intend to connect to another source of energy, an internal or external source of finer, more deeply penetrating energy. This is the case in practices or modalities such as Pranic Healing or Reiki.

The reality that energy precedes matter is one of Albert Einstein's great finding. Some therapies know about this and rely on it. If energy is shifted, moved or balanced, or if good energy is added, a physical, mental or emotional shift.

What is hoped for, and some may say has been shown, is that this energy work will trigger or facilitate healing or at the very least add positively to the body's natural ability to heal.

In principle, the heart will help in two very significant ways with your wellbeing, health and any healing issues or need. s It will directly facilitate greater wellbeing or health and it will guide you in your decision-making.

The heart will also offer immediate additional support to you and help you with whatever health or wellbeing issues that you have. It will enhance your health and wellbeing independently or in conjunction with other modalities; it also has the potential to counteract the sometimes hard to avoid negative side-effects of treatments whether this is the taking of strong pills or chemo-therapy, for example.

You can let your heart help you at the varying degree this works for you while at the same time you continue to use modern medical or alternative therapies or both.

This is very self empowering as it offers more choice and directly and immediately more ways to help you. What is also empowering is that once you have a certain heart awareness, heart understanding and heart strength, you can use this as often as possible. Before looking in more detail into how your heart can offer assistance and be a key element on your wellbeing journey, let us look at two more aspects that are related to wellbeing and health and also to the heart's functions: visualisation and thinking.

Visualisation and your heart

In learning about the heart there is often the question or suggestion about how does visualisation help wellbeing or the heart. There is a school of thought and practice out there that suggests visualisation is beneficial for a range of purposes, including for your wellbeing and health. It is important to discuss visualisation from the perspective of the heart. Once you understand and experience the heart's deep workings you also want to at least be aware of everything supporting or limiting the working of the heart; even in subtle ways.

What is commonly understood as 'visualisation'? Visualisation may spontaneously happen or you may follow someone's directions or suggestions. There are a couple of things that are good to know, with a clearer heart understanding, related to this practice.

Visualisation is about creating something, visualising something that is presently not in your life, or not fully present there or happening. Creating something naturally arises from our day to day understanding of what good health or wellbeing is and how we want our health outcomes to be. This is meaningful and good to some extent. It does not, however, fully recognise and include what your heart, which is the more complete or the whole part of you, knows and wants to facilitate.

The moment you rely solely or mainly on visualising your health outcome there is another crafty thing happening that is taking some of your mind/brain and other parts from the 'here and now' where healing is happening. It is your full presence in every moment that will allow your heart and all healing to be strongly facilitated.

The heart's help is always now, here this moment and every moment. It works in the now. It also brings you into the 'here and now' when thoughts, worries or distractions occur.

Life takes place in the moment and those activities, even when you apply the logic of the mind/brain, will take you out of this moment, every moment. This will somewhat limit your full awareness in every moment, and it will also, to some extent, reduce the heart's ability to help you.

> **Practical Heart Tip 42: Heart-supported visualisation for health ***
>
> *If you practise any visualisation, especially those that are intended to support your wellbeing, health or healing, then it is suggested that you do it from and with a strong heart.*
>
> *The way to do it is to smile to the heart or do full Heart Strengthening (KHH 6) for some time, until you clearly feel the feeling from the heart, then begin your affirmations or visualisations.*
>
> *This means that in your practice the heart and its unique abilities will help or facilitate a deeper impact.*

When asked, program participants always seem to know that any form of visualisation or affirmation is connected to, if not generated, from the mind/brain. This means an involuntary strengthening of an already dominant mind/brain habit or activity. Further, if the heart's help is limited or non-existent, the more you rely on these practices. It is always best to find a balance that feels right to you rather than follow someone's suggestion, directive or experience.

Thinking and your heart

To think is good, natural and normal. Looked at broadly, thinking can be positive or negative. Further, how often you think, or how often you think when feeling or using the heart at the same time, is important. Thinking, its impact on the heart, the heart's role and help and your overall heart strength, wellbeing and health will be explored in the next sections.

Thinking and your body

Over-thinking has already been touched on in the above section on mental health and the heart. A more positive mind-body-heart balance impacts very positively on your overall wellbeing and health. One of these balances is to become aware of your thinking habits and the impact that thinking or over-thinking, has on health and wellbeing in the short, medium and long-term - starting with the tension levels in your body.

The brain and its connection to the nervous system is in place to control and move the body. There is the reverse impact too. The more tension you hold in your body, the more you will be inclined to think and over-think.

To share with you the connection between thinking and the body's response thinking you can do a simple experiment.

> **Practical Heart Tip 43: The thinking - tension connection**
>
> *Lie down and relax (alternatively you can sit comfortably in a chair - so that your head also can be rested). Now take a few moments to relax your body and mind as much as possible. Enjoy relaxing for approximately one to two minutes.*
>
> *Now think of something, whatever comes to your mind - what you intend to do later or tomorrow during the day. As you start to think, feel what is happening in your body. Feel that you become more tense in certain body areas, or overall, because of your thoughts. This can be quite subtle.*
>
> *Now switch a few times between thinking again and then reducing thinking while continuing to relax. Do each for about half a minute. Feel tension levels your body, in particular your hands, arms or legs as you think and relax again.*
>
> *With your current heart awareness and learning you can also switch between thinking/planning something and smiling to your heart/feeling your heart. Bring your awareness to how the body responds.*

What this simple experiment can show is the relationship between (a) mainly your thoughts and the tension your body creates and holds when it is thinking and (b) how there is a relationship between your levels of relaxation and the tendency to think.

The more you think the higher the stress levels can become. Why? Tension in the body is building up, naturally, as we go through the day, hold the body in certain ways, tense muscles to do your work or do other activities. There is a natural balance in all this. Natural means that you relax well, you sleep well and have a form of exercise that keeps you fit, relaxes your body/muscles and maybe stretches your muscles, ligaments and joints.

Over-thinking, or thinking with reduced heart activity or presence, is tipping the scales into one direction: tension in the body will build up. While thinking does create tension and adds to stress or pressure experienced, there is also an energetic impact: energy flowing through your body is reduced. This also means that the body's expulsion of negative energy is reduced. Firstly, this change in healing energy flow will impact medium to long-term on your overall feeling of wellbeing. Secondly, negativity will build up and add to any illness potential over time. This might be too 'out-there' for readers who need more evidence or something more tangible. That is fine, at the very least you have heard about this and know that these energy flows are viewed as essential to human wellbeing and health in, for example, respected modalities such as acupuncture, Chinese Medicine, the Indian Ayurvedic systems and Homeopathy. In fact, most alternative therapies, respected, accepted or less accepted, work on an energy basis.

Energy flow and relaxation often work hand in hand. The more energy flow, the less your energy is blocked, and the deeper the physical and mental relaxation can be. Deeper state of relaxation also promotes natural rejuvenation as a balance to busy-ness and pressures in life.

What you can do instead is to use your growing awareness and both your heart and mind/brain's learning about this to be more relaxed more often and to think less or, more correctly, think only when you need to think. When you do not need to think, do, plan or create something that requires thinking, enjoy the heart, be in your heart and enjoy the pleasant, gentle feelings from within.

There is a risk that after some time, even years, or after prolonged periods of tension, the body will respond more negatively and when illness strikes it can hang around for longer or go to deeper levels causing more problems. There is also no significant illness that develops in a few days. Most serious illness that occurs in adults has a long history.

Positive thinking

Positive thinking, and any approach that you may follow, is in principle helpful to your heart. Any negative thinking will impact on the heart by placing negative, thinking-generated, impurities or burdens round or even within your heart. This depends on the severity of negative thinking and for how long during the day this happens.

Positive thinking - or thinking positively - will help to reduce further burdening of the inner or outer part of the heart. Negative thinking coupled with negative emotions will cause the heart to close.

Positive thinking is just that. Any attempts to unburden the heart to feel lighter, happier and softer through any thinking approaches, will not work. The heart responds directly and only to the natural techniques that you have experienced in earlier sections. The Heart Strengthening and the Heart Meditation practices are the most complete or holistic versions of it.

When you want all the help available to you, all the assistance from your heart in either preventative health or with any health issues, then positive thinking is another ingredient to be aware of. Do not allow negative thinking to be too influential on your heart and therefore your wellbeing.

If you take positive thinking one step further then it can also include the growing awareness of moments when you are or aren't thinking positive thoughts. The ability and power of a clearer mind, helped by your clearing and stronger heart, can help with this. It will help you to be more aware of how you think. These reflections ideally stop you from going in this direction and from following negative thoughts. You feel more empowered, from within, to have the choice to say 'no' to those kind of thoughts and to not follow any past conditioning or rising wants, drives or desires to do so.

It can be hard at first as many of us are so addicted to our way of thinking, mistakenly believing that this is who we are. It is worth the 'effort' you put into it, and the adjustments, as the end result will be amazing. Your heart will be lighter, more peaceful, and you will be happier.

Relaxation

Relaxation is important to our life in general given the almost immediate impact it can have on energy flows and the releasing of accumulated pressures, tensions and negativities.

Relaxation is immensely important for your heart. The more relaxed you are the better able you are to feel your heart or feel it more strongly. When this happens your heart opens and is cleansed instantly. When you are more relaxed the better your heart can be present. This means your heart will be developing more, or more easily, and you will have the help from your heart in times when you are relaxed.

Once you start to practice relaxation it will be easier to be there, be more relaxed in every life situation, because you will also have the presence of your heart to help.

It is wonderful that the more you learn to relax the more your heart will help you in all areas of life. The more relaxed you are the heart will also be able to directly remove burdens and whatever heart-limiting collection of negativities you have around your heart. Some form of regular relaxation practice will significantly speed up your heart's condition and help.

This is a simple relaxation exercise you can practice once or several times a day or week to help to achieve deepening levels of relaxation.

Practical Heart Tip 44: Heart-supporting, tension releasing relaxation (Relaxation II) *

You can do this relaxation sitting-up or lying-down. It further engages the heart because you are encouraged to feel different parts of the body. It will also help you to practice 'letting go'.

Find a comfortable place to sit or lie. Make sure that for the 5, 10 or 15 minutes that you relax you are warm enough and, ideally, are not interrupted. A light or warm cloth can help with heat-loss and an extra sense of cosiness or protection. Once in your position, follow this pattern:

Heart:	*Feel your heart, the spiritual heart ... smile to your physical heart ... and enjoy for a few moments.*
Forehead:	*Feel the whole forehead area ... just intend let go of all tension.*
Eyes:	*Feel your eyes ... (optional: open them once more, then close them gently) ... just intend let go of all tension.*
Top of the head:	*Feel the top of the head ... just intend let go of all tension.*
Sides of the head:	*Feel the sides of the head ... just intend let go of all tension.*
Back of the head:	*Feel the back of the head ... just intend let go of all tension.*
Jaws and Mouth:	*Feel jaws and mouth area ... just intend let go of all tension. Lightly open the temporomandibular joint - the muscle that hold the jaws together - with the lips lightly open or closed.*
Neck & throat:	*Feel the neck and throat area ... let go of all tension.*
Shoulders:	*Feel the shoulders ... let go of all tension. Allow the shoulders to drop, towards the earth/floor.*
Arms:	*Feel your arms, elbows and forearms ... let go of all tension.*
Hands:	*Feel the writs, fingers and whole hands... let go of all tension.*
Chest (upper torso):	*Feel the chest, front, sides and back ... let go of all tension.*
Stomach (lower torso):	*Feel the stomach, whole abdominal area, organs within and the lower back ... let go of all tension.*
Pelvis:	*Feel the pelvic area, front, sides, back and the pelvic floor ... let go of all tension.*
Legs:	*Feel the legs, thighs, knees and lower legs ... let go of all tension.*
Feet:	*Feel the ankles, feet, sole of the foot and toes ... let go of all tension.*

After each section or body part keep feeling for a few moments to give it time to let go and relax. Allow between 10 and 20 minutes for this PHT. Every time you begin you want to feel your heart first, then, while continuing to feel the heart, also feel the body parts. This feeling from within, being within your body, while your feeling and heart are active, will achieve a deep relaxation.

The 'letting go' should be as an intention only, not a doing, will further help. Letting go at the level of the heart is ultimately the key. Letting go from the mind/brain's holding or controlling also offers deepening of 'letting go' learning. While here, in this PHT, 'letting go' is primarily at a physical level, the body, mind-heart unit learns holistically, hence all parts of you will learn to some degree.

Any form of relaxation will directly impact on the heart. With a stronger heart, there is a chance, that you will also be reminded more often that your heart needs relaxation. In turn this will allow the heart to freer, more open and more available to help you.

There is a form of relaxing that will support your heart more. This is relaxing by relying more on both your heart's ability to help you to relax and your body's innate or given knowledge of how to relax. Having the intention to do less, to let the heart do more, to trust the body, will gently and naturally take you there.

PHT 44 is a simple relaxation exercise you can practice once or several times a day or week to help to achieve deepening levels of relaxation. PHT 45 is more intuitive and natural and only available online.

Practical Heart Tip 45: Natural, heart-centred relaxation (Relaxation III) *

There is one more way you can relax your body and mind. The 'natural relaxation' is a blending of earlier relaxation practices. A tuning in with the heart and the heart's engagement are possible from the very first moment you begin to relax. You will find an audio version of this relaxation on the website (www.yourheartcanhelp.org).

Working on relaxing is important. Working here perhaps means to be aware of your life-style, overall tension or pressure levels and to use the mind/brain to make new, better or adjusting choices. Remember and realize that if you consciously choose to relax you are almost half-way there and all the shared benefits of more heart presence will start to be available.

The heart and your body

Any commitment to your heart, to opening and using your heart more, in practices and in daily life, will counteract the tendencies of over-tensing and not-so-helpful, even damaging flow-on effects.

Every time that you do heart practice, do the KHHs that directly activate the heart more, or any of the direct heart supporting PHTs, you will naturally and automatically be more relaxed. Relaxation will stimulate rejuvenation and healing, even alone, although on its own this is limited, especially if illness is present.

Because the mind/brain, body and heart are one unit, any positive steps in one of these parts will also positively impact on the other one.

Relax more often - your body-mind-heart knows how and smile more often! Together a natural release, de-stressing will happen and your inclination to think or to over-think will gradually, at times instantly, be reduced. After some weeks you should see and feel clear results. It will creep up on you, without you noticing it daily, as the tendency to think in situations where it is not necessary.

> *Practical Heart Tip 46: Your heart 'mantra'*
>
> *Make 'relax and smile' your mantra. Relax and smile ...*
>
> - *When you wake up;*
> - *Often or more often during your day;*
> - *When you find yourself having or following negative thoughts;*
> - *When you find yourself having or following negative emotions; and*
> - *As your last thought and action at the end of every day (action here means doing it and feeling the impact).*

What are causes of un-wellbeing, in particular those that relate to or impact negatively on your heart-help, heart journey?

Causes of un-wellbeing

There are very likely many causes of ill-being and illness. The word choice 'very likely' is used to indicate that many different approaches to health and wellbeing have their own theory, concept and empirical data. Yet, perhaps even if all of these were put together, carefully investigated or researched, the full list of causes may still not be fully explored and known.

One clear achievement that modern medicine brings with it is the indirect acknowledgement, too, that both causes and cures still require more search, research and perhaps opening of perspectives, minds and hearts.

In order to better understand how the heart can assist it is helpful to look at some of the known and widely acknowledged causes of ill-being or illness. Only some are discussed, as they relate directly to your heart and heart help.

Discussion of some of these will further assist in pointing to a broader direction of heart-help, including areas where alternative or modern medicine only has partial or no knowledge yet.

The causes of your problems and health issues may be several, complex or, from the viewpoint of your current knowledge, fall outside these lists of possible cause.

Stress

You, like everyone else, will be exposed to varying degrees of stress, tension and pressure. Stress and pressure can be from within us to some extent. The main source is often seen in the external situations, pressures at work or at home.

However, as you are more aware of the different levels of stress and tension that your body-mind-heart holds, you can make new choices that will support your wellbeing and healing regardless of what the ultimate list of causes may be.

There is good stress, too. Good stress may be a level of pressure, timelines, expectation that helps you to perform at your best, to work hard and to find new, deeper levels of commitment to what you do, at home or at work. It also helps us not to procrastinate. This is not the kind of stress to be concerned about.

Any stress that affects, your physical, emotional, mental health and spiritual wellbeing in a negative way, regardless of whether you are aware, partially aware or unaware of this, should be avoided at all cost.

Stress not only contributes directly to any possible ill-being or illness, it also impacts on our emotional world. Have you noticed that the higher the stress levels, the less the mind/brain's natural function is able to hold it together, to limit or stop emotions from surfacing, finding expression and in some instances from running wild. Throughout the book you have learned about emotions and how they negatively or positively affect you, those close to you and your heart. The more stress, the more emotions are likely to surface and impact on others and, in return, significantly add to your stress levels as communication gets more difficult or even breaks down with colleagues, friends or even at home.

Some of the alternative or 'softer' therapies solely aim to help with stress relief and often we love and appreciate them. Practices are, for example, massage and bath routines. These are fantastic tools that can assist. There is also a point where many modalities will not be strong or deep enough to offer sustained or long-term help or change. A change of life style, habits, work routines, environment or a 'change of heart' or attitude are needed.

The harder it is for you to cope with pressure the more you are likely to put pressure on your heart and therefore add more heaviness and burden. At the same time your heart will not be able to naturally or with intention, guide and lead you. Over time you will also feel less and less of the pleasant feelings a light heart naturally generates for you. It is in some way related to the heart's ability to open the outer layers of yourself/or your being and to release pressure that naturally - as you live life - builds up. Active attention to your heart, as introduced in the book, will make the most significant amount of positive change.

This is where your heart directly and immediately assists in returning you to feelings of calmness and inner peace. It also works to reduce the accumulated negativities caused by past stress, and other factors that disallow the right or growing feelings of calmness to fully be facilitated.

This may take some time and will only be felt if your heart practice is correct, with proper attention to the heart, or perhaps if you have made some general heart progress. Equally the heart's broader knowing and ability to help you also does not want you to make radical changes.

Practical Heart Tip 47: Instant stress relief 'heart first aid' *

If you find yourself in a stressful, uncomfortable environment or situation that's hard to cope with, it is best to use your heart. Heart first aid can be any of the following or all of them:

- *Relax with clear intention to do so (PHT 19, 44 or 45) and at whatever level you can feel it, do it or achieve it, feel that it is possible to relax the body and the mind even a little bit more.*

- *Smile to your heart, even a little, so that the heart's balancing, helping abilities are activated and will work instantly and for some time to come, even after you finished your 'heart first aid' break.*

- *Remember to smile to your heart even if things seem or are tough, difficult or stressful.*

- *For this to happen with some quality you may need to take time out. Time out can be whenever it is possible for you to close your eyes, relax, smile to your heart and spend one to two minutes just feeling the heart (even if you can't actually feel).*

- *Intend to be in your heart and feel your heart or area where your heart is.*

When you are triggered and conditioned by the stressful situation you can make a resolution, and place reminders where you will see them, to attend to your heart in stressful moments.

Outside the stressful environment it is really good to do good quality heart practice. Good to commit to regular Heart Strengthening (KHH 6) or a similar complete routine.

If you maintain this practice, regardless of what the pressure is, your condition will not worsen at the energetic, heart and feeling levels. You will come out at the other end, when the stress becomes less in your life, in a good, even better condition than before.

Whether you are at home or at work any sense of peace, calm and 'normality' will be detectable by others and they will feel that you more approachable, likeable and loveable. There will be better relationships, team work and outcomes. You find more about this in the 'work' section.

'Heart first aid' is just that, first aid. Over time you want to get to a point where, even when you don't remember, there is a new habit, a natural smile combined with moments when you relax and feel your heart.

To rely on the heart will be something new to most readers. It is very helpful to keep make notes, put stickers, make calendar entries that pop up and keep a diary or note book. Make a note in your current diary (a) or a Heart Diary (PHT 27) how often you remembered, did the above PHT and other heart practices and (b) how you feel, overall, at the end of the day.

This is not to achieve something or to monitor activity or improvement only. It will allow you also to track any changes, to see that over time there is heart-initiated and heart-supported change. Even if you believe things stay the same or get worse, perception is not always aligned with what is really happening. In addition, ask someone you trust, at home or at work, how do they perceive you. How stressed or calm do you appear to them. Often when we are stressed it is people close to us who notice if any improvements or changes have occurred in us and they can give important, honest and encouraging feedback.

Environments - social, physical and your heart

> *The forest makes your heart gentle.*
> *... no place for greed or anger there. Pha Pachak*

Your social and physical environments have effects on health, wellbeing, healing or any recovery. Your social environment is your work, your home, your family, friends, other social or sporting activities and the wider community. These environments can be more or less supportive to you, your wellbeing and the overall happiness you feel in your heart and life. It also includes the friends you 'hang out with' on social media and what kind of interactions you have in person, over the phone and 'electronically' with your dear ones and any close or loose social groups.

The more your thoughts and feelings are positive or positively enforced in your work or other social interactions, the happier you and your heart will be. Some situations can be changed and some are harder to change. Small changes can make a big difference over time for your heart and wellbeing. Equally important, however, is your response to whatever is happening in your social environment - as discussed in the next section/PHT.

The 'Heart Monitor' will allow you to be and become more aware of your feeling in daily life and how to invite more of your heart in to help you.

Practical Heart Tip 48: Heart Monitor

Draw up a table on a piece of paper or download the version from www.yourheartcanhelp.org.

Set up a basic template similar to:

- *In the left column allow space for the days of the week and events that stand out 'good' or 'not-so-good' in terms of your heart awareness;*

- *Add three (or five) more columns: mornings, afternoons and evenings (or add lunch and dinner time also);*

- *Monitor and assess how you went in terms of being 'heartful' during each of the three (five) stretches of time; and*

- *Plan to 'heart monitor' over a five to seven-day period.*

Every lunchtime, dinner time and before you go to bed leave a brief comment on how you were/felt during each of these stretches of time, for example:

- *How positive overall;*

- *How negative or burdened;*

- *How emotional overall;*

- *How much thinking or how busy as your mind/brain; and*

- *How heart connected, how much were you feeling your heart?*

Over one or several weeks, this will show you where and when you experienced the heart more or more mind/brain or negativity, even if in subtle ways.

Now plan what you can do and make changes that are possible. This may be when and how to remove yourself more from situations or environment, and, what can be done to improve your mind and heart attitude. If you are the 'doer' and add to not-so-good or negative environments or situations, with a strengthening heart and reflection, do less of it.

You can add two additional columns that shows when and where you used the heart or heart strengthening to assist and what was the impact of it, for you, for others in your environment.

Physical environmental conditions are everything physical around you: your home, living condition, quality of physical life-supporting items, such as your home, flat or room, clothing and means of transport. At times it seems more or less obvious that these make us feel more relaxed, more at peace or more stressed. Both social and physical environments have been subject to many research projects, including how they relate to people's wellbeing and health; and allow better planning for social, environmental, town and architectural building to happen.

Your physical environment is also your garden, neighbouring parks and the wider environment within and around where you live. In most of these there are patches or bigger areas of parkland, bush or otherwise natural surroundings.

Your heart likes nature, green, gardens, parks.

The less of this that you have in your immediate environment, the more you can consciously make the time to be there. Do this as often as you can. You may already be aware of this. Naturally, people are drawn to spend time in parks, zoos, by the beach or in other natural settings. People feel that nature, green areas, parks, gardens, a lake or the ocean help in feeling more open, relaxed and at peace. These environments, as one may say, are refreshing 'for the spirit', for the 'heart, mind and body'.

> ### Practical Heart Tip 49: Heart time in nature *
>
> *You can use your Heart Diary to create a simple table or alternatively use an existing calendar to make notes of how often you spend time in nature. This can include walking or sitting in a park, spending time in your garden or at a beach. This will allow you to keep a basic record over a period of time: one week, a month or half a year.*
>
> *What is important and even more heart nurturing is to do the following:*
>
> - *Take your time, sit down and do some form of heart connecting or Heart Strengthening;*
> - *Feel your heart and enjoy whatever you feel, or even follow the feeling; then*
> - *Let your heart, with one intention only, feel and enjoy the nature around you; and*
> - *Sit in this feeling, feeling your heart for some more time. When you feel any shift in feeling, enjoy, keep feeling or follow what you feel in the heart. It is in these moments that your heart will open more, be cleansed, and more ready to help you and all that you do.*
>
> *Every time you do this with some heart-awareness, and really feel it, it will be quality heart refreshing time in nature. If you have any burdens, troubles, challenges or heaviness in your life, the heart's greater activation, by being in nature, will work on these.*

There are physical environments where there is very little green or nature around. If this is your situation the following PHT may help you. You may, however, find that your heart so enjoys nature that you want to use this PHT even in situations where you have some green or nature outside your home.

> ### Practical Heart Tip 50: A green heart spot at home *
>
> *With this PHT you can go 'wild'. Go to an indoor garden store and find one or several plants that you like or that fit your home, space or style.*
>
> *You can also be creative and talk to friends who can give you cuttings, seedlings, an old pot or a plastic pot that carried a plant from the shop to the garden or home. Plants, pots and soil cost money. Let money or time not be an excuse. I found weeds in the garden here in Australia that are sold as indoor green/plants back in Europe. Create some green dots in your home, in all rooms eventually; including next to your favourite heart connection or heart meditation spot.*
>
> *You can then do the previous PHT at home or out in nature. You may find that with more heart and with your heart's radiance, the plants at home will thrive.*

This book is mainly about the heart. However, your mind-brain and your heart need to work together. In the same way, as team work is often better than solo performances.

Sometimes life requires action, steps forward and decisions to create a more positive environment or one that supports you and your heart better.

If you feel to make changes, then you may seek help, gentle advice or self-assess your social, work and physical environmental situation. Make the changes and improvements you can easily make. Of course you want to follow, as best as possible, what feels right to you, your heart.

Bigger or radical changes that push you to the limits or severely challenge others around you may come from the centre of self, ego and negative ambitions. Be aware of it, of the feeling you have - in your heart - as you think about your changes.

Your heart is fast. The moment you contemplate any situation or change, your heart will instantly respond. In a situation, your heart may feel pressure or contraction, meaning the thought, idea and possible choice is not so good for you and all concerned. Or it may feel gentleness, lightness, even expansion, the better choice. As you gain clearer heart-awareness and feeling, and related confidence and trust, make any social or work decisions gently and with care and with love from your heart.

Following Emotions

The way you respond to any situations that trigger your emotions will impact on your heart condition. Sections III and IV cover this extensively. Remember also, that everything that is not well or is ill has a corresponding part in your heart. Further, from section II, emotions are the negative drives that don't feel so good when we or others have them; around us or towards us.

It is in some way normal that negative emotions surface when illness or an accident happens. The grief process that Dr Elizabeth Kuebler-Ross shares in some of her work around serious illness and dying, points to this emotional process, as emotional reactivity, in some of the stages. The main emotions are likely to be around anger and resentment. 'Why did/does this happen to me'? This is often is also coupled with emotions such as resentment, envy or disillusionment 'why me', or 'this is just not right' or 'why me and not others'.

Elizabeth Kuebler-Ross did some wonderful work that you can look up or read, about people who are diagnosed with a serious or terminal illness and how they respond. Some of her key findings are around 'reaction and response'. There is an initial response in situations like this, such as denial, anger or frustration. She also observes that over time people change, accept, adapt and make more reasonable decisions. All this is about grief and the process of grief that is now being used in many other areas of life.

With heightened heart understanding, however, any emotional process is best addressed as soon as possible. The way that you deal with these negative drives is crucially important in terms of your health and wellbeing and how your overall heart condition will be. This means there is a short, medium and longer-term perspective and impact possible, which will be negative or positive in terms of any health, healing and wellbeing.

Seeking professional help, punching a pillow or a boxing bag, going for a brisk walk, talking to a friend and exercising, are a few techniques used to manage these negative drives within.

You know that emotions do not feel pleasant at some level within, equally when they are expressed towards others, they do harm, breach trust and hurt. What is less known is the damage that they do in the long run. Every time you feel, express or have emotion it will limit your heart's ability to help.

Every time that you work to release emotion, and in doing so you experience some or the full breadth of it, it will add to the burdens your heart.

This includes the expression of emotion with good intention, as in sharing it with a friend or punching a pillow or bag to release anger.

Practical Heart Tip 51: Rely on your heart

If you are considering some of the above techniques, it is best they are used in addition to your heart. Going for a walk in nature, talking to a friend with kind feelings, or exercising can be helpful and help - not burden - the heart.

If you punch something, while re-experiencing the emotion, then you are still burdening your heart. It may be much better than punching another human being, yet if you really want to let the heart become strong and the negativity to go, use the suggested Heart Strengthening.

What will happen over time is that you will experience a different and direct level of help from your heart. You will get to a point where this help-input is becoming very clear. From this point on it is good to rely onto your heart as the core, main or foundation practice. Reducing the use of or letting go of other emotion-releasing work is then the feeling or 'voice' from within you.

If you have health issues that you want to resolve, or if you want to grow the levels of wellbeing to new heights, it is important, at least for some time to experiment with a new way of dealing with emotions. In section two emotional intelligence and the heart were discussed. To improve your feeling of wellbeing it is important to put knowledge into practice.

The 'heart monitor' is essential for a more holistic or committed approach. Unsupportive patterns or habits can creep up in everyone. The 'heart monitor' is your quality control, your check-in mechanism to see, day by day, what and how you do. It also helps you to stay on track. You will also see that there are ups and down and yet, you also see, over time, the important longer-term trends and developments.

Practical Heart Tip 52: Heart monitor reminder

If you are serious about improving your heart condition and to do the best for any physical, mental, emotional or other health conditions, use the Heart Monitor over several weeks and together with a heart strengthening routine, monitor your progress and behavioural changes.

You find the Heart Monitor explained in detail in section 5 (PHT 48).

Reaction to illness, injury or un-wellbeing

When something happens to you, when you fall ill, get injured or your wellbeing is reduced, the reaction to it can easily trigger emotions. There is a degree of choice you have in your reaction, in your response. You can positively change with more heart strength.

There is a tendency in all of us to react with some level of emotion when we do not get what we want. In this situation, it is, for example, better health that we want but may not have, get or don't yet have.

Reacting with any kind of emotion, however subtle or strong, will not support your heart and this means also not support you and potential positive changes to your wellbeing.

It is quite normal to have emotional reaction. Emotional reaction as per this book's definition is always a negative one - it has negative qualities or impacts. Have you met anyone in your life with no negative emotions or reactions? You may think of someone you believe is at this place, like a well-respected person in your community or world. Then again, not spending 24 hours and 7 days a week with this person, does one really know?

It can be inspirational to look at others. However, their emotional state or reactivity is much less important than your own. Do you have negative emotions, here and there, subtle, stronger, at the surface or below? Is it clear to you, with up-to-now heart experiences made, that what you feel or follow is heart feeling versus emotion. You can also go back to the discussions and the emotion-list in section II. Perhaps find any emotion(s) you are inclined to experience at times - expressed outwards or not. If you are still unsure, explain to a friend or family member to you the understanding shared in this book about emotions versus heart-feelings and ask for comments or feedback - what is your friend's experience with emotions shown by you?

Emotions commonly would be the negative drives such as anger, frustration, self-pity, disappointment. These emotion or emotional reactions place negativities in or around the heart.

The grief or emotions curve often associated with Dr. Kuebler-Ross's work is showing how one reacts to a significant and upsetting event in life; health-related or not. What the heart offers is to make the wave of this emotional curve and experience 'smaller' or flatter. Wellbeing is to experience shorter times and less intensity of heavy emotional experiences. Your heart can help you to get back on track quicker and, in addition, for all of the heart's abilities to be available in their fullest ways.

The next PHT is immensely important to bring you back on track, to facilitate the heart's help in any 'emergency' situation. Emergency situations are, for example, the presence or diagnosis of a relatively severe illness. Any illnesses, and certainly medium to serious ones, are unsettling and upsetting.

Emergency situation, in your heart's view, is any time that you find yourself emotional, emotionally reactive or triggered to go into emotion.

> **Practical Heart Tip 53: Pull the emergency brake ***
>
> *You find yourself emotional, emotionally reactive or triggered to go into emotion.*
>
> - *Every time you feel this state coming on, emotion rising or overwhelming you;*
>
> - *Stop whatever you do; and*
>
> - *Sit somewhere reasonably quietly or undisturbed and do Heart Strengthening.*
>
> *Experiment with this for a particular length of time. For example, make the resolution to 'pull the heart-emergency brake' for one week. Note any observations in feeling and wellbeing.*

This is the truer meaning of 'following your heart'. Your heart is not leading you in some romantic of mushy way. It has an immense capacity to lead you and to help you towards a purposeful, wonderful, joyful and well life. This wellbeing is always related to, and relative, to your past and your condition.

Ultimately, in addition to all the practical and real help that your heart gives, when your heart is deeper in calmness, in a loving state and in a quiet joyful place, you will be there too, regardless of anything going on within or around you.

At yet another level of help is your heart's greater connection. When a particular emotion arises there is an opening created, in your heart, that allows for your heart, its connection to Divine, to deeply clear. This then works not only on the emotional expression, but also for deeper, inner held blockages, traumas or negativities. An underlying cause of un-wellbeing or illness, as it is associated with the heart, can be cleared.

This is an opportunity to make significant progress in terms of your heart, heart feeling and growth, in terms of improving your health and wellbeing, that is always energetically directly connected to your heart and its impurities.

Heart-help and heart-work it is never about suppressing emotions when they surface. It is about letting go, and for some time to let the emotion be free, to fully surface, for several moments/seconds, but not get caught up in the emotion. Then let your heart help you and do the deeper work.

The emotion may stay for some more minutes, or sometimes longer. It will, however, and undoubtedly, become less, even disappear during your heart 'sitting' in the moment. Over time it will be fully cleansed. It may take you several weeks or months of doing this with your heart working noticeably or unnoticed in the background.

The emotional reactivity, whatever emotion you experience, the regular or familiar, are in some way like a plant, a tree. What you 'see' is the emotion, the experience of emotion, what is visible and has risen above the ground. Then there is an intricate and at times deep root system operating. It is the heart's unique ability that can work through all of this, plant and root system, and leave 'behind' only wonderful feelings within or to share with others.

Numerous people have struggled with a particular emotion or set of emotions for years and then they started to practise choosing the heart when emotions surface. After some time, they had forgotten that they even had these negative drives or responses, as they disappeared. What is always left is your heart's improved ability to experience and share joy, happiness, spread calmness and feel love.

Practical Heart Tip 54: Remind your heart - parts I and II

Part I: Reminding your heart is really reminding your heart-mind/brain unity. This will be unusual for a few days. Similar to earlier PHTs place reminders around your home, office, shed, kitchen, bathroom, workshops, everywhere to remind you to use your heart. Every time you see the reminder, relax a little (more) and smile to your heart. Feel your heart too.

Part II. Have others remind you, help you.

- *Ask people whom you love, trust and respect and who would be willing to help to remind you to use your heart; and*

- *Perhaps, also, to remind you when you follow the old ways, such as following emotion, to be more heart connected.*

Some friends and family members purchased cheap smiley or heart sticker and place them 'strategically' onto items as reminders.

This is a little harder and it is easier when it is someone who also understands about the heart's importance and help. It is very effective and helpful. Make sure that you do not react or 'explode' if they remind you. The best is to ask them from the heart to remind you with love. In turn respond with love and gratitude - from your heart.

The Heart Monitor alone will not be enough. It is not always easy to be aware of changes that you experience going from day to day. Ask others every now and then how they perceive you and how they notice your changes.

For any serious illness or health condition very regular Heart Strengthening (KHH 6) will build the foundation. You can do this several times a day. If followed by heart meditations (KHH 12/13), once or twice a day, the foundation will be even stronger and your heart will also improve significantly. You can then spend some time smiling from the heart to any symptoms you experience and related causes (KHH 9). The last step is important. It also teaches you to rely on the heart in new ways and to trust the heart. You can compare it with the warmth or love you feel from someone close to you. First you need to feel it, only then can you know it is present or real.

The heart works well in tandem with any medical or alternative therapies that you are using. Any heart workshops that you can manage to attend further deepen the way your heart can assist you.

Workshop facilitators and your first workshop steps will help to open deeper levels of heart-learning and heart-help that is available. This is likely to be needed for any deeper lying or serious condition.

You will find some clear and wonderful examples in the following sections of how the heart has assisted others with a range of illnesses and issues, including some quite serious conditions around physical or mental health. The stories are particularly clear in how the journey of the heart is unfolding for these individual and how they relate the changes to their wellbeing to the heart.

The four ways your heart will help

1. The quality of energy flowing through your heart

Through your heart flows the finest, most blissful and most refined energy. When your heart is open, the finest, most blissful and most refined energy flows. This energy will naturally, as your heart reaches a certain stage of opening, radiate first to the organs and body parts close to the heart, including the physical heart and lungs. Then this radiation flows and expands to other parts of the body until eventually all of you is within this radiant healing energy. This energy and some of the qualities is not fully unknown to us. It has love-like quality and can feel like the feeling of love that you know or remember, healing love, unhindered by other influences such as emotions or mind.

A friend shared recently that 'the most touching moments I remember were moments when I was unwell and my mum would be close to me hold my hand or cuddle me. There was a deep feeling of love, being loved. I knew the world was okay, all would be okay and I would be well again soon.

Some of the stories and sharing throughout the book also point in a similar direction or indicate this. More important is to understand, or even 'believe', that once you start the suggested practices you will feel this radiance starting to occur. It is one of the most blissful experiences. Your heart has no belief, it simply knows at a deeper level, feels and connects to truth and wisdom; the heart just 'is'.

2. The heart-impurity - illness connection

Your heart is unlikely to be completely pure and free of any negativity or burdensome 'collection'. Wherever you have a physical, mental, psychological or emotional health issue, there is a direct link, a direct and corresponding connection to something in your heart that is also not pure, holding, not allowing, nor fully accepting its natural openness, function and radiation.

In other words, an impurity in the heart is holding or covering the illness, not allowing it to heal in the best way or not to heal at all. If you commit to opening your heart, using Heart Strengthening and the deeper, more effective Heart Meditation, then these parts, over time, will be changed, cleansed and eventually removed. Healing, or better health, can occur naturally.

This occurs in most cases without you consciously experiencing the heart-process at work. It is best that you trust your heart, let go, focus on heart strengthening and clearing in the ways suggested. A further step would be to consider entry level heart workshops to support you.

Practical Heart Tip 55: Feeling well - now and ahead

Every time that you attend to your heart and develop its capacity more, whether you do it for health reasons or any other reason, will be an investment in feeling well now and into your health future.

If your aim is to feel more kindness towards others, more calmness and happiness within, then regular Heart Strengthening and daily attendance to your heart may be enough for you.

The depth of feeling your heart can facilitate, the foundation-help needed via your heart for health and wellbeing, make any attention to your heart, pay off in the short, medium and long-term.

While the mind/brain is still strong, then 'trusting the heart' and similar statements seems a bit fluffy, and from this angle rightly so. Use your discretion, make a journal and in doing your heart practices, diarise whatever change you feel, in particular in connection with any health or wellbeing issues. Over time you will be able to notice the patterns changing and improvements happening. The mind/brain that likes to see empirical data will gradually be more on the heart's side.

3. The core of your heart - your higher, deeper knowing

Only the heart knows how to find what is precious.
Fyodor Dostoyevsky

The core of your heart has what has been called the Inner Heart, cosmic consciousness, atman, super or supra consciousness and other names that all point to the same thing, something deep, wise and beyond your normal ability to know, understand and perceive is in your heart. What you call it is of limited or no importance. Names can never reflect the completeness of what this essence, the core of your heart, truly is.

It is also not important to explore this or to fully understand this with the mind-brain. Higher consciousness, deeper knowing, understanding and realising have been discussed in spiritual, religious and self-help books extensively.

The term deeper knowing is used instead of higher knowing. While the heart may have a higher knowing, it is never about higher or lower, it is about all parts of you working together in the way they are designed to do so and to help you in the best possible way.

The more you are connected to this deeper self which lies at the core of your heart, then the innate depth of knowing and being from within will guide you in two ways:

- Spontaneously and with no conscious awareness; and
- Planned, access by you: you feel with your heart, as you intend to let the heart and Inner Heart reveal, show and help you.

Note that whatever your heart and Inner Heart will reveal or show you will ever only be in the form of a feeling.

Spontaneously your heart and Inner Heart will bring to the surface feelings. The heart and Inner Heart are so in tune with your whole being and what is going on in your life, that any thought, intention, internal event or external event will trigger a heart feeling. You can be guided by this deeper knowing. The more positive experiences you make, doing more of what feels right, will feel normal and natural. PHT 'Feeling well - now and ahead' and the one below will assist you in practically learning to do this. Your heart will assist you to make decisions that will better support your journey into health and wellbeing.

The commitment to live your life with more heart will open the connection from your heart to your Inner Heart to some extent.

The growing use of the Inner Heart is something immensely profound and helpful. It can perceive a greater or more universal truth. It also strengthens everything 'heart'. The heart is meant to be used in this way.

You can accelerate this connection-opening through the heart workshop program outlined in the back of the book. Open Heart Workshops five and six cover Inner Heart learning. Your growing connection to your heart/Inner Heart will improve intuition and deeper feeling-wisdom available to you, for your wellbeing, growth and relationships.

> ### Practical Heart Tip 56: Tapping into the heart's deeper knowing *
>
> *After some time of Heart Strengthening, and as you feel the presence of your heart with some clarity in your daily life, you can ask your heart/Inner Heart questions for guidance:*
>
> *For example, when you have two therapies to choose from, you can ask:*
>
> - *'How is the feeling from the heart/Inner Heart if I choose therapy/therapist option one? Feel the feeling for some time. Then repeat for ...*
>
> - *Therapy/therapist option two and feel the feeling. Feel the feeling for around the same length of time.*
>
> *It is recommended to ask if there is a third option or person even if you don't know of it or believe there isn't such a third option. Remember the heart knows more, and a bigger picture, than the mind/brain.*
>
> *Where you feel the gentler, deeper or most widening feeling then this is how your Inner Heart and heart are guiding you. If option three is the strongest one, then it may be best to wait, move through your life without acting or making any decision for now. This is, if you can afford to do so, and perhaps pray, in the way you pray, or use affirmation to ask for guidance and insight to realise what another option is.*

Every person is different and the above PHT is solely a tool that gives some structure and to realise how we, as humans, ideally or naturally, should be: following the heart in all matters and using the mind/brain to express and execute action. It is also good practice to use the heart regularly this way for important decisions. You will still learn and make experiences that will guide you and improve trust in your own heart/Inner heart ability.

What is further important is to realise that the answer is at times less important than the regular use of the heart. To go with what is offered, or what feels right or what naturally happens in terms of any therapy choices, and to use the heart's help in addition.

Every person is different. You may have come across a friend, colleague or family member who uses their feeling already quite a lot, including in making moment-to-moment decisions. Perhaps that is even you. Hopefully the discussions so far have assisted to clarify or deepen this natural way of being and using the heart.

4.   The core of your heart - your connection to radiant, unconditional love

> *When you begin to touch your heart or let your heart be touched,*
> *you begin to discover that it's bottomless, that it doesn't have any resolution,*
> *that this heart is huge, vast and limitless. Pema Chodron*

The core of your heart, the Inner Heart, is referred to in many religious, holy books, poetry, songs and related literature as something very special, something God-given.

The ability of God directly to assist humans with illness and disease has often been referred to. To receive 'blessings' or the 'Love of the Divine', is something that seekers, spiritual people and people in need have aspired to for centuries. It is also a field of huge speculation, hope, trust, belief and competition, and everything that comes with it. There is more about the heart and the core of your heart in the section on spiritual growth in this book.

The power of Divine's Love or Blessing may resonate well with you if you are reminded of special moments when you were so loved by someone that all your problems, including health problems, seemed small and insignificant.

Whatever your perception and belief, whether in your daily practice or in your occasional thoughts that there is a Divine Being, God, a higher power and good-willing force, is not so important. It is not the purpose of this book to discuss this. What is important to point out to you is that the heart is something very special and the exquisiteness of this specialness and the heart's natural connection to a higher force, to the Source of infinite love, the Divine, God, Brahma or Allah, can help.

In the past people asked why is this not working automatically, this connection to the Divine and the flow of a deeper, helpful energy or blessing?

> *An analogy may help. In some way, human interaction, human life is the micro aspect of this macro connection. It is only when you realise, listen or 'hear' with your heart, that someone else is on the other line, like in a normal phone, skype or mobile phone call, that one will begin to realise, interact, accept the incoming call and all it means.*

Regardless what your belief or dis-belief is, the more that you connect with, feel and give your heart credit to be something of a profound and special nature, a deep understanding will grow. The more this happens in turn your heart can bloom and work with you as part of a very capable support mechanisms, helping you with illness or lingering health issues.

***Practical Heart Tip 57: Deepening levels of heart realisation and help ***

The next practice does not make sense to the mind/brain or is a small matter for our mind/brain understanding. It is introduced here to offer another deeper level of help in situations where there is a deep-lying root cause of someone's illness un-wellbeing or where there is serious illness.

It is suggested that you do some of the key heart practices (KHHs and PHTs) for a period of time until you can clearly feel the pleasant, gentle and calming feelings from your heart.

Then, during a time when you do Heart Strengthening or follow most of the key steps to connect to your heart:

- *Let your heart realise that the pleasant feeling in your heart is the blessing of the Divine, Source or True Source** (1-2 min);*

- *Let your heart realise that the pleasant feelings or deeper feelings are generated by your heart, (20-40 sec); then again*

- *Let your heart realise that the pleasant feelings in your heart are the blessing of the Divine, Source or True Source (1-2min or longer).*

You can repeat this sequence a few more times. The times in brackets are only a guide for you. In moments when your heart realises that the pleasant feelings are a/the 'blessing', and when you feel a deepening, sweetening or expansion of the feeling, allow yourself to be there for longer, and follow, with your heart, all the beautiful feelings.

This means that your heart is realising by feeling it and as a result accepting a deeper level of help. It is now of course helpful, after this PHT, to continue with any of the heart and health-related practices suggested in this section, and with the KHH 9 'Let your heart smile to your health problem'.

** Source of your true self. This term is used to reflect the Divine, or Divine Source, as the source of your own true self. Change the term used for the Divine according to your belief, or to what feels right to you.

The heart, as the key to self-realisation and to connect to the Divine, offers access to deep levels of health support. What may be helpful here is to allow for some level of openness, without a need to believe or trust. Your heart can help, your heart is very, very special, and it can have understandings of its own. Over time these will revealed to you. The discussions and exercises in the Spiritual Growth chapter may further assist; linking mind/brain and heart's understandings.

Ultimately, deeper learning and understanding will be through and from your own heart.

Your heart can connect you more directly and often instantly to a greater source of energy than any other modality can. It can replenish, transform and remove blockages in an instant; by its very nature it is unlimited. Energy is not the right word for it once you experience the depth, exquisiteness and the way by which the heart, all of you, is being touched.

The heart has always been the centre of feeling that feels shares, gives and accepts love. Love is an energy, too, and has healing qualities. That is why we feel love. All that the heart does or passively receives, naturally connects to qualities of love for our healing and growth.

This growing realisation of the deeper nature of your heart, as well as the quality of your heart's connection to Divine, can assist your healing journey immensely and it can lead you to the wonderful life that you perhaps feel deep inside you should have but perhaps don't have … yet.

Heart, health and healing

And you would accept the seasons of your heart
just as you have always accepted that seasons pass over your fields
and you would watch with serenity through the winters of your grief. Khalil Gibran

The heart is immensely intelligent and as such functions like a potent computer processor and hard disk. It holds all the memory of all your life's experiences, positive and negative, and it governs every part of the being: physical, emotional, mental and non-physical functions and body layers.

The concern when something is wrong with us is often to focus on the physical matter. At times this may be the best response. Sometimes this is the only option, yet at other times there is a much wider array of help available. In some way the heart will always offer you an inclusive option, it will rarely be a black and white suggestion or approach.

Until you clearly know what is best for you to heal perhaps the best and most logical approach would be to use all the tools that you have, all medical interventions suited to your condition, and your heart.

This is not written lightly, and it is shared with you, especially if you suffer from a serious or life-threatening illness. Within a limited amount of time you often only have one or a few chances to get it right. This means that you have a to make the best choices, seek the best help and then hope that what you have decided will make a positive difference within, what always is, limited amount of time.

There are stories shared in the following segments where friends did just that, they sought the best medical advice, used heart and mind to choose, and then followed it. At the same time, they also committed fully to the journey of their heart, for the heart to be in the best condition, and in turn to have the best heart help available to them.

Jonathan's sharing is one of these examples. There are other stories too, where the focus was mainly on known, acceptable interventions available and the heart was either used on 'the side' with very limited focus or not at all. Often progress and healing was less smooth, stagnant or did not happen.

In all your hopes or endeavours for greater health, healing or wellbeing give your heart some credit. Trust your heart and its potential to work for you in a way that you would trust a new person in your life, a new friend, whom you give credit. The only difference will be, if you truly let the heart help you, that it will never let you down. At the very least, it will add positively to your journeying.

The closest truth that reflects my humble learning is that any healing is a blessing from the Divine. Whatever we know, hope for and do to the best of our abilities, health or healing directions and outcomes are often not known or know-able.

In saying this it is, however, important to do the best of what is available to us. Do the best individually in your approach and attitude, including our emotional and heart wellbeing, and then let go, surrender, affirm or pray wholeheartedly for Blessing, guidance and help.

In the following sections you find discussions and stories of the heart's help with emotional, mental, physical and serious health issues.

Heart Based Therapeutics work - emotional clearing and wellbeing

The impact of emotions on your heart and your wellbeing and health are discussed in the 'causes of illness' section above and throughout the entire book. Experiencing, harbouring or following emotions is related to high levels of stress and negative thinking, all of which have been shown to negatively impact on health and wellbeing. This is one aspect. The other aspect encompasses past experiences, conditioning, social or family environments, trauma or other significant events. They can cause inner patterns of behaviour, burdens, trauma or post-traumatic stress symptoms that can be hard to access, work with or heal. Emotional patterns, thinking habits, mental health and overall health and wellbeing are closely interrelated.

In early 2010 a doctor of psychology, Ed Rubenstein, who had been working with the heart as a therapeutic tool and had experienced profound results, founded the Heart Based Institute. Work led to the development of Heart Based Therapeutics (HBT) work and practitioner training. A first course was offered in 2016. The course aims to offer coaches or therapists the tools to include a deeper form of heart-based therapeutic work to their tool box.

Megan's story below shows the working of HBT in relation to issues or challenges that she experienced in her life. Megan shared about her post-natal depression and how, over time, it negatively impacted on the relationship with her partner. In her own words the relationship, instead of being an avenue for sharing joy and love, became a source of stress, burdening feelings and concern.

> **Megan's Story**
>
> *When Megan first shared why she came to a HBT session she mentioned her relationship as one of the causes of her current unhappiness.*
>
> *'My relationship now is not the happiest. I feel scared to express myself and unhappy.'*
>
> *Megan further shared that in particular 'joy' had left the relationship. Megan had attended a small amount of heart meditations at a regional centre and it was here that she heard about the heart-based therapeutic work.*
>
> *In one session she was able to let go and allow the heart to work. A couple of days later Megan shared her experience and the flow on effects from the one session:*
>
> *'I felt connected to my heart all evening, very peaceful and happy. This morning I feel free of the past, able to connect to my true self & still very calm and happy. This is a very powerful experience and the answer I have been searching for.'*

Megan booked a second session several months later. The theme or issue in this second session was different which also showed that any of the very burdening feelings, Megan had given up on being able to ever shift, had not returned.

At the centre of the HBT training is the deep Emotional Clearing Process (ECP). This is in recognition of the strong impact emotions have and that through emotion, deeply lying issues or causes can be cleared, with the heart's help.

In the United States, upon completion of the comprehensive 8-day training program, licensed mental health professionals are granted status as Certified Heart Based Therapeutics™ Therapists and non-licensed mental health professionals are granted status as Certified Heart Based Therapeutics™ Practitioners.

So far HBT and ECP work has shown quite promising and profound impacts or changes in the first months of being available as a new therapeutic tool. A range of positive impacts were initially shown as case studies in the inaugural training program. In total, during development and early HBT/ECP work, conditions, situations or issues that the heart, via these professionally facilitated processes, could work and help with, were:

- Improved health by decreasing the negative effects of stress;
- Eliminating the feelings of burnout, compassion fatigue and exhaustion;
- Reduced emotional reactivity;
- Responding and no longer 'reacting' to stressful situations;
- Becoming more immune to negative emotions;
- Things previously perceived as stressors no longer having the same stress-inducing effects;
- Reduction of conflicts in interpersonal relationships;
- Enhanced experience of intimacy, honesty and genuineness in relationships;
- The ability to forgive those who have hurt us in any way;
- Letting go of patterns of guilt, shame, and unworthiness;
- Becoming more patient and accepting of the imperfections in others and in ourselves;
- Letting go of problems and burdens, especially those that are beyond our control;
- An enhanced experience of heartfelt gratitude;
- The ability to establish healthier boundaries in our relationships;
- Letting go of sabotaging patterns; and
- Recognising and neutralising unproductive belief systems.[9]

Leading into the next section, a mature age female heart workshop participant also added to the training a small set of HBT sessions. She attributed some of the most significant changes to her wellbeing and improved mental health to these interventions. This is what Nora sent a few days after her session:

'I am forwarding this to you to give you an idea of what has been happening to me. One thing that was absolutely AMAZING were heart-based therapy sessions. In these a lifetime of depression was ENDED.'

It is important to note that Nora had already used her heart with greater depth by attending several levels of the heart workshop program and practising regularly. This would have, without doubt, made the HBT interventions work deeper and smoother to some degree.

Help for mental health issues

Mental health is a topic and an issue that has increasingly found its way into homes, workplaces and individual's lives, as it seems to occur more. Mental health has made mental health matters an issue for anyone in society, similar to cancer, because anyone, at any time can be effected by it. While some research shows that people from lower socio-economic circumstances or communities are more likely to be having mental health issues or illness, everyone can be affected by it, from any background or location.

Over the years many have disclosed that they came for a session, a workshop or to try heart meditation as a way to look for additional, non-medication focussed help for mental health issues.

Where there was a clear commitment to their heart individuals shared noticeable to quite significant improvement in both their condition and in their ability to cope with the challenge of suffering from a mental health condition.

Clients or participants with a mental health condition seem to have two tendencies that are more at the surface than in other participants or clients: the strength of how they use the mind/brain and a lesser developed ability to let go. This letting go normally means two things. The first is to let go of thoughts and thought patterns that are not helpful, are negative or are lasting without a need to last. The second is a lesser ability, once the heart work begins, to let go of the normal dominance of the brain and to drop into the heart, and then of course to also drop deeper into the heart. This is only partially based on small research projects conducted. It is mainly an observation as a practitioner and session/workshop facilitator working with the heart for over 10 years quite consistently and almost exclusively.

The heart helps to bring your centre of being to the present moment, more into the heart's zone where it can help.

You can be, for example, fully in your heart, 100% and your mind/brain will also fully function. However, if you learn to be in your heart more and over time much more than in your mind/brain, some of the causes or worsening influences that the mind/brain have on mental ill health, such as, for example, the generation of worries and excessive thoughts, are reduced. This includes

---

[9] The list of issues, symptoms is taken with kind permission from the Heart Based Institute's website www.heartbased.org.

negative thoughts, self-damaging, self-doubting, related emotions and related levels of stress or anxiety. Whatever your situation, this means that you can have some respite from yourself when you are more connected to or in your heart.

> ### Practical Heart Tip 58: Think less *
>
> *Over-thinking is stressful in any situation and for anyone. In relation to mental health it can either worsen a condition or can trigger an episode.*
>
> *To go on a journey of thinking less you don't need to know what thoughts are or where they come from. Your heart works for you, without knowing, thinking or analysing. As you have started to read this book and done some of the exercises, you may have also started to, knowingly or not, trust your heart.*
>
> *To think less is all that you need to be more in the natural heart connection. How to let go at some level of mind-control, for this to happen through the very process of thinking, is only possible in a limited way. It is a paradox: use the thinking process to think less. The more that you use your heart, the less you think to start with: How ...*
>
> - *Relax and smile more, more freely, always, in your daily life and when you practise;*
> - *When you find yourself thinking excessively or unnecessarily, do more of this;*
> - *Allow yourself to drop into the heart-zone, heart-feeling; and*
> - *In addition, do Heart Strengthening in a complete form daily (at least 1-2 x a day) and shorter versions of it every time you find yourself thinking or over-thinking issues. At least do the shorter version 4-6 x a day in addition). Each time will only take you 3-5 minutes.*

There is only some formally researched mental health and heart study work. Several colleagues, some of them medical doctors and others with psychology degrees or doctorates, are currently working on this, using this approach. Hopefully, there will be more findings and experiences ready to be shared on the book website yourheartcanhelp.org, over time.

For now, the experience that Ivan had is one solid example of an individual who had three compounding mental health challenges. The heart clearly supported his wellbeing and health-promoting journey. Ivan directly attributes profound improved wellbeing and health to the heart-help that he found.

Ivan met with me a few months back and started a conversation as to how the heart learning, heart supporting practices and heart meditations could be offered to a wider mental health field. There was an initial surprise about his motivation. He had had a long struggle with mental health issues. Initially he dabbled only in heart work. It was only when he committed to regular heart practices that significant shifts and improvements happened.

Ivan suffered from bi-polar, schizophrenia and depression. At a time when Ivan's bi-polar condition was the worst he spent a number of weeks in hospital following two manic episodes. He was then heavily medicated. Following each manic episode he experienced debilitating depression which lasted for about a year at a time, and he struggled to work in his government job.

Ivan has advanced academic training and is highly intelligent. He agreed to share the essence of his experience in the book, first as an alias, then later he changed it to have his name printed.

> ### Ivan's Story:
>
> *'I have lived with a mental illness for almost four years, and in the beginning I found it extremely difficult to cope. I was extremely depressed and found it difficult to get out of bed, to go to work, to smile. It was hard to interact with others as my personality had, at least on the outside, changed. I felt alone and like no-one else really understood what I was going through.'*
>
> *Ivan further shared: 'As a result of my illness, my performance in a whole range of areas of life, including work and sport, was very poor. And the worst thing was, I was having very little fun, which is the name of the game as far as I can tell.'*
>
> *'After trying various things to help my condition, I grabbed an Open Heart meditation CD out of the cabinet, as I had tried this meditation on a very occasional basis in the past but had never persisted. I vowed to listen to the CD every day, and attend meditation sessions on a weekly basis. Looking back now this was quite possibly the best decision I have ever made in my life.'*
>
> *'I am happy to say things have turned around for me in the past six months since I made that decision. After three weeks of regular meditation I barely recognised myself, and I'm now the happiest I have ever been.'*
>
> *'I am happier than I could have ever imagined, and I believe much of this improvement is due to my regular (heart) meditation practice.'*
>
> *'What are some of these changes? My mind travels slowly now, the world goes slower, and I feel calm. My heart is open, and I can smile. I jump out of bed in the morning, I'm enjoying my previously stressful job, and I can concentrate better. I love interacting with people, I laugh regularly, and the world feels like a truly amazing place. I am optimistic about the future and the possibilities for my life. And the best thing is, whenever I want to connect with my heart and feel that nice feeling, all I have to do is smile.'*
>
> *'I believe that I have come across a real solution for people with a mental health condition. I think mine is a story that demonstrates clearly that people with a mental illness do not need to suffer. They just have to meditate daily, using the heart more, and the rest will take care of itself.'*

Ivan's experience is not unique. Ivan is not fully cured in medical terms or in relation to medication needs. He states that he is now off most medication and only on medication for schizophrenia; and even this dosage is much smaller than it was several months ago.

Ivan has since started a small business on the side which he calls *Happy Ground*. In the absence of his mental health issues and challenges the main benefit he has found since using the heart to help him is:

I have never been happier in my whole life.

In the *Happy Ground* program he introduces participants to a range of wellbeing promoting activities, including the heart. Heart Meditation features as one of several meditations presented.

Sue offered to openly share her heart experience and mental health journey, motivated by the potential she saw in helping others by doing so. She lives in Hobart, is a mother and, after a recent career change, now works happily and successfully in aged care

In 2000 Sue was diagnosed with 'schizoaffective disorder'. Schizoaffective disorder is a condition in which a person experiences a combination of symptoms of schizophrenia, such as hallucinations or delusions and also mood disorder symptoms, such as mania or depression. It is a mental health condition that is not as well understood as others. She has been living with the illness for around 15 years at the time she shared her experience. She had practiced and used the heart for four to five years by then.

Sue's Story:

'I have a combination of schizophrenia and bipolar. What that meant in my situation was that from the time 2000 to 2009 I was thinking a lot, continually thinking. One of my main and continual delusions was that I was the 'millennium bug'.'

'This is kind of funny but personally this was very frightening for me. My family and my doctors were quite happy because I was a good patient, I was taking my medication. Externally I was functioning quite well ... making others happy as I was functioning quite well. For me it was quite difficult living with that.'

'In was in 2009 that a friend talked to me about the heart, the spiritual heart, and I went along to a session that was for the public.'

'Things started to change for me then. It felt good to meditate using the heart and to use the heart in daily life also. Feeling some of the changes, even not very clear from the very beginning, my aim has been to be in my heart as much as possible from that time on.'

'I think so much less now ... it is amazing really ... and I have less anxiety. I am also much more confident. My relationships are better with my daughter, my family and my friends. Everything has improved. I am also not as critical of myself and others. My health is a lot better now.'

'I am very happy now, the heart is really good and I try to stay in my heart as much as I can.'

Sue's sharing is simple, beautiful and in some way to the point. She clearly connects her thinking and over-thinking to higher levels of stress and anxiety.

Sue is a very regular attendee at weekly heart meditation sessions and has also participated in heart workshops during the past five to six years. This is not uncommon. Once individuals experience the benefits they naturally 'want' more. Clear progress is possible without the workshops, however. With a persisting condition almost everyone pre-dominantly lives life from the mind/brain or at least with focus on it with the intention to gain some level of control, feeling safe or well.

Feeling can have many directions and sources. It is when feeling is from the heart or heart-directed that the heart-help unfolds. Beautiful, safe feelings surface which help to calm the mind.

An introduction to the heart, Heart-Based Therapeutic work or heart-related workshops offer a pathway towards a greater balance.

Sue's improvements and her happiness shine through clearly on the short video clip she eventually said 'yes' to taking. You can view it on the web-site. Sue is also now a community volunteer heart meditation leader at the Lotus Centre in Hobart, to share her story and the heart's benefits with others.

Your heart and serious illness

For everyone with a serious illness the heart can offer additional help. In many ways your heart may be the key to your possible recovery, or at the very least to whatever progress or state of being is possible or the best for you. The above sections indicate some of these avenues of help.

A complicated or even simple surgery can become a problem. It does not have to be a serious illness. Health or healing happens, at times miraculously. If everyone would be honest and truthful to the deepest levels of understanding and insight, then one would have to admit that we do not know fully why and how healing and recovery happens. This admission can be a first step to healing, to surrendering more to the heart's knowing and abilities.

The best example is two people, in similar circumstances, suffering from an identical or very similar disease, a cancer or tumour. One recovers, the other does not. These outcomes are not logical from the mind/brain perspective. If any part of you can understand, then it is something that is beyond our outside limitations of the mind/brain consciousness.

With the heart you add another element to what is available to you. You can help yourself. After all, you know yourself the best. You know your environment, past days, weeks or months intimately. It would have to be a very compassionate, attentive and caring health practitioner that has more interest in your health and wellbeing than you do. Even then, they will lack information to form a complete picture in their mind.

Many with an interest or passion for healing, health and growth, or with a passion for understanding who we are, can notice changes in awareness, attitude and perhaps consciousness. People rely less on what an expert says, believe what a medical or alternative health practitioner suggests, look at alternatives or good practice, and to then, at least partially, put things into their own hands. This a wonderful time where it is very easy for most to do some research, google questions, and then look at options. This, and well-intended help from friends, can send you, your heart 'into a spin', as Jonathan shared, too.

This is empowering for individuals and also makes professionals much more accountable. In addition, there have been movements like consumer engagement and client-centred care that clearly acknowledge the important contribution anyone can make to their health, wellbeing and healing, including the client or patient.

The keys are, in an environment where there are treatment and wellbeing options, to know what the options are and to have the best possible decision-making tools available. Heart and mind are needed here.

Serious illness is a serious interruption in life, to the flow that there is now or to the flow that has been happening up to now. Serious illness offers you the chance to stop, to stop all busyness that seems so important. Often, quite naturally, people realise that there is something more to life than all this busyness; it can now be seen and realised when illness strikes.

However, unless it has been an accident, it is commonly known that serious illness never just strikes. There are years of tension, over-thinking, negative emotion, unhealthy forms of diet or exercise and other recognised causes that, over time, lead to mal-function of organs and the degeneration of body functions or body parts.

Jonathan's story is a touching example of how the heart together with appropriate interventions, helped Jonathan not only to fully recover, but to also go through a very difficult time with cancer in a light, supported and clear way, being guided, being helped by his heart.

Listening to and writing down Jonathon's story created goose-bumps, special feelings at several points for me. You will also see that in Jonathon's story it is not about an 'either-or' situation - 'either' this approach to health and healing 'or' that one. For him it was a matter of his heart guiding him to feel and realise what the best option was for his issues and needs.

Jonathan, now 57 years old at the time, works full-time in an office using his business degree and expertise. He has further fine arts qualifications and helps people as a photographer and in developing graphic art documents. Jonathan also has an interest in spirituality, which has deepened since he started to learn about the heart.

He had started attending heart meditations and initial workshops around 4 years prior to his health issues surfacing. In that way he had a 'head-start', or more accurately a 'heart-start' in relying on his heart in addition to other more known supports and interventions offered to him.

Jonathon went to the doctor after noticing physical problems. To his shock he was diagnosed with bladder cancer and an initial biopsy turned into an emergency surgery to remove a growing cancer.

Jonathan's Story:

'It was around three years ago when I noticed something was wrong. There were symptoms that clearly showed it. I went to the doctor who immediately sent me to have scans done.'

'The scan found a growth inside my bladder, the size of a golf ball. A biopsy was scheduled to take a sample, to understand its nature, benign or cancerous, and to remove it.'

'I procrastinated, was stuck in my thoughts about what to do and so by the time the biopsy took place two months later it had become the size of an apple. This kind of growth is normally a clear indication that it is aggressive and not benign. It was removed and when the results came back they confirmed the cancer.'

'When I came back out of the procedure the team of doctors told me that this would not be the end of the interventions and that the cancer would grow back.'

'The surgeons strongly advised me to have the bladder removed and said 'it would save my life. Despite this they could still not give me a guaranteed survival assurance and that this would remove all of the cancer. They said that the removal of the bladder would mean a 70% chance of success.'

'My first response was ... I don't want the operation ... and I felt that if there was anything natural to do, I would do it. I was inclined to try the natural therapy way. I also had a mindset that I can do it myself.'

'People were giving a lot of suggestions and advice, which was well intended. It sent my mind into a spin and I became very busy with all the possibilities, trying to find something that I could to. At the same time it did not lead anywhere and no decisions were made.'

'One night, I remember clearly, I woke up sweating and in fear. I got up and started a recorded heart practice that went for almost 1 hour. This was 3am. At the end of it everything had just fallen away, everything not important. There was only one clear thought and answer: just trust, follow the heart and be within the pure radiance of the love from the heart often or always.'

'All thoughts had melted away; all the fear had gone too. I knew I had to have the operation. I rang up, said I would go ahead and the appointment was made.'

'The heart helped me to realise that I had a lot of concepts around natural healing and natural medicine. And while they were good and had different roles in healing, they were just concepts and not helpful right now, nothing to hang on to.'

'I was scheduled in for a six-hour operation, two weeks in hospital and a three-month recovery period. I was in my heart almost all the time and the whole time was about trusting and using the heart. It changed my whole experience into a time to meditate, pray with the help of the heart and let my heart radiate to all around me in the hospital. I felt instead of being a sorrow patient I would let the heart help me and others and to let the heart's radiating energy flow through me and to all around. This made the whole stay in the hospital very enjoyable.'

'At one point after the operation the team of surgeons and supporting doctors and nurses came around. They said that they could not tell me yet if they had gotten all the growth. Yet, immediately after they walked away I could clearly feel in my heart that everything was fine. This was confirmed several days later. Since the operation I had 3, 6 and 12 month tests, all coming back with clear results.'

'Recently I bumped into one of the hospital doctors in my supermarket and we talked casually. During the conversation he mentioned that my case was one of the best outcomes they had seen for a while.'

As part of the interview Jonathan shared how grateful he was for the support from his friends from the heart community. He felt carried through the time with a lot of love, support and practical assistance. One person in particular took it upon herself to coordinate the team of helpers during that time.

This and other stories around illness or serious illness reveal another need for a clear and helping heart. Let the mind/brain to one part with all information at our finger-tips, on the net, via note-pads, notebooks or computers at home, even on the road, even while we are in medical consultations.

You will want to use your heart to really feel, either ad hoc or using PHT 56, to feel what is best for you. No situation, no body, no condition and its history and no healing journey is identical to another one even when it looks similar or even the same to the eye.

Advice given by others, from close ones or professionals, can be meaningful and helpful. It can also be a cage you are comfortable in accepting, a cage of past knowledge and experience of others that will not be the best for your situation or condition.

If there is a significant illness, your commitment to your heart's journey, to the opening of your heart in some way must match the severity or intensity of the illness or problem.

It is important also to look at all not as an 'either - or' situation. You can let your heart guide you, practically help you. At the same time follow other interventions or the advice of others, natural or modern medicine directed; similar to Jonathan's story.

If you are suffering from a serious condition and clearly feel drawn to all that your heart can offer on your journey, then look for a heart-learning centre near you (see appendix 5) and speak to one of the coordinators, teachers or facilitators. This is helpful in guiding directly, to deeper heart awareness and help.

'Heart time' is not the same as the time the mind/brain knows. If Sue or Jonathan had several years prior experience of heart-learning, then 'heart time' means that you can be at a same level of heart-help in much less time.

An experienced teacher or heart-focussed therapist can significantly assist in making the full capacity and spectrum of the heart available.

Your heart and physical conditions

Let us look at stories shared by clients, workshop or meditation session participants. David is one of them. David first came to heart sessions in 2007/08. His initial encounter was an immensely deep and touching experience for him. As he had long-standing and unresolved health issues he decided to learn more, have more treatments and enrol in heart workshops.

David's Story:

David has his own business. He is an entrepreneur. He designs and produces innovative aluminium boats for the Tasmanian and wider Australian recreational boating and fishing markets.

David is hardworking and creative. His work over many years has involved exposure to and inhalation of toxic fumes. David described his story in this way 'I had overdosed on aluminium fumes after many years welding aluminium in confined spaces'.

The physical work lead to the deterioration of his joints, and combined with the exposure to toxic fumes contributed to his condition, which in his own words left him 'almost constantly in immense pain. It brought me to meditation. Prior to learning about the heart I had meditated in search of help and relief for 25 to 30 years'.

The reason for David's first session was this intense, almost constant physical pain. He later shared that he also suffered from regular panic attacks and that he felt deeply unhappy in his life, even though, at the surface, he had everything. There were times of depression, too. The feeling at the time for David was 'I felt betrayed, let down by everyone around me.'

He said he had suffered from depression for some time. In the period leading up to his first session David reported that the depression had become 'very fierce'.

The first session offered so much relief to David that he signed up for the first heart workshop. He lives out of Hobart and it was less practical for him to come to the daily shorter Heart Meditation sessions.

David described his experiences of the first session as 'I could feel the depth of my heart opening, feeling the absolute beauty, the peace.' This expanded as he joined the first full day workshop: 'During and after the workshop I completely lost for some time all the pain in my worn-out joints.'

Journeying through the days and weeks after David further shared that this relief happened 'only' when he was more connected to the heart, not neglecting it. He said: 'Some of the panic attacks continued yet less often and less severe. Each time I went to a practice, repeated the workshop or did the next workshop level, I felt strong improvements.'

To help himself, David for some time had developed an interest in alternative healing methods, and had tried many of them. He realised that even with the heart-help an instant cure would not be available. He shared about his realisations that 'my health issues showed me how much I needed the heart, how much better I was when I attended to it. I also realised that I was still at times running away from the heart, all the help, the beautiful feelings, the peace and the joy.'

'I realised that the heart was something much deeper than healing for my health problems, I had looked for the heart and all it meant to me for a long time, I was deeply touched, often tears welling up, flowing down my cheeks when deeply in the feeling from the heart during group practices and workshops, being so deeply moved. At the same time there were many uncountable times of laughter and deep joy, bliss.'

'Each time I went to practice with other hearts I felt strong improvements. After the third workshop I felt the radiance and deep love from my heart so clearly that I felt so deeply and fully enveloped .... It was the most wonderful feeling that will stay with me forever.'

'It did not stop there. The next stages, attending further workshops, were even more beautiful. At home, as my wife did not join the practice or workshops, I was at times questioned as to why I had such an interest in the heart. Overall, as the weeks and months went by, I found myself even at home laughing, smiling and deeply joyful during my practices and meditations'.

'The more I opened my heart my body followed and healed also. My joints, whole physical body are in good shape now and I am pain-free and very grateful. My feelings of stress, pressure and anxiety are immensely reduced, too.'

'I am more determined and committed than ever to follow my heart. I am grateful to have found this practice and learning and realise the depth of what is possible to achieve. At times it feels like I have only explored the first few layers of my heart.'

David's story was quite amazing in a way that he experienced help with the issues he sought help for and with other issues that he did not talk about in his first consultations. This is normal and has to do with the stigma that is attached with any mental health issues. It is uncomfortable to talk about.

As with other clients it took David some time to acknowledge the full potential of his own heart, to really follow it and to let the realisations of his experiences guide him in such a way as to let his heart help him with its fullest capacity, and in a more ongoing way. Ultimately it led to dramatic improvements of his physical and mental wellbeing.

David is near retirement age and he enjoys his heart and regular heart meditation in his daily life. Being very talented with his hands he now makes customised wooden meditation chairs to help, to give back and to stay in touch with other fellow heart friends around the island of Tasmania and Australia.

Exercise, sport, your fitness and your wellbeing

The practice of sport is a human right. Every individual must have the possibility of practicing sport, without discrimination of any kind ... ... (it) requires mutual understanding with a spirit of friendship, solidarity and fair play. Olympic Charter

To be well, to keep your body in shape, you know that it is good to move it regularly and be involved in some form or exercise.

The condition of your heart and your whole wellbeing can be further supported by doing some form of strenuous or aerobic exercise. Strenuous for you can mean a brisk walk, a swim or whatever gives you a good work out that ideally also challenges your cardio-vascular system .... it gets your heart pumping, gets you breathing deeper.

Negative energy is dispersed as you do this regularly, once or several times a week. It will also further free your heart space and allow your heart to open more and easier, as you follow the suggested practices.

The feeling in your heart will guide you as to what is right, what is enough for you, what form or exercise will help you and what will add to your happiness, health and wellbeing. Exercise with feeling and feel the wonderful motion of your body, breath and every part of you and trust when intensity or length of your workout is enough. Every time is different, every day. With more heart strength it is also important to be strong in the presence of friends, coaches and others and to clearly know when you have had enough for now. This will be even more important with growing age and related risks of injury, (physical) heart issues.

As in all aspects of life a tendency to have emotions, to follow the drives that burden your heart, can be there. Firstly, the longer-term perspective is that your overall health and wellbeing will be more supported as you recognise these drives, even in your fitness regime and any sport that you may do.

Secondly, you may surprisingly find that your heart will help you in three ways:

- You will enjoy what you do, what you perhaps already do very well, even more;
- You are brought 'into the flow'. As you enjoy more naturally, a new rhythm and lightness can emerge. You can only ever 'be' in the flow, you feel when you are. This means the heart is involved; and
- You will improve - directed by your heart. A lighter heart and less emotion-caused tension frees you from mental, emotional and related physical tension. Your 'game', whether it is tennis, badminton, soccer, volley or basketball, Pilates, an aerobic or yoga work-out or the way you jog, snow board or ski, in terms of effectiveness and efficiency, will also be freer.

You have an immense potential that is non-physical, not yet explored fully, to improve, advance and perfect your exercise or sporting program. Naturally your wise heart's input will bring more joy and lightness and often will also lead to more success, whether 'success' is personal or performance, competitive goals.

Tim's story is a wonderful example of how more heartfulness can improve both performance goals or hopes in your sporting activities, and even more of your movement, its refinement and related skills. Tim picks up on the term 'being in the zone' which perhaps is either being in the heart or being in a similar deeper place where higher awareness, movement, knowing, timelessness and performance meet.

Tim's Story:

'From early childhood sport has been a big part of my life. Some of my fondest memories are playing cricket and soccer in the back yard with my brother, and shooting hoops followed by some rollerblading at the local school.'

'During the late teens and early twenties sport was a central part of my life, it was the source of friendships and confidence. Having grown up with a sporting background I was able to play at a high level in the prime of my physical ability, and this formed my strongest identity - 'the athlete'.'

'My apparent need to maintain this identity as a top athlete drove a highly competitive attitude toward playing sport. Even though I was performing well, my experience playing was not enjoyable as it had been in childhood.'

'The need to win, and be the best, manifested anger when I was not playing well, created a stressful feeling of pressure to perform, led to arguments with team mates, umpires and opposition players and drove a consistent judgemental attitude towards myself and others.'

'In my late twenties I was introduced to open heart meditation. About 12 months into practising this meditation many areas of my life began to change in very positive ways, including sport.'

'Slowly but surely my identity as an athlete has dissolved and feelings of lightness and peace are replacing the strong negative energy experienced prior to meditation.'

'The need to win and be the best is fading, allowing me to have fun and enjoy playing regardless of my performance or the performance of my team.'

'My sporting experiences have deepened through the heart, in terms of enjoyment, performance, and detachment from outcomes. Peak experiences for me have been moments where time stands still, the sport is happening through me, and everything has a beautiful flow about it. I think these moments are what many elite athletes have called 'the flow' or 'being in the zone'.'

'Although these peak experiences aren't consistent, heart meditation helps make an off night an enjoyable experience. Since committing to the practice I've rarely felt anger or frustration while playing, and have let go of the need to win and be the best. I now see my team mates and opponents alike as people to enjoy a sporting experience with. This new attitude has not only improved the feelings I experience while playing, it has also greatly improved the relationships I've formed through sport.'

To enjoy your exercise program more, and to become better at it, will have short and long-term benefits. In the end to become the fittest, strongest, most flexible or the best in your team, community or the world is not a goal for everyone. Healthy and solid competition can be something enjoyable, or it may not be.

With the heart you are adding something else to your sport, fitness or competitive program. The heart will bring you into 'the zone' easier and more directly. In my view, when the heart is the dominant presence, is the zone.

When you focus, when you are absorbed in the perfect moment or perfection of a move or movement, when the mind/brain are no longer busy with other matters, there is in some way only one other place to be: your heart.

This is not new knowledge. Many exercises and/or sports have to do with movement. The refinement of movement is governed less by us knowing in our brain how it works, but more by an acute sense of how it feels. Innovative tuition approaches such as 'Inner Skiing or the Inner Game of Golf or Tennis' build significantly on this.

For some sport is solely exercise. However, sport can offer more if you can also discover new aspects of yourself. Sport with heart-awareness can help to deepen experiences of joy, relaxation, wellbeing and achievement. Exercise or sport become something beyond fitness and health. The gaining of deeper understanding in your leisure time can also flow into your work and social life.

The ultimate joy is in a good life, good health, profound and deep levels of happiness, care and connection to others, in all that you do. This should also be at your exercise location, in your sport program or at highly competitive events. Your heart will always offer new ways to help you the best and to improve your routine and its impact, on you, on your surroundings and gently, even through your regular exercise or sport program, lead you in this direction.

The way you walk - the 'Secrets of Natural Walking'

Related to physical condition, physical health is the way one walks. 'Secrets of Natural Walking' (SONW) walking is much more than that. The way that you hold your body, the way that you walk, can be profoundly supportive to your health and wellbeing. A more natural and heart-supporting way of walking can immensely benefit and support your heart and in turn benefit your health and wellbeing.

Walking for some is a regular form of exercise. For some it is the only one possible. Walking can be very enjoyable, whether it is on your own, with a close friend or with your dog.

Any tension caused by incorrect walking will cause pressure and over time will lead to changes to your joints, ligaments and bones. In almost all instances of incorrect walking the spine is affected, too. In Chinese medicine it is commonly known that everything that is not right or out of shape, mal-aligned or a problem with your spine, in turn has negative impacts on associated organs. In the same way walking also impacts on the two hearts you have.

Numerous clients have sought help over the years for lower back and spine-related issues. In a comparatively short period of time 'natural' or correct walking can stop those and reverse any negative impacts of the past. Your non-physical structure, for example your meridians - where an acupuncturist inserts the most of the needles - and your heart are affected by the free-ness, lightness of your walking.

At the time of writing this book SONW had been about two years old. It spread fast and widely. You will find centres in many parts of the world now. There are many approaches and techniques where you can learn to walk lighter, more appropriately, and in a way that supports your structure, your skeleton, your muscles and everything related. SONW is a new approach that acknowledges and utilises all of the above plus it brings the heart in, too. This means that you practise your heart, your heart will help you more while you walk, and works for all health-related matters, whether it is prevention or treatment.

Connected to SONW are walking clinics where you can have your walking style assessed and more importantly, where, in a short workshop significant adjustments can be made to the way that you walk.

The aim is for your walking to become more natural. Walking naturally will also free your heart and allow you to use your heart easier for all the benefits associated, including your health and wellbeing. The often surprising positive health, wellbeing and healing impacts are well documented on the main web-site and on related social media pages.

For more information on where a natural walking instructor or centre is near you visit www.natural-walking.com . SONW offers you health and wellbeing assistance, correction of old habits, patterns and pressure-causing ways of walking or standing. It also offers a direct and powerful heart-supporting practice or exercise form, holistic and, for some sufficient enough, for your exercise needs. You can say that after learning to walk in this way, you give yourself a reflexology-acupuncture/acupressure treatment each time you practise.

Your heart and Reiki Tummo

Since 2003 in Melbourne and in Hobart at the Lotus Centre new forms of Reiki workshops have taken place. Reiki Tummo attracted different people and wider groups of people. It taught about Reiki and about the use and benefits of the heart.

Reiki is something a bit exotic, unusual for some, and for myself many years ago, it was too esoteric, unusual and intangible. Every form of Reiki, if the atunements are facilitated by an accredited and capable 'Reiki Master', will enable the workshop participant afterwards to channel a refined form of energy that can be used in support of health or wellbeing goals.

Reiki is purely about work with energy. In this way it is similar to the more widely spread practices such as Acupuncture and Homeopathy. They also work with the goal to free patients from energy blockages, so that energy begins to flow again. Perhaps where Reiki can help additionally is through its access to a finer and lighter form of energy that also has its own intelligence. It is these qualities that allow the Reiki to not only penetrate deep into organs or body parts that require healing, it also will flow naturally to parts that are related or even are the causes of an illness. Because of the depth of treatments that can be facilitated, and because of the energy's own high form of intelligence, Reiki is also referred to by some as 'Divine' energy.

In this way Reiki Tummo is similar to any other forms of Reiki. However as part of Reiki Tummo's curriculum there is access to an even finer form or energy the so-called 'Shing Chi' energy. For any one that is sensitive to energy the upgrade to Shing Chi (several levels) is a profound step and achieves better results.

The unique aspect about 'Reiki Tummo' is the inclusion of learning about the heart. Once the heart is present, open and involved, the different and deeper form of Reiki flow, supported by the heart, makes the heart even more available, cleanses it even more and in turn can be immensely helpful for any health issues or problems.

As Reiki Tummo incorporates learning about the heart participants have extra realisations that make them one more aware and sensitive towards the energy body, energy flows other than reiki and other non-physical parts of who we are. This includes the heart. Learning Reiki Tummo can assist someone's heart-learning or the deepening of it.

A wonderful and generous part about the Reiki Tummo workshop program is the fact that anyone with a serious or life-threatening illness can make an application to receive workshops level 1 & 2 either for free or for payment of a small donation, much smaller than the actual workshop fee. In the next level of the Reiki Tummo workshop finer and deeper reaching, healing form of Reiki is available, Shing Chi.

One among a long list of remarkable stories is the help and support Thalia received after her Reiki Tummo 1 & 2 atunements.

Thalia's Story

'I have been using the Reiki a lot on myself, often all day long for the pain. My life has turned around since the Reiki atunement. I have a full-time job and the Reiki keeps me going. I am happier and have a better outlook on life.'

What is important to note is that Thalia, at the time of her atunements, was only 22 years young and had been diagnosed with several cancers. She found this level of support despite the fact that she did not attend the full workshop days, normally two full days. She only attended the atunements that are around 30-40 minutes in length and it is those that then enable the Reiki energy to flow. Normally the impact and help is greater when the full day of workshops content is utilised in Reiki, channelling to oneself or to others. Most people with a serious illness start to benefit if they do a full Reiki self-channelling twice a day.

Reiki Tummo also offers free Reiki atunements to a wider community and all who are interested to receive this. As with the heart's help that is or should be utilised, in this way Reiki as an energy channelling tool is also available to anyone in need with any serious health or wellbeing issues or problems. It is also empowering. Whatever your issues are, you can daily support yourself, do something, in addition to any expert advice or help.

This means that the deeper heart abilities and all its help are available faster and deeper. It can be wonderfully combined with daily Reiki self-channellings to support whatever else you do for any illness or healing goal.

Health and your whole journey

If your heart is a lamp, let it lead you to your true path. Rumi

Health and wellbeing, physically and mentally, will generally become less strong and 'perfect' as we grow older. Depending on what the nature of your condition is, 'healing or wellbeing', may be the ability to be at peace, to feel love, joy, bliss and a sense of aliveness, despite the existence of your illness or condition.

It is always good to focus on good health, wellbeing and preventative activities and attitudes. Your heart will help. Your heart will also help with a deep level of calmness, so deep, that whatever your concerns, illness, real or perceived ill-being.

Heart-facilitated calmness can grow so deep that its blissful and 'at-peace-feelings' will engulf all else. It will be difficult for other unpleasant feeling to be present, whatever the severity of your condition.

It is that feeling and quality that will guide you in the darkest of hours, the biggest challenges and in wonderful ways through your life, including to and beyond the physical existence in this body.

Allow your heart, in all the practices and heart-supporting suggestions, to guide you help you and lead you. New doors, not seen yet, not known about yet, not considered real, will open up. If you are unwell, you will naturally focus on your healing journey, the heart will always offer to bring the peace into your doing, your efforts and your being with it all - a very important balance to maintain.

Health, Wellbeing, Bliss

I have come to drag you out of yourself and take you in my heart.
I have come to bring out the beauty you never knew you had
and lift you like a prayer to the sky. Rumi

Some more about this bliss. Being well is more than being healthy or the absence of illness. Events, encounters and experiences in life can feel nice, great, magical. They are moments dear to us, dear to the heart, according to one common saying. The depth to which you feel these moments greatly depends on the condition, opening and depth of your heart, the very centre of feeling with which these are perceived and felt.

Some time ago a colleague booked a set of heart-therapeutic sessions. Later, ad hoc, this feedback arrived:

> *I have just been quite excited ... I was wondering how I have not heard about (it) before ... the open heart method seems so simple that it could potentially assist lots of people with anxiety, depression etc. Client/practising clinical psychologist*

It indicates the heart's ability to help in deep and at times surprising ways. Whether there are known issues, such as anxiety, stress or depression or whether unknown emotional, mental or psychological patterns limit or block you, the heart has an innate ability to recognise and transform these. From there it will guide you and take you to deeper levels of health, wellbeing and bliss.

It indicates the heart's ability to help in deep and very often surprising ways. Whether there are known issues, such as anxiety, stress or depression or whether unknown emotional, mental or psychological patterns limit or block you, the heart has an innate ability to recognise and transform these, even if your mind/brain does not. From there it will guide you, and take you, to deeper levels of health, wellbeing and bliss.

In your heart, and all of your understanding, it is not only helpful to realise that the most wonderful, sweet, joyful and blissful feelings are possible to feel in every moment in your life, including times when you are on a healing journey. The very nature of your heart will bring you gently, continuously moving forward to this place: where you feel the many moments every day with a depth of joy, bliss and wonderful feelings that are beyond words.

You would have felt this at times in the past during a special moment, with or without a reason for you to feel so. There are two perspectives possible here. One is that special moments can be just that, special moments that we are blessed to experience in rare moments in life. The other one is that special moments are experiences that the heart is able to feel. With a heart condition that is able to feel to this depth all the time, many more moments in life can have similar quality and feeling to them.

As the quote from Rumi implies, there are parts in you, you may have a sense of, a distant memory, a feeling, where you need to trust and make a leap of faith that it is possible, that it is a part of the human ability to feel wonderful, in-bliss, when all parts who you are work together.

> **Practical Heart Tip 59: Heart-leap of faith**
>
> *This leap of faith is small or short ... into your own heart. Out of all leaps of faith you may have been invited to, perhaps, or without doubt, this is the safest one. Jump.*
>
> *You may notice or have already experienced clearly, that, as you do the heart strengthening, heart opening practices and suggestions in this book, something of this bliss, wondrous joy and very enjoyable, nurturing calm is surfacing to point the way.*

Many people I know, from many walks of life, social or professional backgrounds, have moved towards a life with more heart-mind balance, with more heart presence or have chosen to live a heart-centred life. Everyone of them, in their own way, having realised that these special heart moments can happen very regularly and daily.

What is more important is for you to take stock, to feel where your heart practice has taken you so far, to realise changes within and to act positively forward guided by this. If you have practised even half of the introduced KHHs and one third to quarter of the PHTs regularly, you know and feel your progress at some level of your whole existence. This is the validation within, with your heart, and how you perceive truth and can follow truth and helpful choices.

It is not uncommon to make clear steps in the direction of feeling deeper and realising that wonderful, special, profound and exquisite experiences are in many moments every day. Have started to feel this in some way with your heart progress up to now? In your heart you know, or start to know and feel, if it is a beautiful and meaningful direction.

Practical heart help for health and wellbeing

Heal your heart.

The following is a detailed outline of how you can let your heart, in practical steps, support your health, wellbeing and healing. It is also a summary that brings together some of the content, learning, PHTs and KHHs from earlier sections. These work well and can be used whether you have some small, niggling issue, or a major health challenge. They are preventative and active steps to ensure your heart's help for both direct help and guidance on what to do to support you the best.

Your health and wellbeing are the foundations of all of your life. When unwell, you need to give it your best shot. Here a suggested summary practice and approach:

- Read the introduction chapters, I to VI, and also the rest of the book. All practices build on each other. Practice the KHHs and PHTs that speak to you, feel right or important;
- Practice the suggested relaxation exercise often (KHH 3 and the PHTs 19, 44 and 45);
- Practice Heart Strengthening often (KHH 6);
- Based on regular Heart Strengthening and a continuously opening heart, practise regularly the KHHs 3, 4, 5, 7 and 12/13;
- Download the Open Heart Meditation (KHH 13). Follow that to open and cleanse the deeper layers of your heart for deeper peace, heart feelings and resulting help from your heart; and
- Practise the KHH from this section 'Let your heart smile to your health problem' on its own, or much better after you have done Heart Strengthening or Open Heart Meditation. Do this several times a day. Once the feeling is pleasant, you can feel your heart clearly, then do the KHH for several minutes, even up to 5, 10 or more minutes.

This is a suggested sequence and approach to a solid practice routine. You will progress even more in a workshop or training environment, as heart learning and proper heart use is not what one naturally does well or well enough. The online yourheartcanhelp.org training or a heart workshop near you will assist further. Use your own feeling and growing heart strength to decide this and to choose from any of the introduced practices and helpers that seem to work for you.

Key Heart Help 9: Smiling to health issues

This KHH 'Smiling to health issues', or letting your heart smile to your health issues, is introduced at a later stage. Hopefully by now you have developed some trust in your heart's abilities. Remember from earlier discussions your heart is something immensely deep. This may be backed by clear and quite wonderful experiences, for example people starting to respond differently to you, based on your regular use of the heart.

You can greatly enhance this practical help, or benefit from your heart's ability to help as soon as possible, by doing some Heart Strengthening (KHH 6) supplemented by regular Open Heart Meditation (KHH 13). Both will improve your heart ability immensely over time, at the very least in a feel-able way.

The practice of this KHH is not limited to the physical parts of your body. Your heart can connect to every function of your body, your emotional state or drivers, your mind, your mental health issues and their causes and anything else that you feel you need help with or that are issues for you. The simple intention to smile from your heart to whatever problem or health issues that you have - and everything related - will direct your heart's radiance to these parts. Do this even if you are not sure what it is or whether your personal or any professional diagnosis is right or wrong or a bit off the mark. Your heart will only ever add positively to it all.

There is something of immense depth associated with your heart. It is often talked about, you may have found this reflected in your own reading, or some of the quotes in this book may have resonated with you.

Whatever the circumstance or level of understanding, trust in your heart or 'belief' is, the following practice is very helpful for when you want the radiant, blissful and deeply touching energy from your heart's help with health issue.

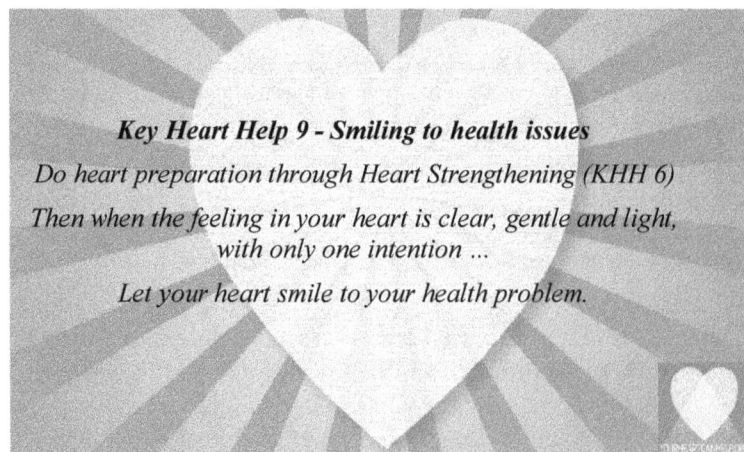

Key Heart Help 9 - Smiling to health issues
Do heart preparation through Heart Strengthening (KHH 6)
Then when the feeling in your heart is clear, gentle and light,
with only one intention ...
Let your heart smile to your health problem.

You can use this as treatment or as a preventative measure. For prevention let your heart smile to health issues brewing somewhere or not yet feelable or diagnoseable.

This KHH could also have the title 'letting the heart smile and radiate to heal or to support healing'. This KHH is easy to do, and looks simple. It is something very nurturing to do, too. What is wonderful and helpful is that you can make this a very regular, daily or several-times-a-day brief meditation.

Smiling with intention to any health issues is just like smiling to your heart. In smiling to your heart there is the intention for it to work. That is enough for the connection between the smile and the heart to open and for all heart-function to open subsequently. Smiling to your health issues will work in the same way. Just try it. What is likely to happen is that there is a pleasant feeling when you do your heart prep. Once you let your heart smile to your health issue, this feeling will deepen and become more beautiful.

The full KHH 9 - Smiling to health issues

Do heart preparation through full Heart Strengthening (KHH 6) or a slightly shorter version. When the feeling in your heart is clear, gentle and light, with only one intention, let your heart smile to your health problem. Then, if you feel a pleasant or light feeling, follow the feeling for the duration of this KHH. Enjoy.

Here are some additional guidelines:

- *Sit connected to your heart for some time (1-3 minutes);*

- *Once you feel your heart or deeper heart connection, smile from your heart to the problem you know (Do this for 3-5 minutes or longer);*

- *What is really helpful, and with your heart you can feel this at some point, is to smile to the 'problem (e.g. my physical heart or large intestine) and to all related issues, matters and causes; and*

- *It will take some time of dedicated practice for your heart to radiate to a level that you can feel it and to feel the impact it has. It can reach all parts of your body no matter how far from your non-physical heart.*

It is important to realise, that this practice is not limited to just physical parts of your body. Your heart can help other parts of you: your emotional world, your mind or mental health issues.

It is essential with this KHH that proper heart preparation through full Heart Strengthening or a shorter version of it happens. This is flexible and when you leave one or two steps out during the day, then it will still work fully and in the best way. What is more important is that you bring the quality to the heart strengthening exercises you do, for the purpose of this KHH, and ideally all the time. Quality means that you take your time, you feel your heart, what is happening, and follow the feeling, while at the same time letting go, focussing on feeling and not so much on watching, trying or wanting to help. The latter three will limit the feeling and your heart's capacity and ability to help.

Do not be concerned when you feel a pleasant feeling in your heart even though you let the heart smile to something not considered a 'nice' or pleasant. The feeling is pleasant for a number of reasons. One reason is that your heart knows and will be more active if there is a need to help. All feelings from a more active and expanding heart will be beautiful.

Your heart knows what is going on and when you ask it for this kind of help its natural response is to become more active and glowing.

Another reason is that the heart also knows the entire journey and the pleasant feeling is part of the heart's help-package. The body is aging, has health problems, and yet, within this, heart-centred joy, calmness, love and sharing, and other positive or enjoyable aspects of life, can always give a foundation for purpose, beauty and fulfilment. This will be clearer and more obvious with an active heart.

The heart will also become stronger in its natural connection to the Divine, a higher realm or dimension including all the flow from this connection. If you do this KHH properly and regularly you and your heart will feel quite amazing.

There is an additional way that you can deepen this KHH and the associated benefits. When you are at the point where you let the heart smile to your health issue you can add additional intentions. If you use this KHH for health prevention the intention could be something like:

Let the heart also smile to all health issues not yet known, including all the causes, roots and everything connected.

If you use it for one or several health issues, use these or similar words as an additional second intention:

Let the heart smile to all health issues known and not yet known including all the causes, roots and everything connected.

This will generate a deeper, even sweeter pleasant or expansive feeling. Feelings from your heart are just that and it will be a sign that your heart knows, knows what is needed and where, beyond the ability of the mind/brain's abilities. The moment it is invited into action, this will just happen. Enjoy.

Low investment high yield

There is no mistaking love. You feel it in your heart. It is the common fiber of life,
the flame that heals our soul, energizes our spirit and supplies passion to our lives.
It is our connection to God and to each other. Elizabeth Kuebler-Ross

The heart is a wonderful tool that you can have instantly available, at low or no cost, and its easily and always accessible. The heart's role in your preventative health, healing or overall wellbeing is very important because:

- It is special and has immense depth; and

- It carries within the essence of who you are. As you get closer to understanding and living with the heart, the less you are in resistance with natural laws, with a natural flow of your life within a greater life, world, the universe and even beyond that. Loping back to point one, the depth of your heart, you can say, is infinite.

One further helpful aspect is that the referred practices require only little knowledge and no special knowledge or skill. The heart complements, without side effects, any of the healing journey that you may be on, any treatment or medication that you may be receiving.

Do not be fooled by this play with words or economic description of the heart and its help for you. People say that the 'answer is closer than you know'. Yet often you don't find it, find the help you look for or need. The question is, have you looked at and into your heart? It is certainly very close to you, always available and because of its specialness, a small investment may just be that 'high yield' for your health, wellbeing, healing or extra support for challenges you face.

Summary - a healthier heart - more health from your heart

Your heart is special, deep and limitless. Your heart has been waiting to help you and to do its part with current health issues or in preventing any future ill-health. The heart can also help you with overall wellbeing, ongoing and severe health issues. Heart-Based Therapeutics has shown profound impact with mental, psychological, trauma or unsupportive emotional or habitual patterns.

Your heart is an essential part of you, as are your body, mind, mind/brain and emotional world. It is natural to use the heart, practically and in real terms, to help with any illness, unwellbeing or unhelpful patterns and stories from the past. Directly related to health and wellbeing these practical heart-steps offer a broad suite of choices and assistance:

1. The main ways in which your heart will help you is through:
   - Guidance in relation to existing or past health issues;
   - In your choice of proactive health measures; and
   - In its direct working on any health issues and their causes or related matters.

2. Your heart, mind/brain and emotional habits are all connected, interdependent. This means that the cultivation, practice and improvement of positive or more positive thinking is important, mainly to help the heart in its abilities to help the best. You can use the suggested Heart Diary, the above PHT 'The thinking - tension connection' or the PHT 'Heart Monitor' (a few pages ahead) to look at your thinking habits, to reflect on them, to make changes that you realise are necessary or supportive or both. If you are familiar with your heart already use the PHT 'Heart Mantra' to engage the heart's help.

3. Management of any negative emotions, replaced by heart-generated positive feelings, will support your health and wellbeing journey. Your attendance to your heart overall, good quality heart developing KHHs, PHTs and Heart Strengthening, are essential to develop and maintain the best heart-help that you can have.

4. The practice of visualisation and of affirmations are mind-based techniques. It is helpful to add the heart to it to equally engage the heart's help. The PHT 'Heart-supported visualisation for health' will help with this.

5. It is helpful to establish and feel the connection between thinking, and too much thinking, and tension levels in the body. Use the PHT 'The thinking - tension connection' to realise this and while doing it, at the same time, improving your relaxation levels. The aim is to improve the thinking (brain) and feeling (heart) balance that is right for you.

6. Your state of relaxation is of immense importance to general heart presence and even more so for any heart help when there are health issues. Several relaxation exercises KHH 3 'Relax more', PHT 19 'Heart - breath - intention relaxation' (both section IV) and the PHT 'Heart-supporting, tension releasing relaxation' are designed to give you heart-centred practices to assist your relaxation and heart.

7. In PHT 'Natural, heart-centred relaxation' a further relaxation is introduced. This natural, heart-centred relaxation is a blend of earlier relaxation practices tuning in with the heart. It is available as an audio recording from the book's website (www.yourheartcanhelp.org).

8. The PHT 'Heart Mantra' is really not a 'mantra' per se. The more often you remember the heart throughout the day, the more active it will become and assist you with your health and wellbeing. Combine this PHT with the KHH 2 'First casual try' and the PHT 'Remind your heart', parts I and II (a few pages ahead), where you place heart reminders around the house/office and invite others to remind you, too.

9. The PHT 'Instant stress relief 'heart first aid'' is a simple tool and practice that will help in times when you or your environment are not in the best circumstance or condition. Using these internal and external situations or irritations as a positive trigger, you learn to choose the heart. Over time the full(er) heart ability will be working for you.

10. The PHT 'Heart Monitor' invites you to reflect on your own patterns of responding negatively, in terms of thinking or emotion, to your environment or situation. Let a strong heart help you to bring more joy, and more, into your life.

11. Growing heart awareness and equally growing beautiful, special or helpful heart experiences will make you enjoy being in nature more. You may also feel with more clarity that being in nature or being surrounded by more green at home, in every room and at your work place, will not only make your heart happier, it will make you happier. It will also make your overall heart feeling lighter and stronger. PHT 'Heart time in nature' and PHT 'A green heart spot at home' suggest that you surround yourself with green, nature, plants and plan regular trips to a local park, beach, nature strip, meadow or forest.

12. Being in nature will not be strong enough to work with the deeper lying tendency to have negative emotions or drives. These can have a real hold on our heart, damage relations around us and pour negativities into and around the heart. The negative effects also affect body tension, organs and overall energy flows. Learn, with a stronger growing heart, to (PHT) 'Pull the emergency break' each time you are aware of these tendencies in you. This is possible when they surface. In this is a gift, as they normally lie deeper in the heart layers. PHT 'Remind your heart' is the complementary practice and reflects a commitment to your overall heart strengthening and help.

13. The PHT 'Feeling well - now and ahead' is a reminder to integrate your heart into your daily life.

14. The PHT 'Tapping into the heart's deeper knowing' is another invitation to let the heart help you or 'comment on', always in the form of a feeling, as to what health, health modality, treatment options or treatment additions to choose.

15. The PHT 'Deepening levels of heart realisation and help' invites you to use the heart in its more complete of full way. The heart can recognise things above and beyond the human mind/brain ability. In moments when you let the heart feel and realise that the energy at work in and through the heart is a/the Divine blessing, then it can profoundly deepen the heart's work in terms of health issues. The heart has learned something and will use it.

16. Secrets of Natural Walking (SONW) is showing incredible positive impacts for people with current or old-standing health issues. SONW is a unique combination of heart-opening walking that also opens and activates the body's energetic system in ways that many people have been able to experience profound, fast health improvements and healing. You can find more information in the contact section in the back of the book.

17. Heart Based Therapeutics work has shown very promising results within a comparatively short period of time. If you have been struggling with personal issues, deep, unpleasant emotions, even trauma, then to find a practitioner and book a set of session may be one of the heart-helped options to find a way back to a lighter existence, to more joy, calmness and love in your life.

18. The PHT 'Think less' is one tool to reduce access or over-thinking. Thinking and feeling are ideally in balance. Most aspects of life we enjoy feel 'good' or special. Let the heart become the balancing tool and the clearer centre of feeling it already is.

19. Reiki Tummo is one avenue for you to have extra and immensely deep help available for your health issues and at the same time for your heart. Any help that the heart facilitates will also be deepened through this. The learning of this or any reiki is another step towards health autonomy and your empowerment. Once attuned, once you have completed a workshop, you can use it daily or several times daily.

20. For any serious illness, serious health condition, old health issues or impacts of old accidents or injuries, a clear, strong and regular commitment to your heart is required. Even if you use SONW, HBT or Reiki Tummo, every additional heart-learning and practice will assist.

21. The heart's help has produced clear and wonderful results for people suffering from a mental illness. The heart's additional unique abilities to help with letting go, to reduce over-thinking or excessive thinking is an important support. The heart and its calming qualities contributes to reducing anxiety and related symptoms. Similar to serious health issues, as Ivan's story shows, mental health issues are best helped by a personal commitment to heart work.

22. Part of a clear commitment is Heart Strengthening (KHH 6) several times a day, combined with heart meditations (KHH 12/13) once or twice a day. They can be combined with any medical or alternative therapy treatment.

23. The next heart learning and heart help step would be the attendance at any of the Padmacahaya Institute's Heart Workshops starting with level 1 (and possibly up to level 6). This will not only deepen immensely the way that your heart can assist you, it will also be a fast-tracking of your heart learning; hard to achieve - but possible - without the help of the workshops.

24. The guidance from your heart is possible in two ways. In the way that you follow PHT 'Tapping into the heart's deeper knowing' and in the way that your heart will recognise the quality of the heart-radiance that is flowing through and from your heart and offer you 'on-the-go' guidance (section 3 - PHT 31). These combined allow you to verify, to realise, that the heart is helping, and even helping more, when illness is present. It always takes time to develop trust, including into the heart's guidance and help. The more this trust grows you access the heart's guidance more naturally and automatically: you will feel what feels right, less right and what not.

25. The heart also is simple in the way that it works and 'suggests' to be worked with: until you clearly feel the feeling from the heart and know what to do next or not to do anymore, or do more of, commit to an overall heart-supporting, heart - strengthening routine.

26. This guidance, together with this section's KHH 'Smiling to health issues' will be of significant help for any health, wellbeing issues. The more that you realise and recognise with your heart, as opposed to with your mind/brain only, that the heart is an infinite source of love, light, blessing and radiant healing qualities of these, any healing, plus all other positive feelings or help from the heart, will deepen. This is the nature of the heart and it has been recognised and referred to in songs, poetic writings and well-known books, including spiritual, religious and personal development literature.

27. The PHT 'Heart-leap of faith' invites you to rely on your heart-experiences up to now, to be more committed to your heart practice and to let your heart help you, at least in parallel in the same way as other health or wellbeing efforts you make.

Chapter 6

Work - Is Your Heart In It?

The market controls everything, but the market has no heart.
Anita Roddick

Imagine a colleague at work who wants to help you, support your program or project and says 'my brain is in it'. It would be unusual, strange and unclear. If the same person would say 'my heart is in it' you would instantly know a range of things. The meaning of this would be known - the person is interested, quite committed and you could rely on him or her. You also know that you could trust that person in some way.

Every situation, every interaction at work, is unique. In exploring the heart's help at work, it will become clearer what it means 'when the heart is in it', when you 'whole-heartedly' attend to your work, team or customers or when 'in the heart of hearts you know what to do'.

The modern work place

The mind cannot long play the heart's role.
Francois de La Rochefoucauld

The modern workplace offers an amazing spectrum of opportunities that can lead to fulfilment, growth or enjoyment. Naturally there can also be limitations: your abilities, or lack of access to work, training or career opportunity. Changes such as those relating to growing internet-related interactions, the fast-paced nature of change and a worldwide competitive market have created choice and flexibility but also challenge, pressure and stress.

The workplace is further characterised by a massive flow of information. Pressure and stress can be because of this flow or because of external circumstances, such as competition, fast-changing technology, or changing consumer behaviour. It can also be caused by internal circumstances, such as change, work place culture or difficult relations with colleagues or key stakeholders.

These challenges can amount to significant burdens for individuals or teams. It can make being at and managing work hard, and success an unreal or impossible expectation. Yet at the same time work can also be immensely rewarding, enjoyable and fulfilling. Your heart can assist in making a distinct line between those two opposites. This is one of the key and ongoing themes of this chapter and you find it also reflected in the ending section 'from stress management to happiness.'

The work chapter is very likely relevant to you whether you work:

- In an organisation;
- From home;
- Are on the road a lot;
- Are self-employed;
- A student, a volunteer, part-time or casual worker; or
- Are working as a mum or dad, as a house-wife or house-man.

This chapter is also about the heart's help with difficult, soft, intra- and interpersonal issues. What are the challenges that are heart-related and can these be helped by more heart? What are some of the ingredients to working well with others, to manage well, to communicate, and to lead effectively? And what are ways to remain open, attentive, joyful and engaged with growing feelings of purpose and fulfilment? This section explores these questions.

Projecting heart intelligence and heart ability to work environments enables your heart to directly and positively impact on areas such as:

- Communication;
- Assertiveness balanced with softness and working with conflict;
- Delegation, supervision and how to be supervised or managed;
- Decision making from a place of deep insight, analysis and vision;
- Self-management;
- Time management;
- Inner strength or resilience;
- Refining your emotional and heart intelligence;
- Abilities to work with change;
- Work under pressure;
- Work self-motivated;
- Self-directed work, or work with limited or no supervision;
- Work or cope mentally or emotionally with over-the-top supervision or micro management; and

- Work in an environment where mental health issues enter the work place and staff and managers need to learn to work with individuals or self, when affected by mental ill health.

This is not a complete list. What seems to stand out is that these are 'other' skills, qualities or abilities, soft skills, not related to technical, subject or professional knowledge or skills. Typical for possible heart contribution, they are connected to how you function and feel within, no matter what the situation, and how from here you relate to others and engage with the world of work. You know about this last point, perhaps.

There are people at work who, no matter how difficult all seems, smile, are positive and positively engage others and get things done.

Whatever you do in your daily work, if you cannot feel light, joyful or happy while doing so, means that work is a chore, a burden or just a lot of time spent waiting for happier moments later or during a two-week annual holiday. The heart offers new approaches and solutions.

Feeling well is a crucially important foundation. From there the heart goes further and offers access to a deeper form of knowing, wisdom and ability to create. Intuition, wisdom, ability to connect dots faster than the linear-working mind/brain are all supported by an inner knowing, the heart's ability to intuit and all of the heart's functions.

Feeling emotionally well, having reduced personal agendas and positive personal behaviour patterns are important aspects of leadership and team work. They add qualities to your input at work that have shown to help you and individuals or teams around you in profound ways. The heart's unique emotional clearing ability will surface also in the work chapter, with specific practices to apply in daily situations.

The ability to innovate, add value, be creative and work with those qualities are a strong foundation to success, recognition or just to feeling good about yourself at work. If you find yourself being more innovative, creative and all-round making better decisions, it means that your heart and mind are working together in new ways.

At the heart of the matter is the lack of heart
A change of heart is needed.

The above list of aspects, issues or challenge areas in the workplace relate to the heart, to emotional intelligence and yet also to wider existence as a human being. Technical or skill training, accumulated knowledge and experiences made are only partially relevant to success and fulfilment at work. Heart capacity supports a vast field of communication, interpersonal skills, soft skills as well as trained or innate behaviours and attitude. These are domains of the heart. The question is how much of your possible heart-training, heart-capacity is being utilised in the development of technical and soft skills.

With much training and educational emphasis being on the learning of skills and techniques, there is a risk for not fully or not really accessing the potential of the heart.

One key problem is that training programs tend to cater for technical or knowledge-based up-skilling for productivity, effectiveness and efficiency.

This is okay where it is about learning something technical or where more knowledge is needed. However, where the aim is to improve relationships, communication or any softer qualities, any mind/brain-centred training somehow needs to be translated into heart-felt and heart-facilitated qualities. This can certainly happen; however a bridging of heart and mind needs to take place for this exchange to become a reality.

There have been positive changes in workplaces in terms of greater focus on people, staff and their wellbeing, regular staff wellbeing survey or programs, efforts to improve culture, and the recognition of life outside work and that it can negatively impact on work. Progressive organisations support staff, including in their private or personal challenges in reflection of a more holistic approach to staff support, engagement, performance and long-term team building.

Within this lies another potential problem. When soft skills are being looked at, trained for and supported, there is an intention to bring in more positivity, warmth or heart. However, as soon as these initiatives are department or organisation-wide, the prime effort is to improve the cognitive, mind/brain understanding around these aspects. Then it is hoped that staff, managers or leaders will translate these into attitudes, new behaviours and overall greater insight and wisdom.

There is another missing puzzle piece: almost every role or function at work now is critically reliant on good relations, either internally, with key stakeholders, or externally with suppliers, clients, customers or patients. Effective refinement of relationship capabilities, and underpinning qualities, are critical to all-round positive and growing relations. Heart facilitated qualities seem to be key in adding quality and warmth to work relations or customer service. Authenticity and genuineness in what one thinks, feels, says or does impacts on effective and sustained team work.

What can be missing, in the workplace and in training efforts, is what the direct work with the heart can offer: the translation of values, principles, hopes and good ideas into genuine, heart-felt qualities, connection and care.

It is the heart shown to you through the stories or your own experiences, that can directly and positively impact on relational, emotional, attitudinal and behavioural qualities.

To be there, to work more with your heart, requires a heart and mind/brain balanced in equilibrium. To get there, let a 'change of heart' assist in accessing your heart and in making this transition.

The following sections will discuss four potential significant interferences with 'good' work, positive workplace cultures and interpersonal relations where people flourish. These interferences offer a view of workplaces issues or challenges more from the perspective of the heart.

Four interferences

I listen with all my heart.

The four interferences can be called 'core' interferences: they can reach a deeper inner core, be hurtful, or interfere with our work. They reflect discussions, observations, personal research and experiences working with heart-capacity building elements or programs in workplaces.

These interferences can deeply challenge and be present in many work situations or work places. If they are present at your work, or in you, it is very likely that in some way you are affected by them and it will take away from the goals outlined above: success, happiness, fulfilment and wellbeing. They also hang around, become niggling issues or burdens, at work and beyond work.

Core interference also means that the chance for them to trigger an emotional and less productive response is more likely. If this is so then they move us away from a mind/brain focussed, heart-centred or heart-mind balanced state of being at work. They can escalate into a need to seek professional help. Needs to debrief informally rise, coupled with risk for things to slide into very frequent ad hoc debriefs, gossip and unproductive time wasting. The implications can be less effectiveness, less efficiency and less enjoyment. In many such situations more time is spent trying to work something out in our head, which can be better dealt with by an active heart.

These interferences, some of which you have experienced in the past or face at work now are harder to pinpoint, identify and to work with. The four core interferences are:

1. **Emotional interference** - where emotions interfere with focus, collaboration or other positive/natural functioning at work.

2. **Heart - mind/brain separation** - where logical, thinking and over-thinking is out of balance with the innate wisdom of your heart.

3. **Conflict at work, difficult situations, challenging interactions** - where interpersonal conflicts, disruptive team dynamics or conflicts nearby absorb energy and attention away from work.

4. **Busyness/culture of 'doing'** - where people who look busy or do a lot of work are easier acknowledged than those who innovate, work hard and smart, and produce outcomes through working effectively and productively as team members.

1. Emotional interference

Emotional interferences at work can be any of possible emotions discussed in earlier chapters. Work related emotions, triggered by past events in this or a previous work place, hang around, burden individuals and take up space. This means that they distract and lead to other activities in search for release or venting.

At work, too, emotions are the not-so-good or not-so-helpful drivers that determine attitudes and behaviours. When cognitive control or heart-strength are low, to balance or transform them, emotions negatively impact in the work place; on oneself and on the team.

Emotions or emotional interference, as in normal day-to-day life, may be harder to identify at work. Emotions, when present at work, commonly are experienced as the opposite to something pleasant, positive, productive or helpful by self or by others.

Emotions can be at the surface, visible and expressed, or hidden. In either case emotions interfere. It is harder to identify interference when someone feels angry towards a colleague, a client or customer and does not show it. Emotional interference happens in four ways and several directions:

- Emotions will limit heartful interactions;
- Emotions are at the other end of the spectrum of 'being whole-heartedly' focussed or present;

- Emotions will burden own feeling and heart as causes of un-wellbeing and reduced happiness; and
- Emotions, expressed or not, will alienate customers or clients and more likely will lead to loss of business, good service outcome, or loss of business with the customer in the future.

This is critical to realise and act upon if you plan to run a successful, positive or growing business or operation. Emotions, shown or not shown, will be felt or perceived in some way or other by everyone around.

Any form of internally felt or generated emotion or externally-caused emotional reactivity will always do two things in a workplace: it will, over time burden your heart, make you feel heavy, more easily stressed and increasingly unhappy, and it will also be dis-engaging and dis-connecting in terms of any relationship with colleagues, stakeholders or with clients, customers or patients. The first PHT in this section 'heart warmth to keep your cool will' assist with this.

At the positive end of the spectrum if you are light in your heart, and looking after you heart and become increasingly lighter, then you will be more attractive, easier to approach and have other qualities that will attract attention, friendship and support.

To show and follow emotions may be normal workplace behaviour and can be seen role-modelled for example in magazines or TV shows. However, if you follow the thread of this book, if you follow the exercises given, you will feel clearer the 'no' from your heart to emotional indulgence and the 'yes' to positive, heart-directed alternatives.

2. Heart - mind/brain separation

A strong or dominant mind/brain means less of your heart's help and insight is present. The US based HeartMath Institute has done ground-breaking research in this field for many years. A mind/brain controlled approach to work appears safe, rational, clear and a 'good' road to success. This may be an illusion. Mind/brain control is often equal with the utilisation of knowledge and experience. Knowledge and experience are always from the past. Every current situation is in the present and may require new approaches and slightly different decisions, too. It will be shown below that the heart is needed to be in tune with this moment to moment reality.

The mind/brain's expertise is to (a) compare, to (b) judge and to base current situational requirements on (c) knowledge and experience from the past where not all situational factors were the same. Let us look at what these three main heart - mind/brain separation interferences mean.

Comparison

To compare situations, pieces of work or the work of individuals can be of use. It is helpful and meaningful to look at what you or others do well or don't do so well. From here you can work on plans to improve your own work, your team's performance, or, as a team leader, how to inspire and lead others to better performance. This applies to whole-of-organisational improvement efforts, too. They can be based on comparison or benchmarking exercises.

Comparison with an active or present heart will help in these three ways:

- In any comparing there will be understanding, care and calmness. This means that you will access your heart's intelligence and analytical, bigger picture abilities;
- Comparing also can trigger emotions such as irritation or anger. Heart-felt care will limit and minimise this; and
- Comparing can be a short or a long process; stretching over hours or days. You can use mind/brain only or add the heart's presence and help every moment along the way.

The tendency of the mind/brain, even though a situation or work program of comparing is completed, is to keep comparing. This is neither logical nor helpful.

This somehow over-comparing can distract you from doing the work. It is helpful and important to find a way by which this mind/brain tendency is stopped or reduced before you begin your work.

Comparison may positively nurture competition. This is true and can be the case. However, you may have experienced situations where ambition, for the sake of winning can take over and the real purpose or tasks at hand are falling by the way side.

Any form of comparison, if not balanced with heart qualities such as understanding of each other's' needs, shared understanding and learning or improvement, carries the potential to cause interruption or disharmony. In a high-functioning team comparison needs both, mind/brain and heart. The mind/brain can express, with openness, honesty and trust, findings that are based on sound comparison. The heart facilitates and engages in orchestrating in balance necessary comparison with understanding, recognition and respect. Everyone at work has expertise, is normally working hard and is human; and it is in this human-ness that everyone makes mistakes at times, too.

In comparing anything, with heart present, you continue to maintain, if not build, strong foundations for high performing, happy, well and enduring teams.

Judgement

Being judged by someone else or others is always tricky. Being judged is very often experienced as something unpleasant. Even when being judged for what looks like the right reasons, for a slip up or mistake, it can cause a reaction or some form of emotion. The mind/brain often wanders there and judges others.

Judgement is often based on someone's truth against someone else's truth. Judgement is the mind/brain's way to create or maintain separation. In moments when you judge you separate from that person, team or situation in terms of idea concept, and also energetically, unless there is a balancing force. While separation can be helpful, it can also be a stepping-back from being involved, engaged, committed and fully present.

Excess judgement often only happens in the absence of understanding, compassion or heart. It can raise its head when performance has not been managed in a supporting, careful and continuous manner. Judgement can equally be self-judgement. It can be around what you could or should have done or done better.

A strong, dominant main/brain, by tendency separating from the heart, can also be tricky and uphold judgement over one's own potential to learn, change and grow. It is easier to judge and stay in belief, emotion or what looks like fact. It is easier to remain the peer, manager or leader that maintains tendencies to judge than to look at one's own weaknesses or improvement opportunities.

One of well-known Dr Edward DeBono's very meaningful findings is that being in a state of judgement, being critical of something or someone, does not mean one has added anything purposeful or helpful to a cause. In fact, when solely in this state, it is often used for self-promotion or other non-creative, unhelpful directions. What he promotes instead is lateral or parallel thinking, where the critical mind is put in the background and thinking that creates, adds value and generates new or solution-focussed ideas is trained.

A heart and mind/brain balanced assessment of what is happening may also be judgement. Yet, it can be a more balanced approach of looking at realities, facts, figures, events and qualities of interactions with logic and with feeling or care. The heart takes emotions out of judgement and, in this way, makes it more what it is, what you have seen or what the facts are. It changes it from judgement to assessment.

When a strong heart does any form of work-place situational assessments or observations, then over-thinking and emotions are more likely to be kept at bay. Others will feel support and heart-to-heart connection and these qualities will continue to build feelings of care and support, in turn promoting contribution and team work.

Knowledge and experience

From the perspective of the heart there are helpful, positive aspects to knowledge and experience and those that are less helpful and less positive. Knowledge is what you know at the mind/brain level of remembering. Experience is what you experienced that allows the mind/brain to access this and transfer it to a new situation. This works well when your work is repetitive or when past and current situations are similar in nature. In relation to experience the question exists 'what is the ability that translates experience and applies it appropriately to a new situation, the mind/brain only or are there other abilities involved'?

It is when there is enough difference in circumstance that neither knowledge nor experience will offer you a good-enough foundation for making a sound decision or the best choice. Culture, weather, people around the table or the customer you are interacting with are all adding to the difference that limits knowledge and experience. New approaches are required and needed, outside your knowledge and expertise.

A very simple and yet to the point example is a project management situation where I worked with a senior executive of an organisation establishing the equivalent of a 500-million-dollar operation (construction and service). The executive had successfully done a similar project overseas: successful meant, completed the project and achieved a positive return earlier than expected. The executive maintained a firm position based on this, did not consider all the environmental factors and did not invest more in the start-up phase as he was advised to do. The operation had significant early operational difficulties, re-investment had to be very significant, and the difficulties were so great that he lost his job.

Knowledge is generally good and in many work situations knowledge, whether it is specific, detailed or a wider, broad, strategic knowledge, is immensely helpful and positive. Knowledge, however, needs an 'as well as', something else or a yin and yang, where in the yin or yang of knowledge is something else that can work. There is a turning-point where knowledge that one person has can be too rigid, as illustrated in the above brief story. More softness, perception, listening, understanding or an ability to intuit is required. This can be driven from a mind/brain or from a heart-intelligence ability to do so.

Knowledge, if not balanced by heart, warmth and softness, can be also be overpowering and dis-engaging. The more you or a senior, superior person knows, the less another employee needs to know or contribute. It is knowledge buffered by a wise and attentive heart that ensures that others are invited to comment, add, or challenge any current or planned course of action. The PHTs 'Listen with your heart' and 'Stop, feel, heart, listen' will assist with this tendency or habit.

The approaches where a project manager, manager or leader shows a balance between interest, leading with questions, encouraging dialogue and seeking first to understand before making oneself understood[10], all point in a direction where s/he can only find out essential, core, key or current information and gain deeper understanding by mutually engaging in open and trusting interactions.

A strong heart is needed here to put any existing knowledge and experience aside and not only to listen and receive but also to be criticised, challenged or confronted with ideas that would not have been considered otherwise. With a strong or light heart it will be easier to say 'yes' to this and to allow the right ideas, adjustements or innovations to be incorporated without bruised egos. Liz Wiseman's work the 'multiplier effect' adds to this discussion.[11]

Knowledge and experience, together with a more separated heart - mind/brain, by tendency will also find reasons or justification to promote self over team more: whether this is general self-worth or the greater worth of one's ideas or contributions; even if in reality there is more of a balance. The reality is that even to overlook one important comment or suggestion can cause significant damage or loss of revenue or loss of public credibility if your heart and mind do not work together and with others in a more dynamic way.

Knowledge and experience, and an overall mind dominance, are harder to bring together with qualities like support, openness, collaboration and genuinely caring work relations.

> *Recently I talked to a colleague who works on a major, state-wide health project. She said that she loves her work and that she has never been so productive. When asked why, her plain and instant response was 'we have a new very supportive manager'. There was no mention of the manager's special knowledge or experience that he or she very likely also has.*

3. *Conflict at work, difficult situations, challenging interactions*

It is normal to have good times and not so good times at work. However, when times are not-so-good or when there is conflict, when difficult, challenging or very challenging situations or interactions happen, then our time at work can be draining or a disturbing, heart-wrenching experience.

Conflict resolution, dealing with difficult situations or people, finding ways out of difficult situations, is an often-seen workshop topic. Many of the approaches come from a cognitive, mind/brain-centred perspective. Other than the development of better communication or coping/resilience tools, mind/brain strategies will need to be translated to 'heart' or otherwise emotional clearing plains for workshops to be impactful at an emotion-level, in terms of clearing of burdens or reduced emotional reactivity.

> *It is the overall condition and strength of your heart that determines how you respond to conflict and difficult situations or challenging interactions.*

The more difficult, traumatic or deeper-emotional the difficulties are, the more risk a sole mind/brain approach or remedy risks secondary or repeat emotional burdening or trauma. This will not work as effectively as the heart or a balanced heart/head unity with an issue. The below KHH 'Surrender burdens - individuals, situations and related emotions' will significantly assist at work and beyond if based on overall heart capacity development.

Better outcomes are achieved when difficult situations, challenges or upsetting interactions are attended to with all the tools and facilities you have available; including your heart. It is normal, logical and perhaps the best to use a clear mind/brain, supported by a strong heart in team work. Ideally the way you work with a difficulty, challenge or conflict is in such a way that allows you to continue to work effectively, to grow as a person, to have continually good relations, and not damage your heart more. The how to from the perspective and capabilities of your heart will be discussed in the following heart-help sections.

4. *The culture of busy-ness*

> *... have heart stand still.*

There is something of a 'busy-ness' mantra in the world today. If you ask a colleague or friend 'how are you', in many instances the answer will be 'I am busy', as if to say that being 'busy' is a statement of wellbeing, quantity and quality of work done, of quality of team contribution or a sign of overall achievement.

> *It can be good to be busy or not good to be busy.*

When a person is busy it can easily be interpreted as the person is hard working, effective and a good employee or worker. This may be true, however it is equally possible that someone who is working hard may not be working particularly smart and effectively. The same person may in some ways work in a wrong direction or for a portion of self-interest; namely their own agenda. Working hard can also mean 'it is hard' because of a possible lack of team work or being overwhelmed by the workload.

---

[10] Stephen R Covey, The seven habits of highly effective people, New York: Simon and Schuster, 1989.
[11] Wiseman, Liz, Multipliers: How the Best Leaders Make Everyone Smarter, Harper Collins, 2010.

Being 'busy' is one of a dominant mind-brain's not-so-helpful expertises that will gradually burden the heart, and lead away from connection, calmness, effective and caring relations and a joyful and fulfilled life. There is no quality in busy-ness.

Even a small shift in the direction of less scattered or overwhelmed busyness would bring more of the person's energy to the team, use more team effort and tap into inner innovative abilities that achieve the same or even better results with much less effort.

What is this busy-ness? It can have a wide range of meanings. At one end of the spectrum it can mean that one is overwhelmed, totally snowed under with work and is highly stressed. This is not so good. Being busy can be just right, a reflection of a full day and a day of work where things are achieved or where people are served well. At the other end of the spectrum being busy can be an appreciation of having work, having something or enough to do that fills the day and something that gives meaning and joy to a day at work or at home. Here, being busy is to do something, to integrate, be in society and a participating part of the community. In addition, there are deeper inner drivers that create an urge to do, act and think almost all the time. These are mind/brain associated and can be strong, in particular when there is a lack of the heart's balancing energy. There is an overall sense 'it is hard to stop', even when you get home from work.

At the difficult, high-pressure or not-so-good end of busy-ness, the efficiency or quality of work can drop significantly. There will always be some tasks that can be dropped. Every bit of heart-centredness can assist here to reduce any feeling of being overwhelmed. At any level of workload and pressure the heart helps to feel calm, centred, clear and in connection. All of these qualities are important to do most tasks or roles well. General heart strength is helpful prior to a really busy time and the PHT 'The to-do-review' can further assist.

> **Practical Heart Tip 60: The to-do-review ***
>
> *The heart-based 'to-do-review' invites you to slow down, be more heart and mindful and engage the heart in both decision-making processes and your interactions with others. The review in action is:*
>
> - *Every moment you are inclined to act, interact or do something;*
>
> - *Pause and connect to your heart (if you are regular in your practice, connection to your heart will be quite easy or become easier over time);*
>
> - *Feel your heart for a few moments, then feel ...*
>
> - *Is there a 'yes' (expansion, gentleness or light feeling);*
>
> - *Is there a 'no' (tension, pressure, contraction or heaviness);*
>
> - *Is there a 'neutral' feeling (none of the above, no movement, no feeling from the heart -*
> - *it stays as it is or was before you felt the feeling); then*
>
> - *According to what you feel, act, do, speak or don't do, be silent, or invite the other to do or speak.*

The PHT will facilitate a being-gently-coached by your heart in one of the key leadership quality directions 'humility'. One can only be humble in a very limited way. Being truly humble is a mindset, some would say. In reality it is equally, or more so, a 'heartset', a quality that is you, reflecting how you do or approach work or others, genuinely.

This PHT will also reduce the stress levels that are based on doing too much and doing when doing is not really needed. It will further function as a balancing force within a culture or addiction to busy-ness. In this way, the PHT will also help those who have an inclination to micro-manage, at work or at home, and take pressure off others, freeing up the 3P's, their true or greater potential, passion and productivity.

You will make new experiences deciding this way. Why not add your heart's growing abilities to the decisions you make or how you lead others? You may at times do this on your own or rely on your heart in a team situation. There is always a chance that an idea or decision is looked at carefully, through the minds and hearts of the team, or people who are treated as equals, and a balanced or better decision is made.

Busy, if not monitored, can also mean being or feeling 'scattered', un-centred and pressed for time. A leader, manager or staff member who makes you feel that they have no time for you, is not necessarily a good person to work with, for, or to have in the work team. The energy that someone gives out in cases like this can make them harder to approach. There is likely to be an impact if their potentially important input is less utilised or their knowledge of a difficult or important situation is not given.

There can be addictive qualities to being busy or too busy. The driver of what I like to call the 'Busy-Bus', might have habits that self-perpetuate, a story of 'I am not good enough unless everyone sees how busy I am' or self-inflicted escapism from problems elsewhere. It may further be pain or emotional pain, or a general mind/brain or emotion-dominance not sufficiently balanced by the heart. It can be a symptom of a lack of ability to work with others, to prioritise, delegate, focus or an expression of a current or overall inability to do the work.

At a high level of busy-ness there is also a good chance that any real, self-inflicted or perceived levels of busy-ness translate into stress, or excess stress, and long-term work or health problems.

There are colleagues who are 'always' centred, open, available, kind, attentive, focussed and who still communicate in a gentle way despite high levels of pressure, stress or busy-ness. Some of this is facilitated by the heart, the inner, innate and natural centre of calmness, centredness that just works, as soon as you allow it too, when it can do what it naturally does.

There is a time also when things get too busy, too overwhelming and an important step needs to be taken to make a workforce, team, structural or workflow change to remedy the situation. PHT 'The Stress buster' may offer an additional way to manage better during these times.

Your heart is the part of you that can help to monitor any healthy or un-healthy busy-ness in your life. The heart can ground or centre you while everything else is pulling you in a hundred or many different directions, putting you at risk of busy-ness beyond manageability. The heart is also the source within you that can keep you calm, in the eye of the storm, in heart-centred attentiveness to self and others and the present tasks or interactions.

How the heart can help - smart work and heart work

When all is said and done,
the only change that will make a difference
is the transformation of the human heart.
Peter Senge

In our personal lives and at work we have tried numerous programs or approaches. We have said things, we have done or tried different approaches and often something is missing. There can also come a point where work is not flowing or just feels harder than it should be. Senge's above statement implies that heart is needed to complete the overall situation at work.

This, the heart, is logical, as it is really only when all of who you are, and the heart is in its right place, that best performances, collaborations and achievements can also follow.

What the heart offers is a continuum of learning, and being. It will help you to approach a state where what you work on or with is in the 'now', heart-helped, with a clear mind, and what you think or do is the sum-total of all you are and bring to work.

With the heart more at the centre of your existence at work everything at work can become meaningful and a very enjoyable, blissful, insightful and fulfilling time, no matter what you do.

This might seem unrealistic, unbelievable and a somewhat crazy or irrational statement. Well, yes, from the perspective of anything that the mind/brain knows, has experienced or can do- yes. Almost undoubtedly you will remember moments where you have had joyful and light experiences at work. What is hoped for is that the following sections, and the stories shared, give you an indication, a feeling or an insight, of possible progress in this direction and where your heart wants you to be.

Let us look at how the core work-related heart functions help in addressing some of the aspects of these four interferences, and how, in this way, this bigger heart-helped picture can unfold. The heart has profound, potent and unique abilities to help. Three balancing qualities and abilities, discussed below, are an expression of these. They will work towards balancing the four interferences or, very likely, more.

Three balancing heart qualities

You will find that the issues described above relate to the following three balancing heart-at-work qualities:

1. Heart-emotional intelligence;
2. Heart-centred communication; and
3. Support, care and love.

These qualities will activate and bring your heart into action, its wisdom and abilities, to counteract the four interferences, as well as any personal short-comings or unsupportive habits. It will further balance any parts or qualities within that make out a well-rounded person in the work place: someone with positive, relevant and refined attitude, behaviours, competencies and deep intelligence.

A strong and present heart - in balance with the head - will also be an important foundation for everything you do at work. When you are well, resilient in times of stress and when you are overall healthy, you will be behaviourally consistent at work, and in your performance. When you are light and joyful you will additionally be approachable and pleasant to work with. When your heart is active at work it will impact positively in two further ways supporting your:

- Wellbeing, resilience and health; as well as
- Happiness and enjoyment.

Past the foundation and the core heart qualities is a further layer of heart-support. It is in relation to decision-making and creativity. Heart-intelligence will support whatever decision-making abilities you already have. You tap into a larger wisdom and analytical source that is within your heart. Longer-term and easier-to-engage with decisions are possible. The heart-at-work will help your:

- Ability to make frequent daily decisions with clarity;
- Ability to be creative and innovative; and
- Ability to make good, forward-looking and all-aspects-considered decisions.

These balancing heart qualities, and other aspects, are discussed to some extent also in the next sections. A more detailed heart at work book will follow 'Your Heart Can Help'.

Heart-emotional intelligence

Heart-emotional intelligence (HEI) is not only a form of intelligence from the heart. This intelligence, on its own is hard to comprehend or relate to, depending where, on a continuum of heart and mind/brain intelligence understanding, learning or collaboration, one is at.

Heart-emotional intelligence as an intelligence and capacity is explored in the following sections as a response to the four interferences at work. The sections are:

- Self awareness;
- Own emotions are cleared;
- Emotionally availability;
- Intelligence, wisdom and decisions;
- Dealing with difficulties;
- Overcoming boredom; and
- Heart-engagement at work.

Self awareness

Understanding of oneself or greater self-awareness is integral to the work of psychologists and other similar professionals or experts. It is integral to everyone as you are the centre or hub of all interactions at work.

One foundation element of HEI is to look at all of what a human is, the physical and non-physical building blocks, and then to look at the behavioural aspects they represent. From there, with the heart re-gaining its natural place, it is about integration, balance and refinement of all parts and aspects.

Common self-awareness centres around the mind/brain as the hub. It is from here that you understand who you are, what you are not and how you can possibly get from A to B, in terms of professional development, learning or workplace projects, based on certain steps, efforts or insights gained.

In the work section, as well as in all other Heart Book chapters, the heart's contribution is to clarify 'self', who we are, once a clearer heart presence and role unfolds, and how, from there, we connect and interact with our environment and others.

Heart-centred self-awareness also requires you to be candid and open with yourself. This can also mean being willing to look at weaknesses, emotions and un-helpful patterns and then secondly to be willing to look at them in a slightly different light. The aim is not so much to solely look at them, analyse, compartmentalise or even judge them or yourself. The more complete and self-aware 'you' can bring them to the transformative abilities of your heart. It is then that the heart can facilitate a smooth transition towards greater work place effectiveness, growth and enjoyment from the inside out; widening continuous understanding of self and others from the expanding and helping viewpoint of the heart.

Self-awareness is more complete with the inclusion of the heart. When you understand and experience the heart then it is also more logical too. The heart, in its wisdom, is accessing a greater logic. The heart is quite frequently referred to by known and respected leaders who have often seemed to be ahead of their time such as: Anita Roddick, Jim Collins, Stephen Covey and Steve Jobs.

Own emotions cleared

Commonly known emotional intelligence work is often focussed on a mind/brain direct emotional intelligence (EI). Some of the work and understanding is on one section of the brain that holds memory about trauma or other significant emotional events or function, the amygdala. In terms of heart-emotional intelligence the mind/brain has a similar role. Mind/brain guide, control and initiate more heart and yet, an additional powerful 'emotion'/intelligence centre is additionally activated and used, the heart. From here emotional regulation and refined growth is facilitated.

Have you ever tried to clear emotional patterns, emotional reactivity or emotional habits? Mind/brain control and direction will help. You can achieve a degree of mind-control, which is the focus of most EI models. If you have tried before you will have realised that it is not easy at all to achieve. Emotion controlled and not expressed is also emotion not yet cleared.

The mind/brain can control emotions to some extent but it does not have the ability to clear them. The amygdala is the memory of emotions or trauma and can recall these. It needs the mind/brain in a controlling and dominant role.

Recalling an emotion or an emotional event often means there is a partial re-experience of the emotion or even the trauma if there was one. Emotion held as memory in the amygdala is triggered by associated events and if too strong, or if mind/brain control is not strong enough, there will be a further emotional reaction. Emotional reaction is emotional reaction even if it is not expressed. This means there is still 'reactivity' and you will still burden your heart.

Every emotion you experience within - or let loose - even if you feel you have the right to, will burden your heart. The negative impact is here not only in terms of, for example, current or future work interactions, it will in some way impact on your whole life too.

There are deeper levels of deposits made when emotions or traumas have been experienced in the past. These are stored within or around the heart which are not supposed to be there. These are impurities or negativities which reduce your heart's capacity and function. You can view these as a deeper form of memory, which is similar to the memory that the amygdala holds and which can trigger a related negative and unhelpful response in a work situation.

The heart facilitates emotional clearing. It is smart enough to know what needs to go and what needs to stay. This is done in a similar way to which your digestive system would filter out the good stuff and eliminate the not useful or bad stuff at a physical level.

If the potential for emotion reactivity remains it can be detrimental to you and your career and it can be damaging to the organisation.

The importance of emotional intelligence and emotional-non-reactivity has long been recognised in customer service organisations. If a customer behaves normally his or her statements or behaviours can trigger an emotional response. Customer service teaches us that even if a customer is very difficult or rude, to stay calm, to be polite and to complete the interaction as positively as possible. Most likely you have experienced this. Warm and attentive customer service feels nice, it can even calm you down if you are agitated, annoyed or upset, for example how you were treated by your mobile phone provider or the parking law enforcement officer.

Outwardly, in a work, commercial environment or customer service situation, it is acknowledged that emotional reactivity is damaging and potentially can significantly discredit the organisation. At project, management and leadership levels the same is happening. Any emotional reactivity will cause a dent, or even a break, in relations and will make it harder or near impossible to engage and re-engage. At a surface level, engagement and collaboration may continue, however, at a deeper held emotions level, the break is real, collaboration will be lip-service and opportunities to dis-engage, leave or block may be used.

Emotional reactivity occurs when mind/brain or common knowledge is overridden by a subtle or strong emotional reaction. In accessing the second emotional centre, your heart, you can bring yourself back into a heart-centred presence. In heart-centred presence any following responses will be characterised by an overarching feeling of calmness, centredness and understanding of self and others. Your heart will - in this very moment - help you, reduce the level of reactivity and dissolve any existing disposition to react in the future, too. In this moment it will help work focus or any interactions with the team members, clients or customers.

Practical Heart Tip 61: Heart warmth to keep the cool *

Use this PHT for situations at work where you are likely to lose your calm - a little bit, just on the inside only, or a lot. Use it in any situation where you react with emotion, expressed or not.

When you are in this situation, when you feel emotion rising ...

- *Stop (even silently say this to yourself), or simply don't follow this habit;*
- *Pause what you do or say for a few moments or as soon as you can;*
- *Realise and remember the heart can help;*
- *Do the five core heart-connecting steps - even if you only do every step as one-word reminders: 'relax', 'smile', 'touch', 'feel', 'follow'; and*
- *Stay now in this heart-centredness ... and act, speak from the heart as much as possible.*

You can use this PHT to prepare for a situation where you know you are likely to be emotionally reactive.

There will be times when you can't attend to your heart in this way, in that very moment. Do the PHT as soon as you can after the event or after the emotional reaction.

It is normal that things get difficult, challenging or even near impossible to bear at work. There will be very difficult interactions, situations where many follow emotions or talk negatively about others. This is the one way of testing your heart-strength and to learn to make a heart choice, not following a negative impulse, with all its benefits; short, medium and long-term.

If a situation challenges you deeply, is heart-wrenching, then it will be helpful to remove yourself from the situation as soon as practical and to do the full Heart Strengthening (KHH 6) as part of this PHT. Equally, a solid overall heart strengthening program will assist to do more systemic and preventative emotional clearing. This sounds like a big effort here yet the essence of emotional patterns or habits can run back a long time and hence lie very deep within.

Utilising the heart strengthening and heart-clearing activities from this book, or the online program, will ensure that any existing emotional 'package' or habits will be cleansed consistently. It also means that any new and daily deposits are also taken care of.

This emotional clearing is taking care of whatever are known or unknown emotional storage, patterns and habits. Over time you will find that difficulties you experienced with certain people or certain groups of people will become fewer.

It is not uncommon for unsupportive or boycotting emotional patterns to disappear completely with the help of an overall committed heart program.

Disengagement based on difficulties at work or difficult interactions with individuals at work will turn to joyful, heartfelt re-engagement at work and with the wider team. Where there are already warm and productive relations, these will become even more enjoyable, productive and creative.

The end-result will be a freedom from emotion and from emotional reactivity. All good emotions, termed feeling throughout the book, will be strengthened, such as feeling light. Within this lightness, an innate, deeply-lying joy, will grow. Joyful people are easier to approach. When it is you, people will be drawn to you. When the joyful, calm, wise and 'real you' emerges, this will give you a wonderful new meaning in life, at work and in all interactions at work, which are, at their core, heart-to-heart encounters.

'Emotional' availability

When your heart is overall freer, with fewer emotions occupying the heart-space, you become emotionally more available to everyone at work. This emotional availability is of greater importance than what it may look at first glance. The heart facilitates and offers a wholehearted attention to a person or situation. This is a very significant internal resource that you have available. It will counteract the turning away from the perhaps one essential piece of information given by a situation or a person that you would otherwise miss in a busy day or moment. Possible examples of this are:

You are in a team leader or senior role. To attend to your full work schedule with as much focus as possible you only allow certain people to see you, talk to you or have the ability to make an appointment. Emotional unavailability is expressed in this way.

You are not only busy, but also emotionally processing a challenge, an upsetting situation. In this moment you will lack the clarity and freedom that more heart can give to see or connect with the right person.

You 'made it' and you are in a better position than some of your colleagues. Even though you try to stay connected, there are the emotions from others. There are subtle emotions of pride or arrogance that take away from the lightness of being and the emotional availability that you had before.

You have an open-door policy. Great, and you are talking to someone who came to see you. Yet, your mind is very busy and it is hard to concentrate on what the person is saying. Or, you don't really like that person. More heart will calm you down. You feel in the deeper connection less of the likes and dislikes that can surface. It will allow you to focus on the person more and to hear what is being said, even if the person has difficulties articulating themselves or the core issue at hand.

In the above examples, more heart will calm everything down. In moments where you interact with others you will be more present, emotions will be kept at bay, and your full mind/brain and heart existence can be present.

When you are heart-emotionally available and present it will affect others. People will feel heard and attended to. If not in this situation then in future situations they will more likely feel welcome to approach you and bring important information, or seek important guidance, advice or information from you.

Your own heart presence will also alert you to time wasting. With your heart you will feel when to say that you have to move on or, attend to other matters, or your work again. A strong heart will give you the confidence to say this and at the same time ensure that it comes from a place of care and heartfulness.

A greater heart-centredness is not only helpful when you call on it in moments of need. When you are overall calmer there will an aura of approachability. You are communicating in an energy-sense to others that you are available if needed. There is always the chance to be approached and to politely say no to an interruption now, to postpone it or to refer it to another person. Let the KHHs from this chapter and the PHT 'Softening the edges' help.

You may find that a stronger heart and heart-facilitated emotional availability brings events, people and situations into the work place that otherwise would not have happened. It is not exactly 'emotional availability' in the way emotions are defined in this book. It is heart-warm, heart-centred care and concern for others that invites others in with clarity. Perhaps it is better described as a 'heart-based law of attraction'.

Intelligence, wisdom and decisions

The mind/brain is directly associated with intelligence and the ability to make good decisions; some would say with wisdom, too. The past decades have seen wider intelligence sources being recognised, our innate emotional, physical and spiritual intelligence. It can be a helpful start to let go or be open to challenging the mind/brain's strong hold on being the sole or main source of intelligence.

Even since my days at university the insights of other parts of us that can help or know were vividly discussed: intuition and higher intelligence. Your mind/brain can be beautiful. What role does your heart play in relation to all this, even if, right now you consider yourself a good decision-maker already? If the mind/brain is the sole intelligence, there is a risk as the mind/brain:

- Tends to be scattered, distracted and overthinks;
- Is easily influenced by:
    - Concepts you have learned or hold;
    - Perceptions you have of others, situations or things together;
    - Past experiences you have had;
    - The world of emotions within; and
- Is not clear where, for example, good ideas come from.

The nature of the mind/brain is to go on and on and to be undisciplined. Even one of the brain experts, Edward DeBono says 'we are undisciplined thinkers'.[12] With your heart added, calming and influencing you, there are likely to be two benefits:

- You will have more room to think about what you really need to think about to make the best decision; and
- You create the thinking space to allow other good ideas, from within, or from others to enter that space.

Concept, approach, truth or experience are at times only as good as they served you in the past. Any of these, applied to a new or current situation, may not be the perfect match you hope it to be; it may only partially be, or not at all. The business establishment example above in the 'knowledge and experience' section is one such example.

Past experiences are a major issue in decision-making, when, within, you are not free to think, see or feel the current situation or bigger picture. People now, perhaps more so than in the past, have derived authority and power from a gathered wealth of experiences. Unfortunately, the more significant and positive such experiences are, the more one tends to hold on to them as a universal truth that always applies. The reality is that no situation is ever the same again: there are different people around, different quality of goods or services or the client or customer behaviour and profile have changed.

Negotiating a heart-emotional intelligence program for staff and team leaders in a medium size organisation the CEO said:

I know what you say ... when staff come to me and say 'I have a good idea on how to do this or that' there is a part in me not listening fully, not being very interested. When, however, a staff member approaches me and says 'it feels good to try this or to do this' then I listen, respond and often it leads to action.

The heart, as the source of intuition, gut-feeling, other intelligence or your gentle good sense, is another tool to use to follow a more complete picture and data set of information. This is useful for moment-to-moment decisions or when bigger, strategic organisational decisions are made and when, despite a strong volume of information and data, there is still flexibility to take route X or Y.

Emotions that you hold can prevent you from making the best decisions.

For example: you like person Y more than person X. Both offer you a business partnership and you can only go with one. You trust this more emotional like as a sign for a more beneficial future business relationship. This may be the right decision or it may be an emotional trigger situation, being led by something other than the heart or good logical mind/brain processes. How much you like or dislike a person can be based on a wide range of factors and it is not an indicator as to how well a transaction or business relationship will unfold.

The heart never seeks to win or become the new boss. The heart is looking for its own natural place within and from there to best support you. In moments when your heart is making its intelligence and innate wisdom available to you, judgement and comparison will be used appropriately; balancing mind/brain with heart intelligence and with care and concern for others.

The heart's intelligence working within will naturally shift you away from whatever you know or don't know is a more self-centred position. In turn, others will feel equally freer to support you, trust you and engage with you, making their fuller potential available to the team, the situation and you. Your heart's radiance when clearly there will allow them to let go of whatever they are holding that is not supportive of an overall, heart-supported, work environment.

---

[12] Edward makes this statement in several of his publications. He made this statement in person over a lunchtime meeting/discussion while he was visiting Australian DeBono centres in early 2000.

Your heart's intelligence is always working in tandem with your already gained knowledge. It knows you. 'Learning something by heart' is the commonly used expression of this.

Your heart knows everything you have ever done or experienced. The problem is that most people are comparatively disconnected from the heart.

Once you start to realise this you can then focus on being with every situation on its own merit, every situation as it presents itself, and every person with moment to moment attention, care and insight. It is the same intelligence that will allow you to be free from your knowledge and experience, unattached from parts or aspects that would lead to wrong decisions or courses of action.

Dealing with difficulties - situations, interactions and conflicts

Your role may be in a complaints department or similar. However, dealing with difficulties at work, difficult individuals or both, is a fairly normal occurrence. A large or excessive work load can be such a situation, or an otherwise difficult work situation, interaction with others, or 'difficult' individuals. At a first glance the heart can help you to keep you relatively calm, be less impacted by stress or pressure and be non-reactive.

In any conflict situation, the often clearly better response is to remain calm, attentive and be caring towards others; which means, knowingly or not, to rely strongly on heart qualities and abilities.

This is common sense, known by experts, trainers, supervisors and staff. Knowing about it is one thing. It is only when you truly have managed to stay calm and feel calm that this calmness is a full reality, your reality. It is then also transmitted to others and can have a positive effect. Some people have a wonderful skill to behave like this; for some it is an effort and for others near unattainable.

The more heart you can bring into situations of difficulty, the more this calmness will be genuine and deeply felt within you. Your heart is an ultimate resilience source and will make, when it is strong and light, work profoundly enjoyable, no matter what happens around you. The heart will make whatever work you do lighter, less burdensome, and everyone you engage with will be affected by this calmness and heart radiant, light energy.

Naturally, and as taught in assertiveness training, this does not mean to give in or to not come forward with suggestions or ideas. It is when your heart is light you can be clear. Emotions will not have a hold on you. From there, inside strong, you are able to say 'no' without blurring from other parts within or from outside/others. In this way, at this inner, heart-emotional level, any of your responses to a difficulty can have a greater chance of being productive, attentive, focussed, caring. This will further support building a sustainable and long-term work relationship with team members or customers; or you allow customers to build their own positive relationship with your service or organisation.

Your heart will help you, when you are heart-centred, to have less or no emotional reactions or outbursts in difficult situations or interactions. You know or may have experienced that even one such reaction or outburst can be very unhelpful in terms of career possibilities or positive, productive work relations.

A heartful response to conflict at work, difficult situations and challenging interactions also brings with it clarity and awareness that no action can be the best in situations when emotions are present. It is in these moments, when a heart-centred presence is added, that the heart can work 'behind the scenes'. It will clear or at the very least build a foundation for the resolution of the issue in the future.

Overcoming boredom and disengagement

To your heart's content.

Boredom and disengagement are experienced at the level of mind/brain more than anywhere else. For a constantly moving mind/brain anything repetitive or anything it knows that could be better has the chance to create boredom. Engagement can be caused by boredom or by an emotional reality, past or present, that becomes cemented in a mind/brain held attitude, especially when emotions or heavy heart-deposits made are not cleared.

The mind/brain requires stimulation to be engaged, not bored, and in some way 'happy'. The more the mind/brain is disconnected from any heart feelings the more chance boredom and disengagement can be present.

Boredom or repetition is something that is not appealing to the mind. The mind/brain will get bored, will want to get into other things and, by tendency, will think about other things.

At the other end of the spectrum are commitment, quiet enjoyment, gratitude and fulfilment, ultimately heart-feelable qualities. They are as intangible as the heart itself or the core qualities 'love, connection, calmness or happiness'.

Any efforts to improve a situation of boredom through self-talk or mind/brain centred interventions will only go to a certain point, as you move within the parameter of the mind/brain and not outside it. The positive, not-bored feelings are much more connected to heart feelings.

What a dominant mind holds or knows is that excitement at work is related to somewhat exciting tasks or times. Feelings of disengagement are less 'feelings', they are either mind/brain held concepts or perceptions based on emotion. Your heart processes are independent from the nature, level, complexity or simplicity of the work you do. Whatever your skill level, role or level of positive work challenge, the pleasant, engaging and connective heart feelings can always be accessed.

Practical Heart Tip 62: Boredom buster *

The boredom buster invites you to look towards your heart every time you are bored or feel disengaged. As you 'feel' bored or 'disengaged', one solution is:

- *Do what you need to do to be more heart connected;*
- *Feel your heart for a few moments and just enjoy these heart-feelings; and*
- *Then stay in these feelings and a clearer heart-centred presence as you continue your work.*

Feel, now or over time, whatever you do will be enveloped by the growing gentle joy and a level of enjoyment that your heart can facilitate and feel in literally every moment at work.

It may take a little while to feel the joy surfacing. It should be easy to feel calmness and other pleasant feelings from your heart by now in moments of heart-connection. You can combine this PHT with other heart exercises too, such as smiling from your heart to others around you (KHH 7) or to someone who you are about to call.

You can turn a negative into a positive. You can use boring or disengaged times as chances to be more heart connected and to build your heart-capacity and heart-intelligence.

In this way, you let your heart practically assist you to overcome feelings of boredom or disengagement and use them as 'investment times'; investing into your heart as a profound, long-term and useful resource. This investment will pay off in the short-term, too: instant greater heart-clarity and heart-strength and boredom, disengagement dissipation.

Heart-engagement at work

Engagement at work is a significant issue. Staff wellness surveys now include, or have fully moved in the direction of, staff engagement surveys. Degrees of disengagement happen at every level of an organisation. It also happens every moment, even though a general attitude, and resulting behaviour, will be the dominant force at play.

It is commonly accepted that feeling engaged at work and feeling happier, more enthused, better motivated and fulfilled at work are related. How can your heart help you on your path to re-engagement or to experiencing deeper levels of engagement with your role and everything that is happening at work?

Firstly, whether the cause of the degree of disengagement is external, to you, internal or even not known, the heart's abilities can improve engagement or re-engage you again. Secondly, the heart will always shift you more towards a 'what can I do to help, what can I do to improve my attitude or behaviour, or what can I do to be more heart-strong', compared to looking at others for solutions.

There is a positive mind/brain choice in this, too. The more you choose, with your head, a strong heart attitude, and engage the heart in doing so, you will be an example of positive attitude 'no-matter-what' is happening. The radiant heart energy will also touch others. As a 'side-effect' your enjoyment and all that the heart offers will be more present in your life, at work and at home.

When the cause of lack of engagement is associated with an emotion of 'I have had enough', 'I am bored', 'I resent being treated this way' or 'I always give and never get back'' the heart can help quite directly. You have two choices to work with this:

- To commit to or intensify your overall heart program; or
- To let your heart directly surrender specific burdens and associated individuals, situations and emotions or emotional patterns.

Key Heart Help 10: Surrendering burdens

This KHH will facilitate more specific help around surrendering. This can be surrendering as a letting go of something you can't control, you can only partially control or you have limited ability to do something about to solve the situation.

An example is that you have a team member or superior person at work who behaves in a way that is not the best in support of good team dynamics or particular work outcomes. That person might be popular, have strong alliances or have an emotional disposition that makes discussions regarding their behaviour not a viable option without some form of risk or consequence.

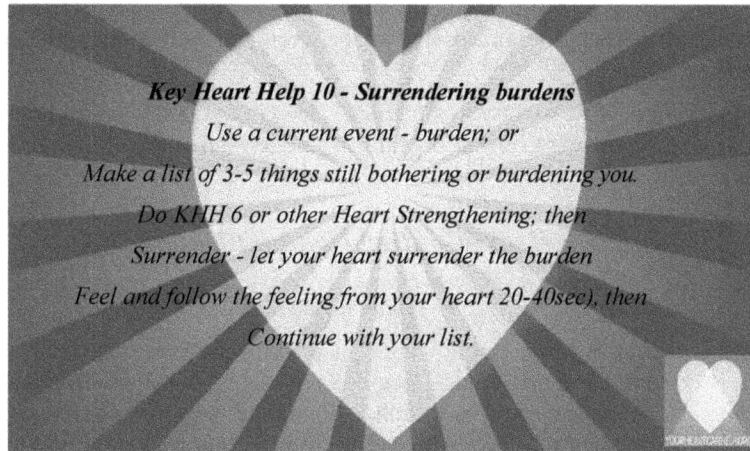

Key Heart Help 10 - Surrendering burdens
Use a current event - burden; or
Make a list of 3-5 things still bothering or burdening you.
Do KHH 6 or other Heart Strengthening; then
Surrender - let your heart surrender the burden
Feel and follow the feeling from your heart 20-40sec), then
Continue with your list.

The full KHH 10 - Surrendering burdens - individuals, situations and related emotions

This KHH is quite effective. The better outcomes are achieved if you combine the two heart program choices. To improve your overall heart condition do this KHH. Here are the steps:

- *Make yourself aware of the burdensome situation or the burden that you want help with. Alternatively, as a good daily routine, make a list of 2-5 burdening items, then proceed.*

- *Do general heart strengthening (full or shortened version of KHH 6);*

- *In brief ... be aware of the situation and individuals involved. Briefly recall the situation, your emotion, reason for disengagement (if known); then*

- *Intend to surrender from your heart the situation, everyone involved and everything related such as burdens, negative emotions, etc.; don't follow any inclination to help or to 'do', let the heart do it;*

- *Wait, smile, relax and feel the feeling from your heart. Even though this is about surrendering something burdensome, the heart will shift everything towards the innate pleasant, gentle, peaceful, even joyful heart-feelings;*

- *If you feel a pleasant feeling in your heart, follow it with all your heart and feeling (20-40 seconds); then*

- *Repeat again.*

If there is only one item/situation, repeat 2-4 times; if you have a list of items go through the list one-by-one.

When finished spend a few moments either enjoying or being grateful from your heart, or both.

Surrendering a problem from your heart can be further meaningful even if you can do something about it. Why? It is in moments when you surrender from the heart that the heart's abilities are further engaged and another layer of help can unfold.

The heart has been discussed briefly in chapter IV as the part of you that connects to the Divine, God, the Creator. If you are okay with this, feel to try, then insert after 'Intend to surrender from your heart the situation … to the Divine, God, the Creator or the Divine Being' of your practice or belief. If you are not sure here, do not have a name or being of belief, you can still let your heart do this and 'Intend to surrender from your heart (the situation or burden) to the Divine Being my heart recognises.'

This KHH is in the work section. The possibility for past events or events of the day or the week to have left you with a burden is always there. This is a deep practice that can teach you, more so your heart, to trust the heart more. At the same time let the heart help you to clear your heart and mind of something from the past, or just today, that you don't want to carry anymore.

Engagement or lack of engagement is more complex. It is related to the individual relationships around you, the management or leadership style and how supportive they are in nurturing team work, fulfilment and other positive work aspects. It is important to realise that individual events are solely triggers and a chance to let the heart do its work. It is ultimately your emotional or heart-emotional intelligence that will see you through any period of disengagement.

Sometimes the upset, hurt or block around disengagement, whether you know or don't know the full cause, can be quite significant. General heart strengthening will facilitate greater readiness and willingness to re-engage again.

If you still have difficulties with others or situations, given the depth and potential of your heart, you can let your heart smile, after heart strengthening, and often ad hoc during the day too, to these situations or individuals similar to KHH 7. If it happens to be a group of people there is no need to list them all in your head. A list somewhere on a piece of paper or in a note book can help to then just smile to 'everyone on my list' and then just enjoy the heart feelings. The outcome of this process has the potential to clear burdens, emotions or otherwise energy-impurities that are between you and others. It is ultimately freeing to these relations and your heart, emotions and mind.

The heart is always after the creation of win-win-win situations. Helping yourself is the first step. The next section on heart-centred communication includes a segment on how you can continue to help yourself and also others with their engagement or other work challenges.

Heart-Centred Communication

When the heart speaks, the mind finds it indecent to object.
Milan Kundera

The need for refinement and improvement of communication in workplaces often ranks very high in staff satisfaction or staff engagement surveys. This is normal as so many work matters need to be done together with others, and for this to happen communication is paramount. The better the communication is, the better team work can occur. Your heart-feeling ability will become finer. You may already know or feel when someone is either absent minded, present, mindful, focussed, light, free or heartful in talking to you.

You can perhaps feel when someone is trying to be present, or even attentive or caring, and yet something is missing that is more than the mind/brain's willingness to be this way. This 'doing or trying' is often mind/brain initiated. When the heart is additionally engaged, when your heart or the other person's heart is working, or both, then connection happens. This is another, additional, deeper and more profound level of connection, where understanding and engagement are facilitated and it completes what may have been missing before.

Heart-centred communication is more. When this heart-to-heart communication is taking place ideas come, doors open and long-term trusting, growing, even thriving and joyful work relations form.

The heart is multi-functional. As you communicate from the heart multiple layers of connection will happen. These are 'side-effects', positive ones, that may be of interest to you.

The heart naturally, and at a subtle level, positively affects all work relations that you have and supports any focus on being effective, efficient and successful.

From a heart perspective, this makes perfect sense. What you see and what someone communicates is never the full picture. In the same way as someone can communicate regularly, be at work long hours, be on time, be seen as busy and yet still can under-perform, the opposite can be the case too: you can do all of the above and yet work heart-smart, enjoy and perform.

Two of the next sections focus on speaking and listening from the heart, the two main and active forms of communication. The heart can help, in what you say, how you say it and in when to speak or when not to speak. In addition, the heart can help as the heart's quality, energy and radiance of care, concern and positive regard will travel with words of sharing, advice, words that challenge inappropriate behaviours or performance and other difficult communications. The result is often engaging, connecting, relationship enhancing and at times the positive result of it will be unexpected.

Foundation, tool and language of engagement

Heart warmth is the magic ingredient in our healing intentions
for ourselves and all life that it touches. Doc Childre

For many at work, communication is multi-directional and multi-layered. At work you have colleagues, close colleagues or friends. You are likely to have a supervisor and maybe people report to you. There are others, too, people from other sections or external individuals or groups, such as customers, clients or patients. Naturally, sometimes interaction is also ad hoc with people you just happen to meet, be in a particular room with or meet via a phone call. Within this group there are some who you 'have' to meet, talk or interact with and it is less easy, light, less pleasant or even a challenge.

In every work situation it is quite normal to make a 'judgement call' when interacting with others, what to say, not to say, what to do, not to do, how much to push or force or how much to stand back, wait or listen. There is also the call of who to talk to more or less. This can in principle be a positive call: 'it is good to talk to this individual', this key person or promising, affluent or willing looking customer. Solely mind/brain initiated judgement is perhaps not sufficient, or the best use of all that you have available, and it can comparatively easily slip towards negative expressions of judgement, where one assumes or where emotions come in and blur. This may be in the form of 'this interaction is or will be not-so-good' or when an irritated client or patient looks 'difficult' or has a reputation of being difficult. The principle can then become an 'it is pleasant to talk to this individual' and you may miss out on important information or interaction. Good mental strength can control these potential slips in some way.

When you feel, and follow the guidance from your heart, then 'judgement' moves over to following your heart, following the deeper intelligence and guidance it offers, to support the team, a project or a customer better.

When heart and mind are in balance, the heart will add a greater ease with which a positive mental attitude can be formed and grow. You will feel a lighter, more heartful approach towards the people you interact with.

With this greater balance any interaction becomes an opportunity to 'practise' and improve heart-mind balance. It should not be much of a practice. Firstly, every moment you are connected to your own heart and interact from there, you will be in a more attentive, relaxed, calm and caring space. This will benefit you, your wellbeing and presence to the work, care or business interaction. The mind will also be influenced by this calmness. Additionally, more heart will support your creativity, innovation ability and intuition. Very likely your results will improve this way and over time. Secondly, any stress or discomfort that the other is experiencing, whatever the source or cause of it, will be influenced by the radiance from your heart. The person will find it easier to engage with you. Any of the above indicated 'good' aspects that you or your mind/brain can see will be enhanced and any of the not-so-good aspects will be softened by the qualities of this heart radiance.

When you speak from both, the heart and the mind, then there is a comparative calmness in your voice and energy. This will allow others to also be calmer, feel, engage and connect and perhaps most importantly it will invite them in … to share their needs, issues, hopes, concerns or ideas. This is in fact something we all appreciate. No matter how good you are, your service, your product, your skills, if there is heart-enhanced engagement, balance, connection and shared time of speaking and listening, then the other will be less overwhelmed, feel sufficiently heard and, more likely, will experience more engagement.

Where the mind/brain plans, assesses or judges, the heart is a tool for greater engagement, it just 'is'. In this being it can connect, be the 'connection-foundation' as nothing else takes the heart from this moment. It is in the moment, the now, where engagement and connection occurs.

From the heart, or in a greater heart-mind balance, you can be personal, focussing on an individual, and it will feel genuine. There will be some degree of neutrality to more heart, such as less excited passion. This calmer state of being, which still involves having passion and love for what you do, will be more heartful. It is a deep way of engaging more equally and genuinely with everyone. When someone loves one group or some individuals more than others, for example, has favourite customers, and is more indifferent towards others, then it is likely that the same service is not provided to everyone. In any team or customer service situation people will feel this at some level and there is a risk that they will look elsewhere for service or products.

Will your work place direct you to attend to internal or external customers in different ways, give at a foundation level preferential treatment to some, but not to others? For your heart every person is unique and so is every situation. In this 'heart state' you can be fully attentive, caring and present towards everyone and everything. A busy mind, trying to work the next sentence out, the next logical or smart step, or a mind that is busy with other thoughts, will struggle to have this same presence. Other forms of mental practices will give you focus ability. What will be less strong or missing will be the heart-warmth, a like-ability and a feel-able care and lightness from your heart.

There is this anecdotal story of Cat Stevens, the popular and famous singer of the late 70s and early 80s, walking into a Rolls Royce dealership. The sales person very unlikely coming from a place of heart, did not serve him and even had an emotional, condescending comment for him, not knowing who he was. Apparently, Cat bought the same model car from the competition.

All communication, verbal and non-verbal, when the heart is active, will engage more deeply, equally truthfully. It will facilitate more choice in the person you interact with, empower them and in you at the same time through more presence and access to the deep intelligence of your heart. You perhaps know that when you have choice, when you feel you are invited to come in, into a project, or a sale, that you will be committed, present and more whole-hearted; very often in it for the long-term.

Listening with your heart

Listen with your heart. Common saying;
Pocahontas Movie - Sound Track

Attentively listening to anyone is one of the most powerful or impactful things you can do. To deeply or truly listen from the heart is also one further step in engaging with a client, stakeholder or team member. When you do this from the heart, and this always means that the mind is more likely to be more present also, then there is deeply feel-able sincerity, care and connection.

It is for similar reasons that the popular and equally respected consultant and author, Stephen Covey, made listening, or in his terms 'listen first' one of the seven principles of successful people. Stephen's work is ground-breaking and wonderful. While there is heart in his work, the heart is often mentioned in his work, there is limited awareness or knowledge about what direct heart-help can do to advance his quite profound insights. In his words the principle 'seek to understand first, before wanting to be understood' looks similar, yet at a subtler level, it is pragmatic, a technique that is mainly directed by the mind/brain. When you add the heart component to it, then there is feeling, warmth and the connecting, all-important genuineness or sincerity that people appreciate so dearly and feel when it is there.

This is particularly precious when you are in need, in an emergency or crisis at a hospital or similar place. What is loosely and commonly being expressed as 'listening with your heart or listen wholeheartedly' then becomes immensely precious and valuable.

This is trainable; do-able, and you will also experience the impact it will have. It is valuable and helpful in any work or life situation. Medical Doctor Paul's story in the work section is a matching example of this.

A well-developed ability to listen is found in good-practice and therapeutic approaches. Listening, letting others tell their story or experience, can have clearing, healing or therapeutic impacts. Years ago a management/leadership survey was presented at a workshop and the number one listed skill of a good leader was the ability of senior staff to listen.

What can the heart add here, to your existing practice? Listening is one way to learn. It is a channel in for data, information, words and insights. In this quieter form of communication mind/brain and heart intelligences help to hear, process and work towards answers or solutions. If you practise a form of active or advance listening already, simply add the heart to it, experiment with more heart, while doing it.

Listening more whole-heartedly, with your heart active, four things will support your listening, dialogue, conversation and any interaction:

- More of you will be present;
- A calm mind will allow you to hear more what is being said and what the other feels - his or her emotional state;
- The heart's radiant, energetic presence will be felt by the other person, deep, free, engaging and productive relations can form; and
- Any response from you will be more heart directed - your overall response, or your next point will be informed by the wisdom, greater knowing and an overall better heart-mind processing of what you just heard.

In moments when you listen more with heart and mind, you will additionally perceive or feel the wider situations and circumstance; and be more present or ready to act more in accordance with this wider perspective. This response will also be noticed by the person you speak with, your team and your customers. This is the invaluable intuition capacity successful entrepreneurs and leaders refer too. It is like it, and it is refine-able and trainable. A friend and colleague shared:

The feeling of calmness and peacefulness from the heart has kept me very productive at work and very focussed. At the same time there is also a feeling of being very relaxed most times. My mind seems very clear when the heart is strong. I often need to listen to clients and team members in my role. Now and after a longer time of practice, it appears that experiences of stress at work have almost vanished.
Portfolio Manager, Banking Industry

Practical Heart Tip 63: Listen with your heart *

Decide on a program of practice where, at work at home or in social situations, you practice both your heart presence and your skills of listening with your heart.

If you have time, do the full Heart Strengthening (KHH 6), or a shorter version of it, before you enter the situation, then.

- *Make the best use of Stephen's wise and important words ... listen first/seek first to understand;*

- *Even before you meet think of a couple of questions you really feel to ask;*

- *Ask opening questions and one or two of the questions you feel to ask;*

- *As you listen to the response, remember your heart, do basic, simple and natural techniques to be heart present, in your heart; and*

- *Let your heart smile to the other(s); especially once you start enjoying being in more heart presence and feeling.*

When the person has finished what they want to say, take even here a bit of time, be heart connected, feel, feel what to say, and even in replying say your words while feeling the feeling from your heart. Continue to interact this way for e.g. one or two conversations in one day, or for whatever time or target you have set. Diarise your experience for a period of time (for one week or one month and make it habit no 9 if you like).

This listening from the heart becomes even more valuable when there is conflict or difficulty in an interaction or whole team situation. The closer this conflict or difficulty is to you, any past similar experiences, or your own issues, then there is a higher likelihood for you to be busy with thoughts, responses or emotions, as you try to listen. This naturally reduces heart. It is exactly in this situation, if you remember and attend to your heart, that the heart is helping you and the person you listen to. Focus on your heart, as you listen to the other person or group of people and let the heart help you to:

- Keep your own responses, reactions and trains of thoughts calm and in control;
- Listen with both mind/brain and the heart; and
- Let heart help you in accessing and formulating a response that is calm, kind and compassionate.

Sometimes where there is difficulty, and you are not swept away by emotion or reaction, then it can even be easier to focus on the heart, to be in more heart connection or presence.

In times that you are less able to be in the heart you may benefit from practising this PHT. It will bring back some level of heart-engagement. Your calmness, presence and listening will improve.

> **Practical Heart Tip 64: Stop, feel, heart, listen ***
>
> *If others enter your space, your office or work space with a conflict or difficult situations on their mind, burdening them, they do not necessarily want you to give just an answer or a doing-response. You also do not want to take on what they bring.*
>
> *You can use this 'conflict or difficult situation' brought to you as a prompt to attend to your heart first, or at the same time, as you attend to the situation. If you 'listen first' you can easily do this.*
>
> *Even a little bit of heart will keep you in a stronger balance and clarity, for this situation and for all you still need to be and do for the remainder of the day.*
>
> *So, whenever there is conflict, just stop, feel, feel your heart, listen ... learn for the first response, heart-helped, to not do or say anything, to react or go into the head (mind/brain).*
>
> *Unless it is an emergency or other responses are needed, feel your heart and be there for a while first, smile to your heart or do more of the heart strengthening. Listen with more heart from the onset. Only then start to respond, act or interact with others. The delay in you responding may only be seconds, half a minute or a minute.*

Engaging your heart more, listening with more heart is one way to improve how much of 'your heart is in it' at work. When you listen with your heart, you will be able to learn by heart. What you need to learn or remember will have another 'brain' to assist, your heart. Listening with your heart automatically activates the heart's qualities and they will assist your interaction with the other. These heart qualities work in the background, and in gentle ways engage even more. In a customer service situation you provide a better service, more with what the customer really needs or wants. In a service situation, for example in a health service setting, you or the patient will be able to be shifted from a set position, towards more flexibility. Perhaps a better referral, diagnosis or more responsive counselling can occur.

With your heart helping you always in all areas of life, more time spent in your own heart will allow the heart to grow, be more present and in turn inform your responses or actions from the wisdom or innate heart-intelligence. Paul's sharing in the work section is an example of this greater engagement that naturally happens and that mutually benefits you, the listener and the other, in Paul's case as a medical doctor, are his patients.

Listening, including more with an active heart, is one step further in being less driven by other agendas; including your own that do not support you. It is logical that they need be turned down a little or even suspended for some time, to be more present to the other, to listen more. More about this heart-directed selflessness follows.

The heart connects

> *Prepare your mind and heart before you prepare your speech.*
> *What we say may be less important than how we say it. Stephen Covey*

Connection can help you to be more successful. Connection is special, a gift when it happens, something that, when it is there, immensely adds to the enjoyment, meaning and outcomes at work. When you connect you just know and it feels right, or you feel there is a lovely connection.

Any connection made by logic, reason or intention will be enhanced by the heart. With some of the heart qualities being warmth, clarity, lightness, openness and unconditional positive regard, with no judgements, others will find it easier to approach, relate and connect with you. What often happens is that better outcomes follow.

With a clearer and more intentional heart connection to your own heart any connection has the chance to also be more heart-to-heart. The heart has cleansed much of what, within you, would trigger even the smallest emotional reaction or expression. This also means that something light, joyful, playful and heartful can be present and be exchanged heart-to-heart. It is this level of connection that you, in reality the heart, feel that will make you walk away from a shopping or customer service experience and say something along the lines of 'wow, that was so nice' or 'I did not expect this'.

> *Many years ago, I had just done the first year of managing a training and employment program which in terms of space was covering two-thirds of Melbourne with four locations where staff had offices. A well-known US based and delightful customer service consultant had been hired by the 600 plus organisation that my team of around 25 staff was part of. I was initially critical of customer service, not seeing its value nor importance. After a short time of being in several training sessions and presentations the penny dropped and so did any cynicism. I participated in the sessions, asked questions and not long after the facilitator referred to me and started to tease; in a very pleasant way. At a later point we had a long and in-depth, purpose of life type discussion over the phone. I am sharing this story as I remember two statements from her she said to some people: 'I like your energy' and, after our conversation, we parted and she said 'wow, we really connected'.*

When you connect, when you or the other person feel connection, then there will be a greater willingness to engage, to participate, to contribute, to commit or to buy. This is commonly known and many clever and helpful techniques are out there. However, with no or little heart, with little or no feeling of truly connecting with another person, another heart, it will be very difficult to create depth or a longer-term relationship. Your growing, glowing or radiating heart will add valuable elements of genuineness to all your connections.

Speaking from your heart

Speak from your heart.

At work speaking from the heart can become a profoundly impactful tool. Paul's sharing, as a doctor, speaking from the heart to his patients, is what speaking from the heart can mean, to a professional, to you. For him it meant more effectiveness, care and a greater level of fulfilment in his work with and for his patients. In speaking from the heart, all of you will be more integrated, brought into play, and will work for you and the person you interact with or your audience.

One of the examples is Paul's experience. He worked in a high-pressure role in a major hospital in Australia as a medical doctor and anaesthetist from overseas. He came to heart meditations several years ago when he was working for two and a half years at the Royal Hobart Hospital. The heart helped Paul in a range of areas, including with long-standing health issues. This story is in the work section for the changes in his approach to work and speaking with his colleagues and patients.

Paul's Story:

One of the first improvements that stood out for him, Paul mentioned, were the changes to his sleep. 'The quality of my sleep, the depth in particular, was very noticeable. I started to wake up feeling rested and very refreshed.'

'In my work I would often take home unresolved issues. Before learning about my heart, my sleep was not very good and aggravated by working long hours, often through the night.'

'This often left me with a fatigued body and mind. Being tired led me to being more irritable with patients and colleagues. I was more disengaged than I would have liked to have been. Sometimes I would get angry with my colleagues which might have involved differences of professional opinion with the surgeon in the middle of an operation.'

'As the years went by, in order to sleep better I had taken a range of natural supplements and prescription medications. In addition, I spent a lot of time and money on body work, and alternative therapies.'

'I always had a spiritual interest. What grabbed my attention was 'it is about the heart' it is not about a teacher or a special technique. Intuitively my sense was that this must be good, safe and trustworthy.'

'Learning to open and experience my heart was what I had been looking for, for a very long time. My issues at work and my sleep problems began to improve: I felt much more relaxed and my irritability was also reduced. The heart meditations gave me a simple technique I could immediately use at home and apply at work too. With this alternative technique the need for body work and massage and the debriefing sessions became much less.'

'Now, after several years of opening and using my heart, I find it easier to enjoy being with my colleagues. There are less barriers, less arguments and less conflicts. When I am in my heart there is connection, a calming simplicity and less stress in all that I do. I think less where I don't need to, worry less, and work flows better. I believe that at times these effects overflow to my patients.'

'There is a deep peace within ... and it is not uncommon for patients to say to me 'I feel peaceful'. It seems they connect to the quality of the heart, the calmness and peace it has given me. For my patients, this means something special, in a way that there is a peace within them, despite their situation, which can be serious and stressful. The day before an operation, especially for major surgery, can be extremely stressful.'

'I can be in my heart easily now, speaking from the heart. I don't add to their anxiety and fear in any way. I let them express their concerns. More often now, patients reply with comments like 'what you said to me made all the difference'. One lady recently even wrote a letter to the hospital saying just that.'

'Working more from the heart, there is an ability to be gentle, and calmer. It affects everything that I do, the speed with which I perform my duties, and the interactions with colleagues, staff, patients and their families. It has significantly improved my ability to be present with everyone; especially the patients.'

'Sometimes I teach patients how to use the heart when they are worried. I simply share the first steps with them, to touch the heart, to feel it, to gently smile to it and be within that feeling, in the natural calmness from the heart.'

'I have changed a lot in the past years since learning to use and be within the heart more. It now seems something more like a blessing to relate to colleagues and to patients in this way. It can be a joy to go to work and to be there all day. I can clearly recognise the changes in me.'

'It is also a wonderful blessing for another human being to discover their own heart, this essential part of their self.'

Paul returned to his native country of Ireland after his years in Hobart and Australia. The heart learning left such an impression on him, that he now offers 'heart meditation' in his home town outside work.

'Now, I open my home to the general public so they have the opportunity to experience heart opening meditation sessions, and I help to organise and coordinate workshops with international teachers for anyone who wants to discover more about the heart.'

He is also training to become a registered and fully endorsed teacher of the Open Heart workshops and he is listed as a contact for the United Kingdom/Ireland in appendix 5.

Listening and speaking from the heart will take some time to learn and refine. It is more than solely the intention to do so. You will need a clear heart strength, an overall good heart-connection and you then, ultimately, want to feel every single word or letter vibrated through your heart and to carry the fuller energetic qualities from it.

You can adapt the next PHT 'Speaking from the heart' to your work, social or home environment. Speaking from the heart means that more of you is engaged in what you say, express and what the heart's intention and sincerity is. It will naturally be a more complete whole of you. To be genuine, sincere, authentic, passionate and compassionate are important, if not critically important qualities in our daily work communications. Even from the heart this can find a quiet, calm or strong expression. It will however never be likely to overwhelm or force and there will be an inviting calmness in your voice and overall energy. In moments when what you say is from an active, and even better, actively-radiating heart, then others will feel this gentle and positive energy too. To practise more specifically the next PHT will help to emphasise this more.

---

*Practical Heart Tip 65: Speaking from the heart ***

For any heart involvement it is good to prepare your heart. You can do heart-preparation (KHH 6 and maybe a brief Heart Meditation if it is a more significant presentation). Prepare even before you go to work. Then repeat KHH 6 or a shorter version of it several times a day in the office, and again just before you plan to speak with others.

Preparation once will work, too. After you re-connect to your heart just before you speak, feel some of the gentle heart feelings, stay calm (by intention) and heart-centred (by continuing to feel), then:

- *Keep feeling the heart feelings equally to what you say;*

- *Focus more on the heart initially than on what words come out;*

- *Feel the heart, feeling, smile, words you speak unite and a vibration or feeling going through your heart as you speak;*

- *Keep on feeling the warmth, calmness, gentleness and flow or vibration in the heart- as you speak;*

- *In moments when someone else speaks back to you, relax again, smile a little and feel to stay or become even more heart-connected; and*

- *Follow the feelings for the duration of your speaking.*

This may not be easy initially. At the beginning, it is helpful to practise, even on your own, speaking really slowly or only a few words and focussing on the heart-feeling while you speak. When it is clear to you when the heart is active, integrate it into your day at work. Let your heart be and stay active while you speak.

Practice will make it natural over time. If your work situation does not allow you to have relaxed, informal and practising conversations, then practise at home or in your social settings and move it to work when you are confident and feel clearly.

Jeremy's story in section V is another example where the heart seemed to guide a difficult work presentation, and, according to him, created a better response and outcome. His staff heard the things he said in a different light and accepted the difficult message, even with gratitude.

Move by being moved by your heart

Moving by being moved by your heart is perhaps the most unusual way of letting the heart help you. Unusual only from the perspective of the mind/brain. It is heart-logical, and in some way mind/brain logical too, that if you listen and speak while the heart is present or directing, then movement can also carry the heart's radiance. Intentions, emotions and heart-feelings are an avenue for the heart to connect, share, be moved and generally interact in a more wholesome way: body, mind/brain and heart work together.

The next PHT and exercise will allow you to experience this wholesomeness and in turn strengthen your heart and the quality of relations in your life. Practise it regularly to integrate it effectively into your life.

---

*Practical Heart Tip 66: Move by being moved by your heart ***

Prepare your heart as outlined above. Then ...

- *Feel your heart and your whole body;*

- *Smile from your heart to your whole body to bridge body-mind-heart;*

- *As you start to move your body, feel the response in your heart;*

- *Keep moving your body while maintaining the feeling of warmth, calmness or gentleness in your heart; and*

- *Follow the feelings for the duration of your movements or practice.*

It is important that you move your body slowly or slower than usual to maintain the feeling in your heart. Over time a profound feeling of calm and joy will surface and continue to grow.

How much you feel will depend on your overall heart-routine or heart-condition. Be diligent and committed to your heart and this refined body-heart-mind connection will become clearer and more blissful.

It will be interesting to notice that when you move your body in this way, your heart in return will be stimulated clearly, even strongly. It will impact strongly on your overall energy or energy-radiance. Your body will absorb the energy or radiance from your heart with a chance for it to glow and radiate beyond your physical body.

People may say we are one, one system, all within is connected or one unity. If you experience this, then you start to feel this more clearly while at the same time improving your heart and your wellbeing.

When your body is more connected to your heart, when your heart is further stimulated by the movements of your body, all of you will be more engaged and active. This will energise you and invite others to engage more with you. There will be an alignment in your communication, too. This alignment can change and be in tune with what you have learned in the past, with any conditioning that is present in your body-mind-heart unity, and align it to your heart's wisdom. If you feel to deepen these alignment processes, Secrets of Natural Walking, discussed in the Health and Wellbeing chapter, will offer significant steps forward.

Your innate heart intelligence is present

In the above first section 'heart intelligence' is discussed. Emotional and heart intelligence share one common goal to make choices that are positive, engaging and wise and that support you and, ideally, others around you.

When talking about heart intelligence the main advancing leap from emotional intelligence to heart or heart-emotional, heart intelligence is the expansion from a mind/brain understood intelligence model, to one that accesses the innate abilities and wisdom of the heart. Greater heart presence and knowing informs every thought, choice of action, action and interaction.

What is added is the heart and inner heart, core of the heart, as an infinite information processing computer of intelligence, wisdom and one that has a negative or unhelpful thought-emotion deposit tray function.

The second and third sections, or balancing heart qualities, further discuss that this heart-presence or heart intelligence is a constant interplay between the mind/brain's ability to process in coloration and in balance with the information that the heart gives you. This information will only ever be in the form of feeling. To engage your innate heart intelligence you need to be relaxed, feeling, and have an awareness of your heart: what does heart-feeling feel like.

It is in this 'feeling mode' that you will perceive situations in a new 'light', the radiance and capacity of your innate heart intelligence. It is via feeling that the heart's wisdom and insights are accessed whether this is by intention or a more natural, flowing state or process.

Facilitation of more connection and engagement

It is actually the magical connection between your heart and his/her heart. Rumi

The quote from Rumi reinforces the essence and working of your heart's help in workplace communication, activity or interaction. When things are said or done with heart present then proportions of truth, positivity, clarity and integrity are added, making these 'magical' and equally more effective.

It is the magic of more heart - a clear, light, active and radiant heart - that will build or strengthen bridges, magically improve the connection you already have and from this place of connection it will engage and bring others in. There is almost no piece of work that can be done in the modern workplace that does not involve some form of contribution from others. It is this heart-felt sincerity in you that brings your own fuller presence and engagement capacity to the surface. It also engages others and invites others in. They will feel comfortable, in their own heart and all that they are. In addition to getting this done, this degree of heart input builds positive, light, sustainable and joyful relations for longer-term work, service or business outcomes.

Love, Care and Support

It is care and support felt from peers, others or the 'manager' that staff appreciate. In many conversations staff have shared that the periods of times they enjoyed the most in a workplace, or excelled the most, were when they felt cared for or supported.

In one of these conversations I asked a colleague, 'how are you going in your new role'? He answered, 'I have a great manager, I have a degree of freedom, and I feel very supported by him.'

Love is a bit harder to talk about in the workplace. Love at work, if the term 'love' is used, is the unconditional appreciation, positive regard and deep connection of care that can exist between colleagues. Perhaps in this way the term love becomes more acceptable and is quite clearly differentiated from any form of romantic love or romantic interest.

I recall reading in Jim Collin's book 'Good to Great' that, when one of the 'great' managers or leaders passed away, 'there was a lot of love in the room' at the wake.

Care, support or love, if only mechanical, technical or expressed by giving something to an individual or team, risks being hollow, shallow or even uncaring. It is good to be given resources and whatever else materially needed to do the job. How can you love someone at work? This love has to find other ways to be expressed. When practical or material support is from the heart, given with feelings of genuine care, then an energy, a quality of love, is travelling within this. The perception of how even the exchange of material things happens will be different, enveloped in heart-energy, and as a result deep and trusting relationships can form. The meaning behind 'my heart is in it' is in this, too. More correct would be to say that 'things or words exchanged are in my heart'. In work situations, when you give - time, things, listening space or an open door- from the heart, when your heart is in it, then there is feel-able care, or love.

The KHH of this chapter is to do all that you do at your work, whenever you remember, with feeling from the heart. Every time you do this, the capacity and intelligence of your heart will be activated.

It is in these heart moments that you are embarking on a continuous improvement program.

Everything you do with feeling from your heart will improve how you relate to your work. It has direct influence on how engaged, passionate, committed and heart-emotional intelligent you are. It can even improve how much you love your work. It is one of the sayings used around work that has the 'love' word in it when someone says 'I love my work'.

Key Heart Help 11: Do all with feeling from the heart

The KHH is both a regular re-connecting to the heart and a practice program to ensure that you not only connect to the heart but that you also stay there, keep the connection and keep the heart engaged.

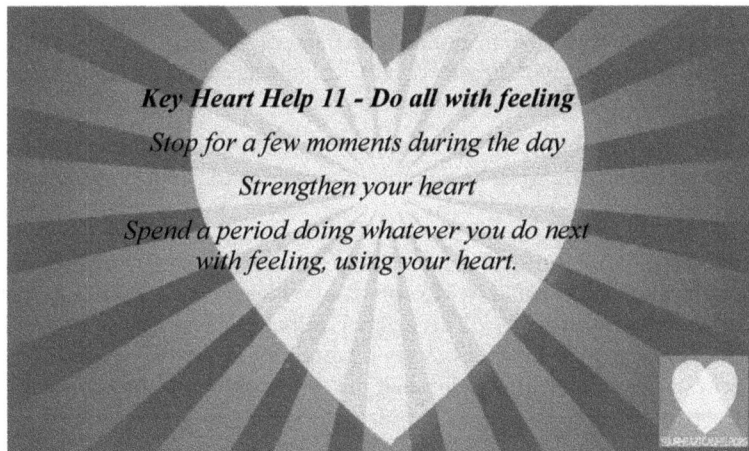

Key Heart Help 11 - Do all with feeling
Stop for a few moments during the day
Strengthen your heart
Spend a period doing whatever you do next with feeling, using your heart.

The full KHH 11 - Do all with feeling from the heart

The KHH invites you to actively integrate the heart into your work and to keep a diary record for some time in order to stay on track. Give quality time to your heart at work and at home:

- *Stop 5 - 15 x per day;*
- *Relax and smile (10-30 sec);*
- *Smile to your heart (20-60sec); and*
- *Spend a period doing whatever you do next with feeling, using your heart.*

The key is now to maintain the feeling. It is only then that you keep staying in heart-centred presence and the heart can continue to help.

Use your Heart Diary or any other method to make a brief note in relation to (1) the frequency of your 'stops', (2) the length of them, (3) what you felt and, at your next entry, (4) add anything else you noticed between these heart sessions.

This KHH looks simple, easy and almost less significant than some of the earlier ones. Remember, it is introduced here as you have already done regular and core heart-connecting and heart strengthening exercises. Every moment you connect to your heart, then continue to stay heart-connected by continuing to stay feeling or in the heart-felt feelings, both your intelligence centres, your mind/brain and your heart will be collaborating. You are extending the heart's help into periods of work beyond an active heart-practice.

What you really want is the heart's presence and help during every moment at work.

Natural, as opposed to romantic or mind/brain generated, feelings of love, care and support for others will grow. Whatever you feel will be communicated automatically, in your voice, and energetically, in your attitude, behaviours, movements or body language.

Remember, these greater feelings of unconditional care, support and love will be felt by the hearts of everyone around you, too. Any unconditional love, care or regard you feel, like that of a parent towards a child, will also allow you to stop, be clear, say 'no' and make sharp and, if needed, unpopular yet important decisions.

> **Practical Heart Tip 67: Heart-to-heart at work ***
>
> *Continuing from this KHH you can make any giving, any receiving, any communication and any interaction a heart practice. You may, for example, solely hand a document to a staff member, peer or client a document, or some of your time. In each task, each interaction is an opportunity to be remembering that it can be with the heart or from the heart.*
>
> *When you are in an interaction or dialogue at work:*
>
> - *You can practise the above KHH and combine it with the suggestion in this PHT; and*
>
> - *Act, listen, speak, feel, smile, interact more from a place of feeling and heart.*
>
> *In these moments, when your heart is active and involved, no matter what the content of your interaction is, the relationship will be nurtured by unconditional positive regard and related feelings such as mutual respect, care and appreciation.*

Love, care and support for others can easily be an undervalued aspect at work. If it is valued, then how is it best expressed, verbalised or talked about? How often have you heard 'I don't feel appreciated or acknowledged'? How are associated goals set and strategies put into place around 'love' and how to improve relations or interactions?

The following sections look at this and the heart's potential. Hopefully this can assist in undoing any pre-existing concepts, concerns, beliefs or habits and let the heart's work bring more love, care and support to the surface.

Being strong in being soft

Becoming soft or weak is one of the, if not the, greatest concern expressed by leaders when discussing the heart. Being perceived as strong seems easier to accept than being soft. Being soft is often seen as a weakness. Yet, being soft and strong from the perspective of the heart, looks somewhat different. There is a trap that one can tap into believing or following an approach that favours strength over softness, firmness over kindness or giving directions over receiving instruction. In a western world of male or 'yang' dominated approaches or paradigms it is easier that the 'yin', softer qualities miss out.

Everything strong is likely to have an opposing weakness, one of these being the generation of resistance by triggering emotion. On the contrary, everything soft can bend more yet needs strength to not be over-powered in wrong circumstances.

From the perspective of the mind/brain and within an interplay of soft - strong, gentle - tough, kind - firm it depends what you believe, what you have experienced or what you favour. Your personality or make up may favour either the more yin or the more yang qualities. Still from the perspective of the mind/brain, to be effective, efficient and to successfully relate, a balance is needed between these qualities.

When you live in the moment, with mind/brain awareness or attentiveness, or with heart-centred clarity, or both, then this balance is just that, a moment to moment act and achievement.

If you feel that you have been too hard, too much focussed on being strong, tough and living the more yang qualities, the next PHT can help to soften some of these harder edges and offer new experiences.

> **Practical Heart Tip 68: Softening the edges ***
>
> *Be overall more aware of your heart at work. A few times during the day practice Heart Strengthening (KHH 6), even if it is a shortened version of it.*
>
> *Let this greater heart presence now invite you, guide you, to:*
>
> - *Feel situations more;*
>
> - *Listen or look with feeling while being within the gentleness of heart feelings;*

- *Feel and enjoy the heart-felt feeling of softness, gentleness and other related feelings; then*
- *When you speak, speak from the heart (PHT 65); and*
- *Take notes in your 'Heart Diary' (PHT 27) what you observe, within, or in others.*

You can add to this PHT, in moments when you listen, feel, speak with heart 'letting feelings of love, care and support flow through you/your heart' and feel the heart feelings as you make this resolve.

This PHT will be useful just for that, to soften any hard edges. Over time, becoming more familiar and more natural in using the heart, you want to be just how the heart, in collaboration with the mind/brain, is guiding you to be.

Remember, too, that the heart is smart and any hard aspects, in the moment, or as part of your character, will not be overruled or changed. You will then be soft or strong, gentle or tough, kind or firm, or any quality between those, exactly how every single and new situation is requiring you to be. When you are guided in this way by more heart, by the heart's innate intelligence, it will not be surprising when medium to long-term interactions within your team, your department or your general work or client environment, yield better results.

Your heart's help is offering you a third choice. In following your heart, you move beyond what a duality of 'strong or soft' represents. You will be somewhere on a continuum between two qualities and at the same time make decisions that have a sustainable, far-reaching and best-outcome-for-all quality to them.

One supportive person

The more your heart will bring love for others, care, and willingly given support to the surface, the more you will be able to support others.

You can also look at past situations when you worked hard, or beyond expectation - for a team or a team leader. What were aspects or qualities that invited you in, that made something in you respond positively with commitment? It is not uncommon that the softer, kinder qualities make others more approachable and in turn invite people in. Heart-generated, from-the-heart, also means that these qualities are genuine and carry a feeling of love, care and support. Feel-able by everyone assists in building environments where people can flourish. When you feel supported, loved and cared for, when some of these qualities are present, then the courage to be, to contribute or just do your work well, have a bigger foundation to 'stand' on.

It needs only one person who is willing to be supporting, helpful and kind that gives permission to others to also let these qualities unfold and find expression in their work relations.

The unity of mind/brain and heart will always be present to help, every moment, to know when it is right to support or when it is good to let individuals or a team be on their own, to work things out, to experiment or just to do it on their own. However, even then, when you are in a leading role, the feeling of your presence in willing supportiveness may be all that is needed for people around you to excel.

Practical Heart Tip 69: One supportive person *

Use this PHT to increase moments of heartfulness at work, to access your heart's help and to let growing gratitude give additional strength to the heart/mind/brain unity.

Right now, or when a memory of having been supported in a special way by a colleague comes up ...

- *Stop for a moment (close your eyes if you can);*
- *Relax your body and mind;*
- *Let your heart/mind/brain unity remember or recall the situation; then*
- *Enjoy the feeling your heart remembers and generates for a few moments (smile); and*
- *Stay in this enhanced heart-based presence for as long as possible.*

Support, based on genuine love, care, support or appreciation is often what has brought us forward to where we are now.

It may have been a teacher at school, a friend and mentor at work or someone outside work, a friend or counsellor, that functioned as a supportive or encouraging sounding-board-like person. Often one supportive person, one significant other as some experts would say, can be sufficient to help someone out of self-doubt or hesitation, or towards their best performance.

If you feel that lack of support in this way has hindered any success at work then let your heart take you on a journey of more heart, heart-supported existence, which will make you freer, lighter and naturally more like-able and love-able. Use the above PHT and find even the closest possible example of some support. In addition, more heartfelt gratitude is one avenue to attract more goodness, love or support.

Another avenue is to offer your support to others. With an open and light heart you find it easier and more natural to genuinely do so. In turn your heartfulness at work will attract more support and make success an easier journey. With growing heart awareness, and a light and free heart, it can be you who is that one supportive and caring person for others.

Love and your team

Love and the function of your team is a continuation of the earlier whole chapter on team work. Love also can have deeper widening expressions than care and support. Love or qualities that branch off from work characterise and determine all our relations. It is simply that at work the term 'love' seems less appropriate or less frequently used.

This is what a young person, a professional reporter, shared recently on social media:

> *I always get the urge to say 'love you' at the end of a phone conversation ... even in business calls at work.*

When the heart is free you feel a deepening, caring connection with a growing number of people. There is something not quite right to talk about love or to say 'I love you' at work. Another way to describe this love quality at work may be as 'unconditional positive regard' or 'unconditional positive appreciation of others'. Ultimately the quality is love and the feeling is one of love. Yet in the work place you express it differently than at home or in friends' circles and also how it feels right to you, as an individual.

This has to be viewed in the light of earlier discussions around the opposites of 'strong and soft'. From your heart you can have this unconditional positive regard and yet negotiate a redundancy with someone. The 'positive' element will be that none of the own mind/brain or emotional interferences will be there. There is the seed-opportunity for any interaction to be in the full presence of positivity, clarity and care/love and support.

In addition to caring for and supporting your team and others, people function well when they feel appreciated, recognised or valued. When these feelings are sincere then something within minimises emotional or mind/brain caused interferences. A willingness to work or just to get on with things is created by these heart qualities.

When you understand, in theory and practice the function of your heart, this makes perfect sense. The invitation to you is, through the KHHs and PHTs in this section, to let understanding of these heart-team qualities be transformed into an energy, into energetic qualities that others can feel and that you can feel.

Coherence, collaboration and commitment to the team are inner or foundation qualities to effective and consistent team work. In this way they are indirect performance-enhancing ingredients. Energetic connection, engaging heart-to-heart with your close colleagues, wider team members or customers, creates energetic coherence that connect and give people feelings of being attended to. There is more than just attention: they feel looked after, cared for, supported and in the purer form of love quality, they feel loved.

Heart warmth engages and nurtures. Many of the innate heart-enhanced or heart-facilitated qualities promote engagement and collaboration.

Care, love and 'like' between team members make it easier to work together. Your experience most likely by now has also been that when dominant mind/brain aspects or interfering emotions are reduced, then the joy of working together naturally is more present. Collaboration then not only becomes something that happens, in your heart you feel the joy of being in this state of flow, creativity and connection.

The more the heart is in balance with the mind/brain, the more the heart helps you at work and commitment to the goals set by the organisation or your team are 'lighter' to follow. Can you imagine or feel what it would be like when, supported by the heart, all irritating or heavy emotions experienced in a day or week would be gone? In moments like these you would feel commitment to your work, your team and your organisation, perhaps even close to unwavering.

Feeling also can provide 'fuel', in the form of caring and appreciating feelings towards others, that propel everything towards equality, while still fully recognising positions and roles.

> *For example, when a hierarchically lower-positioned team member has a better idea, a better contribution or is challenging a more senior team member the focus will be on the working together with each other, based on deep respect, fuelled by attentive, caring and loving relations.*

The recognition of values such as love, care, supportive or unconditional positive regard offers glue-like strength to team-cohesion and collaboration. In one other situation this is immensely valuable: when things go wrong. Internal or external challenges occur; mistakes are being made; difficult tasks face you, such as the need to down-size, deal with performance issues or communicate the loss of a job to someone.

It is the presence of these feelings, when felt by the other, the recipient of difficult or 'bad' news that maintains the positive relationship and a feeling of connection. When an ethical and organisationally-right decision has been made the recipient will feel this connection, even when personally, emotionally it is hard to accept.

Stephen Covey described this wonderfully in the relationship bank account analogy. In work, in any human interactions, there are deposits and withdrawals. It is worth reading up on. Just add the heart to it, so the analogy and practice will become richer.[13]

The heart added to situations like this is not only of importance to the individual recipient of challenging news. With mind/brain and heart the entire team will watch, too. An organisational or management integrity can stay intact.

This wholeness of every individual will see and feel how a difficult or personally challenging situation is being worked with or 'managed'.

The mind/brain and the hearts of everyone on the team will watch, analyse and feel the situation, leading to confusion, uncertainty or clarity and security.

Indicating the role of the heart's help, showing how a mind/brain and heart balance supports the very qualities that make teams function well, in turn indicates that sole mind/brain or cognitive programs will struggle to achieve improved team dynamics, team cohesion and whole-hearted engagement.

From Stress Management to Happiness

Everyone responds differently to stress which means that the inner capacity differs. The same amount of work-related or relationship stress at work will cause different degrees of stress in individuals. When stress is experienced at work, whatever the cause is, then the degrees of collaboration, productivity and enjoyment are likely reduced. Going to work can become a burden and if the experience of stress is not caught or stopped, then, at a personal level, and at an organisational cost level, the impact can be significant. The 'cost' is paid time off, treatment of some kind or loss of good staff; by individuals and an organisation.

In those times, to 'manage' stress seems the only way to improve and perhaps is, in the same way, like a non-performing staff member needs to be managed. In allowing the heart to lead you, work-life can be much gentler. The heart can function as a stress-prevention tool stopping stress from becoming 'negative stress'. Heart-strength is inner strength or resilience. Your heart wants you and others at work to be happy, and to help in this way.

What is stress?

Stress is acknowledged as one of the main causes of illness and un-wellbeing. At work some stress or positive stress, can help you to work with focus, more discipline and more commitment. When stress at work, caused by work or brought from home to work, is too much or negative, then it can interfere with the same issues: there is less focus, less discipline and with it less commitment or clarity.

When reduced to its essence then this negative stress causes an individual to be unable to cope with pressure, work load, relational or emotional issues. Once stress exists there is a flow on effect, noticeably or not, that impacts negatively on performance, health or wellbeing.

Causes of stress

Causes or sources of stress can be categorised, in parts from a heart perspective, in four ways:

- Pressure, demand and culture of busy-ness and doing is getting to a point where one's ability to manage or to cope is exceeded;
- Relationships with others at work, the team, a senior person, line manager or customer are difficult or there is significant conflict;
- Hard to resolve or unresolved emotional issues within the team, in you, or happening elsewhere, such as in the family; and
- Emotional trigger situations such as job security, lack of direction, lack of consistency or lack of ownership.

One of these can be enough to cause burdensome stress. Given the complexity of many work places, it is likely that several stress-causes co-exist at the same time. Within these causes the nature of the relationships at work play a very significant part. If there are, for example, poor relations with peers, a critical manager or if relations are stretched, and they are characterised by emotions such as irritation, resentment, anger or jealousy, then stress levels rise and the existing inner strength or resilience may be exceeded: the experience of stress is negative.

Work-life balance is also cited in research and literature as a reason for growing experiences of stress. When there is too much work, when time spent away from work is not offering sufficient 're-creation' or balance needed then stress levels increase.

Lack of engagement, lack of inner engagement with work that you do, or lack of engagement with others also contributes to stress. This is also closely associated with lack of real or perceived control, poor communication and organisational change. Change,

---

[13] Google 'Stephen Covey emotional bank account' if you feel to read more about it.

change at times for change sake, or without enough consideration, can lead to additional pressures. Change related pressure adds to any existing pressures such as work load peaks or deadlines.

Friends, colleagues, peers and clients have shared that stress caused through emotional issues at work are far worse than any other form of pressure or stress.

This, for example, is any form of bullying by senior staff or peers; being side-lined; being singled out for unclear reasons; performance discussions; job insecurity; change projects; mergers; people talking behind someone's back; feeling micro-managed or feeling unsupported by others, the supervisors or the team, in times of hardship or pressure. Emotions are easier caused by these or can flow into interactions.

The more issues are personal, the more they 'go to the heart', which here actually means they trigger emotions or are felt as being un-reasonable. They can reach deep and cause severe experiences of distress and stress.

Your work load, pressures, and levels of stress at work may be so high that you feel that none of these discussions or exercises will work.

If the pressure you experience is so high that you believe nothing will work, or you are just too busy, then then the next PHT is designed to assist with this. This PHT 'Stress buster' is the bare bone starting program to make inroads in a day, week or routine where the pressure or stress is so high and where it seems not possible to add anything else to the schedule.

Practical Heart Tip 70: Stress buster *

Use the core Heart Strengthening (KHH 6) once a day, ideally before work, then continue with similar or slightly shorter version of heart strengthening. Aim to do it for a few minutes (2 to 5min) each session. Also, aim for quality, not just quantity.

Set your computer calendar or mobile phone alarm and follow this session routine for 21 days:

First three days:	three times a day
Days four to six:	four to six times a day
Days seven to nine	seven times
Days 10 to 21:	seven times
Days 22 onwards:	continue! Feel and decide what is a good number to continue to support you.

When you use the 'stress buster' follow the 80/20 'rule'. Ensure and diarise the 80% of heart sessions that you have and be okay with not managing to do the other 20%. For example, days 'four to six' the goal is four to six times, then aim for 3 to 5 times. Be kind and accepting if you fall behind a bit. However, aim to be between 80 to 90% most days.

Do the 'heart check' at the beginning of the period and decide to redo it, re-score your heart-intelligence levels, which is also an indicator of your feeling and stress levels/resilience.

Ideally, write a brief Heart Diary note, too. Record the number of times, how whole-heartedly you do it, for example use a rating from 1 to 5 (one is low, five is high) and make a few notes on how you felt during and after each session.

The heart's role: inner strength, resilience building, prevention and cure

The heart has an innate capacity to lower the levels of stress that you experience. It builds inner 'heart' strength and improves stress resilience in this way. The heart's intelligence can detect stress and causes of stress, and remove parts that are experienced as stress. The heart can also work with parts, aspects or causes not known, or not yet known or experienced as stress. Because of these innate abilities, the heart can help with your inner strength and resilience, and function as prevention and cure.

Inner strength

Inner strength is the ability with which you manage to continue to work, enjoy and perform at high levels. Inner strength really is how you are able to have another capacity within you that manages all the interferences such as high workload, unreasonable clients and colleagues or senior staff, while you still have energy or strength to focus on the task at hand.

Inner strength is directly related to your heart condition and capability. Any form of workplace pressure will add to the tension or pressure that you normally experience in your life. If there is a heavy heart, then the pressures will increase emotional reactivity that is either directed towards self, in the form of self-doubt, sadness or anger, or it is directed at others. You snap, show your irritation towards peers or are short with customers.

Resilience building

Every moment you attend to the heart you will build exactly the resilience needed that lets you continue to perform and enjoy at work. Resilience is to stay heart-centred, to stay in the positive feelings, energy and vibration from your heart, no matter what the outer world throws at you. If you have practised most of the practices up to now you will have no doubt already felt positive changes in terms of your inner strength and grown resilience.

When your inner strength and resilience have grown from within your heart, and offer you a deeply-felt calmness, you will still be challenged by extra workload or pressure. This extra challenge will, however, not rock you to the core or penetrate so deeply that you struggle to cope. If you already work from the heart, in addition to the use of your mind and brain, then the joy of connecting with others, the joy of working and the enjoyment of working in a team will always, even if quieter, be present and balance pressures or stress.

Prevention and cure

It is heart-logical then that a strong heart is prevention for difficult, pressure and stressful times. Any burdens, impurities or 'collection' within the heart, when at low levels, means that there are less receptors within that can react or make you feel stressed.

If you have been exposed to a lot of pressure and stress in the past, then it is likely that some heaviness from it is still stuck around or in the heart. Attend to your heart, do regular Heart Strengthening (KHH 6) and any versions of the suggested direct heart-improving practices and you will find that familiar feelings of lightness and gentle joy can come back after some time.

Calmness at work

When someone can stay calm, even at busy or stressful times, there also remains an ability to stay focussed, to get the work done and to relate with attention and warmth to others. In fact, when you 'lose your calm', even as the common saying suggests, it will be less pleasant to work with you. There is further risk that relationships suffer, people are alienated by any 'lost-calm behaviours' and, depending on the degree of emotions expressed, members of the team or others pull back. There is less help available. Potentially this is a downwards spiralling scenario. When a connection is lost in this way it can take a lot of work, and often quite some time too, to bring it back to the same level of trust, warmth and function.

Calmness at work is also about the ability to make good decisions. You have felt already by now, being more relaxed and calm, that your heart has a voice. You feel more and your heart can support you in your assessment of situations. More in-tune decisions have an ability to add to success and to your wellbeing. You will have to rework less because others find it easier to support you, as they feel the rightness of decisions you make. More time and energy are freed up to improve what you do or to do more.

Anthony's story is one example of how the heart assisted after a career change and in a first role in the new job. After ten or more years in one role, Anthony decided to study nursing. After university he immediately found employment and started his new career. Like many others perhaps too, he found that the excellent academic training, and some work placements, were not enough to fully prepare for the role.

Anthony's Story:

'I remember before the opening of my heart that if I was placed in a position or situation where I did not know what do to or how to do it, I would try and work it out all on my own. Even if I was unsure or did not know, I would do it myself with whatever knowledge I had.'

'This was very hard and I remember it often didn't work. This put immense pressure on me, knowing that what I did at times was very improvised and not the best for a client, myself and the team.'

'I was stressed and anxious as a result and I did often not enjoy what I was doing, even though on the outside I appeared calm. On the inside I was distraught and merely focussed on getting IT done, the task at hand, getting somehow right. Thus, there was not much joy or enjoying in what I did or was asked to do.'

'Now with the help of the heart I still feel the same anxiousness rising, especially in a new role and a totally new environment. I notice the significant difference now. I am much more relaxed, at peace, I am comfortable, which is very new, to ask my more experienced colleagues. This it makes all much easier. Colleagues and patients often comment on how much I smile, giggle and laugh at work. In fact, I have to remind myself to not do this too strongly, especially when patients with serious issues are around me. Many positive comments are made and this lightens everyone and everything up a little.'

'So, when anxiousness arises, I remember the heart, I know there is guidance through the heart that the heart's knowing is guiding me also. Often answers come spontaneously to help in new or difficult situations.'

'This enables me to follow the heart and feeling and not the anxiousness. Often something or someone will turn up, helping miraculously.'

'Last week in a serious situation with a patient, simply a colleague walked up and offered help.'

'I realise now that I am more centred, calmer on the inside and I am not afraid to ask nor to admit I need help.'

'Work is a lot more enjoyable for me this way. I interact more naturally with everyone and I can feel my heart free and light. Work and interactions with everyone flow freely and there is a lightness in all.'

'What is very clear to me is the direct connect in the way in which the heart is part of this, and how people respond to me. People are very open towards me. They share their problem and hardships, the enjoy my company. Colleagues and patients seem to enjoy my presence. They feel at ease with me ... affected by the heart's radiance.'

'Patients share the deepest things with me. I don't make any effort in this. I feel guided through the heart in joyful and wonderful ways. My trust in the heart's help has grown a lot in the past months. It is amazing. At times when I feel and know that I don't follow the heart as well as I could it still seems to do its job. It naturally helps me and others around me. This is also the case at home. When I come home after a long shift at work, working with difficult or very unwell patients, I feel open, light and loving.'

Anthony is a friendly, helpful and joyful person. In his sharing he indicated that he struggled to ask for help. It is logical that this causes anyone stress and equally does not produce the best outcomes for the team, clients, patients and the individual.

The heart offers and brings out natural qualities and aspects like patience, care, supportiveness and genuine self-less action. The combination of these, even just more of this 'energy' invites others in, and facilitates team work and can lead to better outcomes or services.

Anthony, with the help of the heart, has been able to overcome his anxiety. He has become very calm. Heartfelt or deep calmness invites people in and draws them towards you. This may lead to assistance for the work you are supposed to do or to better client or customer outcomes.

In Anthony's case it became evident that patients were drawn to him and naturally trust him. This led to him being asked to work in more trusted roles with more responsibility and an increased salary within a short period of time. What also is coming through in his story is the growing joy in his work, starting from the foundation of heart-centred calmness and an active heart.

Happiness is in your heart

In some businesses the state of the happiness of everyone is a primary goal. Somewhere in people's goals and aspiration, obviously or less obviously, is the search for happiness, love and purpose or fulfilment. If what you or your team does is solely coming from the mind/brain, unless it sinks somewhat to the heart, it will be hard to be felt by yourself or others. If vision, values and goals are also perceived and expressed from the heart, and you genuinely work towards it, fulfilment, purpose, happiness and love, qualities that the heart can feel, have the chance to touch others and you.

Organisational visions, values and goals developed in this way can support your happiness. When you are happy, when any member of staff is happy, then it will be harder, if not impossible, to feel stressed.

You can let your heart help you to feel happier using the following PHT to remember a past happy moment and then stay in the heart-feelings for some time. Then let these lighter and more joyful heart-feelings shift you more towards happiness, choosing the heart and letting the heart help you even more.

Practical Heart Tip 71: Happy moment - happiness - stress *

This PHT may also be a quick 'on-the-go' heart charger. Earlier in the book (KHH 1 in Section II) you were introduced to connecting with a joyful, beautiful or happy moment in your life. In PHT 12 you were invited to make a 'list of joyful moments'. Let us repeat KHH 1 and then add to it.

Relax on a chair or in a sitting position. Close your eyes and if you feel like run through one of the relaxation exercises introduced. When you are relaxed, with or without additional heart preparation, intend to:

- *Remember a special, joyful, beautiful or happy moment in your life;*
- *Feel and re-experience the feelings you had in this special moment;*
- *Feel the feelings more than the thoughts that come up;*
- *Realise the feelings, keep relaxing, gently smile, follow all the beautiful feelings that you feel;*
- *If you feel them in or around your heart, follow the feelings from your heart (spend 2-3 minutes enjoying the feeling); then*
- *Realise and feel how stressed you feel or how the level of stress, pressure or general life burdens feel right now.*

Alternatively, you can feel, in the last part of the PHT, how stressed or burdened you felt earlier in the day or before the PHT and how do you feel it now?

What can happen is, depending on your current heart-strength, you clearly feel in moments when your heart is triggered by a beautiful memory, that any stress, burdens or pressure will find it harder to penetrate you and even dissolve. The problem, issue or challenge will still be there, perhaps, but it will not penetrate as deeply, not be a burden, and distract you less.

With this PHT you only get an indication of the fact that, when heart strength and joyful feelings in your heart grow, this growth can continue in relation to how you attend to your heart and live in heart-mind balance. Problems will always be there, at different times, so you might as well be happy when solving them. 'Happy or unhappy' does make a difference to the problem and to you.

Ultimately any level and depth of feelings of happiness are determined by your heart strength. After all, you 'feel' happy. Mind-based and heart-based wellbeing programs or tools at work are generally aimed at minimising stress levels. Your heart, will not be happy with an objective of solely minimising the 'negative', stress. If you attend to your heart, if you use your heart in daily life more, following this chapter's KHHs and PHTs and others in the book that speak to you, change in this direction will invariably happen.

Your heart will take you to a point where feelings of happiness are so profound that stress cannot find a toe-hold anymore.

You will still be in a job and there will still be external pressure and stressful moments. However, the feeling inside you will be at a minimum 'low or no stress and no unpleasant pressure feelings' and even growing feelings of gentle joy just for being in every moment, while being in the heart and being helped by it.

Heart-based wellbeing and resilience programs

In the absence of a heart element, wellbeing programs are either using familiar cognitive approaches, physical exercise or meditation-associated efforts, or any combination of these, to achieve improved staff wellbeing.

There is a high likelihood that elements that bring about the heart's help are missing or only indirectly touched on. Direct heart-learning, direct and practical heart interventions being comparatively new, often wellbeing activities and programs are limited to a mind, physical, emotional and at times spiritual focus.

Feeling well or resilient are ultimately feelings where you feel well or resilient. A feeling of health, energy, lightness, emotional freeness, freedom from burdens, mental calm or clarity and other positive feelings are some qualities associated with wellbeing. Your heart is the centre of feeling. It can not only receive or feel the end-product of any wellbeing efforts, that you or your employer make in improving wellbeing, it can also actively and directly help.

Your heart practices up to now, following the KHHs and PHTs, very likely have given the following experiences:

- Your heart helping you to become calmer, lighter, freer and emotionally less reactive;
- More heart helping you to balance a tendency to use the mind/brain often and within this to find a new balance of calmness, clarity and relating softer to others; and
- Your heart opening quality of relations to others at work, at home, building new connection and adding warmth, care and genuine interest without losing sharpness of mind and overall clarity.

These aspects will improve how you work, often with a direct impact. How you are and feel, at the level of mind/brain, heart and emotion, and physically, is the very foundation upon which a day at work is built.

Heart-based wellbeing and resilience programs implemented in workplaces, have shown what the heart promises to do and can do: to change the way people feel in terms of overall wellbeing, feeling inner strength/resilience and having more energy.

Figure 17.: Impact of heart-based wellbeing programs at work

Measured Impact	Before	After	Change	In %
Feeling well	*58*	*85*	*28*	*48%*
Feeling resilient	*50*	*85*	*35*	*70%*
Feeling positive	*70*	*90*	*20*	*29%*
Feeling energy	*63*	*90*	*28*	*44%*

Wellbeing at work, when the heart has cleared interfering or blocking emotions, is essential to well-flowing team work, to positive client-customer-staff interactions and for the mind/brain to be focussed and clear. When burdens, negative emotions or impacts of past hurtful events are cleared by an active heart, then the purpose for interacting with others becomes the main event that takes place, untainted, clear and joyful. This also means that work flows, service is professional or heart-felt, attention given is genuine, and a gentle love and quiet joy touches everything.

In addition, with an active heart, these interactions will feel gentle, caring, attentive and open in a way that listening and talking will find a new balance, often 'just right' for every situation. This means that you use mind/brain initiated learned or personal communication techniques together with the heart's energy to connect, show care, and maintain clarity.

Wellbeing at work, how healthy, balanced and happy staff are, is an important ingredient in how productive, effective and engaged staff are, including managers and senior managers. The impact of stress and related absenteeism is very significant, in terms of cost for an organisation and overall service delivery, growth and the ability to maintain competitiveness.

Emotions and an over-active or dominating mind are two negatively impacting forces in that they are not adequately balanced. With reduced interference from the broad possible range of emotions, whether this plays out openly or is hidden, the joy of working together, the abilities to do the job, to do it well and to make even wider positive contribution opens to a new plane. A calmer mind will reduce an overall tendency to be driven internally, to burn out, to not be able to stop or to have a mind that races for racing sake, including past 'pit stops' where it is important to feel, listen and recognise a new idea, new way of doing things or a new way of responding.

The reward of this freer, healthier and more creative way of being at work is priceless. Broader studies and longer term research will hopefully be conducted to verify what has been shown clearly and often in very short times in many pilot-like activities and workshops.

Wellness and resilience are the very foundation of every day at work, in the office and at home. Heart-balanced wellbeing takes care of all the building blocks of who you are: emotions, mind/brain capacity, body, and deeper inner/spiritual aspects. The innate capacities of the heart and its refined intelligence have shown to be at the hub of this, facilitating profound wellbeing shifts and positive impacts, and all in a comparatively short time.

It is all about relationship

If we learn to open our hearts, anyone,
including the people who drive us crazy,
can be our teacher. Pema Chodron

'It is all about relationship', is a statement made by a dear colleague, friend and executive HR Manager from Europe. At that time she was on a sabbatical in Australia as a young, senior and successful HR Manager in her early 30s.

At the time the statement was surprising at a first glance, as her background was predominantly in production environments. She clearly grasped the importance and meaning of more heart at work and in all work relations, and generously volunteered her insights in putting workplace heart programs together.

The extent, quality and overall flow with which this working together happens is equally mind/brain and heart directed. Perhaps, by now, reading more about the heart and its capabilities, and having made direct, even clear experiences, you may say that it is the heart that has a much greater influence on the quality of your work relations.

What are some of the qualities that underpin effective, efficient and above-average work place or team relationships and relate to the heart? The heart enjoys simplicity, focusses on the essence of issues and from there helps you to make good decisions and sound steps forward. Qualities that underpin good work relationships are:

- The development of positive work and work relations supporting attitudes and behaviours;
- Well-developed emotional intelligence and overall maturity that keep the four potential interferences at bay; ideally this is coupled with an active heart to:
    - create enough awareness of your own agendas and to balance your own with organisational agendas;
    - offer an awareness of your emotional world and how to work with it and with more heart, reducing emotional reactivity - expressed or not expressed;
    - bring to the surface any unhelpful heart-mind separation and develop full heart-emotional capacity;
    - shift towards genuine team relations;
    - assist with more effective or less effective dealing with difficult situations;
    - shift you from times of boredom or disengagement to heartfelt commitment or enjoyment; and
    - move you away from any guarding and disengaging behind busy-ness; and
- A balanced heart-mind/brain personality that minimises comparison, judgement, knowledge and experience in ways that are productive, value adding and not de-motivating or burdening to self or others.

The heart's help in building and maintaining your work relationships is potentially quite profound. You add another component to all your relations and with this you enhance the heart-to-heart interactions you have. Heart-to-heart here means you add all the qualities of the heart in refined ways. This may be more clarity, more focus, more support, more insight, more wisdom, more strength in kindly saying 'no' or just a heartful presence that radiates an energy of understanding, care, reliability or companionship.

Pat's experience in using her heart through her work at an aged care day centre highlights some of this. It also shows the profound impact that a strong heart can have in helping with personal issues; especially so that these issues do not affect performance and the quality of relationships at work.

Pat's Story:

'At the time I experienced a lot of emotion, a lot of change in my life, a lot of upheaval.'

'I was very grateful to be able to go to the heart workshops and to feel that things began to change. Over the next couple of years I continued to experience upheaval and change but less emotion. Everything felt smoother and easier and for that I was grateful.'

'I work in a day centre for elderly clients. They either have memory loss or are very frail or are socially isolated and they are still living at home, not in a nursing home, because of the care they receive.'

'It is an amazing difference to use what I know now about the heart. Especially in the way I relate to the people I am with. I find that my attitude with them is so much calmer and present. And, honestly, I am really happy to be with them and it is less like job and more like sharing all the time.'

'It goes both ways. They respond so beautifully, too. It is not limited to the clients there. I find it is a lot easier to relate to the staff, my co-workers, from the heart as opposed to from the mind/brain, as I would have done it several years ago. I find myself less trying, trying to get something or trying to make things work. Instead there is a flow and things are a lot easier and smoother than they used to be. I am very grateful for these changes and they keep coming.'

What Pat's story shows is that the more any emotional or negative or interference patterns are cleared, there is less interruption, focus on work is improved and the circle of professional relations can widen. These additional colleagues or friends will not just be additions. There will be heart-warmth and attentiveness for existing and new 'team members'. This widens the team that helps you and your work. Even in solely mathematical terms, a greater number of professional relations will increase the likelihood of more support, better collaborative outcomes and growing numbers of clients or customers, who in turn talk to others.

The importance of good, effective and long-term work relations is widely recognised. Relationship-enhancing programs for team building, cohesion, collaboration, customer service, sales promoting and conflict resolution training programs are offered. The heavier stress or accumulated burdens or emotions such as anger, resentment or disillusionment are, the clearer it will seem now, from a combined mind/brain and heart perspective, that sound heart interventions will take much better care of intra-personal, inter-personal or relationship-enhancing issues or obstacles.

It is hoped that the examples and stories and your own experiences with more heart have shown in some way that the heart offers a valuable addition to all that is 'relationship' at your work place. It is also hoped that the examples, stories and exercises from other chapters of the book have also added to this picture. The value of your own practice and experience is two-fold: In attending to your heart, you will feel within you the heart-felt feelings of calmness and lightness. It is also very common that participants of heart-based programs notice a change in how others relate to them and how work suddenly flows smoother. This is the secondary working of the heart for you, and never just for you. Others will be touched, gently changed or invited to change by the soft, gentle and transforming heart radiance.

Summary - is your heart in it?

You may work in an organisation, from home, on the road, self-employed, as a student, volunteer, part-time, casually or you may be working as a 'mum' or 'dad' in the home. Bringing more of your heart into what you do will offer additional support, guidance and enjoyment.

You can change how much of your heart is in your work, how whole-heartedly you do things and how deepening heart-to-heart connections enhance what you do at work. Practical heart steps in the 'work' chapter are:

1. You can be strategic about heart-centred professional development: where are your issues, challenges, strengths and growth opportunities? Where do you stand in relation to the four interferences and the three balancing heart-qualities?

2. Reflect on, and make notes, about the three balancing heart qualities, how they can assist you further, and expand to the additional qualities such as wellbeing, happiness, customer service and relationship.

3. The first PHT 'The to-do-review' is in the 'culture of busyness' section. Impulses to do or act will make others quieter or less forthcoming. To monitor and review what you normally do offers new ways of interacting with others and inviting others in. You also let the heart add wisdom. It will help with any internally driven busy-ness also.

4. The PHT 'Heart warmth to keep the cool' is in the heart-emotional intelligence section. Emotional reactivity at work is a detriment to facilitating win-win situations. Accessing the second emotional centre, your heart, brings you into a heart-centred presence with the help of this PHT. Your heart will, in acute or crisis moments, help you to dissolve tendencies to react. Interactions with the individuals, the team, clients, customers or any internal or external stakeholder are bound to improve.

5. Not every task at work is exciting. Mind/brain get easily bored, no matter what the task or situation. The heart is always present and you can enjoy the beautiful heart-felt feelings every moment. The PHT 'Boredom buster' is a down-to-earth tool to bring more heart-presence to your work day and to minimise experiences of boredom. More heart will also assist in engaging or re-engaging again if needed. From there, smiling from your heart to those around you, can further assist you and your work environment.

6. An overall commitment to your heart, regular heart strengthening and any of the KHH or marked PHTs (*) will help you to be emotionally available, escape the culture of busyness, and offer more direct, more frequent access to your heart's innate intelligence, wisdom, decision-making ability and guidance.

7. Be heartful when working with difficult people or in difficult situations. A strong, light and present heart assists in those moments. It will also assist you in taking less or nothing home. The heart's clearing help will ensure that no accumulative burdening occurs. In turn this ensures your attendance, performance and related rewards through the help of the heart.

8. Engagement at work can be a significant issue, for you, the team or an employer. It is hard to assess the engagement of others. It is easier to know and to admit when you are disengaged and you want to take steps to change this. KHH 'Surrender

burdens', or individuals, situations and related emotions, is a powerful tool to let go of whatever problem you have, especially when you can't solve it with reasonable effort, or it is out of your control to change the relationship or situation. This is a more structured way to surrender, and should work deeper, than the earlier introduced PHT 'Surrendering from the heart' in section 3.

9. Listening is one of the most powerful and impactful ways to communicate. When listening from the heart the core of you is present. The heart's radiation makes additional connection, and, at this level, new outcomes, solutions or ways to connect can happen. Use the PHT 'Listen with your heart' to master this skill, to engage the heart and to be even more whole-heartedly present, with feel-able sincerity and care.

10. The PHT 'Stop, feel, heart, listen' is an extension of the listening PHT. Let it function as a helpful tool in difficult, conflict, high-pressure or high-stress situations. You can also go back and review the 'emotional rescue guide' in chapter V.

11. Utilising the PHT 'Speaking from the heart' at work, or at home, you can experience new impacts in your presentations, during meetings or in any interactions. When you speak from your heart a calm, genuine, sincere, authentic and caring energy will travel with your voice and words enveloping what you intend to communicate. It will generate trust, engagement and willingness to collaborate or build the bridge to a solid, long-term relation.

12. The full potential of your heart at work, helping you and those around you, would not be complete without the use of your body, a body that is in some way moved by the heart. During quieter moments, or at home, practise the PHT 'Move by being moved by your heart' to ensure the energy, radiance and quality of all that your heart is can also flow through your body's movements.

13. The section 'Love at work' has the KHH 'Do all with feeling' within it. Using the heart more directly in this way, your mind and heart are integrating and emotions are more likely to be kept at bay or cleared. The KHH invites you to actively integrate the heart into your work and to keep a diary record for some time to stay on track.

14. PHT 'Heart-to-heart at work' expands KHH 11 into something dynamic - into a giving, receiving, communicating and interacting from a place of feeling and heart. You may, for example, give a staff member, peer or client some of your time. Make it a heart-present time, as one way to give or to show heart-felt care, appreciation or unconditional positive regard.

15. A brush with Chinese philosophy, Yin and Yang, shows that in strength can be weakness and in weakness or softness can be strength. The PHT 'Softening the edges' invites you to welcome softness or gentleness as genuine heart-feelings into your day at work. Taking diary notes will assist in realising new strengths unfolding from within this softness.

16. The PHT 'One supportive person' is an additional way to improve heart capacity at work.

17. Practical aspects of the 'Love and your team' section are to be kind and loving as two of the core heart qualities and feelings. Experience being in loving heart-radiance, kind and within an unconditional positive regard for all around you at work. Let KHH 10, 11 and PHTs of this section assist you to be within this loving state, with elated sweet, joyful feelings, to attend to all that needs to be done with wisdom, clarity and heart.

18. The heart's help is such that you are being moved by the heart's unique capabilities, from managing stress to 'managing' happiness. The PHT 'Stress buster' of this section is a powerful tool that combines some of the key heart tools of the entire book to ensure that stress levels you experience, at work and outside work, are reduced. Commit to this PHT for a 21-day period, or for however long it is needed.

19. The PHT 'Happy moment - happiness - stress' is an 'on-the-go' and quick heart charger. Every time you have a moment, every time you feel pressure or stress building up, you can apply this tip and tool. It will also move you away from negative thinking or emotion and re-focus on a positive event, at work or otherwise.

Chapter 7

Personal Growth - Connecting the Dots

I feel therefore I am.
Heart workshop participant

In the following chapter personal growth is explored and how a heart-supported, heart-centred approach can offer additional perspectives, avenues of help and levels of fulfilment.

Human beings are something quite incredible. Abilities to think, plan, love, interact, create, and enjoy are quite amazing characteristics. When connecting with this we can realise how wonderful and refined these characteristics or abilities really are. They are also highly complex. For instance, consider the complexities of:

- The entire human body and its functions: the nervous and cardio vascular systems, glands or digestion; and
- The interconnectedness between us, as humans, with the earth, society, the solar system and universe around us, all in support of life and growth.

The human complexity is so vast that, as one example only, less than 10 per cent of the brain's functions are known. In relation to the interplay between mind/brain and the heart the physical reality, combined with metaphysical questions such as 'who are we' or 'who am I', are age old quests and queries.

The level or layer of help that the heart offers to any of your personal growth plans or efforts is one of purpose-alignment and fulfilment. Unless personal growth is somewhat connected to you, a deep you, it will perhaps only ever produce a certain degree of inner satisfaction. Equally, if personal development does not generate clear feelings of growth, positive change on both an inner and outer level, too, then what is its worth?

Personal growth, with the heart involved, is naturally more about the inner aspects of personal growth, less about what you achieve on the outside, at work, socially, physically or financially. It is about connecting the dots: inner and outer and short to long-term. The aim of it is to achieve short-term happiness and ease, medium-term alignment and long-term profound and feelable satisfaction, purpose and growth.

Previous chapters have been around ability to grow and to develop as a person with the heart increasingly involved. This chapter is about more specific areas of life that are commonly associated with personal growth ranging from being a better person to reaching new realisations, insights or truths.

You will find a brief discussion around what personal growth is and the introduction of the Kaleidoscope of Personal Growth. This shows the interplay between areas of growth, inner aspects of growth, past influences and impacts from outer factors, such as our community, culture and family, and wider social and physical environments.

The heart's role in personal growth is not only able to align any growth efforts but it can also function as your own and wise inner quality control mechanism. No matter what personal growth is now for you, no matter what others say or believe, and no matter how successful in your eyes, or the eyes of others, you are right now, the question can be there 'how happy am I', 'is this it', or 'is this who I really am'? And in some way there is always 'something else' until growth and the deeper or deepest inner you connect - until there is a feeling of unity or completeness where family or social life, work, learning, deep in-sights and all that life is flow harmoniously.

When the inner connection to the real you is only there in fragments, or not at all, then the question is, what is personal growth if not every part of you is considered and involved, including your heart?

In return, with the heart actively involved, it can guide you, facilitate and ultimately feel any longed-for feelings of joy, peace, contentment, completion, purpose or fulfilment.

The facilitation of more connection has a range of aspects. The clearest one perhaps is that all personal growth achievements will be in some way meaningless if they are not connected to what the inner-most knowing within, the inner-most desire or longing within also wants or knows.

More heart may also assist you in finding new approaches to better connect, or where needed to disconnect from a range of possible personal growth helpers in life. These helpers normally start with our parents, then teachers and then as we grow older shift to work place coaches, good friends, mentors or life coaches.

The direct heart help in personal growth will cover the heart's abilities to offer greater clarity, intelligence or wisdom and the heart's direct growth facilitation.

To begin with let us look at what personal growth is or can be all about. You may feel that it only is important to you in relation to some of the items discussed above, or on the Kaleidoscope of Personal Growth chart, or more growth areas exist for you. It is hoped that the discussions, examples, experiences and practices will first show the potential of your heart and how to use it even more.

What is personal growth?

It is meaningful to first look at what personal growth is: what are elements or aspects of personal growth, how do these relate and where does one fit in, within a wider definition of personal growth: growth also as part of a social network, community and even wider?

At a first glance, personal growth is about the growth of you as a person. What this looks like, your growth, in some way is also just that, 'personal' to you. From this angle your growth is what happens to you overall, and also as a result of the sequence of many events that unfold with more or less intention. From this perspective, personal growth involves what you plan, what you decide and do, and how all of this unfolds, depending on insights, plans and actions.

There is another angle too, where personal growth is the betterment of you personally in direct interaction or direct relation to the environment. If, for example, you are not very successful in your area of work, if you live in comparative poverty, if the circle of friends is very small and if your key family relations are not good quality, then some would question the personal growth achieved over the years.

Personal growth will further be enhanced or limited in terms of where you live, what country or region and what happens globally - for example, in terms of the economy, the environment or world peace. This means that even in relation to 'personal' growth there are bigger picture aspects where you are tied into an organic system, a huge world or universe that a limited mind/brain can only perceive in limited ways. Personal growth can significantly be enhanced by the wisdom and abilities of the heart.

Why personal growth?

Why do we grow, long to grow or embark on personal growth journeys? Growth and personal growth is something that is aspired to by many. There seems to be an inner program that looks to be tapped into. Hence we look to grow personally. Some people do a significant amount of planning for this kind of growth and others happen to be taken there or get involved by accident. Whatever the starting point or reason, most people consider it as a 'good thing' when it happens.

Perhaps as an evolving society it feels right to grow, to learn to develop and to grow personally.

The importance of personal growth is illustrated by the emergence, over the past decades, of a whole industry of growth-helpers: coaches of all sorts, psychologists, psychiatrists, general counsellors, mentors and facilitators. All this is pointing to a strong need and interest base for personal growth.

This phenomenon is perhaps an expression of an innate yearning within of wanting to grow, develop and learn. If you read this and it feels right to you then you could say that a longing to grow aligns with the truth from your heart.

Whether it is planned or unplanned, it is difficult to grow without help or support from others. One of the most important aspects of this help is the relationship between you and the person who provides the support, regardless of whether this support is actively invited, arranged, bought, intentional or given-freely. It is also important to recognise that our personal growth also involves others, such as our friends and family. When we are attempting to grow, we need the help of others.

The occurrence of personal problems may be a reason why individuals seek to change or grow. Problems or challenges tend to take us out of a comfort-zone, out of a routine or pattern of behaviour or existence that seem normal and then suddenly is interrupted. At first this is not easily welcomed; at least not by most people. However, people often say, when reflecting on past challenging or un-welcomed events, that a stronger, more mature, wiser or softer person or self has evolved as a result.

From another angle, however, difficult challenges also provide a chance to look at one's life, to feel what needs to be changed and to be open to new developments and growth.

The model of growth that one has may also be understood in our mind or brain. There are two alternative approaches to understanding growth:

- Growth that moves us toward something in some way; or
- Growth that also reaches inwards, that touches and transforms the deep inner structures of who we are.

Personal growth according to the second view is also offering a transition to new ways of being, feeling, interacting with others and perceiving the world. This includes all layers of growth: personal, spiritual and whatever else may be on your radar of growth.

Heart-based and heart-facilitated growth is more like the second way of growing, which then also facilitates a more fulfilled and more successful life.

As you open your heart you will obtain access to and guidance from the heart and inner heart, which will pull you in a direction that is more who you really are. Over the time of growth, over a whole life, this will generate deep levels of fulfilment, satisfaction and connection.

Heart-based and heart-facilitated growth will, however, also help you in terms of guidance and action to achieve what you want to achieve. The heart often has a better picture of what this is and even if you want a lot, the heart will be the quality control and often facilitate something that is better and more wonderful.

This quite specific role of the personal growth supporting heart becomes even clearer when looking at the Kaleidoscope of Personal Growth.

The Kaleidoscope of Personal Growth?

Why the term kaleidoscope? The Kaleidoscope or Spectrum of Personal Growth intends to show that personal growth is a combination of aspects that has inner, outer, relational and environmental aspects; all with a quality, feeling, attitude and behaviour focus. It also shows there is a difference between inner-quality and feeling aspects of growth, and outer-quality 'doing' or materially manifested of growth. The kaleidoscope also is the reflection of a dynamic model of growth, and, as a more heart-centred personal growth unfolds, it will look different for everyone.

The Kaleidoscope of Personal Growth is a visual illustration of the discussions around the connecting and facilitating qualities that your heart brings to the personal growth aspect of your life.

Figure 18: Kaleidoscope of Personal Growth

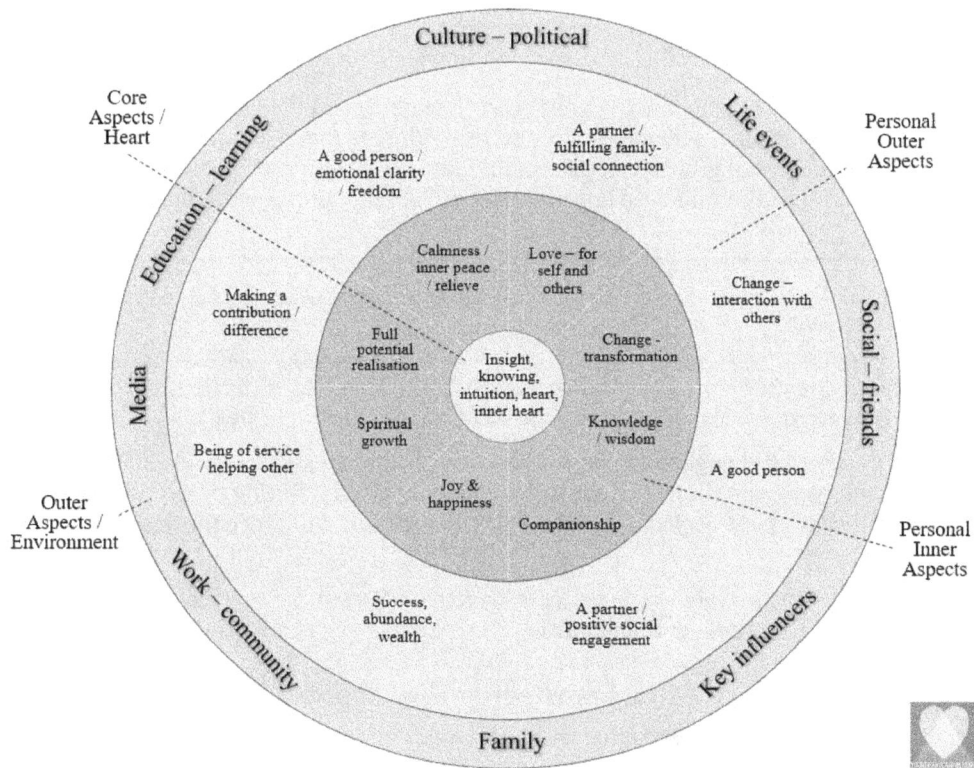

The kaleidoscope also shows the 'dimensions of growth': the personal-inner dimension and the personal-outer dimension. The personal-inner dimension and its aspects are more directly influenced by your heart, and in turn, the personal-inner dimension and its aspects are influenced by the quality that your heart brings to the personal-inner dimensions and from there to the outer ones. Depending on the strength or clarity that exists within these inner and outer circles and their aspects, a person is more or less influenced by the outermost circle, social and cultural influences. This existing or growing clarity is a strong foundation for fulfilment in all ways you engage with life.

The hub of the wheel, influencing, radiating into all the areas, shedding light to them, is the heart. The kaleidoscope also clearly shows a core inner centre of self and growth as 'the centre of insight, knowing, intuition, heart, inner heart' to which ultimately all areas or aspects of growth connect to. Your personal growth can, in expanding ways, be directed from there - from your heart - and no doubt, to some extent already is.

The kaleidoscope further shows the existence of an outer circle of influencers: current or past social or cultural influences and their aspects such as upbringing, life events, physical and social environments, wider family, friends, school, work places, the political situation and the media.

As with most charts or models, the Kaleidoscope of Personal Growth can never be complete or all-embracing. It intends to show two things: your personal growth is complex; and in addition to any material, tangible goals, there also the qualities of being, depth of feeling within. Personal growth will always also be an interplay between the visible aspects of growth (third circle) and the invisible growth aspects (the inner two circles).

The heart brings together and connects these dimensions and aspects of growth, including any related tangible, material aspects or goals. This means all results, successes and other expressions of growth will be what they are, and have value as such. They will, however, also connect back to the core of you, the real you. They will also connect, within this inner kaleidoscope, to clear and deep feelings of fulfilment, realisation or insight and purpose.

It is hoped that the kaleidoscope offers a visual expression of an inner purpose of growth and that you are able to reflect and then re-focus on qualities, values or purposeful goals that create deeper, inner-felt, heart-centred levels of fulfilment, experiences and realisations for you.

It is perfectly normal and okay to want to have success in the outer or visible world. However, it is not emphasised in the kaleidoscope for two reasons:

- Personal growth means growth as a person in all ways and areas that make the whole-of-us grow - hence the focus on non-physical growth aspects; and
- Success as it is commonly understood is also not emphasised, as no amount of wealth, success or status will ensure you have a fulfilled, happy and love-filled life.

However, when you have your inner or core centre - your heart - connecting all the dots that are your personal growth, then any wealth, success or status will be authentic, genuine, and connected within, to this core. The degree of success and abundance will matter less than in any tangible degree of growth that your mind/brain perceives. From there you will have a chance to share, help others and be socially, personally and spiritually abundant - and all with love and warmth that in turn nurtures your heart and the hearts of others.

The core heart question in all this is ... to what extent do growth, success and purpose connect back to you and give meaning to the inner most truth you understand or hold?

The inner centre of the circle, the centre of insight, knowing, wisdom, deep idea or feeling, is your heart to which all connects. Ideally, personal growth is directed, or at the very least somewhat connected to your heart.

The kaleidoscope shows, as personal change in the light of the heart is discussed, that any deeper connection to the inner centre, your heart or inner heart, will resonate well, will be smooth and will give you a feeling of 'going in a right direction'. When it is really heart-connected it will be the right personal growth for you. The heart will prove the wiser director of change or growth in the short, medium and long-term.

What the kaleidoscope doesn't show is that there is a deep connection between the way that your heart is linked to your personal growth, fate, or your God-given disposition or foundation.

Disposition or foundation

It is important to at least briefly look at the disposition and foundations of personal growth. Disposition and foundation represent all the genetic, given or learned abilities that you have right now. The heart perspective is positive: significant change and personal growth is possible even if personal or environmental circumstances don't look so promising.

Foundation is about the skills and genetics that you have been given, your 'starting resources' if you like. It is further what you learned from your parents and others while growing to adulthood and developing as an adult. Common foundation aspects are intellectual abilities or IQ (intelligence quotient). This IQ is built on by what is learned when young - at school, while training for work, at home or in any other way. Of course, into play here comes also what one did not learn and opportunities missed.

The term 'disposition' is used here to indicate even more than in the foundation part that there are aspects to what we are, where we are now, that is mouldable and flexible. This includes your skills, attributes and qualities. What you learned or did not learn in the past can function as a realisation, and hence incentive, to now be more diligent, motivated and disciplined, if it is something that seems important or purposeful. The dispositions can become mouldable from teenage years on, when you can decide to learn from others and break out from any boundaries adopted from parents or family.

What the key heart-ingredient here is ... is the fact that any plan, any hope and any rational assessment of what can be, without the active support of the more-present heart, will never be as good, high or wonderful compared to what your heart wants to facilitate or what your heart knows.

Or in other words your heart can overcome limitations or add immense value in relation to your foundation or disposition in quite amazing ways.

One way to connect with this more is to look at friends from high-school, depending on your age or at friends from some years back. Some had more potential than others based on their foundation or disposition. Often, surprisingly, it is not always those who seem to have the better foundation or disposition that have done well. There have been other factors involved.

The fact that the heart can facilitate outcomes beyond what a logical assessment of foundation or disposition looks like may sound strange, dreamy or whatever label comes to your mind. It is also not new, especially since insights and work in the areas of emotional intelligence and spiritual intelligence have broadened perspectives.

This is the reason, also, why perhaps one of the most profound and fascinating stories, the story of Daynis, transformation from a MacDonald's worker who was not very respected by his peers, to an internationally operating IT consultant, is in this section below.

Daynis is a young man who arrived to Australia as a migrant at the age of 15. He lacked English language skills and an Australian cultural background and values, which affected his ability to communicate with his peers at high school. He grew up with his mother and his grandfather.

In his story Daynis discusses his lack of focus and inability to multi-task. In his casual jobs after he left school this became a major obstacle. He also found himself becoming an outsider at work because of it. This affected not only his self-esteem, self-worth and social integration, but also his work performance. With a lack of acceptance and overall poor performance at work, team integration and team support became near impossible.

Daynis's Story:

'I remember when I was younger, after we had just arrived in Australia, it was difficult for me to be with others, to connect to others, to make friends easily. During my school years I was being teased and there were times when I had no friends.'

'Once I started working I noticed one of my weaknesses was that I could not hold things together. I could not multi-task easily. I became confused and I must have appeared scattered to others around me. My colleagues and supervisors noticed this, and in my first hospitality job I was soon being monitored for efficiency. I was even put on notice.'

'Every one of my early jobs required me to multi-task. This was very hard to do and sometimes I simply couldn't do it. In addition, I also had problems concentrating. This led to my work hours being lowered and I got less shifts than others. I was the odd one out and the people at work wouldn't talk to me freely, I was perceived by my team members as a non-performer. The stigma of being the odd one out prevented my attempts to bond with the collective and become a part of the team. This made my early work life very difficult, and a career impossible.'

'Once I started to do the heart meditation I immediately applied the practice to my work: I was servicing customers while smiling, and then, after a while, would let my heart smile to every customer all the time. It was not to achieve something or do something but to simply let the heart work more and help me, and to just give this new technique a go. The first few times doing the meditation were quite pleasant experiences and I realised that I wanted to improve my heart further.'

'The immediate change was that people opened up and talked more freely and sincerely than before, first the customers, then the staff, too. I felt more accepted by the team, too, as I continued. As there was more acceptance by the team, the team members in turn then helped me to improve my technical work and my work skills. I became much better at what I would do in my various jobs. The changes were very quick in a way. All I was focusing on was being in the heart and being happy in the heart while at work.'

'The experience at work began to spiral upwards. Two years into working with the heart more, I found myself working as a sales person in a major electronics shop. My performance was improving continuously and not long after I was finding my name being frequently listed amongst the top 15 nationwide sales people.'

'I was appreciated by my team members, they were happy to support me and I was liked. In turn I became better at my job. All these positive happenings have improved my confidence and my self-esteem. As a result, the quality of my social life started to improve as well. I also started to help my friends from the heart meditation group with their computer problems. Shortly, I found myself being employed by my friends to do small IT projects, computer repair work, and designing websites.'

'Dealing with work and any work issues became easier. I became more comfortable, more natural at work and gradually able to multi-task quite easily. This improved a lot over the past 2-3 years. Now I am able to project manage, run several small to medium IT projects parallel, plus work with new, potential clients and supervise up to 15 IT support staff in subcontracting roles.'

'At this stage I am very grateful as my colleagues and clients seem to feel very comfortable around me and they trust me. They seem to feel a degree of attention and care that they did not experience from other IT consultants.'

> *'I know that this is in a big way due to the changes that the heart-learning started and supported, in particular as people did not trust me, could not relate to me and would struggle to work with me in the past. Now they easily feel a heart-to-heart connection and work flows amazingly from there.'*

At the time of the completion of the book Daynis was 26 years young and a successful IT project manager and business owner. At times he manages up to 10 contracts and a team of up to 15 individual sub-contractors who do parts of the bigger projects that Daynis coordinates.

Daynis also offers his skills as a volunteer, assisting not-for-profit and personal development projects with his general IT and creative web-design skills and passion.

Daynis's story illustrates that to use your heart without knowing its potential is not enough. It also shows that dispositions and foundations that do not look very promising can be transformed, or transformed easier, with the help of the heart.

Daynis's story is particularly incredible when you further consider that English is not his first language. He is one of several individuals - who in feeling the depths of what the heart can do - committed sufficient time and effort to their heart development; in turn getting significant personal development and personal growth help from it.

Our nature

Our nature is something very personal, beautiful and wonderful. It is deeper than personality and also deeper than foundation and disposition. It is shining through, in some people more often and clear than others, and for many it is one indicator of who we really are. In particular, it shines through to ones who love us, have always loved us, or spontaneously love or like us. One can feel it, too, when loving another person or really liking others.

This feeling or state of being may be quite regular or almost permanent in your life, or you may have felt this only a few times. This inner, beautiful nature is close to where the heart is or where your heart energy and quality shines through.

These moments of being your purer or truer nature can also be of help. They can be a guide to let you realise that there is a wonderful and beautiful part within that can shine more; beautifying your life in terms of how you feel, and beautifying the life of dear, close ones around you; and all your relations. To long to be there, in this feeling, more can be one of your heart-guided, heart-based personal growth aims.

You can plan to let your heart, and all of you, work towards a change in this direction. Moments and stretches of time when you are being changed by the heart in this way, from the inside of you outwards, will only ever be in the gentlest of ways.

> *The more this heart-centred nature rises to the surface, the more it will help you feel more like how you truly are and who you truly are. Interacting from this place with others, to be in a more natural state, to be at the centre of all personal and wider growth, is a true gift.*

If this speaks to you and you feel to add this to your personal growth goals then you can perhaps also connect with the reality of an inner knowing, an inner existence that is your heart, and only your heart can direct or help the transformation in this way.

Our nature, this deeper human nature, is not to be confused with 'persona' or 'personality. Persona can be impressive, charming, fluttering and more. There is also a lack of sweetness and lightness and it is easier to use it for a goal, purpose or direction. There is a risk of it being self-centered and excluding others. 'Persona' meaning mask in Greek already somewhat indicating it is not the real you.

Good and not-so-good circumstances

Already implied in the above, there may be circumstances in your life that you look at as good or not-so-good in your relations. Some may also say, when looking at the successes or personal growth of others 'oh, there were just a set of positive coincidences'.

The law of attraction, the ability to materialise things, as presented by some, is based on notions that with the mind/brain you can do all sorts of things that support growth and success. What is lesser known and shared is that any mind/brain planning or intent will have the heart either in support of it or blocking it. The only way that the heart will block anything good for you is when the heart is full of collection-items and can't feel or help.

> *To any input, inspiration, positive stimulation or help, there is a risk that a heavy heart will experience a collection-reaction instead of a heart-smart interaction and filtering. Somewhat 'naturally' these not-so-helpful reactions are stronger when difficult events happen in our lives.*

It is the collection-items around the heart, negativities and other burdening particles, that create reaction instead of allowing the wisdom of the heart to do its job. These parts within or around the heart prevent positive attraction that the heart can facilitate - for you and others.

Whatever you would consider as not-so-good circumstances in your past, with a clearer, lighter and more active heart, it is unlikely they will look and feel the same. A light and free heart feels differently, and it attracts different energies, different people, and all the positive responses discussed in the work section. Of course this will not only happen at work. If you are at home with family or children, the heart energy will also create a softening and en-lightening of all interactions; something quite valuable and beautiful. In any social settings you will be more popular. People will feel the deeper beauty in you and, as your heart has changed, this beauty will also be expressed in actions, words and feeling.

The heart's own radiant energy and power, not limited by space or time, has the capacity to dissolve current inner blockages, past events and negative deposits. It also has the power to pave the way forward and beyond circumstances that are difficult, and may appear impossible to change.

Growth and problems

Having problems of course is not so pleasant, and naturally, people hope to have fewer problems or a 'problem-free' life. The reality is that some degree of challenge or problem will always exist. However, if you live a heart-centred life, or let the heart help you more, you can use the problem to slow down or stop, and then tap into your heart's help.

The moment you stop, any worries, burdens or over-thinking you will also be likely to find some rest. This will not happen naturally though, as it is you who needs to make the decision to stop. When you have a problem, you may have experienced already that as you pay more attention to your heart, the heart can help, guide and facilitate change. The next PHT is the problem first aid to personal growth.

> ### Practical Heart Tip 72: Problem first aid *
>
> *When you have a problem, or when you feel that a problem is burdening you, follow these steps:*
>
> - *Use the actual problem as a trigger or 'stop sign';*
>
> - *Stop everything, pay attention to your heart and with no planning or thinking. Do that and ideally do full heart strengthening with good quality;*
>
> - *Connect to the heart and after you feel a stronger heart presence stay there for some time in connection to your heart with your feeling;*
>
> - *Look at your situation again now, with greater mind/brain and heart balance;*
>
> - *Then make a plan or work out steps for what to do next to improve the overall situation, to improve your response to it - now or in the future - and write it down; and*
>
> - *Feel or feel with your heart - this may take some time - what steps or actions feel right or good to take that are in accordance with the greater knowing in your heart.*
>
> *You can do this PHT together with the next PHT 'Planning for personal growth'.*

This is a very important approach and step to take, engaging your heart's help, not only when you have problems that are in relation to personal growth, but every time that you have a problem, challenge, or experience any form of emotional response in you to what is happening in your life.

The key steps in this are to connect to the heart. Then, with or without intention or direction, the heart can help. You are allowing the heart to disconnect you from emotion, and the risk of following emotion instead of following a heart-based path of more clarity. With a stronger heart you will be more relaxed, and the mind/brain will also be able to think clearer.

In moments like this, when you are more heart-grounded, you can look at the overall situation, what happened, what has caused the problem, what led up to it, what is 'my part in it' - and extract the learning from it for your personal growth.

Extracting the learning means that you use the ability to reflect - mind and brain - together with a clear emotional state - heart-centred - and look at a problem situation to learn, to extract what life or the situation is showing or teaching you.

Once realised and 'seen', make the learning part of your experiences. In this way an experience becomes a valuable lesson and will help you to make better decisions in similar situations.

Within a short period of time, even while you follow the above PHT, you may find that with a stronger heart problems seem less over-whelming or challenging. Over a longer period of time you see and feel that life is no longer a play between good times and bad, but a chance to live the natural mind/brain and heart-balanced life. With growing heart strength calmness and other positive feelings will be present, no matter what the outer life is presenting to you.

It is often the case that problems we perceived to have, or have in real terms, are connected to other people. Other people can of course also have a directly helping role in relation to our personal growth, and in this way have a positive influence or function. Let us have a look at what this can look like with the additional perspective from the heart.

The role of others

To be helped by others is natural, normal and more often than not it is a very beautiful, special experience. We are interconnected beings and with no help from others it would be impossible to survive. This is most obvious when we are just being born. However, imagine if a world would exist with no doctors, no farmers or no people around who build and maintain your home. How easy or possible would it be to grow, even to survive?

Can you recall moments when you were helping someone and the help was given freely and joyfully? It is a wonderful experience in most cases, especially when your efforts were met with some degree of gratitude.

It is equally wonderful when we are in a situation of need or urgency, and we lack the necessary skill or experience, that someone shows up and freely offers their time and help.

At times, the best help is offered when you feel, listen, are present, and just show the heart-felt care within. It is not always about doing something or being an expert.

Our experiences are even more positive when what is given is genuine, authentic, and from the heart, with the intention to help and when other agendas are low or non-existent.

Whether we are aware of it or not, it is those other agendas that can blur helping situations. There are without doubt endless examples that can show how agendas interfere in those situations. Sometimes agendas rise to the surface or grow within as time goes by. For example, when you help a colleague at work and you expect, with or without awareness, that one day the favour is returned, then your giving is not as free as it could be.

As interconnected, social beings it is always good to offer help and to help others. However, the more you feel with your heart when to help and how to help, the more beneficial, agenda-free and smooth it will be. It is really only when you give, with a free and pure heart, that giving and helping will be free for the other person too. No ties, no burdens, no expectations and no emotions are present or being created.

Expectations arise when there is an agenda that is playing itself out. While this is normal, some awareness about how to reduce your own agendas and how to manage your own expectations, will lead to a life of more freedom and joy. Expectations are by-products of the mind/brain, and they are often coupled with emotion. As your heart-strength grows, your own emotional agendas will naturally and automatically be reduced, also influencing the mind/brain. Furthermore, when others approach you their feelings and behaviour will no longer penetrate, affect or hurt you. A strong heart is an alert heart to someone approaching you with a high degree of agendas or hidden agendas, that are not good for you, will make you feel pressure in your heart, which is a 'no' or caution from the heart.

The role of others can also be tricky when you pay for the expertise of a mentor, consultant, coach, life coach, psychologist or other professional. While in most cases advice will be given with the best intentions, the reality is that you are receiving help from another human being. In situations like this, despite the perceived greater experience, they may or may not have the full spectrum of wisdom and truth of greater, higher intelligence, to ensure that any advice or help given will work for you. This level of ability to help is very hard, if not impossible to achieve.

The outsourcing of important parts of life, personal life, work life and personal growth in this way is one of the great possible pitfalls.

You may find that after doing what many others did, after doing something for a long period of time in order to grow, that your needs, interest or your deeper truth was of a different kind. As a result you may find that the expert advice, or the advice of someone dear or near to you, is not working out at all for you. Good or even the best intentions will not be enough to give advice as no one situation is identical to another, when you look at all supporting or environmental circumstances. In addition, as the section below 'what others know and what we know' also covers, knowledge of any situation will always have some form of limitation.

I recall a simple situation from my own life. At the age of 19 I was in a bar, talking to the partner of a friend. He would have been around 45 to 50. Naturally and unfortunately I attributed experience and wisdom to him. After expressing to him, having just finished school, the intention to study architecture, he made a range of strong statements around recession, negative growth in the building industry, and that anyone studying architecture now would be in a bad situation at the end of their course.

What happened in reality was different. Five to six years later the country experienced a building industry boom that was beyond any expectations, and in some instances architects were head-hunted out of universities.

It is in these situations like that the heart is of immense value. No matter what the expertise, age or status of the person providing advice, you can it run through your heart, too, and feel the heart's response: is the advice useful, partially useful, or not useful.

When you are the expert, helper or the one offering advice or a hand, then your heart will also guide you. Offering help will feel light in the heart when it is the right thing to do, no matter what comments the brain may have. The heart may also show you a 'no' or caution to be engaged in this way. So without the mind/brain knowing yet, it may help the other person involved to be more independent and to be empowered to find their own solutions. Equally, this 'no' or caution may be for you, helping to drag you away from an important piece of work already in front of you, or not yet in front of you. Put simply, your heart already knows. The key is to use the infinite wisdom of your heart as often as possible.

In relation to any personal development or personal growth advice, or for that matter any advice given, there is an issue or dilemma to be aware of. Before looking at the heart's role and help, let us look at growth dilemmas.

Personal growth dilemmas

Dilemmas in planning for, or embarking on, any personal growth does not only lie in the advice given or help offered. Looking at a variety of dilemmas enables us to understand the importance of a deeper inner check-point. These dilemmas can include:

- Others giving or offering advice or help
- Looking at what others know and what we know; and
- Looking at the complexities within and around us.

Others giving or offering advice or help

It is wonderful and important to offer help and advice, and to act on it. It is perhaps one of the most beautiful aspects of being together, working with others, studying at school in a group, and in other family or team-like scenarios.

Without going into too much detail - as this is more the expertise of psychologists or related professions - any advice or help given is always influenced by the individual's own background, experience and specific set of circumstances. It is also impacted by what the person perceives as your set of circumstances or background.

Limitations of other people's advice become more obvious. A professional person or expert will have their own expertise and wealth of background and experience. However, even the most professional or experienced person can't know the full breadth and wealth of your experience or background. They have not lived your life or been a direct part of it. In some situations this distance and objectivity can work, in others it will work less or backfire.

To illustrate, the more that a person is a close or a long-standing friend, the more likely the person is to know a lot about you. The downside of this situation is that they may not be objective, and thus their assistance can be limited. A bigger picture perspective of a more professional, expert view may be missing.

You may ask, what if a close person is also a professional of some sorts? Some of the best shared ventures, home or work projects have been with experts who were also friends. When there is friendship there can be a fantastic synergy, but there can equally be a slackness, relaxedness and care-free approach. The friend/professional may not care about your project, instead preferring to concentrate more on those that pay more or feel more inclined to work harder for un-known others who pay the same.

'The path to hell is paved with good intentions' is a common expression that seems to want to tell us that best intentions, often based on a strong mind/brain, are not enough to do what is universally or long-term the best or to create good outcomes.

What others know and what we know

Close to this is an objective view around what we know and don't know. When you have the courage to include this view or reality in your personal or business planning, then, in some way, you can get to the point that knowledge, experience and insights are limited. They are never enough to make a really good decision and to know things will work in best possible ways.

Other people know some things well or are experts in particular areas. You may also have some additional knowledge to the expert. This part-knowing somewhat compels us to work together, to offer and give each other advice and help each other. However, when we restrict ourselves to rational mind/brain beings, it can be difficult to plan our lives and understand the full picture.

Our perception is a mind/brain activity. For example, in organisational strategic planning, often a combination of what was, what is now and what is hoped for or seen as 'could be', is part of the process. Not dissimilar, we can plan in some strategic way for our personal or whole-of-life growth.

Strategic planning is an interesting example. While it is clear that a group of people put their minds and brains together to look ahead, based on past experiences, data and other facts, it is also an attempt to look at what could be. It is perhaps in this synchronicity of minds and hearts that both sources of knowledge or knowing is accessed for longer-term, positive results. You can use strategic planning in a similar way with a small group of close friends or colleagues. Yet equally be aware of the limitations of what others know and what we really know. In everything let a strong heart be equally involved.

Looking at the complexities within and around us

Personal growth is naturally focussed on us, on the growth we can hope for, feel is within, see is possible, or wish to have. The opening to this chapter and the Kaleidoscope of Personal Growth indicate some of this complexity. Then there is the wonder of us, as human beings and the interconnectedness between us, and, the possible positive expressions of this inter-being, as humans, with each other, a community and the earth - all in support of life, human life and growth.

For some people's understanding the picture is even bigger than this. This complexity can only be perceived by the brain in parts and worked meaningfully into personal growth activities. The mind/brain can be a bit tricky here, too. As a simple example, you may build a personal growth plan on the experiences of your own, a friend's or an expert's past experiences, on what worked at another time. Not only has time changed, no situation is exactly equal to an earlier situation, even though certain aspects or principles will apply and work. How a family, work team, a community, the weather, stars or other external factors influence your planning is difficult to grasp; perhaps impossible for mind/brain only. With or without an active heart there is guidance, change and growth already somehow facilitated in the background. With an active heart you have a chance to tap into this more directly, purposefully and for your growth benefits.

Personal growth and our connectedness to all this is part of the complexity within which we exist. The complexity of personal growth, as part of a Kaleidoscope of Personal Growth, shows that solely relying on the linear ability of the mind/brain will only achieve limited and more linear results. It will much less likely bring in, utilise or capture processes that are interwoven, interconnected, have not happened yet or are layers within that are not accessible as yet.

The next brief PHT should give you in-sight into an inner unfolding that is taking place, sometimes regardless of levels of awareness or planning.

Practical Heart Tip 73: The now and then stocktake

Take a moment, in this present moment, to tune-in, feel and connect with who you are now: how you live, function emotionally, how you see others, how you live your life, how you interact with others and how caring, loving or supportive these interactions are. Write brief statements in your Heart Diary.

For a more complete perspective you can use some or all of the life sections covered in this book. If this list is not complete, then add other key aspects and qualities of your life to it. What are your truths and insights around this now? Spend 2-5 minutes on each life section.

Then go back 5, 10, 20 or more years of your life and look at you then, your insights, truths and qualities then. Only choose one of these suggested time spans at a time to keep it simple.

Do the entire PHT from the heart with heart strengthening beforehand and feeling your heart while you do it.

After you felt aspects/sections of your life you can by guided by questions like: How have I changed? How have insights, truths and personal qualities, behaviours or values changed? How is it now, compared to what you hoped for or expected it to be?

Make notes in your diary and repeat the PHT again after several months of heart practice.

You can combine this PHT with the KHH 15 'Grateful from the Heart' and spend some time letting your heart be grateful for what has changed in a positive way, for challenges that helped you grow, even for aspects of your life that are difficult and remind you to be the best you can be.

This PHT can show that changes take place and that the quality of our life and our insights have changed. Some will have changed as planned, some will be because of forced change, due to life circumstance or challenges, and some have come into our life as a surprise. Many good things can and do happen in life, coming from somewhere, which we don't exactly know or which are based on actions we did not connect with a positive change or outcome.

Looking at all this, it becomes clearer that actually neither us nor any experts know absolutely everything about personal growth. The heart guiding, feeling and helping, to add heart-intelligence to this overall equation, looks like a purposeful approach. Any heart input is likely to be valuable, more valuable than solely following a rational, limited-linear thinking mind and brain, in managing the complexity within and around us.

It is hoped that, in briefly discussing these dilemmas of personal growth, the existence of and the direct involvement of the heart will make more sense and in some way offer new perspectives of logic, logic of the consciousness and capabilities of your heart.

The heart's role in personal growth

Don't listen to anything but your heart. Jesse Martin

The young Australian Jesse Martin sailed around the world, solo, unassisted and non-stop at the age of 19. On a video clip he wrote the quote above. It is also on a picture card given to an admirer of his. His book had a related title 'Lionheart: A Journey of the Human Spirit'.

The main heart function in personal growth is that it offers you a facility to tune in and check what is right for you and what is not. It can guide you, help you and fulfil functions that are somewhat outside of what many would consider 'personal growth'.

Quality control

To make personal growth relevant for you, the heart can help to connect every aspect, input, idea and decision. This is the essential, important and overarching function of your heart, helping you with both planned and unplanned personal growth.

This quality control is a check of all aspects of your personal growth with the innermost core of you, your heart and your inner heart. This inner core or heart check will allow you to feel with your heart, run through your heart. Use the PHTs 31, 35 or 56) to empower your choices and empower you in accepting, adapting or rejecting any advice or help offered to you. This is holistic and structured and, with the mind/brain also involved, initiates the check.

In reality your heart is responding to everything that happens in your life. Where you really want to be - in any situation - is to use the heart by feeling it and feeling its very response to every event, suggestion, invitation or advice.

Initial heart feelings will be expansion, light feeling when something is good or the 'right' thing to do or follow. There will be pressure, heaviness or contraction of the heart feeling in other instances. In moments when you are in your heart, and when feeling it, too, there may also be no response at all. This means that you can do either or. In moments when you feel answers from your heart, do not stop feeling once you perceive an answer. Beyond initial feelings is the heart's ability to give profound and detailed answers. There can be a sequence of feelings from the heart showing you developments over time in relation to your questions or choices.

One example of this sequence of feeling was when I had planned to buy a new car. The car I wanted to buy was an older one and I realised I was a bit attached to having it. I rang a friend and asked her to feel whether the car was a good one to buy. After a few moments, connecting deeper to the heart and feeling it for some time she said: 'Good ... initially some pressure, but then good.'

At that time I had no idea what this meant. Following my own feeling in the heart, too, I bought the car. Two months later a major fault occurred in the engine and a $1,000 repair was needed. After four years it was time to sell the car again. There were no other significant repairs, I had hardly done any servicing and sold the car for a similar amount as it was purchased for, so overall the result was good for an item that normally loses a lot in value.

An additional inner check, quality control or safety check can be undertaken with your heart. This becomes a valuable ally to you in looking at any well-intended help or advice offered by others, and your own ideas. Using your heart brings you a deeper truth that your heart can realise and feel.

In this way the heart is a hugely empowering tool or ultimate inner wisdom check for things that are right for you, directions that feel right to take, and that no one else can know or feel for you.

This is based on the simple reality that no other life situation is identical to anyone else's, and that any advice given, with the best intentions or with the broadest experience-base or knowledge, will always be limited in some way.

Equally, one step towards maturity, responsibility and personal or spiritual growth is to become aware of moments or times when we 'outsource' our life. Outsourcing our life is tempting. It means we give away our responsibility in planning for our personal growth, and all that we do in our lives. There may be situations where the outsourcing has worked or will work, when the person helping, by chance or by their own heart-connection, has connected to a greater, broader truth or wisdom and things relating to their help will unfold positively.

The trap, however, is that this deeper understanding may not have been present, and things will not unfold so positively. In cases like this you are likely to struggle two-fold: with a challenging or difficult life situation, and with a lack of ownership of having made the decision in the first place.

When you follow your heart as best as possible, when you plan, decide and take action and all of this is connected in a clear and healthy way to you, then it will be easy to take responsibility and go through life positively and with a learning spirit or heart.

Personal growth is about you growing as a whole person. Whatever building blocks you believe or feel you are or have - mind/brain, body, emotional or feeling world, heart, spirit, soul - personal growth means the growth of all these parts of you in a positive, purposeful and truthful way.

The heart can additionally be of use, actively assisting personal growth through the following four functions: clarity, direct help, intelligence and connection.

Clarity

Living your life, moving continuously within your Kaleidoscope of Personal Growth, an innate ability to have clarity or access to clarity is important. The core clarity is emotional clarity, or an overall lightness of being that gives you a clarity of decision-making in all matters of personal growth.

It is emotional blurring or emotional attaching that interferes with the deeper inner realisation and heart abilities that already are guiding you, and want to fully guide you. The clarity, connection, lightness and purpose are priceless.

Emotional blurring means that in any period of time, or in any moment when decisions are made, or when you respond to an outside event that is related to personal growth, you will either not see it fully or your feeling will be blurred. It may be blurred by past heavy, unclear or burdening experiences that still cause a reaction, by parental or any other relational conditioning. It is this reaction that steers in a direction of growth that is not you, flying off course, or 'negative' growth, which is growth part-directed or driven by a difficult or painful experience.

Emotional attaching is very similar. The memory of uncleared emotion like 'wanting' or 'past hurt' will again influence what you plan for or what is brought to you. It will also impact what is happening in some way, where reaction is less pure than the clarity of action directed from the freedom of a light and cleared heart.

An overall heart-commitment will naturally lead to a clearer heart and therefore inner centre. From here the experience will be two-fold:

- Challenging and difficult situations will still allow you to see clearly, to feel clearly and with little or no emotion, offer an ability to extract the learning and to make good decisions regardless; and
- In daily life or when you plan for personal growth, you will be directed from the inner centre and your heart.

This means that all you plan for, and eventually embark on, will not only feel right, but will be a deeply-felt and wonderful set of experiences of change and growth.

Help and feeling

The heart's help is represented in the all-connecting key, your heart. It helps further in being able to recognise a greater truth every moment in life or when being given advice.

The heart has this ability to know, to recognise and to facilitate processes, such as the clearing of interfering influences. In this way an active, light and open heart is helping all the time.

This help is invaluable as it is then that the heart's help will be more available in all the functions. It will enable progressive clearing, remove obstacles, build bridges, facilitate and guide.

When your heart is actively helping, it provides a calmness as well as feelings of gentle joyfulness and the growing love for others. It will bring you to inner places of being that will give meaning and direction to your personal growth. This meaning will be from within, your core. This deeper joy, love, calmness and feeling will give a special, beautiful and truthful sense to personal growth, and exceed the ideas that are trends of the time, ideas of others, or ideas that are not fully agenda-free.

Intelligence

The refined or additional intelligence that your heart can offer you will allow you to use your heart more as the all-connecting tool. The active, 'intelligent' heart has the ability, like an alert mind and brain, to filter out information, to realise, and to make decisions.

It will take time to trust this form of intelligence. As you experience that guidance in this way from your heart, it is possible that you will use it with more intent and it can produce better personal growth results. The heart's perspective and guidance will always be according to the greatest possible picture. This may mean that heart-directed and heart-facilitated personal growth, where you listen to your heart, will not be as clear short-term, as it is in the medium to longer-term.

The insight, wisdom and intelligence are a part of the wonder of our human abilities and existence. Importantly, we all have been given an ability to use it.

What can this look like? Imagine that you make decisions about a workshop you know - in your mind/brain - and feel - in your heart - is good to attend. Others, even experts or 'wise' people around you, may oppose such a decision. However, it will only show over time that your choice was the truly wise one, for you and those around and close to you.

Connection - the four bridges

The heart will build four types of bridges that are an important part of your personal growth journey. Building a bridge means strengthening the heart and the connection to these four aspects. The connection to the bridges can grow over time, so can the dimensions of growth shown in the Kaleidoscope of Personal Growth.

The four bridges are to:

Bridge 1:   to your inner core, the real you;
Bridge 2:   to all the aspects of your personal growth shown in all the dimensions within the Kaleidoscope of Personal Growth;
Bridge 3:   to the social, physical and wider environment around you; and
Bridge 4:   to the Divine, the Creator or to the place/being of your understanding, faith or belief.

The first bridge, connecting your personal growth to your inner core, is important. For all personal growth, the heart is the centre and bridge of all you plan and do. Connecting you in your personal developments to the innate inner wisdom within, and to directions and guidance the heart feels, perceives and connects, is essential. This bridge will give the personal inner-most meaning to what growth is and means to you.

The second bridge is in linking your personal growth to all the aspects of your personal growth, as outlined in the Kaleidoscope of Personal Growth. The vast spectrum of options, the vast possibilities of direction that the kaleidoscope shows, require an equally vast depth of intelligence and bridge-building. Therefore, all the components, tailored to your growth and learning, can be connected, tied together, loosened or whatever is needed. A strong heart can do this well: it will help you with what to focus on. It will balance several aspects at once or over time, and it will facilitate heart-centred growth, ultimately connecting the important parts to the inner core and to the outer influences and environment. This will occur in a constant moment to moment flow of growing joy, calmness, peace-of-knowing and love. These qualities will be feel-able to you and your heart. The peace-of-knowing will be a heart-felt peace, of all that is connecting up between the growth levels. It will provide a degree of confidence and trust that will become increasingly unshakeable by outside events and the ups and downs of life.

The third bridge is connecting your personal growth to the social, physical and wider environment. The heart has an inner and an outer focus. Focus means the heart will bring together 'what can be and what is' in you, with 'what can be and what is', in your social, physical and wider environments. This connecting can be via your heart showing you a resource, a person or an event that feels good to engage with as part of your personal development plans. It could also be your heart showing you to behave in a certain way, when you interact with the environment around you, for the best outcomes. Your heart will facilitate, nurture and grow the radiant, gentle feelings of joy, calmness, peace-of-knowing and love. At home, personal goals of more kindness, love and support for each other will be realised more easily. Similarly, at work or in social settings, your radiance will make it easier for others to connect, approach you, and for you to naturally grow a support-team.

The fourth bridge, connecting your personal growth to the Divine, the Creator, or to the place/being of your belief, is a type of connection that is discussed and illustrated in more detail in the next chapter on spiritual growth. Within this fourth bridge is the notion that the universe works in a particular way. It is perhaps sufficient to realise that this connection is of meaning and purpose and that the heart knows, or knows better than the mind/brain. Any universal meaning may be a set of universal rules, a place where people aspire to be in the life beyond life. Or it may be experienced through the guidance, love, direction and support given by a Creator, God or Divine Being of someone's choosing. The heart is deeper than belief, given it is a more refined 'tool 'and a connector, offering a truth, that can be beyond logic, rational thought and anything the mind or brain can perceive, hope for or do.

If there are such things as universal rules, then the connection to these in your planning, and pursuit of personal growth, would be quite meaningful.

Daynis's story perhaps is one example of such rules. When you work in a certain way, as he did initially at McDonald's, then the support from other people around you will be limited. Lack of attention, focus and commitment to a role will create, universally, a poor response from others. However, friendly, committed and knowledgeable customer service followed in his second role, once he began to live from the heart. How can the heart, connecting to a place of spiritual or heart-recognition, be of help in your personal growth? Similarly, how can the heart's connection to the Divine be of any significance? Put simply, any personal growth that is aligned to the will, love, wisdom and support from an all-knowing Creator or Divine Being, must have more support - to be helped, and to facilitate personal growth of greater depth and longevity.

Over 15 years ago my own marriage fell apart. It was perhaps the most difficult time of my life.

For several years there has been discussions, counselling and other attempts to remedy the marriage. Two still quite young children were also involved. Without a doubt it was the most heart-wrenching time of my life. This was not even the hardest part. Feeling the suffering of the children was even worse. I remember times, not really having a particular belief, when I would look up and say or pray 'please help to make sense of this all'. The level of distraught was deep. Especially after tens of years of welfare and counselling, natural therapy work, teaching meditation and helping others. There had been a hope that personal development and all-of-life would have been more progressed and free of this level or pain. It was at that time a dear friend sat with me and said 'better learn some Reiki'... and 'you need some Divine guidance'. It was at this moment, with the mind/brain surrendering, that the heart understood something. Three to six months later opportunities for heart-learning surfaced, and gradually a deeper sense and guidance grew.

The heart's ability to help has been referred to extensively in spiritual, holy and religious books, not in accordance with any particular belief, but in line with the mystics of these sources or beliefs which transcended to a higher, deeper and more compassionate form or understanding and being.

Strengthening your heart and you

Starting to refer to these deeper and more refined abilities of the heart, through more in-depth practices and more commitment to your heart, will facilitate these abilities and functions.

This section's KHH consists of the introduction of a 'simple heart meditation' that can be used to give strength to the heart, and to achieve a natural and personal balance. This will balance the training of your mind, with a greater influence from the heart.

You can give it a different term than meditation if you prefer. You can call it 'sitting-in-silence', 'sitting in-heart-space', 'sitting in heart-felt feelings', 'heart-intelligence activation', or any other name. What it is named is not important. What does matter, is to bring together your current experiences with the previous KHHs and supporting PHTs, to deepen your heart-connection, and all that your heart is longing to give in return.

Key Heart Help 12: Simple heart meditation

This KHH combines the KHH 6 'Heart Strengthening', with a couple of extras, to turn it into a heart-centred or heart-based meditation. You will also find extra pointers and tips that can assist this meditation.

It may look simple, yet you will very likely find that meditating using the heart is much easier than focussing on a place, an item such as a candle, a dot on the wall, or on a point of the body. Popular places are the centre of the forehead, the nostrils, or the flow of the breath. Why is this so? Focussing on something will calm the mind, which is one of the great goals of meditation. Then you need to ask what is next? If only if the mind is calm, then you want to be somewhere else. Different meditation approaches talk about the heart as something deep, yet they use the mind to do all. With the heart becoming an equal if not greater player in this, in meditation, the growing and feelable peace, joy and love will make it easy, eventually much easier, to be in this meditation.

The combination of the heart strengthening, then adding a period of sitting in silence and feeling the heart and following the feeling, works well. This expands the heart, strengthens the heart, and allows us to go deeper into the full depth of the heart.

Fuller depth of the heart is written here to indicate that the heart has many layers, and that the meditation today can deepen the next day, and for years to come. Feeling deeper into the heart also means that you are living with more heart, and all the heart's abilities will grow and be more available to you. You will be more aware of what the heart is and how it works in more detail. With it you will feel more of the positive heart feelings too.

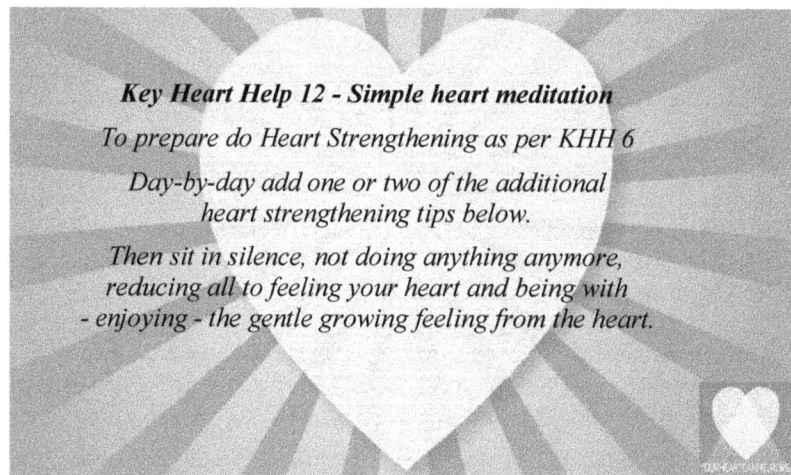

Key Heart Help 12 - Simple heart meditation

To prepare do Heart Strengthening as per KHH 6

Day-by-day add one or two of the additional heart strengthening tips below.

Then sit in silence, not doing anything anymore, reducing all to feeling your heart and being with - enjoying - the gentle growing feeling from the heart.

How to improve your heart meditation

Here are a few more practical tips that you can include, one at a time, in your sitting in silence, sitting with heart, inner calm, or meditation with heart practice. In sections II - V and in the family section these heart supporting approaches were discussed:

The natural way the heart works the best is if:
- You don't do anything else;
- You have an attitude of 'letting go'; and
- You just let this natural heart-process unfold.

The full KHH 12 - Simple heart meditation

Relax your body and mind before you start. Create a quite environment. Then:

- *Start with one of the relaxation techniques from PHT 19, 44 or 45;*
- *Do Heart Strengthening as per KHH 6; then*
- *Then sit in silence, not doing anything anymore, reducing all to feeling your heart and being with - enjoying - the gentle growing feeling from your heart.*

To deepen your experience, day-by-day add one or two of the additional heart strengthening tips below to support this Simple Heart Meditation:

- *Remember the keys are to 'relax and smile' in the best way that is possible now. Often the body is holding some tension that you are not fully aware of. Utilise and regularly repeat the relaxations provided. Downloading an audio version from www.yourheartcanhelp.org will allow you to close your eyes and have a less stimulated mind/brain.*

- *Smiling freely is not easy and some would say not normal. It is not ... initially. Most of us need extra help. Use a mirror and look at the smile you do when you meditate and smile to your heart. Repeat exactly the same smile. Then ensure that you have the best possible smile that feels as natural as possible and as free as possible, too. Practise in front of the mirror and then 'export it', that same smile and feeling, to your meditation spot or when you do this KHH.*

- *Focussing, watching (inner observation), trying more, helping the heart and other good ideas or additional heart helpers invented by you or others are in most cases activities of the mind/brain or mind/brain activating. Let the heart do it more and more. Feel more, when you find yourself doing some of these extras, let go, relax more and come back to the free, gentle, natural, even slightly joyful smile.*

- *When the feeling in your heart is becoming gentler, sweeter, expanding slightly or continuously, when gentle joy arises and when any thought processes are minimal or even not present for periods of time, you know you are on the right track.*

It is somewhat remarkable how we can discount or reduce benefits for ourselves, even though we really want it or long for benefits, growth, joy and other wonderful feelings. One more approach that can help is pretending being on camera or 'TV smile'.

*Practical Heart Tip 74: The TV smile ***

Follow the heart strengthening instructions, your efforts in doing Heart Meditation, or any of the KHHs as if you were on camera or national television.

Use any similar 'scenario' that works for you. In this way you will add an additional positive trigger to improve your smile. It will work for you, your heart, your personal growth and in a heart-way for others around you too. When the joy from your heart is clear enough, in moments you connect to it, then it is good to use triggers like this less.

Feelings that you are likely to experience over time are a deepening of any wonderful, gentle or joyful feeling flowing from the heart and gradually flowing through other parts of the body; then the whole body; and growing from there. At the same time you may be experiencing some cleansing every now and then too.

In all situations, what will always help is to remember that while you do this KHH, the two keys are to relax fully, smile freely, and not to add anything else to the practice.

If you have any additional or better 'ideas' or if you have some 'fantastic or creative' thoughts of how you can do it differently, you know which part of you this is: your mind/brain.

There will be thoughts coming up as you sit. This is very normal. Seasoned meditators hope that all thoughts will cease, so that a deeper level of inner being can be achieved. These are often associated with steps towards an overall higher being.

Your heart's intelligence in helping and actively assisting in our personal growth has several angles. It can facilitate and actively help. It also coordinates, filters, guides, and has its own ability to recognise, know, build bridges and connect.

This KHH will not only give strength to your heart in a sequential or linear way. Every time you practise it, the clearing, deepening and growing ability to facilitate all personal growth aspects will be enhanced. All other aspects discussed in previous main sections of the book will also be impacted, due to the complexity, wonder and win-win nature of the heart.

The heart strengthening will give strength to your heart and all its doing, connecting and perceiving. It will also strengthen you. A strong heart will make you more resilient to life's natural ups and downs. You will feel more clarity in easy-flowing, and challenging situations, and as your heart-focussed life progresses. You will feel the gentle and beautiful feelings in your heart all the time. This is what one part of personal development can be like. It allows you to have a wonderful, sweet, productive and potential fulfilling life, facilitated by all parts of who you are, including the profound abilities of your heart.

Heart-centred personal growth

Personal growth can be heart-centred and heart-supported. The more your heart's potential is realised, the more purposeful and wonderful your personal growth will also be.

The complexity of the Kaleidoscope of Personal Growth makes it clear that a multitude of drivers, directions, areas and pulls - helpers, friends or parents - exist. Each of them can support or hinder personal growth.

The wonder of the heart is that no matter what your life situation is now, no matter what your foundation or disposition is, the heart has an immense ability. This ability may be clearly active, or more passive, in an 'undercurrent-kind-of-way'.

The heart's intelligence, together with its ability to facilitate, can connect all the personal growth dots. It can connect the dots better within you, and in interaction with the world around you. What the heart does is to connect all that back to you, to your inner-most centre, the core of who you are. Being your centre of feeling, the heart makes sense and gives an assurance that no one else can give.

Personal growth is not personal growth when you live life through the experiences or successes of others. These others may be heroes, celebrities or mentors, guides, coaches, life coaches, a good friend or authors of self-help books. The personal growth, facilitated by the heart, will also gradually free you from these dependencies, patterns or the use of others as replacement-experiences or crutches.

Growing up at the level of the heart is in some respects like growing up from children to adults. Learning about the heart provides us with the ultimate guidance or verification-tool within, which makes life more do-able. There is a freedom within this, too - an emancipation or freedom in a deep, spiritual and life-supporting sense. You will be able to make all decisions from this place of inner freedom, and experience true personal growth - related to you and a deeper core of you.

When your decisions, outside guidance and support from others connect to the real you, based on an innate inner tool, then overall responsibility - or the ability to better respond and be response-able in all sorts of life situations, is an empowering and profound gift worth realising and using.

Sailing around the world at a young age in harsh conditions may or may not be the true and real following of the heart. On the one hand, it could be the following of ambition, an inner lack of worth, and a desire. On the other hand, it could be an illustration of a person guided by, and following, their heart. For this reason, it is important for you to regularly check your heart, to see that you are following a path that is supported and directed by your heart.

Being really empowered by your heart, and following the heart in action, means to achieve new levels of freedom and independence within, in all that is personal growth. It is perhaps that only from this refined level of freedom that a truer purpose of growth can be 'seen', felt and realised. From the perspective of the heart, this freedom also means to make choices that represent and show a mature, clear and life-enhancing responsibility. You will be independent and interdependent, able to relate to others with clarity and from your heart centre. Engagement at profound levels will be possible and more natural, including the ability to help others and to accept help. Your personal growth will become a 'team effort' without inner compromise that is unclear, disruptive, hurtful or unsupportive.

When the heart is strong and clear, then the role of others can be realised at a quite deep level. The role of others, even if they are our parents, mentors or guides, is more enjoyable, has meaning where there is meaning, and all else can be filtered out by the heart, often in light and joyful ways.

Life often repeats in patterns. When one watches one's own life carefully and with awareness, then repeat patterns of learning are obvious. At times these patterns are enjoyable. In most instances, however, these patterns mean some form of pain, letting go or a tougher life segment is happening right now.

With the help from the heart in all areas of personal growth, people have gradually experienced that life's tough lessons are valuable, and even enjoyable at a deeper inner realisation-level. Most important, perhaps, the lessons can be seen and realised, and any painful effects can be minimised. The more that the heart melts away inner-held blockages and wrong concepts and beliefs then the more a natural flow can follow supporting your growth and, in the wisdom of your heart, all around you, too.

In looking again at the Kaleidoscope of Personal Growth, it is your heart that is taking care of the connection of all that you plan, do and achieve. It will also provide balance to the inner core of who you are, the real you, your heart and inner heart in ways otherwise hard to achieve.

From this core or being the heart reaches out and facilitates. Over time it ensures an inner unfolding, the realisation of inner, perhaps not-yet known abilities, or important aspects of you. In turn it will nurture inner realisations which are ultimately the growth that you are and can be.

Personal growth with more heart enhances our ability to tap into inner guidance and wisdom. If we are faced with apparently conflicting directions, conflicting choices or conflicting focus areas in life, the heart offers an additional tool to use. Lower level wants, hopes and desires are replaced with heart-realisations and insights. These realisations lift life, personal growth and the interconnectedness of all, to levels of growing enjoy-ability and individual balance. They also support the connection to people close to us, dear to us, or affected by our personal growth decisions.

The real secret

Within this heart-helped personal growth approach lies a greater secret or 'the real secret'. It is a commonly held beliefs are around whatever you plan for, belief in and push hard enough for, will be achievable. This may be true and yet, you are moving within a small circle that does not include the heart or inner heart's wisdom and ability to connect all. These goals and aspirations are often children of the mind and therefore limited.

Your heart has an innate, often so easily accessible, and huge potential to facilitate and offer you a bigger picture in the form of feeling, realising and gradually being taken there by the heart's very unfolding. Then the heart will facilitate, as the hub, the connection of your plans, goals and aspirations to the inner-most core of who you are. It is only then that deepest forms of happiness and fulfilment and love can happen. No earthly achievements will change the way you feel, unless they touch, open and deepen how your heart, as the centre of feeling, will be and feel. In using your heart in your growth plans and efforts you will be quality assured and any planning, working towards goals, and being in the joy of moving closer your goals and inner realisations in parallel, is a profoundly exquisite journey. It will further be meaning, fulfilling and you will be successful at the same time. The happiness and fulfilment your heart wants to facilitate will always be more than any other part of you can plan for, hope for or aspire to.

When personal growth becomes shared growth, when you realise more, grow and offer insights relating to your growth to others, then all 'personal' growth becomes an even deeper experience of joy, connection and synchronicity. Growth then is nurtured within a refined or realised mind/brain and heart unity. It involves the growth of oneself, the growth of family or close friends, and the growth of the communities around us, directed towards a better, more heart-centred world.

Summary - heart-facilitated personal growth

Your heart can guide and facilitate growth. Your heart is a part of you which, with its unique intelligence and ability, can recognise, facilitate and connect all the dots in your personal growth spectrum. It adds another tool, if not the missing ingredient, to your personal growth efforts. In a practical sense the heart can help in these ways:

1. Understanding and realising that the heart is an inner quality control tool is important. The more that you use your heart, the clearer the difference between mind/brain and mind/brain/heart planning, pursuing of goals will become.

2. The 'Kaleidoscope of Personal Growth' has one practical function: to reflect on any past personal growth and equally on current personal growth plans, aspirations and steps-in-motion. It helps to align them with your mind/brain and heart-understanding. The key is to appropriately include the heart and its innate wisdom.

3. Personal growth efforts, in the same way as life itself, is not without challenges, difficulties or problems. The PHT 'Problem first aid' allows you to stop, connect to the heart, and use the heart in re-aligning your personal growth direction, efforts, or both.

4. The PHT 'The now and then stocktake' invites you to do a brief and yet detailed inventory of how you perceive life and how you live it. The key within this is to also feel and assess how you interacted with others then, with what qualities and how do you interact and work with others now. This is a powerful tool to view yourself, any changes, and to give them a heart-centred, heart-helped direction.

5. KHH 12 'Simple heart meditation' is one of the key practices that will offer you access to the heart's infinite depth and ability to help. The more you give quality attention to your heart, the more quality time you sit deeply in heart connection, the more the layers of your heart can open, unfold and offer its full potential - to your growth and all your life's aspects.

6. The PHT 'The TV smile' is a light exercise to improve the smiling. Smiling more freely and really stretching the lips will make a difference. It will give an extra boost to your heart and in turn will deepen your 'heart times' or 'heart meditations'.

7. When faced with the opinions of others your heart provides the ultimate way of quality control. Do this in the ways suggested in the PHTs 31, 35 and 56 which are all about getting answers from the heart. It is the planned or on-the-go way of using your heart. Use your heart every moment and in any personal growth situation by feeling it, and feeling your heart's very response to any event, suggestion, invitation or advice.

8. The heart can assist your personal growth in an active and passive way. Commitment to your heart naturally engages the heart more. The active help will be through an ability to clearly recognise a heart-felt truth when faced with situations, when being given advice, or when planning. Passive heart help will be in the form of clearing of all internal interferences and of reactions to outer influences, where the reaction interferes.

9. Overall, the clarity of your heart will directly support your personal growth in four ways or 'bridges', which can be strengthened, renovated, built or re-built.

10. The first bridge will be to directly connect your personal growth to your inner core. This will mean a connection of all your personal developments to the innate inner wisdom, and to a centre within that can guide, lead and give direction. This bridge will give the personal inner-most meaning to what growth is and means to you.

11. The second bridge involves your Kaleidoscope of Personal Growth. The heart will lead you to and through the vast spectrum of options and possibilities. It will tailor your growth and learning to what is needed, in accordance with your heart. Peace-of-knowing will be a heart-felt peace. It will equally be a confidence and trust that becomes increasingly unshakeable by outside events and life's ups and downs.

12. The third bridge is the connection to the social, physical and wider environment. This will connect you, the core of you, not solely to the world around you, but also to a fuller potential in you.

13. The fourth bridge is the connection of your personal growth to a Divine Being, the Creator, or to a holy place of your belief, from which you receive guidance, purpose, love and support. Within this bridge will be your heart-realisations of the universe working in particular ways, providing a clear meaning and purpose to all of existence. This universal meaning, from where you are now, may be a set of universal rules, a place where people aspire to be in the life beyond life, or the guidance, love, direction and support given by a Creator, God or Divine Being of someone's choosing.

The heart's help here is of a different nature, as it has the capacity to perceive more than what the mind/brain can. It bridges the world here and now, to the world or realm of belief. It recognises higher places and higher guidance. In a way that is a more refined tool or connector to a truth - a truth that lies beyond logic and rational thought. If there are such things as universal rules, higher places and a benevolent, loving Creator, then the connection to these in your planning for and pursuit of personal growth, would be profoundly meaningful.

Chapter 8
Spiritual Growth - Feeding the Light Within

And as we let our own light shine, we unconsciously give other people permission to do the same.
As we are liberated from our own fear, our presence automatically liberates others.
Nelson Mandela

Spiritual development or spiritual growth for some is very important. For others it is an unusual, uncomfortable topic. This may be because spiritual matters concern the non-physical and are harder to grasp. Spiritual growth is about different kinds of growth of a deep, inner nature that is potentially, and in reality, hard to measure. Because of this it is often a matter of hope, aspiration or belief and as such can vary from person to person, group to group, culture to culture.

Spirituality can be closely related to 'religion'. It can be within religion entirely or partly, or be non-religious, or a blend of both. It can also be related to the knowledge, experience or expertise of a holy person, a saint, minister or monk. While it is more than natural for some to have such an expert or trusted person in their life, as in personal growth, there are risks. One is that some form of imbalance occurs that a fraction too much responsibility and inner truth is outsourced or handed to someone else, who ultimately can't live life for you. The other is that even though solutions are offered, the person offering advice may actually not know if their advice will take you closer to the goal, a higher truth, enlightenment, the Divine or God.

Kent's story is a beautiful amalgamation that shows the longing within unfolding, guidance that is around us, trust in a feeling within and changing direction and career. He also shares how more heart and clarity came into his life.

When I met Kent I was surprised by his kindness and calmness. Kent had left his career, trade and training and bought, against some people's advice, a small and comparatively unsuccessful alternative gift and bookshop.

We stayed in touch over several years. Apart from running his own business it became clear that Kent had an interest in healing and spiritual exploration of different traditions and faiths. His interest was deep and his research meticulous. In a short time the choice of books in the shop had grown into a substantial and diverse range. The bookshop had also become quite successful.

There had been difficulty in Kent's early life. His family was of a particular faith that did not allow anyone to look outside this framework. In time, Kent was dis-fellowshipped, losing contact with his family and childhood community, of which he had been an integral part.

In sharing, Kent mentioned that from a young age he always had a spiritual interest and felt inquisitive in this direction.

Kent's Story:

'In my teenage years I began having unusual physical and also non-physical experiences. Many times I found myself, or some part of me, leaving my body and having certain non-physical experiences while retaining normal awareness. These experiences were a completely new experience and outside my past learning. They intrigued, excited and propelled me into a search for meaning and for understanding of these unusual happenings.'

'I had trained to be an electrician but decided to leave this profession to travel. The central and most profound experience was the chance meeting with a man in the UK who I ended up living with. This friendship restored a lot of trust in life and faith in the better attributes of human nature. It was in many ways a healing time.'

'I strongly remember the amount of love I felt he had for me, for others and the times he spent in silence, being topped up from some invisible well. He spent enormous amounts of time with me, helping me from a psychological and spiritual perspective. All this help was given freely and without condition, with an understanding that something deeper was unfolding in this exchange.'

'He had extraordinary insight or vision. At the time I was not sure what it was. He shared with me many things that he felt or knew about me, which he could not have known about me or my family. These insights and new perspectives helped me a lot to come to terms with the path that I was choosing, and the loss of family that I had experienced. Looking back now on my life I can see that he had some specific insight about certain events detailing the direction of my life.'

'The time in London was very healing and mind-opening, however in leaving, an old feeling of separation and loneliness appeared, not in any obvious way, but in some place not easily defined, like a spiritual ache or knowing that still, something was missing.'

'In the 10 or so following years, I encountered a lot of varied spiritual practices. There was intensity, excitement, laughter, tears and funny stories. What still eluded me was the peace, the calmness and the sweetness of feeling, which at that time still, was unknown and inaccessible to me. This experience, a more continuous and sweeter feeling at a finer vibration, was just around the corner.'

'When I first came across the heart meditation, its simplicity surprised me. It was very light and gentle so there was some initial scepticism that such a practice could really touch some of the more deeply held and repressed things in me.'

'However, in a short time, I felt changes that were going very deep. Over time I came to understand that love is the most revealing of all energies. I realised and felt that through the heart the Divine Blessing is working and that the less that I do, the more it is that happens. It became a sweet, gentle surrendering to this love, to this gentle energy, that restored that deep sense of peace and feeling of connectedness.'

> *'The practice was natural, real and gentle. The healing that happened was deep. Before starting heart practices and workshops, I had awareness of many physical problems and also energetic ones. These issues started to lessen, many of them disappeared completely.'*
>
> *'My life always had felt it was given for some spiritual purpose, and now, through regular meditation, that deeper peace was emerging. The peace was also the knowing in my heart that there is no need to look anywhere else other than in my heart and to let the heart, be the eyes through which I live and share in this life and world.'*
>
> *'I had searched for so long, read many books, but now I was experiencing the answers close and direct, in my heart. It was more than a glimpse that other practices, meditations and healing approaches had offered. It was becoming a continuous day to day reality, not some mysterious blessing bestowed at some unknowable moment, which, by the way, I remain very grateful for. Life is more solid now. There is an inner knowing, an almost permanent exquisiteness of feeling and beauty, to be shared with others.'*

Not long after learning about the heart, Kent felt so deeply moved that he started to offer workshops in his home town of Hobart, inviting friends and family. He began to share in his community by offering a weekly heart practice and heart meditation in the rooms above his second book and gift shop.

With no paid or any significant advertising, Hobart's Lotus Centre now runs over forty weekly heart practice sessions and meditations. Fifteen of these are visible online and for the wider community, the others are for intermediate or advanced heart practitioners. Hobart has become one of the most thriving heart-learning centres in the western world.

Several years into Kent's heart practice he learnt that his father had fallen ill and it was clear that he would soon pass away. Kent was invited for the first time to see his father again. He later shared how he sat with his father, heart to heart, reconciling all the pain and hurt we feel when we separate, cut off - which both hearts feel, whether you are cut off or you are the one being cut off. It was deeply touching to hear and to feel the peace that both were able to share and hold in these special moments and while his father passed away. Kent felt that he was able to help in the way of the heart even during this time.

What is hoped for in this next section is for some demystification of spiritual growth, for heart-centred spiritual growth to be something tangible, feel-able and normal, as a natural and beautiful extension of your personal growth.

Starting from you, as a person, as an individual, there is often already some awareness or feeling of the existence of something deeper within, or that which you are part of. This may or may not be coupled with a longing to grow, to be connected or to be part of something bigger. This something may be described as a spiritual goal, aspiration or a belief. Life sometimes shows that spiritual experiences, a spiritual existence, is part of the very nature of who we are.

> *Some examples of this can be that you connect to a person, a situation or a feeling within in ways that only you know is special and it is normally hard to find words to express this. The birth of a child, the passing of a loved one or other key events often hold those feelings within.*
>
> *An example is that you may think of someone and that person walks around the corner, or sends a text or calls you. Different individuals have tried to explain these occurrences as being 'synchronicity'.*
>
> *To explain this, to open a connection to this, in corporate heart workshops I regularly invite people to think of, or more so, feel their age. What is interesting is that around half the group say their real and current age, while the other half starts to connect with an inner age and come up, usually, with an age range between 17 and 25. To understand what is happening here it is important to know that the average age in these groups is often around 40 to 45 years of age.*
>
> *Another example is when you love, admire, adore or simply have a very dear and close friend. In moments when the feeling is deep, sweet and wonderful, the feelings of beauty, lightness of being, of connection, awe and love are way beyond what logic or physical being of this other represent. This can be combined with feelings of deep connection, much deeper than mind/brain logic can explain, and even like or love can express; it's a connection of heart, spirit, soul, of something deep within.*

Spiritual growth may be about esoteric, religious, out-there, inner-deeper, untouchable and unreachable matters. It doesn't have to be. What the heart offers is two-fold:

- Spiritual growth as a step-by-step exploration and opening of all the layers of your heart and the spirit within its core; and
- Opportunities to realise and live spirituality, as a down-to-earth heartfulness in normal, daily, tangible and experience-able aspects of life.

In its gentleness the heart offers you a choice to focus on neither of the above two items, on the first or on second one, or on both. What is shown as part of this chapter is that in the moments when your heart grows, the spirit within also grows. This is spiritual growth and it happens organically, naturally.

> *In a sense, in moments when you use your heart you fulfil a spiritual aspect of you no matter what you or others hope for, believe or have experienced.*

This is a more direct, down-to-earth, real-life and empowered access to a rounded or more holistic growth. This more integrated growth, once the heart is actively involved, realising and facilitating, becomes a new quality of life experience. This is ultimately your experience and fulfilment.

You may connect to the example above using this PHT 'Feel your inner age' from section IV. It is just one way to feel that there is another part within that is learning and knowing. When you do this PHT you naturally want to intend to feel the age and then let go. You know your physical age, the day and year you were born. This PHT works well when you are relaxed and not agitated by emotion or under pressure. These are moments when your mind/brain is less dominant and another feeling or reality emerges. This age that many people then feel is often younger, between 16 and 25 years.

Your heart, so directly related to 'spirit' as a quality, word or understanding, has already started to help you in earlier KHHs, PHTs and exercises. In all the previous chapters, in particular in chapter IV the heart has been described in this way in more detail.

Using your heart more in daily life, you will grow and develop more fully as a person. Every moment you use your heart in the way it is designed to help, your spirit will respond positively. You and your spirit at the core of your heart grow. You grow spiritually.

What is spiritual growth?

The heart offers a simple and yet profound and empowering perspective and approach to your spiritual growth. The heart is you. The heart is one of the key elements of who you are. Every natural or positive involvement of all parts will nurture all your learning and growth, including in spiritual matters.

The depth and unique abilities of your heart can help your spiritual growth plans, efforts, hopes or beliefs. The heart is gentle, personal and you can add more heart to your practices, meditations, affirmations or prayers and it will only ever refine, purify and beautify them.

Spiritual growth can be threatening. It can be the powerful expression of ideas, concepts, hopes or beliefs, often written in some important book or document, which, when you are not sure or don't believe it, produces pressure - internally or externally caused. This can be from a family member, friend or social group, or pressure felt within due to the lack of feeling the same way as people around you.

Commonly understood spiritual growth is often mixed in with a dominant view, an established religion, or spiritual cultural practices that have evolved over a long time and things are 'just done this way'. To the heart some may make sense, others may not. Some also clearly, when feeling with the heart, do not feel so meaningful, helpful or truthful.

As you would use a word-processor these days for writing most of your documents, it can be similar to existing spiritual practices. Just because they are old does not mean they are truthful. Like a typewriter they may be out of date, no longer aligned with a greater or Divine truth, a truth our heart can feel and align to.

Then again, at times to write a document on paper with a nice pen or to get an old manual type-writer out may just be the right thing to do. In this way, how to be spiritual is what connects you to a greater truth, a truth that can be verified, followed by your heart, whether it is an old way of doing things or whether it has never been done before ... in your heart or centre of your heart you know. This, even most holy books state.

Spiritual growth with heart is simply the growth of the spirit that resides in the heart. It is how you live life with more heart expressed in your interactions with others, thoughts, attitudes, behaviours and in your meditations, prayers. In return your heart can grow even more. This gives meaning to life on earth and the way it can be lived using heart, mind/brain and body.

In some way this is just another idea or concept being given. True. There is also the chance to look at holy books, personal development books, poetry and music where you find this reference to the deep and important nature of life. It resonates well with the heart, too, and with its functions: the heart as the core to feeling, growth as well as deep, beautiful and helpful connections to others and to the Divine, as the key to spiritual growth. Again, even if you complete your own piece of research here, in some way it is largely mind/brain knowledge.

This may help as mind/brain and heart work together. The stronger your heart, the more you will start to feel a resonance, a feeling in your heart. This is, when the feeling is gentle, expansive and light, your heart showing you direction of growth and truth.

It is the heartful, beautiful, joyful feelings facilitated by your heart that are transformative. With the feelings comes a growing love for self and others. There is a realisation that spiritual growth and the overall growth of who you are, in connection to others, is directly related to your heart.

If you aren't sure about where you stand in all this, whether you have a spiritual vein within, whether you feel to, want to or not want to grow spiritually, perhaps this following 'check' can offer some clarity or direction.

One PHT or exercise can help. When you connect to where you want to be at the end of this life, which we know is one of the natural events or outcomes in life, it can help, even in a simple way, to gently bring a spiritual element into daily life.

> **Practical Heart Tip 75: End-of-life check**
>
> *Relax and ideally do some heart strengthening before starting to ensure both heart and mind/brain are involved.*
>
> - *Without thinking too much write your intended achievements on a piece of paper, in an electronic file or in your Heart Diary. Be spontaneous; and*
>
> - *Write five to 10 statements.*
>
> *Then feel, realise and reflect on what you want to or feel to do - including in terms of spiritual development - to move in this direction, or to be there, at the end of your life.*

You may or may not feel to do this. Contemplating the end of life, even though it is a clear reality, is not everyone's 'cup of tea'. You may want to come back to it later. After a few weeks or months of regular heart practice you may become comfortable with this PHT. In your heart you can realise a bigger picture. It is natural that we are born and that we die. Mind and brain alone cannot make sense of this. When all of you 'work' together then life and death simply become one larger, realised and well-arranged picture or plan. Repeat this PHT, too, as you may feel after a second or third time that your priorities, goals and insights are changing.

The empowering heart-way of spiritual growth

There is something that just feels right or natural about being empowered, feeling in control of your life. In health services this has found a strong expression in what researchers or experts call 'social determinants of health'. What this approach and related research has found is that when people have a sense of control in their lives their health issues or challenges improve equally, or even more so than targeted medical interventions.

It is not the place here to start any new arguments or discussion. The best is of course to have excellent health care and medical intervention available to you and to also feel and in reality be empowered to make decisions that affect your health, wellbeing and your life. The common way of spiritual growth, in the absence of clear and direct access to your heart, is often not very empowering.

The moment another significant, 'important person' or expert is involved, or becomes the key figure, there is a risk that either you give them more power than they perhaps should have or they claim more power, based on their position, age, role or perceived experience. If you are lucky this will work.

This common way to pursue the fulfilment of an innate and inner longing to grow is flawed. You would not walk down the street, ask any retired person how to raise your child and then just do it that way. In the same way, it is not the best to listen to any self-declared spiritual leader, nor to any spiritual leader or teacher that society has put in front of you, and then to automatically trust in all matters completely or totally. A spiritual teacher in the form of a friend, older person, a guide or religious leader.

The 'Common Way of Spiritual Growth Support' figure also shows that the heart or deeper 'inner heart' is being used on the side, only partially, and if the mind/brain is very strong or has been developed with a lot of focus, then the heart has no role at all.

Figure 19: Common way of spiritual growth support

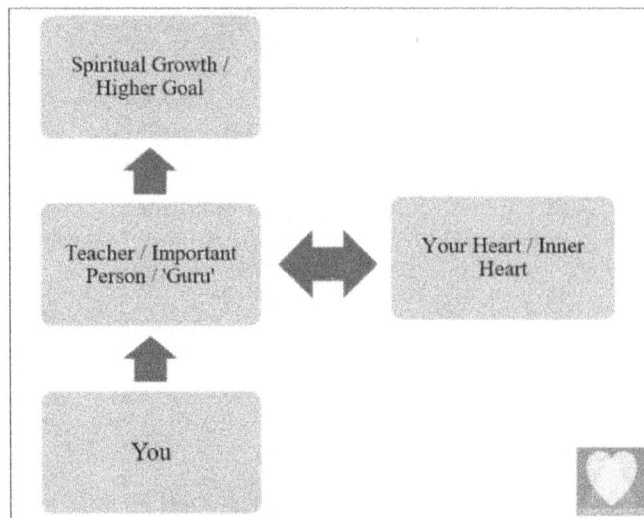

In this model there is a risk to give the teacher, guru or important person too much power or influence. If another person or group comes into your life, s/he may also potentially have significant influence. This may happen in a subtle way or not be obvious. This risk is real whether you are aware that influence is happening or not.

Even in 'good' situations, where, say, 90% of all advice given is good, or good for a vast majority of individuals, it may not be good or right for you. Even if 10, 5 or less percent is good or truthful, then in spiritual matters this can sometimes be celebrated as a huge success. When a teacher doesn't really know, does not have the experience, or worse, has an agenda of their own, then there is trouble: potential for dependency is high, for feeling dis-empowerment and risking not seeing what your heart is showing or wanting to help you with.

If a shop keeper tries to persuade you to buy a brand of satellite navigation device for your car that works perfectly in 90%, 80% or 20% of the cases when used, would you buy it or would you keep looking for a better one. The answer for most is simple. You apply a similar approach to your spiritual direction: the 100% working device ultimately is your own heart and inner heart.

When you start to look at often self-declared or popular teachers or facilitators of spiritual growth you will find that many of them do far less brilliantly over time than their image or statements suggests. When you research their broader life, over some time, what you find are lives far less perfect and some don't even follow their own teachings or advice.

It can be very helpful to follow someone for some time. There is dilemma and potential pitfall when spiritual advisors state they know the essence, all, or are fully realised. No matter what a teacher says it will be different from really having experienced it or being there. Let your heart be your guide to start with: if there is gentleness, kindness, love for you and a wide circle of others, then you are on the right track.

It is good to have a teacher who empowers you in action, and it is even better to have the inner teacher, truth compass, an active and clear heart to ensure that in all aspects of life and in spiritual matters you stay on track.

If they are truly there for you, then this is wonderful, you have found a treasure that will guide, support and help you. However, do you know what they have seen, experienced or 'where they come from' in terms of their teaching? Or whether it is complete or suited to you? It is here that the other approach and model, using your heart at the centre, becomes valuable.

Figure 20: Heart-facilitated way of spiritual growth support

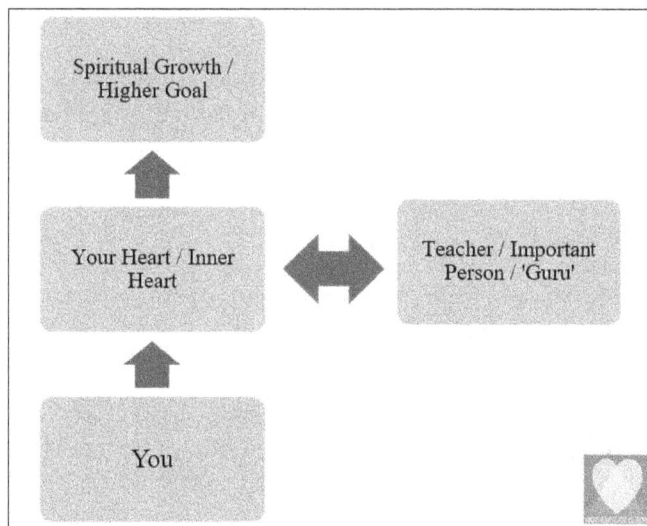

The heart way here is offering another win-win situation. You can have both, a wise and guiding person in your life and also feeling with your heart. It will show you when and if the advice is right for you and when paths or opportunity arise.

How many spiritual guides or teacher will be happy for you to go and learn somewhere else? Perhaps this is a sign of their maturity if they do, if they don't need you, or if they deeply respect your wisdom and choice.

Personally I appreciated spiritual teachers who were honest and said 'I can help you here a little' or 'I have some knowledge about this or that but overall I do not know if you will achieve spiritual growth through it or reach an ultimate goal'. There are some who do so and say this in refreshing humility. Some claim to have far too much insight, which, with a clear heart becomes felt quite easily, quite early when using the heart.

In some spiritual branches or religious groups emotions play a strong role. If this is so, then it is somewhat problematic. Any nurturing of emotions blurs both your mind/brain and the heart.

The key here is that with an active heart, the role of another person or practice is to be a facilitator. Quality control is with you or more directly with your heart.

From a mind/brain and feeling point of view the more a teacher insists that only his or her view is the right one the riskier the journey will be. The more confident and able a teacher is that his or her way is truly touching your heart, then if it is truly beneficial, everyone's heart will be touched. The more the teacher can let go and allow your heart to choose, will build your heart confidence and equally a feeling of freedom.

When you reach the end of your life and the inner-most learning and longing has not been fulfilled then no teacher will be there to console you, hold your hand or make some last-minute changes to fix it all. It will be down to you, your choices and your commitment to all that life has shown or offered.

It makes good sense to attend to your heart from here. It is equally good to commit to a journey, a path and a particular practice. However, at every point, let your heart guide and help you too. The trust in your heart will grow. Following it in small daily matters will help when or if it is time for an old belief or hope to be adjusted or let go of. Every spiritual practice often has some wonderful truth within. More often than not it is a matter of adjustment, it's about letting go that will nurture the heart and you.

The heart will demystify both spirituality and religion. Any wise or heartful group or teacher will be at peace with this. In the heart many people already feel that it is not the group or congregation, the building or individual people in high spiritual or religious positions, that is important, it is the relationship that we have with our heart. Over the course of your life the heart will never let you down. It may take some time to feel deeper stronger and clearer feelings from the heart, but it will always guide you as to the best way over a period of time and for your whole life.

Spiritual Goals

Differing understanding or insights gained around the purpose of spiritual growth can easily lead to arguments or disagreement. When larger groups were involved in disagreement in the past, it led to national conflict. It is not easy to determine a goal without knowing what the clear direction is or what a possible continuation and 'non-physical journey' after life will reveal. First let us look at what some of these goals are or can look like.

Reaching a Place

One group of spiritual goals involves a destination in the afterlife such as heaven, Nirvana, the Kingdom of God, paradise, Sukhavati and other places. What is very interesting is that in two of the same beliefs or religions there are two different places or goals: Heaven or Kingdom of God for a Christian or Nirvana and Sukhavati for a Buddhist. If they were earthly places, and they don't seem to be, and you were to set your car navigation device to these places, you could only hope that they are the same. We will never know until we get there.

Close to the Divine

Other spiritual goals centre around being close to or returning to the Divine, the Creator or God, either in relation to place or about being close in spirit and as an ultimate reality. A Christian and Muslim would associate with this. For a yogi the term Divine Union is the deeper understanding of 'yoga', not the set of exercises that are practiced. It means to be with the one or highest Divine Being again. Even though for a Buddhist the highest goal is a place such as Nirvana or Sukhavati, there are Buddhist texts indicating that the very fact that these places exist, someone, a being of even higher nature must have created them. These are solely intended to be examples of the limitation of wanting to 'know' or being at peace with what others know or have found out. What is common to these two types of goals is the rising upwards, even while alive, to the higher place, or to be with the Divine.

Calmness Within

Related to the goals of achieving a rising upwards or ascension, during life or after life, is the goal of calming or even total stilling of all mind and brain related activities. Why does this goal exist?

The mind/brain's activities, perhaps outside its normal tasks, have a tendency to jump around, to go backwards in time, forward, and to randomly be driven to activity and thoughts.

The mind/brain is also of a physical nature and hence limited to the physical or earthly world. The heart/spirit nature, on the other hand, the real 'you' can change form, expand or be in several places at the same time.

However, even though this may seem exciting to some, spiritually it is less meaningful where you are, than how you connect to the deeper part that exists within that can help and guide you more. Over the centuries, calming the mind and brain has become one main focus, to attempt to connect to this deeper part by default; hoping or believing that when the mind/brain stops, even for short periods of time, the other, deeper self automatically shows. In meditation, prayers and specific exercises are the chosen vehicles. With more presence or awareness, living more in the current moment 'here and now', it is hoped to connect even more to this deeper centre.

Being a Good Person

A heart of gold.

For others, spiritual purpose is connected to being a good person or having a good life. Sometimes people who share their spirituality find expression or fulfilment when they are in nature, where they feel a deeper, and more peaceful connection to self.

Somewhat related to this, and suggested by some, is the spiritual goal or direction, to be happy or to become happier and to find inner peace. While being happy and peaceful are beautiful states, they connect to others, help others, in indirect ways only. When you are happy, peaceful, others can also let go a little more, find more peace, joy or relief, indirectly or through the heart connecting to this.

Finding a Greater Love

To find love and to be loved is an additional state or way of being also offered as a spiritual goal.

'Love your neighbour', 'have love and compassion for every living creature' or 'do not to seek for love, but merely find all the barriers within yourself that you have built against it.'

… are some expressions of this goal to find a greater, unifying, all-embracing and unconditional love; a love not just for 'self' but also to be shared with others.

To make a difference, or to discover a deeper meaning in life, or who we are, can be another aspiration. Making a difference for most is perhaps related to doing something in life, or with one's own life which is in tune with a higher goal, something profoundly meaningful and lasting. In discovering the meaning of life or in answering the question, 'who am I' it is also hoped that the events of life, any challenges or 'suffering', all positive experiences and ultimately life itself will offer meaning or resonance within.

Naturally, there are also people who do not have any desire to find the meaning of life. Or they can be individuals who sit on the fence, looking at different spiritual growth options and do not feel to decide or commit. Others see some of the chaos between different groups and some do not feel that there is any relevance or meaning in having spiritual growth or spiritual beliefs as part of life.

Spiritual Pointers

The heart can be happy within many situations and doesn't look for radical or big changes.

Whatever your spiritual situation, feeling or belief or no-belief is, from the perspective of the heart it is more important to use the heart, to be connected to the heart, lead a heart-centred life in all aspects and dimensions of life, than to follow any approach, system or belief.

The following section on spiritual pointers is intended to show that the heart has been part of realisations and deeper understanding about who we are for a long time.

Holy books

Some time ago, out of curiosity, I googled one or two online bibles and within them searched for 'brain', 'mind' and 'heart'. Although it is too long ago to remember any of the details, what was clearly present was that there was no hit for either 'mind' or 'brain' but over 20/30 hits for 'heart'.

This is not intended to be a scientific or research example and the bible is only one of many profound and highly-regarded, highly-respected holy books. You will find that, when looking at these books, the indicators of the importance of the heart are in all of them. There is a vast body of literature out there that is intended to help others in relation to spiritual growth, regardless of the faith.

If you have read some holy books you may recall that many make direct and at times profound references to the importance, meaning and even key functions of the heart.

Some give instructions on how to live a more heart-centred life and mention the need to balance heart with the mind/brain existence. Having looked at publications over the past decade or so through a more heart-aware lens it has been heartening to see that anecdotally an increasing number of references to the heart appeared: in stories, song, work-related matters, spiritual and general publications.

Near death experiences

Near death experiences (NDE) are situations where individuals have clinically been dead for a short period of time and yet they have 'come back', lived again to tell about their experience, which is very individual. NDEs are one pointer into a world that is opening to humans at the edge between life and death; death of body and our normal mind/brain knowing or consciousness.

In brief, there is one group, having had a NDE, that have not had any notable experience of any kind. Then there is the second group that shares about a channel of light, beautiful feelings and overall about a very positive, light and uplifting event. It is this second group that also shares that the gift given to them through this experience was quite significant. Some didn't even want to come back.

Almost all come back with two messages ... to love more and to learn more.

Without a doubt many of these individuals would have been very loving mothers, fathers, grandparents or friends, already taking care of close or loved ones in special ways. However, for some reason not enough focus or emphasis must have been given to this to receive such a piece of advice. From the viewpoint of the heart this is simple. With an in-principle endlessly deep heart, how much love is enough, how unconditional is it, how free is it, how free is it able to extend to everything and everyone in the right ways? These are only some of the love-centred questions.

The centre of feeling, receiving and giving love is your heart.

At a first glance there is a first layer or circle we share our love with: family, partners, dearest of friends. The heart also is offering a second circle of loving. This is a love that can radiate and flow in ever-widening circles, and ultimately to everyone, no longer distinguishing between close or not close, near or far, friend or non-friend.

NDEs also offer some insights around knowledge. Knowledge is loosely described not as the accumulation of more information, but as knowledge that is about wisdom, learning what we truly are supposed to learn and what gives meaning to our lives and the lives of those around us. Knowledge is perhaps, more likely to be what is commonly called 'wisdom', something deeper or something that has been verified or run through the heart in accordance with the above Celtic quote.

NDEs can offer some very profound insights about us and this greater spiritual reality. The insights that come from them, if accepted, can be completely life changing for those who have had the NDE, and for those around them.

The heart itself

'The awakened heart is like a luminous sphere - just giving without thought to any who may come close.'
Meister Eckhart

The very function and capacity of the heart is one of the clearest indicators of what the purpose of spiritual growth is. The heart itself is there, it is present and offers you help and clear experiences - at least over time - that are somewhat special and profound. These experiences are both deep and quite beautiful. They are outside the limitations of the mind/brain, in particular, in the light of the declared goal to become more mindless or to still the mind.

The heart's direct clearing of emotions and emotional reactivity is one way to still the mind. It is emotional activity that can trigger significant mind/brain activity or make it hard to still it.

Hopefully by now you have experienced that the actual function of the heart is doing just that. The more of you that is outside the unwanted, unhelpful, uncaring and unnecessary negative feelings the more you will feel present, connected to others and can be taken deep into meditation or prayer. You will also feel beautiful, joyful and at peace.

'Mindlessness', or a completely still mind, can swiftly occur when the heart is the other active and working centre.

Mindlessness, or a completely still mind in meditation or contemplation practices, can occur when emotional distractions or an active mind become stiller. It can also happen when another centre, the heart centre, becomes more present and active. In fact, the heart can become the centre from which you live and feel, work and interact within everything and everyone in your life. At that point the mind/brain are still and only called upon when needed, but they are still important. If allowed to operate through the heart, the mind/brain operates more effectively.

The heart offers a deep and loving connection to others. The heart is about a greater, universal or Divine love.

The heart, in so many ways, in poetry, song, dance and theatre, is associated with love. The heart also can symbolise the growing of love and often with a deeper, sweeter and wider love that is beyond the love for a loved one or small group of close ones. Nurturing your 'heart garden' will also nurture the abilities to grow this love and while this love is for everyone, it will always be special for some, your close ones and the wonderful feeling will flow through your heart, each time and always.

The heart is a way to perceive non-physical parts of us and as such can be a gateway to happiness, inner peace and more.

Spiritual growth as well as spiritual goals, are often about parts of us that are non-physical. They are equally about the understanding or realisation of a longer-term even eternal existence. The mind/brain is physical and naturally logical in its design and function. The mind/brain is for the physical life-related functions: to move the body, to plan, write, think and also from here offer a bridge to the non-physical and to the heart.

The heart is one of the non-physical parts of us. In terms of our search for love, happiness and freedom it is no less important because of its 'non-physicality'. It is with the heart that non-physical parts of us, such as love or care for others, and their life-enriching qualities can be perceived. The main function or quality is in the form of feeling. You feel certain things again and again when you use your heart more or when you use it for spiritual practices. The heart is equally 'scientific', even if solely for you, as it shows you direction, deeper realisation and deeper connection.

The heart is your tool, should you feel drawn to use it, to go into deep meditation, to still the mind and body and in prayer.

When this other centre, balancing mind and brain, is active, a deep connection to all that is, the entire creation, within understanding and beyond can be felt. This is perhaps comparable to the latest model computer which can, in spilt seconds, solve complex formulas and offer answers and insight; even if this program was written over years. Your heart has similar and better abilities, after all the computer was developed by human mind/brain abilities. The heart has the ability in this way, too, to connect with and perceive places within that know, places outside the universe and any higher being that may be part of your spiritual goal.

When you look at the profound, special and wonderfully peace and joy-giving qualities of the heart, then it seems almost natural to look at something within, something God-given, something that empowers, helps and connects as the guide to deep, underpinning aspects of your existence and growth.

How can the heart have these abilities? As indicated in the introduction sections, the heart carries at its core the true self, spirit or Divine spark. Indicating it here has little or no meaning. It is when you are using it, when you let your heart help you, that any aspect of life and your spiritual growth will become part of it and will feel and realise this natural and logical heart ability. It is in this way that your heart can offer a way to connect to, and in return be guided by, a Divine Source.

Describing the heart as the key to your connection to the Divine, or as the connection, risks just being technical and another concept or belief, lacking feeling or realisation. The next PHT is for your heart. If you let your heart feel this divine connection, if the heart is learning or in its language is 'feeling' and 'realising' this, then it is your heart's realisation or truth.

When your heart feels its innate divine connection, it will realise its deeper existence.

Repeat this PHT several times or regularly as you become more familiar with your heart and heart-feelings. The clearer and lighter your heart has already become, the depth and clarity of feeling in this PHT will also deepen.

> ### Practical Heart Tip 76: Heart realising connection and 'blessing' *
>
> *Find a quiet place, do a brief relaxation and ensure you have some uninterrupted time.*
>
> - *Do Heart Strengthening (follow all the steps - allowing each step to work);*
>
> - *Feel any expansion, lightness, calmness and any other pleasant feelings*
>   *(enjoy these feelings for some time, being aware not to try, do more, or observe - 1-2 minutes);*
>
> - *Then let your whole feeling, your whole self be pulled into this expansive, light feeling, follow all your feelings (2-3 minutes);*
>
> - *Then let your heart realise and feel that the expansive, light, calm and other beautiful feelings are from the natural presence of the blessing of the Divine within your heart (as you feel, continue to feel or feel any deepening ... follow your feeling, any shifts in feeling ... 1-2 minutes);*
>
> - *For a few moments let your heart NOT Realise ... then*
>
> - *Let your heart realise and feel that the expansive, light, calm and other beautiful feelings are from the natural presence of the blessing of the Divine within your heart (as you feel, continue to feel any deepening, expansion or any other pleasant feeling ... follow your feeling or any shifts in feeling ... 1-2 minutes).*
>
> *You can repeat the last two steps two to three times. This allows your heart to deepen its realisation and the experience. Deeper levels of clearing, cleansing, healing and overall heart help can also happen now, for this PHT, and in previous or upcoming heart practices.*

It is good to remind yourself that the heart has its own refined intelligence outside any expert's or own perception. Whatever your heart does or 'sees' will also solely be in the form of a feeling. If you feel, even a subtle or slight shift of a deepening or expansive nature during this PHT, it means that your heart is recognising this connection and the help given in the form of a 'blessing'.

Blessing is just one term you can use. Alternatively, you may call it a 'gift of love', 'healing light', 'blissful energy' or 'love and light'. In Hinduism and Yoga the term 'amritam' is used to point to a flow of special or 'divine energy'; it is also referred to as an element or path to immortality or salvation. Now, or if you persist with your heart commitment and practices, you will feel this feeling of being filled by an exquisite and blissful feeling fairly soon. No need then to wait until you are a 'holy being'. Just enjoy living with and through your heart.

What it is called is of lesser importance than letting your heart feel and realise it and to let it work for you. When you enjoy these feelings, and let the realisation fill your heart, this gift will continue to work and help. It is in these moments that you receive the help, blessings or love from the Divine, the Creator, the Source of Infinite Love in deepening ways.

Practical Heart Tip 77: Letting the blessing work *

Do Heart Strengthening KHH 6. Follow each of the steps - allowing them to work; then continue and ...

- *Feel any expansion, lightness, calmness and any other pleasant feelings and follow your heart feelings. Enjoy these feelings for some time, being aware not to try, do more, or observe (1-2 minutes).*

- *As your heart continues to expand and grow, keep on following the pleasant feeling for one minute or longer to let your heart and feeling become even stronger and deeper.*

Do the next steps with your eyes closed, while staying relaxed, touching your heart and smiling continuously and freely to it.

- *Let your whole feeling and your whole self be pulled into this expanding, light, calm, peaceful feeling. Recognise how the more you follow and allow the pulling into the wonderful sensation, your heart and feeling are becoming stronger. Continue this process without stopping for two to three minutes;*

- *Realise that the joyful, expanding, light, calm, peaceful feeling you are experiencing is from Divine's blessing within your heart. Feel how your heart and feeling react as soon as you realise this. Keep on following the shifts in your feeling, which will strengthen your heart even more;*

- *Also realise that Divine's blessing within your heart is helping you in so many ways. Feel clearly how your already strengthened feeling is becoming deeper and more beautiful;*

- *Now, stop realising that Divine's Blessing is working within your heart. Recognise how your feeling that was strengthened by the realisation now weakens, and the way in which the feeling radiates also diminishes;*

- *Then, realise again how Divine's Blessing within your heart is helping your heart, in everything. Recognise how your feeling is becoming strong again, and begins to radiate so wonderfully. Follow the changes in your feeling, to allow it to grow and strengthen further;*

- *Repeat the last two steps ('stop realising' - 'realise again') several times until your feeling is strong and free; then*

- *Conclude the session by continuing to follow the changes in your feeling during a 'realise again' sequence while staying relaxed and smiling sweetly and freely to your heart for 2-3 minutes or longer.*

'Realise/realise again' and 'stop realising' are included as variations to help you to feel, understand and follow your feeling more naturally. This 'on' and 'off' will help the feeling to be clearer, the heart will learn and the 'blessing' will work deeper. Your heart and its abilities will improve at the same time.

The next section explores the heart's role in practical ways so that your spiritual practices can benefit from more heart ultimately empowering you through your inner heart-ability to experience, feel and verify a truth that is outside the realm of mind or brain.

The heart's role in spiritual growth

The heart's role in helping and actively assisting in spiritual growth is multi-fold:

- It can facilitate and actively help;
- Guide you to feel, help you to understand and realise at deeper levels;
- Help you to realise the earthlier spiritual goals such as becoming more peaceful, happier and joyful; and
- Lead you to an exquisitely love-filled life.

The heart's connection to and help with love is profound. In many common sayings and ways love is associated with heart. The clearer your heart, the gentler and sweeter love is perceived and given. This love is also mixed with less emotion.

Understanding and using your heart will by default let a deep, widening and gentler love flow through your heart and all of you over time. The essence of what the heart is and connects to is a greater, all-embracing love. In its recognition of the Divine, the heart connects to the Source of infinite, pure and unconditional love.

This is something quite blissful, healing and exquisite. We often strive for a deep inner longing for 'more' love. In truly connecting heart-to-heart any hope or longing for the sharing of unconditional love with others becomes a reality guided by an opening and purifying heart.

The increasingly profound guidance from the heart will bring about gentle realisations, profound changes and engender a deepening of the beautiful feelings that give confidence, from the inside out, about the rightness of your spiritual direction or purpose.

Guide to active help

Spiritual goals can be closely related to your life now, your aspirations, relationships to others and how you feel in daily life. While your heart, as previous chapters discussed, can directly help, it can also guide you in ways that you would normally not think of.

Every event in life is a huge amalgamation of events and coincidences. The more you are looking at your own life through the eyes of the heart, which really is your heart feeling, you will notice that most of them, if not all events, are profound in purpose and give you a chance to learn, realise and grow.

One simple example would be that you walk along the street window shopping and you will stop, look at a book or a workshop being advertised that normally you would not stop for or even look at. This may be an indication of a change-of-heart or your heart is stopping you and making you see this. The more accurate heart guiding here, as a second step, would be if you would additionally feel with your heart and notice the direct heart response.

Strangely and wonderfully you become more mindful with more heart and you will be drawn to see possible ways to be helped through following more the feeling in your heart.

Guide to deeper understanding and realisations

Spiritual growth, when viewed from the perspective of gaining wisdom, is about the development of something that is more than repetition of what other people have said or written. Wisdom in this way is something that resonates deeply within you and in others also when shared.

You may recall a moment when you spoke with a dear friend or colleague or when someone was speaking to you about something personal. Sometimes this happens in distressing or challenging times. These are heart-moments, when you or the other person experiences the specialness of having someone who will listen or be listened to, to really be there and say few words. Perhaps you can also relate to the same or other moments when too much was being said and it did not feel the same way.

When words spoken come from a place of feeling, compassion, care or love, then they come quite likely from the heart. Often, what is being said, is just perfect for a difficult or heart-rending situation.

Deeper understanding and realisations are not limited to the interactions between two people. The heart can understand and realise every moment and every aspect of life. When your heart is present and open it wraps its coat of wisdom and love around those concerned and the situation, in such a way that expressions and words become wise, and learning or realisations happen.

With less heart it is meditation and prayer that can prepare for or offer these bliss-moments. For example, when you meditate in a certain way or when you pray in a certain way, over time there will be particular experiences or outcomes. These outcomes may be in ways that you have changed and how others perceive this change. In moments when these 'certain ways' are connected to your heart or from your heart, the change will be clearer, to you.

Another example is the PHT 6 (in section IV) feeling how old you are within as a spontaneous way to connect to a higher knowing or deeper realisation within. One of them is your heart and in moments when you can let go a little, feel, use the feeling from your heart, it can shine through.

Happiness and inner peace

It is quite wonderful to be happier and to feel free inside, free in terms of feeling calm, peaceful and free from burdens and everything that reduces happiness, joy or inner peace.

The heart is the very centre of your feelings of joy, happiness, calmness, freedom and inner peace.

The heart's capacity is to generate more of these feelings by facilitating the clearing of anything that is not those or other beautiful feelings and the heart is the part of you that will make you feel happy or peaceful or both.

A small example and exercise may help. The next PHT will show you the difference between mind/brain generated calmness or inner peace and the one from your heart.

Practical Heart Tip 78: Inner peace from mind/brain and heart *

Find a quiet place and make sure that you have a few minutes of uninterrupted time.

Part 1. Inner Peace from Mind/Brain

Being mainly helped by your mind/brain tell yourself to be calm and peaceful. Do this over a 5 to 10 minute period. Speak silently and quietly in any way that you know is helpful, perhaps in a slow, auto-suggestive way. Say something similar to 'I am calm and peaceful in every possible way' then wait 30 seconds to 1 minute, then repeat again.

At the end of 5 to 10 minutes feel the impact or result.

Part 2. Inner Peace from the Heart

Use the core Heart Strengthening (KHH 6). Allow it to take 3-5 minutes and then sit for another 3 to 5 minutes in whatever heart-presence you feel or are connected to after heart strengthening.

At the end of 5 to 10 minutes feel the impact or result of each of the practices.

Look for two main impacts:

How calm are you overall; and

How busy is your mind/mental activity overall and compared to normal?

Initially it may be difficult to feel a difference between the two. The stronger your heart is the clearer the difference will be and your stronger heart will facilitate a clearer result. To get a clearer difference between the two do part 1 and 2 straight after each other.

It is quite likely that after part 2 the 'inner peace from the heart' exercise there is noticeable reduction in the mind/brain's tendency to jump from one thought to another. You may also find that the volume of thoughts is reduced. There is a likelihood too that in doing the above PHT there may be feelings of joy bubbling up.

The heart will always want to facilitate or give more, beyond and outside our intentions or plans.

Heart-generated joy and happiness are equally wonderful and gentle. They have the ability or seed within to change not only you but also your environment. When you watch the video clip stories of some of the people who shared in this book, on the web, or on social media, you will feel, even when people talk about a challenge or a very difficult time in their lives, there is a gentle radiance of joy and peace. This is the happiness and peace that the heart generates; in your heart you can feel both past challenges and how the person has been helped by the heart to grow, learn and let go.

Deep, widening and gentle love

On a continuum that reaches from strong unpleasant emotion to deep and beautiful radiant love, most people at some point in life feel a deep and unconditional love, and long for more of this wonderful feeling. It is also common that during special moments when you experience this there may also be a feeling that you know love or know love from the past; it is familiar.

In the absence of unpleasant or burdensome emotions there is naturally a vast and fertile field upon which love can grow. This love has more to do with your heart than fulfilment through others.

This will be more love for self and for others; it will also connect to infinite love as the Divine glue that holds everything together, including us. Imagine for a few moments a world where love and the more direct love-related qualities are the only qualities that exist. There would be kindness, friendliness, courtesy, giving, forgiving, understanding, helpfulness, care, gentle attention, open listening, freedom from excessive judgement or criticism and other sweet, enjoyable, connecting and freeing qualities. What the heart can broker, connect with and expand into, in relation to love, will at some point of your heart journey no longer be describable in words.

There is a time, as you use your heart in action, that love will fill you, your body, your being in the most exquisite feelings of bliss, wonder and gentle joy.

This is normal and will become more regular as you engage with your heart and with the deeper heart practices more. This love has a special quality, too, similar to known love or a less expansive love. When you feel it and try to have it or hold it or make it more it will fade, and in moments when you let go, surrender into it, the feeling can grow infinitely.

The ability to love and receive love is given to every human being. It is something quite wonderful regardless of an overall mind/brain focus in education. People who have had a near death experience have shared that the amount of love felt, received and given is what counts during and towards the end of one's life.

Naturally the heart is associated with love. The opening of the heart brings love back or brings you into a deeper flow of love that is at times overwhelmingly beautiful and heart-touching.

At any point in life, in any life situation, at any age, with or without a romantic or love partner, the spiritual meaning of love, to live a love-filled life, is possible.

Every feeling of love needs to start with the heart, inside you, giving or receiving it. From there a spiritual love-opening can happen, whether this is the growing love for others or the growing and deepening love in your relationship with the Divine. Fulfilment of whatever love you long for will be fulfilled, facilitated and arranged by the heart.

Making a difference - Living for a greater purpose

Making a difference is a wonderful goal to have. With the heart being at least as logical as the mind/brain, making a difference is only meaningful if that difference is in a universally positive way.

Firstly, using the heart is a positive step in this direction, and as you find out about this key part of you, everything you do, becomes a more authentic reflection of the whole-of-you.

Secondly, when you use the intelligence of your heart, whatever you do will also be in tune with a wiser you and a more complete sense of understanding and wisdom.

> **Practical Heart Tip 79: Purpose in daily life**
>
> *As with so many things in life it can be very helpful and meaningful, to make first small steps.*
>
> *If you feel confident enough that you have started to use your heart and that you can feel feelings from your heart you can try the following:*
>
> *Write down in your Heart Diary or somewhere else your responses to:*
>
> - *What are some of the qualities in your relations to others that give meaning or purpose to these?*
> - *What can you do today to bring more of these positive qualities into these relations?*
> - *List other things, behaviours or attitudes that you could do as options that you haven't done so far; and then*
> - *Use the feeling from your heart in*
> -   *(a) eliminating qualities or aspects that are less supportive of you and others in your relations; and*
> -   *(b) make a list of priorities that you should focus on more.*
>
> *Make an additional note at the beginning of this PHT around how things are and how you feel about them. Make a note every 2-3 weeks of how you progress and feel and of any overall changes (observations and feelings) in your relationships.*

You can do this either in your daily work, in your other work (as a volunteer, working on a hobby) or in being with your family or friends. What is important here is to let your heart and feeling help you to connect with any heart-facilitated changes. This includes changes in understanding and in how your heart has guided you to connect to a more purposeful way of being or in your interactions with others.

You will notice a focus on you and changes within as part of this PHT. Some time ago the saying crossed my desk, 'if you want to change the world, bring your own house in order first'. It made perfect sense to me then and still does. This means that you also bring your heart in order too, as part of the whole house.

There is very little credibility in doing big or purposeful things out there, in business or otherwise, and not having a balanced heart-mind-emotional existence in smaller ways too.

When one is successful in the outer world of work, business or in a social/welfare way and yet the same person is emotional at home, then something doesn't feel quite rounded or right about it. Loving others more, supporting, encouraging and helping them, from the heart, is a core observation in many spiritual or holy books. This is about the qualities of relations that you have with people around you.

Finding a deeper meaning in life, in exchange for offering your services or expertise, as a professional, volunteer or in any other capacity, and to do this from the heart, can offer a more refined way of making a difference. The whole next main chapter is on this bigger picture working or existing. It is often that this existence is connected to growing inwardly in a spiritual way.

Empowered learning and growth

Spiritual growth with the heart's help becomes another way to have a meaningful, joyful and purposeful life while also being of help to others, at home, at work, wider social environment and even on a global scale.

When your heart is in action it can be very freeing and empowering and you may find that many of your ideas and beliefs are less rigidly held.

This is why in some traditions or beliefs spiritual growth is equal to freedom. A deep inner freedom that allows you to make the right spiritual and earthly-meaningful moment to moment choices.

This quasi-marriage or separation between you and a good idea or important concept or belief when mind/brain are supported by your heart, becomes easy and more like a natural flow, as water flows from one boulder to another one in a river or creek. Water will always flow, no matter what the obstacles or temporary blocks are. In the same way the truth and freedom will become clearer and following the right steps or ideas will be easier.

The heart will also empower you to make choices that are otherwise hard to make. Age, position, particular clothing, having read book x or book y or having sat in meditation or prayer for x amount of hours may have impressed you before. It is very refreshing when you feel a sweeter, greater and more life-supporting truth in your own heart.

No matter what anyone says, suggests or threatens you with, in moments when you feel with your heart and follow your heart it will support not only you, your personal and spiritual journey, it will also support the dearly loved ones around you.

In a similar way, whatever you perceive now as spiritual being or growth and whatever goal you have in relation to it, can and naturally will, change over time, even if this change is just a small adjustment to what is now, what you feel now or what you believe now. You can trust heart-directed change, perhaps more than anything else.

This makes spiritual learning simple, relevant and demystifying. There is nothing that the heart can't perceive, understand and realise, including a truth and insight that even the most learned spiritual teachers or holy persons have longed to understand though the ages. It is a particularly special time right now, where the heart's importance is surfacing, and where heart-facilitated inner learning and growth is possible.

Heart's role in your spiritual practice

Your heart can support you directly in your spiritual practice. This can be in two ways

- In whatever you do now or will do as 'your spiritual practice'; or
- Simply in living a heart-centred life, every day.

Living with more heart awareness in your life can be your sole or main spiritual 'practice'. This is not a practice as such, it is living a heart-centred life in action and experiencing the meaning, beauty and growth through just that.

Living with your heart in action, living with the heart as the core, centre, 'brain' and deep inner wisdom guide is at the core of a natural spiritual life. 'Natural' here can mean pure, simple, un-influenced by others while equally being of profound depth, joy and fulfilment. Certainly, holy books refer to the importance of the heart, and a growing number of self-help and personal growth books and online resources do point in this way.

There is humility in this too. As well there is a lack of ability to be, or hide, under the umbrella of a large group, association, hall, church, temple or belief. It is no problem at all to be part of any group and to use the heart as a hub, support, connector or wise facilitator to deepen and beautify all of you in your environment. Any group that also allows enough freedom of being, freedom of thought about the heart and for your heart to blossom, will support you and the more whole you. Suppressing the heart is perhaps similar to suppressing the mind/brain, or not to have freedom of speech in modern society. We know there is freedom of speech, yet some will not enjoy this right, even try to avoid it to happen. In the same way the deeper freedom that the heart is offering and facilitating may be uncomfortable to others.

There is also a vulnerability in which you are what your heart is or how you have integrated this wise part or self, this knowing and loving part, into daily life as part of both, a 'practice' and a heartful human being. It is however perhaps the same vulnerability we experience when we reach the end of this life, 'knock at heaven's gate' or are who we truly are at that point.

The heart is to be used in daily life, every moment, similarly to the mind/brain you may associate with awareness or attentiveness.

The more special practices introduced in this book, such as meditations and prayers for the heart, mainly function as fuel stations for it, as times to strengthen it and to return stronger, clearer and more heartful to the rest of your life.

The next three sections show that a spiritual practice supported by your heart is about life, all of life, your life and a down-to-earth existence in this quite incredible physical human form.

Life

The emphasis on 'Life itself a spiritual practice' can be found in many sayings in books or is said by spiritual or wise leaders; at times it is stated as a path, even a goal. Life and your heart can form a profound and growing partnership. Life, when perceived mainly via the abilities of a strong mind and brain, is often like a pendulum swinging between good times and hard times. In a way this is the function of the brain, to distinguish and to compare. It is good to use those functions and to be clever in observing, reflecting and making better choices next time.

The heart as the centre of feeling and your spiritual centre offers ways to equally be in partnership with your mind and brain too. When the heart is not only present, but also has been cleansed and 'enlightened', then the direct and beautiful feelings are naturally always present. This means that when life is good you feel peaceful, joyful and a gentle love-connection to everyone around you. When life is not so good it is exactly the same, you still feel peaceful, joyful and in love.

Naturally we are not machines and when life is good, kind or when we feel better the natural or true heart feelings are also easier to feel or have a deeper and sweeter depth.

Looking at spiritual growth this is the direction that the heart offers and that the heart facilitates in every moment you choose your heart. You choose your heart when you are more relaxed, smile gently to it and feel it, or during most of the suggested heart exercise, meditations or prayers.

The mind/brain is literally always on in daily waking moments. In the same way your heart can also always be on.

You connect to the heart via 'feeling' and using the feeling from your heart. The mind/brain is used and stimulated by anything physical and through five senses.

Looking at spiritual maturity then becomes a matter of the quality of heart that you can bring to every moment, every situation in life. This kind-of-test is valuable when life is not-so-good or positive or when one is in emotion. Life then becomes a teacher or mirror. It is not really a test, it is much more a reminder that our heart awareness, heart opening and purity of heart is not at the best stage yet, and it is wise to be more committed to a clear and clean heart.

A grateful heart is also a lighter heart. In life situations, or phases when life is good or even wonderful, then let your mind/brain remember that gratitude is one of the heart-supporting and heart-advancing qualities. Let your heart be grateful often, feeling it, spending quality time connected in heart-space or just feeling your heart with more intent and enjoy whatever beautiful feelings that brings. You can use the grateful versions in KHH 15 to assist with this.

When you look at life this way, when you approach life with all of your heart, and with your mind/brain in full support, then the life you live is spiritual in a down-to-earth and simple way. It is also 'complex', full or rich, as the full depth and the full range of abilities of your heart will come to your aid.

Kindness and love

A loving heart.

Being compassionate, being kind, being loving and letting love radiate to others are some of the qualities or goals that people may aspire to in the name of spiritual growth. This is a wonderful inner aspiration or goal to have. Imagine an earth where there is more kindness or when only kindness is the dominant feeling or emotion.

A goal is of course something that is assessed by the mind/brain as something worthwhile. In this instance it is clear that goal and reality are two things. Having the goal or mental vision and actually being kind and loving are not the same - with the help from the heart let them become one.

When kindness and love flow through the heart then with an opening heart, over time and naturally, all you become is love and everything that is love.

When these or any related qualities are anchored within this way, then they become not only felt and real for others too, they also become a genuine and authentic part of who you really are.

To make kindness and love a part of daily life you may look at KHH 4 again 'Doing everything with love' and remind yourself of its key elements.

> **Practical Heart Tip 80: A day in love ***
>
> *Choose a day when you decide to do everything with love and from the heart. Work out a system of reminders or ways that help you to not forget too often and to be reminded in as many situations and moments as possible.*
>
> - *Use the feeling from the heart and by intention do everything with love;*
> - *Review your day;*
> - *Compare it, solely for learning and realisation purposes, to the previous day or other similar days; and*
> - *Briefly summarise your day in your Heart Diary.*
>
> *Establish a 21-day 'day in-love' or 'in-the-love' program. If you like the feeling, benefits or impacts on yourself or others, make it an integral part of your daily life.*

A day in-love or in that greater Love that your heart connects to naturally means a day in the heart with all its wider benefits. It will be better to repeat this day as a regular pattern, maybe each weekend or second weekend to strengthen the heart and this deeper, greater love-feeling within.

You may already be more aware of the subtler heart feelings within. Also be attentive to the responses of your surroundings, your family, friends, neighbours, colleagues and others who you see on a regular basis. With the heart being something so deep, using the heart-feelings in this way, subtle and yet clear and positive changes will happen in you and in others.

A good person

Goodness comes from the heart.

To be a good person and to have 'been a good person' as a general or spiritual goal in life, hardly anyone would dispute. To be good from the perspective of the mind/brain is in essence a good idea, a good concept or what is known to be good. Without doubt you have experienced situations, or made decisions where you had the best intentions to do the right thing, to 'be good' and yet, given all circumstances, it did not work out the best.

It is good to be good, but it is perhaps better to be aligned with a greater and heartfelt truth that is good and that also connects to a bigger picture.

Being a good person solely using the mind/brain is like being a person with only one leg available to walk onto wants to go from place A to place B. Whatever the intentions, hopes and aspirations, in such a condition, one will be late and once having arrived there, will be less time to do things and even when there, there will be a chance because of the temporary dis-ability that less can be done overall.

Working or being in life with little or no heart involved is not just like a temporary limp. It is not only the slowness or incompleteness of moving about in life. It is the lack of using all that is available to you, to make good decisions, to perceive a bigger picture, and to be guided by the built-in centre of wisdom, intuition and higher or Divine guidance.

The heart can connect to a more complete truth and at the same time you can remain a 'good person'. The heart at times will show you to say 'no' or to not help someone at home or in the office, in a kind way, for whatever this greater purpose is. You may not be perceived as good. For parents this is a normal situation.

The family invitation to a BBQ story in section IV is one of such examples. In that moment the decision made was not being 'good' or nice to our friends and yet, having had the heart's wisdom and foresight, it was being good to our child who later became really unwell. The seed for this sickness was already there; invisible to the human eye and its nerve connection to the mind and brain.

With the direct assistance from your heart, the active engagement of it, being a good person will be more wholesome. A deeper level of goodness will flow from the heart into what you do. You will be gently moved, from the wonderful start of having the intention or longing to be good, to a finer and more complete truthful enactment of what it is to be a good person.

Meditation

In meditation go deep into your heart.

Over the past decades, meditation has gained growing popularity in the Western world. Some of the practices stem from the West, most of them from Eastern traditions, beliefs or practices.

The reasons for meditation can range from seeking help to relax via managing stress to gaining insights to the quite targeted practices or searches for ascension or transformation of consciousness. In other words, the second group of meditators are reaching for high or the highest form of insight, wisdom or consciousness, and related states of being. Ascension is more associated with a rising upwards, after life or during life, of the parts of you that can rise, which are the non-physical aspects.

Every time you are busy in the outside world, busy in the mind/brain, too, the heart, an integral part of you, will also be engaged in this busyness, unless you direct the heart otherwise.

Realising this, every form of meditation is useful and in some way, even if very indirect, will help your heart. There are endless definitions, approaches and practices of meditation. Some of these are rooted in particular beliefs, some are old, established forms, while others are more modern, creative or free-style.

It is highly likely that any form of meditation will support you overall and also your journeying with more heart. During times when you are more relaxed, when your mind/brain is less active, naturally feelings of more peace can rise. Sitting in meditation, with the intention to do less, often by itself brings feelings of calmness or relaxation. It will also reduce pressure on the heart and in turn allow the heart to have more room and freedom to express itself. It will then allow the heart to have a chance to grow, open and develop. This will increasingly happen as you become more heart-aware and in fact use the heart in more targeted ways. In these moments, a more helping heart will promote depth, enjoyment, peace and freedom. The heart will actively clear some of the disturbances that can be present in the form of unnecessary thoughts or emotions.

Being relaxed and being peaceful go hand in hand. You can use the heart, as suggested in the next PHT, to practice a heart-based and heart-centred meditation. In moments when you are directly using your heart the goal, stated even by deeper meditation or spiritual practices of calming or completely stilling the mind, is naturally approached.

Even if your goal is simply to be calmer, more relaxed and more peaceful then your heart will facilitate this in an immediate and direct manner.

Practical Heart Tip 81: Meditation for a strong and clear heart *

This PHT is a simple combination of the PHT 'Letting the blessing work' from above and added time at the end to turn your time of being in heart-centred calmness into a meditation.

You can do the full version of the above PHT or shorten it by omitting the last two bullet points/instructions. At the end of the PHT 'Letting the blessing work' continue:

- *Smiling, relaxing and following all the gentle, pleasant heart-felt feelings;*

- *Stop doing anything. Stop listening to anything, stop reading or giving yourself further instructions;*

- *Just keep sitting and staying in the feeling of being pulled into the expanding, light, calm, peaceful feeling from your heart;*

- *Follow the feelings from your heart and enjoy the gentleness, calmness, radiance or expansive feelings; and*

- *Sit for an additional period of 5, 10 or 15 minutes at end of your last instructions.*

If you maintain the feeling from your heart you can extend it even further. It is best to stop your meditation when you find yourself thinking or following thoughts or emotions. Try again later or the day after.

In moments when you stop everything, when you stop giving yourself instructions, the heart will have an even greater chance to open, unfold and gain the full clarity and strength needed to help you.

It is not uncommon for meditation and prayer to be closely associated. Belief, faith and hope are not part of you, your mind/brain or the purer heart-form that exists at birth. These are given or adopted from others or our surroundings as we grow older. From the perspective of your heart, meditation and prayer are not related to any practice or belief. It is about you and your heart experiencing more of what you and your heart are. In that sense with the help of your heart you are being brought towards the answer or realisation of 'who am I'. In return, whatever your belief is, aspects of it that are truthful, more heart will strengthen, deepen it and often give you experience 'talked about' or 'hoped for' in books or by others.

In Tibet, Nepal and other Asian countries which have a strong meditation practice there are endless rows of prayer flags too. From the little knowledge about Buddhism read about in the past, being taught or from what people shared, these prayers are not directed to a particular being. So there is no absolute higher Being, Divine or God and yet there is the practice of prayer. Perhaps with a similar mind or 'mind and heart set', with or with no belief, you can let the heart do both, the meditation and prayer, in the following KHH 'Open Heart Meditation', which contains three elements: heart-preparation/heart strengthening, a heart-centred prayer and meditation.

The 'Open Heart Meditation' was originally written by the founder of the Padmacahaya Foundation for Inner Studies. The combination of heart strengthening, prayer and meditation is serving the heart well and, if you are able to let go and really let the heart do it, then your experiences will deepen significantly over time.

It is really important here to emphasise that the meditation and prayer shared here are to be from the heart and with the use of the heart. It is about adding something more or learning something new in prayer and meditation by using the heart in real terms.

If you consider your heart as something similar to what the mind/brain can do, then you can let the heart do the meditation and prayer. The difference is that heart has no belief or faith it just connects to truth, truth that just is, including the truth that belongs to your faith, belief or concepts. Whatever these are, it is okay to be within them, and to let your heart be the additional element.

Meditation and prayer from the heart is meant to be 'experiential'; meaning something you feel, something you have a deepening experience with. With the core of the heart being your inner heart and spirit, spiritual growth, either through prayer or meditation is or 'has to be' related to the heart's involvement.

You can do the following Open Heart Meditation in two ways.

- Read the preparation, prayer and meditation to yourself; or
- Record your own or use a recorded version from www.yourheartcanhelp.org.

A. Pre-KHH-Meditation preparation
- Preparation: find a comfortable and peaceful place to sit
- Make sure that you have a sufficiently uninterrupted stretch of time ahead of you
- Ideally, turn mobile phone, landline phone and any other sources of interruptions off
- Have any children supplied with activities or snacks
- Follow all the given instruction as best as possible or as they feel right to you and your existing practice or belief
- If you have an existing belief you are very welcome to replace the term used for the Divine being with the one that you use in your faith
- Remember the two foundation keys: relaxed/be relaxed and smile freely
- Do all this while continuously feeling your heart … letting your heart do it.

B. Reading the meditation - prayer to yourself
- Use the provided text below and read it to yourself
- Always to start with heart strengthening, which is included in the text below
- As you move from paragraph to paragraph close your eyes between each of them and take some time to feel, feel with your heart without trying, looking for the feeling, doing something or watching any process, and follow the feeling. Use this feeling time as a time to let go, to surrender and to just relax, smile and feel
- For as long as you feel the pleasant feelings from your heart, growing or expanding, you can keep your eyes closed. Open the eyes again, continue to read the next paragraph, when you feel the feeling fading, or just after some time - 20 seconds to 1 minute - or download the Heart Meditation audio recording from the website to have a practical example of timing
- At the end, allow yourself several minutes to sit in silence, in meditation and in a space of more heart-presence, more heart-radiance, where your heart has connected to the greater and all embracing, radiating love of the one source, Divine Source of infinite love
- Allow yourself to dissolve in all of the beautiful heart feelings
- When you are ready, open your eyes, staying connected to a clearer heart-presence and continue your day (or go to bed if it is that time).

C. Download a version from www.yourheartcanhelp.org or record your own version during one of the first times you read it out to yourself
- Follow the pre-preparation as above
- Press play and stay being relaxed and gently, naturally smile the best, freest way you can
- There will be a part at the end where you sit in 'meditation' and allow yourself to dissolve into the beautiful heart-felt feelings.
- The recording will end and when ready open your eyes, staying connected to a clearer heart-presence and continue your day (or got to bed if it is that time)
- You can stay and sit for longer in the clearer heart-presence, even continue letting yourself dissolve more in the heart radiance and greater love.

It is helpful, and you will clearly feel a difference over time, if you manage to do this regularly. We are not used to being heart-connected as we go through life. Some are gifted and have some form of clear heart presence already. In most instances, however, this is not the case, and an idea or hope that we are in the heart is not the same as really using it.

Over 21 days of Open Heart Meditation you are very likely to create enough of a shift, calming the busy or strong mind/brain, to facilitate a feelable and clear heart awareness, with gentle, true heart feelings.

Key Heart Help 13: Open Heart Meditation

This Open Heart Meditation (OHM) links previous exercises and KHHs and is an even more profound heart-clearing and heart-opening tool. For all the deep and exquisite help that you can get from your heart, in all aspects of life, the best heart condition is needed. Regular OHM is important.

At a micro level, spiritual and life learning is between the elements of who we are: mind/brain, body, heart and, if you know, believe or feel that there are other parts, then your heart will include these too. In this intimacy it is important to realise that if there are still moments when you experience any form of emotion, going back to the short or more complete lists of what they can be, then there are still parts of your heart that need cleansing or healing.

At a macro level your heart will understand the Divine, God, the high place of your spiritual knowing or aspiration and your personal, heart and whole-being connection or relationship to these. The opening of the heart is to the Source of Love, the Divine Source of the true and eternal self within. In relations to others around us the intent and purpose is to share this greater or growing love, unconditionally.

The opening of the heart is to the Divine Source, Creator or God of your faith and choosing. This makes it safe and risk-free.

In this way, as discussed in the early sections of the book, it is safe to open the heart. The heart's nature is to open to the eternal father, mother or Divine Being and to share the greater, deeper and more complete or unconditional love to everyone else.

If you are not a spiritual seeker, then that is okay too. A pure heart will offer you a good and prosperous life, and most importantly of all a fulfilled one. Where you and the deeper part within are aligned in harmony or in sync. This deeper part is your heart and inner heart in a dual role: the spiritual brain and the tool or facilitator to continuously align, guide and navigate.

For micro and macro to work in the best ways for you, the Open Heart Meditation is one essential part of a regular and deep heart-centring, heart-opening heart-practice.

The full KHH 11 has three parts to it (A) heart preparation (a variation of Heart Strengthening), (B) a prayer component and then (C) a meditation part. All three work together well and aim to maximise heart clearing, heart opening and learning how to stay in the feeling, connected to your heart for a while. Then, ideally, you open your eyes afterwards and continue with the rest of your day, staying more heart-centred and heart-connected.

The full KHH 11 - Open Heart Meditation

(A) Preparation Part:

Find a peaceful, quiet place to do this meditation, where you won't be disturbed or interrupted.

Sit down and relax, keeping your spine straight without tensing yourself.

Place both palms on your lap, with your palms facing upwards.

Close your eyes so that your mind/brain is not active.

Relax and smile ... to do this OHM the best way, let your whole self be here and now completely.

While relaxing and smiling, inhale deeply without forcing yourself and then exhale through your mouth ... let all burdens from your mind be expelled as you exhale. Feel and enjoy this moment when your thoughts are becoming more relaxed, as you continue to smile freely.

Inhale deeply, and exhale though your mouth, letting all tension in your body be removed as you exhale. Feel your whole body as it becomes more relaxed. Enjoy moments like this, when your whole self is relaxed, and let yourself smile even more freely.

Inhale deeply, and exhale though your mouth, allowing all remaining thoughts and tension in your body to be removed.

Your body and mind are now very relaxed.

Smile, enjoying this moment when you are completely relaxed .... body and mind.

From now on, breathe normally, inhaling and exhaling from the nose.

Now, place your fingers or one or both palms on the centre of your chest where your heart is located, and smile to your heart. Do not think or try to find the exact location of your heart, just smile freely, while listening to the instruction.

Keep on smiling freely to your heart, with all of your feeling. Realise you are becoming calmer. Enjoy while continuing to smile .... this is the moment when you are letting your heart become stronger.

Keeping your fingers or your palm(s) on your chest while smiling freely to your heart and enjoying the calmness from your heart, let us now pray from the heart to the Source of True Love asking that emotions from our heart be cleansed, so that our heart becomes lighter and open even more ...

(B) Prayer Part - Open Heart Meditation

Source of True Love please bless my/our heart so that all arrogance is replaced with love & light ...[14]

Source of True Love... please bless our heart so that all anger is replaced with love & light ...

Source of True Love... please bless our heart so that all selfishness is replaced with love & light ...

Source of True Love, please bless our heart so that all envy & jealousy are replaced with love & light ...

Source of True Love ... please bless our heart so that all greediness & cunningness are replaced with love & light ...

Source of True Love, please bless our heart to help us to realise that our heart is the key to our connection to You ... that we must keep our heart clean, because our connection to You is the most important thing ... please bless and help us to forgive others sincerely ...

[Now, for one minute, forgive everyone sincerely, although the same person has been doing the same negative things repeatedly and is still doing them. Remember that keeping negative emotions in you will simply create more pressure and burdens ...]

Source of True Love, by forgiving those who have done us wrong, please bless our heart so that all hatred, grudges, resentment, dissatisfaction, and all other negative emotions are removed, to be replaced with love & light ...

Source of True Love, please bless and help us to realise all of our mistakes to you or to others. Help us so we can regret them, and ask for forgiveness sincerely ...

[Now, for one minute, realize all of your mistakes to Source of True Love and to others ... regret them and ask for forgiveness ...]

Source of True Love... please forgive all of our mistakes to You and to others ....

And having been forgiven, let all burdens, fear, worries, and all other negative emotions caused by those mistakes, be cleansed from our whole heart and whole self to be replaced with love & light ...

Source of True Love, please bless our heart, so that all worries and fears caused by the lack of trust in you be cleansed and replaced with love & light ...

Source of True Love ... with negative emotions removed from our heart, please bless our heart to open better to you, and to also be directed even better to you ... let love and light flow more abundantly into our heart, so our feeling becomes stronger, so we can feel the calmness, peace, and beauty of love and light even better ...

Source of True Love, let love and light fill our whole heart and whole self, so that our whole heart and whole self are filled with calmness and peace... So we can rely more on love and light ... So we are always within our heart, and within the love and light ...

Source of True Love, Thank You for Your love that has removed the negative emotions from our heart and our whole self. Thank You for opening and directing our heart even better to You, so that our whole heart and whole self are filled with love and light even more ...so we can feel and enjoy the calmness, the peace, and the beauty of love and light even better ...

Thank You Source of True Love ... Amen.

---

[14] You can use my heart or our heart. Feel what feels nice or nicer, gentler for your heart and then continue using 'my/our' or 'I/we'.

(C) Meditation Part - Open Heart Meditation

Now feel and realise your whole heart and whole self have become lighter, freer, even more joyful

Enjoy whatever your feeling is within your heart or whole self ... keep smiling gently, naturally (1-2 minutes)

Let the Love, Light, Blessing or radiance from your heart work ... within and beyond your heart, whole self (1-3 minutes)

Let your heart and whole self dissolve into the Love and Light ... while keeping on being relaxed, smiling and enjoying (1-3 minutes)

While enjoying peaceful and wonderful moments ... let your whole heart and self dissolve continuously ... let go of all else, just let go (1-3 minutes)

Now feel and realise how your whole heart and feeling are filled with wonderful feelings ... from the Love, Light and all radiance from and through your heart ...enjoy and be grateful (1-2 minutes)

And while you smile and enjoy wonderful moments and feelings ... staying connected to your heart, staying in the Love, Light and heart radiance beyond this Open Heart Meditation ... move your fingers slowly, open your eyes, smile, let your heart smile through your eyes and all of you ... to share the Love, Light, deeper heart love and all heart radiance to everyone around you.

You can take this script and it will work for you and your heart. The more you have already worked with your heart the deeper the beautiful feelings and continued opening. If you are quite new to it, you can make significant progress in all matters 'heart' in a comparatively short time. The ball - your heart - is in your court.

It is less about what you do than what your heart is facilitating while you do the meditation/prayer.

It will deepen your experience if, after each paragraph, you close your eyes and reconnect deeper to your heart for a few moments. Just be feeling it and following any heart-feelings from it. With your eyes closed, and with the earlier outlined approach, you will let go more, into your heart. Then, when you feel to open your eyes and read the next paragraph. The times in brackets in some sections are only a guide and perhaps at those places stay with your eyes closed a bit longer.

Similar to physical fitness, if you go for one first large brisk walk, one jog, one swim or one gym or aerobics session you will very likely just get sore. The beautiful feelings here also come from longer practice and commitment.

Despite the depth of this prayer/meditation combination it will take some time for you and your well trained, well-used mind and brain to let go. Commit to doing it regularly, perhaps every day, every second day or a few times a week, in total 10, 20 or 30 times. Then take stock to see how it works for you. That will give you a much better picture than trying it only once or twice only.

It could be good, too, to read over the book's 'letting go' section. It is in moments you let go that a shift towards more heart, and your heart working for you, can happen more easily.

Give your heart some credit, too. It is perfectly fine to pray in your own belief if you have one, or if not just let your heart be free to allow it to happen and to experience. Feel and let your heart be cleansed and opened more and to feel close to the Divine in ways only your heart can.

Additional Comments

Turn 'hard times' into 'heart times'.

It is helpful, in a small way, to sit at the same spot each time for your heart or OHM activities. Your own heart vibration, overall vibration, will change and if you have a chance to sit at the same spot you will benefit from this.

Create your special meditation or sitting place. This can be as simple as a chair in a corner solely used for your heart times.

Negative emotions are the tricky parts that take us away from the heart and the pleasant and gentle feeling. While we all have a collection of emotion-related negativities, if you are quite relaxed, smiling freely and not doing anything else, you will only ever experience a very small fraction of the emotional deposits or even traumas that are being cleansed.

If you feel some of these emotions, relax more, smile more feely and continue or repeat again. Alternatively have a break then start again.

Turn 'hard times' into 'heart times'. Every time you struggle with something or someone, do whatever helps you or helped in the past. However, also spend time connecting to your heart.

Thoughts are natural, too. If you are free of thought while meditating or praying you are either asleep or you are a holy being already, according to some beliefs; it is very unusual. If you find yourself thinking just recognise this, relax more - to reduce tension-triggered thinking - and smile more to calm the mind while also strengthening the heart.

Do not follow your thoughts as best as possible. Just notice them and let them pass.

The terminology used for the Source of Infinite Love that the heart connects to, can be Divine Source or the God of your belief or choosing. It is really up to you and it doesn't matter. In the book and the associated recordings, it works better to have a neutral term in use. Exchange this term with your familiar term every time it is written or recorded.

Forgiving others is not about the other person or any emotions experienced at that time. You can almost totally detach from the other person, the past you had with the person or what is happening now in that relation or connection that you share.

It is good to be remorseful as an attitude, not as an emotion, so that the full openness to all deposits and all clearing can be there.

It is then that the heart can more easily facilitate deep cleansing of all that surrounds any event or person. Forgiving is much less about the event, more about emotions generated around or after an event and associated deposits. When you choose to forgive, from both heart and mind/brain, then the deeper clearing of any deposits, such as traumas and other negativities, can happen easily and more swiftly.

Forgiving yourself is equally important to do in a sincere way. Again, the event or what you did is not the focus, it is rather a facility to admit and to let everything related come to the surface. The heart, in its connection to the Source of Infinite Love, can cleanse and clear in a deeper way.

Forgiving and thinking. It is normal to want to think about events, persons, situations when prompted to forgive or be forgiven.

Write a personal and private list, only for you to see, of persons you feel to forgive as part of the Open Heart Meditation. Also make a list of your mistakes.

Put the list away somewhere safe. In the OHM, when it comes to these forgiveness parts, the one thought is enough 'whoever is on my list' or 'whoever and whatever situations are on my list' and then let the heart do the rest and clear any still lingering, burdening emotions or associated limitations or blocks

Helpful tips

Your heart is smart and capable. The best really is to:

- Just relax;
- Smile feely; and
- Let go.

You will find this is not that easy to do for the entire meditation. So be kind to yourself when you are struggling with these three approaches or attitudes. Do your best and then let go. It may help at times to go back to the sections of the book where the key heart helpers (KHH 2, 6) are discussed.

Be aware of what we normally like to do. We like to 'try', 'watch' or add other ingredients. While this is perfectly normal and 'ok' to do in other aspects of life, the heart does not need these additional ingredients.

Practical Heart Tip 82: 'Try more' or 'watch the heart' *

Do the standard Heart Strengthening KHH 6, or any of the direct heart-practising PHTs or KHHs introduced, and enjoy the pleasant feelings in your heart and beyond for a few moments.

- *Then, from within, try to make the heart bigger to make the feelings stronger, bigger. Feel what is happening when you do so; then*

- *Just relax, smile and enjoy the feelings from your heart again. Feel what is happening.*

Now do the same PHT and replace 'try to make the heart bigger' with 'watch your heart' ... watch or monitor your heart and what is happening through an internal process of looking. When you do this, notice a stronger connection from the mind/brain area to your heart.

Repeat each of these experiments 2-3 times.

You can have quite different results and gentler, more expansive feelings with less trying or watching. You may feel this the first time or over some attempts clearly. In the beginning, you may feel that very little is different by trying or watching things improve.

In moments when you try, watch or add other 'doings' to your heart practice a subtle form of pressure, holding or blocking is created that limits the nicer feelings. Why? Most of these are mind/brain related or initiated and more mind/brain at an early stage will limit the heart.

With dedicated and good-quality heart practice you will be able to 'have' both, feel the heart all the time, even continuously opening, while using the brain for complex thoughts.

This initial switch between more mind/brain use and more heart involvement in the PHT above and in all heart practices is quite helpful in the beginning. It assists in understanding clearer when the heart and when the mind/brain are more active and engaged.

What to be aware of

In the Open Heart Meditation is only a sample list of negative emotions, such as arrogance, anger and jealousy. Some of these may be too strong for your liking or you believe that you don't know them or feel them. Here the best is to let the heart do it. Applying some logic can help too: if you are really free from these, it will do no harm. If, even at a deep level, there are still remnants of these emotions, or related blockages in your heart, then the OHM will work on them. What this can mean is that even in an extreme or very difficult situation where many people would react, for example get angry or upset, it will be hard or not possible to have this reaction.

In some way the so-called negativities or blockages in the heart are 'good'. They show that the heart is working and they function as a reminder to look at the quality and function of your practice, meditations or prayers. Sometimes the best is to repeat what you just did with more quality, more whole-heartedly. Other times it is enough and you know that repeating will not result in better quality. For example you are tired. Then having a break and starting again will be the better approach. Start to trust your heart and feeling.

Life is not always perfect and sometimes when you sit and do your meditation or full Open Heart Meditation you may have made the best plans to have a peaceful and un-interrupted time. At home, at work or in a park something may happen that will demand your attention.

When you meditate, tell the children what you are about to do and arrange things so that the children will most likely be happily occupied for a time. If you are interrupted at some point then respond in a way that is natural and heartful. You can gently open your eyes, respond slowly, from the heart, or invite the child onto your lap, then continue. Children often respond well to their parents meditating and adjust well.

It is very common that children feel to sit with the parent for some time and then leave again. Feel what feels right in your heart, let them come and go freely. Heart and love never force.

They will also feel, in their own hearts, that you will become even softer, more kind, lighter and even more beautiful in other ways and will then support you more freely or directly in your heart meditation or prayer times.

Prayer

I pray we'll find your light ... and hold it in our hearts.
Andrea Bocelli & Celine Dione 'The Prayer'

Have you prayed before any time in your life? Prayer is an interesting phenomenon. It is closely related to some of the main faiths on earth, on the other hand it is something that we remember, children do naturally or they just spontaneously say 'yes' to. At certain times in our lives, often when stuck or deeply challenged, we remember, look up and pray.

The heart likes to pray. And with the heart you have all the flexibility you need, want or feel to have. Angela's story later in this section is a lovely example of this.

A brief personal note before continuing. There is no intention to promote any belief, faith or spiritual path more than any other. Naturally, having grown up in a central European country and now living in Australia, by default there was more exposure to Christianity than any other religion. There is only the hope that whatever your faith, belief or non-belief is that more heart and a lighter heart will facilitate a wonderful and purposeful life for you and everyone else. I am grateful, too, that from an early age I have recognised a similarity and beauty in all the different faiths and approaches rather than the differences. We know, too, that unfortunately and sadly these mind/brain perceived or knowledge-differences have often led to arguments and conflict, even on large scales.

If you have no faith, belief, even if you are a convinced atheist, you can let your heart pray and 'experiment' with the feeling, help, depth and the outcomes of your heart-prayers.

If you have a set belief, a strong faith or belief, then, hopefully, you can find in your heart, the flexibility or strength to add and use the heart in your prayers. After all it is the holy books that refer to the heart's importance in many places and yet, a modern teacher, your current minister, rabbi, imam, nun, monk, priest, pundit, guru or saint may not be aware of this.

Prayer traditions and the normality of praying

There are quite a lot of references to the heart in the main religious books. The bible talks more about the problem we have when our hearts are not pure. However, it has some indirect references to praying from the heart.

> *'When you are on your beds, search your hearts and be silent.'*
> Psalm 4

The Koran talks in quite a beautiful way about the heart. Some of the scholars describe it as the inner, spiritual or metaphysical heart. It is considered to be of 'utmost importance'. Mohammed the Prophet is stated to have said, further pointing to its significance:

> *'Let this be known, inside the body there is a piece of flesh. If it is sound, the whole body is sound and if it is spoiled, the whole body is spoiled. Beware! Know that that piece of flesh is your heart.[15]*

The Koran shows in other places that the heart can perceive a greater truth and that it is emotions that blind the ability to see this truth.

> *'In prayer, it is better to have a heart without words than words without a heart.'*
> Mahatma Gandhi

Gandhi declared himself a Hindu and yet respected and embraced individuals of all other faiths. Connected to Hinduism, together with other holy books, are the Upanishads. A very beautiful quote is in the oldest Upanishad:

> *'There is a light that shines beyond all things on earth, beyond the highest, the very highest heavens. This is the light that shines in your heart.'[16]*

The same section of these Upanishads explains that this light, this inner most core of your heart, is the 'atman', which in their religion, as in Yoga, is considered to be the equivalent of the core of every human, or the spirit. It is this part that can recognise the Divine, communicate beyond words or mind/brain limitations and is ultimately the one 'merging' with, or returning to, the Divine or the Divine's residence, heaven, paradise or the kingdom of God.[17]

The Sufis, often perceived as the mystics of Islam, are listed separately here. It is perhaps because they have used the heart with more clarity or dedication than other groups, they have produced an almost endless and quite beautiful list of heart-related insights:

> *'I have come to drag you out of yourself, and take you in my heart. I have come to bring out the beauty you never knew you had and lift you like a prayer to the sky.'* Rumi

These books are clearer about the 'results' in terms of the help from the heart in prayer, all of life and to achieve a good life.

> *'Blessed [are] the pure in heart: for they shall see God.'*
> Matthew 5:8

> *'And the Garden shall be brought near ... for everyone who comes with a contrite heart; enter it in peace. This is the Unending Day.'[18]*

> *In the assembly of Allah in the hereafter, the only benefiting will be a purified heart. This awesome day when neither wealth nor children will profit anyone except him who brings to Allah a pure heart.'*
>
> Surah Shu'ara, verse 88, 89

In Judaism the heart is also given an important role and function. Prayer forms part of the relationship with God. Service to God is supposed to be 'with your whole heart.' One of the services performed is prayer with the heart.[19] The heart is also the source of a greater inner ability to be conscious in a different way and to perceive truth.

> *'It is in the heart that the heart becomes conscious of itself and of its own operations.'*

It seems normal for many individuals, with or without a particular faith, at times to pray. Let us look closer at the help that the heart can offer.

Before doing so, let me here also apologise to you and your faith group if you are not listed here. Make it your own 'research' to find out where the heart's role or importance finds expression in your faith, in words or in action. I would love to hear about it.

---

[15] The Koran, citation from Bukhari, Muslim, Tirmizi, Abu Dawd and Nasayi.
[16] Chandogya Upanishad 1.13.7.
[17] The term merging is being used here as 'yoga' means to merge. Even the practice of Yoga, often understood as physical exercise with some spiritual aspects also, describes yoga as a goal, to have the heart and essence of who we are to return back home, back to the spiritual home.
[18] Surah Qaf, verse 31-34.
[19] This is in accordance with the 'Talmud Bavli' one of the central books in Rabbinic Judaism.

Does the prayer reach - does God listen?

Does my prayer reach the Divine or God? Does God have the time or even bother to listen? This can be burning questions for the faithful or for someone even casually praying. In the heart of hearts you know. This and other questions are what the heart can answer. It's ability to perceive, to know, has no limits.

It will take some time, perhaps five, ten or a few more years. Yet, when you reach a state of heart openness and heart clarity, then answers to deep questions or some of the world's or the universe's secrets can be revealed. In the same way, with the help of the suggested heart-preparing Heart strengthening practices, the KHH below and the related PHTs, you will feel answers, in the form of feelings, to those questions within.

It is when you feel the truth, reality and feeling in your heart while praying that you know beyond what others say or what others said, even what so-called holy people have said.

It becomes a deeper truth or an unshakeable inner knowing that can deepen your practice, beautify your life and give profound meaning to your spiritual existence and growth; in meditation or prayer or in daily life.

Using the key

Prayer can be just to pray, to feel closeness, connection or to fulfil a requirement according to faith or guidelines. For people who pray less regularly prayer is often triggered by an event or a situation. For some this may be a time when they are particularly joyful and grateful for others. It may a time when divine or higher level intervention is longed for.

The following KHH and the PHT around the main heart strengthening are structured the way they are so that an experience of heart or more heart in prayer can be had.

At times in sessions where all the facets and helping aspects of the heart are covered, the role of the heart in prayer is also discussed. An analogy is used that many people easily relate to. You feel to make a mobile call to a dear loved one in a faraway location or country. You have a wonderful mobile phone (a physical body and more, your whole self), you have signed up to the phone company (your faith, feeling or spiritual group) and now you expect to be connected and have a dialogue. A small oversight occurred. You forgot to activate and use the sim card (your heart). The sim card is the key, one part that enables the call and that has the information or program, even to dial the right person.

What the analogy illustrates is that a connection with the Divine is possible only when using the tool given for it, the heart. The following KHH, in combination with the PHT afterwards, offers an opportunity to experience this and as your heart grows and opens more, to experience this deeper and deeper. In your own prayers, as you experience it, your heart will be more naturally this connector, the sim-card and the receiver. It will also help your heart meditations to be taken deeper into the bliss, radiant heart energy and Blessing that can flow continuously to and through the heart.

Key Heart Help 14: Praying from the heart

I see this life like a swinging vine
Swing my heart across the line.
One Republic (song)

The key to experience a prayer from the heart is to just have a similar approach and attitude in using the heart as in any of the previous heart exercises and meditations.

In the way that the heart is introduced in this book, and will naturally work for you, it can deepen any existing experience, practice or belief. The heart is just the heart. It is not about a group, belief or new approach. Kalila's Story shows how an existing and devoted practice of prayer and belief can be enriched by more heart presence. She grew up in a Catholic household and found this a beautiful and enriching experience. It was through the heart that another world started to open.

Kalila's Story:

'I started to first learn about the heart at a Reiki workshop[20]. I had tried many workshops, however, I felt that something was still missing. The workshop taught me how to directly connect to my heart centre and to the nice feelings in the heart. I was so happy. Other workshops talked about the heart but didn't connect me to it. It was what I had been searching for all these years.'

'Before opening my heart my life was very good as far my physical surrounding was concerned. I had a great family and job. But, it was the feeling inside me that wasn't right. I very often felt anxious, restless, was seeking for something but didn't know what. There was also a lot of sadness.'

'Once I started to use my heart I was starting to experience more happiness, calmness in my life. I also felt a lot of relief because a part of me knew that I was here on earth for a greater purpose but wasn't sure how to execute this. I have always loved helping people, so once I

---

[20] The workshop Kalila attended was a Reiki Tummo workshop. It is the Reiki Tummo and Open Heart Workshops taught by the Padmacahaya Foundation for Inner Study that teach about the heart in this way. It is open for anyone. Other programs may also state that they work with the heart, help it to open, yet their knowledge or experience may be quite different.

realized I could help people by just sharing the love in my heart, this all made sense to me. It was so simple, so deep and so beautiful. I realized that I didn't have to go to anywhere or really do anything extravagant to make a difference to the world and that by connecting to my heart and sharing the Divine love within with others was all I needed to do - what I was here on earth to do.'

'I also further deepened my connection to God in my prayers and really all the time. I began to feel a more direct connection with God, a feeling of being taken care, comforted, loved, so yummy and difficult to describe in words. My mother always prayed with me as a child and instilled a lot of faith in me about God. I did pray often before opening heart. I did trust in God, however I also had a lot of fear in God. After continuing to open my heart, and with the guidance of our teacher, it was clear that God always loves us and never is upset with us. This allowed me to open my heart even more and allow myself to receive all the love and abundance that God wants to give us.'

'By having opened my heart, I have also let go so many of my worries and fears, so now I am able to move through whatever challenge there may be, so easily and quickly. Now there is joy whatever it is I am doing and beautiful moments of real happiness that sometimes I start giggling out of the blue and my colleagues or family wonder why I am laughing. My life also is flowing more smoothly and everything that I need just seems to show up at the right time.'

'I really feel how much God really wants to give us everything that we need and that we are the only ones that limit ourselves. I also experience moments of bliss, a feeling of like almost being in love. It is something to be experienced and words do not give it justice. I have also noticed that when I stay within these beautiful feelings, people around me also soften up, smile more and my day at work flows easily. I am more grateful for everything that I have, and to have found my heart.'

Kalila's sharing indicates some of the changes that the heart can naturally facilitate, in relation to prayer, in our connection to the Divine, God and in relation to the greater love and connection our heart feels to everyone.

Praying from the heart is something very beautiful and deep. An experience of closeness, love, being loved, being in deep peace becomes clearer over time and with deepening heart involvement.

Every time you pray using your heart the heart will open more, and the more your heart is opening, your prayers, meditations and all of life will become more beautiful.

Praying from the heart is not exactly right as a description. It is more natural when all parts work together and while you can pray without words from the heart it is equally normal, natural and all right to have a prayer formed in thought and then for it to be helped by the heart. The best really is when all parts, mind/brain, heart and all else work as a team.

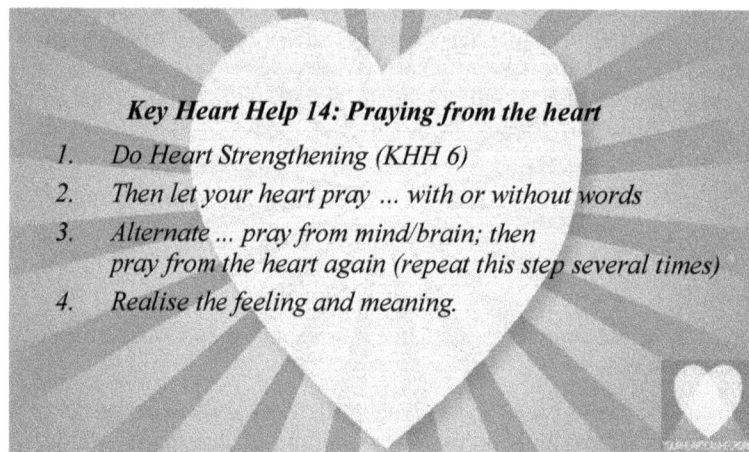

Key Heart Help 14: Praying from the heart

1. Do Heart Strengthening (KHH 6)
2. Then let your heart pray ... with or without words
3. Alternate ... pray from mind/brain; then pray from the heart again (repeat this step several times)
4. Realise the feeling and meaning.

The full KHH 14 - Praying from the heart pray I - no words are said

The best preparation for your heart is always the complete Heart Strengthening (KHH 6) even if you feel your heart is already naturally active, present and open. The deeper preparation is the PHT 76.

- When you clearly feel the heart feelings, while staying relaxed and smiling feely;

- Let your heart pray without words. (Here it is important just to have this one intention and no words to follow, and then for the heart to pray); then

- Feel and enjoy or follow the feelings - your prayer - from your heart.

You may have a feeling or reaction from your heart. This may be an expansion, pulsing or something being pulled upwards or flowing upwards. This is the prayer from your heart. In moments you feel these feelings, follow them with all your heart and feeling.

In some way this PHT is a warm-up. It offers a chance to feel that the heart is there, the heart has its own knowing, connection and ability to pray, very similar to the more standard mind/brain formulated prayer.

If you are relaxed enough, trusting your heart, you should clearly feel a response, a reaction and expansion of some sort. The heart knows its natural Divine connection. Similar to the above mobile phone analogy, once the sim card is programmed, it will just work. Also the flow of information, communication, care and love is never only one way. It becomes a two-way communication. It is natural that praying in this way, even with no words is a touching, deepening and quite special feeling and experience. In moments when you pray from your heart you are connected, in two-way communication, in touch and you can send and receive.

> ### The full KHH 14 - Praying from the heart pray II - with words
>
> *Prepare with Heart Strengthening or PHT 76. Then ...*
>
> - *From your heart (one intention is enough) as a prayer, call the (name of the) divine (in one or two words) or pray by saying one or two prayer lines;*
>
> - *After you have called the Divine or said one/two lines of your prayer, give it time, feel, relax, smile;*
>
> - *Every time you say something, reconnect with the heart, heart feeling and follow the feeling. It is in those moments that prayer becomes a dialogue or exchange; and*
>
> - *Use the feeling from the heart all the time. Give more emphasis or meaning to using the heart-feeling than the words or exact words you want to say or 'should' say.*
>
> *It may be helpful, to work more with the feeling, to only use one or two words initially, to feel the quality of using the heart, to let the prayer work, to feel and to give it time.*
>
> *When you feel the feelings clearly in your heart as you pray in one, two word prayers only, then expand your prayer to more lines. After each set of one to two lines, pause, be in the feeling, heart-connected, then continue.*
>
> *At the end of your prayer remain in heart-centred presence and gratitude for a while.*

This looks simple, and for some, too simple. A little logic may help to illustrate that even praying one or two words from the heart can be meaningful. Why does someone pray? The answer here is normally to have a better connection, to be closer to the Divine or to be helped. So what is more important, the prayer, your prayer or the response and help from a loving divine being or Creator?

The less you do the more you can allow the other flow and help to naturally be stronger. When you are connected in this way, and with love, feeling and from your heart call the name of the Divine, these feelings can even deepen.

Past experiences with this way of praying or Open Heart Meditation have shown that when there is no perception, history or concept in relationship to the name of the Divine then terms like Divine Source or True Source allow for an even deeper experience.

Perhaps be at peace in your heart here. Moments when you call the Divine from your heart, using your heart, the Divine knows and will help, make corrections and will make sure it works.

Praying from the heart can expand the meaning, feeling and experience around your prayer-practice. Hopefully this is all neutral and natural enough for you to include somehow into your existing practice. The analogy of the sim card and mobile phone may look very simple and yet the invitation is to let your heart be the key or the missing link. If you use the heart already, let the exercises help you 'learn by heart' and for everything to become deeper still. Often outcomes and help facilitated can also change and improve.

Friends, clients, workshop participants have changed hugely in this way and have naturally found a balance between being free-spirited, doubtful, a meditator or with a praying practice to someone who now combines all. They have also realised that their best intentions and ideas always carry within them the seed for improvement. This has gently taught them that it can be very helpful to make the prayers more open and less driven by 'I want' and 'I need'. Do we really know what we really want or need? And, after all, the logic of the heart and mind often are that we need help and pray to a higher source, power, being or the Creator of us, of all.

If you feel to, add to your prayer words or lines such as ... when praying for your family or loved one 'please bless and help so that all our interactions can be loving and kind, with understanding and in support of each other and whatever is in accordance with your love' or when you pray for your work situation 'please bless and help so that all can be facilitated or arranged for work to run smoothly, or for a new job to come along at the right time, all in accordance with your love and will.'

Be prayer-wise and use your heart. Be prayer-smart and pray for the best you can think. Be in sweet surrender to the God of your faith to guide, help and facilitate, which often is the reason for the prayer in the first place. Don't solely send your prayer, relax, smile be heart-present and also receive the return-call, help or blessing.

Within and beyond the heart - summary

Your spiritual existence, your spiritual growth, daily life is something that can add wonderful meaning to your life, the relationships around you, and offer a depth to how you experience life.

The heart fully empowers you here, too. It does not have any 'must dos', 'rules' or any other similar guidelines. Yet, the heart requires some degree of maturity. Following the heart is, when you really follow it, the ultimate guide to doing the right thing, to living life meaningfully and successfully as determined by every moment.

The way that the heart can build bridges to your own future, the way it knows 'by heart' all your past, and the way it brings you to the moment, the often cited 'here and now', is unique. It is rightly considered important, this 'here and now', as all of life takes place there, every moment.

Being heartful is at the core of being a human being. The heart does not benefit from you trying more. Human doing is less helpful for the heart. Trying is effort directed from the mind/brain: our plans, intentions, ideas, wants, hopes or desires. The heart knows what is needed and perhaps even more so the very Creator of every heart and of the universe we live in within the heart's natural divine connection. All planning and hoping is a questionable attempt to try to control what will be in an hour, next month, next year or past retirement age. Meditation and prayer then become a sweet and gentle surrender to what is and what will be at the level of your deeper inner existence and wisdom. In the physical world you use the heart's insights, guidance and all its abilities to do, to do with love, heart and all that the heart has shown so far and still will show in all its depth.

The heart is unique and can connect to the present and the past. It can also connect to a mouldable blueprint of the future. Feeling the heart now, when you make plans or decisions, is all that is needed to be in tune.

Heart-centred spirituality is simple and yet profound. By finding trust in something that is non-physical, your heart, the often priceless, non-physical, intangible and non-purchasable life qualities, such as love, peace, wonder or joy, can be felt clearer.

The heart offers you a wonderful opportunity to be at the centre of a joyful, safe, amazing, heartful and purposeful life - and to feel, experience its reality.

Who you are will naturally be clearer with more access to and wisdom given by your own heart. When and how this will happen depends on many factors, one perhaps being how much you use and open the heart to gain full access to it. Spiritual growth will have another depth to it with this deeper understanding of who you are. Opening the heart can be greatly assisted with the workshop program described in the appendix section of the book. Your heart will or may know when, where, how and if that is part of your heart journey.

The heart has been described in books, poetry, song and stories as something greater than us, something that can help to understand matters beyond the mind, brain, hopes and dreams, including those of deeper personal, spiritual or faith nature.

What is again wonderful and beneficial is the taking-out or influence-adjusting of the outer powers from the past, the teachers, gurus, experts, ministers and anyone who tells you what they think the truth is. They may or may not be on the mark; or only partially be on course. With your own heart you can feel a bigger picture, you can feel and connect to a much greater or profound truth in personal, family, relationship, social, work and spiritual matters. This allows you to follow a direction that will benefit you, your heart and others around you. It will offer you an inner peace that is based on deeply feeling within, realising, and therefore knowing this truth.

Summary - the core of your heart - the light within

Connecting more heart-to-heart to others is one of the most exquisite feelings in life. In moments like this, a deeper light within can shine with feelings of sweetness, connection and shared growth. This heart-to-heart works also in terms of the relationship with the Divine and the Creator. Here are the main aspects of your heart's possible help for you to be connected, to grow as a whole person and spiritually:

1. You can connect to a part in you that knows, feels and has another deep or deeper intelligence by feeling your inner age (PHT 6 'Feel your inner age' in section IV).

2. The PHT 'End-of-life check' invites you to write statements in your Heart Diary about where you want to be at the end of your life. It then allows you to let your heart also feel these and show you a feeling as to where your heart wants you to be, what the deeper, wiser you longs to achieve. Repeat this several times over one or more years. Check earlier entries to realise how, with the heart's continued opening and help, goals, perspectives, insights and truths shift or change.

3. You have followed some of the KHHs and PHTs in the book or online. Have you noticed the depth in feeling that your heart is gently facilitating? You can deepen this by letting your heart realise that it is connected to infinite love, a limitless source of love and a finer form of exquisite feeling, energy or blessing. Let the PHT 'Heart realising connection and blessing' and PHT 'Letting the blessing work' guide you so that your heart can realise this more. In return your heart will facilitate deeper opening and even more profound help.

4. Inner peace is wonderful to have and to feel. In PHT 'Inner Peace from Mind/Brain and Heart' you can let yourself be taken from perceiving calmness, peace or 'inner peace' from the mind/brain and from the heart. Every heart use, every heart exercise, is heart-learning and a deepening of everything 'heart'.

5. With more heart-presence the purpose in daily life will shift. PHT 'Purpose in daily life' will guide you to realise this clearer and document this in the form of diary notes over time. In turn changes in your life, helped by more heart, will be clearer and you will find it easier to commit to your heart more.

6. The PHT 'A day in love' is a practical step of integrating heart-presence into an average day.

7. Use the PHT 'Meditation for a strong and clear heart' as another way to deepen the heart's connection to the Source of Love, Divine or the God of your belief or choosing. Directing the heart more to the Divine is something the brain does not know, nor can do. Trust in your heart and the guidance in your spiritual existence or direction can grow profoundly in this way.

8. The next KHH 13 'Open Heart Meditation' combines three key heart-supporting exercises: heart strengthening, letting the heart pray and heart-centred meditation. This simple, yet profound practice can be the most direct route to a clear, light and wonderfully free heart.

9. There are two parts to KHH 14 'Praying from the heart'. In the first part, after your heart preparation, you solely intend to let your heart pray and then feel/follow the feeling. You can experience that your heart knows how to pray. In the second version, you are invited to use words and yet still engage your heart. Experiment with both as two ways to pray. It will develop your heart capacity and the special feelings from the heart. You may also find that your prayers will be more effective.

10. There has not been one person who did not have any form of cleansing while doing heart strengthening or further practices introduced in the second half of the book. This is a wonderful sign that the heart is working, that the heart is needed to cleanse burdens or heaviness. Persevere, do another round of practice or rest, then start again. This is the approach that will work.

11. You have a practice of prayer or meditation, or you don't have one, or you are not sure. Once you have the core understanding and first heart experiences and intend to use your heart in meditation or prayer, it will be doing it and help you. They will become special, beautiful and heart-opening, heart-cleansing experiences. Following the instruction from the PHT 'Try More' or 'Watch the Heart' will deepen all your meditations and prayer and all else that you hope your heart will do for you and others, dear ones around you.

Chapter 9

The Bigger Picture - In Your Heart You Know

*The release of atomic power has changed everything except our way of thinking ...
the solution to this problem lies in the heart of mankind. If only I had known,
I should have become a watchmaker. Albert Einstein*

Why would anyone want to be part of a bigger picture, what are reasons or motives? Not everyone longs to do so, and yet, in some, this longing is clear and strong. One trend seems to be, as people get older, wiser and gather more experience in life overall, it can become more meaningful to contribute to or be part of a bigger picture. For some this 'bigger picture' existence becomes their declared main purpose in life.

Is your heart a part of all this? If so, what helpful role can it play in connecting you to a bigger picture? Can your heart assist in directing and fulfilling this urge and perhaps most important of all, in making sure there is deep, long-term and lasting meaning? While the ability of your heart to understand a bigger picture was touched on in earlier chapters, the following sections will explore these questions in detail from the perspectives of the heart.

For some people there is a sense within, that being part of a bigger picture is important, such as being part of or contributing at a community, state, national or global scale. For others, a bigger picture is just reaching out from within and extending to a closer, social, family or neighbourhood environment. For others, again there is no such sense at all.

When you look at a bigger picture from the mind/brain perspective only, then there is a risk to solely look for big items. Work for the whole community, whole state, whole country, world-wide or global looks good and in some way, is being part of something bigger or very large. From a heart's perspective large is different. Items that people in general, from the mind/brain perspective, like or associate with 'big picture' will be run through a growing heart intelligence and wisdom. You may find that a physically 'big picture' first becomes smaller, like attending to and growing your heart capacity, and then, from there, an adjusted outward course is taken.

By now you can, hopefully, relate to what the heart can offer here: a refined form of guidance towards what to do or what not to do, and how to do it - with your heart involved.

The first step is to use the heart. That is being within a bigger picture. The heart can then further assist directly, gently and in deepening ways to be part of an outer bigger picture.

The heart may guide you to be active and out there, to search for deepening meaning and to be of service. Alternatively, it may guide you to just be at peace, to find a deepening peace; perhaps in meditation or prayers for others you know, or the entire world.

The question is, what can the mind/brain know on its own, about what we should learn, and what our role, purpose or contribution is supposed to be like for oneself, or any other person? Humans are wonderfully complex beings and it would be really hard to work out exactly what is someone else's bigger picture. Some people make these kinds of decisions for others and they give the impression that they know. However, in line with 'bring your own house in order first', perhaps good work in the world is done in harmony and flow with growing heart clarity. One part of it may be, 'to bring your own heart in order', to en-lighten and clear the heart, to polish the lens through which you perceive yourself and the world. With this 'eye of the heart' you can then look, feel and adjust and engage more heart-to-heart with others.

Your heart will help you to learn from its innate wisdom, and as such you can gain greater awareness about what is natural and what is intended for you. But it is much less important how big this picture is. It may be quite small or very large, this is up to the heart, in team work with the mind/brain to decide.

The following sections discuss in more detail what a bigger picture may look like at a personal level and in relation to our connection to others. It will also look at, from a heart's perspective, the important interplay between external issues, concerns like 'peace' or 'environment', and the inner heart role, your inner deeper self or being.

Steve's story below is a wonderful example of how more heart awareness and presence has created a shift in someone who always has been longing to make a difference, to help and to be of service within a bigger picture. In Steve's sharing he set out to work for the environment and gradually with more heart, was able to shift his focus to see a bigger, more beautiful picture.

Steve's Story:

'I grew up as an environmental activist. I was always in the Australian bush catching lizards and other creepy crawlies from the age of about 4 - or so I'm told. Nature was the place where I felt most connected and grounded.'

'The incredible discovery of the heart helped me to deepen this relationship in a way I never thought possible. What I realised through the experience of my heart opening was that I was in direct relationship with the Creator of everything in the entire Universe and beyond... which put me in direct relationship with everything in a very different way.'

'As my heart opened through the open-heart practice, I began to experience a shift in my perception of reality. To our mind, being separate from each other and our environment is a physical fact, and yet, strangely, physical separation is immaterial from the perspective of an open heart. Feeling connected to others, and knowing somehow that we are a part of 'one reality', is the experience that began to dawn on me as my heart opened.'

'I realised over time that it is us who creates our separation from each other and our environment. We reinforce that separation by the choices we make every moment, which, often, happen at such a rapid speed that we can't even see them as choices. These reaction-responses are part of the fight/flight mechanism buried deep within our DNA, the engine room of which is fear. Slowly I began to realise what an incredible blessing it is to have our hearts open, because as our hearts open, we are able to receive more Love and Love replaces fear and changes our lives dramatically.'

'So, this is what happened. As my heart opened I automatically began to trust people and situations more. This trusting was automatic, almost as a by-product of my heart opening. And as I trusted more, my very reality also changed. I felt more connected to everything. Things turned out better more often. I stopped losing things, I started remembering things and my relationships with people were smoother and more loving and open.'

'Seriously, it was like a magic wand had been waved over my life! I had spent my whole life up to this point wondering how come some people had more and others had less. I began to realise that we all have everything... in a strange way. Having it all simply means that you stop wanting for things that you don't have. It is fear which drives that wanting because it is part of the primitive survival mechanism within us.'

'In the years since my heart began opening (and it just goes on and on!) a 're-scripting' has taken place within me at the deepest level. Choosing love over fear now happens naturally. Deep peace and joy is now an everyday part of life and is something so precious and yet, miraculously, it is also our very birth-right. Our Creator is simply waiting for us to accept the gift of love so that we can become who we are all supposed to be.'

'Strangely, opening our heart is more like a process for remembering our true nature - the way we were created in the first place.'

Steve also talks about his passion or longing for social change, to be a facilitator of change. He also realises over time that without heart there is a risk of becoming a 'justice warrior' and what is being done is a reaction to events or to injustice. However, often in going out to war and fighting something or someone, if there is emotion like fighting with anger, there is the risk of overtly or under-the-surface simply creating another injustice. There will be one powerful side effect - the step-by-step burdening, even closing of the heart.

What Steve is implying in his story is that any readiness to fight, a willingness to be inwardly and outwardly angry, to have any kind of emotion, in doing good or righting a wrong, can be counterproductive to all that the heart is and stands for. The following sections explore a more heart-centred pursuit of a 'bigger picture'.

Heart choices

The bigger picture is often viewed as something outside of us. From the perspective of living a more balanced or heart-centred life, to make the vital connection between all of who you are and any bigger picture there needs to be a 'hub', or something that can do this 'connecting'.

The world around us is present and, by coincidence or design, its existence and our need to interact with it or to be within it, naturally takes place. At some level there is no need to plan, think or have a 'bigger picture' concept or goal. Yet, equally, many of us use our mind/brain to plan, think, direct or reflect on your role within a neighbourhood, community or the world. But is the mind/brain, on its own or as the dominant force, sufficient to facilitate a purposeful life? Let us look at some of the possible big picture activities to illustrate the heart's role more.

Social issues - our community

To work with social or social justice issues is one expression of purposeful bigger picture work. To be an active member of a community, to have concern for social issues is something wonderful and often comes naturally; even if it is just in the form of helping a neighbour out. There is heart and care in it. Who would send away a neighbour knocking at the front door asking for help, for a helping hand? Who would ignore someone during an emergency, who needed a ride to the doctor, a nurse or dentist, or just for something she or he currently is lacking, like a lawn mower, a tool or a food item?

Being active, being engaged meaningfully in a social or community setting can be quite simple and fulfilling at deep levels. Activities may be voluntary work at the local soup kitchen, a second-hand clothing outlet, at your church group, youth work, aged care work or personally helping a neighbour who is unwell or suffers from a permanent or temporary disability. This low paid, temporary or unpaid work may be in a health or charitable organisation doing whatever is necessary, or be very specific, doing highly skilled tasks.

Medium to larger social, social justice or community issues may see you involved in some form of committee role, involved in boards or regional/state committees, due to your background or experience. It may be around social, environmental, political or other broader, bigger picture issues. The key is not so much how big or how 'important' your role is in terms of status, it is about how much and how clearly is your heart in it.

The heart is happy and at peace whatever you do as long as you do it from your heart and in accordance with it.

This kind of work you feel drawn to do, and often someone will say 'this person has a big heart' when recognising your contributions. Indeed, many social support events or welfare services could not do their work without volunteers with a 'big heart'. The list of possible social issues to be involved with is, without doubt, very long. But a big heart will feel a call to help. If we follow this call and our heart is also open, we can remain light and give the best, from our heart, and avoid the potential of also feeling upset, angry or disillusioned.

It is wonderful if you feel to help and to contribute in this way, and even better if you have time and energy to do so. You can help anywhere, at any level and any time. The key, however, is if you want it to help yourself and others the best, do it 'whole-heartedly'; meaning really use your heart practically and as much as possible, while 'at work'.

The more you feel and realise from the depth of your heart, the more you will naturally want to use the heart with more precision to make these choices, and decide how and where to contribute, which place, what organisation or area, and what attitude and heartfulness to bring to it. In bringing to this your heart's feeling and guidance there is increased likelihood that your contributions will be better. There will also be more fulfilment and purpose for you too, based on your unique skills and qualities, some of which may yet have to open or fully unfold.

Political

The word political may sound a bit too 'formal' or 'important' than it needs to be or is. The political field of being and working is almost endlessly wide, and in some way, everything we do or not do can be seen as a personal political activity or statement.

Opinions or thoughts that you hold are all political expressions. The ways you find to help in expressing these could go in any direction, stemming from upbringing, learning, influential people around you and whatever your opinion, belief or truth around issues are.

The heart is very helpful in terms of any political statement and doing. It can help to look to the past to realise that a deep understanding is needed. You will find examples where governments or organisations did things that seemed good or meaningful then, yet now we know they were not so good then, or failed to consider the longer-term. An example far enough away in history is perhaps Gandhi's sense that England should not own India. He followed his truth and heart, perhaps more than even others, in finding non-violent ways to say 'no' to occupation and related political and economic exploitations. Now we know with growing political awareness, that it is not right to invade or occupy another country for economic reasons.

Environment

It is spring again. The earth is like a child that knows poems by heart.
Rainer Maria Rilke

Environmental issues are one other area where people can feel to focus on. In years gone by, in particular in the 80s, 'the environment' was a huge concern and strongly in the minds of many people. It was around that time that environmental groups and green parties around the world formed and started their work.

It appears that at present environmental issues such as pollution, energy consumption, use of non-renewable resources, the ozone layer and many local environmental issues are less on people's minds and less on community, political and the media's agendas. While this may be the case the reality of the state of the planet is one where pollution still occurs, wildlife, nature and humans suffer because of it, and attention to improve guidelines, legislation and attitudes are perhaps still needed.

When you feel the state of the whole planet with your heart, now and in comparison, 50 years ago, or 150 years ago, it has not improved and is currently not in a good condition. From the perspective of the heart, environmental or political environmental activity can be good. With more heart perhaps more creative and sustainable inventions or changes can be made to improve the life of all humans, animals, plants and ecosystems on the planet. Perhaps these 'inventions' will equally assist economically, businesses, employees and governments. And perhaps, with more heart, the hearts of people who hold onto destructive patterns by following fear, concern or other emotion, can also be touched and invited to change - as Steve shared earlier.

One way to help and improve the situation is at a local, even personal level (as discussed further later in this chapter). One action that feels right to your heart is much better for your heart than many words or long papers written from the mind/brain only, or long discussions how things could be improved. This will also help your heart more.

You can feel what feels right to do, in the home, your garden in relation to how you manage environmental issues such as waste, energy consumption and others, and act more in accordance with your heart.

If for example you are a writer, then to write on environmental issues is not only your unique skill, but it is one way to make your heart happy. If you a gardener or hobby gardener then your contribution will be of a more practical nature, like planting trees, helping with weed control, or offering your advice.

Make big issues small

The more open your heart is, the more you will feel where there is a need, where there is pain or suffering, or where your bigger picture service can help. You will feel this with heart and not emotion, or with a heart comparatively free from emotion. There will also be less over-thinking of issues or possible related action. You can make any kind of decisions in harmony with mind/brain and heart's knowledge and wisdom.

For this decision the size of the big picture work matters less than the application, which is inevitably local. This can be a little clearer if one asks how bigger issues can be tackled by us in the best ways, at smaller picture levels, in the personal or family life?

It doesn't matter how small or big the issue or playing-field is within you or your work. What matters is that we integrate, smoothly and heartfully, the big picture work, with all that is 'small', routine or part of our daily interaction. This applies at home, at work, everywhere, and in this way another big picture circle can close.

This is not that hard. Outer motive or reason is one trigger for you to become active. To look for the bigger picture there is naturally some form of inner response that it is based on. The question for which you need to find the answer in your mind/brain and heart unity is:

Is what you do or plan to do predominantly driven by mental perception, by emotions or by what feels gentle, pleasant, expansive in your heart?

Getting to know more about who you are and how you function, including around the heart's role, can be helpful to see clearer why you do certain things, why you get involved in certain activities or groups, and to reflect on the depth and clarity of those involvements or past experiences.

Using some of the examples, you can perhaps connect with a reality that some of the political, social or environmental activities may be motivated by:

- Good ideas - meaning our mind/brain and more rational or logical reason;
- By emotion - the drivers or motivators are fear, worry or concern; or
- By the heart - feeling deep and gentle concern for others and feeling to act, respond or help.

While these look like three separate possible drivers or motivators, the reality is often a blurring of two or three of them. Just be aware of these and follow your heart and feeling more, to be more on the side of your heart's wisdom and help. By tapping into the flow of your heart's wisdom and abilities, you can open new ways of working in the world and with others, in ways that the mind/brain does not know or does not know yet.

The analogy of the emotional response to another person, when you are triggered by someone's actions towards you in a more personal situation, is not dissimilar to the larger, bigger picture emotional or clever mind/brain analysed events. There is a risk to get to the end of a period of time, the end to a work or volunteer life, and to realise that the deeper purpose and bigger picture contribution was not what the heart felt or longed for - it was not deeply enough aligned to a bigger picture or truth.

The heart's role

Nothing can dim the light which shines from within. Maya Angelou

How exactly does the heart help you to connect to a bigger picture in a way that is more organic, natural and more according to the heart's innate wisdom? How does the heart facilitate this connection, driven by an inner longing to be fulfilled, to make a difference, to be part of something bigger, and to make sense of it all? This section will explore your heart's role in this.

Personal growth-related

Your vision of making a bigger picture contribution may be in conjunction with or driven by your personal growth intentions and plans. You may know within that the full potential of who you are or can be is not yet fully reached. It is good and logical to really feel into this.

A first level of knowing what this is or can be may be dawning once we have certain skills or qualification. Yet it is more likely to surface once these skills are confirmed in the form of experiences or personal qualities that surface clearer over time.

At the same time your mind/brain may not or will never fully know what this really is, and how this your personal growth can help a bigger picture can unfold. The reality is that any vision, hope or plan will depend on variables that the future will bring. This future is never known now, and while it may unfold as planned or hoped for, it is equally likely that life will throw in other variables that may shape your plans.

In the same way, as the stories placed through the book tell, there are gradual and at times fast changes. In moments when you use your heart and are heart-connected, then the heart's planning, vision-support, ongoing guidance and active help will support you in keeping on track. It may also lead you off largely mind/brain created plans, such as for example personal or skill perfection, towards a path where the heart is added to your plans.

There is almost never a full separation between all these parts of who we are. Most likely, what you feel already to be or to do and how to make a difference, will connect at least in parts to your heart.

The greater depth of your heart's knowing is a longing to grow and live in such a way that there is a bigger picture part to life. For this to unfold it would be logical to use all that you are. This means more attention to develop the heart, as for most of us it is less developed than the developed strengths and abilities of the mind/brain.

It is good to make a first step or the next new step and to trust that more heart will mean more help and guidance. Many steps outside of the heart are steps into the unknown. However, stepping more into the heart should be safe, easy and into more know territory - you. It is a step inside, into what is you, accessing the fuller inner potential and from there to then create more fulfilment at an outer level. Personal growth, inner realisation and bigger picture living are deeply intertwined.

There can be a range of inner drivers when we aim to grow personally and consider the bigger picture at the same time. However, the driver source is somewhat connected to where you are at now, and the match between your long-term fulfilment, purpose and link with the bigger picture will unfold. The degree of personal fulfilment and enjoyment hinges on this too. In all personal growth there can be more of a focus on:

- Self, self-development and learning;
- Growth, development and learning exchange, interaction and shared learning with others;
- Focus on others more than self; and
- No focus, development and growth as a natural process.

The heart's contribution is not so much in ways of creating a line in the sand or establishing scores as to how much of your bigger picture 'doing' is in either one of these four areas. It is not about how personal, self-focussed or focussed on others your efforts are. The heart is solely there to be present and helpful and to facilitate the right blend. It will work in the way it does, it will guide you and will ensure that personal growth is ultimately unfolding in alignment with an outer reality, or bigger picture or purpose.

The depth of the heart is vast. The lighter, more present and purer your heart will become, the more you will be taken gently from self-development and learning for yourself, which can be one part of a bigger picture, to an even bigger one. There will be no focus needed.

'No focus' simply means that you, your mind/brain, no longer needs to focus, plan and to control the direction of your contribution to the big picture. While from the heart's perspective you will need commitment and hard work, if you follow your heart you will simply and easily be directed by the inner 'Company Director' or 'General Manager', your heart and inner heart.

The heart will also ensure that whatever is happening for you with your 'outer' activities, such as achievements and visible contributions to a perceived bigger picture, is heart-directed.

Knowing this or not knowing this is less important than a strong and clearing heart to just be there, to be present, and to move with some confidence. This also then means that you move through life with a more bridged or collaborating heart and mind unity. Over a period, when heart-connected to a bigger picture that the heart also knows, a natural alignment happens more and it will be in heart-sync with a bigger, universal picture. With this, deepening levels of purpose are revealed and deep levels of fulfilment and enjoyment happen.

In meditation, moments of insight, prayer or premonition, and more so in moment when you are deeply heart-connected, you have a chance to feel this as a guiding light. Progressing with the heart's help you will feel a deep, even overwhelmingly calmness or peace of being on track, being connected or 'at one' in a feeling kind-of way, as the part of a growing puzzle and big picture.

Fulfilment

If you wish to be a mine of jewels,
open the deep ocean within your heart. Rumi

The quote from Rumi points towards this chance and the joy of making a personal and positive contribution to the world, as well as the depth and preciousness of the heart.

The depth of the heart's work means that everything you plan and do will invariably trigger and facilitate a response in the direction of fulfilment.

Any degree of personal growth, insights and heart-realisations will add more to the quality, depth and feeling of your contributions. The gem, all of you, will be polished continuously and can shine like a bright spark. In doing, in being and in the most unusual places and situations, you can become that radiant jewel that your heart wants you to be. It is then that whatever knowing, wisdom, urge or longing is within can also be touched and fulfilled.

Some contributions or directions to follow look good and seem meaningful. The chance the heart offers here is to add additional depth to a mind/brain level of knowing. In addition to knowing that 'I have made a difference', there can then be a deeply felt and realised sense along the lines of 'it feels beautiful, right, truthful and in tune with a bigger picture'.

You may or may not know what this bigger picture or plan is. In feeling it deeply within your heart there is the heart's feeling and with it a deep and growingly unshakeable peace and fulfilment.

You may help to build a big bridge, a well or a children's playground and gain a degree of satisfaction from it. The deeper fulfilment is one that you will ever only feel within. While our mind has limitations, it is at this inner, heart level, where the knowing or truth is unshakeable.

Albert Einstein's quote at the beginning of this chapter serves as a more telling example. For an ambitious scientist to develop something new or find something that has never been discovered looks like a great contribution. However, longer term this may look very different. Other examples throughout this book also point to this. The more you follow or are guided by your heart, the more your bigger picture workings in the world will be of a clearer, genuine and sustainable goodness.

Spiritual growth related

Bigger picture existence and fulfilment for many would be about bringing our inner qualities into the world. At the same time, to live a happy, purposeful and fulfilled life is not about 'outer or inner'. The separation of an outer and inner world, the polarisation of everything, is one aspect, one principle often created by an overly strong mind/brain. The sweet flow of life is more like a permanent pendulum swing between the two of them or as an 'as-well-as' happening of all that life is. The heart can connect these two aspects. For some this one-ness is part of a bigger picture.

An inner focus on bigger picture items, on making a difference can be a somewhat strategic approach. Spiritual growth is often related to this inner world, the inner-most part of us that grows, does something or just is. Given they are within us, in the short or even medium term your spiritual progress or achievements may not be clear or obvious. There is a likelihood no one will see any development, in the form of an achievement or reaching a goal. This is because when we undergo spiritual growth related to a bigger picture, it is about non-physical aspects, qualities within and how they connect to spiritual goals or aspirations. Feeling, for you to feel, for others to feel the quality of any interactions is the domain of the heart. These qualities or feelings, which are the domain of the heart, are somewhat 'known' or have written about in very similar ways, in holy books and other works.

Sitting in silence, meditation or prayer is widely practiced. With it there is an acknowledgement of the importance of being loving and kind, finding inner peace and being connected as a means of being authentic stemming from an inside core.

For your heart there is purpose in having as your big picture goal to be kind and loving. While this is clearly stated in some of the beliefs systems or religions there is a part within that can connect with this too. Steve's sharing about his heart's learning and realisation is about this greater love that comes from the heart.

The greater the love you have in your heart, the more you feel it, the more every interaction is also filled with love, care and understanding, at home or at work. You know that a loving family life is meaningful, you also know that appreciation, care, support and flowing team work are meaningful at work and help our lives.

This most beautiful love can't be created by hope, want, vision or other mind/brain directed ways. While the mind/brain can assist, the ultimate feeling, depth and the vastness of it can only be felt and shared by the heart.

When you open your heart, others benefit as well. You have perhaps felt or seen that people around you thrive in their own way when you just love them, support them, be kind to them, and have unconditional love or unconditional positive regard for who they are.

Peace within and on the outside

Peace or deep feelings of calmness within may look like a similarly humble bigger picture goal. When you are at peace, it is hard to start a fight, have unrest at work or at home, a community argument, a bigger conflict or war. To be part of such a bigger picture is the hope for some, such as those who live in active conflict zones around the world.

There is selflessness in both being loving and being peaceful. It is the qualities of selflessness and humility that extend so easily beyond our self, touch or reach others, silently, with no words and often also with no action needed.

Perhaps, therefore, we are called 'human beings' and not 'human doings' to remember that these silent, quietly helpful human-to-human qualities are so easily appreciated and as such, meaningful.

You have learned and experienced that a clearer or lighter heart will not only have more calmness and love to share, it is also more peaceful within. The heart's ability to be a hub of calmness inspires other hearts. You are helping others in this way, heart-to-heart to soften, let go and to be more at peace. Finding more inner peace is one way to create a different world - starting from within. The more your heart develops these feelings, the more you will feel this as a possibility and reality.

If at the end of your life you and your heart are at peace, and, in many daily interactions you exemplified this peace, planted seeds of understanding, compassion, care, support or love, and others have felt it too, can you say that the life has been lived well or for a greater purpose?

Being connected - positive relations - belonging

Every human being is somewhat different in relation to their social life. Some are very social while others prefer to live more like a hermit. Regardless of where you are on this scale, there is something beautiful, joyful and wonderful when you connect to another human being, when you enjoy positive relations around you. No matter how different you may perceive yourself or others to be, all of our hearts long for connection and the fulfilment of something within that enjoys being in touch, interacting and loving. The heart's contribution here is to shift all experiences more towards quality and depth, and away from numbers, for example, how many friends, associates or social media contacts one has.

To be in touch with others, to have contact, is often not enough. This may at times be clearer when there is conflict or disharmony at home or at work. It doesn't feel so pleasant. You may also have had a great experience socially, or at an event, that touched you and others deeply, and still something is missing. Something doesn't yet feel right, something within is still longing to find a more complete balance or picture.

Being and feeling connected at a heart level, and having beautiful, positive relations, is one way to live a more fulfilled and big picture life. It can also be an incentive for you to start to use the heart more, by being in your heart more and practice interacting more with others from the heart. General regular Heart Strengthening and the KHH 11 from the work section will assist with this.

From this place of connection a deep sense of belonging can be revealed - a depth of feeling, safety, being at one with the world, and an acceptance of what will be. This belonging, based on the longing in the heart that seeks fulfilment, is the bridge between the longing within and what ultimate fulfilment of a bigger picture and plan will mean.

With a strong heart it matters less when and how often you see a close one. It is when you meet or interact with dear friends or family members that the deeper heart sharing will naturally balance what is often a reality now: dispersed families, friends who can only be seen a few times over a period. There is peace, calmness and deep joy in these ways to be and connect. More heart will give more depth and meaning to every one of these precious connections. The more heart that you can bring to these experiences, the more likely these relations will blossom and for more heart-to-heart time to be experienced. In all these interactions, even in thinking of each other from afar, there is a heart facilitated help unfolding. This can be immensely meaningful as Anna's story shows.

Anna had only started to learn about the heart and in a conversation shared that her brother had personal difficulties, including contact with the law, substance abuse and other challenging personal issues. While there had been no contact for some time with her brother, suddenly with a more active heart there was an openness again to connect, to be in touch and to forgive.

Anna felt a strong urge one day to write to her estranged brother. However, unfortunately she did not follow it, only to hear on the following day he had attempted suicide.

Anna's Sharing

'For some time now I did not have contact with my brother.'

'We are of similar age and yet things happened between us that made me pull back and not be in touch with him for quite some time now.'

'Late last week I felt to write to him and even sat down and wrote a long e-mail. I didn't quite trust the feeling and let it sit for a day or two, perhaps not trusting to send it either.'

'There was a clear sense that it was now time to re-connect, to forgive, to let go ... I really felt to connect.'

'I was shocked to hear the day after, that he had attempted suicide. It was to all a cry for help. I am very glad to hear that he was not successful. I asked myself, too if, would he have done it.'

'He replied since to my e-mail and was thrilled to hear from me, accepted, acknowledged many of the things I shared, from my heart, with him and I now look forward to a new beginning.'

It is not possible to know if there would not have been a suicide attempt if the e-mail was sent earlier. At the very least Anna felt that there was a possibility. Anna also vowed to follow these feelings now more often as they occur. This experience helped her to trust the heart more, to follow these feelings more, knowing that they are from the heart and that they are in support of her and others around her.

The feeling to not have been in touch and to have made a difference in someone's life can be heavy. In a situation, as in Anna's story, it can be hard to forgive oneself if a feeling, the heart's voice, and an opportunity to connect is missed.

Sometimes in life there is one chance to get it right. And yes, some chances are given again and again, but as in Anna's situation, if the brother's attempt had been successful, this chance to share more and to reconcile any heaviness or emotions from the past, and to move on from there, would have not been possible anymore.

With more heart, and following your heart, it will be quite difficult not to have a positive, deep, meaningful or wonderful time of connecting and sharing.

Whatever difficulties arise there is at least your stronger-growing heart, which can stay in peace more, allow for things to be aired, and for the heart to transform the interaction. This can happen because it has - ideally - already transformed you. Anna's story may also be a pointer that time is precious and that we should attend to the heart and what it tells us about the precious relations around us.

When you connect more heartfully with others, there is a further chance to grow using your heart innate ability. This includes any realisations around your purpose and its links to any deeper picture that includes your social, family or work connections. When this profound 'heart-to-heartness' unfolds, in ways that no doubt you have felt in moments in life before, a gentle flood of love and wonder will start to flow through you and from you. This at least is the heart's direction of connection and positivity. When there is a purer or unconditional love in your heart, the joy and bliss is for you and naturally to share. Even in times of disagreement, argument or heavy discussions, the peace or love will hardly ever leave.

Meditation and prayer

There can be a deeply felt longing within to connect, to make a contribution that is not only beneficial to us, but also to others. It finds expression in a somewhat spiritually grounded urge to be good and, to connect to goodness, in the light of the biggest possible picture or frame of reference.

This for some is one reason for their practice of meditation or prayer to connect either to deeper consciousness or to a Divine being, God. The sitting in meditation is to be in stillness, perhaps to clear disturbing influences of mind or emotion, and in this stillness to perceive a greater insight, truth or to attain deeper wisdom in order to then fulfil this longing.

Sitting or being in prayer is not dissimilar even though some would draw a deep 'line in the sand' based on past experiences around prayer. From a place within we seek connection and prayer is either an expression of this search for meaning or connection, or a call for help for self or for others. Connecting to the Divine, or realising similar things as is hoped for in meditation, can be one purpose of your prayer. What is further hoped is that we will be guided by a higher Being, God, the Divine of your belief, not only with day-to-day guidance, but also to be guided on or onto a path in life that is in alignment with a greater picture, plan or a Divine plan.

The nature of your heart is to want to connect to and fulfil a big, if not the biggest possible, picture.

The heart can connect and will reveal in growing clarity what you know, is unknown or partially felt within.

The heart likes to meditate and pray, or both together, and its very function is to deeply bring together the program, or longing within, for connection of your outer living.

Being within a larger plan

Making a difference, being of service, making meaningful contributions or being part of a big or very big picture may not be for everyone. Yet sometimes we do not seek this, as it can happen almost by accident. There is a risk, however, that in society focused on 'doing' and 'performing', this can also be just another expression of performing well, doing more or being seen to be active, busy or of importance. This is less important than the need to live a life connected to what resonates deep within you, at the level of your heart.

From the perspective of the heart you are much less a human 'doing' than you are a human being. Qualities such as kindness towards self and others, being at peace with yourself and others, and giving to the world by feeling joyful, happy and fulfilled can be wonderful if not profound gifts to the world.

The previous book chapters are all pulling you in this direction. The KHHs and PHTs offer ways to practically use the heart to enable you to feel these unique and beautiful human qualities. These innate heart qualities are quite inclusive too. When you are kind, at peace and joyful you can still work, be a student, be a parent, be an athlete or whatever else your path or work is now.

Being within and being part of a bigger picture then becomes something that is simple, profound and quite achievable. Another extension to this is to be in connection and 'in love', in a greater, deeper, free and supporting love; loving in ways the heart shows and naturally facilitates more, whether by yourself or with others.

Over time the heart can bring clarity to bigger picture discussions about topics such as evolution, a Divine Plan and the greater purpose of life, some of which has been the topic in the spiritual growth chapter. These realisations open from the heart and become your gifts to the part within that is longing to know, learn, understand and realise its place in a larger world, universe or whatever the biggest possible picture or reality is.

The mind/brain will struggle to perceive anything beyond the physical universe. Even within this universe only parts are known. This can illustrate the heart's role and its necessity. As a non-physical part within, it can perceive both physical and non-physical realities. The more you know your heart, or the real you, there is a decreasing need to convince or sway others. What the heart offers is feelings of quiet and clear confidence, self-esteem and ultimately deep, unshakeable peace of being part of a big picture and greater evolutionary or Divine plan.

Down- to-heart - for the heart and with more heart

... have best interest at heart.

Life is a wonderful gift to experience something quite special at times, and to also learn or 'be with' challenges. Accidents and natural disasters can be hard to grasp and cope with - without feeling emotions such as overwhelmed, sad, shocked, disillusioned or any other heavy emotion.

Look at life, there is a naturalness of being born, living and then passing on. Logic tells us that this all goes according to natural laws. As we are born, great grandparents move on and pass away and then normally, or naturally, our grandparents. It is our turn too, sometime in the future. Even though life and death are natural, normal and a given, logic is not enough to be at peace. The mind/brain unity will wonder and worry about this much more than the heart.

It is with the heart that a deeper existence and peace can be felt that transports your existence beyond these events, or what may be limiting occurrences, like the end of life and death. Somewhere inside you know or feel that a life, with focus or intent to live for a bigger purpose, often leads to more peace and more acceptance of all that life is. This is because the heart is about connection and building the greatest possible connection to all. It can help in finding purpose in our relations to others and all that defines us, as human beings; including the full journey that we go through. The heart also helps us to realise also that it is okay to retreat, to be a hermit or to seek solitude. And, despite this, our heart often naturally brings us back to a social setting or family. This is because our heart longs for connection and expression of what this connection means - to your heart and to everyone's heart. Indeed, this need for connection is evident when we consider that people who are strong and independent, and a leader of some sort, also need others. For instance, if this describes you, it important to realise it would not have been possible to be here, now, in this life without at the very least the willingness of your mother to bring you here; and often a team of family members, a partner or husband and medical or nursing staff.

The heart will connect, even, or in particular, in times of disconnect or distress. You need to give a voice, more so, listen to it. You may be the sole leader of an organisation or group, or you may be living in an isolated or new area with very few contacts, family or friends nearby. The heart will help you and make it incredibly easy and light to find social and heart-to-heart connection. For the heart it is not important if you are a leader or worker on a shop floor. Imagine a country solely with political or business leaders: there would be no medical staff or no farmers to grow food, and thus life would not be possible.

There is a purpose in your heart, the purpose of 'doing' is here perhaps the smallest one. How you connect, interact and how you realise the heart's full potential, is the next big step to take or make.

As outlined above, events such as natural disasters or other traumatic occurrences can be very difficult to come to terms with for the mind/brain. But fortunately, in every moment the heart realises, learns and can make sense of a bigger picture. The heart helps us to make sense of things, even if this is only one level. However, more importantly, if you make a commitment to a strong heart, this will enable you to be the best you can be in times of hardship or challenge. And even further, if you let your heart guide you, it will facilitate new ways that you can help in emergencies, hardship or challenging times.

Your exposure - act local

Given we live in a technological, information and media age, the flow of news and information can be overwhelming. In order to maintain a healthy and clear heart, it is important to choose what, when, and how much you expose yourself to this flow. This is because too much information or exposure to disturbing news or images can burden you and your heart over time. This can be information that you get via newspapers, television, social media or in any other form. This is particularly helpful early on your heart journey. It can also be good to reduce yourself to information flows that are not necessary and that stimulate the mind/brain more than required, or away from a desired greater heart to mind/brain balance. So always ask yourself, do I really need to know about this information or event?

Fortunately, the stronger the heart is, the more heart and mind/brain are in balance, the less negative impact any event will have on your emotions and subsequent wellbeing. You can then listen to or watch more of these kinds of events, without being affected. You will also probably also find, however, that the stronger your heart is, the less news of this nature will be of less interest.

To maintain a good heart, it will be beneficial to make some form of program that reduces exposure to events you don't need to know about, and which you can't do something about to help, reduce the impact.

You, your heart will want to spend more time on doing what is meaningful and what you are able to contribute. What is good for the heart is to look around, in small or medium circles, and to attend to situations that can do with your help. Any action, act of help, care and love will support your heart in turn. Yet, here it is time to share your heart with others, to really help from your heart. It is easy to find welfare or charity groups that need another pair of hands or hearts, your professional expertise, or simply to help where needed in very practical and heartful ways. There are heart benefits where you give or help at additional levels:

- You help others in situations of urgency or need;
- You help, heart-to-heart, others who will feel at some level a form of heart help or heart boost also; and
- You helping with more heart, will slow down thinking, overthinking and the often-related heavy thoughts, in turn keeping your heart light and free.

Now that your heart is present and that you know how to strengthen your heart, you can also apply 'doing things from the heart' to such situations by using the KHH 11 and, for example, PHTs 15, 16, 37, 63 or 79. There will be something for you in this. You will not only feel empowered to do something, you also see, feel and know that you make a difference. The feeling, joy and gratitude that you can not only experience but also share, is something quite magical. This more whole-hearted way of helping others will also be very feel-able to people in need, offering another level of relief and peace.

This relief and inner peace will be because of your heart's radiance and help. The more it is present it will alleviate stress, burden or trauma in others - without any words or doing. While words and actions can clearly help, our touch is deepest when hearts radiate to others, and we give or feel heart-felt actions or words from others. In moments including those of crisis, your heart can help one person, a whole group or community. The depth and spread of the heart's radiant and healing qualities are not limited by time or space. The bigger your heart, the more it can reach, in each and every situation.

> ***Practical Heart Tip 83: Let your heart smile and radiate to others - in widening circles ****
>
> *You can go back to revisit KHH 7 'Let your heart smile and radiate to your partner/others'. Prepare with smiling to your heart for a few moments, or do the Heart Strengthening - KHH 6. Once you feel your heart becoming more active, responding and radiating, then*
>
> *Smile from your heart to:*
>
> - *The group of people around you; or*
> - *Individuals affected by a crisis or emergency.*
>
> *Keep on smiling freely and with feeling for some time. As long as you stay in the feeling from your heart, heart-connected, it will work and help your heart and people you let your heart smile to, too.*

The stronger your heart the wider you can make this circle. Experiment with this by adding more and more people to your, list or circle of people around you, that you let the heart smile to. Another way to expand your practice and heart is to add not only more people but everything physical and all events around you; also in widening circles over time as your practice and heart-capacity deepens. The love, calmness and wonderful feelings flowing through your heart during such moments will be exquisite.

Be the change

In the same way that you may strive for a greater mind/brain and heart balance at an inner level, it is meaningful to be mindful and heartful of the big goals on the outer plain. What is your personal big picture visions? And what are actions or activities you already know or have in place to align them with bigger picture life?

> *When I was about to go to another country to sit and meditate I was challenged by my father as to why. The reply was simple. I acknowledged that he and others had a big vision and purpose ... to rebuild a country destroyed by war, to build their own homes and a good life for themselves. I then said to him that in learning to meditate I hope to find what needs building or renovating within, to then lead a life that has purpose and meaning where the inside and outside connect and work together. I also said to him that I had read and felt that it is easier to climb Mt. Everest or to achieve almost anything on the outside, physical or career goal levels, than to face oneself and all the mountains and challenges within. After that he never asked nor challenged me again, ever; despite many more opportunities or reasons given to do so.*

All this happened for me before the discovery of the heart. For many years the chance to climb that personal mountain, to clear what needs to be cleared, to gain access to a form of wisdom that allows for a purposeful and fulfilled life - indeed seemed unsurmountable. Yet, somewhere within, it was an important goal to keep alive.

To have access to the heart seems such a wonderful and special gift now, and yet every human being has the ability to use this gift. The heart is also gentle and kind in its make-up, never judging. So, you may not be there, you may never be in a perfect equilibrium, and yet to have the heart that is allowing you to feel when the outer and the inner are not in balance, to guide you back into a greater balance when needed, is precious. You can then attend through the heart to home, office, social or work situations that require attention, and that can then give renewed strength to go out again to give, contribute and live your purpose or be part of a bigger plan. In this way you can be the change you want to see in the world through the eyes of your heart; being guided by the heart.

The importance of being a role model can be seen in a new light when the heart is there, too. Others will see, hear and feel what you do, and they will share what you do with others. Whatever you do, radiate into the world, or represent, it as a profound joy to be the change you want to see in the world. This is most likely to happen when our mind/brain, heart and physical self are all working well together.

Be grateful

When you are grateful, the heart radiates outward sending the vibrational message
that you have everything positive in your life and so you will
in turn attract more positivity into your way. Brian Tracey

Connecting to gratitude and allowing more gratitude into your life, will connect you to a bigger picture. In heartfelt gratitude your heart swells and you invite others in because gratitude always connects. Your heart likes gratitude and being grateful. Perhaps you can relate to this when you do something for someone else and you get a thank you for your efforts. It just feels pleasant, even if you really don't need or didn't want it.

It is gratitude that opens the heart to another layer of feeling, being and to a bigger picture that the heart is and can connect to. In moments of gratitude, for good things, the present life situation and even more, the heart can facilitate a bigger picture unfolding within and around you even more.

Day-to-day gratitude is easy to relate to. When a colleague, friend or family member says 'thank you' it can make our day. If the children say 'thank you' you are likely to cook with more joy and love the next time, even though this may only be a small shift inside.

When your team leader or superior at work is grateful for what you did for the team, there may be a small shift inside. The engagement, commitment and heart-to-heart connection is likely to grow and expand. This exchange will be one aspect that will make you more committed, dedicated, passionate and most likely accomplish more. It is one step closer towards a beautiful, connected existence, which can also create more efficiency at work.

What is the other important aspect to gratitude? When good things are happening, which is often based on some form of relationship, and when you are being grateful, there will often be a strengthening of this connection. Every connection has the potential to connect you to a bigger picture or at least to another step forward.

The more you feel your heart, the more you express gratitude freely, the more you can practice and feel for the two, gratitude and heart, being and working as one.

When we are not being grateful, there is the other choice too: more mental busy-ness and more busyness with ourselves instead of maintaining and building connection to others and to a bigger heart picture.

It is easy and good to feel gratitude for the good things in life. Nevertheless, while this is harder to begin with, you can also benefit when you learn to be grateful for those things that aren't as pleasant or positive.

Practical Heart Tip 84: 50 things to be grateful for *

Make a list of 50 items you feel to be grateful for; on a piece of paper or in your Heart Diary. This can be anything in your life, people around you now or in the past and any events, situations and any personal, family or team successes.

You can write this list in one sitting or over 2-3 days. There is a chance when you write it in one or two sittings that surprising items surface, too, items that you didn't 'think' you wanted to or could be grateful for.

This is a wonderful warm-up exercise for the following KHH and other practices. At times, it is just nice to re-connect with pleasant, special, joyful, beautiful and wonderful aspects of your life. The more you feel and use your heart, you may even experience the sweet and wonderful feelings in your heart as you write these items down.

Being grateful from the heart is an additional step to offer positive or negative aspects of your life to the abilities and transformative power of your heart.

In offering these items or aspect of your life to your heart, it has a chance to add, work with and transform any associated emotions and more. It will open more each time you do so, become more active and connect to a bigger flow or picture. In your gratitude is a recognition that laws greater than the mind/brain's understanding can be at work. In letting your heart acknowledge this through gratitude your heart will be filled with deeper heart feelings, be able to open more to the bigger picture your heart is naturally more attuned to. Life is likely to become more flowing, easier, lighter and filled with successes and abundance.

If you feel to experiment with being grateful for not-so-nice or difficult events in your life, this will not be the same as turning a blind eye. You use your heart to feel the situation and hence reduce the hold it can have on you. In letting your heart be grateful, any burdens can be dissolved. You can still see, reflect and learn from it. You will also see in greater clarity how to perhaps solve or resolve issues and what are new ways forward, directions or goals.

If in life or in your interactions with others you did not do the best, the heart can make amendments for you to learn, and even for the very events to improve. There is a sweet surrendering in this, too. You are acknowledging a greater inner wisdom and you may also acknowledge within your gratitude, a greater universal or Divine working.

Grateful for good things is the final KHH in the book. It is a practice that initially focusses on you, your heart and the further growing of your heart experiences and heart-centred life. Then, you can practise it in your interaction with others. And, should you feel to, you can make it part of your spiritual practice too.

Key Heart Help 15: Grateful from the heart

Gratitude from your heart outward will profoundly work inward and deepen your heart's understanding and abilities, and the heart's help for you and all around you will grow.

You can do the next KHH in two ways. One option is to choose any items from the above list of '50'. Select these randomly or work your way through the whole list. You may feel different qualities or depth of feeling for different items. Remember the main aspect is to feel the feeling and to follow it, and to not follow any thoughts or analysis or what is felt and why. The second option is you connect with what you feel to be grateful for today or at the end of your day.

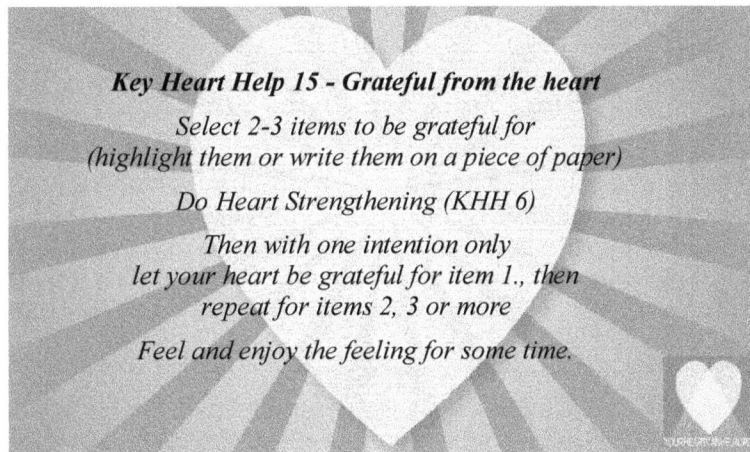

> ### Key Heart Help 15 - Grateful from the heart
>
> *Select 2-3 items to be grateful for*
> *(highlight them or write them on a piece of paper)*
>
> *Do Heart Strengthening (KHH 6)*
>
> *Then with one intention only*
> *let your heart be grateful for item 1., then*
> *repeat for items 2, 3 or more*
>
> *Feel and enjoy the feeling for some time.*

The full KHH 15 - Grateful from the heart

Heartfelt gratitude is important to improve and refine all that your hearts is and can do for you. Like almost all in life, heart-felt gratitude can be developed. This is a full heart-practice routine.

Prepare by doing Heart Strengthening:

- *Close your eyes to decrease the activities of your brain;*
- *Completely relax your body and mind;*
- *Touch your heart with one or more fingers;*
- *Smile freely to your heart without thinking how;*
- *Feel any pleasant, light or expansive feelings and follow the feeling;*
- *Relax even better more and smile more freely;*
- *Once you start experiencing calmness, lightness or joy, follow your feeling while continuing to relax and smile ... and let yourself dissolve into all gentle and pleasant feelings (one to two minutes or more); then*
- *While staying in the beautiful heartfelt feelings ... look at the first item you want to be grateful for; then*

- *Just let your heart be grateful, don't do anything, just feel and continue to feel the gentle or changing feelings in your heart for some time - take your time; then*

- *Continue with point 2, 3 or all points on your list.*

When you are finished just stay being grateful and connected to your heart. Experiment with the variations suggested below to deepen your heart's understanding and growth.

What you will notice is a deepening feeling of the sweet, gentle and wonderful heart feelings almost every time you do this. This means your heart is opening more, cleansing itself more, its surroundings, too, and the heart's capacity and ability to help you in all aspects of life will unfold more.

If you are happy to experiment, then after a couple of times, let your heart do more and the mind/brain less. Still make a list of some items to be grateful for. Then, do the KHH, but do not look at your list anymore. You can just say, in trusting your heart more, 'let my heart be grateful for item one', and then item two, and so on, on today's list.

Another experiment, if you have an existing spiritual practice, you can add another element to the last to extended KHH 13: replace 'let the heart be grateful' with 'let the heart be grateful to a/the universal 'Source of infinite Love', 'Divine' or 'Divine Source' and then continue as suggested. You can replace the terms 'Source of Infinite Love', 'Divine' or 'Divine Source' with the divine being of your belief, practice or religion. If that is not offering enough option you may also use a sentence like 'let the heart be grateful, in the heart's understanding, to the highest or most loving, helping or caring being'.

For your heart the picture that develops through gratitude exercises like these is likely to be bigger than any perception, idea or wisdom elements that the mind/brain knows alone. In this way you allow gratitude and in-gratitude-connection or relationship building to be a greater heart, big picture and spiritual plain or level of working.

Aligning mind/brain, heart and body to a bigger picture
Grateful from the bottom of my heart.

Aligning all simply means to let your heart play its role as the refined intelligence hub in aligning your life to a bigger picture. Working with the mind/brain, the heart and inner heart always look for ways to move your life towards one of deeper fulfilment aligned to a bigger picture. The role of the body-mind-heart unity is then to put it into action and to continuously adjust course.

This adjusting is necessary, as heart-mind-brain intelligence and wisdom develop over time. Whatever unfolds in this trinity will feel natural, 'right' for you and in tune will all around you too. In the same way as it is logical and meaningful to be part of a bigger picture from the mind/brain only, it is meaningful when all parts or aspects of any one of us is more aligned to. Logically, or as a consequence, when the heart joins this process, all planning and all doing will also be more aligned. It is possibly a huge disappointment to find out that a life's work of hoping to make a difference by adding positively to a bigger picture, was lacking alignment to the best possible impact, purpose or truth.

When you use the heart, when the heart is becoming the more influential driving wisdom, consciousness or 'brain', then the chance to find profound fulfilment, purpose and related inner peace is at the very least better than with limited heart or no heart involvement at all.

In this way, your greater strength of heart has an immense and wonderful, immediate ability to help you to be the change many hope to see in this world … leading naturally and through your heart to less destruction, less violence, less injustice, less corruption, less power imbalance, abuse or misuse of others, less negativity and less environmental damage.

I have walked a long walk to freedom … it has been a lonely road … I know that my country was not made to be a land of hatred. No one is born hating another person … because of the colour of his skin … people learn to hate … they can be taught to love, for love comes more naturally to the human heart than the opposite. Nelson Mandala

Nelson Mandala is perhaps someone who walked a heart-path for some time, always or often focussing on gentleness, forgiveness, clarity and equality and not in the easiest of circumstances. This quote and every quote, every analogy and every story will have within them the potential to speak to your heart, for your heart to connect, feel and remember its own wisdom.

This is such a wise and profound quote from someone who with much trust and faith lived with vision, passion and purpose; despite finding himself living within a difficult personal, political and social time in his country.

It is perhaps timely to again point out that everyone's quotes, sharing, stories, no matter how unknown or famous the person is, are solely intended to be a pointer or a reminder of the importance, functions, endurance, and deep inner knowing of your own heart.

Everyone's heart is beyond special in its abilities, in its wisdom and in its ways to uniquely assist your life, every minute or second from here on. Nelson Mandala and everyone quoted in this book, according to someone's mind, brain or heart may have failed or been successful - or been weak or strong. Only deep in your heart or inner heart is there a deeper clarity around this. More important is for these quotes to inspire you to lead a heart-centred life or, at the very least, a life that is perfectly reflective of your own personal or bigger picture mind/brain and heart balance.

For the heart, and all of who we are, the question then is less what we do, but how is it being done, how is the engagement with our family, community or a larger picture? More than anything else, it is perhaps how much heart wisdom is in our actions, which defines our ability to fulfil our real and bigger picture purpose in this world.

'Checking out - checking in'

There is a degree of trust needed in letting your heart guide in reality, in action and beyond talking about the heart.

Your heart has its own 'shopping list', what it longs for, which are the stepping stones for a fulfilled, joyful and love-filled life. There is a unique purpose and alignment that happens when these items are ticked off when every life is moving toward the 'check out'. This analogy is not dissimilar to a feeling within to be part of a bigger picture, to make a difference, to leave a legacy to be remembered for the good things we have done.

It is in ticking off your heart shopping list that a deeper longing, urge and wisdom within can guide you towards even greater and more profound alignment to a bigger picture.

In life, when you get to the 'check out', contrary to the supermarket line, there is no chance to run back for a few items overlooked and missed.

The heart knows, in your own heart you know, and the heart will help to collect these important life-purpose items along the way.

These life-purpose items are about learning and sharing, and about a life filled with loving and love. All these are kind-of heart items, where the mind/brain can help but never really be the main player. It is only through the heart that we can truly connect to the bigger picture.

The end of this book is not intended to be any kind of check out. The examples, stories and practices introduced in this book have worked for many people, individuals, families, work groups, and groups of friends. The use of the heart in the way is designed to be the ultimate and final missing piece to really check-in - into life and into all that life is, can be and ought to be.

The invitation is to you to use your heart and all you are to equally and appropriately use all the building blocks that you are. Being more heart-focussed, attending to the heart more, will be a necessary first period of time to balance over-focus, over-educating and an over-use of the mind/brain. From there your balance, and more importantly the full use of the heart, will be there to help you in all areas of life. In the same way, when you look back at plans, ideas or concepts held - maybe a few years back, 10, 20 years - compare these to what is now, how you feel or think about it now. Often these have changed in some way or even very significantly. This is a reflection of the mind/brain's limited way to perceive, plan and 'run the overall show', your life. Checking into the heart more in its essence means to have all its help, all its unique and profound abilities available to you, and to be in a smoother flow of all that life is. Enjoy with all your heart!

Summary - a big heart making a difference

Your heart's bigger picture can have several aspects. It will less likely lead you somewhere where, at the end of the line, you realise you were not really supposed to be or you have forgotten something important. 'Put your heart into it' is under one of the sub-heading and quotes in an early section of the book. Everything you do, with heart-presence or a helping heart, will connect you to a bigger picture more:

1. Interact more from the heart with others, everyone. Connection to all that is in your life will be a deeper version of connection if facilitated by the heart. As Anna's story shows in a more personal way, with a strong heart it matters less when and how often you see a close one. It is when you meet or interact with a dear friend, family member or colleague that deeper heart sharing will naturally balance what is often a reality: dispersed families, friends who can only be seen a few times over a period, or conflict and disagreement.

2. Connection from the heart means attention to detail and inclusion of a bigger picture. There is calmness and joy in these ways to be and connect. More heart will give more depth and meaning to every personal connection and to the bigger picture of all that you do.

3. Feeling love, feeling at peace, feeling gently joyful are practical experiences that give meaning to life. In a small or more personal way your heart is bridging the parts within that are non-physical and purposeful. Every moment in the heart, being kind, at peace and sharing heart-to-heart with others, including helping others from the heart, will nurture this wholeness.

4. The PHT 'Let your heart smile and radiate to others', even if similar to other practices, now is the invitation to you to let your heart do its part in sharing the blessing, so that pure or deep love from your heart can radiate in ever widening circles to all around you, to all. The stronger your heart the wider you can make this circle. Experiment with this by adding more and more people to your list or circle of people around you, that you let the heart smile to. The love, calmness and wonderful feelings flowing through your heart during such moments will be exquisite.

5. Use the PHT '50 things to be grateful for' to make such a list on a piece of paper or in your Heart Diary. This can be anything in your life, people around you now or in the past or any events, situations and any personal, family or team successes. You can write this list in one sitting or over several days. This list can help you with the next KHH.

6. Commit to a 'program' of being grateful from your heart. Use KHH 15 'Grateful from the heart' and earlier practices that work for you and your heart to expand your overall gratitude. The nature of important aspects of life, such as love, joy and a feeling of connection or belonging are not easily achieved by the ways of relying on the abilities of mind/brain. A grateful heart will help immensely to improve all 'heart' and steadily take you there.

7. The mind/brain's strength is to 'know already', to 'judge self and others' and to have limits. A clear commitment and workplan to the KHHs and PHT will take you into a deepening heart connection. From this connection, the heart can recognise and facilitate a gentle yet steady journey towards these immaterial or non-physical purpose-giving aspects of life. Within the fulfilment of these is a bigger picture alignment or goal realisation.

8. There are often key moments in life - important decisions, turning points, invitation to join a group, a person or a project. These or other key moments can be an invitation to change, reflect a need to change or to turn towards people and directions that the mind/brain struggle to recognise. In heart-centred presence there is a greater chance that you are relaxed enough to see and not miss key moments. The heart will want you to recognise these, too, and will make this known as a feeling.

9. Use the feeling from the heart often. One day you will naturally be heart and mind aware all the time. In this way the heart becomes not only an invaluable ally in finding purpose and a life connected to a meaningful bigger picture, it will become part of the real and more complete you.

10. The greatest possible 'big picture', spanning across a wider spectrum of your life, from back in time to reaching forward in time, is what the heart can connect to; it always does, as its ability to perceive via feeling has no limits. All that your heart connects to, means it will do something to help and facilitate in the background. A strong heart, in a clarity greater than thought, facilitates this being within a bigger picture as something that is gently unfolding and quietly achievable.

11. Use the heart to feel and realise. Over time, normally much more subject to discussion, hope and speculation, the heart can connect and pull you towards a universal or Divine Plan, or whatever you feel to call such an ultimate picture. This picture is beyond vision, hopes, dreams and aspiration. This greater picture and purpose of life, some of which has been the topic in the spiritual growth chapter, is one that offers deeper levels of fulfilment, too, as the picture is bigger and heart realised. These heart realisations then become gifts to be within a larger picture, world, universe or existence.

12. In the first chapter of the book is a quote 'follow your inner heart and the world moves in and helps'. No matter what you do in this world, there will be a limit to what one person can do, achieve or change. When the world, others, the universe, the Divine Plan, all heart-facilitated, come to your aid a bigger job or picture can be fulfilled.

13. The aim of the book and online resources is to inspire, invite and assist in practically using the heart more, to achieve a personal mind/brain and heart balance or working-together. Whenever your heart is involved, not as an idea, but in action, in the ways your heart is opening, clearing itself of all that is holding, limited or blocking, then a bigger and more purposeful picture can be connected to. In this unfolding is also your alignment to a greater plan or picture that will initially naturally, automatically and then with more inner heart or heart-felt clarity, open to your heart's greater ability to know. Purpose and fulfilment and the alignment to a deeper inner heart-knowing will open.

Chapter 10

In Closing

You have learned about the essence and detailed functioning of the second, non-physical or true heart. In following the practices and exercises you also had clear, and very likely quite profound experiences, of your heart's presence and help.

No matter what your life looks like right now, what it feels like, how wonderful it is already or how significant your challenges or problems are, the heart can offer another layer of help, learning, transformation, depth in quality or enhancement. It offers more than that. In the section on personal growth the heart's role as a super-intelligent, capable and connecting hub is introduced as the 'real secret', the part of you that can connect all the dots and enable gentle shifts, growth and profound levels of purpose, realisation and fulfilment.

The book shares the sweet exchange between Pooh and Piglet where Piglet asks 'how do you spell love' and Pooh answers 'you don't spell it, you feel it'. Love and important qualities or feelings in life are directly connected to your heart, which is also your centre of feeling. You feel them with the heart.

As for love, happiness, calmness and fulfilment, the transformative energy of your heart will gently and steadily move you to feeling these clearer and in more beautiful ways. These feelings are more closely connected to your heart than to the knowledge or experience that is held in the mind/brain or head. If you have not felt this deepening of your heart yet, which is normal in the beginning, re-read the introductory sections, read up on 'letting go', then repeat all the KHHs.

Love for oneself and for others is the foundation and enveloping quality of all relationships that we have - at home, at work or in social settings. The feeling of love is mouldable. It can grow or diminish. In most instances the experience of love is broader than solely romantic love. At work the love quality is the care, support or unconditional positive regard for colleagues or clients. At home love is the support, love and lightness in being with family, loved ones, friends or a partner.

'Your Heart Can Help' has shown, shared and offered you experiences that relate to life, to most areas and aspects of life, and that whatever happens in life is a 'matter of the heart' as well as the head. When you truly 'follow the heart', when your 'heart is in it', when sincerity of your interactions are heart-centred, then the heart's help unfolds and the full use the three God-given human building blocks work together: the mind/brain, the body and the heart.

In life, in the multitude of life's interaction with others, constantly, there is no perfect human being. In this way, everyone is learning. Happiness and love-reducing patterns or habits are revealed with more clarity from the heart. From there steps can be taken, heart-assisted, towards positive change. One of those key unhelpful or damaging patterns is the following of emotions, the heavy feelings, as per the definition of emotion in this book, instead of 'following the heart'.

The deeper meaning of following your heart is to practically use it, have its help fully available and be guided by it. There is a heart reason why, as people grow older burdens, heaviness and negativity can grow, too. When these occupy the heart there is also less space for all the positive feelings possible to have, or to have a memory from the past.

It is here where the heart has one of the most profound impacts. These patterns and the impacts of emotions are discussed in every chapter of the book. The book's exercises are based on proven, natural methods and ways to unlock this full heart-potential offering shifts from heavy emotions to free and positive feelings.

For additional revealing of your heart's help or when you feel to make the next heart-learning steps, there is the online two-level training program at www.yourheartcanhelp.org. Level 1 is designed to make the book's main exercises available as an online, self-paced course, including further learning. Level 2 is designed as a progression and deepening of what you have learned through the book.

Additional progression is possible by attending informal heart or heart meditation sessions near you. There are also the Padmacahaya Institute's heart or open heart workshops and the 'Bridging Heart and Mind' workplace programs. (www.innerheartsolutions.com) The Heart Based Therapeutics training program is designed for counsellors, coaches and other professionals to deepen their heart capacity and to assist others in this way. (www.heartbased.org)

It is not all about you, me, one person. Sharing with someone, caring for a loved one, exchanging with others can help your own heart journey and yet often 'heart-to-heart' is one of the most wonderful ways of relating. If you have used this book, the KHHs, PHTs, and the online resources and, if your life has been changed by this special heart of yours, then please let others know: talk about the heart, this book and the other avenues of heart-learning referenced in 'Your Heart Can Help', so they too, can bring the heart's full help into their lives.

Helpful Lists (Appendices)

1. List of Key Heart Helpers (KHHs)

Just one smile immensely increases the beauty of the universe.
Sri Chinmoy

2. List of Practical Heart Tips (PHTs)

3. List of Figures/Chart/Tables

4. Useful Resources and Links

The following book and web-sites offer further reading and avenues to continued heart learning.

'Smiling to the heart meditations' by Irmansyah Effendi

This book is by one of Amazon's best-selling meditation book authors. In terms of books, this would be the next step to take. It is a concise and step-by-step introduction to the heart. It then moves quite fast to the heart's deeper layers of helping: the ability to realise. It offers a 'learning by heart' experience where the mind/brain work alongside the heart. The book guides, shows and gently facilitates the ways that the heart as a meditation method works and that any stillness in the mind comes from a clear, open and strong heart.

'Let the Love Work' by Raewyn Somer

The association 'heart and love' is age old. Through the heart a deeper, greater, sweeter and unconditional love works. Raewyn's book is a short and to-the-point introduction to the heart. It contains early exercises and heart strengthening to make heart-learning and a more heart-centred life available to everyone.

'Psychology of the Heart' by Dr Ed Rubenstein

Ed's book is a practical hand book that coaches the reader gently, yet in profound ways, through the heart's deep emotional clearing ability. It addresses unsupportive habits as well as growth-limiting thought-patterns and beliefs.

Useful links

www.padmacahaya.org.au

The Padmacahaya institute is a central heart learning organisations. Many of their branches, like this one in Australia, are not-for-profit and have a vision to share about the importance of the heart.

www.natural-walking.com

'Secrets of Natural Walking' is the inaugural program of 'Natural Way of Living'. Within only three years it has reached over 20 countries and has over 150 instructors. Participant testimonies show its ability to reverse the clock and powerfully re-awaken participant bodys' natural healing capabilities.

www.lotuscentre.org

The Lotus Centre has become Australia's largest heart-learning centre. Over 40 weekly sessions are run there, including 15 of which are open to the general public as well as other heart-centred practice events for people at the next stages of heart learning. Heart, Reiki Tummo and Natural Walking workshops are offered at regular intervals.

www.heartbased.org

The US Heart Based Institute is a group dedicated to pioneering new healthcare and other programs through their main modality and approach of Heart Based Therapeutics™. The group advocates the benefits of the heart and promotes heart-centred living to allow the heart in guiding daily choices and responses, leading to overall greater health, well-being, peace, joy, and fulfilment.

www.innerheartsolutions.com

The Inner Heart Solutions (IHS) founders realised that the heart and its capacity was missing in the world of work and the direct impact that more heart has on integrity, passion, communication and fortitude. IHS's unique approach is built a business framework to assist individuals and teams with day-to-day and strategic agendas.

www.heartmath.org

Heart Math are another institute committed to researching and sharing about the heart. It seems that only in recent years their focus shifted, based on their research findings or insights, from the physical to the non-physical heart. I personally love their research. However, I found their heart training approaches less developed than others.

www.lotusheart.de

This is one of the European heart-learning and heart-resource pages. When writing this book, some of my friends from central Europe regularly asked for a German version of Your Heart Can Help. This page has information, contacts, meeting details and current heart workshops listed.

www.yourheartcanhelp.org

This is the Your Heart Can Help book's own website. You will find some of the book's stories as video clips here, additional materials and resources that complement various exercises of the book.

5. Heart-Centre Contact Details

Connecting, sharing and practising with others can be very beneficial for your heart-learning journey. The following links to contact persons and experienced heart-practitioners are useful. If they are not near you, they very likely know the nearest other person or group. Sometimes you find only one person per region, like Deb in North America and yet there are activities in most larger cities. Then Deb, or Yvonne in Germany, will be able to provide further information and contacts. Unless the name is in the actual email address you find the name of the contact person listed in brackets.

Heart-Centres/Heart Learning Groups - In Australia and NZ

Tasmania
South - Hobart
Kent@lotuscentre.org & Amanda@lotuscentre.org
North - Launceston
(Caroline) Padmacahaya.tas.north@gmail.com
North West
(Gill) Padmacahaya.tas.northwest@gmail.com

New Zealand
North & South Island
(Jane) Janehughessnz@gmail.com

Mainland Australia
Melbourne - VIC
(Annie) Amhutchins@gmail.com
Sydney - NSW
(Carolina) Padmacahaya.sydney@gmail.com
Northern Territory
(Vanessa) Openheart.alicesprings@gmail.com
(Shar) heartsindarwin@gmail.com
Western Australia
(Melky) Melkyherlina@gmail.com
South Australia
(Trish) Trishm30@adam.com.au

Other parts of the world

Europe
United Kingdom - Ireland
(Paul) Pmcdur@yahoo.co.uk

Germany - Austria (Central Europe)
Yvonne.kury@gmail.com

South America
(Martha) taluza.atkinson@gmail.com
Canada
(Selina) selina.lotusheart@gmail.com

North America
(Deb) Deblafon@gmail.com
Russia
(Tatiana) Awesomehome@gmail.com

Singapore
(Jessica) reikitummo.singapore@gmail.com

Asia All Other - Africa
(Tetty) Tettyj@gmail.com

Inner Heart Solutions - Workplace Heart Programs
World-wide
Bernadette Halloran
Bernadette@innerheartsolutions.com
Australia – New Zealand
Stuart Hayes
Stuart@innerheartsolutions.com

Heart Based Therapeutics - Practitioner and Workplace Training
Heart Based Institute - info@heartbased.org

www.ingramcontent.com/pod-product-compliance
Lightning Source LLC
Chambersburg PA
CBHW080355030426
42334CB00024B/2885